Movies and Mental Illness
Using Films to Understand Psychopathology

Movies and Mental Illness

Using Films to Understand Psychopathology

Danny Wedding
Missouri Institute of Mental Health
School of Medicine
University of Missouri-Columbia

Mary Ann Boyd
School of Nursing
Southern Illinois University Edwardsville

Ryan M. Niemiec
Saint Louis Behavioral Medicine Institute
School of Medicine
Saint Louis University

HOGREFE

Library of Congress Cataloging in Publication

is available via the Library of Congress Marc Database under the
LC Control Number 2005922397

Library and Archives Canada Cataloguing in Publication

Wedding, Danny
      Movies and mental illness : using films to understand
psychopathology / Danny Wedding, Mary Ann Boyd, Ryan M. Niemiec.
-- 2nd rev. and expanded ed.

Includes bibliographical references.
ISBN 0-88937-292-6

      1. Psychology, Pathological--Study and teaching--Audio-visual aids.
2. Mental illness in motion pictures. I. Boyd, Mary Ann II. Niemiec, Ryan M.
III. Title.

RC459.W43 2005   616.89   C2005-901256-0

© 2005 by Hogrefe & Huber Publishers

PUBLISHING OFFICES
USA: Hogrefe & Huber Publishers, 875 Massachusetts Avenue, 7th Floor, Cambridge, MA 02139
              Phone (866) 823-4726, Fax (617) 354-6875; E-mail info@hhpub.com
EUROPE: Hogrefe & Huber Publishers, Rohnsweg 25, 37085 Göttingen, Germany
              Phone +49 551 49609-0, Fax +49 551 49609-88, E-mail hh@hhpub.com

SALES & DISTRIBUTION
USA: Hogrefe & Huber Publishers, Customer Services Department,
              30 Amberwood Parkway, Ashland, OH 44805
              Phone (800) 228-3749, Fax (419) 281-6883, E-mail custserv@hhpub.com
EUROPE: Hogrefe & Huber Publishers, Rohnsweg 25, 37085 Göttingen, Germany
              Phone +49 551 49609-0, Fax +49 551 49609-88, E-mail hh@hhpub.com

OTHER OFFICES
CANADA: Hogrefe & Huber Publishers, 1543 Bayview Avenue, Toronto, Ontario M4G 3B5
SWITZERLAND: Hogrefe & Huber Publishers, Länggass-Strasse 76, CH-3000 Bern 9

Hogrefe & Huber Publishers
Incorporated and registered in the State of Washington, USA, and in Göttingen, Lower Saxony, Germany

Printed and bound in the USA
ISBN 0-88937-292-6

Dedication

For Lester R. Bryant, MD, ScD
Mentor, model, scholar, friend.
DW

For Jim
My viewing partner.
MAB

For my *transformed* Father, *compassionate* Mother,
captivating Brother, and *endearing* Sister.
RMN

Foreword to the Second Edition

John Milton, in *Paradise Lost*, tells us that we must "strike the visual nerve, for we have much to see." So, too, in this present work, do Wedding, Boyd, and Niemiec admonish us that there is much to learn by seeing with the mind's eye what these well-chosen films, by turns sad and silly, offer us in illuminating the psychopathologies set forth in the Diagnostic and Statistical Manual of the American Psychiatric Association.

Ranging from such classics as the depiction of alcoholism in *The Lost Weekend*, to relatively obscure films perhaps known only to the aficionado of foreign films, Wedding, Boyd, and Niemiec have achieved a work which may itself become a classic in this genre, particularly with respect to its intended purpose of teaching how the various psychopathologies might play themselves out in an approximation of real-life, real-world situations of which these films are a simulacrum.

Wedding, Boyd, and Niemiec provide a brief synopsis of the particular film in relation to the major category of psychopathology being covered in a chapter, and they relate the manifest and latent content of the film to the various diagnostic symptoms within a category, such as childhood disorders, and further provide an illustrative case study to assist in the process of generalizing from the film to actual diagnostic work.

As a didactic tool, the work by Wedding, Boyd, and Niemiec should have a salutary effect in engaging the attention of the student, as well as in engaging the affective response of the student to the vicarious identification with the film characters portrayed and, hopefully, enhancing the learning process of what otherwise tends to be a rather tedious pedagogical adventure for most students.

The authors provide a lively expository style, and the use of epigraphs for each chapter is a particularly happy device for setting a tone for each chapter and for capturing a pithy bit of dialogue that may cause the reader to engage in some cognitive restructuring, as when one of the characters says, "I recall every fall, every hook, every jab" in the chapter on the dementias, a quote which instantly evokes an image of the prizefighter with organic brain damage. Other such examples abound and contribute significantly to the teaching potential of the work.

On balance, this is a work that is likely to become a classic of its type and a particularly useful teaching tool for the diagnosis and understanding of the various psychopathologies for students of the helping professions. I commend it to the reader, be the reader student or professor.

Allan Barclay, PhD
St. Louis, Missouri

Preface

"Mental health movies are often like going to the zoo. They can be wonderful but you go with the normal person surrogate and together you view the person with mental illness. You see the disease from the outside in, and it does a disservice to our ability to empathize and understand. If we saw the world the way the people who suffer see it, we would understand them differently. The hope being that if one person came home from the movie theater, just one, and saw somebody screaming at empty air on the street corner and related to them differently with understanding then we would have done our job."

Akiva Goldsman, screenwriter of *A Beautiful Mind*,
in the DVD's section titled
"Development of a Screenplay"

We wrote *Movies and Mental Illness* because of our conviction that films are a powerful medium for teaching students (in psychology, social work, medicine, nursing, and counseling), engaging patients, and educating the public about the fascinating world of psychopathology. In addition, we wrote the book because we genuinely love watching and talking about movies. It is important to understand that while this book's title is *Movies and Mental Illness*, we also discuss serious problems that do not reflect mental illness *per se*, including mental retardation, physical or sexual abuse, and violence.

We have made several changes to this edition. We have added hundreds of recent films to Appendix G, expanding this resource to nearly a thousand films that can be used to illustrate psychopathology. We plan to maintain this Appendix on the internet (http://mimh.edu/danny_wedding) and hope it continues to be a useful resource for students, teachers, lecturers, consumers, mental health professionals, and people simply interested in psychology and mental illness. Although it is impossible to list every film depicting every disorder, we feel we have chosen the most important films that illustrate psychopathology. You will find many of these recent films discussed in more detail in the relevant chapters in this book.

In response to requests for expanded coverage of psychopathology, we have added a new chapter on "Sleep, Eating, Impulse Control and Adjustment Disorders." We expanded the "Sexual and Gender Identity Disorders" chapter to include discussions of sexual addictions and sexual dysfunction, and the "Violence and Physical and Sexual Abuse" chapter has been expanded.

Many chapters now include a section on "International Films" that depict particular disorders. Often these films are more powerful and accurate than anything the United States has produced. We hope this will entice readers to watch more foreign films.

In discussing psychopathology, we occasionally reveal endings or surprise twists to films, and we realize this may spoil the film for some readers. We apologize in advance if this occurs.

The book is also designed to supplement core texts in abnormal psychology; if the book is being used in this way, the relevant core chapters in the primary text should be read *before* reviewing the corresponding chapter in *Movies and Mental Illness*. (However, it will usually be helpful to review the "Questions to Consider" section that introduces each chapter on psychopathology before seeing the recommended film.) We will occasionally present information about mental illness, but this information is almost incidental to the discussion of the films themselves, and we have tried to avoid redundancy with the many fine textbooks that already discuss psychopathology in considerable detail. We assume the reader will look up unfamiliar terms or discuss them in class, as we have not always defined each new term.

Each clinical chapter is introduced with a *fabricated* case history and Mini-Mental State Examination. We have developed composite presentations linked as closely as possible to the character being portrayed in the film being discussed. In every case, the diagnoses we present reflect hypotheses, not facts; the case studies are designed to generate ideas, enliven discussion, and stimulate learning. Our diagnoses and character descriptions are always derived from our own judgment and clinical experience, and our fabricated evaluations are anchored in the events portrayed on screen, even when films are based on actual figures (e.g., the character of John Nash in *A Beautiful Mind*).

Although educated and trained in different disciplines (Clinical Psychology—DW and RMN; Nursing—MAB), we are all clinicians and educators who have found that the judicious use of films dramatically increases students' and patients' understanding of abnormal behavior. For example, when lecturing about alcoholism, we might supplement our lectures with a "demonstration" of delirium tremens using *The Lost Weekend*. Before a lecture on bipolar disorder, we'll ask our students to watch *A Woman Under the Influence* or *Mr. Jones*. Both films have richness and an intensity that simply cannot be captured by a classroom lecture or the printed page. Likewise, when working with a patient going through a divorce who becomes incensed over the behavior of his or her spouse, we might recommend watching *Kramer vs. Kramer*. We have found that the discussion of relevant films offers a wonderful way to open clinically relevant areas that have not previously been explored.

We discuss a variety of films throughout the book; however, we usually use one or two films as *primary* illustrations of each disorder. These "primary" films are movies we have watched repeatedly. In many cases, they are popular movies that students are likely to have already seen on their own (e.g., *Fatal Attraction*, *A Beautiful Mind*, *Matchstick Men*).

Usually the connection between the films being discussed and the chapter is immediate and direct, but we occasionally include obscure films when a small section relates in a meaningful way to the points made in the chapter. There are other classic films such as *A Clockwork Orange* that have tremendous pedagogical value, and we take great pleasure in introducing a new generation of students to these films. In addition, films such as *Pelle the Conqueror* are occasionally included, even when there is no direct connection to psychopathology, because the films are provocative and moving and are good illustrations of psychological phenomena, even when they do not address psychopathology per se.

Films can be integrated into courses in abnormal psychology and psychopathology in a variety of ways. The particular approach selected will vary from course to course, depending on the needs of the instructor and the interests of students.

First, students can be asked to take responsibility for seeing many of these films on their own. Because we have selected popular films as the exemplars for each clinical chapter, students can easily rent them from any number of commercial sources. Costs are minimized if students choose to see the films in small groups. This promotes the intellectual camaraderie, discussion, and debate that characterize effective learning. We recommend that whenever possible students see the films *before* coming to class to discuss the corresponding topic.

Second, we have used films in classes that meet twice weekly. The first class meeting is devoted to seeing the film; the second is spent discussing the content of the related textbook chapter and determining whether or not the film accurately represents the disorder being discussed. It is ideal when such courses can be team taught by a mental health professional and a literature/drama professor.

Finally, most professors choose to use class time to show selected vignettes from pedagogically powerful films, and they encourage students to view the entire film and other related films on their own time. The goal with this approach is to augment lectures with relevant in-class discussion while minimizing the total amount of class time spent watching films. Using a film vignette that vividly depicts a psychiatric disorder circumvents the ethical issues (confidentiality, securing releases and permission, etc.) associated with using real cases and clients as illustrations in the classroom.

When films are used in the classroom, it may be necessary for the educational institution (or the members of the class) to pay a fee for public usage. Most colleges and universities have audiovisual departments well equipped to handle such administrative details.

Many readers will disagree about the ratings we have assigned films included in Appendix G. However, it is important to remember that our ratings are based primarily on the utility of the film as a teaching tool and only secondarily on the film's artistic merit.

We are including our e-mail addresses below so we can get feedback about the book. We hope those readers who share our enthusiasm about cinema as a teaching tool will recommend additional films that we can include in the next edition of *Movies and Mental Illness*.

Danny Wedding, PhD, MPH
danny.wedding@mimh.edu

Mary Ann Boyd, PhD, DNS, APRN, BC
mboyd@siue.edu

Ryan M. Niemiec, PsyD
rmjn@lycos.com

Acknowledgments

Many special people contributed to our efforts over the decade we spent watching movies, reading reviews, and thinking about films as we prepared the first edition and the new edition of this book. Many of our ideas and the selections of films to be included in *Movies and Mental Illness* grew out of discussions with our friends, especially those who are mental health professionals and interested in the fascinating ways in which psychopathology is portrayed in film.

Rob Dimbleby at Hogrefe and Huber is an extraordinary editor and a valued friend. We appreciate his vision and his enthusiasm for publishing a second edition of this book.

Vicki Eichhorn, Jill Meyer, and Christine Pearce all helped with the preparation of the manuscript. Vicki was especially valuable as she managed the myriad details associated with formatting, citations, and permissions—all with cheerful alacrity and consistent good humor.

Special thanks go to Kris Copeland, Bradley Daniels, Jean Kehlinbrink, Dante Mancini, Kelly Mazonne, Gary Mitchell, and Jeanne Richart for their helpful suggestions, clarifications, and ideas during earlier drafts of particular chapters.

Ryan Niemiec also acknowledges those who have contributed to his interest and passion in films over the years: (1) "Ms. Schneider" who first taught him that movies have a significance that extends beyond the plot; (2) film professors Bill Vincent (teacher of Spiderman director, Sam Raimi) and Ken Harrow of Michigan State University who taught him how to explore these deeper levels; (3) Bob Godley of the New York state psychiatric system who taught him to integrate and express these deeper levels; and (4) Danny Wedding who supported his interest in films by creating his position as film editor for *PsycCRITIQUES: Contemporary Psychology—APA Review of Books*.

Table of Contents

A film index is available for download at *www.hhpub.com.*

Chapter 1

Films and Psychopathology

If it can be written, or thought, it can be filmed.
Stanley Kubrick

For better or worse, movies and television contribute significantly to shaping the public's perception of the mentally ill and those who treat them.
Steven E. Hyler

Introduction

In all of human perceptual experience, nothing conveys information or evokes emotion quite as clearly as our visual sense. Filmmakers capture the richness of this visual sense, combine it with auditory stimuli, and create the ultimate waking dream experience: the movie. The viewer enters a trance, a state of absorption, concentration, and attention, engrossed by the story and the plight of the characters. This is exacerbated in movie theaters where the viewer is fully enveloped in sight and sound. Many consider movies to be the most influential form of mass communication (Cape, 2003).

Hollywood took the original invention of the cinematic camera and invented a new art form in which the viewer becomes enveloped in the work of art. The camera carries the spectator into each scene, and the viewer perceives events from the inside as if surrounded by the characters in the film. The actors do not have to describe their feelings, as in a play, because we experience what they see and feel.

In order to produce an emotional response to a film, the director carefully develops both plot and character through precise camera work. Editing creates a visual and acoustic **gestalt**, to which the viewer responds. The more effective the technique, the more involved the viewer. In effect, the director *constructs* the film's (and the viewer's) reality. The selection of locations, sets, actors, costumes, and lighting contributes to the film's organization and shot-by-shot **mise-en-scene** (the physical arrangement of the visual image).

The Social Influence of Films

Film has become such an integral part of our culture that it seems to be the mirror in which we see ourselves reflected every day. The widespread popularity of DVDs, the addition of movies by mail (e.g., Netflix), the use of unlimited rentals for a monthly fee (e.g., Blockbuster), and the availability of literally thousands of films in every corner video store have greatly expanded the influence and accessibility of this medium.

When someone is watching a movie, an immediate bond is set up between the spectator and the film, and all the technical apparatus involved with the projection of the film becomes invisible as the images from the film pass into the spectator's consciousness. With the best films, the viewer experiences a sort of dissociative state in which ordinary existence is temporarily suspended. No other art form pervades the consciousness of the individual experiencing it to the same extent and with such power.

We believe films have a greater influence than any other art form. Their influence is felt across age, gender, nationality, culture, and even across time. Films have become a pervasive and omnipresent part of our society with little conscious awareness of the profound influence the medium may be exerting.

Films are especially important in influencing the public perception of mental illness because many people are relatively uninformed about the problems of people with mental disorders, and the media tend to be especially effective in shaping opinion in those situations in which strong opinions are not already held. Although some films present sympathetic portrayals of people with mental illness and those professionals who work in the field of mental health (e.g., *The Three Faces of Eve*, *David and Lisa*, and *Ordinary People*), many more do not. The victims of mental illness are portrayed most often as aggressive, dangerous, and unpredictable; psychiatrists, psychologists, and other health professionals who work with these patients are often portrayed as "arrogant and ineffectual," "cold-hearted and authoritarian," "passive and apathetic," or "shrewd and manipulative" (Wedding & Niemiec, 2003).

Films such as *Psycho* (1960) perpetuate the continuing confusion about the relationship between schizophrenia and dissociative identity disorders (multiple personality disorders); *Friday the 13th* (1980) and *Nightmare on Elm Street* (1984) both perpetuate the myth that people who leave psychiatric hospitals are violent and dangerous; movies such as *The Exorcist* (1973) suggest to the public that mental illness is the equivalent of possession by the devil; and movies such as *One Flew Over the Cuckoo's Nest* (1975) make the case that psychiatric hospitals are simply prisons in which there is little or no regard for patient rights or welfare. These films in part account for the continuing stigma of mental illness.

Stigma is one of the reasons that so few people with mental problems actually receive help (Mann & Himelein, 2004). The National Institute of Mental Health (NIMH) estimates that only 20 percent of those with mental disorders actually reach out for help with their problems, despite the fact that many current treatments for these disorders are inexpensive and effective. In addition, there is still a strong tendency to see patients with mental disorders as the cause of their own disorders—for example, the National Alliance for the Mentally Ill (NAMI) has polling data that indicate that about one in three U.S. citizens still conceptualizes mental illness in terms of evil and punishment for misbehavior.

Cinematic Elements

A film director must consider countless technical elements in the making of a film, often orchestrating hundreds of people, many of whom monitor and pass down orders to hundreds or thousands of other collaborators. There are three general phases involved in making a film.

The time spent prior to filming in **pre-production** is often seen as the most important. Many directors "storyboard" (draw out) every single shot and choreograph every movement for each scene to be filmed. Countless meetings with each technical supervisor (e.g., cinematographer, costume designer, set designer, electrician) are held to prepare and coordinate good integration. The director will also scout out locations, work with casting appropriate actors and actresses for the various roles, and may re-work the screenplay.

In the **production** phase, the director attempts to film his/her vision, working closely with the actors and actresses to encourage, stimulate, guide, or alter their work, and carefully monitoring camera angles, lighting, sound, and other technical areas.

In **post-production**, the editing process and the laying out of the musical score and background sounds are major areas of focus. The director integrates each of these elements while working to honor the original purpose, message, and underlying themes in making the film.

Of course these three phases exclude countless other tasks involving financing, budgeting, marketing, and other business, administrative, and legal aspects. Some of the most important cinematic elements are summarized with film examples in Table 1.1.

Directors attempt to artfully integrate the technical elements of sound, camera, and lighting fluidly with the plot, themes, pacing, and tone of the film while ascertaining quality acting performances. Danis Tanovic, director of Best Foreign Film, *No Man's Land* (2001), about the Bosnian-Serbian war speaks to many of these elements as he describes the shock and disharmony of the war that he attempted to depict in his film:

"This shock is something I have reproduced through my film. On one side, a long summer day—perfect nature, strong colors—and on the other, human beings and their black madness. And this long, hot summer day reflects the atmosphere of the film itself. Movements are heavy, thoughts are hard to grasp, time is slow and tension is hiding—hiding but present. When it finally explodes, it is like fireworks—sudden loud and quick. Panoramic shots of landscape become unexpectedly mixed with nervous details of action. It all lasts for a moment or two, and then tension hides again, waiting for the next opportunity to surprise. Time slows down again."

For the most skilled directors, virtually everything that the camera "sees" and records is meaningful. The sense of subjective experience produced

Table 1.1 Film Elements with Movie Examples

Film Element	Explanation	Classic Example	Recent Example
Themes	Overall meaning, messages, motifs	*It's a Wonderful Life* (1946)	*House of Sand and Fog* (2003)
Cinematography	Visual appeal, framing, camera-work, lighting	*Lawrence of Arabia* (1962)	*Lord of the Rings: The Return of the King* (2003)
Pacing	Movement, fluidity	*M*A*S*H* (1970)	*The Hours* (2002)
Sound	Music, score, sound effects	*Ben-Hur* (1959)	*The Matrix* (1999)
Mood	Tone, atmosphere	*M* (1931)	*Life is Beautiful* (1998)
Art	Set design, costumes	*Star Wars* (1977)	*Moulin Rouge* (2001)
Dialogue	Conversation, modes of communication	*Annie Hall* (1977)	*Lost in Translation* (2003)
Acting	Character portrayal, depth & quality, casting	*The Philadelphia Story* (1940)	*Mystic River* (2003)
Editing	Continuity, transitions	*Citizen Kane* (1941)	*Memento* (2000)
Screenplay	Story-line, plot	*One Flew Over the Cuckoo's Nest* (1975)	*American Beauty* (1999)
Direction	All elements together, quality of film overall	*A Clockwork Orange* (1971)	*Amelie* (2001)

by a sequence of **point-of-view** shots facilitates the audience's identification with the film's characters, their perceptions, and their circumstances. Extreme **close-up shots** and a variety of **panning techniques** facilitate the importance of an emotional expression, inner conflict, or develop pacing for the film. High-angle and low-angle shots give emphasis to character control, power, strength, weakness, and a variety of other dynamics. For example, in *American Beauty* (1999), high-angle shots are used at the beginning of the film on Lester (Kevin Spacey) to indicate a passiveness and submission to authority before his transformation to a strong-willed, commanding character.

Each viewer possesses unique perceptual preferences, prior knowledge about the film's content, and preconceptions about the images the film contains that mediate his or her perceptions and experience. Rarely, if ever, do any two viewers have an identical experience when viewing the same film. Each viewer subjectively selects, attends to, and translates the visual and acoustic images projected in a theater into his or her own version of the story. Often audiences are affected by or identify with the film's characters so strongly that it appears clear that the defense

mechanism of **projection** is present. This process is facilitated when the audience can anticipate the story line, the plot, or the outcome. The avid moviegoer quickly realizes familiar themes, similar settings, and "formulas" for plots and endings across a variety of films. The more one views films, the easier it becomes to identify a specific film type, or **genre**.

The Close-Up

When we see an isolated face on the screen, our consciousness of space is suspended and we become vividly aware of all the nuances of emotion that can be expressed by a grimace or a glance. We form beliefs about a character's emotions, moods, intentions, and thoughts as we look directly into his or her face. Indeed, many of the most profound emotional experiences (such as grief) are expressed much more powerfully through the human face than through words. Consider the dynamic film, *Amelie* (2001), in which director Jean-Pierre Jeunet purposefully chooses characters (as he does for all of his films) that have very expressive faces. There are numerous close-ups on several of the characters' faces throughout the film. He says he wants to have characters that are interesting for the viewer to look at. In turn, this enhances viewer interest and character development.

This ability to share and comprehend subjective experiences through empathic interpretation of the language of the face is clearly evident in early **silent films**, and these films still have the power to evoke strong emotions. In fact, many early directors of silent films, confronted with the development of "talkies," feared that the addition of sound would place a barrier between the spectator and the film and restore the external and internal distance and dualism present in other works of art.

The principles of observing emotional nuances can be extended from the human face to the background and surroundings in which the character moves, and a character's subjective vision can be reproduced by a film as objective reality. For example, film can show the frightened, paranoid individual, but also the distorted, menacing houses and trees which the protagonist views. This technique was used in the expressionist film *The Cabinet of Dr. Caligari* (1919).

Even with vastly improved technology and the addition of sound and color, the essence of film still remains its visual content. Gestures and facial expressions convey inner non-rational emotions that cannot be expressed in spoken or written language. They also express emotions that lie in the deepest part of the self and which often cannot be adequately expressed by words, which are mere reflections of cognitions. What we see in a facial expression is made immediately apparent to the spectator without the intermediary of words, and a good actor can convey multiple emotions simultaneously.

All this is achieved through the skill of the actor. It has been found time and again that real people playing themselves are less convincing than actors. This is true with instructional films, advertisements, and docudramas, as well as feature films. In *Ordinary People* (1980), the director, Robert Redford, attempted to cast an actual psychiatrist in the role of the therapist, but the effect was unconvincing. Redford decided to cast actor Judd Hirsch in the role and the film ended up winning an Academy Award for Best Picture and Hirsch received a nomination for Best Actor.

Identification

As a film is being projected onto a theater screen, we project ourselves into the action and identify with its protagonists. At one time it was thought that, in order for the audience to maintain the attention of viewers, a film had to have a central character and theme. At times this central figure has been an "anti-hero." However, directors such as Robert Altman and Quentin Tarantino have experimented with techniques in which they rapidly shift among short vignettes that may be only loosely linked with a story line or central character. Altman's *Short Cuts* (1994) and Tarantino's *Pulp Fiction* (1994) are two examples of this approach.

Filmmakers have also experimented with other means of holding the psychological continuity together, such as making an inanimate object or an animal the center of the story. Most films, however, use a single character to hold the film together as a psychological whole.

The classic question posed to students regarding films in introduction to cinema classes—"Are movies merely art imitating real life?"—is perhaps unanswerable. For some viewers, seeing movies takes on such importance that it seems as if films and film characters have supplanted their lives.

Suture

Viewers integrate separate, disjointed photographic images into coherent scenes and different scenes into the whole film experience without conscious effort or any appreciation for the complicated psychological processes involved. "**Suture**," to use a medical metaphor, occurs when cutting or editing occurs and the resulting cinematic gaps are "sewn" shut by viewers.

According to suture theory, instead of asking, "Who is watching this?" and "How could this be happening?" viewers tacitly accept what is seen on the screen as natural and "real," even when the camera's gaze shifts abruptly from one scene, location, or character to another. Suture works because cinematic coding makes each shot appear to be the object of the gaze of whoever appears in the shot that follows. The most commonly cited example of suturing is the **shot/reverse shot**, in which each of two characters is alternately viewed over the other's shoulder.

The Representation of Psychological Phenomena in Film

Film is particularly well suited to depicting psychological states of mind and altered mental states. The combination of images, dialogue, sound effects, and music in a movie mimics and parallels the thoughts and feelings that occur in our stream of consciousness. Lights, colors, and sounds emanate from the screen in such a way that we readily find ourselves believing that we are actually experiencing what is happening on the screen.

In *Secrets of a Soul* (1926), German director G. Pabst dramatized psychoanalytic theory with the help of two of Freud's assistants, Abraham and Sachs, and depicted dream sequences with multi-layered superimposition (achieved through rewinding and multiple exposures). Freud himself did not want his name connected with the project and had misgivings about the film's ability to convey the nuances of psychoanalytic process. In a letter to Karl Abraham, Freud wrote, "My chief objection is still that I do not believe satisfactory plastic representation of our abstractions is at all possible." Freud himself remained skeptical about the cinema all his life.

Film is frequently used to objectively portray subjective states such as dreams. Perhaps the best example of this is Hitchcock's collaboration with Salvador Dali on the dream sequence in *Spellbound* (1944). Hitchcock wanted to "turn out the first picture on psychoanalysis." He was determined to break the traditional way of handling dream sequences through a blurred and hazy screen. Hitchcock wanted dreams with great visual sharpness and clarity, and images sharper than those in the film itself. He chose Salvador Dali as a collaborator because of the architectural precision of the artist's work. Hitchcock originally wanted to shoot *Spellbound* in the open air and in natural light, but he wound up shooting the film in the studio to cut costs. *Spellbound* depicts the cathartic recovery of repressed memories, an emotional experience intense enough to eliminate the hero's amnesia. This is a psychological process that has been depicted in film since its early days.

Films can also be used to interweave fantasy and reality, and a director may intentionally set up situations in which the viewer cannot tell if the film portrays reality or the unconscious fantasies of a character. Examples of this technique include Ingmar Bergman's *Persona* (1966), Frederico Fellini's *Juliet of the Spirits* (1965), Luis Bunuel's *Belle de Jour* (1966), and Robert Altman's *Images* (1972) (Fleming & Manvell, 1985). Director David Lynch has made this approach his trademark with such films as *Mulholland Drive* (2001), *Lost Highway* (1997), *Blue Velvet* (1986), and *Eraserhead* (1977).

Processes such as thinking, recalling, imagining, and feeling are not visible, but the language of the **montage** and camera techniques such as **slow fades**

can suggest these invisible processes. Also, the film can be edited in such a way that the viewer is forced to think about psychological phenomena. The inclusion of images with symbolic meaning, such as a hearse passing by or the well-known chess game with Death in *The Seventh Seal* (1957), can evoke certain moods or prepare the viewer for events that are about to occur. Symbolic sounds, such as a baby crying, can have a similar effect.

Another symbol often used in film is the mirror. When a character is filmed looking in the mirror, it often represents self-reflection, insight, a new identity emerging or changing, or even a narcissistic preoccupation with oneself. *Monster's Ball* (2001) uses mirrors and other reflective objects to symbolize self-distortion and negative self-perception in the two lead characters who are numb to their own lives. Mirrored images depict a broken and distorted Marlon Brando character in *Last Tango in Paris* (1972), self-deprecation in *American Splendor* (2003), self-criticism in *Soldier's Girl* (2003), deterioration in *Focus* (2001), and externalization of blame in a dramatic, comical scene of *25th Hour* (2002).

"Beyond all physical and palpable reality another dimension defined only in painting, a mirror which deforms life… an instant reflected… a magical reality where all is possible."

Goya in *Bordeaux*

Films offer numerous examples of unconscious motivation and **defense mechanisms**, involuntary patterns of thinking, feeling, or acting that arise in response to the subjective experience of anxiety. For example, in *sex, lies, and videotape* (1989), Cynthia, who is having an affair with her sister Ann's husband, inadvertently loses a pearl earring after a sexual encounter in the home of her sister. The earring is discovered and the discovery forces Ann to confront the fact that Cynthia is sleeping with Ann's husband. **Acting out** is present in *Intimacy* (2000), *You Can Count On Me* (2000), *Lantana* (2001), and in Michael Douglas' response to the stress in his life in *Falling Down* (1993). **Altruism** can be seen in *Patch Adams* (1998), and the character of the doctor who devotes himself to the indigent people of India in *Streets of Joy*

(1994). **Denial** is dramatically illustrated in Katharine Hepburn and Ellen Burstyn's gripping roles as drug addicts in *Long Days Journey into Night* (1962) and *Requiem for a Dream* (2000), respectively, as well as most townspeople in both *The Village* (2004) and *Dogville* (2003). **Intellectualization** is present in *Lorenzo's Oil* (1992) and **suppression** is apparent in *The United States of Leland* (2003), *Kill Bill, Vol. 2* (2004), and is commonplace in *Gone with the Wind* (1939).

"I'll think about it tomorrow. Tara! Home. I'll go home, and I'll think of some way to get him back! After all, tomorrow is another day!"

Gone with the Wind

The Depiction of Psychological Disorders in Films

This book organizes categories of psychological disorders with appropriate film examples. Table 1.2 presents an overview of well-recognized and accepted disorders and some of the best representations of them in cinema. Each is discussed in this book.

Psychopathology in Different Film Genres

The depiction of mental illness in films most commonly appears in three popular genres: the drama, the horror film, and the suspense film. Often the most effective portrayals of mental illness are those that infuse surreal and expressionistic images into a montage that is realistic and plausible, powerfully conveying the "interior" of a character's psyche. For a skilled director, convincing perceptual aberrations such as visual hallucinations are easy to construct and to project to an audience.

An early film that served as a prototype for **horror** films, Wiene's *The Cabinet of Dr. Caligari* (1919), is highly expressionistic and established a precedent for setting macabre murders in mental institutions. Like dozens of films that followed, it linked insanity and the personal lives of psychiatrists and implied that mental health professionals are all "a little odd." Evidence of the enduring effects of these themes is found in the successful

and highly acclaimed film *The Silence of the Lambs* (1991), in which Anthony Hopkins plays a mentally deranged and cannibalistic psychiatrist.

The seminal films of Alfred Hitchcock provide the best examples of the **suspense** genre. They are unique in the way they engage the viewer and pander to his or her anxieties in subtle, unrelenting, and convincing ways. The majority of Hitchcock's films, noted for their stylized realism, invariably evoke a sensation of vicariously pulling the viewer "in" to the plight of the characters as a not-so-innocent bystander, through a carefully edited montage of a variety of objective and subjective camera shots and angles. Hitchcock's filmography reflects not only a fascination with pronounced and extreme psychopathology (e.g., *Psycho*, 1960), but more important, an appreciation of more subtle psychological phenomena such as acting out, reaction formation, idealization, repression, and undoing. These defense mechanisms are depicted in Hitchcock's films *Shadow of a Doubt* (1943), *Spellbound* (1945), and *Marnie* (1964). Hitchcock's style is immensely popular and has been imitated frequently by other directors such as Brian DePalma and Roman Polanski.

The popular genre of **drama** is perhaps the most fertile ground for psychopathology to be portrayed in movies in a very realistic, engaging way. Every chapter in this book has numerous examples of drama films depicting psychological disorders. The range is vast from the slow-moving drama of *The Human Stain* (2003) and the disjointed, complex drama of *21 Grams* (2003) to the affectively engaging dramas of *Love Liza* (2002) and *Mystic River* (2003).

Mental illness is also depicted, although less often, in the genre of **documentary** films. Frederick Wiseman's *Titicut Follies* (1967) and the recent film, *Capturing the Friedmans* (2003) are clear examples of psychopathology being depicted in documentaries. It is interesting to contrast the former movie with the horror film *Bedlam* (1945) or the "docudramatic" films such as *The Snake Pit* (1948), *Pressure Point* (1962), and *One Flew Over the Cuckoo's Nest* (1975), all dealing with mental institutions and the treatment of people with mental illness. At least two heralded films, *The Three Faces of Eve* (1957) and *Sybil* (1976), provide viewers with full-scale case histories and the struggles between patient and psychiatrist. John Huston attempted to portray Sigmund Freud's personal struggles with and professional inquiries into the human psyche in his biographical film *Freud, the Secret Passion* (1962), the only complete cinematic work devoted to Freud and his work.

Table 1.2 Psychological Disorders and Movies that Portray Them

Category	Classic Film Example	Recent Film Example
Disorders of Childhood and Adolescence	*Kids* (1995)	*Thirteen* (2003)
Mental Retardation	*Sling Blade* (1996)	*I Am Sam* (2001)
Autism and Pervasive Developmental Disorders	*Rain Man* (1988)	*American Splendor* (2003)
Neuropsychological Disorders	*On Golden Pond* (1981)	*Memento* (2000)
Substance-Related Disorders	*The Lost Weekend* (1945)	*Love Liza* (2002)
Schizophrenia	*Clean, Shaven* (1994)	*A Beautiful Mind* (2001)
Mood Disorders	*Ordinary People* (1980)	*The Hours* (2002)
Anxiety Disorders	*Vertigo* (1958)	*Matchstick Men* (2003)
Somatoform Disorders	*Persona* (1966)	*Hollywood Ending* (2002)
Dissociative Disorders	*Psycho* (1960)	*Identity* (2003)
Sexual Disorders	*Lolita* (1962)	*Secretary* (2002)
Gender Identity Disorders	*Boys Don't Cry* (1999)	*Normal* (2003)
Eating Disorders	*The Best Little Girl in the World* (1982)	*Center Stage* (2000)
Sleep Disorders	*My Own Private Idaho* (1991)	*Insomnia* (2002)
Impulse-Control Disorders	*Marnie* (1964)	*Owning Mahowny* (2002)
Adjustment Disorders	*The Wrong Man* (1957)	*Best in Show* (2000)
Personality Disorders	*Fatal Attraction* (1987)	*One Hour Photo* (2002)

The **comedy** genre has its share of films portraying psychopathology. *Drop Dead Fred* (1991), *What About Bob?* (1991), *High Anxiety* (1977), *Hannah and Her Sisters* (1988), and *Scotland, PA* (2001) portray psychological aberrations with quirky humor that is used to defuse the sense of anxiety that is produced by the behavior of the lead characters in each of the films.

Misconceptions and Stereotypic Themes in Films

Otto Wahl, an authority in media psychology, summarizes the media's portrayal of mental illness in *Media Madness* (1995): "Overall, the mass media do a poor job of depicting mental illness, with misinformation frequently communicated, unfavorable stereotypes of people with mental illness predominating, and psychiatric terms used in inaccurate and offensive ways" (p. 12-13).

Steven Hyler (Hyler, Gabbard, & Schneider, 1991) has provided a compelling analysis of the portrayal of mental illness in films. In the 1991 article, Hyler and his colleagues describe six common stereotypes that perpetuate stigma. The first of these is that of the mental patient as **rebellious free spirit**. Examples of this portrayal can be found in films such as *Nuts* (1987), *The Dream Team* (1989), *The Couch Trip* (1989), *Francis* (1982), *An Angel At My Table* (1990), *Shine* (1996), and perhaps most clearly in *One Flew Over the Cuckoo's Nest* (1975).

The stereotype of the **homicidal maniac** is present in most of the slasher/horror films described earlier. However, the authors point out that this stereotype can also be traced back as far as D. W. Griffith's 1909 film *The Maniac Cook*, in which a psychotic employee attempts to kill an infant by cooking the child in an oven. *Sling Blade* (1996), a well-intentioned and sympathetic film about a man with mental retardation who commits a second murder after leaving a psychiatric hospital 25 years after murdering his mother and her lover, perpetuates the myth that people with mental illness and mental retardation are dangerous.

The patient as **seductress** is seen in films such as *The Caretakers* (1963) and *Dressed to Kill* (1980) and most clearly, in the 1964 film *Lilith*, which stars Warren Beatty as a hospital therapist who is seduced by a psychiatric patient played by Jean Seberg. The stereotype of the **enlightened member of society** is linked to the work of writers such as R. D. Laing and Thomas Szasz and is illustrated in films such as *King of Hearts* (1968) and *A Fine Madness* (1966). The **narcissistic parasite** stereotype presents people with mental disorders as self-centered, attention-seeking, and demanding. It is reflected in films such as *What About Bob?* (1991), *Annie Hall* (1977), *High Anxiety* (1977), and *Lovesick* (1983). Finally, the stereotype of **zoo specimen** is perpetuated by films that degrade people with mental illness by treating them as objects of derision or a source of amusement or entertainment for those who are "normal." Films that exemplify this stereotype include *Bedlam* (1948) and *Marat/Sade* (1966). A variation on this theme occurs in Brian De Palma's *Dressed to Kill* (1980), in which a psychotic and homicidal psychiatrist murders a nurse in a surrealistic amphitheater-like setting, with dozens of other patients sitting in the gallery and watching in silent approval.

Hyler (1988) describes three dominant themes in film that help establish stereotypes about the etiology of mental disorders. The first is the **presumption of traumatic etiology**. This theme reinforces the belief that a single traumatic event, most often occurring in childhood, can have profound ramifications on later life, often precipitating mental illness. Examples include the amnesia experienced by Gregory Peck that was eventually shown to be related to his role in the childhood death of his brother (revealed by Hitchcock in a dramatic and unforgettable flashback scene) in *Spellbound* (1945), and the dissociative identity disorder that resulted when a child was required to kiss the corpse of her dead grandmother in *The Three Faces of Eve* (1957). Other examples of this theme are found in films such as *Suddenly Last Summer* (1959), *Home of the Brave* (1949), *Nuts* (1987), and Robin William's character in *The Fisher King* (1991).

Hyler's second theme is that of the **schizophrenogenic parent**. This is a widely held myth that holds parents (most often, the mother) accountable for serious mental illness in their children. The National Alliance for the Mentally Ill (NAMI) has worked hard to dispel this unfounded

but pervasive belief, but it is deeply rooted in popular culture and commonplace in films. Examples include *Agnes of God* (1985), *Face to Face* (1976), *Sybil* (1980), *Carrie* (1976), *Frances* (1982), *Fear Strikes Out* (1957), and *Shine* (1995).

"Insanity runs in my family. It practically gallops."

Cary Grant in
***Arsenic and Old Lace* (1944)**

The final myth discussed by Hyler is that **harmless eccentricity is frequently labeled as mental illness and inappropriately treated**. We see this theme most vividly presented in the film *One Flew Over the Cuckoo's Nest* (1975). Jack Nicholson's character, Randle P. McMurphy, is charismatic, flamboyant, and colorful. The only diagnosis that seems at all appropriate is that of antisocial personality disorder, although it is not even clear that this is justified. However, once in the system he cannot get out, and he is eventually treated with electroconvulsive therapy and lobotomy, presumably as a way of punishing his misbehavior in the name of treatment. The same theme is found in two films released in 1996, *King of Hearts* and *A Fine Madness*, and in the more recent film *Chattahoochee* (1990). A related theme, that treatment in mental health facilities is actually a form of social control, is reflected in the work of Thomas Szasz (e.g., in books such as *The Myth of Mental Illness* and *Psychiatric Slavery*). It is also reflected in films depicting excesses in treatment such as the aversion therapies portrayed in *A Clockwork Orange* (1971). For a full list of misconceptions perpetrated in movies accompanied by film examples see Appendix E. Appendix F looks specifically at the mental health profession and delineates a list of both "balanced" and "unbalanced" portrayals of psychotherapists.

Psychopathology and its representation in films will be discussed in some detail in the chapters that follow. In general, we will follow the nosology of the American Psychiatric Association's *Diagnostic and Statistical Manual, Fourth Edition (DSM-IV)*. Appendix G includes a filmography broken down by diagnostic category. Readers who will take time to review some of the films included in Appendix G will find that the experience will supplement and enhance their understanding of psychopathology.

Chapter 2

Anxiety Disorders

I don't like being outdoors, which I know is called agoraphobia, right?...
I don't like it when people put shoes on my carpet. Obviously I have a lot of tics.
I find that very frustrating to say the least.
Certain things distract me; make me feel sick to my stomach.
Nicholas Cage in *Matchstick Men*

Questions to consider while watching *Matchstick Men*

- To what extent do/could medications help Roy's condition?
- If you were treating Roy, what type of therapeutic interventions would you utilize?
- Are there obvious inaccuracies in Cage's portrayal of OCD?
- Roy experiences symptoms of several anxiety disorders. How common do other anxiety disorders co-occur with OCD?
- What is the treatment of choice for OCD? Do Roy's comorbid symptoms compromise this treatment?
- The psychiatrist in the film gives Roy a nutritional supplement to treat his OCD, leading him to believe it is a psychotropic medication. Is this ever ethical? Are placebos ever clinically useful?
- The film suggests Roy's OCD, tic, and panic symptoms result from his estrangement from his daughter and the dishonesty of his profession. Would changing his profession and reconciling with his daughter result in relief of his symptoms?
- How important a role does avoidance (both cognitive and behavioral avoidance) play in the manifestation of OCD?
- Roy states he has been taking illegal medications to manage his symptoms. How common is it for patients to obtain medications outside the United States for treatment?
- How would you describe Roy's mental status in the final scene? Is the portrayal accurate?

Patient Evaluation

Patient's stated reason for coming: "I just found out I have a daughter and I don't know what to do. How am I supposed to know how to be a father? Oh yeah, my shrink sent me."

History of the present illness: Mr. Roy Waller is a 42-year-old, Caucasian man. He reports numerous obsessions and compulsions; these have been present for the past fifteen years. An example of one of his obsessions is the perceived need to do things a particular way for fear that "bad things will happen" if he completes the task incorrectly. He responds to his anxiety by performing a verbal, mental, and/or behavioral act such as counting to three in French while opening and closing a door three times before entering or leaving.

Roy experiences severe panic attacks related to perceived germs, dirt, messiness, or disorder in his life. He frequently hyperventilates at these times; he copes with these episodes by breathing slowly into a paper bag. He engages in extensive cleaning behavior when he is under duress. He dislikes being outdoors, near open windows or windows with the blinds drawn, and he avoids groups or virtually any gathering of people. His anxiety also manifests through tics in his left eye; under extreme stress, the tic appears in both eyes. At times, his entire body jerks and he makes grunting noises.

Past psychiatric illness, treatment, and outcomes: There is a family history of psychiatric illness in Roy's family. He stated his mother seemed to have many OCD qualities although she never sought treatment. Roy admits he has avoided interactions with mental health professionals for over a decade; he states his disdain for mental health professionals is the reason he turned to black-market medication.

Medical history: Roy recently depleted his supply of the (still undetermined) illegal medication he has been taking to treat his OCD symptoms. He currently takes one medicine for OCD and one anti-anxiety medicine to be used as needed. He has not been evaluated by a primary care physician in eight years. Roy's health status is very poor. He is a chain-smoker, smoking two packs of cigarettes per day. His eating habits are rigid and limited. He is plagued by insomnia.

Psychosocial history: Roy is a very isolated man. His last intimate relationship was over 14 years ago. It was with his wife of two years who divorced him when she became pregnant. He has not had contact with her throughout this time. He had made no effort to make contact with his daughter until she contacted him two weeks ago. Roy claims to have only one friend who is also his business partner. He reports being employed as an antique dealer for the last 20 years and describes the work as satisfying and enjoyable.

Drug and alcohol history: Roy repeated a strong history of alcohol use while he was married. He currently drinks small amounts of alcohol on occasion for "business meetings."

Behavioral observations: Roy arrived for the interview wearing a dark suit with a handkerchief in his pocket that he uses "for doorknobs, phones, and other miscellaneous objects that arise in my environment." He was agitated and restless throughout the interview, particularly when speaking about his daughter or ex-wife. He stood up and paced around the room at these times. His eye contact was fair, but he avoided eye contact when speaking about his job in the antique business. Affect and mood were anxious. Although generally cooperative, Roy would sometimes raise his voice in the middle of sentences in a mildly threatening way.

Roy seemed very precise and rigid in his movements and body language. He frequently mumbled to himself and displayed tics as he reflected on his responses. He was immediately bothered by the therapist's open window and said he could not continue until it was closed. During the interview, Roy pointed out numerous flaws in the office: a slightly crooked picture, areas of the carpet that were worn, and books misaligned on the bookshelves. He became upset when he was not allowed to smoke in the office.

Mental status examination: Roy is fully oriented to person, place, time, and situation. There was no evidence of thought disorder or psychotic processes during the examination. Roy denies homicidal and suicidal ideation. He was able to repeat serial sevens without difficulty. Short- and long-term memory appear to be intact. There are no difficulties with naming or repetition. The patient can follow both verbal and written commands. He writes well, and there is no evidence of construction dyspraxia. He attained a perfect score of 30 on the Mini Mental Status Examination.

Functional assessment: Roy is able to adequately take care of himself, however, this ability is seriously compromised as his stress levels elevate and symptoms exacerbate. At times, his obsessions and compulsions become so debilitating that he escapes by staying in bed for several days at a time—this has happened on three occasions that he can remember. This occasional inability to work has a dramatic impact on his work life and keeps him socially isolated.

Strengths: Roy is very excited (though also anxious) about the prospect of developing a relationship with his daughter. They seem to have gotten along well on the two occasions when they have met. Roy is a bright and clever man and has some motivation to get better. He has sufficient insight into the reality of his psychological conditions to be able to change.

Diagnosis: Obsessive-Compulsive Disorder; Tic Disorder NOS; Panic Disorder with Agoraphobia (Rule Out); Antisocial Personality Disorder (Rule Out)

Treatment plan: (1) Weekly psychotherapy to first establish better rapport and trust, followed by education on OCD and OCD treatment, and skill-building in the arenas of cognitive, emotional, and behavioral skills to manage anxiety; (2) Creation of an appropriate exposure hierarchy to implement in vivo exposure and response prevention for various anxiety symptoms; (3) Lifestyle adjustment to improve nutrition, sleep, and self-care habits, particularly as anxiety elevates; (4) Continued regular meetings and medication management with his psychiatrist; (5) Consultation with a primary care physician for a medical evaluation to rule out any undiagnosed physical illness.

Prognosis: Due to the particular strengths mentioned above, Roy's prognosis is good. I'm concerned that his motivation may be situation-specific, which will limit his prognosis. This issue needs to be explored further.

Anxiety Disorders

Aaron Beck (1976) wrote "Anxiety is generally considered not only a universal emotion but a mark of a man's humanness" (p. 132). Most psychologists and philosophers would agree with Beck. The experience of anxiety is often a normal reaction to a situation or stressor, a motivator for performance, and a healthy warning signal of danger or something that needs attention.

Panic Attacks

Panic attacks result in extreme fear and discomfort, and the individual experiencing the attack may believe that he or she is literally going to lose control, go crazy or die. Panic attacks occur with many of the anxiety disorders. Essentially, a panic attack can be said to occur when an individual experiences intense fear or discomfort with accompanying symptoms such as palpitations, accelerated heart rate, sweating, trembling, shortness of breath, a feeling of choking or smothering, chest pain, nausea, dizziness, lightheadedness, derealization or depersonalization, fear of losing control, fear of dying, numbness or tingling sensations, and/or chills or hot flushes.

Panic Disorder

When panic attacks occur on a regular and unpredictable basis, a diagnosis of panic disorder may be appropriate. These episodes are not associated with any particular situation or event (such as public speaking); instead, they seem to come from nowhere. The fact that they seemingly occur anywhere and anytime is one of the reasons that panic disorder is such a debilitating condition. Many patients can vividly recall their first panic attack.

Some people will have daily panic episodes, while others may be able to go for weeks or months without experiencing panic. People experiencing panic disorder frequently believe they are having heart attacks or experiencing symptoms associated with some other undiagnosed medical problems. In fact, many people with panic disorder wind up being treated for unrelated conditions before their true problem is diagnosed. Likewise, patients with genuine medical conditions, such as **mitral valve prolapse**, are sometimes erroneously diagnosed as having panic disorder.

Robert De Niro plays a mob boss with panic disorder (without agoraphobia) who meets with a psychiatrist, played by Billy Crystal in both *Analyze This* (1999) and *Analyze That* (2002). Paul Vitti (De Niro) believes he is suffering a heart attack, but Dr. Ben Sobel (Crystal) explains the important difference between a panic attack and a heart attack and eventually helps Vitti get in touch with the deeper pains and sufferings that trigger his attacks. Though Vitti resolves some important issues in his life, this therapeutic approach risks misleading the viewer into believing this is the typical treatment for panic disorder; in fact, empirically validated treatments for panic look very different than the treatment Vitti receives.

In the popular HBO television series, *The Sopranos*, New Jersey gangster Tony Soprano (James Gandolfini) is treated for panic attacks by psychiatrist Jennifer Melfi (Lorraine Bracco). The series portrays realistic psychotherapy settings, and it illustrates the process of **transference** in Tony Soprano's frequent sexual fantasies about his therapist.

In *Something's Gotta Give* (2003) Jack Nicholson experiences panic attacks on two separate occasions. This film makes the point that panic can often present with symptoms very similar to those accompanying a heart attack; the cause of Nicholson's panic appears to be relational stress with co-star, Diane Keaton.

In *Panic Room* (2002), Meg (Jody Foster) and her young daughter, Sarah, move into an extravagant mansion on the Upper West side of Manhattan and while spending their first night in their new home, three crooks, expecting an empty house, break in hoping to steal millions of dollars. Meg and Sarah find refuge in the steel-plated, impervious "panic room" which holds both the money and their safety. The viewer sees Meg experiencing symptoms of a phobic disorder as she shows difficulty breathing and her face expresses fear when she becomes enclosed in the panic room for the first time in a non-threatening situation and her daughter says "Mom you're not gonna wig out, are you?" When confronted with a dangerous situation, Meg shows resiliency and her panic is justified. It is interesting to note that the stress of the situation triggers Sarah's anxiety and causes a hypoglycemic response so severe her faces changes color.

In *Lady in a Cage* (1964), Olivia de Havilland stars as Mrs. Hilyard, an upper class woman who is trapped inside her home elevator when the electricity in her house goes out. In making a call for help, she attracts thieves who rob her and try to hurt her.

The film melodramatically and metaphorically represents claustrophobia and panic attacks.

Panic attacks are also frequently depicted in a realistic way but with only a minor role in the overall story, as in *Das Experiment* (2001), *My First Mister* (2001), *Monster's Ball* (2001), and *Hannah and Her Sisters* (1986).

Agoraphobia

Individuals who are agoraphobic are afraid of being vulnerable and experiencing an anxiety attack in open, insecure places. More specifically, the individual suffering from **panic disorder with agoraphobia** is afraid of the perceived consequences of a panic attack (e.g., losing control, going crazy or dying) and finds ways to limit his or her life to avoid panic attacks. The avoidance can be quite subtle (e.g., these individuals may be able to leave the home comfortably if they leave with a person perceived to be "safe" and whose presence would somehow magically protect them from the catastrophic consequences of a panic attack). Although the word agoraphobia comes from the Greek work for fear of the marketplace, the idea that people with agoraphobia fear all "open places" is incorrect; the person may associate any number of situations or places with fear of panic attacks. This should be differentiated from the individual with **agoraphobia without panic** who may experience catastrophic fears related to other physiological experiences such as fainting, vomiting, headaches, etc. These individuals are not fearful of panic attacks; however, the avoidance seen in these situations can be identical to the avoidance in those who are attempting to avoid panic attacks. With both disorders, the individual is literally housebound and cannot leave the perceived safety of their home. In extreme cases, people with agoraphobia are unable to leave their bedrooms.

An important diagnostic consideration is illustrated by Nicholas Cage's character Roy in *Matchstick Men*. In addition to OCD, it is clear Roy has panic attacks and avoids public places: nevertheless, these symptoms are not sufficient to justify a diagnosis of agoraphobia. There must also be an intense fear of experiencing panic attacks, and it is unclear from the film if Roy has this fear. If the latter criterion is not met, it is more likely he is experiencing *situational* panic due to his fear of contamination.

Sean Connery's character William Forrester in *Finding Forrester* (2000) could probably be diagnosed with Panic Disorder with Agoraphobia (he also has characteristics of Avoidant Personality, an often challenging differentiation to make with Anxiety Disorders). Forrester does not leave his apartment (in part out of a fear he will have a panic attack in public), is socially awkward, and experiences panic when he is required to go into a public place. He does what many people with agoraphobia do—he has his groceries delivered so he does not have to leave his apartment. The film captures the subjective experience associated with Forrester's panic attacks when the camera shows Forrester's "spinning" feeling, and sound is blurred. In the throes of his anxiety, Forrester wanders off and gets lost. At the end of the film, the viewer sees the potential for successful treatment of agoraphobia when Forrester is shown riding his bike on busy and crowded streets.

One of the best cinematic portrayals of agoraphobia is found in Robert Taicher's movie *Inside Out* (1986). In this film, Elliott Gould plays Jimmy Morgan, a New York businessman with marked agoraphobia who has not left his house for ten years. He has food delivered to him, arranges for call girls to come to his apartment for anonymous sex, places bets over the phone, and almost never ventures out of his house until forced to by circumstances beyond his control.

It is important to differentiate between true agoraphobia (which is driven by a strong desire to avoid the perceived catastrophic consequences associated with symptoms of anxiety that occur whenever one leaves a safe area) and the isolation, withdrawal, and seclusion that result from thought disorders such as paranoid schizophrenia. One of the authors once ran an evening support group for a group of high-functioning patients with agoraphobia. When an announcement of the group was made in the local paper, one person called and requested an opportunity to participate. However, a brief telephone interview disclosed that the woman was genuinely concerned about being eaten by aliens if she ventured far from her home. This was *not* agoraphobia.

Specific Phobia

Specific phobia occurs when a person has an excessive or unreasonable fear of an object or situation and the anxiety-provoking stimulus is avoided. Various subtypes of this disorder include animals (i.e., dogs, insects), natural environment (i.e., storms, water), blood-injection/injury (i.e., medical procedures), situational (i.e., bridges, elevators), or other miscellaneous stimuli (i.e., situation that might lead to choking).

Vertigo

Vertigo (1958) is a classic Alfred Hitchcock film that stars Jimmy Stewart as John Ferguson, a San Francisco police detective, who is paralyzed by his fear of heights. The phobia has a traumatic etiology: while chasing a criminal across a rooftop, John almost falls to his death. A fellow officer, trying to aid John, is killed when he plunges to the street below. John, overcome with guilt, develops **acrophobia**, a debilitating fear of heights. The term *vertigo* refers to either marked dizziness or a confused, disoriented state of mind. Both meanings apply in this complex and engrossing film.

At one point in the film, John designs his own behavior modification program, stating, "I have a theory that I can work up to heights a little bit at a time." He puts a stepladder near the window, stands on the first step, waits, gets down, stands on the second step, waits, goes to the third step, becomes frightened and dizzy, and then falls to the floor.

The plot of *Vertigo* is complex and detailed. John is hired as a private detective and given the job of trailing Madeleine (Kim Novak) around San Francisco. He soon falls in love with her. Madeleine eventually leads him to a mission at San Juan Batista. She ascends the bell tower and inexplicably jumps to her death. John, unable to assist in any way because of his paralyzing acrophobia, watches helplessly.

John responds to Madeleine's death by becoming so anxious and confused that he has to be hospitalized. When he leaves the hospital, he becomes enamored with a woman who appears to be an identical twin to Madeleine. Later in the film we learn that the woman *is* Madeleine, and that the earlier suicide had been faked.

Trying for a second time to treat his phobia, John insists that Madeleine accompany him as he confronts his fear and ascends the mission bell tower. However, when they are at the top, a nun dressed in black appears and startles Madeleine, who jumps back from the figure and falls to her death. John has overcome his acrophobia, but only at tremendous personal cost.

Anxiety, Fears and Phobias

Anxiety is a normal part of life, and specific fears are sometimes justified. Spiders can bite us;

people do fall from high spaces; and even small cats can scratch us. Existential writers and psychologists have made the point that anxiety is an expected part of the human condition. However, when anxiety becomes socially or occupationally debilitating, a psychiatric label and treatment may be justified.

Fears are labeled as phobias only when specific conditions are met. Marked anxiety must be present in the presence of the phobic stimulus and must routinely occur with exposure to the stimulus. In addition, the phobic individual must generally be aware that the magnitude of the fear response is excessive. Most people with specific phobias will avoid the stimulus situations that leave them fearful to avoid the extreme distress they experience in these situations.

Many phobias are triggered by a specific traumatic event (at least traumatic to the individual experiencing the event). This was clearly the situation in *Vertigo*. Specific phobias will occasionally remit spontaneously in the absence of treatment, but this is relatively rare.

Mel Brooks' character in *High Anxiety* (1977) suffers from severe acrophobia which generalizes to a fear of planes, escalators, elevators, higher numbered floors in hotels, and any high places where he can look down. He experiences dizziness, nausea, and vertigo in these situations.

Social Phobias

Intense and persistent fears of criticism and rejection characterize social phobias. People with social phobias experience anxiety in response to the possibility of or perception of thoughts of negative evaluation or scrutiny, and consequently they avoid situations in which they are likely to be observed by others. The disorder can take many different forms and occurs in situations that require public speaking, public performance, test taking, or social skills. Some male patients with social phobias are unable to urinate in public places (also called **paruresis**), as shown briefly in *Roger Dodger* (2002); other patients are unable to eat in public for fear they will make a mistake and be ridiculed. The disorder is related to common phenomena such as performance anxiety, stage fright, and shyness. When fears relate to almost *every* social situation, the social phobia is considered "generalized."

The onset of social phobias typically occurs in childhood or adolescence and the clinical course, if left untreated, is usually chronic, unremitting, and associated with significant impairment. Few people with social anxiety seek professional help (Van Ameringen et al., 2003).

Social phobics sometimes experience panic attacks in anticipation of social interaction or during the experience. The symptoms of social phobia include tachycardia, trembling, sweating, blushing, dizziness, and hyperventilation. Even more distressing is the sensation of impending doom that frequently occurs. Finally, patients feel an overwhelming need to escape from the social situation that is causing their distress.

Anticipatory anxiety about social situations often sets up a self-fulfilling prophecy. The phobic individual worries excessively about the performance demands of an upcoming event, loses sleep worrying about the situation, becomes tremendously anxious just before the event, and in fact performs poorly in the actual situation because of the high levels of anxiety. This poor performance then confirms the individual's beliefs about his or her inability to perform adequately in these situations, and their fear is exacerbated, causing them to perform even more poorly in similar situations in the future.

Social phobias are portrayed or implied in numerous films. In *Coyote Ugly* (2000), a young woman, Violet, moves to New York City to try to make it as a songwriter. Her social anxiety disorder keeps her from reaching her full potential so she takes a job as a "coyote" bartender at a wild nightclub. At this bar she begins to perform in front of large groups, deliberately "exposing" herself to those situations that she fears; moreover, her boyfriend helps desensitize her by having her sing in the dark. It is this exposure that helps her manage and work through her anxiety symptoms. In the film's climax, she begins to get stage fright while performing and attempts to leave the stage; however, when the lights are turned off she is able to perform and she continues performing when the lights come back on. Violet believes the etiology of her social phobia is genetic; her mother also went to NYC to be a singer but left because of her own social phobia, and Violet believes she is carrying a "gene" for her inability to sing in front of others and her other avoidance symptoms. After she is able to perform, Violet learns it was her father who encouraged her mother to move home, and her mother never had a social phobia.

The painfully shy woman is a common film motif found in *Amelie* (2001), *Lonely Hearts* (1981), *Rocky* (1976), *The Fisher King* (1991), and *I've Heard the Mermaids Singing* (1987). Shy and socially unskilled men are portrayed in *The Shape of Things* (2003), *Dummy* (2002), *Marty* (1955), *Untamed Heart* (1993), *Awakenings* (1990), *Goodbye, Mr. Chips* (1939), *Howard's End* (1992), *The Remains of the Day* (1993), and all of the Charlie Chaplin films in which he played the Little Tramp. The ways in which two shy adolescents come to grips with their emerging sexuality and a racist society are portrayed in a wonderful Australian film, *Flirting* (1990).

Obsessive-Compulsive Disorder

People with **obsessive-compulsive disorder** are troubled by obsessions and/or compulsions. These thoughts and/or behaviors take up a significant amount of time, cause considerable distress to the individual, and frequently interfere with occupational or social adjustment. In severe cases, an obsessive-compulsive disorder can come to dominate virtually every minute of an individual's life.

Obsessions are defined as "recurrent and persistent thoughts, impulses, or images that are experienced . . . as intrusive and inappropriate and cause marked anxiety or distress" (*DSM-IV-TR*). These experiences are of greater magnitude than the everyday worry that is part of almost all our lives. Although people with obsessive-compulsive disorders try to suppress these thoughts, the very act of suppression serves to exacerbate the condition. Finally, it is important to appreciate that people with obsessions experience the thoughts as disagreeable and alien to their own sense of self (i.e., ego-dystonic).

Common obsessional themes include harming others (especially children or helpless individuals), contamination with germs or feces, exposure to toxins or infectious diseases such as AIDS, blasphemous thoughts (such as thinking the Virgin Mary is a whore), and sexual misbehavior. Obsessions can also coexist with post-traumatic stress disorders and may sometimes have traumatic etiologies.

Compulsions are repetitive behaviors or thoughts that serve to reduce the discomfort associated with the obsession. Sometimes there is a logical connection between the compulsive behavior and the event it is supposed to prevent (for example, repeated hand washing *may* help prevent contamination from germs). However, in other cases there is no logical connection between the two (e.g., the patient who feels a compulsive need to sing the first few lines of a popular commercial before pulling away from every stoplight knows there is no meaningful connection between the behavior and the likelihood of an accident).

Either compulsions or obsessions are sufficient to justify the diagnosis of OCD; however, it is common for these two problems to occur in tandem, and the vast majority of patients present with both problems. It is often evident that the compulsion addresses the individual's need to find some way to cope with his or her obsession. For example, one patient had an obsession that involved the belief that he would drive over the body of a child lying in the road. In order to cope with this distressing image, he would circle the block whenever he hit a bump in order to ensure that he had not hit a child. This patient would spend hours getting to work each day because of his compulsive need to check and recheck every bump in the road.

In addition to *Matchstick Men*, another excellent portrayal of a person with obsessive-compulsive disorder is found in Melvin Udall, the character Jack Nicholson plays in *As Good As It Gets* (1997). Melvin is a misogynist and a homophobe, and he has a pronounced obsession with cleanliness. He eats every day at the same restaurant, sits at the same table, insists on the same waitress (Helen Hunt) and always orders the same meal. Udall always brings his own paper-wrapped plastic utensils to this restaurant, so he does not have to risk contamination from unclean silverware. Whenever anything disrupts this well-established routine, Udall becomes anxious and belligerent. He wipes off door handles before opening doors, and he carefully avoids stepping on cracks as he walks to his therapist's office. Nicholson's obsessions are his repetitive thoughts about germs and disease; his compulsions are the ritualistic behaviors he engages in as a consequence of his thoughts. Patients with OCD frequently have multiple obsessions, and the film *As Good As It Gets* presents a realistic presentation of the disorder (with the possible exception that a patient with an obsession about cleanliness as severe as that present in Nicholson's character would be unlikely to handle a small dog).

It is extremely rare to find a film that depicts OCD patients who are compulsive hand-washers. One exception is a short film called *Waiting for Ronald* (2003). It is a simple film about a man, Ronald, leaving a supervised residence to take a bus to live in the community with his friend, Edgar. Both men have developmental disabilities. Edgar has OCD and he is a compulsive hand-washer. He is very precise in the way he places his hat, fixes the folds in the hat, and places objects in his bag. He arrives early at the bus stop, and since Ronald misses the first bus, Edgar has to wait longer. Meanwhile, Edgar has a strong need to use the restroom which he finally does, knowing he might miss Ronald's arrival. Edgar begins to wash his hands and continues repeatedly even though he has heard the bus arrive. He wants to stop washing but cannot; his anguish is palpable. He winces and struggles, moaning in mental pain. He washes his hands harder, crying, trying to push himself away from the sink. The viewer can clearly see the pain and suffering the hand-washing causes him. Edgar coaches himself over and over (with the words and name of his therapist), "You can do it. Joe says you can do it… just breathe." Eventually, he slowly pulls his hands away from the sink one hand at a time.

The comedy, *What About Bob?* (1991) stars Bill Murray as a patient with multiple problems, including overwhelming anxiety when he cannot be close to his therapist, played by Richard Dreyfuss. Hoarding, an occasional symptom of obsessive compulsive disorder, is portrayed in Harvey Pekar, the comic strip artist portrayed in *American Splendor* (2003).

For details about the treatment of OCD (and other anxiety disorders) as depicted in films and movies used to treat OCD via the strategy of *in vivo* **exposure and response prevention**, see Chapter 15: Treatment.

Post-Traumatic Stress Disorder

Post-traumatic stress disorders (PTSD) occur after exposure to traumatic events. The individual with a post-traumatic stress disorder must have personally witnessed or experienced some event that involved actual or threatened death or serious injury and must have responded with "intense fear, helplessness, or horror" (*DSM-IV-TR*). The traumatic event is then re-experienced by the individual in the form of nightmares, recurrent recollections, and flashbacks or as physiological distress. The PTSD victim works hard to avoid these recurrent experiences. In addition, the individual usually experiences sleep disturbance, irritability, difficulty concentrating, hypervigilance, or an exaggerated startle response.

Military combat is a common cause of post-traumatic stress disorder, but the disorder can also occur in response to earthquakes, fires or floods, mugging, rape, the witnessing of violence, or any of a variety of other traumatic situations. Often, seemingly innocuous stimuli will cause an individual to relive the anxiety-producing experience; for example, hearing a car backfire may trigger a terrifying war memory of combat for a war veteran.

Many victims of combat or natural disasters experience what is sometimes referred to as **survivor guilt**. People might feel guilty when they realize that their lives were spared while those of more "worthy" individuals (e.g., children, young parents) were taken. Consider Tom Cruise's character Ron Kovic, who would meet the criteria for PTSD, in *Born on the Fourth of July* (1989). Kovic's guilt about the death of his buddy "Wilson" is an example of survivor guilt.

Suicide and suicide attempts are common in patients with post-traumatic stress disorder. In addition, it is essential to assess for comorbidity (especially substance abuse) in cases of post-traumatic stress disorder. Nearly all post-traumatic stress disorder patients who are suicidal will be found to have a concomitant psychiatric condition.

The movie *Fearless* (1993) provides an interesting picture of a somewhat unusual reaction to trauma. Jeff Bridges is one of a small group of survivors of a devastating plane crash. Bridges assists a number of other passengers and is celebrated as a hero and a saint. He becomes convinced he is invulnerable, and he grows increasingly impatient with the banal concerns of his wife and child. After a near-death experience precipitated by an allergic reaction to strawberries, he returns to normal and reestablishes a loving relationship with his wife and son. The movie includes a very interesting segment in which a psychiatrist (who is employed by the airlines because he has written a best-selling book about post-traumatic stress disorder) leads a discussion group for survivors of the crash.

Kevin Spacey's portrayal of Prot, a spiritual man who claims to be from another planet, presents a diagnostic enigma in *K-Pax* (2001). One way to view the film (other ways are discussed in Chapters 3 and 9) is that this character has PTSD. The viewer learns through flashbacks that Prot is Robert Porter, a man who experiences trauma when he returns home to find his wife and daughter murdered and the killer still in the home. Prot/Porter re-experiences the trauma under hypnosis and displays highly significant physiological arousal (e.g., a racing heart rate, elevated blood pressure) when his psychiatrist (Jeff Bridges) forces him to recall the traumatic incident. Porter engaged in extensive avoidance following the

trauma—denial, estrangement from his home town, inability to recall information, and a restricted range of affect.

In *The Fisher King* (1991), Robin Williams plays a former college professor who becomes homeless and psychotic after witnessing his wife gunned down in a restaurant. However, the sort of active, well-formed, and specific hallucinations Williams experiences (e.g., a red knight riding a horse in Central Park with flames shooting out of his head) would be very unlikely to occur as a result of a traumatic experience. The character Jeff Bridges plays in the same film, a disc jockey who withdraws from life and abuses alcohol and drugs after a traumatic event, presents a far more realistic portrayal of post-traumatic stress disorder. Although *The Fisher King* is imprecise and confusing in the way it links trauma to psychosis, post-traumatic stress disorder is common among people who are homeless. The prevalence of posttraumatic stress disorder in persons with severe mental illness is estimated to be 34%. However, the prevalence of PTSD is even higher in patients who are young, white, homeless and unemployed. PTSD may actually contribute to substance abuse, psychiatric and medical comorbidity, and psychiatric and health service utilization (Mueser et al., 2004).

The stressors experienced by homeless people are illustrated in the films *Ironweed* (1987) and *The Saint of Fort Washington* (1993). *Ironweed* (1987) is a compelling film in which Jack Nicholson plays an alcoholic whose drinking is apparently related to his guilt about dropping and killing his infant son. Many of the symptoms of PTSD have become obliterated by Nicholson's alcoholism, which has become the dominant theme in his life. *Ironweed* illustrates the way in which alcohol abuse can develop as a secondary problem in response to trauma and then can become the primary psychological problem as abuse progresses to addiction.

Dozens of movies have been made about the Vietnam War, and many of these (as well as other war movies) illustrate either acute stress disorders or, more commonly in those that follow the hero home after the war, post-traumatic stress disorder. Some of the most powerful of these films are *Born on the Fourth of July* (1989), *Coming Home* (1978), *The Deer Hunter* (1978), *Apocalypse Now* (1979), *The Killing Fields* (1984), *Platoon* (1986), *Hamburger Hill* (1987), and *Full Metal Jacket* (1987).

In the original version of *The Manchurian Candidate* (1962), Frank Sinatra plays a brainwashed trauma victim who has recurring nightmares. He wakes up screaming with extensive sweating and a recollection of traumatic dreams that seem real. In a recent remake of *The Manchurian Candidate* (2004), director Jonathon Demme updates the film by including contemporary politics and more recent wartime experiences. Denzel Washington plays a Major who returns from the Gulf War with PTSD, paranoia, nightmares, and memories he cannot understand. He displays flat affect when he describes events surrounding the war, and he experiences intrusive memories. He becomes obsessed with trying to uncover the truth about what happened to him and his men. He hallucinates blood oozing from the forehead of a woman and has a flashback to a time when he was seeing a hypnotist; this symbolizes a real memory coming back and triggers a panic attack. He slowly begins to put together the sinister pieces of a political plot that involved extensive trauma and torture as well as physical and psychological abuse and brain-washing.

PTSD symptoms are also displayed by Nicole Kidman's character in *The Human Stain* (2003), *Open Hearts* (2003), *The Princess and the Warrior* (2000), and *The Pawnbroker* (1965). The latter film portrays a defeated concentration camp survivor who has become numb and indifferent in response to wartime experiences that included seeing his wife raped and his children killed.

Acute Stress Disorder

Acute Stress Disorder is in many ways similar to post-traumatic stress disorder. However, acute stress disorder occurs relatively quickly after the traumatic event (within no more than four weeks) and may resolve quickly or develop into PTSD. In contrast, the symptoms of PTSD by definition have to last more than a month, and the onset of symptoms may occur months or even years after exposure to trauma. Marisa Tomei's character in *In the Bedroom* (2001) experiences a traumatic event when her boyfriend is murdered by her estranged husband. In a later scene, she is shown as depressed and expressionless.

Generalized Anxiety Disorder

Some people are characterologically anxious; they walk around with a sense of apprehension and experience physiological arousal in a variety of different situations. They display what is sometimes called **free-floating anxiety**. They can be very unhappy, and their condition quite debilitating. These individuals frequently receive a diagnosis of **generalized anxiety disorder**; the diagnosis requires that worry and anxiety be present more days than not.

Anxiety symptoms associated with generalized anxiety disorder include the same physiological, cognitive, and behavioral symptoms associated with other anxiety disorders, but the symptoms are chronic. The individual with this disorder may have multiple somatic complaints such as tachycardia, a dry mouth, and gastrointestinal distress. He or she will worry constantly about the multiple things that can go wrong in life and may be irritable and short-tempered because of anxiety. The lifetime prevalence of generalized anxiety disorder in the general population is about 5 percent, but relatively few of these patients actively seek out treatment. Onset of symptoms typically occurs in childhood or adolescence.

Nicholas Cage plays two twin brothers, Charlie and Donald, in *Adaptation* (2002). Both brothers are screenwriters, but one much more neurotic than the other. No makeup or artistic tricks are used to differentiate the two twins; instead, Cage's talent alone is sufficient to portray both the worried and neurotic Charlie and the easy-going Donald. This provides a nice contrast for people studying anxiety. Charlie anxiously struggles with writer's block and he is plagued with self-doubt and preoccupation with himself, both hallmark symptoms of generalized anxiety disorder. In another scene, Charlie is too anxious to approach an attractive woman played by Meryl Streep. The viewer learns about Charlie's anxiety, worry, and rumination not only through cinematic close-ups displaying his anxiety symptoms (e.g., sweating), but also through the voice-over indicating his thought processes. A major theme of this film speaks to how people try to "adapt" to circumstance, problems, and, in this case, anxiety.

Kissing Jessica Stein (2002) explores sexuality and relationships through the character of a New York journalist, Jessica Stein, who is tired of the dating scene and its limited offerings. She places an ad for "women seeking women" and meets a woman who turns out to be a great match. As their relationship develops, Jessica must battle her own neuroses about a lesbian relationship as well as her feelings for an ex-boyfriend who is still in love with her. Jessica experiences generalized anxiety as a worrier and classic neurotic. She is uptight and rigid, and very anxious about anything new or different. She does not have the self confidence necessary to defend herself when she is criticized in public. She rarely stands up for herself and is unable to be honest to family or friends about her female lover. Jessica describes her experiences with panic attacks and mentions various other anxiety symptoms. She stumbles over her words and tries to control situations in which she becomes nervous. After reading a book about lesbians she realizes she is afraid of both sexuality and sensuality. Her anxiety is particularly noticeable at the dinner table prior to a family member's wedding; she is preoccupied with what people think of her and is unable to be honest, covering up the truth with repeated lies. This film emphasizes honesty, individuality and the potential for change.

Most Woody Allen comedies will include at least one character with an anxiety disorder, and many depict characters with generalized anxiety disorder (usually played by Woody Allen, himself). Indeed, neurotic, insecure, and self-absorbed characters and the existential anxiety produced by the need to cope with a complex and impersonal world form the basis for much of Allen's humor. *Annie Hall* (1977) and *Manhattan* (1979) are the Woody Allen films that best illustrate generalized anxiety disorder.

Mel Brooks' now classic film *High Anxiety* (1977) makes fun of numerous movies with Hitchcock-like psychological motifs. Mel Brooks plays Dr. Richard H. Thorndyke, an anxiety-ridden psychiatrist, who takes over a prestigious mental institution, "The Psycho-Neurotic Institute for the Very Very Nervous." Thorndyke must battle unethical and murderous staff in order to save his patients and himself. Meanwhile he struggles with his own generalized anxiety and phobias.

International Films:
Anxiety Disorders

Elling

The Norwegian film, *Elling* (2001) presents an honest and fair portrayal of what it is like to cope with the debilitating effects of mental illness. A small, feeble man named Elling is taken to a psychiatric hospital after his mother, who was his caregiver for 40 years, dies. It is there Elling meets another eccentric, Kjell, who has sexual obsessions about women and problems with anger management. The two men are discharged together and placed in supportive housing under the guidance of a social worker. The film is about their return to the

reality of everyday living. Each man must prove he can live on his own.

Elling states he has two enemies: dizziness and anxiety; "they follow me everywhere." He refuses to leave his house and believes he is unable to answer the phone (even when it is only the social worker checking in). He has learned to be completely dependent on his mother and the hospital staff, so it is a great achievement when he is able to walk to the end of the block to go to a store. Further challenges are met when Elling begins to talk on the phone, eat at a restaurant, and go on a vacation. Elling takes another big risk in battling his anxiety by going to a public poetry reading; arriving several hours early, he befriends an isolated, famous poet. Elling is rigid in his behavior, worries constantly, and is terrified of losing his only friend Kjell to Kjell's new girlfriend. Elling expresses this fear in jealous passive-aggressiveness whenever he feels he has been left out or abandoned. His friendship with Kjell develops and deepens as they sacrifice for one another and stick together through the difficult times. "Hard work pays off" is a theme applied to the psychological challenges Elling and Kjell face. Rather than avoiding their fears, they face them and in turn, find freedom—freedom from dependency, from the hospital, and from isolation.

The interaction between the social worker, Frank, and Elling is noteworthy and inspirational. Frank sets firm boundaries and gives clear directives to Elling, taking a "tough love" approach that emphasizes that Elling must take chances to challenge himself or he will lose his new residence. Frank is accepting and understanding of Elling's eccentric ideas, and tolerant at the film's end when he walks into the home and finds Elling lying on the couch, drunk, and having thrown up on himself. Elling awakens and believes he is sure to lose his house and his freedom; instead, the opposite happens because this all too human behavior confirms in Frank's mind Elling's readiness to live on his own in the outside world.

Walking on Water

In the Australian film *Walking on Water* (2002), an assisted-suicide plan for a man dying of AIDS goes awry and a friend forcefully suffocates the dying man. The friend is plagued by intrusive images and memories of the suffocation; he tries hard to avoid his memories, acts out in self-destructive ways, and displays considerable irritability and interpersonal conflict. He appears to be suffering from an acute stress disorder.

Critical Thinking Questions

- How does post-traumatic stress disorder differ from the problems faced in previous wars that resulted in conditions such as "shell shock" and "combat fatigue?"
- Some existential therapists such as Irvin Yalom and Rollo May have argued that anxiety is an essential part of the human condition, and that it needs to be confronted rather than avoided (e.g., they discourage the use of benzodiazepines after the experience of intense trauma). Do you agree?
- Drugs like Valium can be addictive, as illustrated by the film *I'm Dancing As Fast As I Can* (1982). Have you known anyone who has abused anxiolytic medications? How did you know?
- Do you believe general practitioners are too quick to prescribe anxiolytics for people having difficulty coping with the day-to-day stresses of modern life?
- Does a system that pays veterans who develop psychiatric disorders while in service in subtle ways actually reinforce the illness behaviors and minimize the likelihood of people overcoming these problems?
- Are there some occupations in which it might be adaptive to have an obsessive-compulsive disorder?
- What are the things you fear the most? What differentiates these fears from those experienced by someone with a phobia? Is the difference qualitative or merely quantitative?
- Some people believe you can overcome your fears by confrontation. For example, some parents help their children overcome a fear of water by tossing them in the deep end of the pool. Are these methods likely to be successful?
- Do we normally fear things themselves (e.g., spiders) or what they symbolize?
- Have you ever felt a compulsive need to behave in a certain way (e.g., checking twice or three times to ensure the door is locked before you leave for a vacation)?
- What is the influence of genetics on the likelihood of developing an anxiety disorder?
- How common is it for people to treat their own anxiety with alcohol (e.g., having a drink or two before giving a speech)?

Chapter 3

Dissociative and Somatoform Disorders

> *Matricide is probably the most unbearable crime of all...*
> *so he had to erase the crime, at least in his own mind.*
> A police psychiatrist attempts to explain
> Norman Bates' behavior in *Psycho*

Questions to consider while watching *Psycho*

- Hitchcock's Psycho is one of the greatest films ever made. Is it an accurate presentation of mental illness?
- Do films like Psycho do a disservice to people with mental disorders by perpetuating the myth of the homicidal psychopath?
- Bates' voyeurism seems almost innocuous compared with his other behaviors. How often are paraphilias (such as voyeurism) linked with violence?
- Bates has trouble saying the word "bathroom" when he shows the hotel room to Marion (Janet Leigh). Is it common for people who commit sexual crimes to be uncomfortable with mature discussions of sexuality or elimination?
- How often in a lifetime of clinical experience would a therapist treat a patient with a dissociative disorder? How often would a Norman Bates come along?
- Marion has stolen $40,000. How does Hitchcock manage to make her a sympathetic character with whom we can all identify?
- How can a patient with a dissociative disorder suppress the evidence presented by everyday experience (e.g., the nonresponsiveness of the dead Mrs. Bates)?
- How does Hitchcock's story-line fit with the psychological zeitgeist of the 1960s?
- Would you feel comfortable working with a patient like Norman Bates? Would you insist that security officers be present during your evaluation?

Patient Evaluation

Patient's stated reason for coming: "I had to come. They made me. Of course, I'm eager to get any help you can offer. I truly do suspect you can be helpful."

History of the present illness: Norman Bates is a 27-year-old white male who has been referred for psychological evaluation by the Madison county court. Mr. Bates is awaiting sentencing on four counts of murder. The alleged murder of his mother and stepfather occurred more than a decade ago; the two recent killings are reported to have occurred within the past 30 days.

Past psychiatric illness, treatment, and outcomes: Mr. Bates has a long history of eccentric and odd behavior, including isolation, withdrawal, seclusiveness, and secrecy. These behaviors have been noted by local authorities; however, there has never been any evidence of danger to self or others, and Mr. Bates has never received treatment in the mental health system.

Medical history: There is a history of the usual childhood diseases, such as mumps and chicken pox. Aside from these childhood experiences, Mr. Bates has never seen a physician. He has never been hospitalized.

Psychosocial history: The patient reports that he walked and talked at about the normal times. He has a long history of self-imposed isolation. He is reported to have been lonely and withdrawn in school, and he cannot identify anyone he regarded as a friend when he was growing up. He obtained passing grades, although he dropped out of school at the age of 16 to help run a family motel. When the expressway bypassed the motel, business dwindled to almost nothing. His mother and stepfather died approximately 10 years ago; since that time, Norman has managed the motel and the family home on his own. He manages the books for the motel, and he performs routine maintenance on both the motel and the family home. He has no brothers or sisters, and there are no other living relatives. He reports devoting almost all of his leisure time to his hobby of taxidermy. Mr. Bates has never been married or involved in a significant romantic relationship. He does not date, and he has no regular or routine social activities.

Drug and alcohol history: Mr. Bates denies any history of drug or alcohol use. He believes drunkenness is a sin, and he prefers not to be tempted by social drinking. He does not smoke.

Behavioral observations: Mr. Bates arrived on time for the evaluation, accompanied by a deputy sheriff. He was appropriately groomed and dressed. He was polite to the point of being obsequious. He cooperated fully with all tasks, except for those instances in which his identity would be questioned or challenged. At these points, the patient became resentful and stopped cooperating with the evaluation.

Mental status examination: Mr. Bates was alert and oriented to place and time. He was disoriented to person, however, and steadfastly maintained that he was actually his mother. He became agitated and threatened to leave the room when I pointed out the obvious (e.g., he had male features and male genitalia; she had been buried some years ago, etc.). After I stopped challenging his assertion that he was in fact his mother, he cooperated with the evaluation and was able to answer all other questions on the Mini Mental Status Examination, obtaining an overall score of 29.

Functional assessment: The patient appears to be of average intellectual ability. He has not completed high school, and he has no significant occupational abilities other than minimal bookkeeping skills. However, he appears to have been able to manage on his own for the past 10 years. He has no living family, and there are no friends to provide social support. (Mr. Bates appears comfortable in his isolation and does not appear to be distressed by the solitary nature of his existence.) Mr. Bates' social skills are limited, and he tends to be quite awkward and uncomfortable in social situations. However, his entrenched and well-defended delusional disorder appears to be his most limiting feature, and he is unlikely to function successfully in either occupational or social settings as long as he continues to maintain he is his mother.

Strengths: Mr. Bates has very limited support systems in place, but he is of at least average intelligence and he possesses the skills necessary to manage on his own.

Diagnosis: Dissociative Identity Disorder

Treatment plan: Mr. Bates was referred by the court for a forensic evaluation, and therefore no systematic treatment plan has been developed. Given his legal problems, it is likely that Mr. Bates will be imprisoned for life, and it is unlikely he will be offered the benefits of active psychological treatment in the corrections system. Even if treatment is available, it will require years of daily work before this client begins to understand himself or his problems.

Prognosis: Mr. Bates lacks insight into the nature of his problems or their causes. He resists efforts to change his belief system. He has maintained these fallacious beliefs for the entire past decade, and they are likely to prove intractable. If he is acquitted by reason of insanity, he is likely to be remanded to the state hospital for intensive treatment. However, even then his prognosis is quite bleak.

Psycho and Psychopathology

In the latter half of the 1900s, films began depicting the increasing psychological complexities of the human personality. *Psycho*, Alfred Hitchcock's 1960 film, describes a young man who assumed the personality of his mother after he murdered her and her lover. This film is regarded by many as Hitchcock's finest film. It is a superb movie; unfortunately, it also contributes to the negative stereotype of persons with mental illnesses.

The film begins in a hotel room in Phoenix, with Marion Crane, played by Janet Leigh, who is scantily dressed. She is discussing her future with her lover, Sam Loomis, played by John Gavin. Marion wants to get married, but Sam is unable to make a commitment because of previous financial commitments to his ex-wife. After the afternoon rendezvous, she returns to work, where she steals $40,000. The next morning she heads toward Sam's hometown with the money.

During a rainstorm, she seeks shelter at the Bates Motel, only 15 miles from Sam's home. Norman Bates, played by Anthony Perkins, invites her to dinner at his home behind the motel. Marion hears Norman's mother yelling at him for wanting to bring a girl to dinner. Norman fixes sandwiches for Marion and apologizes for his mother's behavior.

They talk in a room adjacent to the office, and Norman shows off his taxidermy collection. Norman later watches Marion undress through a peephole separating her room from the office. That night Marion is brutally murdered by someone who appears to be Norman's mother. The murder scene occurs in a shower; this scene (with its dramatic musical background) is one of the most famous single scenes in film history.

Norman cleans up the blood from the shower room and puts Marion's body in the trunk of her new car (and unknowingly hides the stolen $40,000 there as well). He then drives the car to an isolated area, where he is able to sink the car and its contents into a swamp.

"I'll just sit here and be quiet, just in case they do suspect me. They're probably watching me. Well, let them. Let them see what kind of a person I am. I'm not even going to swat that fly. I hope they are watching. They'll see. They'll see and they'll know and they'll say, 'Why, she wouldn't even harm a fly.'"

Bates sits in his (her) cell, smiling and thinking to himself (herself)

Instead of telling the police about the stolen money, Marion's boss hires a private detective, Milton Arbogast, to track Marion and recover the money. He traces her to the Bates Motel after following Marion's sister, Lila, to Sam's. Neither Lila nor Sam knows anything about the stolen money. Mr. Arbogast is killed when he visits the Bates home to investigate his hunch that Norman Bates is somehow involved in the disappearance of Marion.

Lila and Sam then contact the local sheriff, who is willing to investigate Marion's disappearance if an official missing persons report is made. He also informs Sam and Lila that Norman's mother has been dead for 10 years and that she killed herself after poisoning her lover.

Lila and Sam return to the motel to solve the case. In a very suspenseful ending, they find that Norman Bates had exhumed his mother's grave, mummified her corpse, and kept the corpse with him in the house for the past 10 years. Bates had always been a disturbed child, and, after he killed

his mother and her lover, he coped with his guilt by assuming her identity.

By the end of the movie, Norman has totally assumed the alter ego of his mother.

Dissociation, Trauma, and Films

Alteration in consciousness can occur under many different conditions. With alcohol intoxication, there is a clouding of consciousness with attenuated awareness of sensory stimuli and diminished attention to the environment and self. Some drugs produce a dream-like state in which the individual is conscious but inattentive. Heightened states of attention, concentration, and absorption brought about through hypnosis, meditation, or relaxation are further examples of alterations in consciousness.

Dissociation involves a separation of consciousness with closely connected feelings, behaviors, thoughts, or memories of events (APA, 2000). In dissociation, events and information that would ordinarily be connected or integrated are divided from one another. Dissociation is often viewed as a normal defense mechanism that can be used in frightening, stressful, or painful situations to cope with stress. It allows an individual to detach from overwhelming fear, pain, and helplessness generated by trauma.

Dissociation can be viewed on a continuum from minor dissociative experiences of everyday life (i.e., daydreaming) to major forms of psychopathology, such as multiple personality disorder (Allen & Smith, 1993; Bernstein & Putnam, 1986). Most people have minor dissociative experiences, such as driving a car over a familiar route and suddenly realizing that they do not remember what happened during all or part of the trip. In some cultures, dissociative states, such as trances, are common and accepted cultural activities or a routine part of religious experience. The development of extreme dissociative behavior patterns has been linked to trauma. For example, in *Sybil* (1976), the lead character's development of 16 different personalities was found to be the result of repeated physical and psychological abuse she experienced at the hands of a deranged and delusional mother.

Numerous films depict characters experiencing a traumatic event and many depict the lead character dissociating from the traumatic experience in order to cope. However, it is unlikely that any of the characters in the following five examples would be given a dissociative disorder diagnosis as there is not enough evidence in the film to meet all of the diagnostic criteria. In *Lilya 4-Ever* (2002), a young girl is prostituted against her will in a country foreign to her and she is neglected and abused; she dissociates during sexual intercourse with a client. In *The Princess and the Warrior* (2001), a man is stuck on a toilet while his wife is killed; his various traumatic reactions include, "freezing," dissociating from reality, feeling tense and shaky and experiencing flashbacks. In *Natural Born Killers* (1994), Woody Harrelson and Juliette Lewis are both victims and perpetrators of various violent and traumatic events; in the film, dissociative pain numbing, dissociative perceptual distortion, dissociative time distortion, and dissociative derealization are depicted. *Swimming Pool* (2002) portrays a young woman exhibiting dissociative amnesia in her inability to remember killing a man. One particular dissociative episode occurs when she thinks she is seeing her mother; she screams when she is told her mother is not there, and then she faints. In the independent film, *Searching for Paradise* (2002), a woman, in the middle of sex with a "fantasy-come-true" man, suddenly stops and states she feels betrayed by the partner; this seems to be a dissociative experience in which she seems to be confusing her father who had left her and this "fantasy" man who has become real.

Another dissociative experience often experienced in traumatic situations is **derealization**. In derealization, the person feels detached from familiar people or places which seem unreal and non-recognizable. The size or shape of objects may be perceived as altered or strange, and people may seem mechanical. During the 1989 San Francisco Bay Area earthquake, 40 percent of the 101 persons interviewed afterward reported feeling as though their surroundings were unreal (Cardea & Spiegel, 1993). Filmmaker, David Lynch's films seem to induce a derealization state for not only other characters but for the viewer as well, and his characters' identities are often confused and locations seem unreal. The films *Lost Highway* (1997) and *Mulholland Drive* (2001) are particularly good examples of this kind of derealization.

Dissociative Disorders in Films

There is controversy in the mental health community about the categorization of dissociative experiences as psychiatric disorders. Dissociation, by itself, does not necessarily lead to impairment and is not necessarily viewed as evidence of psychopathology. However, if dissociative states lead to distress and impairment in psychological, interpersonal, social, or vocational functioning, then they should be evaluated as psychiatric problems. Because dissociative symptoms such as amnesia and depersonalization can be present in other psychiatric disorders such as post-traumatic stress disorder and schizophrenia, no other psychiatric disorders can be present if a person's symptoms are diagnosed as a dissociative disorder. In addition, the disorder cannot be caused by a traumatic brain injury; this is the reason that films such as *Memento* (2000) are discussed in Chapter 10, "Neuropsychological Disorders."

There are four primary dissociative disorders: Dissociative Amnesia, Dissociative Fugue, Dissociative Identity Disorder, and Depersonalization Disorder.

Dissociative Amnesia

Dissociative amnesias are characterized by an inability to recall important personal information, usually of a traumatic or stressful nature (e.g., the death of a child). Such individuals can usually remember events up to the time of the trauma but have memory loss for events that occur after the event. Even though significant personal information is lost with dissociative amnesias, cognitive abilities and the ability to remember new information remain intact. This memory impairment is reversible. In the classic disorder, the person is quickly brought to a mental health provider because of an overt, dramatic change in memory. Persons with amnesia may have intense emotional reactions to stimuli without knowing the reasons for the reaction or the significance of it.

Even though filmmakers do not typically focus on the psychological etiology of amnesia, they have often used amnesia as a central theme. One example is the 1940 Academy Award-winning satire, *The Great Dictator*, starring Charles Chaplin, Paulette Goddard, and Jack Oakie. Chaplin plays a dual role as a Jewish barber and Adenoid Hynkel, dictator of Tomania. This spoof of Adolf Hitler begins when Chaplin plays a Jewish barber in a "Tomanian" ghetto who is recovering from amnesia and wakes up to find himself living under the thumb of Hynkel (also played by Chaplin). He escapes to Austria with a Jewish laundress, Paulette Goddard, who is in love with him. In Austria, he is mistaken for Hynkel, who had recently assumed control of the country. Chaplin then assumes the role of the dictator.

Amnesia is also portrayed in the excellent film *Sullivan's Travels* (1941) starring Joel McCrea and

Veronica Lake and directed by Preston Sturges. The main character becomes amnestic when he is hit over the head and ends up being sentenced to six years on a chain gang. An example of traumatic amnesia triggered by a murder can be found in the film *Dead Again* (1991).

Amnesia allows a spoiled, self-centered, rich women to experience life at the other end of the social ladder in the comedy *Overboard* (1987), directed by Garry Marshall. Dissociative amnesia is also illustrated in the classic films *Spellbound* (1945) and *Suddenly, Last Summer* (1959).

It would appear that the Jim Carrey and Kate Winslet characters in *Eternal Sunshine of the Spotless Mind* (2004) have some form of dissociative amnesia, as they are unable to remember certain events and people, particularly those related to a former significant other. However, because the memories are intentionally erased through the help of a specialist who erases traumatic memories with sophisticated technology, the diagnosis would not apply.

Hollywood movies have reaped some financial gain with action films using amnesia as a plot device, such as the successful *The Bourne Identity* (2002), and the unsuccessful *Paycheck* (2003). In the former, Jason Bourne, a CIA assassin, loses his memory after a failed spy mission and he is left to try to uncover who he is before he is killed.

Mirage

In the film *Mirage* (1965), David Stillwell, played by Gregory Peck, develops amnesia after witnessing the accidental death of his boss and mentor, Calvin Clark. Stillwell, a scientist, had just discovered a method for neutralizing the effects of nuclear fallout. Believing that his mentor was working for world peace, Stillwell shares the information with him. When Stillwell realizes that his formula would end up being used to "produce" nuclear weapons, he sets the formula on fire in front of an open window. In an attempt to save the piece of paper, Calvin lunges toward Stillwell and falls to his death from the 27th floor. Stillwell observes the fall, is horrified, and then calmly picks up his empty briefcase and leaves the office. He has developed amnesia. The lights in the office building go out.

The audience has none of this information until the end of the film. The film actually opens during a blackout in an office building in New York City. David Stillwell appears to be a very calm, rational individual who leads a woman, Sheila, played by Diane Baker, down the darkened 27 flights. He

does not recognize Sheila, but she recognizes him. Upon returning to his apartment, he is greeted by a man who attempts to kill him. Stillwell overpowers the intruder and leaves him unconscious in the servants' quarters. Gradually, Stillwell begins to realize that he has lost his memory, but he becomes convinced that he has been in an amnestic state for two years instead of two days. He seeks help from a psychiatrist, who questions his amnesia and throws him out of the office.

In this Hitchcock-style thriller, Stillwell's belief that he had been a cost accountant in New York was reinforced by his enemy, the Major, who hires thugs to follow Stillwell and get the formula. Stillwell next employs Detective Ted Caselle, played by Walter Matthau, to discover his identity and figure out who is trying to kill him. Caselle attempts to fit the pieces together but is killed in the process. A romance is rekindled between Sheila and Stillwell, who had previously been lovers.

Following the detective's death, Stillwell desperately contacts the same psychiatrist, who is again skeptical of Stillwell's amnesia. By now, Stillwell's memory is beginning to return and he realizes that his memory loss has been present for only two days. The psychiatrist asks some questions that provoke the retrieval of more memories. Gradually, the amnesia for his friend's death lifts, and he is able to face the horror of the event.

Dissociative Fugue

Dissociative fugues are characterized by sudden, unexpected travel away from home or one's customary place of work, an inability to recall one's past, and confusion about personal identity or the assumption of a partial or completely new identity (e.g., a person whose business is failing may show up in a new city with a new identity and no memory of previous problems). With the onset of fugue, a person begins a new autobiographical memory that replaces the original one. These individuals appear normal and will not reveal any evidence of dissociative symptoms unless asked. When the fugue resolves, the original memories are recovered, but the fugue memories are lost. The individual then has a permanent void in personality history. Even though the prevalence of dissociative fugue has been reported as only 0.2 percent of the general population, it may be more common in times of war, natural disaster, and dislocation (Fullerton, Ursano & Wang, 2004).

Some patients with dissociative fugue disorders will travel short distances over brief periods;

others may travel far and remain in a fugue state for months or years. The acclaimed and thought-provoking Wim Wenders film *Paris, Texas* (1984) introduces the character of Travis Clay Henderson, an individual suffering from dissociative fugue. He has been lost for four years and is found wandering in the desert. Eventually, he (partially) puts the pieces of his shattered life back together.

Jim Carrey's lead role in *The Majestic* (2001) would be another example of dissociative fugue had the experience not been caused by a head injury from an automobile accident; Carrey's character has amnesia, has traveled away from home, and readily takes on the identity of a "missing in action" soldier in a small town.

Amnesia and identity are central themes in *Identity Unknown* (1945), starring Richard Arlen and Cheryl Walker. In this film, a soldier develops amnesia during World War II and tries to recover his identity.

K-Pax

Kevin Spacey as both Robert Porter and Prot in *K-Pax* (2001) is a diagnostic quandary. In addition to hypothetical diagnoses of delusional disorder and PTSD, a valid and highly arguable case can be made for dissociative fugue.

From this vantage point, a man named Robert Porter experiences a highly traumatic event. Upon returning from work one day, he finds his wife and child murdered with the perpetrator still in his house; Porter quickly kills the man, cleans up, and jumps in a nearby river. He then travels from his home in New Mexico to New York City under a completely new identity as Prot, a highly spiritual person with great knowledge of planetary rotations. Porter interacts with other people comfortably with this new identity and claims no knowledge of any other past history. Under clinical hypnosis (age regression), the amnesia is lifted and he painfully faces his past trauma.

Dissociative Identity Disorder

Dissociative identity disorder (DID), formerly called multiple personality disorder, is an extremely rare condition characterized by disturbances in memory and identity. The essential feature is the presence of two or more distinct identities, or alter personality states, that assume control over behavior. Amnesia is present in one or more of the personalities. Usually,

the more passive the personality, the greater the amnesia. Dissociative identity disorder is usually believed to be a post-traumatic condition that emerges after overwhelming traumatic childhood experiences (APA, 2000).

The symptoms of DID are associated with many other psychiatric states such as anxiety symptoms (phobia, panic attacks, obsessive-compulsive behaviors), mood symptoms (manic and depressive), other dissociative symptoms (amnesias, fugues, depersonalization), somatoform symptoms (conversion), sexual dysfunctions, suicide attempts, self-mutilations, substance abuse, eating disorders, sleep disturbance, symptoms of schizophrenia, symptoms of post-traumatic stress syndrome, and borderline personality disorder. Since many symptoms of PTSD occur in dissociative identity disorder, some argue that these two are variants of the same disorder (Piper & Merskey, 2004).

There is no evidence of spontaneous remission or integration of personality alters without mental health treatment. Therapy is long-term and involves the establishment of a therapeutic relationship with the individual. Hypnosis may be used at varying stages of treatment. Through the support of the relationship, the original traumas are accessed and examined and the psychological pain is soothed and viewed from an adult perspective. At this point in therapy, internal conflict can be addressed and resolved.

Recent DID Films: *Fight Club*, *Identity*, and *Secret Window*

None of these three popular, contemporary film examples of DID is especially helpful in portraying important and accurate psychopathology information of this disorder, or at least, they are not as educational as *The Three Faces of Eve* and *Sybil* (to be discussed later). In their defense, these films don't pretend to educate viewers about DID; instead, the condition is used as an important plot device to enhance excitement, intrigue, fascination, and entertainment. Each of the three films is unique in its cinematic approach and has something to offer the viewer interested in dissociative disorders, therefore each is worth seeing.

David Fincher's fast-paced, visceral *Fight Club* (1999) begins with the narrator, Jack (brilliantly played by Edward Norton), struggling with insomnia and perhaps depression. Jack begins to deteriorate as he is entrenched in an unsatisfying consumerist lifestyle, feels apathetic at work, and becomes addicted to attending different support group meetings each day just for emotional release. The culmination of his deterioration happens early on in the film when he meets Tyler Durden (Brad Pitt), although he (and the viewer) do not realize Tyler is Jack's alter-ego for much of the film. Tyler is everything Jack is not: flamboyant, exciting, seductive, unconventional, and self-empowering. The two (really just Jack) fight one another (he fights himself) and begin a "fight club" that attracts other disenfranchised men wanting a release. It is interesting to note that there are many clues to Jack's DID given in the film, including one-frame cinematic flashes of Tyler Durden until the full alter develops, illustrating Jack's full dissociation.

Identity (2003) takes a different approach to DID. The viewer sees two stories: one story depicts ten characters (including John Cusack and Ray Liotta) stranded at an isolated motel trying to hide and elude from a mysterious serial killer on the loose in the area; the other story portrays a convicted serial killer, Malcolm Rivers, on the night of his final hearing before having the death penalty carried out. The viewer later learns these two stories are integrated in that Malcolm has DID and that the ten characters represent Malcolm's alters whom he is trying to kill off to achieve integration.

Secret Window (2004) manipulates the viewer and it is not until the conclusion of the film that the protagonist's dissociative identity disorder is revealed. Johnny Depp plays Mort, a man who witnesses the traumatic event of his wife cheating on him in a motel room. Mort confines and isolates himself in the woods to write his next novel and subsequently begins to deteriorate (this is a direct parallel with Jack Nicholson's famous and more overt character in *The Shining* [1980]). Coinciding with his deterioration (which takes the form of angst about his deteriorating marriage, anger toward his wife's boyfriend, an inability to quit smoking, alcohol abuse, and writer's block), is Mort's provocative encounters with Shooter (John Turturro) who wants amends, claiming Mort has stolen his story. These interactions become more dangerous and threatening and Shooter kills various people and Mort's dog. Toward the end, a frustrated Mort throws an ashtray against the wall—the wall and house begin to crack—and he hallucinates the crack spreading around the house; this scene is a metaphor for his own fragility and continuing decompensation. We then see Mort talking to himself and begin to hear his inner voice that then shows up visually and multiplies. Mort had been so afraid of the Shooter part of his personality that he developed it as an alter and suppressed it from his conscious awareness.

The Three Faces of Eve

In *The Three Faces of Eve* (1957), narrator Alistair Cooke prepares the viewer for a documentary of a true story about a woman with multiple personality disorder (DID). This black-and-white film takes place in 1951 in a small Georgia town. Joanne Woodward introduces the viewer to Eve White, a quiet, passive, modest homemaker who begins having severe headaches, followed by "spells." She cannot remember what she did during these spells. Mrs. White is married to a rigid, dull, unimaginative man named Ralph, who is frustrated with the changes in his wife's behavior. Their unhappy marriage is even more stressed by these unexplained events.

During these spells, Eve Black, the second personality, "comes out." Eve Black is a seductive, sexually promiscuous single woman, who buys flashy and provocative clothes, smokes, drinks, and frequents nightclubs. Eve White, who is unaware of Eve Black's existence, is afraid she is going crazy because of her unexplained periods of amnesia and hearing voices. Eve Black, on the other hand, knows of Eve White, dislikes her husband, and their child, Bonnie, and delights in having Eve White feel the hangover following Eve Black's night of carousing. Eve White and her husband seek psychiatric treatment from Dr. Luther, played by Lee J. Cobb, for her headaches and spells.

It is well over a year before Dr. Luther is able to identify the existence of Eve Black. Following an incident in which Eve Black attempts to strangle Bonnie, Eve White is admitted to the hospital. She vows not to be reunited with her daughter until she is well. While Eve is in the hospital, Dr. Luther is able to establish a therapeutic relationship with both personalities and attempts to integrate them into one. The diagnosis of multiple personality disorder is explained to Eve White and her spouse, who both attempt to understand the problem. Ralph is never able to understand the disorder and eventually divorces Eve.

As Eve White struggles to work during the day, Eve Black parties at night. They both continue to be treated by Dr. Luther. Eventually, a third personality, Jane, emerges who is aware of both Eve White and Eve Black, even though neither is aware of her. Following a visit with her daughter, Bonnie, at her parents' home, Jane begins to have memories of playing under the porch as a child. Gradually, through the use of hypnosis, Dr. Luther is able to help Eve recall the trauma (being forced to kiss her grandmother's corpse) that precipitated her personalities splitting. After reliving the memory, only Jane remained.

Sybil

The film *Sybil* (1976), based upon a true story, stars Sally Field as Sybil and Joanne Woodward as Dr. Wilbur. It is interesting to note that Woodward, who received an Academy Award in 1957 for her lead role in *The Three Faces of Eve*, returned almost two decades later to play the psychiatrist treating Sybil. The viewer is introduced to Sybil, a distressed young woman who is working as a pre-school teacher while attending art school. As Sybil is talking with the children, the creaking sound of a swing stirs traumatic childhood memories. Sybil unsuccessfully attempts to attend to her assigned task of organizing the children into a game of follow-the-leader. In the next scene, Sybil is standing in the middle of a fountain, obviously confused. Her supervisor is scolding her for leading the children the wrong way. Sybil returns to her apartment, where she curls into a fetal position, trying to escape her tormenting memories. In desperation, she breaks her apartment window, which seems to give her some psychological relief. Because of her cut wrist, she ends up in an emergency room. Due to her confusion, she is referred to a psychiatrist, Dr. Wilbur, who evaluates her and begins treatment that lasts for 11 years.

This episode represents one of many in which Sybil is initially overwhelmed with flashbacks of traumatic childhood events that lead to periods of irrational behavior followed by a climactic event, such as breaking a window and injuring herself. The viewer gradually realizes that, as Sybil recalls traumatic memories, one of her 16 other personalities, or "alters," gains control and triggers the irrational behavior. Each of the other alters represents a part of Sybil and serves a particular purpose. For example, Vanessa is musical and enjoys playing the music Sybil once played. Vicki is very much in charge of life and is fearless. Peggy is a child who feels the terror and anger of childhood trauma. Marsha represents her despair and is often suicidal.

Through interaction with the different personalities and the use of hypnosis, Dr. Wilbur gradually pieces together Sybil's traumatic past. The goal of therapy is to integrate the personalities by helping the alters remember the past, experience the emotions associated with the traumatic events, and develop an adult perspective on the trauma. Patiently, Dr. Wilbur develops a warm, therapeutic relationship with all of the alters who are able to share their experiences. Dr. Wilbur, in turn, is able to help Sybil remember parts of her life that were previously shut off. Gradually, as the repeated abuse of her childhood is relived, Sybil is able to remember her childhood experiences and integrate them into her whole personality.

The film *Primal Fear* (1996) should also be seen to provide a certain degree of skeptical balance as it portrays a man (Edward Norton) who feigns DID in attempt to evade murder charges. This film reminds clinicians of the potential for malingering in suspected cases of multiple personality disorder.

Dissociative identity disorders are also illustrated in *Raising Cain* (1992) and *Voices Within: The Lives of Truddi Chase* (1990), a made-for-television movie based on the best-selling book *When Rabbit Howls*.

Depersonalization Disorder

Depersonalization disorder is diagnosed when there is evidence of persistent or recurrent feelings of detachment from one's mental processes or body. There is an alteration in the perception of self and often a sense that one is living out a dream. The person feels like an outsider looking in but continues to be connected with reality during the experience. Transient experiences of depersonalization are common in adolescents and decline with age in normal individuals (Putnam, 1985). During a traumatic event such as rape, depersonalization is sometimes experienced by women who report they were floating above their own bodies during the assault (Classen, Koopman, & Spiegel, 1993). Closely related to depersonalization experiences are **out-of-body experiences** in which the individual has the experience of leaving his or her body. Often these individuals are able to describe scenes as if viewed from above and report a sense of being isolated and detached from their bodies.

Since depersonalization occurs as a symptom in a variety of disorders, some authorities have questioned whether depersonalization is a distinct disorder. The cause of depersonalization is unknown. Some authorities speculate that the phenomenon is related to a neurobiological disturbance produced by temporal lobe dysfunction. Others claim that depersonalization is an adaptation to overwhelming trauma. Still other authorities argue that depersonalization is a defense against painful and conflictual stimuli, or that it is a split between the observing and participating selves that allows the person to become detached from self (Steinberg, 1991).

Film examples of depersonalization disorder are found in the fascinating "Film Festival hit" *Tarnation* (2003), *Dead of Night* (1945), *Altered States* (1980), and Martin Scorsese's *The Last Temptation of Christ* (1988).

The Butterfly Effect

It might be a stretch to place the film, *The Butterfly Effect* (2004), under this diagnostic category; however, while it does not seem to fit any category neatly, it can inform us about depersonalization. Evan, a 20-year-old, college student experiences frequent blackouts during highly emotional or stressful times. When he reflects on his amnestic blackouts and reads his copious journal entry of a given memory, he is transported to the actual past memory. He is then able to change the memory with various ensuing consequences on his and others' lives in the present.

Each of the memories he engages can be seen through his detachment from his body; he enters the memory, relives it, and changes it while maintaining reality testing to his world and the new world (due to the changed memory) around him. This process cause him significant personal and social distress as he realizes each of these "detachment" episodes has a profound effect on his own life and on the lives of those around him.

Other Examples of Dissociative Disorders in Films

Dissociative disorders are among the most fascinating forms of mental illness, and it is not surprising that they are often portrayed in films. In addition to the fairly clear-cut clinical examples cited, film history is replete with examples of quasi-dissociative conditions in which one character exchanges personalities (or sometimes even bodies) with another. The classic example is Bergman's *Persona* (1966), in which two characters gradually exchange personalities. A similar theme is found in the Robert Altman film, *3 Women* (1977), in which two of the women appear to exchange personalities.

In the mock-documentary/comedy, *Zelig* (1983), Woody Allen plays a human chameleon whose personality changes to match whatever situation he is in—if he is around black musicians, he talks and acts like black musicians; if he's around politicians, he becomes a politician. Ronald Coleman finds himself merging his own personality with that of Othello in *A Double Life* (1947). The comedy *Prelude to a Kiss* (1992) is about an old man and a young bride who mysteriously exchange bodies after kissing on the bride's wedding day. The film raises interesting questions about what it is that one person loves in another; is it a physical body or

a set of personality characteristics, such as wit, charm, and grace? The means through which the transformation is effected is never specified in *Prelude*. In contrast, it is very clear in *Black Friday*, a 1940 horror film in which Boris Karloff transplants the brain of a criminal into the body of a college professor.

The theme of contrasting personalities in the same person is seen in those films in which someone presumed to be dead returns to his or her old social roles, usually as a vastly improved human being. We see this in *Sommersby* (1993) and *The Return of Martin Guerre* (1982). The dramatic force of both films is heightened by the sexual excitement both women feel as they go to bed with a man who may or may not be the husband who left them years earlier.

Dissociation is also used in a plethora of films that contrast the forces of good and evil inherent in all of us. Oftentimes, the evil is inherent in a twin. For example, the personalities of good and evil twins are juxtaposed in *The Dark Mirror* (1946) and in Brian de Palma's *Sisters* (1973). The latter film adds an interesting twist by making the two women Siamese twins who were separated as children.

Films have often presented the duality of the human personality, usually depicting a struggle between good and evil. In 1920, *Dr. Jekyll and Mr. Hyde* was first introduced as a silent film, starring John Barrymore and Martha Robinson. The 1932 remake, directed by Rouben Mammouliam, was the first sound version of this Robert Louis Stevenson classic. In this film, Dr. Harry Jekyll (played by Fredric March, who won an Oscar for his performance) represents all that is good and kind. He is a well-respected physician who devotes endless hours to hospital charity work. His innate curiosity, as well as his own socially unacceptable feelings, has led him to speculate about good and evil within human beings. He believes that the evil of humans can be captured and isolated. As the film opens, he is engaged to Muriel, played by Miriam Hopkins, with whom he is deeply in love. According to the custom of the time, Muriel's father has set a marriage date that is too far in the future to suit Harry. The audience gets a glimpse of Dr. Jekyll's underlying impulsiveness, his impatience, and the sexuality that he is trying hard to repress.

When Muriel's father takes her away for an extended trip, Dr. Jekyll tests his theory about inherent evils. He mixes and swallows a potion that he believes can isolate the evils of human beings. He then becomes the evil Mr. Hyde, who seduces, abuses, and eventually kills a woman who is his social inferior. Eventually, he can no longer control the "coming out" of the alter personality (Mr. Hyde), and he confides his mistake to his future father-in-law. After attacking his fiancée, Mr. Hyde is caught and killed.

Dr. Jekyll and Mr. Hyde was remade in 1941 and starred Spencer Tracy and Ingrid Bergman. It was filmed again in 1968, starring Jack Palance, and given a new title, *The Strange Case of Dr. Jekyll and Mr. Hyde*. One of the best adaptations of the Dr. Jekyll and Mr. Hyde story is in the more recent *Mary Reilly* (1996), starring John Malkovich and Julia Roberts. A somewhat different twist on the same theme is found in *Steppenwolf* (1974), an adaptation of the Hermann Hesse novel, illustrating the problem of a single individual grappling with these two competing aspects of self.

Critical Thinking Questions (Dissociative Disorders)

- How can an understanding of the phenomenon of hypnosis help us understand dissociative disorders?
- Movies such as *Primal Fear* (1996) suggest it is relatively easy to fool lawyers and therapists into believing you have a multiple personality disorder. How would you assess the likelihood of malingering if you were a clinician evaluating a patient with an alleged dissociative disorder?
- Many reputable theorists believe DID does not exist? What evidence do you find for and against this claim?
- Are there instances where dissociation occurs, but not amnesia?
- Compare dissociative experiences that are culturally acceptable with those that are considered abnormal.
- What are some other causes of dissociative disorders aside from trauma?
- Name a few of the inaccuracies and misconceptions perpetrated in the DID depiction in the film *Identity*.
- Compare and contrast Edward Norton's character in the modern day film *Fight Club* with Joanne Woodward's character in the classic *The Three Faces of Eve*.

Somatoform Disorders

While 80% of healthy individuals experience somatic symptoms in any one week, the following disorders go beyond transient bodily complaints: Somatization Disorder, Undifferentiated Somatoform Disorder, Conversion Disorder, Pain Disorder, Hypochondriasis, and Body Dysmorphic Disorder.

Somatization disorder is diagnosed when there is a pattern of recurrent and multiple somatic complaints that require medical treatment or that limit the effectiveness of an individual, but for which no clear organic etiology can be identified. In addition, multiple organ systems must be involved. Specifically, there must be at least four pain symptoms, two gastrointestinal symptoms, one sexual symptom, and one pseudoneurological symptom for the diagnosis to be made. The enormous economic impact of the medical treatment of the unexplained symptoms has gained international attention. Rarely is mental health treatment sought (Hiller & Fichter, 2004).

Patients with somatization disorder are poor historians, and their complaints may vary from session to session. This problem is complicated by the fact that they easily become dissatisfied with their physicians and may be constantly changing doctors, sharing different parts of their story with each new physician. In addition, since most physician visits result in a prescription of some sort, these patients are often taking multiple medications, some of which produce side effects that result in general somatic distress. This pattern sets up a vicious cycle and makes diagnosis of the patient with a somatization disorder a challenging dilemma.

Diagnosis is further complicated by the fact that some genuine medical conditions, such as multiple sclerosis, hyperparathyroidism, and systematic lupus erythematosus, can have vague symptoms that affect multiple organ systems. Occasionally, patients have multiple physical complaints that appear to be somatoform-like but are not sufficiently varied or of sufficient duration to meet the full criteria for somatization disorder. In these cases, the residual diagnosis of **undifferentiated somatoform disorder** is used. The common diagnoses of Irritable Bowel Syndrome and Chronic Fatigue Syndrome often fall under the "Undifferentiated Somatoform Disorder" category as they do not meet the full criteria for somatization disorder; yet the individual is experiencing bodily symptoms not fully explained by medical tests.

Safe

The Todd Haynes film *Safe* (1995) almost exclusively focuses on a woman with a somatoform disorder. Carol White (Julianne Moore) slowly begins to deteriorate with unexplained symptoms, related to chemical sensitivity, allergy, and somatic complaints. Doctors tell her stress is the cause of her problem, and advise her to learn to relax. However, it is difficult to see what is stressful in her life—she has a loving husband, beautiful home, good social life, and servants to do the cooking and cleaning. Her bodily system becomes overloaded and overwhelmed by fumes, toxins, fragrances and other "pollutants"—deriving from traffic, her shampoo, her husband's cologne, or a new sofa. It is as if she is being attacked by plastics, ozone, chemicals, high-energy wires, pollution, additives, preservatives, and hamburger fumes. Carol continues to get physically sicker and sicker, leaving her physicians baffled. At one point, she is hospitalized due to extensive bleeding.

Carol makes the decision to travel to another part of the country to a specialized clinic that offers group therapy, seminars, and social activities for people suffering from similar anomalous problems. During a casual group session, the therapist asks probing questions of the patients (and metaphorically to society and the viewer): "Why did you get sick" and "What's behind your sickness?" One character speaks to abuse experienced as a child, how she made herself sick to remember, and how she had not forgiven the perpetrator and took it out on herself. For other characters, what they believed was behind their sickness is self-blame or anger, and in one man's case, a drug addiction. Upon hearing other characters speak of coming to terms with their inner self-hatred, Moore's character admits to also having a deep sense of self-hatred. However, despite all of her treatment, she seems to just get worse. The treatment emphasizes simplistic themes of a need to love oneself more, that we all make ourselves sick, and the role of the mind; while these ideas can play an important role, particularly the impact of the thoughts and feelings on the immune system, the approach comes across as trite and misleading, not unconnected with each patient's suffering.

Ultimately, the film is a dark comedy and a satirical social commentary. Todd Haynes cleverly uses the cinematic element of a background hum to suggest to for the viewer that we can never fully escape the impact of the environment.

Amelie and Agnes of God

Georgette in *Amelie* (2001) would probably meet all the criteria for somatization disorder if she were to appear at a doctor's office. While operating a cigarette counter, she complains of various symptoms from sciatica to the discomfort of smoke getting in her eyes. One interesting quote used in the film describes Georgette precisely: "A woman without love wilts like a flower without the sun." When Georgette's mind is not occupied with love, she is preoccupied with enough symptoms to meet criteria for somatization disorder, but when she has a love interest, she feels perfectly healthy and happy.

Another complex film is *Agnes of God* (1985), starring Meg Tilly as a young nun (Sister Agnes), Anne Bancroft as the Mother Superior of the convent, and Jane Fonda as the psychiatrist sent to investigate the apparent murder of a newborn baby who was found wrapped in bloody sheets and stuffed in a wastebasket at the convent. The film juxtaposes reason and faith and quickly convinces the viewer that although Sister Agnes is surely one of "God's innocents," she is just as surely the mother and the murderer of the child.

Fonda uses hypnosis in treating Sister Agnes, and it turns out that she was sexually molested by her mother as a child. It also turns out that the mother was the sister of the Mother Superior. At the end of the film, the court finds Sister Agnes not guilty by reason of insanity, and she returns to the convent, where she will continue to receive psychiatric care.

Sister Agnes' confusion seems very real and the label of insanity seems justified. It appears that a dissociative amnesia may have been present, and one believes that Sister Agnes had repressed the memories of her rape and was genuinely amnestic for the incident in which she strangled the child with his umbilical cord. Agnes begins to experience the stigmata once in a convent room and once in a chapel while praying. **Stigmata** is the name given to bleeding in the hands and feet, presumably from the sites where nails were driven into when Christ was crucified. It is a relatively rare but well-documented phenomenon that is found in people with deep religious convictions. In the case of *Agnes of God*, the blood of Christ, the blood of the murdered infant, and the blood of Agnes all seem to commingle. The somatic element of the stigmata in this film is much more complex, powerful, and integrated into the story and personal life of Agnes than the stigmata depicted in another suspense film, *Stigmata* (1999).

Conversion Disorder

A conversion disorder exists when (1) patients experience significant distress or impairment from motor or sensory symptoms that appear to be neurological but for which no adequate neurological explanation can be determined and (2) it appears that psychological factors have played a significant role in the etiology or maintenance of the disorder. In addition, the clinician must rule out malingering before the diagnosis is made.

The very name conversion disorder is linked to a psychological theory that maintains that unconscious psychological distress can be "converted" into physical manifestations. Interestingly, symptoms are far more likely to occur on the left side of the body (presumably because most people are right-handed).

Conversion disorders are fascinating, in part because the underlying dynamics seem so transparent to an external observer. The soldier who can't fire a rifle because his arm is paralyzed has found a convenient way of avoiding battle; the woman who becomes functionally blind after witnessing a car wreck in which her son was killed can never see anything this awful happen again. In actual practice, few cases of somatoform disorder are this tidy.

Woody Allen's character, Val Wawman, in *Hollywood Ending* (2002) is a clear example of hysterical blindness, a previously frequent but currently rare conversion disorder. Just prior to the first day of directing a new film (in which there is the added stress of his ex-wife being the co-producer with her new fiancé), he loses his sight. This would suggest a neurological condition but an extensive medical examination fails to produce medical or physiological reasons for Wawman's blindness. He goes to see a psychologist who explains this is psychological in origin and supports this comment with individualized interpretations—Val's fears of failure, internal conflicts, and poor relationship with his son. Val also exhibits numerous hypochondriacal symptoms including his extreme fear of getting an illness and preoccupation with illness. He previously thought he had experienced many outlandish diseases (e.g., diseases that only trees can get, the plague, etc.), all due to his misinterpretation of bodily symptoms.

The film *Sorry, Wrong Number* (1948) stars Barbara Stanwick as a bedridden heiress who is partially paralyzed, although her doctors cannot determine any neurological reason for her inability to walk. One evening, she happens to overhear two men planning a murder; later she realizes that she is the intended victim. Much of the suspense of the film revolves around the realization that she must get out of bed in order to save herself.

Persona

Persona (1966), a complex Ingmar Bergman film regarded as one of the greatest films ever made, deals with a famous actress, Elisabeth Vogler (Liv Ullmann), who suddenly, and seemingly without reason, stops talking. Her doctor can find nothing wrong with her and is at a loss to explain her patient's symptom. However, she prescribes rest and constant attention, and Elisabeth spends the summer at a house on the coast in the care of a full-time nurse, Alma (Bibi Andersson). Although Elisabeth almost never speaks, we know that she retains the capacity for speech. At one point, when Alma appears to be about to throw boiling water on Elisabeth, the actress shouts, "Don't."

Although the conversion disorder portrayed in the film is fascinating, the more interesting element is the merging of the personalities of the two women. There are a number of interesting dream sequences, and one scene presents a face on the screen that is a composite of Elisabeth and Alma (one-half of each woman's face is shown). In selecting the title for the film, Bergman was likely thinking both about the masks worn by Greek actors in classical theater and of Carl Jung who used the term to refer to those parts of our personality that we show to the outer world. Perhaps Elisabeth quit speaking because she had resolved to stop acting and wear no more masks. The ending of the film is somewhat unclear, but it appears Elisabeth returns to acting, Alma returns to nursing, and the personalities of the two women do not remain merged.

Pain Disorder

Patients with somatoform disorders often present with pain as a symptom; in fact, the presentation is a necessary condition for the diagnosis of somatization disorder. However, some patients will be preoccupied with the experience of pain, and their activities will be dramatically limited by the presence of pain, even when there is no lesion, history of trauma, or other objective medical data that could account for their suffering. According to the American Pain Foundation, back pain is the leading cause of disability in

Americans under age 45. Over 26 million Americans between the ages of 20 and 64 experience frequent back pain and two-thirds of American adults will have back pain during their lifetime. In many of these cases, psychological factors play an important role in the cause, exacerbation, and/or maintenance of the pain experience.

A large number of associated disorders can be comorbid with pain disorder. In addition, it is common for patients with chronic pain, whether due to medical or psychological reasons or both, to become depressed, anxious, or angry in response to their pain. Psychological tests such as the **Minnesota Multiphasic Personality Inventory** (MMPI) and questionnaires such as the **McGill Pain Questionnaire** may be helpful in determining the extent to which psychological "overlay" is present in a patient's report of pain.

In the black and white thriller *Pi* (1998), the lead character is a computer wizard and mathematician who suffers from excruciating migraine headaches. His pain becomes so debilitating he bangs his head on a sink and eventually drills into his head. If seen in a psychology clinic, one of this character's diagnoses would be Pain Disorder associated with both psychological factors and a general medical condition.

Hypochondriasis

The hypochondriac is preoccupied with thoughts of disease, infirmity, and death. This person worries that simple, benign body sensations or symptoms may be indicative of a serious disease. In the extreme, a hypochondriac might interpret routine stomach pain as cancer of the bowel, headaches as a consequence of a brain tumor, and/or misplaced keys or glasses as an undeniable early indication of Alzheimer's. The preoccupations persist despite physical exams, lab tests, X-rays, and other examinations suggesting there is no illness present.

Some patients who have been labeled as hypochondriacs are later found to have bona fide medical disorders. This is especially common with disorders that have vague symptoms and a slow progression (e.g., multiple sclerosis). In addition, patients who are initially believed to have hypochondriasis are sometimes later found to have somatic concerns related to anxiety, depression, or another psychiatric disorder.

Hypochondriasis is easy to ridicule, and there is something comical about the person who goes through an "organ recital" when describing his or her health. However, the concerns of these patients are very real and deserve sympathetic attention and empathic understanding.

In *Dogville* (2003), one character is a hypochondriacal doctor who misinterprets lumps and various other physical complaints; he is someone who needs the constant reassurance of others to convince him he is not dying.

Bandits

In *Bandits* (2001), Billy Bob Thornton plays Terry Collins, a bank robber with hypochondriasis. Terry is convinced he has various illnesses despite his physician assuring him there is nothing wrong. While in prison, he ruminates about how helpful garlic is and becomes upset when it is banned from the prison cafeteria; in a later scene, he incessantly screams in the prison yard about ringing in his ears. In his leisure time, he reads a medical dictionary and while driving listens to *Merck Manual* cassette tapes alphabetically defining diseases.

After escaping from prison and robbing a bank with his cohort in crime, Joe Blake (Bruce Willis), Terry's arm becomes numb, he complains of seeing spots, and makes weird noises with his throat. When challenged by his partner, he exclaims, "I have sanitation issues, Joe."

When under duress, Terry experiences a sneezing attack and a tic in his left eye. He then begins to talk fast and speak in medical jargon. He also becomes preoccupied with one pupil being larger than the other. Each of his senses is affected in some way throughout the film. In addition, he suffers from food allergy, lactose intolerance, and various obscure phobias such as a fear of getting smaller, a fear of antique furniture (Billy Bob Thornton is reported to have this fear), a fear of historic figures, and a fear of black and white movies. He experiences numbness in his arm, lips and legs that leads him to collapse and flail about on the floor in one scene.

Hannah and Her Sisters

Hannah and Her Sisters (1986) is one of Woody Allen's funniest and most gratifying films. Allen plays Mickey, the role of a neurotic television executive, who is a classic hypochondriac. He is on his way to get a blood test when the film opens, and we soon realize that he is preoccupied with doctors, hospitals, and his own fragile mortality. He works in a high-stress job and early on in the film he remarks, "Has anybody got a Tagamet? My ulcer is starting to kill me." (Director Woody Allen has a remarkable sense for the prevailing concerns and habits of the American public. A decade earlier, he had amused his viewers with a similar line about Valium.)

"This time I think I really have something... It's not like that adenoidal thing, where I didn't realize I had them out."

Woody Allen discussing his hearing loss with his physician in *Hannah and Her Sisters*

Mickey has experienced some hearing loss and is convinced that he has a brain tumor. He suspects that his doctors have known this all along but "they don't tell you [these things] because sometimes the weaker ones will panic." He awakens in the middle of the night, terrified, crying out "There's a tumor in my head the size of a basketball." With each new test, he grows more apprehensive. When his computerized tomography scan turns out to be completely negative, he is at first elated and then plunges into despair as he realizes that this is just a temporary reprieve and that eventually he must die.

Questions to Consider While Watching *Bandits* and *Hannah and Her Sisters*

- How can nonmedical therapists rule out organic pathology?
- Does *every* client with a psychological problem have to be worked up medically to ensure that there is no medical disease present?
- How common is it for a patient who has headaches actually to have a brain tumor?
- Should patients be able to insist on expensive tests (such as CAT scans and MRIs), or is this decision ultimately up to the physician? Should it matter if a patient has insurance?
- Is the percentage of clients who visit psychologists for what are eventually determined to be medical problems about equivalent to the number of patients who visit physicians for treatment of what are ultimately determined to be psychological problems?

- Do the symptoms of hypochondriacs worsen under stress?
- Is the reassurance typically offered hypochondriacal patients going to be possible in a world of managed care? Will these changes in policy exacerbate or ameliorate the patients' concerns and symptoms?
- What is the optimal approach for a physician or medical professional to take in working with a person with suspected hypochondriasis?

Body Dysmorphic Disorder

When somebody becomes so obsessed with a perceived physical imperfection that he or she is unable to function successfully interpersonally or on the job, a diagnosis of body dysmorphic disorder may be appropriate. Individuals with this problem may spend hours each day looking into a mirror and brooding about their perceived inadequacy.

A rare, quality example of body dysmorphic syndrome is found in Gerard Depardieu's portrayal of *Cyrano de Bergerac* in the 1990 French film by the same name. Cyrano is deeply in love with his cousin Roxanne but cannot profess his love because he is too ashamed of his long (and to him) deformed nose. Instead, he writes long love letters for his friend Perez. The letters are successful, and Roxanne falls deeply in love with the romantic Perez. Perez is killed in battle and Roxanne enters a convent, where Cyrano continues to visit her. Fifteen years later, as he is dying, Cyrano recites one of the last letters from Perez by memory and Roxanne realizes that he has been the one whom she has really loved all this time.

In 1987, Steve Martin played the role of a modern-day Cyrano in the film *Roxanne*. However, in this film his nose is truly of grotesque proportions and he would not qualify for the diagnosis of body dysmorphic disorder (which requires an imagined defect in appearance). In the French film, Depardieu's nose is elongated but not grotesque, and one suspects that his concerns are at least as much psychological as real.

The artistically eccentric Peter Greenaway directed the film *The Belly of an Architect* (1987) in which the viewer is introduced to Stourley Kracklite (Brian Dennehy) who is a prominent American architect putting on an exhibition in Rome. Kracklite is too preoccupied with himself to care much about his wife's flirtations with a younger man. In particular, Kracklite becomes obsessed with his stomach. This begins to occupy all of his attention. His doctor states it is nothing more than gas and egotism. Kracklite examines other options—dyspepsia, fatigue, over-excitement, lack of exercise, too much coffee, too much constipation—but his stomach obsession continues. He makes photocopies of a statue of Augustus, obsesses over the statue's stomach region, and compares it with his own. In a memorable scene, Kracklite's obsession with his stomach extends to his covering his entire room including the floor with photographs of bellies. The film presents an interesting diagnostic challenge and the need to distinguish the features of somatoform disorders, OCD, and delusional disorder. Support for a diagnosis of hypochondriasis is found in his unshakable belief that his body is being consumed by a tumor. There are other psychological elements contributing to his disorder: fear of being embarrassed, fear of death, isolation, psychological stress, and narcissistic factors of grandiosity and self-preoccupation.

Differential Diagnosis

Patients with somatoform disorders will often experience some amount of **secondary gain** as a result of their medical problems, such as extra care and attention from others, worker's compensation benefits, reduced expectations from family, or avoidance of difficult activities. It is important to be cognizant of normal secondary gain factors while separating a given somatoform disorder from both malingering and factitious disorder. In **malingering**, a person deliberately "fakes" his or her symptoms in order to achieve a clearly understood goal (e.g., one character in Memento). A death row inmate may feign symptoms of mental illness—for example, believing that the state cannot execute someone who is not mentally competent. Likewise, a small child may complain of stomach pain, remembering that the last time this occurred he or she was allowed to stay home from school and eat ice cream.

In contrast, **factitious disorders,** a completely separate diagnostic category, involve feigning illness with the specific intent of assuming the sick role. Some patients with factitious disorders will present with predominately psychological symptoms while others will have predominately physical symptoms. **Factitious disorder by proxy** occurs when symptoms are intentionally produced in another person, the classic example being the mother who makes her child sick so the child can assume the "sick role."

The term **psychosomatic** is often used as a derogatory term for people suffering with the disorders mentioned in this chapter. The term usually refers to physical disorders in which emotional processes play a role indicating a mutual influence of physical and psychological factors; the generality of this concept can be applied to not only somatoform disorders but most medical and psychological conditions as well.

Critical Thinking Questions (Somatoform Disorders)

- How do somatoform disorders affect the national health care budget?
- How are people with somatoform disorders affected by the adoption of managed care practices?
- What percentage of major medical illnesses are missed when they are being mislabeled as psychosomatic?
- What particular mind-body treatment strategies are most useful with these disorders?
- What personality characteristics are most closely associated with somatization disorder and hypochondriasis?
- Why is pain one of the most common and least understood problems facing the medical profession?
- How does the film Safe both add and detract from the understanding of somatoform disorders?

Chapter 4

Psychological Stress and Physical Disorders

I'm in love with you. And I'm in love with your beautiful woman.
And I'm in love with your kids. And I'm even in love with your unborn child.
I'm even in love with your anger! I'm in love with anything that lives.
Mateo, a man dying of AIDS, desperately seeking connection in *In America*

Questions to consider while watching *In America*

- How does the stress of Mateo's disease influence the manifestation of his symptoms?
- Even though it is not formally mentioned in the film, what evidence is there that Mateo is suffering from AIDS?
- What are the indications in the film that the disease is progressing?
- How does AIDS interact with psychological problems such as depression, anxiety, and anger?
- Mateo is a character who is highly isolated. How common is isolation for persons with HIV/AIDS?
- Mateo has a refrigerator full of medication. Is this realistic for someone with AIDS? Why is so much medication needed?
- Explain how Mateo redefines his view of himself and his illness. How common is this type of dramatic change?
- Why does the director choose not to explore Mateo's past, including how he contracted HIV?

Patient Evaluation

Patient's stated reason for coming: "I can't cope with this disease anymore! I'm sick and tired of being sick and tired!"

History of the present illness: Mr. Mateo Kwame is a 42-year-old, Nigerian man who is suffering with AIDS. He was first diagnosed as HIV positive four years ago. His feelings of anger and depression have worsened over the last year. He has experienced a constant underlying depression throughout the course of the illness, and he experiences frequent episodes of anger. He engaged in self-harm on two occasions in the last three months during periods of rage; in both incidents, he used his own blood to color paintings on which he was working

Past psychiatric illness, treatment, and outcomes: There is no past history of psychiatric illness.

Medical history: Mateo has been living with HIV/AIDS for four years. He states he goes to his physician two times per month although he has been encouraged to make more frequent visits. His entire refrigerator is full of medications that help him manage symptoms and pain. Mateo is compliant with his daily regimen. He experiences chronic fatigue and occasionally faints. He has been diagnosed with hypertension.

Psychosocial history: Mateo has lived alone in an apartment for the duration of his illness. He was married for twelve years with one child until his wife and daughter were tragically killed in an automobile accident ten years ago. He never remarried and states, "I would not betray that love." He earned a bachelor's degree in Artistic Design and worked as an art gallery administrator for several years until the onset of his illness. After his diagnosis, he quit working outside his home, moved into an apartment, and began to paint. Occasionally, he has sold his paintings but he is not interested in painting as a full-time occupation; he says, "I paint to release my insides." Mateo is socially isolated. He did mention that he is beginning to establish a relationship with some Irish neighbors who recently moved in his apartment complex. He described a particularly meaningful connection with the two young girls who are part of this family—"I see so much life in them."

Drug and alcohol history: Mateo denied any significant drug or alcohol history other than experimenting with marijuana as a teenager and drinking alcohol in college.

Behavioral observations: Mateo was casually dressed and on time for the interview. He answered questions but did not elaborate. He displayed a stern, tense expression on his face, as if he was deliberately trying to blunt his affect. Affect ranged from high agitation to deep dysphoria. He was tearful at two points during the interview—once when he spoke about the loss of his wife and daughter and once when he spoke about his long-term isolation from people. He is aware that he has paranoid thoughts, and he referred to people attacking him and beating him up (it should be noted that he does live in a dangerous neighborhood). He denied homicidal and suicidal ideation and plan, as well as any thoughts of self-harm.

Mental status examination: Mateo has normal cognitive functioning, and there is no evidence of psychosis. He earned a score of 30/30 on the Mini Mental Status Examination. The MMSE was unremarkable.

Functional assessment: Mateo's self-care has been steadily diminishing over the last three months. He claims his apartment is a mess and that he no longer bothers to clean up after he has an anger outburst. His sleep and appetite are poor, and he has lost 10 pounds in the last six months.

Strengths: Mateo appears to be a resilient person. His interest in connecting with his new neighbors is a positive sign; he spoke about them with genuine animation and excitement. He continues to look for meaning and purpose in his life. He has a deep appreciation for his African heritage, and he enjoys painting for self-expression.

Diagnosis: Major Depressive Disorder, Single Episode, Moderate; Intermittent Explosive Disorder (Provisional)

Treatment plan: (1) Supportive psychotherapy is recommended to manage any future self-harm behaviors, to help Mateo continue to adjust to the limitations of his illness, and to help him make changes in his lifestyle. (2) It is recommended Mateo contact Hospice for additional support, monitoring, and care. (3) It is important he maintain more regular contact with his primary care physician and immunologist to monitor changes in his health status.

Prognosis: Guarded. Mateo did not seem interested in following the interviewer's initial recommendations and stated he would "think about it" when asked to return to therapy. The prognosis would improve if Mateo could accept his illness and become more comfortable asking for help.

In America: AIDS, Emotional Turmoil, and Healing

The film *In America* (2003) is loosely based on director Jim Sheridan's personal life and story. It is about a family who emigrates from Ireland to the United States following the death of a family member (a two-year-old child). Each member of the family grieves in his or her own way, with the father having the most difficulty in letting go. After finding a home in a dilapidated Hell's Kitchen apartment in a drug-invested area of New York City, they befriend the downstairs tenant, Mateo, a Nigerian painter dying from AIDS. Djimon Hounsou was nominated for an Academy Award for Best Supporting Actor for his performance as Mateo.

Mateo is known by the apartment tenants as "the man who screams," and he displays intermittent episodes of rage where he intensely cries out in anguish, throws objects in his apartment, and violently slashes his paintings with a knife. The introduction to Mateo is a frightening one: he is depicted as stern, with a tense appearance and periodic tortured screams. "Keep Away" is painted on his door, and he bellows a threatening "Go away!" to two little girls trick-or-treating. However, Mateo soon softens to the girls and is very kind to them. The girls see Mateo's entire refrigerator is stocked with medications and no food; it is then the viewer learns there is a good reason for Mateo to scream. The girls tell Mateo the story of their younger brother, Frankie, who had died of a brain tumor. Mateo cries upon hearing this story—the child's story seems to parallel his own disease.

Every physical illness has a psychological impact. In addition to anger and rage, Mateo is isolated and depressed. It is visually apparent his emotional stress mutually interacts with the physical illness and complicates his coping abilities. Mateo's condition further deteriorates as the chronic fatigue of having an immune disease leads him to pass out and experience shortness of breath. In the latter stages of AIDS, Mateo develops blistering lips, facial sores, temperature sensitivity, and exhaustion, leading him to fall asleep when talking to others. Underneath Mateo's rage and hatred toward life is a gentle softness and wisdom. The Irish family, particularly the two youthful, energetic girls, help Mateo re-discover his ability to love and connect with others. His screaming and anguish subside. He begins to accept the reality of his disease and embraces death and suffering in a magnanimous way, continuing to reach out and influence the lives of others until the day he dies.

Behind the Red Door (2001) is another recent film about a man suffering and dying of AIDS and his psychological response is intermittent, explosive anger that vacillates with depression. This film stars Keifer Sutherland as Roy, a person with AIDS; unlike Mateo, Roy does not write "Stay Away" on his door, but Roy's narcissism pushes people away just as effectively. As with Mateo, Roy is connected with others (in this case a previously estranged sister) and this helps Roy to cope psychologically, which brings him to accept his illness in a deeper way. Both men transition from fighting to embracing death.

"I have sex with men. But unlike nearly every other man of whom this is true, I bring the guy I'm screwing to the White House and President Reagan smiles at us and shakes his hand."

Al Pacino as Roy Cohn, a Washington powerbroker who does not see himself as homosexual, despite the fact that he has contracted AIDS from having sex with another man in *Angels in America*

In Tony Kushner's *Angels in America* (2003), directed by Mike Nichols, Al Pacino plays the role of Roy Marcus Cohn, a high-powered lawyer who has contracted AIDS but who steadfastly denies his homosexuality. This scene in which Cohn's doctor tells him he has AIDS is a an illustration of the power of denial.

The Dynamic Nature of Stress

Stress is ubiquitous. It is a multi-dimensional phenomenon that can result from various internal and external factors and affect the body and mind in a multitude of ways. Stress is also protean; it can be both cause and effect and it can manifest in the following forms: physical, cognitive, emotional, behavioral, social, and spiritual. Each of these major domains interacts and each affects the others. Stress affects physical illnesses in at least three ways: (1) Stress can **cause** the illness. This seems to be the case with medical diagnoses like irritable bowel syndrome and tension headaches. (2) Stress can worsen or **exacerbate** already existing conditions. Migraine

headaches and other chronic pain conditions are clearly exacerbated by the presence of stress. (3) Stress can also **inhibit** improvement or keep an illness from improving. This is illustrated by the man with cardiovascular disease who continues to subject himself to the stress of working 60 hours per week.

Interestingly, the four leading causes of death are stress-related conditions: cardiovascular disease, cancer, stroke, and respiratory conditions. Managing stress helps people avoid or manage these and other illnesses.

Psychological Stress

Stress can be understood from a variety of theoretical perspectives. The **behavioral** perspective views stress as a consequence of an illness. How one copes with an illness is determined by whether or not "illness behaviors" are rewarded. For example, if a person receives attention while experiencing the stress of adapting to a wheelchair, the attention is rewarding. The individual then may be more likely to seek out situations in which a wheelchair can be used in order to receive attention.

Cognitive theorists emphasize what is going on in a person's thinking, as well as his or her behavior. This approach relates stress to the meaning of the illness or the person's control over it. If the illness were serious or terminal, according to cognitive theorists, that person would more likely experience stress. An example of a cognitive approach is represented by the work of Richard Lazarus and his colleagues (2000). Lazarus argues that stress depends on the relationship between a person and the environment that is "appraised" by the person as taxing—the more threatening the environment, the greater the stress.

Psychodynamic theorists focus on interpersonal relationships and family interactions. They believe that, the greater the dysfunction of the interpersonal relationships, the greater the stress.

The **sociocultural** perspective says that stress is a result of the society in which the person lives. Social disruption, such as a divorce or the death of a family member, precipitates stress in an individual.

The **biological** perspective would argue that impairment in physical functioning could result from changes in the immune system. These physiological changes follow stressful events. During stressful periods, illness symptoms can get worse in chronic diseases that are sensitive to the immune system. It is hypothesized that emotional upsets, common in interpersonal relationships, seem to be related to changes in physiological functioning (APA, 2000).

The stress associated with everyday life is convincingly portrayed by Michael Douglas in *Falling Down* (1993), while the stress of the business world is apparent in films such as *Jerry Maguire* (1996), *Glengarry Glen Ross* (1992), and *Death of a Salesman* (1951/1985).

Characters experiencing stress can be seen in many films. Almost any film dealing with war will address the physical and psychological consequences of prolonged exposure to combat stress. Films like *The Caine Mutiny* (1954), starring Humphrey Bogart as Captain Queeg, illustrate the stress of confronting and challenging inept leadership, while other classic films like *Twelve O'Clock High* (1949) document the stressors associated with military life.

There is an interesting illustration of the psychosomatic consequences of stress in *The Secret Lives of Dentists* (2002). One child experiences a high degree of family stress; some is overt stress (the parents yelling, blaming, cursing) and some is covert stress (the parents keep secrets from one another, become isolated, and spend less time with each other). This child begins to develop body symptoms with no known origin and eventually gets the flu; as a result, the entire family gets sick.

This example speaks to the body becoming more vulnerable due to stress (i.e., resulting in lowered immune system responses) with sickness following. Vulnerability is explored in a different way in M. Night Shyamalan's thought-provoking film, *Unbreakable* (2000). In this film, Elijah (Samuel L. Jackson) has a rare genetic bone disease and is highly vulnerable to breaking a bone with any action or movement he makes. His character is directly contrasted with David Dunne (Bruce Willis), who is a "superhero" archetype—he is practically invulnerable as he has never been sick, and he is the only survivor (seemingly untouched) after a deadly train crash. This character contrast sets up interesting questions regarding a continuum of low susceptibility to disease or injury versus high susceptibility to disease/injury and the role that stress plays with this continuum.

A very similar bone disease is depicted in the character of "The Glass Man" in *Amelie* (2001), who is unable to leave his home because he could easily shatter his bones.

Stress and Coping

There are a variety of different styles of coping, and how a person copes with and manages stress depends largely on his or her attitude and approach. Some people cope by internalizing their stress to their body,

e.g., Woody Allen's characters in many of his films somaticize stress and develop bodily complaints. Others deny stress, e.g., all three lead characters reject offers of help from others in *The Station Agent* (2003); still others remain stoic and hardened in the face of stress, e.g., Western hero, John Wayne; and some people externalize or blame others, e.g., Annette Bening in *American Beauty* (1999).

The Station Agent explores the various coping strategies the characters use to handle their stress and suffering. These coping approaches range from dangerously maladaptive to positive and healing. Alcohol abuse, isolation, denial of help, and suicide attempts exemplify the destructive approaches, while friendship, developing a hobby of train watching, communal dinners, and painting are some of the healthy coping strategies.

A particularly interesting and unique form of coping is displayed by Ann, a 23-year-old woman dying of ovarian cancer in *My Life Without Me* (2003). She decides not to tell her husband or children she is dying and lies to them when they ask about her doctor's appointment. Despite feeling alone where "lies are your only company," Ann decides to live her life more fully and prepare her family for when she is gone." She creates a "to-do list" which includes making tapes for both of her children's future birthdays, making a man fall in love with her, and picking out a future mate for her husband. In many ways her coping is maladaptive, manipulative, dishonest (she creates a double-life), and selfish; in other ways, it is inspirational, thoughtful, and transformative.

Stress and Physical Disorders

Stress is a normal part of everyday life. This stress is compounded when a person has a physical illness, disorder, or disease. Internal stress (anxiety of the future, self-blame, regret for actions taken, depression over current health), external stressors (work, school, family environment), and the stress of the illness (limited mobility, decreased work hours, loss of relationships) all interact and increase the burden of coping.

My Flesh and Blood

My Flesh and Blood (2004) is a documentary of a woman, Susan Tom, and her caretaking for 11 special needs children. Many parents can vouch that caring for one special needs child is extraordinarily stressful, and, as the sole caretaker, the stress Susan is taking on is mind-boggling. One child has a rare genetic skin disorder, another has cystic fibrosis and serious anger problems, one is a severe burn victim, two do not have legs, and others have developmental disabilities. Susan slogs on, taking one day at a time. When a child dies, she quickly adopts another. Why does she do it? Her mother says Susan is filling "a void" of loneliness by taking on responsibility for raising these children. Susan's explanation is that she was driven to be a caretaker at an early age and that her parents were not very nurturing.

This film is also about "people with abilities." We see one boy who's barely able to move and in a wheelchair performing in the school play, girls without legs ice skating on their hands and others skating in wheelchairs, most of the children swimming, and some interacting normally with other children at school. The film intentionally provides fascinating dichotomies and heartbreaking contrasts: the director frames some of the children happily swimming and then immediately cuts to another child in the hospital getting respiratory therapy; another example depicts one child in tremendous pain in getting his bath while others are laughing and jumping freely on a trampoline outside the bathroom.

Duet for One

In the film *Duet for One* (1986), a chronic, debilitating illness, multiple sclerosis, is the major stress in the life of Stephanie Anderson. In the early stages of multiple sclerosis, there are abnormal sensations in the extremities or on one side of the face. There are also symptoms of muscle weakness, dizziness, and problems with vision such as double vision and partial blindness. Later in the illness, there may be **emotional lability** (rapid shifting of moods), **ataxia** (staggering gait, poor coordination), and difficulty urinating.

Stephanie Anderson's symptoms in *Duet for One* are more characteristic of someone moving into the later stages of MS. She suffers from the lack of sensation in her hands and she also has a problem with falling; in response to the stress of her illness, she has confined herself to the wheelchair. Throughout the movie, Stephanie vacillates between very good feelings (euphoria through denial) to extreme depression and suicidal thoughts. Part of her mood swings can be explained by the meaning of the devastating illness to her career and her lifestyle. Some of her mood changes can be attributed to her illness.

Duet for One portrays the plight of a middle-aged woman whose life changes dramatically in a few short months. Anderson goes from being a famous concert violinist, married to a well-known, glamorous composer who is blatant about his womanizing, to living in the country with a new husband, her former psychiatrist. Her struggle with her illness becomes an identity crisis. Her self-esteem had been previously tied to being rich and famous. When her illness forces her to give up the stage and her concert life, she tries to find meaning in her new life. Her husband, who doted on her when she was famous, rejects her in illness. His romantic attachment to his secretary leads to his eventually leaving Stephanie. In an attempt to validate her attractiveness, Stephanie takes a married lover. This relationship quickly ends, and she is more alone than ever.

"I'm healthy and I'm normal and I'll be alive after you die!"

Alan Bates confronting Julie Andrews with the reality of her illness in *Duet for One*

There are a variety of ways to understand Stephanie's responses to her physical illness and her experience of stress. From a strictly **behavioral perspective**, Stephanie can be viewed as a woman whose achievement as a world-class violinist yielded positive rewards throughout her life—success, money, and marriage. These rewards became reinforcing and, now that she will lose her ability to perform, she has no system of rewards. She cannot cope because the rewards are no longer there. Consequently, her stress increases and she is seeking new experiences that are rewarding.

From a **cognitive perspective**, Lazarus' stress model would explain Stephanie as someone who is experiencing an environmental event (loss of ability to perform), and she appraises this loss of functioning as extremely threatening. She in turn is trying to cope with the threat of the loss of functioning. Her inability to cope in turn negatively affects her health status.

The **psychodynamic perspective** focuses on Stephanie's feelings about herself and her affliction with a chronic, progressive illness. The anger that is evident throughout the film in her interactions with her husband, student, manager, and domestic housekeepers represents the anger toward the illness and the changes that are occurring. Her personality is that of a high achiever who is self-centered and ambitious. For someone with this type of personality, a chronic illness is devastating because it strikes at the very core of the personality.

The **sociocultural perspective** becomes particularly evident as we observe an attractive woman who is losing her physical functioning to aging as well as a chronic illness. Her sexual conquest of the junk dealer represents her developmental struggle with aging and the disease process. Stephanie has surrounded herself with people like herself: self-centered high achievers. People in her life also are attracted to her because of her fame and money. They are not likely to provide her with the emotional support that she needs when she is no longer a celebrity. Instead, they become alienated from her and eventually leave her at a time when she needs them the most. In the end, like all of us, she faces death alone.

Another film, *The Waterdance* (1992), starring Eric Stoltz, Wesley Snipes, and Helen Hunt, offers a convincing portrayal of what life is like for someone confined to a wheelchair after a biking accident. The film deals very convincingly and sympathetically with the sexual concerns accident victims often face after their injuries. At one point, one of the hospitalized patients clearly articulates a question the new patient, Joel Garcia (played by Eric Stoltz), has been asking himself: "How long is it going to take before that pretty little girl leaves you for someone who can tune her engine?" The patients in the hospital are divided by race, values, and social class; however, they are united in a profound way by the devastating reality of their injuries and the resulting physical limitations, and ultimately these similarities prove to be far more significant than the trivial differences that separate them. Many of the same themes had been effectively portrayed by a wheelchair-bound Marlon Brando in *The Men* (1950), a film cast with real paralyzed veterans from a California Veteran's Administration Hospital.

Jimmy Stewart is confined to a wheelchair and subsequently develops an interest in voyeurism in Hitchcock's *Rear Window* (1954). The psychological adaptation required to adjust to life in a wheelchair is portrayed in *Born on the Fourth of July* (1989) and *Coming Home* (1978), and somewhat less convincingly in *Crash* (1996). Pathological adaptation to paralysis is presented in *Bitter Moon* (1992), *The People vs. Larry Flynt* (1996), and *Breaking the Waves* (1996). The stress associated with caring for someone who is wheelchair-bound is presented in *Passion Fish* (1992); the stress parents

experience with a chronically ill or dying child is poignantly illustrated by the film *Lorenzo's Oil* (1992). *The Accidental Tourist* (1988) is a film in which William Hurt plays a man unable to cope with the death of his son. Samuel Goldwyn's film *The Best Years of Our Life* (1946) depicts the changes that occur in the life of a sailor who comes home from the war missing both hands.

Successful adaptation to a degenerative disease such as amyotrophic lateral sclerosis is documented in films such as *Pride of the Yankees* (1942), the life story of Lou Gehrig, *Tuesdays with Morrie* (1999) and *A Brief History of Time* (1992), an examination of the life and ideas of cosmologist Stephen Hawking.

A rare depiction of the very common gastrointestinal disorder, irritable bowel syndrome, is depicted in a Coen Brothers' film, *The Ladykillers* (2004). The man with IBS is depicted mostly for comic relief, but some of his suffering is shown and it exemplifies how symptoms can strike at inopportune moments.

The stress of migraine headaches is dramatically and skillfully portrayed in Darren Aronofsky's *Pi* (1998). The protagonist does whatever he can to try to stop or prevent his pain, including drilling into his head. Aronofsky skillfully uses the cinematic element of sound—piercing, screeching, and droning during the headache episodes to enhance the experience of suffering.

International Films: Psychological Stress and Physical Disorders

An Academy Award winning film from Canada, *The Barbarian Invasions* (2003), is about life and coping with an illness marking the end of life. A narcissistic man, Remy, is dying of cancer and his family and friends gather around to show their support. Remy is a university professor who has been separated from his wife for 15 years because he insisted on having sex with students and mistresses, and he has previously taken great pride in his sexual prowess. He has a poor relationship with his son, Sebastian, and he is overly critical of Sebastian's highly successful work with video games. Remy stubbornly argues and criticizes Sebastian, as well as society, while lying in the hospital bed. Nevertheless, Sebastian does whatever he can to help his father cope; he makes various accommodations for his father, including getting him an entire vacant floor in the hospital for just his father, bribing his father's students to show support and care, and purchasing heroin for pain management. Remy begins to smoke the heroin in the hospital to cope with his pain; he experiences serious withdrawal when he goes one day without it.

"Only idiots refuse to change."

Sebastian arguing with his dying father in *The Barbarian Invasions*

The Eye (2002), from Hong Kong, is a suspense-filled thriller about a young woman who undergoes a cornea-transplant and regains her sight. She immediately begins to see and experience ghosts, labeled as the souls of the dead who are forced to relive their death and die each day every day until resolution or forgiveness takes place. The woman comes to realize she has been given the eyes of one of these ghosts and must go on a journey to bring resolve and healing. The film addresses the interesting theme of vision recovery and speaks to not only the patience needed but the fear involved in such a process. It also addresses the challenges such a person would face, such as shifting from a well-developed kinesthetic memory to visual memory, even with simple objects. *The Eye* illustrates this challenge in a scene in which the woman tries to use a stapler. Regrettably, this film, like so many others, features a psychologist who crosses professional boundaries in the name of love.

The Danish film *Open Hearts* (2003) depicts a random accident in which a man, Joachim, is getting out of his car and is hit by another speeding car, leaving him paralyzed from the neck down. Joachim's reaction is anger and resentment toward his girlfriend, nurse, and society. His girlfriend, Cecilie is stricken with confusion, hurt, and grief, as is the female driver who hit Joachim. Cecilie, feeling rejected turns to support from the driver's husband, and an affair develops. The movie forcefully conveys the powerful emotions that result from physical injury and explores the impact of such an injury upon loved ones. It also shows what happens when coping is compromised and the emotional confusion, loneliness, and pain that can result.

Italian for Beginners (2002) is a story about a woman in extraordinary pain who is dying from pancreatic cancer. She copes through externalizing blame onto others, is mean-spirited, and insists upon

morphine injections for her pain. Another Italian classic, *Cinema Paradiso* (1988), portrays the friendship between a projectionist and a young boy; the projectionist becomes blind as a result of a fire, but must continue to live his life as fully as he can.

The powerful role of stress is emphasized in *Son of the Bride* (2002), an Argentinean film about a man whose heart attack seems directly related to the amount of pressure he is under as well as the denial of family and support in his life.

Critical Thinking Questions

- What kind of support would Hospice offer Mateo in *In America*?
- Is the role of stress even more significant for people with immune system diseases?
- What are the most successful medical and psychological approaches in slowing down the progression of AIDS?
- What is the best explanation for Stephanie Anderson's reaction to her illness in *Duet for One*—behavioral, cognitive, psychodynamic, or biological?
- How common is it for someone to react to a devastating diagnosis (such as multiple sclerosis) by beginning an affair?
- How would paralysis affect your life? What would you do to facilitate your adjustment to your new circumstances?
- Is there stress with *every* illness, disease and disorder?
- How can mind-body therapies help the various physical disorders mentioned in this chapter?
- What type of coping style is most difficult to treat?
- What advice would you give to a woman like Ann in *My Life Without Me* who has decided not to share with her family the fact that she is dying?
- Are films such as *Falling Down* accurate in their suggestion that contemporary American life is becoming more stressful? Support your answer with evidence.
- When a person like Michael Douglas' character in *Falling Down* "snaps," is this suggestive of mental illness? Can this occur without an underlying or unaddressed psychological problem?
- In *Unbreakable*, how has Elijah's physical illness impacted his life? Is this meant to be believable?

Chapter 5

Mood Disorders

The woman has come here and tried to take her own life. We must help her.
She's a bird, a broken one. Your grandfather used to say the bird which
flies into your house is an angel. You must look upon its presence like a blessing.
Sir Ben Kingsley giving advice regarding Jennifer Connelly's
first suicide attempt in *House of Sand and Fog*

Questions to consider while watching *House of Sand and Fog*

- Based solely on the film, does Kathy meet the criteria for a diagnosis of mood disorder?
- At what point would hospitalization be recommended for Kathy?
- What are the negative automatic thoughts likely to occur in Kathy?
- What is the relationship between alcohol and depression in this film? How commonly does alcohol and drug abuse co-occur with mood disorders?
- How much more likely is a depressed drinker to commit suicide than a depressed non-drinker?
- Describe the ways characters react to Kathy's suicide attempts. Are these reactions typical?
- What suicide signs are evident for Kathy? Compare and contrast the suicide risk factors for Kathy and Behrani?
- What is the purpose of the film's title? Does it relate to depression or addiction?
- Some reviewers have described Kathy as a weak person. Do you agree?
- What are Kathy's healthy and unhealthy coping strategies?

Patient Evaluation

Patient's stated reason for coming: "I've lost everything...my home, my family, my life. There's nothing I can do."

History of the present illness: Kathy Nicolo is a 37-year-old, Caucasian female who referred herself to this outpatient clinic for problems with depression, recurring thoughts of suicide, and circumstances of loss mostly surrounding the seizing of her home three weeks ago because of her failure to pay her taxes. Kathy has driven by the house several times and viewed a new family moving in; these trips exacerbate her depression and suicidal thoughts.

Past psychiatric illness, treatment, and outcome: Kathy has experienced depression for most of her life with exacerbating episodes occurring every couple of years. She received one month of inpatient treatment for substance abuse and depression two years ago. This hospitalization was triggered by a suicide attempt in which she mixed alcohol with a friend's Valium.

Medical history: Kathy was placed on a trial of Fluoxetine (Prozac) during her inpatient treatment. She was not compliant with this antidepressant and found it to be of minimal help. There is no significant history of medical illness, injury, or disease.

Psychosocial history: Kathy maintains contact with her mother and brother, however both live out of state. She was particularly close to her father, who died eight months ago leaving his house to Kathy and her brother. Kathy has lived alone in this house (the same that was seized) for the last eight months; she also lived in the house as a child. Kathy notes she has had few close friends over the years and has not made any efforts to maintain close relationships with them. This social isolation exacerbates her feelings of depression and loneliness.

Kathy has worked as a house cleaner for six years. She states she does not find this to be fulfilling work but comments, "I have to work somewhere."

Kathy is currently separated. She claims her husband of nearly eight years left her for another woman two years ago and they have not had any contact since he left. It appears this event triggered her previous suicide attempt. Kathy does not have any children. She had not dated anyone after her husband left until recently when she began an affair with a married police officer who has been assisting her with her domestic troubles. She does not believe this relationship will continue.

Kathy denies engaging or enjoying any particular hobbies, activities, or areas of interest, saying, "I have lost motivation for all those things. I probably have some. I just don't know what they are."

Drug and alcohol history: Kathy relapsed with alcohol on two occasions last week. There is a significant history of alcohol dependence. Kathy completed a 30-day treatment program two years ago. She had been completely sober until last week. She attended Alcoholic's Anonymous three times per week for a year and a half following her hospitalization, but attendance has diminished significantly over the past six months. She has experimented with marijuana and cocaine, but denies recent use of either drug.

Behavioral observations: Kathy arrived on time for the interview. She was unkempt and disheveled. She acknowledged she had not showered in three days. Affect and mood were dysphoric. Eye contact was fair, although much of the time she looked down. She cried when she spoke of her recent alcohol relapse. She became visibly angry with voice elevation and rapid speech when describing the loss of her house.

Mental status examination: Kathy was oriented to person, place, time, and situation. The Mini Mental Status Examination was administered and she scored 27 out of 30, which is in the normal range. She did not receive perfect scores on object recall or serial sevens.

Functional assessment: Kathy's self-care habits have greatly diminished, particularly in the last three weeks. Sleep, eating, and other health strategies have decreased. In addition to alcohol relapse, Kathy has begun to smoke cigarettes again, a habit she had stopped for nearly two years.

Strengths: Kathy has an interest in relationships with others; however, her depression, fatigue, ennui and malaise often preclude her from developing these relationships. Her self-referral to this clinic is a definite strength in that she is able to acknowledge she is having problems and that she wants to get help.

Diagnosis: Major Depressive Disorder, Recurrent, Moderate; Alcohol Dependence

Treatment plan: Three areas require immediate attention. Following success with these three areas, a new treatment plan for individual psychotherapy will be devised.

1) Managing suicidal and depressive patterns: devise a "no suicide" contract and plan, including building a support network, keeping emergency phone numbers handy, stopping triggers such as driving by her former house and drinking alcohol, and eliminating lethal or dangerous objects. Psychiatric referral for another trial of anti-depressant medication is recommended, but with appropriate caution due to her history of overdosing on prescription medication.

2) Alcohol sobriety: make a commitment to stop drinking; return immediately to AA three times per week; find an AA sponsor; maintain accountability with a psychotherapist.

3) Continue to take action with the immediate stressor of the seizure of her house: consultations with local and state government professionals as needed and additional legal support seems necessary.

Prognosis: Good if she follows the above recommendations. Poor, if she discontinues this treatment or continues to relapse with alcohol as this will exacerbate depressive and suicidal symptomatology.

House of Sand and Fog

Vadim Perelman made his directorial debut with *House of Sand and Fog* (2003), which is based on a popular novel by Andre Dubus. This film is a modern day tragedy about life and death that is profoundly emotional and poignant. The movie stars Jennifer Connelly as Kathy, a depressed, recovering alcoholic, Sir Ben Kingsley as Behrani, a former, high-ranking, Iranian colonel working hard at two menial jobs to create success for his family, and Ron Eldard as Lester, a married police officer who protects Kathy and wants to start a new life with her. Perelman succinctly describes the dynamics of each character's psyche as follows: "Behrani wants up, Kathy wants in, and Lester wants out. Those are their motivations." Kathy's house is seized due to tax payment delinquency and Behrani wins the house in an auction, thus beginning a complex web of morality, conflict, individual needs, and pursuit of one's dreams.

Kathy lives alone in a house she and her brother inherited from their father. In one of the opening scenes, Kathy is sleeping when she is awakened by her advice-giving mother on the phone; after discussing the need for her to attend support group meetings, Kathy ends the conversation with a lone tear streaming down her cheek and hangs up the phone. She then rises from her shaking waterbed (an early symbol of her instability) and begins to walk around her unclean house that includes an unfixed, dripping faucet and a large stack of unopened mail blocking her front door. The opening scenes set up a depiction of an unsteady woman with a history of alcoholism who lives a sedentary, isolated, and unmotivated life. These scenes set the stage for Kathy's battles with alcoholism and depression.

Kathy seems to have an underlying depression quality marked by agitation, numbed and blunted affect, and social isolation. Early on, she alludes to her struggle with depression and remarks "I'm trying not to harp on the negative." Kathy also has financial problems, she is unable even to afford a motel for two days and she begins to live and sleep in her car, turning the engine on for heat. She finds some comfort and escape from her loneliness through an affair with a married man. As stress increases, she begins to smoke cigarettes again. There is a clear link between alcohol and depression, yet this begins with denial. Kathy says, "See, when I think of my sobriety I don't think about wine, alcohol was never a problem." She then begins to drink wine with a subtle smile. This is a break in her two years of sobriety and it rapidly results in physical and emotional deterioration. This is a serious and severe relapse for Kathy, clearly triggered by the stress and chaos in her life.

Kathy's overt "cry for help" comes when she calls her brother, pleading with him to visit and support her: "I just feel lost, Frankie, I just feel lost." Her brother, a typical busy American, claims there are new things needing attention at his job and quickly gets off the phone. Kathy despairs even further. With tearfulness and blood-shot eyes from crying, Kathy purchases several mini bottles of whiskey and some gasoline. She drinks the bottles while driving and crying. Her depression and helplessness then lead to two suicide attempts. While despairing over the house she lost, she tries to kill herself with a gun, pulling the trigger several times. The gun is unloaded. She is found, taken in, and cared for by her rival Behrani, and his family, and she attempts suicide a second time, swallowing several bottles of unnamed prescription medicine. She is again saved, this time because she is found early and forced to throw up most of the medicine.

Metaphors for depression abound in this film. The emergence of the moon and the setting or rising of the sun represents character transitions and shifts into different mood and mental states. As the title suggests, sand and fog are important elements in the film; one possible interpretation is that both represent the symptoms of depression. Sand is a naturally unsteady element representing the sinking nature of suicide, and sand is mentioned in Behrani's tragic decision to cut down trees on the beach. As Kathy sinks deeper into depression, fog is seen in many scenes, becomes thicker and more concealing until in one scene it completely surrounds the house. There are several camera shots of "moving fog" in which the fog quickly covers trees, mountains, water, and homes. This is similar to the rapid clouding associated with the negative thoughts, helplessness, and self-destructive behaviors one finds in depression. The film opens with life being cut down (trees) and concludes with a shot of a tree surrounded and protected by a fence.

The viewer is particularly challenged with this film, as he/she can empathize with both characters and can see the needs of both sides. As tension rises and conflict continues, this challenge becomes more complex, even to the point in which a state of helplessness is induced in the viewer which mirrors the helplessness portrayed on screen.

Mood Disorders

Periods of depression are normal in most persons' lives. For example, failing an examination or ending an affair often precipitates a predictable period of sadness. In addition, the feelings of high energy that accompany major events such as a graduation or marriage are also common in everyday life. However, some illnesses involve affective states that resemble these normal periods of depression or elation, but in fact they are very different. The individual experiencing a mood disorder is consumed by negative emotions and is unable to alleviate them through normal coping mechanisms. These illnesses are characterized by emotions that are so intense they dominate a person's life. Mood disorders include many different cognitive, emotional, and behavioral manifestations, but the overriding symptoms of all mood disorders are *emotional* in nature. The *DSM-IV-TR* categorizes types of mood disorders as **depressive** and **bipolar**.

Depressive Disorders

Depressive disorders, one of the most common types of mental disorders, occur in an estimated 16 million people in the United States. Most surveys show that depression is twice as common in women. There is a relationship between depressive disorders and social class, and depressive symptoms are more prevalent in individuals with fewer economic advantages.

A **major depressive episode** is associated with depressed mood and a loss of interest or pleasure in daily activities. Sleep, eating habits, appetite, concentration, motivation, self-esteem, and energy level are areas most often affected. An episode can range from mild (few symptoms) to severe, and major depressive episodes can be accompanied by delusions and hallucinations. Some people experience a **masked depression** where they unconsciously mask their depression as the experience of physical aches and pains rather than the traditional depressive symptoms. These physical manifestations of depression are often misdiagnosed as physical illnesses. Others experience an **agitated depression** where frustration and anger seem to dominate and cover up depressive symptoms. If chronically depressed moods, low self-esteem, and feelings of pessimism, despair, or hopelessness are present for two years without suicidal thoughts or limitations in functioning, the diagnosis of **dysthymic disorder** is made (APA, 2000).

In *American Splendor* (2003), comic strip writer, Harvey Pekar illustrates the chronic, low-grade elements of dysthymia. His depression is expressed through agitation and negativity, and he kicks and breaks objects and sees life through a very pessimistic filter, frequently describing himself as "a nobody." He has a chronically furrowed brow that emphasizes his agitated affect and frustrated view of the world.

"Now there's a real disappointment."

Harvey Pekar upon looking in the mirror

Harvey has few social skills; he is socially distant, unfriendly, awkward, inappropriate, and has poor eye contact. Despite success with his comic books, he maintains unchangingly cynical attitudes and behaviors; this theme is emphasized when he repeatedly appears on the David Letterman show and presents as highly defensive and cynical. Harvey denies having any sense of spirituality. Loneliness is a significant experience for Harvey and he makes the quick decision to marry after one meeting with a woman who travels from out of state to visit him; to the viewer, it seems obvious that these are two lonely people covering up their pain. Nevertheless, Harvey seems to have found a good match in his wife (Hope Davis) who also has a dysthymic quality; she is easily agitated, highly somatic, pessimistic, and suffers from hypersomnia.

Various coping strategies are exhibited. When diagnosed with cancer, Harvey explores creative expression of the disease through comics. On a less healthy note, Harvey has some characteristics of hoarding: his residence is unclean and covered in clutter; there are stacks of comic books everywhere; and he regularly goes to thrift stores and garage sales to acquire more "stuff."

In the emotionally intense *Monster's Ball* (2001), Hank (Billy Bob Thornton) and Leticia (Academy Award winner Halle Berry) are two lost, self-hating people who become even more lonely and raw after each loses an only child—Hank's son commits suicide in front of him, and Leticia's son is hit by a car. Both parents had been physically and verbally abusive to their sons as they attempted to work through their inner turmoil and struggles. The film emphasizes how both characters are trying to escape from their internal hell; in some ways, the prison itself is a metaphor for their inner pain, loneliness, isolation, and futility. Hank literally leaves a prison (he works for the Department of Corrections in a death row prison), realizing the emotional toil his job had taken on his personal life. The relationship of the racist Hank and the beautiful Black woman Leticia begins following an act of kindness by Hank when he aids a screaming Leticia he finds on the side of the road; he explains that he just felt like "doing the right thing" and that he is trying to get outside of his "insides." After drinking to intoxication, they engage in raw, uninhibited sex "just to feel." Both are emotionally numb and overwhelmed by their personal pain; scenes of the two lovers interacting are interspersed with flashes of human hands reaching into a "cage" to release a bird desperately flapping its wings. Through their connection, which becomes more intimate and genuine over time, both characters find meaningful, expressive outlets for their depression for the first time.

The Cooler (2003) is about Bernie (William H. Macy), an "unlucky" man, who works for a traditional, antisocial, casino boss (Alec Baldwin). Bernie's job is walking around successful casino patrons to bring them bad luck. Bernie is "the cooler" because he turns winners into losers; simply his appearance at a table is enough to make a winning patron quickly go bankrupt. He claims he can do this easily; "I just be myself." He is stuck in the past and trapped by it, unable to move on since he is forced to use his "bad luck" to pay off his extensive gambling debt or be killed by the casino boss. When we look deeper beyond the plot, the viewers see that Bernie's personality is very self-critical, self-defeating, and negativistic. His "unlucky" quality is a self-fulfilling prophecy. He is isolated, lives alone, and is too passive to take action in life.

This film presents a classic depressive triad: the protagonist is hapless (unlucky), hopeless, and helpless. A cognitive therapy approach emphasizing the impact of one's thoughts, beliefs, and attitudes as affecting mood states is highlighted. Upon falling in love, Bernie's luck changes, he becomes assertive, and his presence at casino tables enhances the success of others. The power of attitude is an overriding theme, as we see Bernie's negative attitude closing him from love and luck and the positive attitude bringing him good luck and success.

In many ways, the story is clichéd—the fight for love to the death, escape from the tyrannical boss, and tremendous luck in the end saves the heroes from their seemingly inevitable demise.

In *Scent of a Woman* (1992), Lieutenant Colonel Frank Slade experiences many of the classic symptoms of a major depressive episode and would probably qualify for the diagnosis. He has both a depressed mood and a loss of interest and pleasure in everyday activities (**anhedonia**). Slade's angry comment "I have no life, I'm in the dark" clearly suggests depression as well as blindness, and the sentence captures the lack of meaning and purpose in his life. His daily activities, sitting alone and drinking himself into oblivion when he is not tormenting his· four-year-old niece, are clear indications of his loss of interest in life.

People who are depressed are not pleasant, and they can be quite difficult to be around. They are often irritable and easily angered. This serves to hide their underlying need for help. Colonel Slade is irritable, intimidating, and verbally abusive to anyone who approaches him. Expression of this type of anger and abuse has a distancing effect on others, who naturally withdraw from unpleasant situations. Charles Simms did not want to stay with

Slade after meeting him, and Simms dreaded the weekend he was forced to spend with the Colonel.

Additional Questions for Discussion (*Scent of a Woman*)

- Do depressed people ever use alcohol to assuage their depression? If so, can it help?
- The Colonel decides to shoot himself while in uniform. Would his previous military experience increase the likelihood that Slade would actually kill himself?
- Does the true likelihood of suicide increase because Slade is blind?
- Would the risk of suicide be higher if Slade were African-American?
- Who should determine if a decision about suicide reflects an accurate appraisal of life and its likely rewards?
- Who is qualified to determine if the decision is the consequence of a disease such as depression?
- Should physicians and psychologists be empowered to involuntarily hospitalize people who are believed to be at risk for suicide?

Another interesting film depicting depression is the 1971 Academy Award winner *The Hospital* starring George C. Scott as Herbert Bock, a middle-aged, depressed, suicidal physician who is trying to cope with the mayhem of a crowded and disorganized institution, where negligence and confusion result in a series of deaths. Bock's personal life is also a mess. He is recently divorced, alienated from his children, and suffering from both personal and sexual impotence. He had been believed to be a medical genius in his early career; at the point we are introduced to him in the film, he is washed up and discouraged. At one point in the film, Bock is seen sitting in his office, preparing to inject a fatal dose of potassium.

Bock demonstrates the classical symptoms of a depressive episode. His depressed mood is expressed through his explosive angry episodes and chronic irritability. He is anhedonic and expresses no interest in his patients, his profession, or any of the activities of daily living through which most of us find meaning and purpose. Bock cannot sleep, he feels worthless, and he is plagued by recurrent thoughts of suicide. Dr. Bock's behavior is remarkably similar to that of Lt. Colonel Slade—it is similar because both men are clinically depressed.

Marlon Brando plays a depressed man trying to come to grips with the meaning of his wife's suicide in Bernado Bertolucci's powerful film *Last Tango in Paris*. The character of the coach's wife in Peter Bogdanovich's *The Last Picture Show* (1971) is clearly depressed, and her affect and behavior offer good teaching examples of depressed affect for students learning how to give a mental status examination. The despair that overcomes a man when he is abandoned by his wife is presented in the Australian film *My First Wife* (1984). Finally, Joanne Woodward presents a memorable performance as a depressed housewife in *Summer Wishes, Winter Dreams* (1973).

Hyler (1988) has pointed out that many of the characters who appear depressed in films would meet the DSM-IV criteria for **adjustment disorder with depressed mood** rather than major depression. The examples Hyler cites include Jimmy Stewart's character in Frank Capra's *It's a Wonderful Life* (1946) and Henry Fonda's character in *The Wrong Man* (1956). In the latter film, Fonda develops a reactive depression after he is unjustly accused of murder.

Bipolar Disorders

Bipolar disorder occurs less frequently than depressive disorders but affects approximately .5 to 1 percent of the population. Unlike depression, bipolar disorders occur equally often among males and females. Like most mental disorders, the prevalence is greater in the lower socioeconomic groups, in part because these illnesses interfere with a person's ability to work and in part because the cost of the illnesses quickly depletes the economic resources of all but the very wealthy. Even wealthy clients can quickly become impoverished, however, because of the poor judgment associated with manic episodes.

A **manic episode** is a distinct period of an abnormally and persistently elevated, expansive, or irritable mood, lasting at least one week, during which the mood disturbance causes marked impairment of work or functioning. The manic episode may range from mild to severe and may be accompanied by psychotic features. A **hypomanic episode** results in a period of sustained elevated mood, lasting at least four days. This change is obvious to others and alters a person's level of functioning. However, by definition, a hypomanic episode is *not* severe enough to impair work or social functioning.

People with bipolar illnesses are often very likable. Their basic personality is usually outgoing, and they often work in people-intensive occupations such as sales. During a manic episode, they feel good about themselves and their moods are contagious. They are often very generous and may buy strangers expensive gifts. During a manic episode, judgment is typically very poor. Individuals may gamble away their life savings or charge all their expenses on an expensive vacation. They often have multiple sexual partners within a short period. They also seem to have endless physical energy, appear to function perfectly well without sleep, usually eat very little, and may lose 30 or 40 pounds within a few weeks. The potential for physical exhaustion during a manic episode is very real, and the long-term consequences of a manic episode can be devastating for families. For example, it may take years to pay back a debt or forgive infidelities.

Bipolar I illnesses are diagnosed when a person has both manic and depressive episodes and cycles from one to another. The depressive episode may last three to six months before the person swings to a manic phase. The diagnosis **bipolar II** disorder is reserved for those who have primarily depressive episodes, with occasional hypomania. These patients do not have full-blown manic episodes. **Cyclothymic** disorders are found in individuals who never experience a major depressive or manic episode but who have hypomanic and depressive symptoms.

Mr. Jones

Alan Greisman and Debra Greenfield's 1993 film *Mr. Jones* is about a musician, Mr. Jones, played by Richard Gere, and his psychiatrist, Dr. Libbie Bowen, played by Lena Olin. *Mr. Jones* is a clear-cut illustration of Bipolar 1 disorder. The film portrays Mr. Jones as elated, seductive, and euphoric. He is a charismatic man with tremendous personal charm. He persuades a contractor to hire him, proceeds to the roof, and prepares to fly after rhythmically pounding a few nails into the roof. Before climbing to the front of the roof, he insists that Howard, his newfound friend, accept a $100 bill. After realizing that Mr. Jones really believes that he can fly, Howard persuades him to move away from the beam where he was teetering. The ambulance arrives and takes Jones to a local psychiatric emergency unit, where he is released after a few hours. At the hospital, he is misdiagnosed and given inappropriate medications.

Next, Mr. Jones goes to a bank and withdraws $12,000; he seduces the teller in the process, and then goes on a spending binge. He purchases a baby grand piano, checks into an expensive hotel, and then attends a concert. He is arrested and returned to the hospital after he disrupts a symphony concert by attempting to take over for the conductor as the orchestra is playing Beethoven's "Ode to Joy;" Jones is convinced that Beethoven would have wanted the piece played at a much faster tempo. Mr. Jones is once again hospitalized in a state of manic exhaustion, and this time he is accurately diagnosed and treated by psychiatrist Elizabeth (Libbie) Bowen.

Jones knows he has manic-depressive illness. He was first diagnosed in late adolescence and had several hospitalizations. However, he refuses to take his medication, which makes his hands shake. It is during the "highs" or the manic phases that he feels best about himself. The rest of the time Mr. Jones is lonely and depressed. His lows are life threatening and result in suicide attempts. The viewers are able to gain some insight into the impact of a mental illness on the promising career of a classical musician. In addition, the film illustrates the ways in which interpersonal relationships are affected by a condition such as bipolar disorder. Mr. Jones' one important relationship ended when a woman he loved could no longer deal with his mood swings.

Unfortunately, the rest of the movie involves the romantic relationship that develops between Dr. Bowen and Mr. Jones. Even though Dr. Bowen resigns from the hospital, underscoring the unethical nature of this doctor-patient relationship, the true impact of the psychiatrist's behavior is never addressed in the movie.

Additional Questions for Discussion (*Mr. Jones*)

- Why does Dr. Elizabeth Bowen question the resident's admitting diagnosis of paranoid schizophrenia?
- At what point is the doctor/patient relationship first compromised? Are there early warning signs that should have alerted the psychiatrist to her countertransference to this patient?
- Does Mr. Jones' history of a previous suicide attempt increase the likelihood of another attempt?
- Is an affair between a doctor and a patient more serious than one between an orderly and a patient? Would it have mattered if the patient had been discharged? Why?

- Is it ethical for a psychiatrist to visit a university to get historical information that may be relevant to a patient she is treating?
- Should patients with illnesses such as bipolar disorder be required by the courts to take medication, even if they dislike the effects of the medication and find it dampens their creativity?

Some films describe characters with bipolar disorder and do not show them as symptomatic. In *The Last Days of Disco* (1998), for example, one character is stereotyped as "looney" and "crazy;" however, he also is depicted as compliant with Lithium, and is shown to be stable, kind, and balanced. In contrast is another fairly balanced character portrayed as bipolar in *Garden State* (2004). He spontaneously becomes noncompliant with his medication and finds that his life improves dramatically without exacerbation of his bipolar symptoms. While **drug holidays** might be recommended by physicians on occasion, films of this sort mislead the public and suggest that these important decisions can be made without medical consultation.

One of the best films depicting a bipolar illness is *Call Me Anna*, a 1990 made-for-TV movie starring Patty Duke, who plays herself in this adaptation of her best-selling autobiography. The film traces her career and her battle with a bipolar disorder and vividly portrays her mood swings and the accompanying personality changes she experienced. In real life, Patty Duke has become a vocal advocate for persons with mental illness.

Gena Rowlands plays a woman who appears to have a bipolar disorder in the John Cassavetes film *A Woman Under the Influence* (1974). She is quite convincing during a manic episode, and there is a memorable scene in which a neighbor stops by to drop off his kids and then decides that it is not safe to leave them with Rowlands. He does not know exactly what's wrong, but it is clear to him that *something* is not right. Unlike *Mr. Jones*, the actual diagnosis is never specified in *A Woman Under the Influence*, despite the fact that Rowlands spends six months in a psychiatric hospital.

Another example of an apparent bipolar disorder is found in the Harrison Ford character in *Mosquito Coast* (1986), although Ford's eccentric habits and obsessional style are probably adequate to support multiple diagnoses. The biographical film *Mommie Dearest* (1981) suggests that Joan Crawford had a bipolar disorder.

Examples of the type of rapid speech, quick thinking, and impulsive behavior associated with a hypomanic episode can be seen in the college president character played by Groucho Marx in *Horse Feathers* (1932) and in *Good Morning, Vietnam* (1987), in which Robin Williams plays an Air Force disc jockey with a rapid and clever repartee that endears him to his military audience.

Theories of Mood Disorders

There are three main theoretical explanations associated with mood disorders: the **genetic**, which is useful in understanding familial tendencies; the **biologic**, which explains the physiologic changes and the rationale for pharmacotherapy and electroconvulsive therapy; and **psychological**, which give direction for understanding behavior and psychotherapy treatment for the impact of the illness. The environment and external events are an extremely important factor in the manifestation of mood disorders, i.e., loss of a job or a recent divorce.

Genetic Theories

Twin and adoption studies have documented that there is a genetic vulnerability to mood disorders. Family studies have demonstrated the degree to which a disorder is actually familial. Bipolar disorder, in particular, has been shown to have a very high heritability estimate of 93% in identical twins (Kieseppa, Partonen, Haukka, Kaprio, & Lonnqvist, 2004).

When researchers compared the incidence of mood disorders in identical twins (who share the same genetic code) with that of fraternal twins (who have different genetic material), the concordance rate was 67 percent for the identical twins and 15 percent for fraternal twins. The high concordance for identical twins has also been found in twins who were raised in different environments. Clearly, there is a significant genetic component in mood disorders.

Biologic Theories

The biologic approach to mood disorders focuses on the activity of the neurotransmitters in the limbic system. The neurotransmitters involved include **dopamine**, **serotonin**, **acetylcholine**, and **norepinephrine**. In depression, it is believed that there are fewer available neurotransmitters in the synaptic junction; in mania, there is an excess.

The limbic system also regulates the pituitary hormone, a key element in the highly complex endocrine system. Changes in the endocrine system also influence mood. There have been many studies documenting the changes in the functioning of the pituitary and thyroid that occur with mood disorders. Some depressed persons have been found to secrete an excessive amount of cortisol, a hormone produced by the pituitary. Additionally, persistently low thyroid hormone levels have been noted in some cases of depression, and an elevated thyroid hormone is present in some rapid cycling bipolar disorders.

Psychological Theories

Psychological theories have always played an important role in the understanding and treatment of mood disorders. While the depressive and bipolar disorders clearly have a biological basis, the psychodynamic conceptualization of these disorders provides a different way of understanding the behavioral and emotional problems associated with these conditions. Many of the psychological features of depression are readily apparent in films.

The early psychoanalysts (e.g., Freud, Abraham) noticed that people with depression experienced **ambivalence** toward significant persons in their lives. That is, they often acted as if they loved and hated the same person. In *Scent of a Woman*, Lt. Colonel Slade is both affectionate and antagonistic toward his niece, brother, and other family members. He also becomes antagonistic and aggressive when Simms tries to help him.

Introjection, the unconscious "taking in" of qualities and values of another person or a group with whom emotional ties exist, was also identified as a characteristic feature of depression. In *Scent of a Woman*, Slade introjected the values of the military and continued to treat everyone as if he or she reported to him. Interestingly, Slade had been discharged from the military because of his overbearing behavior. Most "nondepressed" persons would not have become so entangled with their job.

Regression, another characteristic of depression, refers to a return to an earlier pattern of behavior. During a depression, childhood behavioral patterns may appear, and a person may act less mature. In *Scent of a Woman*, Slade's ongoing battle with a four-year-old is not acceptable adult behavior for a retired Colonel.

Denial, ignoring the existence of reality, is characteristic of persons experiencing a manic episode. They often stop taking their medication because they believe that there is nothing wrong with them. They reject any advice from family members and may become belligerent at any suggestion that there is something wrong. Mr. Jones had been hospitalized multiple times after he discontinued his medication in *Mr. Jones*, and he is smart enough to know it will happen again. However, each time he convinces himself that this time will be different. This is a classic example of denial.

Cognitive-behavioral theorists have contributed significantly to the understanding of the experience of depression. Aaron Beck has described a cognitive triad that is common in these patients. The triad consists of (1) perceiving oneself as defective and inadequate, (2) perceiving the world as demanding and punishing, and (3) expecting failure, defeat, and hardship. These "automatic thoughts" are readily apparent in *American Splendor*, *The Cooler*, *Scent of a Woman*, *The Hospital*, and Julianne Moore's character in *The Hours*.

Mood Disorders and Creativity

There is compelling evidence that mood disorders may be related to the creative process, and numerous artists, poets, and composers have been diagnosed as depressed or bipolar, or have biographies that suggest that these disorders were present. Examples of poets believed to have experienced mood disorders include William Blake, Lord Byron, Alfred Lord Tennyson, John Berryman, Sylvia Plath, Theodore Roethke, and Anne Sexton; examples of painters and composers with mood disorders include Vincent van Gogh, Georgia O'Keefe, and Robert Shuman (Jamison, 1993). Sylvia Plath's difficulties with depression are detailed in the film adaptation of her semi-autobiographical novel *The Bell Jar* (1979), as in Gwyneth Paltrow's portrayal in *Sylvia* (2003). The troubled life of Beethoven is portrayed in the 1995 film *Immortal Beloved*. Vincent van Gogh's life, work, and mental illness (which may have been bipolar disorder) have been documented in the films *Vincent* (1987), *Vincent & Theo* (1990), and *Van Gogh* (1991). However, none of these match the artistic achievement established by the 1956 film *Lust for Life*, in which Kirk Douglas plays van Gogh and Anthony Quinn plays the supporting role of Paul Gauguin.

Shakespeare was fascinated by people who took their own lives, and his plays and their film adaptations provide a useful and fascinating way to approach the study of suicide. Major Shakespearean plays in which suicide is a prominent theme includes *Romeo and Juliet*, *Julius Caesar*, *Hamlet*, *Anthony and Cleopatra*, *Macbeth*, *Othello*, and *King Lear*. There here have been multiple film adaptations of each of these plays.

Additional Questions about Creativity

- Are people with certain mental illness more creative than people without such disorders?
- How do you make sense of such a significant split between dramatic creativity and complete chaos and disorder that often mark such individuals' lives?
- What are your own views on van Gogh? What behaviors support a diagnosis of mood disorder? What evidence suggests a seizure disorder may have been present? Are there any other competing hypotheses?
- If you had the power to cure someone like van Gogh, but you knew that the treatment would destroy his creativity, would you proceed?
- What other artists and writers have experienced mood disorders?
- Can you name other artists, writers and poets who have committed suicide?

Suicide

Suicide and Depression

Suicide is the eighth most frequent cause of death throughout the world, but suicide rates vary widely among different countries. Generally, the suicide rate is low in the less prosperous countries and highest in the more affluent ones, such as Germany, Switzerland, and Sweden. However, the suicide rate is also high in all the Eastern European nations. The suicide rates in the United States and Canada are in the middle range. Among adolescents, suicide is the third most frequent cause of death. While men are more likely than women to commit suicide, women attempt suicide more frequently than men. Men are more successful in their attempts because they are more likely to choose a more lethal means (e.g., guns).

Mortality rates for suicide are generally higher in urban areas, and prevalence rates for suicide have been shown to be positively correlated with the size of cities. Although suicide has a low incidence in closely-knit rural communities, the problem is more common among the elderly, in areas where agriculture is in decline, and among workers who are immigrating to the cities. The incidence of suicide increases with age, with the elderly population having the highest suicide rates (NIMH, 2003).

One of the best predictors of who will attempt suicide is a history of a psychiatric disorder. Those who are at the highest risk for suicide are those who have no hope. People who express hopelessness are more likely to commit suicide than those who have some hope for the future. The association between suicidality and hopelessness is stronger and more stable than the association of suicidality with the presence of depression and substance use disorders (Kuo, Gallo, & Eaton, 2004). The lead characters in films discussed earlier—*Scent of a Woman*, *The House of Sand and Fog* and *The Hospital*—have a strong sense of hopelessness.

The Hours

The Hours (2002) is a film of enormous psychological, emotional, and cinematic proportions. The film was nominated for Academy Awards as Best Picture, Best Director, and Best Adapted Screenplay. The all-star cast includes Nicole Kidman, Meryl Streep, Julianne Moore, Ed Harris, Claire Danes, Jeff Daniels, Toni Collette, John C. Reilly, and Miranda Richardson. Music is brilliantly composed by the renowned Philip Glass, and the script is adapted by David Hare. Ironically, one of the least known figures in this film is perhaps the most important, the director. This was director Stephen Daldry's second feature film, though his extensive work and awards in the London theater show he was more than equal to the challenge.

> **"If I were thinking clearly, Leonard, I would tell you that I wrestle alone in the dark, in the deep dark and that only I can know, only I can understand my own condition."**
>
> **Nicole Kidman as Virginia Woolf**

The film depicts three stories of three women, who are closely connected although they live in different time periods. Each struggles with both serious depressive symptoms and suicide issues.

Kidman plays the now celebrated novelist, Virginia Woolf, struggling to write her soon-to-be-famous novel, *Mrs. Dalloway*, in the early 1900s while suffering with what would be named today as bipolar disorder. The film dramatically begins and ends with the suicide of Virginia Woolf, who drowns herself in a quickly flowing river with heavy rocks in her pockets to weigh her down. Woolf's depression is emphasized in the film though some mania symptoms are depicted, including her agitation, decreased need for sleep, poor judgment and her indecisiveness, such as when she decides to leave her house against doctor's orders with the intention to move to and live in London. She has a history of "fits," problems with mood, she hears voices, and she has made two attempted suicides. Though her life has been set up to protect her, the inner turmoil she experiences is simply too painful. She smokes marijuana to calm herself, focus her thoughts, and to numb the pain.

> **"There are times when you don't belong and you think you're going to kill yourself. Once I went to a hotel. Later that night I made a plan. The plan was I would leave my family when my second child was born. That's what I did. I got up one morning, made breakfast, went to the bus stop, got on a bus, left a note... What does it mean to regret when you have no choice? It's what you can bear. There it is. No one's going to forgive me. It was death. I chose life."**
>
> **Julianne Moore as Laura**

The character of Laura (Moore) is living in a quaint neighborhood home in the 1950s. She reads *Mrs. Dalloway* with interest and passion, finding comfort and inspiration in the lead character. Laura's character is an enigma, but she is clearly depressed and overwhelmed by life and its demands. She is socially awkward and skittish, at times unsure of how to respond socially and at other times standing near the door (after the doorbell rings) but not answering it. She is overwhelmed by easy tasks (i.e., baking a cake) and is self-critical of her mistakes. Laura, like Woolf, feels alone and craves connections though does not seem to know how to make them. She kisses her visiting neighbor, Kitty (Collette), on the lips, clearly trying to connect with another life. She spends a lot of time alone and experiences frequent crying spells. At one point, she decides to commit suicide, leaves her son with a baby-sitter and checks into a hotel—a suicidal dream seems to be the catalyst that changes her mind. Ultimately, life is too much for her to cope with and rather than committing suicide, she travels to Canada to restart her life, abandoning her husband and children.

The third interweaved story is set in New York City in 2001 and involves Clarissa (Streep), a woman trying to impress others and cover up her pain by throwing a party (just as in Mrs. Dalloway) for Richard (Harris), her former lover, a prize-winning poet dying of AIDS. Clarissa is a strong woman who is socially confident and appears sure of herself. Her vulnerability is slowly disclosed through her struggles to help Richard, through her distant relationship with her partner of several years, and in her emotions that rush to the surface when she confronts a former lover (Daniels).

"I still have to face the hours, don't I... I mean the hours after the party and the hours after that."

Ed Harris as Richard alluding to his suicidal thoughts when speaking to Clarissa

---

Clarissa covers her inner pain through self-sacrifice, trying to help Richard cope with his hallucinations, non-compliance with medication, depression, and cynicism. Ultimately, Richard commits suicide by jumping out of the apartment window in front of Clarissa.

Additional Questions for Discussion (*The Hours*)

- Compare and contrast Virginia Woolf's decision to commit suicide and Laura's decision to live but abandon her family. Is one decision healthier? More just?
- Is suicide the right decision for a person such as Woolf who feels trapped in life and consumed by intense inner turmoil, or is suicide a selfish attempt to escape one's pain?

- How might a therapist approach a predicament and character such as Woolf's?
- What is the prognosis for Clarissa at the film's conclusion?
- What depression elements are paralleled in each woman across the generations?
- Can someone painfully dying of AIDS (e.g., Richard's character) still have a life worth living? What can be said to a patient who would answer "no" to this question?

Hopelessness and suicide intent are well depicted in the film *Night, Mother* (1986), starring Sissy Spacek as Jesse and Anne Bancroft as the mother, Thelma. This film is a thought-provoking and gripping film adaptation of a Pulitzer Prize-winning stage play about suicide. The entire film takes place in the mother's home, where Jesse has lived since her divorce. As the play begins it is 6:05 p.m., and Jesse has just informed her mother that she plans to kill herself that night. The two women examine their lives as Thelma tries to protect her daughter from her decision. Ultimately, Jesse explains that she has no hope and ends her life at 7:45 p.m.

Suicide makes for high drama, and it is a common theme in films. Some examples include the unforgettable Russian roulette death of the soldier who remained in Vietnam in *The Deer Hunter* (1978); the suicide by drowning of a young man who feels he cannot please his critical father in *The Field* (1990); the murder/suicide by a Marine recruit in *Full Metal Jacket* (1987); the lead character in the Roman Polanski film *The Tenant* (1976), who becomes suicidal after renting the apartment of a woman who in fact had recently committed suicide; Greta Garbo's suicide by stepping in front of an oncoming train in *Anna Karenina* (1935); and the suicide staged to look like a hunting accident in *Mountains of the Moon* (1990). Japanese novelist Yukio Mishima, one of the most fascinating characters in contemporary literature, committed *seppuku* (ritualistic suicide), and his life and death are portrayed in the film *Mishima* (1985). Peter Finch, playing Howard Beale, the mad prophet of the evening news, announces to the world that he will commit suicide on the air in two weeks and sees his ratings soar in the film *Network* (1976). In the independent film, *Eye of God* (1997), a young boy views his mother's suicide. He is left in acute stress, confusion, and terror, unable to speak and catatonic-like. Shortly after, he kills himself at the age of 14.

Often a failed suicide attempt is a means by which a director can heighten tension or set the stage for future character development. After Olivia (Patricia Clarkson) attempts suicide in *The Station Agent* (2003), her relationship with two other lonely characters deepens and the three complete a close bond of support and friendship. When Pu Yi, the last emperor of China, attempts to commit suicide by slashing his wrists in a railroad station restroom in Bernardo Bertolucci's *The Last Emperor* (1987), we get some insight into his character and a better sense of the despair he is experiencing. Glenn Close attempts suicide by slashing her wrists in *Fatal Attraction* (1987), and the attempt is necessary to establish the extent to which she is willing to go to manipulate and control her lover. When Gary Oldman shoots himself in the chest in the opening scenes of *Chattahoochee* (1990), we learn that he is afraid to die and not genuinely psychotic.

Suicide is sometimes romanticized in film, such as in the hauntingly beautiful *Elvira Madigan* (1967), in which two lovers decide on a double suicide. In a French film, *The Hairdresser's Husband* (1992), the female protagonist jumps to her death by drowning in order not to lose the happiness she has found with her new husband.

Finally, suicide is often treated as a humorous topic. Examples include Burt Reynolds' character in *The End* (1978), the multiple suicide attempts of Harold in the black comedy *Harold and Maude* (1972), the Italian judge who tries to get his sister to commit suicide in *Leap into the Void* (1979), the elaborate last supper for the impotent and suicidal camp dentist in *M*A*S*H* (1970), and the inadvertent death by hanging in *The Ruling Class* (1972).

The Virgin Suicides (1999) was Sofia Coppola's directorial debut. The story involves a repressed family with five daughters who commit suicide in response to their mother's overbearing control and repression. Unfortunately, this film supports the public misconception that suicide is caused by over-controlling parents when in fact it is the opposite that occurs.

Dead Poets Society

Dead Poets Society (1989) stars Robin Williams as John Keating, an unconventional English teacher at a rigid boys' preparatory school. This film was nominated for several Academy Awards. Set in 1959, this drama contrasts institutional values and individual creativity. By fostering "critical thinking" in his classroom, Keating broadened students'

educational experience and their ability to think independently. The students also discovered that when Keating was a student at the school, he started a secret society, the Dead Poets Society, dedicated to intellectual creativity. These students reactivate the society.

One important conflict in the film is between Neil, a student who wants to be an actor, and his father, a domineering businessman who wants his son to be a doctor. Neil's father will not allow him to try out for a campus production of *A Midsummer Night's Dream*. Neil disregards his father's demands, goes to the audition, and is selected for the lead role. Keating encourages Neil to explore the relationship with his father and to enlist his father's support. Neil's father is enraged when he views his son's successful performance. Neil is immediately brought home and, in an act of desperation believing that his father will never "allow" him to become an actor, Neil shoots himself with his father's gun. Keating becomes the scapegoat for Neil's suicide, and the school's administration uses the suicide as an excuse to fire the unconventional teacher. The film ends with the other students protesting Keating's dismissal.

Additional Questions for Discussion (*Dead Poets Society*)

- Would Neil qualify under *DSM-IV* for a psychiatric diagnosis? If so, which one?
- How common is it for someone to commit suicide as a way of punishing someone else?
- Does the presence of a handgun in a house increase the likelihood of suicide?
- Would a daughter have been as likely to shoot herself?
- What else could John Keating have done to reduce the conflict between Neil and his father?

Risk Factors and Antecedents

There are many risk factors associated with suicide. The demographic risk factors include being adolescent or elderly, male, white, separated, divorced or widowed, isolated, and unemployed. Other risk factors include depression, alcoholism, bipolar disorders, and neurological disorders.

Unfortunately, even though risk factors and the antecedents of suicide have been well established, accurately predicting who will commit suicide is extraordinarily difficult. Most clinicians include a suicide assessment in their initial interaction with any client who has an emotional problem or a mental illness. An assessment for suicide focuses on three areas: intent, plan, and lethality.

Intent, or thinking about suicide, is a specific indicator of an impending suicide and probably the single most important predictor. Those people most intent on suicide have worse insomnia, are more pessimistic, and are less able to concentrate than those with less intent. In the film *Night, Mother*, the total story focuses on Jesse's intent to kill herself. Those individuals most intent on killing themselves are more often males, older, single or separated, and living alone. However, experts also know that intent is episodic and that even if there is no intent today, there may be tomorrow. In *Dead Poets Society*, there is no mention of Neil's intent and the viewer is led to believe that he does not intend to kill himself until he returns home, feels helpless, and convinces himself there is no way out of an untenable situation. If someone had recognized his intent or if he had reached out for help (e.g., by calling a suicide hotline), Neil might have been able to identify creative alternatives to suicide.

Most experts believe that even though a person is intent on suicide, there is almost always an underlying wish to be rescued. Thus, a person who is very intent upon killing himself or herself may consciously or unconsciously send out signals of distress, evidence of helplessness, or pleas for help. Some of the verbal cues may be "I am going away" or "You won't be seeing much of me from now on." There may also be unusual behaviors such as putting one's affairs in order, giving away prized possessions, engaging in atypical acts, or becoming socially isolated. These behaviors are all present in *Scent of a Woman*. Lt. Colonel Slade puts his financial affairs in order, visits his family, says good-bye, and has his "last fling."

People who have a **plan** for committing suicide are more likely to actually kill themselves than those who have vague thoughts about not wanting to live. Clinicians are trained to determine if their patients have a plan to kill themselves and how specific their plans are. An individual who does not have a plan is considered to be at lower risk than someone who knows how he or she can commit suicide, and who has access to the planned method. In *The Hospital*, Dr. Herbert Bock plans to kill himself by injecting a lethal dose of potassium. He demonstrates both plan and intent, and, because of his easy access to potassium, he is clearly at high risk.

The **lethality** of the method is also an indicator of the risk of suicide. The more lethal the chosen means, the more likely the person will commit suicide, especially if there is easy access to the method selected (e.g., guns in the home). The most lethal suicide methods are using guns, jumping off buildings and bridges, and hanging. Slashing one's wrists and ingesting 15 or fewer aspirin are common methods of attempting suicide, but they are seldom lethal. Other methods that carry a moderate to high risk of lethality are drowning, carbon monoxide suffocation, and deep cuts to the throat. In both *Scent of a Woman* and *Dead Poets Society*, the lethality was high because guns were the means selected for the suicidal act.

Prevention of Suicide

Since there are no clear predictors of suicide, there are no foolproof prevention strategies. Treatment of an acutely suicidal individual involves protecting him or her and connecting with that part in each person that wants to be rescued. Usually, a person who is suicidal is hospitalized and not allowed to be alone. Even in those instances, if a person wants to commit suicide, a hospital environment cannot prevent it, and many suicides have been completed in a protected environment. In the film *Crossover* (1983), a psychiatric nurse is plagued by self-doubt after one of the patients he works with commits suicide.

Ordinary People

Ordinary People (1980), an Academy Award-winning film based on Judith Guest's novel by the same name, depicts the aftermath of a suicide attempt. Conrad Jarret, played by Timothy Hutton, is a sensitive teenager who has attempted suicide following a boating accident that killed his brother, Buck. Conrad could not overcome his feelings of guilt, attempted suicide, and was hospitalized for four months. The film begins following Conrad's return home and traces his struggle for personal redemption and his futile attempts to communicate with his parents. His father, Calvin, played by Don Sutherland, is a successful tax attorney who tries to respond to Conrad's needs. His mother, Beth, played by Mary Tyler Moore, is well intentioned but ultimately unable to meet the needs of her son. Beth is the nucleus of a family in a crisis.

Upon his return from the hospital, Conrad is inattentive in class and distant with classmates. He is also ill at ease with his parents. His father encourages Conrad to contact a psychiatrist, and eventually he begins therapy with Dr. Berger, played by Judd Hirsch. In therapy, Conrad explores his relationship with his parents. When Dr. Berger suggests that the entire family meet together, Beth refuses. Throughout the movie, Beth's feelings toward her living son become obvious. Calvin begins to question his relationship with Beth and unsuccessfully attempts to reengage his wife in their relationship. Beth eventually leaves her husband and son, who come to terms with Beth's limitations and begin to rebuild their lives around their love for each other.

Other characters play an important role in the movie. Conrad's swim coach quizzes him about his hospitalization, asks him if he received shock treatment, and is demanding during training sessions. Conrad finally decides to quit the swim team.

The other important character is Karen, a girl Conrad met at the hospital. While hospitalized, Conrad and Karen had a completely "open and honest" relationship. When Conrad contacts her at home, she is distant but appears to be in control. She is involved in school activities and maintains she no longer thinks about the problems that resulted in her suicide attempt. She also decides not to see a therapist. Karen's newfound confidence is startling to Conrad, who begins to question his own fragile condition. When he tries to get in touch with her later, however, Conrad learns that she has committed suicide.

Karen's death forces Conrad to relive the boating accident that took Buck's life. At last, he is able to explain his guilt—he lived and Buck did not. Conrad realizes that he was angry with Buck because he did not hang on to the boat. With the help of Dr. Berger, he experiences the intense pain of his loss and resolves his guilt.

If a suicide attempt is survived, the meaning of the attempt should be examined. Even though the viewer is not told whether Conrad has symptoms of depression, it is safe to assume that they were present prior to the suicide attempt. Conrad's suicide attempt was both an attempt to kill himself and a cry for help. His family fails to appreciate or respond to his distress over his brother's death. His mother is unable to relate to anyone, and his father is withdrawn from family interaction. Through a suicide attempt, Conrad got his family and friends to acknowledge his desperate situation.

Every suicide threat should be taken seriously. While attempting suicide is often an impulsive act, it is also an act of communication. If Conrad had possessed the necessary communication skills, he could have discussed his feelings and explored their meaning.

Additional Questions for Discussion (*Ordinary People*)

- How would you describe Conrad's family in Ordinary People?
- If you were a therapist working with this family, how would you proceed?
- Do any of the characters in the film meet DSM-IV criteria for depression?

International Films: Mood Disorders and Suicide

Suicide Club (2002) is a Japanese film that explores the phenomenon of suicide raising more questions than answers. It assesses possible links between suicide and crime, music, violence, group contagion, internal compulsions, consumerism, evil forces, and various external factors. After 54 young girls mysteriously and collectively commit suicide by jumping in front of an oncoming subway train, mass hysteria and confusion develop and several individuals and groups around the country take their lives. One scene depicts a group of students joking about creating a suicide club, and they gather at the edge of a building's roof and chant for each other to "jump." One by one, they watch each other plummet to their death.

Rain (2001) is a New Zealand film about a young girl coming of age as she interacts with family and neighbors on a beach. The film is included in this chapter because of the girl's depressed mother, an alcoholic who acts out sexually and only seems to be happy when she is drinking. The drinking clearly helps her escape from her depression.

The Scottish film *Wilbur Wants to Kill Himself* (2002) is helpful only insofar as it allows the viewer to witness the various stereotypes and misconceptions possible in a movie. Wilbur is a depressed and angry man who curses children, rejects women, and cheats with his brother's wife even though his brother is the person who repeatedly keeps Wilbur from killing himself. The brother is depicted in the role of protector, frequently checking up on Wilbur, supporting him, and removing sharp objects from his home. Wilbur's persistence in his suicide attempts include pills, gas from the oven, hanging, drowning, cutting his wrists in the bathtub, and standing at the edge of the roof of a building. Wilbur's determination to commit suicide ends once his love for his brother's wife becomes mutual. This perpetrates the misconception that love conquers mental illness, extending to severe, serious suicidality. Equally disturbing is the film's blatant stereotypes of two psychologists leading a group; one smokes cigarettes during sessions and comments that the patients would be better off without group therapy; the other violates boundaries with a patient, licking his ear, going out on a date, engaging in sexual activity in a hospital closet, and violating confidentiality.

Critical Thinking Questions

- Are dysthymic disorders, major depressive episodes, and major depressive disorders qualitatively different phenomena, or are they simply different quantitative expressions of a single disorder?
- If you genuinely believe a friend is suicidal, what are your ethical and moral obligations?
- Do your responsibilities to that person change if you are a therapist rather than a friend?
- Is there a suicide hotline in your community? Do you know how to access it?
- How do you distinguish between passing thoughts of suicide and a cry for help?
- The suicide rate for both men and women is much higher in Sweden, Denmark, and Austria than in the United States. What cultural factors could account for these differences?
- Kathy in *House of Sand and Fog* does not receive treatment for her depression. What percentage of depressed individuals go un-treated? About how long does it take a depressed individual to seek treatment following the onset of his or her disorder?
- At one point in *Mr. Jones*, a physician compares bipolar disorder to diabetes. In what way is the comparison apt? In what way is it misleading?
- Patty Duke is a well-known personality who has "come out of the closet" and openly shared the story of her mood disorder (see *Call Me Anna*). Can you think of other celebrities who have been candid about their own struggles with mental illness? Did any of them have bipolar disorder?
- How could you distinguish between someone experiencing a manic episode and someone experiencing the elation and energy associated with amphetamine abuse?
- Dr. Bowen in *Mr. Jones* states, "You're not a sick person; you're a person with a sickness!" What is the significance of this semantic distinction?

Chapter 6

Personality Disorders

It's not going to stop. It's gonna go on and on until you face up to your responsibilities...
I just want to be part of your life... What am I supposed to do?
You don't answer my calls, you change your number.
I'm not going to be ignored, Dan!
Alex (Glenn Close) lays down the law for former lover
Dan (Michael Douglas) in *Fatal Attraction*

Questions to consider while watching *Fatal Attraction*

- Why is Alex Forrest (Glenn Close) so threatened by the termination of a seemingly insignificant affair?
- What advice would you give Dan Gallagher (Michael Douglas) if he were to consult with you about how to handle the situation with Alex? Should he return her phone calls and try to set limits or simply ignore her?
- Are there any characteristics of borderline personality disorder that are not present in Alex Forrest?
- Why is sexual acting out so common in people with borderline personality disorder?
- Is there any relationship between physical and sexual abuse in children and the subsequent development of personality disorders?
- Do you believe Alex is genuinely pregnant or is this simply an attempt to get attention?
- Are Alex's suicidal threats genuine or are they empty attention-seeking gestures? Would you caution Dan Gallagher to take them seriously?
- What is the prognosis for a patient with a borderline personality disorder?
- Can a person have several different personality disorders at the same time?
- Is borderline personality disorder more common in men or in women? Why?
- How is a personality disorder qualitatively different from an Axis I DSM-IV disorder?

Patient Evaluation

Patient's stated reason for coming: "I can't seem to hang on to a relationship. I need to know what's wrong with me."

History of the present illness: Alex Forrest is a 35-year-old woman who has never married. She has dated widely, and she has established romantic and sexual relationships with dozens of men over the past 18 years. However, she has not been able to sustain any of these relationships for more than a few months. Each new relationship is characterized by intense, torrid sexual activity followed by a rapid diminution of interest by her partner.

Past psychiatric illness, treatment, and outcomes: Ms. Forrest has been hospitalized on two occasions following suicide attempts. She took an overdose of Valium from her mother's medicine cabinet when she was 17, following a fight with her boyfriend. She called her mother when she began feeling ill and was taken to a local hospital, where her stomach was pumped.

About five years ago, she purportedly attempted to drown herself by jumping into a public pool while fully clothed following an altercation with a former boyfriend who had just informed her of his plans to marry another woman. She was taken to a local psychiatric hospital, where she remained overnight for observation and was released the following morning. Approximately two days ago, Ms. Forrest attempted to cut her wrists with a razor blade; however, the cuts were only superficial and hospitalization was not required. She denies being suicidal at the current time but has engaged in self-injury behaviors during periods of stress.

Ms. Forrest has been treated intermittently by a large number of psychiatrists, social workers, and psychologists; however, these relationships, like her romantic liaisons, always start strong and then prove to be unrewarding in the end.

Medical history: Ms. Forrest has a long history of nonspecific pelvic pain and pelvic inflammatory disorders. She was treated for gonorrhea at the age of 20. An unplanned pregnancy at age 22 was voluntarily terminated. There is an intermittent history of bulimia, but she has never been hospitalized or treated for this problem. Ms. Forrest had her appendix removed approximately eight years ago. The rest of the medical history is unremarkable.

Psychosocial history: Ms. Forrest is an only child whose parents divorced when she was 11 years old. She reports that her parents were constantly fighting, and her childhood was quite unhappy. She has no siblings and no significant relationship with her grandparents or other relatives. Her mother moved frequently following her divorce, and Alex was often required to change schools in the middle of the school year. Ms. Forrest had relatively few friends and was somewhat reclusive until high school, when she learned that she could use sex as a way to gain popularity and status. She passed each grade on schedule, although there is a recurrent history of disciplinary problems in high school. She was reunited with her father during her college years. He died during her senior year. Ms. Forrest attended the State University at Stony Brook and graduated in 1967 with a bachelor's degree in psychology.

Drug and alcohol history: She reports sporadic use of marijuana, dextroamphetamine, barbiturates, and LSD. After leaving college, she continued to smoke marijuana recreationally for about a decade but discontinued use of the other drugs. Over the past five years, she has intermittently used powdered cocaine at parties. She drinks heavily: almost every evening meal includes a bottle of wine and she sips bourbon all evening long, almost every night. She often becomes intoxicated at parties, and this public drinking has frequently impaired her judgment on numerous occasions. This patient smokes approximately one pack of unfiltered cigarettes each day.

Behavioral observations: Ms. Forrest was attractively, if somewhat provocatively, dressed. She wore an expensive pearl necklace for the interview. She proved to be verbal and articulate. She cooperated fully with the examination. She appeared to have good insight into the nature of her difficulties with men. She seemed genuinely eager to get help with these relationship problems.

Mental status examination: Ms. Forrest was oriented in all spheres. Both immediate and delayed memory were intact. She was able to repeat serial sevens without difficulty. There is no dysnomia, and she can easily repeat both simple and complex phrases. Judgment is intact. She can follow simple directions, read, write, and draw without difficulty. Ms. Forrest denied current suicidal or homicidal ideation. She earned a score of 30 on the Mini Mental Status Examination, and there was no evidence of cognitive difficulty or psychiatric disturbance on the mental status examination.

Functional assessment: Ms. Forrest has changed jobs frequently since graduating from college. However, she has consistently worked in the publishing industry for the past decade, and she is reportedly a good editor. Her on-the-job interpersonal difficulties and several affairs with co-workers have limited her ability to develop a career with a single publisher. Her father is deceased, she has not spoken to her mother in more than a decade, and there are no other significant family relationships. Ms. Forrest has few friends other than the men with whom she has been involved.

Strengths: The patient is attractive, intelligent, and well educated. She has had extensive experience in therapy, knows the language, and appears motivated to change.

Diagnosis: Adjustment Disorder with Disturbance of Emotion and Conduct; R/O Borderline Personality Disorder

Treatment plan: Weekly individual therapy. Establish and develop a therapeutic relationship, and track the cognitions and behaviors associated with the men she is currently dating. Encourage nonsexual friendships and appropriate "boundary setting" with both men and women. Continue to monitor for signs of depression and suicidal thoughts.

Prognosis: Ms. Forrest has the cognitive capacity to identify and understand the reasons she has never been able to sustain a meaningful romantic relationship. However, her long history of unsuccessful therapy suggests her prognosis is guarded at best.

Psychopathology and Fatal Attraction

Glenn Close's character in *Fatal Attraction* (1987) offers one of the best available depiction of psychopathology. Michael Douglas plays Dan Gallagher, a happily married New York attorney who becomes sexually involved with Alex Forrest (Close), a glamorous and sexually aggressive publishing executive. What starts out as a simple, one-night affair for Dan turns into a nightmare for him and his family as Alex becomes increasingly possessive and manipulative. Dan tries to extricate himself from the affair, but Alex resorts to verbal threats, telephone calls to his wife, a suicide gesture (slashing her wrists after Douglas tells her the affair is over), and intimidation of his wife and child. The performance by Close dramatically illustrates many characteristics of patients with a borderline personality disorder: anger, impulsivity, emotional lability, fear of rejection and abandonment, inappropriate behavior, vacillation between adulation and disgust, and self-mutilation. Although people with Borderline Personality can be dangerous to others as displayed dramatically in *Fatal Attraction*, this is not always the case as they are probably more likely to be dangerous to themselves. If the individual has some strong Antisocial Personality characteristics as well (which Close's character does), the risk of danger to others rises.

Types of Personality Disorders

All of us have unique personalities and our own individual personality traits. On occasion, these personality traits get us in trouble. For some individuals, their personalities result in a persistent pattern of recurring interpersonal difficulties. When there is a persistent pattern of inflexible and maladaptive behavior that *continually* gets an individual in trouble or that causes him or her considerable subjective distress, a diagnosis of personality disorder may be appropriate.

People with personality disorders exhibit enduring, pervasive, and inflexible patterns of behavior that deviate markedly from societal expectations. Their behavior seems odd, unusual, or peculiar to most other people. However, to the individual the experience is so ingrained that it is ego-syntonic—it does not bother them, i.e., they have learned to be comfortable with their own pathology.

The ranking of ten personality disorders in Table 6.1 is not arbitrary but is based on a conceptual model that groups all personality disorders into one of three relatively distinct clusters. **Cluster A** (for *odd or eccentric behavior*) includes the paranoid, schizoid, and schizotypal personality disorders. **Cluster B** (for *dramatic, emotional, or erratic behavior*) includes the antisocial, borderline, histrionic, and narcissistic personality disorders. **Cluster C** (for *anxious or fearful behavior*) includes the remaining personality disorders: avoidant, dependent, and obsessive-compulsive.

Personality disorders are rarely diagnosed in children and many of the traits of personality disorder that are common in children (e.g., problems with impulse control in adolescents) do not persist into adulthood. In addition, the diagnosis is inappropriate in any situation in which aberrant behavior results from transient situational factors (e.g., the individual who repeatedly gets his or her tax returns audited may become paranoid about the government). Finally, it is critical that cultural variables be considered when a diagnosis of personality disorder is being considered. For example, the Italian film *Down and Dirty* (1976) includes a protagonist who appears to have an antisocial personality. However, his behavior must be understood in terms of the culture of southern Italy and the debilitating and corrosive effects of poverty.

Some personality disorders are more common in men (e.g., antisocial and narcissistic personality disorders). Others are found more often in women (e.g., borderline, histrionic, and dependent personality disorders). This is quite consistent with cinematic portrayals, as we will soon show.

Cluster A Disorders

These "odd and eccentric" disorders are rare and hence their depiction in cinema is uncommon (unlike other disorders such as Dissociative Identity Disorder, which, though rare in reality, are often shown in movies).

Paranoid Personality Disorder

People with a paranoid personality are isolated and suspicious. They are convinced that others are talking about them behind their backs or plotting against them. The behaviors of others are carefully scrutinized for evidence of intent to harm, and overtures of friendship or good will by other people are rejected as manipulative gestures or parts

Table 6.1 Characteristics of Personality Disorders with Examples from Contemporary Cinema

Personality Disorder	Characteristics	Classic Film Examples	Recent Film Examples
Paranoid	Distrust and suspiciousness about the motives of others	Humphrey Bogart in *The Caine Mutiny* and *The Treasure of the Sierra Madre*	Will Smith in *I, Robot*
Schizoid	Detachment from social relationships and a restricted range of emotional expression	Charlton Heston in *Will Penny* Billy Bob Thornton in	Crispin Glover in *Bartleby*; *The Man Who Wasn't There*
Schizotypal	Acute discomfort in close relationships, cognitive or perceptual distortions, and behavioral eccentricities	Jack Lemmon in *The Ruling Class*	Owen Wilson in *The Royal Tenenbaums*
Antisocial	Disregard for and violation of the rights of others	Malcolm McDowell in *A Clockwork Orange*; Robert Walker in *Strangers on a Train*	Matt Damon in *The Talented Mr. Ripley*; Robert Duvall in *The Apostle*
Borderline	Instability in emotions and interpersonal relationships, inadequate self-image, fear of abandonment, and marked impulsively	Glenn Close in *Fatal Attraction*	Ellen Burstyn and Ashley Judd in *Divine Secrets of the Ya-Ya Sisterhood*
Histrionic	Excessive emotionality and attention seeking	Vivien Leigh in *A Streetcar Named Desire*	Annette Bening in *American Beauty*
Narcissistic	Grandiosity, a need for admiration, and lack of empathy for the problems and needs of others	Gloria Swanson in Sunset Boulevard	Aaron Eckhart in *In the Company of Men*; Campbell Scott in *Roger Dodger*
Avoidant	Social inhibition, feelings of inadequacy, and hypersensitivity to criticism or negative evaluation	Jane Wyman in *The Glass Menagerie*	Audrey Tautou in *Amelie*; Sean Connery in Finding *Finding Forrester*
Dependent	Submissive and clinging behavior and fears of separation	Bill Murray in *What About Bob?*	Renée Zellweger *White Oleander*
Obsessive-Compulsive	Preoccupation with orderliness, perfectionism, and control	Jack Lemmon in *The Odd Couple*	John Turturro in *Box of Moonlight*

of a plot. Ironically, because paranoid individuals behave in peculiar ways, a self-fulfilling prophecy occurs and people *do* begin to discuss the paranoid individual behind his or her back. Paranoid people tend to have few or no friends. They personalize almost everything and misinterpret casual remarks to make them fit into their belief structure.

The character Joseph in *Amelie* (2001) meets the criteria for a paranoid personality, as he is so suspicious of his ex-girlfriend dating and meeting other men that he sits all day in the café where she works and watches her closely. He carries a small tape recorder in his pocket and records her various laughs, comments, and conversations with his own play-by-play and time of day voice-over. The viewer sees this is a pattern (thus providing additional weight for the diagnosis) as he continues similar suspicious behavior with the next woman he begins to go out with and then again with the first girlfriend when the new girlfriend dumps him. Anger and quick defensive reactions are common in the paranoid personality and are additional qualities of Joseph in the film.

Another convincing portrayal of this disorder is Detective Spooner (Will Smith) in *I, Robot* (2004). Spooner is a highly suspicious, judgmental, and angry person, particularly around robots, which are a mainstay in this world of 2046. Spooner takes a shower with no curtain and his frustrated mistrust of robots leads him to push away a friendly robot delivering a package. His misperceptions bring him to randomly chases down and tackle a robot running with a purse, which he has assumed is a robbery even though no robots have ever committed a crime at this point in history. Much of the plot transgresses due to Spooner's paranoia, which other characters recognize. One man (the James Cromwell character) counts on Spooner's paranoia to save the human race from robots. As with many films depicting a paranoid character (also see Mel Gibson in *Conspiracy Theory*, 1997), the psychopathology is often distorted by the entertainment value of the plot which results in a character's paranoia proving to be accurate and justified in the end.

Ben Stiller's character in *The Royal Tenebaums* (2001) displays numerous paranoid characteristics that seem stable over time. He has an underlying anger and rage toward his father, unrealistic fears, and displays excessive concern and hypervigilance regarding his environment and home.

Humphrey Bogart's role as Captain Queeg in *The Caine Mutiny* (1954) is a wonderful illustration of the paranoid personality. Queeg becomes preoccupied with trivial misdemeanors by sailors while he ignores the important parts of his job — such as maintaining the morale of his men. He eventually falls apart under pressure when he is called to the witness stand to testify in a court martial hearing for an insubordinate junior officer. There is a famous scene in which Queeg takes two ball bearings out of his pocket and begins to move them around nervously in his palm, and everyone in the court senses that this man is not well adjusted. Bogart plays another paranoid personality in *The Treasure of the Sierra Madre* (1948) in which he becomes obsessed with the idea that his partners are out to steal the gold all three men have agreed to split between them.

Schizoid Personality Disorder

The individual with a schizoid personality has little interest in and avoids close interpersonal relations. He or she is likely to be described as a loner who lacks meaningful ties to a family, community, or value system. These individuals are unlikely to display strong emotions or tenderness to others; they appear apathetic, diffident, and indifferent. They most often have little or no interest in sexual encounters and few marry.

There are some excellent portrayals of schizoid personality in the cinema. Two examples come from two films named *Bartleby*; both are remakes of a Herman Melville short story, "Bartleby the Scrivener." The 2001 version is a fascinating, cult film about a quiet, passive man named Bartleby (Crispin Glover) hired for a mundane office job. He thoroughly does his job at first but soon begins to refuse doing extra work, repeating the mysterious phrase, "I would prefer not to." This quirky behavior continues as he stares for hours at an air conditioning vent and displays no interest in socializing with his work peers. Schizoid individuals are often isolated from society, and an opening scene symbolizes Bartleby's isolation as he is depicted enclosed and caged on an overpass bridge above a busy, productive society represented by an expressway below. His speech is slow, eye contact is limited, and affect is flat and emotionless throughout the film. At times, he displays an incongruent, distant, random smile or two, but does not engage others interpersonally with smiles or laughter. Often times, there is no understandable reason as to why a person behaves in schizoid manner, and the film parallels this idea as no explanation is overtly given for Bartleby's behaviors, lack of emotions, or social apathy. The earlier 1970 version portrays very similar schizoid traits for the lead character, Bartleby, and the plot is very similar to the new version. This older film is black and white, dark, slow, and gloomy.

Another classic example of schizoid personality is found in the Coen Brothers' film noir, *The Man Who Wasn't There* (2001), where even the title of the film suggests a schizoid quality. Billy Bob Thornton plays Ed Crane, an aloof, taciturn barber who appears disinterested in life, claims he dislikes most things and that his life has been one of "no excitement." He is unemotional with flat affect and a monotone voice. He moves slowly and stiffly, and even the way he smokes cigarettes is a slow, unconscious, steady ritual. His responses to others are dull with heavy sighs, and he is passive when criticized. He does not seem very bothered by the fact that his wife is cheating on him with his friend. He allows himself to be exploited by a traveling salesman. The only relationship he seems to invest emotional energy in is with a young girl; he appears committed to helping her pursue her dream of becoming a musician. Also consistent with schizoid characteristics is that no one "really knows him;" this is reinforced by his inability to share himself with others.

Crispin Glover plays another socially awkward, schizoid character in *Willard* (2003). Willard is isolated from others and his only companions are the rats that congregate in his basement. After one rat, whom he names Socrates, saves him from a suicide attempt, he distances himself further from people and rallies the rats to help him get revenge. In the film, *Heavy* (1995), the lead character displays a schizoid reaction to his mother's death. He becomes frozen, emotionless, sexually disinterested, and isolated with flattened affect. In order to qualify for a diagnosis of schizoid personality disorder, his bereavement would need to be differentiated and his personality assessed prior to his mother's death. The film offers another interesting schizoid description about the lead character's isolation through his belief that you can be as "big as an ox and no one sees you."

The figure of the loner is a staple in western films, and many of these characters would meet the criteria for schizoid personality disorder. They avoid close relationships, prefer solitary activities, lack close friends and confidants, and appear indifferent to the praise or criticism of others. Charlton Heston in *Will Penny* (1968) is one example; Robert Redford in *Jeremiah Johnson* (1972) is another.

Schizotypal Personality Disorder

People with schizotypal personality have "schizophrenia-like" characteristics but do not typically meet the diagnostic criteria for schizophrenia. They hold odd or peculiar beliefs, thoughts, and/or behaviors. They are often very superstitious, have unusual perceptual experiences, and are suspicious and paranoid. Some authorities have suggested the disorder reflects a mild form of schizophrenia. The character of Maude in the film *Harold and Maude* (1972) exhibits the sort of highly eccentric behavior of the type that sometimes leads to diagnosis of a schizotypal personality disorder. However, Maude's flamboyance and exuberance would be very unusual in someone with a schizotypal personality.

Owen Wilson in *The Royal Tenenbaums* (2001) plays Eli, a man who wears flamboyant outfits with his cowboy hat and uses unusual words. He has a quirky tone of voice, odd and eccentric behavior, and often does not have a firm grasp on reality. His apartment has numerous odd paintings covering the walls. It is uncertain how much these qualities result from his drug abuse; regardless, his behavior and interactions are quite schizotypal. Denis Leary plays a truly fascinating man who has paranoid schizophrenia in *Final* (2001). He displays some interesting schizotypal traits as well, but to qualify for a diagnosis of Schizotypal Personality, these traits could not occur exclusively with the schizophrenia episodes.

The character, Ernie, in *Bartleby* (2001) displays many schizotypal traits. He has a poor use of logic and when he gets upset, he speaks in a verbal salad, mixes words, and is somewhat nonsensical. His appearance is disheveled. He is easily overwhelmed by stress. His behavior is often inappropriate for the situation, as he never appears to be working when he is at the office, he displays no reaction after spilling water and copier ink, and he is later repeatedly and genuinely scared by a pop-up spin toy. He presents with a constant paranoid, concerned look on his face and has blunted affect throughout the film.

The schizotypal personality is demonstrated in Flannery O'Conner's novel *Wise Blood* and in the 1979 John Huston film adaptation. The Southern preacher works hard to convince people to join his "Church Without Christ." He has numerous peculiar beliefs, odd speech, constricted affect, strange behavior, and few close friends. These five characteristics would be sufficient to justify the diagnosis of schizotypal personality. Hyler (1988) uses DeNiro's portrayal of Travis Brickle in *Taxi Driver* (1976) to illustrate the schizotypal personality. He feels this film is such a useful tool for teaching medical students about psychopathology that he has incorporated it into a computer program that can be used to teach medical students to perform and record a complete mental status exam (Hyler & Bujold, 1994).

Additional Questions for Discussion (Cluster A Disorders)

- Where do you draw the diagnostic line for these disorders, and how can one differentiate them from similar Axis I counterparts (e.g., schizophrenia)?
- What are some etiological components for schizoid personality (such as for the lead character in *Bartleby*)?
- Is there any validity to the idea that people who are odd and eccentric, as illustrated by these examples, are simply very creative people?

- What is the treatment of choice for someone with a Cluster A diagnosis?
- Do any of the characters in the films discussed above make meaningful changes in their personal, social, or occupational life? Are Cluster A disorders resistant to change?

Cluster B Disorders

Each of the personalities in this cluster is often lively and colorful, fitting the description "dramatic, emotional and erratic." Consequently, individuals with Cluster B disorders are common in movies, as they tend to make fascinating, stimulating cinematic characters. They are often attention grabbing, conflicted, manipulative, charming, and charismatic—many of the qualities the moviegoer typically loves or hates. In addition they often have troubled pasts, and the viewer gets to observe them escape from present pain or make impressive changes, either way making for good drama.

The Talented Mr. Ripley (1999) is a wonderful example of a film's character (Tom Ripley, played by Matt Damon) who displays characteristics of each of the disorders in this cluster. Even the opening credits get at the complexity of this disorder, listing the following adjectives to replace "talented" in the title: mysterious, yearning, secretive, lonely, troubled, confused, loving, musical, gifted, intelligent, beautiful, tender, secretive, haunted, passionate.

Antisocial Personality Disorder

People with antisocial personality break the law, can be physically aggressive, manipulate others, lie, take senseless risks, and have little or no sense of remorse or guilt about the consequences of their behavior. These individuals violate the rights of others and appear to experience distress only when their behavior results in punishment or incarceration. They are impulsive, thrive on the "pleasure principle," and have a great deal of trouble planning their future behavior or anticipating its consequences. Individuals with antisocial personality disorder have a great deal of trouble learning from their mistakes and find themselves dealing with similar legal and interpersonal problems throughout their lives.

Abuse of alcohol and other drugs is common among antisocial personalities. Bar room fights, such as those in the film *Last Night at the Alamo* (1983), often occur. However, the loyalty to the Alamo bar displayed by the protagonist and his friends would be very uncharacteristic of anyone with a genuine antisocial personality.

People with antisocial personality disorder often have multiple sexual partners and tend to use others for sexual gratification, with little concern for the needs or feelings of their sexual partners. They can be superficially warm and charming but become distant and aloof after their sexual conquest. This is evident in David Thewlis' intellectual, philosophical, and antisocial character portrayed in *Naked* (1993).

Robert Duvall plays a complicated, antisocial minister who philanders, abuses and projects his problems onto other characters and God in *The Apostle* (1997). Duvall's character, Sonny, is driven but flawed. He is a "spiritual antisocial" in that he passionately preaches and his manipulation and charm often takes the form of genuinely wanting to help others have more meaningful lives; however, he externalizes his problems by blaming Satan and not taking responsibility to his life. He abuses alcohol, is unfaithful to his wife, threatens her with a gun, throws an object through a window, and, most seriously, grabs his wife roughly by the hair and attempts to drag her away from the baseball game and then hospitalizes his wife's boyfriend by hitting him on the head with a baseball bat. He lies to others about his past, despite their trust in him as their spiritual leader. Sonny certainly embodies the qualities of narcissism as well, with his grandiose speech and in his preaching, and he feeds off others' admiration and his ability to stake out a position in center stage. This film will remind some of the role of the much more psychopathic "preacher" played by Robert Mitchum in the classic film *The Night of the Hunter* (1955).

The fascinating film *Tape* (2001) takes place in one setting (a motel room) with only three characters (Ethan Hawke, Robert Sean Leonard, and Uma Thurman). Despite this simplicity, the film is a complex look at a devious, antisocial personality Vince (Hawke), and his manipulation of two high school friends. Vince is a 28-year-old without a job who volunteers as a firefighter. He presents as unstable, using drugs, jumping and running around the small motel room, "chugging" beers, and throwing the cans around. He has a history of drug dealing and reports that he has "anger tendencies" and "unresolved issues." At times, he is sweet and soft-spoken, but the viewer soon realizes he is purposefully acting this way to manipulate his friends. With extreme craftiness, he secretly "tape records" his friend, John (Leonard) revealing some vulnerable information (about a date rape in high school) after Vince interrogates him in cross-examination style; displaying a total lack of empathy, he blackmails John and calls another old friend (Vince's ex-girlfriend and John's date rape victim), Amy (Thurman), with the hopes of continuing his plotted manipulation.

The true story of Danny Burrows (played by newcomer, Ryan Gosling) in *The Believer* (2001) speaks to the serious love-hate relationship a young man has with himself as he adopts a dramatically contradictory role as a Jewish Nazi. In the opening sequence, the viewer sees Burrows, who presents as a stereotypic skinhead displaying Nazi symbols, seek out and beat a young Jewish man in the middle of the street. He embraces repugnant Nazi beliefs, ranking ordering races by worthiness in the following order: Whites, Asians, Blacks, and Jews. At the same time, Burrows is highly intelligent and articulate, speaking charismatically to adults many years older than him about Nazi order, discipline, and values, articulating "kill your enemy" and "Judaism is a sickness" messages. His aggressiveness and impulsivity lead him to instigate numerous fights. Burrows displays little remorse for any of his antisocial behaviors until, while ransacking a synagogue with a Fascist group, he begins to show concern for how people treat a scroll containing sacred Jewish writings. He brings the scroll home, takes painstaking care of it, and begins to teach his girlfriend Hebrew. From here, his internal contradiction begins to fade, as does his antisocial behavior, yet he still must deal with the consequences of the lifestyle he has created for himself.

Another film illustrating an antisocial personality that is based on a true story is the film *Shattered Glass* (2003) about Stephen Glass (Hayden Christensen), the New Republic magazine writer who went to extensive lengths to fabricate and embellish stories. Both the film and the lead actor do a remarkable job of depicting not only the elaborate deceit, fantasy, and double-life associated with this personality disorder, but also the neurotic quality of the "antisocial in trouble." The latter phrase refers to anxiety mixed with a façade of change that comes about when a person with an antisocial personality disorder is caught or about to be caught. Glass' response is to become emotional, obsequious, and/or apologetic. His manipulations take many forms, from trying to emphasize his need for the editors' support and how important it is (when he is lying) to trying to play others against one another to incessant repetition of the question "Are you mad at me?" Glass

does not see the consequences of his actions as he continues to tell various lies and stories to cover up earlier lies, digging himself deeper into deception with each interaction; we later see the tremendous impact of his behavior on the New Republic.

Another "caught" antisocial is Edward Norton's character in *25th Hour* (2002), who has 24 hours before he must serve a prison term for trafficking marijuana. Since he is caught, he is forced to face some of his shame, guilt, and anger. In one unforgettable scene, he externalizes intense anger, blaring out "fuck you" to every race, group, district, and borough in New York City, as well as his father and girlfriend. We can infer he is saying this to himself as well, especially since he is looking at himself in the mirror while talking, but the acceptance of personal responsibility seems to be missed—as it often is in the antisocial personality. This Spike Lee film brings up important issues of regret and choice and brilliantly leaves many questions open-ended.

Catch Me If You Can (2002) is another film about a character with an antisocial personality disorder. The film is based on the true story of Frank Abagnale Jr., a con man who used his charm and good looks to defraud banks of millions of dollars in the 1960s. The role of Abagnale is played by Leonardo DiCaprio, who successfully impersonates a Pan-Am co-pilot, a physician and an attorney. Abagnale is pursued for six years by FBI agent Carl Hanratty (Tom Hanks), before he is eventually captured, and he winds up consulting with the FBI on fraud crimes.

An interesting contrast of antisocial personalities occurs in *Levity* (2003), a film in which Billy Bob Thornton plays a person with an antisocial personality trying to make amends for his actions (a murder many years ago), and Morgan Freeman plays an antisocial preacher hiding from the police with a fake identity. Likewise, Tom Hanks is a charming person with an antisocial personality who cleverly uses sophisticated speech and extensive rationalizations to manipulate an old woman for his own purposes in *The Ladykillers* (2004).

A somewhat less dramatic illustration is found in the callous manipulation of naive home buyers vividly portrayed by Jack Lemmon, who plays a desperate and unhappy real estate salesman in *Glengarry Glen Ross* (1992). The manipulation of others for personal gain without concern for the consequences of one's behavior is a characteristic feature of antisocial personality disorders. Natasha Richardson and Mia Farrow play two consummate con artists in *Widow's Peak* (1994), although the diagnosis of antisocial personality is incompatible with the character portrayed by Farrow for most of the film. Many films appear to depict antisocial behavior, but it is often unclear as to whether these characters would meet all the criteria for the disorder.

Some actors like Kevin Spacey can make their career out of playing antisocial characters. Though Spacey can play a variety of characters with vastly different personalities, he has played an impressive range of roles that illustrate the antisocial personality; for example, he portrayed an arrogant writer in *The United States of Leland* (2004), an unhappy man who becomes obsessed with "the pleasure principle" in *American Beauty* (1999), a devious serial killer in *Se7en* (1995), a con man in The *Usual Suspects* (1995), and a brutal executive in *Swimming with Sharks* (1994).

Antisocial vs. Psychopathic Personality

Though Psychopathic Personality Disorder is not an actual diagnosis, it is a commonly used term, and there is often confusion when the labels antisocial personality, sociopath, and psychopath are all lumped together. A useful distinction is to consider the previously described characteristics as a description of the more global antisocial personality (i.e., manipulative, rule-breaking, irresponsible). The psychopathic/sociopathic personality has all of the features of a person with an antisocial personality disorder, but these features are present in an extreme degree. For example, the psychopath has no morals, is always self-serving, very aggressive, and lethal. Psychopaths/sociopaths are referred to as having "no conscience," whereas people with a diagnosis of antisocial personality disorder do—it is just covered by deep layers of defenses. Movies can be helpful in making the distinction more clear; consider *Pirates of the Caribbean* (2003) and contrast Johnny Depp's character as the antisocial pirate with the pirate zombies led by Geoffrey Rush's character. The latter are clearly psychopathic.

Likewise, Leonardo DiCaprio's character in *Catch Me If You Can* would be considered to be antisocial, but not sociopathic. Table 6.2 helps make this distinction more clear with the help of contemporary cinema.

Two particularly powerful films pose interesting questions relevant to this distinction: *Monster* (2003) and *American Psycho* (1999). *Monster's* Charlize Theron might be the very rare example of a serial killer who seems more Antisocial than Psychopathic. She is able to express and share love for another (her lover played by Christina Ricci)

and in the film she claims (as did serial killer Aileen Wuornos in real life) that her killings were in self-defense. In *American Psycho*, Patrick Bateman (played by Christian Bale) is depicted as killing many people throughout the film. If we are to take this literally, then he is clearly a psychopathic personality. Interestingly, the film also suggests that all of the murders depicted in the film are in Bateman's thoughts/fantasies, which is supported by plot elements, by his extensive fantasy doodles, and cinematically at the end through close-up shots of Bateman's head. The viewer is left to believe that Bateman is very narcissistic and has heavy antisocial tendencies, but not a psychopath.

The cinema is replete with examples of characters who illustrate the psychopathic personality. Some salient examples include Anthony Hopkins' portrayal of a murdering cannibal, Hannibal Lecter in *The Silence of the Lambs* (1991), Hannibal (2001), and *Red Dragon* (2002); Ian McKellan in *Apt Pupil* (1997), a film that depicts the rekindling of a suppressed psychopathic personality; *In Cold Blood* (1967); *The Boston Strangler* (1968); *Henry: Portrait of a Serial Killer* (1990); Fritz Lang's child serial killer in *M* (1931); and Dennis Hopper (who is often typecast in the role) as a sociopath in both *Blue Velvet* (1986) and *Speed* (1994). Charles Manson, as portrayed in the film *Helter Skelter* (1976), is another example of the indifferent disregard for social values and moral behavior that is found in people with psychopathic personalities. (Manson, responsible for the death of nine people in 1969, has never shown any remorse for his behavior or the deaths of his victims.)

"A door had been opened that couldn't be shut."

Ian McKellan as a reclusive, former Nazi henchman in hiding in *Apt Pupil*

The legendary director Stanley Kubrick frequently depicted psychopathic personalities in his films. Perhaps his most famous is the street hoodlum, Alex, in *A Clockwork Orange* (1971); other characters in his films with strong psychopathic tendencies include the Senior Drill Instructor (Gunnery Sergeant Hartman) in *Full Metal Jacket* (1987), Jack Nicholson's deteriorating character in *The Shining* (1980), the deceptive computer, Hal,

Table 6.2 Differentiation of Antisocial Personality from Psychopathic Personality Through Movies

		Film	Personality Characteristics
Personality	**Antisocial**	Johnny Depp in *Pirates of the Caribbean*	Manipulative and devious though Depp's character does show qualities of trust, care, allegiance, and teamwork
		Edward Norton in *25th Hour*	History of not conforming to laws/rules, impulsive, irritable, and reckless disregard but shows remorse and care for others
		David Thewlis in *Naked*	Deceitful, impulsive, self-centered, lacks empathy, irresponsible; also shows fleeting concerns and care for others and for the betterment of society
		Robert Duvall in *The Apostle*	Heavily deceitful, impulsive, and dangerous in words and behaviors; also shows genuine care for others, love for God, and shows remorse
	Psychopathic/Sociopathic	Geoffrey Rush in *Pirates of the Caribbean*	Kills at will for own gain, embodies seven deadly sins, particularly greed
		Owen Wilson in *Minus Man*	Serial killer with no conscience and no reason or purpose, kills randomly
		Woody Harrelson and Juliette Lewis in *Natural Born Killers*	Torture and kill anyone that gets in their way or bothers them, without hesitation or regret
		Samuel L. Jackson in *Unbreakable*	Complete disregard for human life as he commits mass murder out of a self-serving need to find his "better half"

in *2001: A Space Odyssey* (1968), the obsessed pedophile in *Lolita* (1962), and the generals who confronted Kurt Douglas' character in the anti-war masterpiece *Paths of Glory* (1957).

A classic example of a psychopathic personality is found in Alfred Hitchcock's *Strangers on a Train* (1951). Robert Walker's character, who repeatedly engages in unlawful behavior (including murder), is deceitful, appears to be impulsive (e.g., proposing murder to a total stranger on a train), and there is never any reason to suspect he feels any remorse for the murder he commits or his plan to have his father murdered.

Borderline Personality Disorder

Borderline personality is characterized by unstable but intense interpersonal relationships, labile mood, impulsive behavior, and erratic emotions. These individuals are easily angered, but their anger may pass as quickly as a summer storm, leaving no sign of its recent presence. They become overly attached in almost all of their relationships: when they initially become romantically involved, their partners are apt to feel smothered by the intensity of the relationship and perplexed by the wild swings between affection and anger; when they enter therapy, therapists quickly become concerned about their excessive dependence and inappropriate adulation. These are the patients most likely to call in the middle of the night, insisting on an emergency consultation or late-night office visit. This is most apt to occur when the patient feels isolated or alone (e.g., when the therapist is about to take a vacation). They often vacillate between indiscriminate adulation and active hatred (referred to as "love-hate" or "push-pull"), often within the space of hours (e.g., Glenn Close in *Fatal Attraction*).

Suicide gestures and self-injury are common in people with borderline personality disorders. These gestures cannot be ignored, because completed suicide occurs in about 10 percent of borderline personality disorder cases. However, it is more common for the patient to behave in ways that are more attention seeking than life threatening, such as swallowing 20 Valium and then calling a crisis center or making superficial cuts on the upper arm before calling a suicide hotline. Self-mutilation is also a common and serious problem with borderline personalities. The symptoms of borderline personality disorder overlap with those of both depression and bipolar disorders, and many borderline personality patients respond to treatment with either antidepressants or lithium. Women are diagnosed with borderline personality disorder about three times as often as men are.

In *Divine Secrets of the Ya-Ya Sisterhood* (2002), an emotionally labile and behaviorally erratic mother, Vivi, is played by Ashley Judd (the younger Vivi) and Ellen Burstyn (the older Vivi). Vivi has lived a tragic life; her true love was killed in combat, and she lives a life of despair and anger with a fawning man whom she believes is "lesser." She threatens to leave the family and eventually does after a dramatic nervous breakdown. Though we learn much about her instability through flashbacks documenting verbal and emotional abuse, alcohol abuse, and excessive conflicts, the viewer also sees the remnants of a disturbed woman in the present day. The plot focuses on Vivi's current tribulations, poor relationship with her daughter (Sandra Bullock), the resentments that continue to build because of prior family disarray and instability, and the challenge of bringing a relationship based on conflict into balance.

The intriguing movie *Swimming Pool* (2002) portrays a young woman, Julie, who is seductive, provocative, and has a desire for excitement. She presents as nonchalant and laid-back, but she is also someone who can be easily hurt or angered. She is sexually impulsive and promiscuous, having sex with a different man each night. She throws herself at older men, even when they express disinterest. One night she appears with a bruise on her face around her eye and the viewer is left to speculate as to what sort of danger she had been involved in while staying out the whole night. She is manipulative and jealous when her roommate begins to dance with a man. Julie acts out in anger when she is rejected. Her instability leads to a dissociative episode where she thinks she sees her mother (who is deceased) and expresses happiness at the prospect of her mother's return, screams when she is told this is not true, and then faints. Julie also experiences a loss of memory, in which she is unable to remember killing her lover.

The hospital staff in the film *Girl, Interrupted* (1999) apply the diagnosis of Borderline Personality Disorder to the lead character, Susanna (Winona Ryder). It is difficult to justify this diagnosis, as Susanna only seems to display two behaviors fitting this diagnosis—a suicide attempt and sexual promiscuity. However, she is clearly depressed and has serious relationship problems.

Christina Ricci's character in Woody Allen's *Anything Else* (2003) displays borderline personality qualities in her interpersonal relationships and her affective instability. She has some attention-seeking qualities, is dishonest, manipulatively takes advantage of a dependent man, uses drugs, and is defensive and self-righteous in explaining her decisions and behaviors.

Fear of abandonment is a pathognomonic characteristic of borderline personality. Matt Damon's character, Tom Ripley, in *The Talented Mr. Ripley* (1999), has a tremendous fear of abandonment and commits murder to prevent himself from experiencing the pain of abandonment. Other potential examples of borderline personalities include Diane Keaton in *Looking for Mr. Goodbar* (1977) and several of the female supporting characters in Martin Scorsese's *After Hours* (1985).

Histrionic Personality Disorder

The defining feature of histrionic personality is dramatic attention-seeking behavior. These individuals are self-centered and preoccupied with their own appearance. They feel uncomfortable in any situation in which they are not "center stage," and they can quickly turn their emotion on or off and with little provocation. They resent attention directed at others and will often engage in excessive behavior to have the focus of attention redirect to themselves. They initially seem to be spontaneous and interesting people, not unlike Rosalind Russell's portrayal of the title character in the film *Auntie Mame* (1958). However, true histrionic personalities soon find that others quickly tire of their desperate attempts to remain at the center of attention and are angered by their inability to engage in equitable social interaction.

Annette Bening as Carol in *American Beauty* (1999) is very melodramatic and clearly a histrionic personality. She is unhappy and under-stimulated in her marriage, thus sexually acts out with a man whom she admires for superficial reasons—he is rich, successful, charming, and highly narcissistic. She ruins a rare intimate moment with her husband (Spacey) when she shows obsessive concern that he might spill beer on the couch. She is exact in her appearance, dressing in elegant clothes that make her stand out. At work as a real estate agent, Carol attempts to sell a house by exaggerating the house's appearance to unimpressed customers. She shows excessive emotionality and breaks down when faced with the reality that bright smiles and superficiality do not sell houses, and she goes into an emotional fit, crying, slapping herself in the face, stomping on the floor, and yelling, "Shut up! Stop it! You're weak! You baby! Shut up! Shut up! Shut up!" In social situations, Carol displays a very loud laugh that can be heard across a crowded room. She is socially inappropriate and highly critical of family members, such as when she greets her daughter after her daughter's dance routine, "I watched you closely. You didn't screw up once" with a big smile on her face as if she has just made an important, helpful observation. Her daughter looks at her in disgust.

In addition, rapid shifting from one extreme emotion to another is common in people with histrionic personality disorders. Carol quickly switches from hysterical laughter to blatant seriousness with a man she desires, and later from tearful crying to anger and slapping her daughter's face. Histrionic personalities are often very suggestible as well. Carol displays a ridiculous level of awe for another real estate agent's mantra, "You cannot count on anyone except yourself," and she follows and teaches this as the most important lesson to learn in life. In summary, appearance and style are far more important than substance for the person with a histrionic personality disorder.

One of the best film examples of a histrionic personality is Katharine Hepburn's portrayal of a dying mother in *Long Day's Journey Into Night* (1962). Family life centers around the mother, and her two sons and her husband dote on her. She is extremely concerned with her appearance, openly fishes for compliments, and makes frequent references to her lost beauty. If she were being clinically evaluated, Hepburn's character would be diagnosed as a histrionic personality disorder on Axis II and as opioid dependent (morphine) with physiological dependence on Axis I.

Robin Wright-Penn in *White Oleander* (2002) plays Starr (an appropriate name for a histrionic character), the first mother-figure for a young adolescent, Astrid, whose biological mother has been incarcerated. Starr is a former stripper, recovering alcoholic, and born-again Christian who encourages Astrid to read the Bible and accept Jesus as her savior. At first, Starr is kind and overly helpful in her care for Astrid; soon the viewer realizes these are superficial overtures that develop into a dangerous murder attempt when Starr becomes threatened as she realizes that Astrid's emerging sexuality appeals to her husband.

Zaza, the gay transvestite performer in *La Cage aux Folles* (1978), provides another wonderful example of a histrionic personality. She is dramatic and flamboyant, and almost everything she does is exaggerated. When Renato tells her that he plans to invite his ex-wife to an important dinner with his son's future in-laws, Zaza is highly insulted and announces her intention to commit suicide. Neither Renato nor the viewer thinks for a minute that she is serious about her threat.

Narcissistic Personality Disorder

People with a narcissistic personality have an intense need for admiration, often self-centered, and have an exaggerated sense of their own importance. They may spend a great deal of time fantasizing about success or power. They feel entitled to special treatment and expect that others will automatically comply with their expectations; this often leads to their appearing conceited and pretentious. Their preoccupation with themselves leads them to overlook or devalue the contributions of others. The name of this disorder is taken from the Greek myth of Narcissus, who fell in love with his own reflection. Hence, mirrors are often used in films to symbolize self-reflection, infatuation with self, and distorted or broken mirrors represent a fractured sense of worth or esteem.

Although presenting as confident and secure, people with narcissistic personality disorder have low self-esteem and harbor unconscious feelings of insecurity, unworthiness, and self-doubt. Consider the film *Phone Booth* (2003), in which a highly narcissistic New Yorker is stripped of his defenses and completely unravels at the end, admitting to all his deceits, manipulations, and cover ups, from the expensive clothes he wears, to his deep relationship fears, to keeping a young male sidekick around to feel better about himself. Suddenly, all his grandiosity, entitlement, and conceit are gone. He had never admitted these deeper issues even to himself in a conscious way, and they remained present but deeply embedded. It took an extreme situation to trigger awareness and admission. Of course, most narcissists do not come to such insights about themselves, and when they do, it is not long before they return to their old patterns.

Contemporary cinema is replete with examples of narcissistic personality disorders: Andy Garcia's fascinating character is a narcissistic, struggling writer in *The Man from Elysian Fields* (2001) who eventually realizes his narcissism and subsequent self-inflicted destruction and makes a change by facing his pain; Nicholas Cage's corporate character in *The Family Man* (2000) states his only concerns are for money and power, nothing deeper; Ben Stiller's ridiculous character in *Zoolander* (2001), is too self-absorbed to realize he has been brain-washed; and John Turturro's character is a narcissistic opera singer and performer in *The Man Who Cried* (2000).

In *Roger Dodger* (2002), Roger is a classic narcissistic personality—a womanizer who is teaching a 16-year-old adolescent about how men think and see the world. He teaches the boy to see, think and perceive sex everywhere he looks. Roger creates various "opportunities" for the boy to seduce women—at the bar, at a party, and then with prostitutes. He has no qualms about encouraging the boy to take advantage of a drunken woman who has passed out. Roger displays little true empathy for the boy as he thrusts him to manhood. Underneath Roger's inflated self-image and conceit is his rage at being rejected by his attractive boss (Isabella Rosselini) who has put an end to their love affair.

In *Lovelife* (1997), Alan is a minor writer and professor who thinks he is very important. He seems to care only for himself and his work. He treats women poorly and exploits women through seduction, deceit, and manipulation, and he eloquently explains his approach and craft to a barfly. In denying his own arrogance, Alan believes he is compassionate and sensitive because he has to struggle to manage a relationship with two women (the real issue is that one of the women is not as fawning as the other). He believes women should be at his "beck and call" (one character describes him by saying "he says what he wants and everybody jumps").

"I want somebody to think I'm the greatest thing that ever happened to them and without me they couldn't go on."

A narcissistic writer in *Lovelife*

The film accurately portrays the underlying sensitivity to criticism and inherent low self-esteem of the narcissist (which frequently results in narcissistic injuries). Alan gets very upset, stubborn, and passive-aggressive when his girlfriend does not come to his lecture; he expresses an intense fear of abandonment as he makes a big production about his girlfriend leaving a party

without him, he then grovels on his knees with the girl standing over him, and lays in a girl's lap to receive the motherly nurturance and attention he so deeply craves.

"Let's hurt someone."

Chad in *In the Company of Men*

Director Neil LaBute created unforgettable and cruel narcissists in two of his bitterly satirical movies—*In the Company of Men* (1997) and *The Shape of Things* (2003). Though there are two male narcissists in the former movie, Chad is more pathological as he convinces his friend that they should seduce a vulnerable, deaf woman and get her to fall in love with both of them, only to subsequently dump her. Chad feels entitled to do this, blaming women for being rejecting, controlling, and manipulative, ostensibly believing he and his partner can restore dignity to men through revenge and the pain of the innocent. In *The Shape of Things*, a character named Evelyn transforms Adam, an anxious, insecure, shy person, into a physically attractive, stylish, confident man. Without any qualms, she shocks Adam, the viewer, and the audience to whom she is giving a presentation when she reveals that her relationship with Adam has been a class "project" in which she used a human subject to prove that people are like clay and can easily be molded and manipulated. When talking with Adam afterward, Evelyn has a strongly stubborn, confident, and resentful expression on her face. She believes she made him a better person and thus should have been thanked for her behavior. The characters in each film have strong antisocial qualities evident in their complete disregard for others and social convention and in their pathological manipulation. They are literally predators who consciously sought out their prey—a vulnerable, neurotic individual with poor esteem. The endings of both movies reveal just how pathological both characters are as they reveal their manipulative "game," totally devoid of empathy.

Female narcissists are less common, but include Madonna portraying a grandiose, striking Eva Peron in *Evita* (1997). Eva emphasizes physical appearance, presentation to others, and her posture as critically important features. She manipulates people throughout the film for her own advantage—helping her rise in her career and look better in front of others. In addition, Mena Suvari's adolescent character in *American Beauty* has narcissistic traits clearly seen in her preoccupation in becoming a model, her lack of empathy for a new student who has been hospitalized, and her strong beliefs that she is somehow special and important.

Other classic narcissistic characters include Gloria Swanson in *Sunset Boulevard* (1950) and an (initially) arrogant and self-serving Mickey Rooney in *Boy's Town* (1938). In *The Doctor* (1991), William Hurt plays a self-centered and narcissistic physician who cares little for anything except himself and his career until he develops a tumor in his throat and discovers what it feels like to be a patient. Finally, Warren Beatty plays a narcissistic and self-centered gangster in the Barry Levinson film *Bugsy* (1991).

Additional Questions for Discussion (Cluster B Disorders)

- Why are most film examples of Borderlines women and most examples of Narcissists men? Is this an accurate clinical picture?
- What qualities of the Cluster B disorders make them the most common personality disorders found in jails and prisons?
- Do you agree with the distinction between the Antisocial Personality and Psychopath/Sociopath? State your case.
- Does society have a role in the creation of serial killers?
- One way of interpreting Monster is that Aileen Wuornos is a victim of circumstance. Would Aileen have developed into a murderer if she had not been a prostitute? What would have happened if she had never been abused?
- With which of these disorders is a client most likely to seek treatment? When and why? Who is least likely to ask for help?
- How close does Tom Ripley's character in The Talented Mr. Ripley come to meeting the criteria for each of the four disorders in this cluster?

Cluster C Disorders

As is true in clinical settings, characters in films will have symptoms and personality characteristics that overlap with more than one disorder in each

cluster. For example, it is clear Robin Williams' milquetoast character in *One Hour Photo* (2002) has a personality disorder, however, he has characteristics of several disorders, most of which are found in Cluster C. He lives alone, being too scared to take the risks that relationships require (Avoidant); he is obsessed with a pseudo family (Dependent); and he is orderly and rigid in handling and hoarding photos (Obsessive Compulsive). Add in some depression with psychotic features, a probable history of past sexual abuse, and voyeuristic elements and Williams' character becomes even more complex.

Avoidant Personality Disorder

People with **avoidant personality disorder** have a tremendous fear of being exposed as inadequate and inferior. They are hypersensitive to criticism and shape their lives around fear of rejection and disapproval. They generally avoid intimate relations, convinced that they would be ridiculed as inadequate lovers. They conceptualize the world (and especially interpersonal relationships and interactions) as unsafe and threatening. They have diminished self-esteem and describe themselves as inept, incompetent, and inferior. They are apt to spend much of their time at home and alone, in large part because of their concern that their personal deficiencies will be revealed if they venture out in public. These pervasive feelings of inferiority typically originate in childhood. In Adlerian terms, the person with an avoidant personality lacks the *courage to be imperfect*. However, it is important for clinicians to be sensitive to cultural differences that may affect a client's behavior. For example, in some Asian cultures, self-deprecation and extreme modesty about one's own achievements are normative behaviors and not indicative of a maladaptive personality trait.

This diagnosis overlaps substantially with the diagnosis of **social phobia, generalized type**. The overlap is so substantial that many clinicians find the distinction between the two diagnoses to be meaningless, and the *DSM-IV* acknowledges that the two diagnoses may be simply different ways of conceptualizing the same (or similar) conditions. Keep this in mind as you read about the characters in the following films.

Audrey Tautou's whimsical and endearing character in *Amelie* (2001) has many avoidant personality characteristics. As Amelie, she wants contact with others, especially intimate love, though she is unable to take the risk. The emphasis in the film is on her thoughts and the challenge involved in meeting a man; the key theme, which the movie cleverly portrays cinematically, is her constant avoidance of actually meeting a man who comes into her life. After doing a good deed, Amelie appears nervous and looks away, ignoring an opportunity for human interaction; she simply does not know how to interact socially.

The film is rare in its sophisticated exploration of the causes of Amelie's anxiety and avoidant behavior. It notes she was born and trapped between a neurotic mother (who had "shaky nerves" and was anxious about everything) and an iceberg father, who avoided all feelings. In addition, she had no playmates or social life and therefore became used to isolation, fantasy and imagination. Other contributing etiologies are presented when she is tricked into feeling guilty as the "cause" of natural disasters, when her mother is dramatically killed in front of her, and when she has ongoing problems in relating and communicating with her father.

A common pattern for people with avoidant personality is the problem of self-sacrifice—devoting oneself to helping others and losing sight of one's own struggles and self-care. Amelie epitomizes self-sacrifice as she devotes herself to being a regular "do-gooder," helping others find joy and become "unstuck" from their life patterns. Amelie is personally stuck in her avoidant pattern and does not know it. Eventually, she finds value in reaching out to others for support and developing the courage necessary to face her fears.

Avoidant personality can be distinguished from schizoid personality in that although both avoid interpersonal contact, the avoidant person actually craves the intimacy lacking in life. *Finding Forrester* (2000) is about a high school student, Jamal, who befriends a reclusive, retired professor and writer, William Forrester (Sean Connery), who seems to want more intimate connections. Like *Amelie*, this film is about people who are trying to get "unstuck" from their avoidance patterns. In *Finding Forrester*, Connery's character does not leave his apartment and can only be seen by others when he is cleaning his windows. He wrote an award-winning book 50 years ago but has not been able to get his subsequent work published. He seems to have given up, perhaps because of fear of rejection. He avoids other people and denies being interested in any life other than his own. When he does eventually go out, he has a panic attack when in a crowd. He is socially inappropriate, such as when he closes the

door in the face of Jamal without a "goodbye." There is a fundamental sadness in William's isolation in his apartment; he actually does look for connection as a voyeur, watching others outside with interest and keeping his windows clean so he can continue observing the outside world. The viewer begins to wonder how much of William's isolation is simple loneliness. The protagonist drinks alcohol alone frequently, often while working. He avoids discussing personal issues such as his family history or his work. Clearly, he is reluctant to risk interpersonal sharing, and although this changes significantly as the friendship with Jamal develops, William keeps the secret of his cancer to himself.

"The best of those who have gone before us cannot steady the unrest of those to follow."

From *Finding Forrester*

Sheila McCarthy plays an insecure, socially awkward, temporary worker with avoidant traits in the popular Canadian film, *I've Heard the Mermaids Singing* (1987). She is naïve, socially inhibited, and seems to have a fragile self-esteem and self-concept. The voice-over narration done by McCarthy provides insights into her thinking and feeling when she is interacting with others.

Dependent Personality Disorder

Dependent personalities have extreme difficulty making decisions. They are submissive and look to others for structure, meaning, and direction in their lives. They tend to be passive and clinging. These people lack assertion skills and submit to the will of others. They sometimes submit to verbal, physical, or sexual abuse by their spouses and others. They lack self-confidence and feel they cannot manage on their own. They fear the loss of approval that may occur if they express their own opinions or beliefs. They invest tremendous time and energy in maintaining a relationship with the person upon whom they are dependent. When a close, dependent relationship ends, they almost immediately seek out another relationship that supports their chronic need for succor.

An amusing illustration of a dependent personality occurs in the 1991 film *What About Bob?* Bob, played by Bill Murray, is the patient of a psychiatrist played by Richard Dreyfuss. Bob pursues the beleaguered psychiatrist across the country when the psychiatrist tries to take a short vacation. Almost all therapists have had overly dependent patients, although they are unlikely to have encountered a case as extreme as that of Bob. The film is an interesting starting point for a discussion of transference and countertransference.

In *Lovelife* (1997), a female bartender, Molly, maintains a high level of obsequiousness toward her narcissistic boyfriend, Alan, doing everything she can for him and losing her own identity in the process. Molly believes Alan can do "no wrong" and that he has no flaws; in addition, she subjects herself to his unrelenting criticism. Like many other dependent personalities, she finds herself rejected by her boyfriend who takes up with another woman; when he loses that other woman, he shows up and Molly takes him back.

"I've been seeing myself through him for years."

Dependent personality in *Lovelife*

Similarly, in the Spanish period film, *Mad Love* (2002), a woman compulsively attaches to her husband despite continuous evidence of his philandering. She becomes preoccupied and worried about his whereabouts, yet she maintains a high level of excitement when he returns from a journey that has obviously involved infidelities. In one scene, he resists a warm embrace despite her clinging and affectionate behavior, and she asks him to lie to her about where he has been. Even when she is rejected by him and sent away in isolation for decades, she obsessively continues to love him and believe they will be reunited upon her death.

Renee Zellweger plays Claire, a foster mother with a dependent personality, in *White Oleander* (2002). Claire's submissiveness to her husband, inability to confront or challenge his decisions, and her vulnerability to manipulation by others lead her to commit suicide. Jason Biggs' agreeable, people-pleasing character in *Anything Else* (2003) is so dependent he has to be "tricked" into being alone, asserting his needs, and challenging himself.

"I want to love you even if you loathe me."

A classic dependent quote from "Joan the Mad" in *Mad Love*

Audrey Tautou's character in the French film *God is Great and I Am Not* (2003) has a quirky element of dependent personality (but probably not the disorder) insofar as she repeatedly compromises her beliefs by conforming and converting to the religion of her partner at the time. She is shown trying to dedicate herself to Catholicism and Buddhism before finding a non-practicing Jewish man and converting to Judaism. Her fear of being alone leads her to become suicidal after the end of an intimate relationship.

Obsessive-Compulsive Personality Disorder

A person with obsessive-compulsive personality has enduring, inflexible, and maladaptive personality traits that involve perfectionism, orderliness, and an excessive need for control. They display exacting attention to detail and may devote a great deal of time to making lists and plans. Time is seen not as the fabric of life but rather as an enemy and something to be conquered. All of this psychological energy is expended in a futile attempt to achieve a sense of control over the exigencies of life and the vicissitudes of fortune. Two films that are solid depictions of obsessive-compulsive personality disorder are *The Odd Couple* and *M*A*S*H*. *The Odd Couple* (1968) presents a memorable performance by Jack Lemmon as Felix Unger, Walter Matthau's neurotic roommate who roams the house with a can of air freshener, determined to eliminate any unpleasant smells. In *M*A*S*H* (1970), Major Frank Burns spends the entire war fretting about the antics of Hawkeye Pierce and Trapper John McIntyre and the inability of the system to set limits on their exuberant behavior. He is obsessed with rank and bitterly resents any undue familiarity by enlisted men or junior officers. He also works hard to ensure that the enlisted men do not fraternize with Korean women. He is self-righteous, moralistic, and rigid, despite the fact that he is having an ongoing affair with "Hot Lips" Hoolihan. He becomes furious when he doesn't get his way, and he is totally ineffectual in responding to the cavalier attitudes of his tent mates.

It is important to understand the difference between obsessive-compulsive personality disorder and obsessive-compulsive disorder. The first disorder reflects a maladaptive personality style; the second indicates the presence of a serious mental disorder characterized by recurrent and persistent thoughts, images, or impulses (obsessions) and repetitious behaviors or mental acts (compulsions) that the individual cannot avoid or suppress. For example, an obsessive-compulsive personality may need to be constantly cleaning the house and "picking up." This is maladaptive (when excessive) but may not significantly impair the person's life, and may be mildly adaptive in some roles. However, the patient with an **obsessive-compulsive disorder** (e.g., Jack Nicholson in *As Good as it Gets* and Nicholas Cage in *Matchstick Men*) spends much of the day focused on his or her obsession or engaged in compulsive behavior. This individual is significantly distressed by his or her problem, and realizes that the behavior or thoughts are abnormal and out of control. In contrast, the person with **obsessive-compulsive personality disorder** is far less likely to be troubled by his or her condition.

John Turturro plays Al Fountain, a man with obsessive-compulsive personality disorder (OCPD) in *Box of Moonlight* (1996). Turturro's character is a rigid, overly conscientious, rule-driven man in both his work as a manager and in his family life with his wife and children. Al is rigid about the way his child learns using flashcards and obsessively asks about their use; he seems unable to handle joking, and has to rehearse a social situation before its occurrence. He is awkward and rigid at his job, bossing others around, seems robotic and machine-like, and is stiff in behavior (e.g., walking). The depiction of the effect of these OCPD traits on the family and co-workers is very clear: the family avoids, is passive, or hesitant around him and the co-workers make fun of him behind his back.

Al takes time off work and family to loosen up as he goes on a journey to search out his past. Along the way, two Jehovah's witnesses quickly and accurately get at his pain and sense of loss over the years (perhaps confronting the etiology of his OCPD) but they soon turn religious and proselytizing, which quickly alienates him. In a couple of scenes, Al sees things going backwards—water being poured and a child riding a bike. Does this represent his own life going backwards? It is a fascinating cinematic example of the lack of progress that occurs when one is so stuck in routine that it seems as if one is going backwards. Moreover, it is a metaphor for time, one of the biggest enemies to someone with OCPD.

Additional Questions for Discussion (Cluster C Disorders)

- How close does Robin Williams' character in *One Hour Photo* come to meeting the criteria for each of the disorders in this cluster?
- Since anxiety is a strong component of these disorders, can medication be an important part of treatment?
- Is the treatment the same for a person with OCD as with OCPD?
- What advantages are associated with being OCPD, Avoidant, or Dependent?

Films Portraying a Hodge-Podge of Personality Disorders

Some readers may want to see films that depict several personality disorders in one viewing for educational and clinical purposes. These films present interesting dynamics in their portrayal of interactions between different pathologies. Some examples follow.

Bartleby (2001) displays a classic example of schizoid personality in the lead character, Bartleby, portrayed exquisitely by Crispin Glover. Surrounding Bartleby, amidst a colorful office, are co-workers who are narcissistic (Joe Piscopo as Rocky, a self-inflated womanizer), schizotypal (Ernie, a disheveled man who often speaks in word salad), histrionic (Vivien, seductive and attention seeking), and dependent (the boss, unable to separate himself from a "fired" employee).

In *White Oleander* (2002), we see a young girl under the care of various "mother-figures," each with their own personality flaws. She goes from her biological mother, Ingrid (an antisocial manipulator), to Starr (a dangerous histrionic), to Claire (a dependent personality with low self-esteem), and eventually to Rena (an antisocial personality who forces her foster children to sell clothes on the street to make money). The eyes of each mother seem to say it all, from the penetrating eyes of Ingrid to the downtrodden eyes of Claire.

The Royal Tenenbaums (2001) portrays the ultimate dysfunctional family, with pathologies that include narcissism, dependency, incest, suicidal behavior, paranoia, addiction, depression, and antisocial behavior, along with a schizotypal friend.

Woody Allen's *Anything Else* (2003) portrays an older man with a narcissistic personality disorder who befriends a young person with a dependent personality disorder who is in a relationship with someone with a borderline personality.

French director, Jean Pierre-Jeunet purposefully creates films with very interesting and quirky personalities who play their roles on elaborate, often fantastical, set designs. See *Amelie* (2001), *The City of Lost Children* (1995), and *Delicatessen* (1992).

Critical Thinking Questions

- Is it useful to treat life-long personality characteristics as *diseases* (i.e., should personality disorders be included in the *DSM-IV*)?
- It is difficult to treat personality disorders, and treatment may last for several years. Should insurance companies be required to cover the treatment of these conditions?
- Is the concept of *evil* meaningful when discussing people with antisocial personality disorders?
- How does a personality feature (such as suspicion) differ from a personality disorder (such as paranoid personality disorder) or a disease (such as paranoid schizophrenia)? Are the differences qualitative as well as quantitative?
- *Fatal Attraction* originally ended with a suicide by Alex Forrest, using a knife that had Dan Gallagher's fingerprints on it. However, viewers did not like this ending, and it was replaced with the memorable bathtub scene. Would the original ending have been more consistent with a diagnosis of borderline personality disorder?
- What problems can therapists anticipate when they are treating clients with borderline personality disorders?

Chapter 7

Substance Use Disorders

You can't cut it short. When you're on that merry-go-round,
you have to ride it all the way, round and round 'til
that blasted thing wears itself out and the music comes to a halt.
Don Birnam in *The Lost Weekend*

Questions to consider while watching *The Lost Weekend*

- How does the portrayal of alcoholism in *The Lost Weekend* (1945) differ from that of more contemporary films about alcoholism, such as *Leaving Las Vegas*, *Trees Lounge*, *Drunks*, *28 Days*, and *When a Man Loves a Woman*?
- Is there a biological or genetic basis for alcoholism? What is it that makes alcohol so addictive?
- What examples of denial are illustrated by the film?
- At what point is it clear Birnam "has a problem?" When does the alcohol "abuse" become "dependence?"
- If Birnam's girlfriend drank as heavily as Birnam and became pregnant, what would be the likely consequences for her child?
- How common are hallucinations among alcoholics?
- Is the film's portrayal of delirium tremens realistic?
- Does alcohol increase suicidal ideation? Does it increase the likelihood of a completed suicide?
- Name each of the areas of functioning affected by Birnam's alcohol use. How much are these areas affected?
- Are there medications available now that would have helped Birnam cope with his withdrawal symptoms and his craving? What are they?

Patient Evaluation

Patient's stated reason for coming: "I'm an alcoholic, a hopeless alcoholic. I need to sober up and I need to stop drinking. You can help me with the first problem but not the second."

History of the present illness: Don Birnam is a 32-year-old man who has been admitted to Bellevue for the third time. He is a professional writer who has a long history of alcoholism. Mr. Birnam has pawned his typewriter and most possessions of any value. He reports drinking since age 18.

Past psychiatric illness, treatment, and outcomes: Mr. Birnam has not been treated for any psychiatric problems other than his alcoholism. He has been arrested on numerous occasions for public intoxication, and he was recently arrested after stealing a bottle of rye from a liquor store. Once he

begins drinking, he is unable to stop until he passes out. This is Mr. Birnam's third admission to this unit over the past two years. He presented with auditory and visual hallucinations and delirium tremens on both past admissions.

Medical history: This patient has a history of liver disease secondary to alcoholism. He broke his arm on one occasion after falling from a fire escape while drunk. He has multiple scars from abrasions that occurred during falls while drinking.

Psychosocial history: Mr. Birnam is the younger of two children. His parents are dairy farmers in upstate New York. He did well in school and achieved normal developmental milestones at appropriate ages. There is no history of truancy or delinquency. The patient was a successful writer who supported himself writing for magazines until approximately two years ago. He is currently with a supportive and caring woman (Helen) who appears to tolerate and even condone his drinking. Mr. Birnam lives in a Manhattan apartment with his brother Nick. Nick and Helen comprise this patient's social support system.

Drug and alcohol history: Mr. Birnam has been drinking daily since his early twenties. His drinking has escalated to the point where he currently consumes approximately two quarts of rye whisky each day. There are obvious withdrawal symptoms whenever this patient tries to quit drinking or reduce the amount he drinks.

Behavioral observations: Mr. Birnam was sweating and shaking during the interview. At times, he appeared to be hallucinating, claiming at one point that bugs were crawling on him. The patient appeared anxious and agitated. He had trouble sitting still and frequently got up to pace around the examination room.

Mental status examination: Mr. Birnam was confused and disoriented on the mental status examination. He knew the month, season, and year but not the day of the week or the date. He was oriented to place. He was able to recall only two out of three objects immediately and zero out of three after a brief delay. He could not complete serial sevens. He could identify simple objects and repeat phrases without difficulty. He could follow verbal and written commands. He was able to write a simple sentence, but his writing was barely legible because of his tremor. He also had great difficulty copying intersecting pentagons. His poor score of 18 and his obvious difficulties on the Mini-mental Status Examination are believed to be secondary to his withdrawal from alcohol, and the test will be readministered after several days of sobriety.

Functional assessment: This patient's alcoholism has severely limited his ability to function as a writer. His memory impairment and general state of confusion make sustained concentration and effort virtually impossible. He has also alienated many of his friends because of his drinking. He is obsessed with alcohol and has few interests or activities that are not alcohol-related.

Strengths: Mr. Birnam is an intelligent individual who was once a successful writer. He maintains good verbal skills, although it is difficult for him to concentrate. He is a congenial individual with good interpersonal skills. His greatest strengths appear to be the consistent support of his brother and girlfriend.

Diagnosis: Alcohol Dependence with Physiological Dependence

Treatment plan: (1) Detoxification; (2) 28-day inpatient treatment on the Alcohol Treatment Unit;

(3) Outpatient follow-up; (4) Alcoholics Anonymous

Prognosis: Given this patient's long history of alcoholism and previous treatment failures, his prognosis is guarded at best.

The Lost Weekend and Alcoholism[1]

Billy Wilder's classic film *The Lost Weekend* (1945) is a powerful portrayal of alcoholism. The protagonist, Don Birnam (Ray Milland), is ready to sacrifice his brother's trust, his career as a writer, and the love of his girlfriend (played by Jane Wyman) for one more drink. Early in the film, we see clear examples of denial, believed by many to be the characteristic defense mechanism of the alcoholic. Don Birnam minimizes the significance of his drinking as long as he can, but eventually he realizes that it is ruining his life. A scene in which Birnam watches a bat kill and eat a mouse is an effective illustration of the type of hallucinations characteristic of **delirium tremens**. Birnam eventually hocks his girlfriend's coat to get a gun and then writes a suicide note. However, Jane Wyman arrives before he pulls the trigger, and the film ends with Birnam planning the novel he is going to write and, in a heavily symbolic gesture, dropping a cigarette in a glass of rye.

"One's too many and a hundred's not enough."

A bartender chides Don Birnam in Billy Wilder's *The Lost Weekend*

Despite an ending that is somewhat too pat for contemporary viewers, the film is still a dramatic illustration of the destructive effects of alcohol. Milland won an Oscar for best actor for his portrayal of Birnam, and the film earned additional Oscars for best picture, director, and screenplay. Billy Wilder, the film's director, consulted with Alcoholics Anonymous before beginning work on the film.

---

[1]In this chapter, we use the nonspecific, non-diagnostic term "alcoholism" to refer to both "alcohol dependence" and "alcohol abuse" as in many films the distinction is unclear. When it is clear, we differentiate between the two.

Alcoholism

The use of mind-altering substances appears to have existed almost from the time that humans first became aware of the potent effects plants could have on the human experience of reality. Oliver Wendell Holmes, Jr. once remarked, "There is in all men a demand for the superlative, so much so that the poor devil who has no other way of reaching it attains it by getting drunk," and the use of alcohol can be traced back at least 5,000 years. The relationship among alcohol, drugs, and mysticism has been explored in books such as William James' *Varieties of Religious Experience* and Aldous Huxley's *Doors of Perception.*

Alcohol and the Brain

Alcohol is quickly absorbed into the bloodstream and transported to the liver, which is capable of metabolizing about one ounce of 100-proof alcohol in an hour. If a person consumes only one drink per hour, the liver is able to keep up and alcohol does not affect the brain. However, at consumption rates greater than one drink per hour, the brain is quickly affected, with obvious consequences. In particular, there is rapid uptake of alcohol in the cerebellum, and this results in staggering, diminished coordination, and slower reaction times. Judgment is impaired, and alcohol can trigger aggression in some individuals. Although alcohol may initially

Table 7.1 Symptoms of Alcohol Dependence

Criteria	Examples from *The Lost Weekend*
1. Alcohol is consumed in a larger amount or over a longer period than the individual intended.	Birnam is drinking when the film begins, and he drinks throughout the film.
2. People know that their use of alcohol is and excessive but fail in their attempts to control their drinking.	Birnam has tried repeatedly to go on the wagon has "taken the cure" at least once without success.
3. A great deal of time is devoted to acquiring alcohol, drinking it, or recovering from its effects. else, In severe cases, almost all of the individual's waking hours are devoted to the substance.	Birnam is preoccupied with rye and has hidden it throughout his apartment. He thinks about little and he steals a purse and robs a liquor store to support his addiction.
4. Intoxication or withdrawal symptoms occur at work or in other inappropriate situations (e.g., while driving a car).	Birnam has quit writing altogether and has pawned his typewriter to buy rye.
5. Important social, occupational, or recreational activities are replaced by alcohol.	Birnam's relationship with his brother is seriously damaged by his drinking, and he avoids spending a weekend in the country with his family. He also comes close to destroying his relationship with his girlfriend.
6. Alcohol use persists, despite increasing awareness of the problems it causes.	Birnam describes himself as a "drunk," and he is acutely aware of his declining prowess as a writer.
7. Tolerance develops, and an increased amount of alcohol is required to produce the same effect. (Tolerance is less marked for alcohol than for some other drugs.)	The film shows Birnam drinking approximately two quarts of rye per day, far more than most people could tolerate.
8. Withdrawal symptoms develop when the individual cuts back on his or her use of alcohol.	Birnam develops delirium tremens and hallucinates in the film.
9. After experiencing withdrawal symptoms, the individual begins to drink to avoid these unpleasant experiences rather than to produce the pleasant feelings initially associated with alcohol use.	When questioned by a bartender about drinking so early in the morning, Birnam remarks, "At night it's a drink; in the morning it's medicine."

Table 7.2 Alcohol and Mortality Data

Aviation deaths	32%
Drowning	62%
Falls	48%
Fires	54%
Homicide arrests	7%
Homicide victims	64%
Suicides	37%
Fatal single-vehicle crashes	63%

facilitate sexuality by reducing inhibitions, at higher levels of use there is clear impairment of sexual functioning. In the words of Shakespeare, "Lechery, Sir, it provokes and it unprovokes; it provokes the desire, but it takes away the performance." (*Macbeth*, Act II, Scene 3).

Patterns of Alcohol Abuse

DSM-IV lists seven characteristic symptoms of dependence and requires that at least three occur at any time in the same 12-month period for the diagnosis of substance dependence. Some of the symptoms that apply to Don Birnam's alcoholism are presented in Table 7.1. The symptoms of dependence are the same for all psychoactive substances (alcohol or drugs).

Epidemiology of Alcoholism

The majority of American adults (about 65 percent) drink at least occasionally, and 1 in 10 consumes more than one ounce of alcohol per day. Males tend to tolerate alcohol more easily than females, in part because of their greater weight, and so the definition of a heavy drinker needs to be adjusted for males and females. However, it is generally accepted that individuals who average more than three drinks per day are heavy drinkers. Many individuals will consume far more than this average: ten percent of all drinkers consume more than 50 percent of all alcohol.

It is estimated that more than 7 percent of the adult population in the United States—approximately 13 million people—are alcoholics. Alcoholism is one of our most serious public health problems, costing billions annually in lost

productivity, increased healthcare costs, and accidents. Alcohol abuse contributes to about 30 percent of all motor vehicle accidents, and it is responsible for about half of all traffic fatalities. More information about the relationship between alcohol and accidental death is presented in Table 7.2.

Analysis of Alcohol Dependence in *The Lost Weekend*

About 10 percent of adults seeking treatment by physicians are alcoholics, and about a third of admissions to general hospitals are for alcohol-related problems. The mortality rate of alcoholics is two to three times greater than that of the general population, and the life span of alcoholics is 10 to 12 years shorter. In addition, the children of alcoholic parents are at increased risk for hyperactivity, low IQ, emotional problems, child abuse, and fetal alcohol syndrome (NIAAA, 2000). Despite the severity of these problems, less than 10 percent of alcoholics will receive treatment for their problems.

The Genetics of Alcoholism

Alcoholism runs in families, and both twin and adoption studies have shown that the children of alcoholics are far more likely to become alcoholic than are the children of nonalcoholic parents. Monozygotic twins are far more likely than dizygotic twins to be **concordant** for alcoholism (i.e., both twins have the same status: alcoholic or nonalcoholic), and the sons of alcoholics are about four times more likely to become alcoholic than are the sons of nonalcoholics, whether they are raised by their biological parents or foster parents. The genetic link appears to be sex-related, and the relationship is not as strong in daughters.

Assessment of Alcoholism

The diagnosis of alcoholism is made in accordance with DSM-IV criteria. The **Michigan Alcohol Screening Test** (MAST) is the instrument that has been used most extensively for diagnosing alcoholism, and it is the standard against which all other alcoholism screening measures are judged in terms of validity and reliability. However, in clinical settings, the diagnosis often is based on the "Three Cs" of alcoholism: documentation of

Compulsive use, loss of Control over alcohol consumption, and Continued use in spite of adverse consequences (Veitia & McGahee, 2001).

A number of specific assessment devices have been developed to help clinicians. The simplest of these—and one of the most effective—is the CAGE test. The CAGE test requires that the clinician ask four simple questions of every patient suspected of alcohol abuse: (1) Have you ever felt the need to Cut down on your drinking? (2) Have you ever felt Annoyed by criticism of your drinking? (3) Have you ever had Guilt feelings about your drinking? and (4) Do you ever take a morning Eye-opener? Two affirmative answers should raise the suspicion of alcoholism; three positive answers virtually confirm the diagnosis.

The Portrayal of Alcoholism in Films

Images of alcohol and drinking are ubiquitous in contemporary films, and one is hard-pressed to name adult films in which alcohol is not represented in some way. This may reflect the fact that alcohol affects everyone directly or indirectly.

The early success of *Lost Weekend* (1945) led to other films with alcoholism as a central theme, including *Harvey* (1950), *A Star Is Born* (1954), *Come Back Little Sheba* (1952), *Days of Wine and Roses* (1962), *Key Largo* (1948), and *Cat on a Hot Tin Roof* (1958). Other films include *Who's Afraid of Virginia Woolf?* (1966), *Tender Mercies* (1983), *Arthur* (1981), *Ironweed* (1987), *The Verdict* (1987), *Paris, Texas* (1984), *Under the Volcano* (1984), *Hoosiers* (1986), *Barfly* (1981), and *Clean and Sober* (1988).

In contrast to the sobering representations of alcoholism in films such as *Clean and Sober*, some films portray the alcoholic as happy and carefree. *Harvey* (1950) and *Arthur* (1981) are the two most obvious examples. Writing about *Arthur*, Vincent Canby (1981) noted

> Not since Nick and Nora Charles virtually made the dry martini into the national drink... has there been quite so much boozing in a movie without hidden consequences. Arthur drinks scotch the way people now drink Perrier... When he goes giggling about town, sloshed to the eyeballs, he's not seen as a case history but as eccentric. (p. 10)

Unfortunately, the film presents an appealing model of Arthur tooling about Long Island in his Rolls-Royce. In the film, he has the good fortune to have a chauffeur; most of the teenage audience emulating his example won't be so lucky.

Movies *reflect* social mores as interpreted by filmmakers, and this certainly applies to the use of alcohol. In turn, movies *affect* social mores in a cyclical manner. One of the most recent film presentations of the ways in which families are affected by alcoholism is found in *When a Man Loves a Woman* (1994). Other powerful films about alcoholism and its treatment include *Leaving Las Vegas* (1995) in which Nicholas Cage willingly drinks through graphically depicted delirium tremens until his death, Steve Buscemi's *Trees Lounge* (1996), and *Drunks* (1997). This last film is an especially helpful introduction to Alcoholics Anonymous and is highly recommended to anyone who has not had an opportunity to visit an open AA meeting. In addition, anyone interested in the way in which alcoholism is portrayed in films is referred to an excellent book by Norman Denzin, *Hollywood Shot by Shot: Alcoholism in American Cinema* (1991).

Following Meg Ryan's outstanding portrayal of a woman with alcoholism in *When a Man Loves a Woman* (1994), several films have portrayed depressed women who are either dependent upon or abuse alcohol; some recent examples include *House of Sand and Fog* (2003), *28 Days* (2000), *Rain* (2001), *Walking on Water* (2001), and *Monster's Ball* (2001). Helen Hunt plays an alcoholic working two jobs to pay the bills while secretly drinking in *Pay It Forward* (2000). Even a very small amount of alcohol is associated with violence in Kim Bassinger's character in *Final Analysis* (1992).

Alcohol abuse is evident in several lead characters, such as Robert Duvall in *The Apostle* (1997), Sean Connery in *Finding Forrester* (2000), Billy Bob Thornton in *Bad Santa* (2003), and Matt Damon's character, Rannuph Junuh, in *The Legend of Bagger Vance* (2000) who drinks heavily upon returning from war. Alcohol only exacerbates his isolation and loneliness. Alex and his "droogs" use alcohol to "sharpen up" before committing violent acts in *A Clockwork Orange* (1971).

Alcoholism is particularly common in the Western film genre with saloons, bar fights, whiskey bottles, drunken gunfighters, and town drunks being staples of the genre (Wedding, 2001). *High Noon* (1952), *Shane* (1953), *Stagecoach* (1939), *Rio Bravo* (1959), and *Unforgiven* (1992) are classic examples.

Drug Abuse

Substance use disorders (alcohol or drugs) include substance abuse and substance dependence. **Substance abuse** is defined in terms of a *pattern* of use characterized by *recurrent adverse consequences* related to the use of the substance. The diagnosis requires evidence of impairment as evidenced by one of the four following criteria: (l) failure to meet role obligations, (2) recurrent use in situations, such as driving, in which clear hazards are present, (3) recurrent legal problems, and (4) continued use, despite social or interpersonal problems related to the substance. In addition, the symptoms must never have met the criteria associated with substance dependence.

Substance dependence involves a more complex set of behaviors that include tolerance, withdrawal, and compulsive drug-taking behavior. The symptoms associated with dependence on different drugs are similar (but not identical) across drug categories. Dependence is diagnosed when

clients present with three or more of the seven criteria listed in Table 7.3 at any time during a 12-month period.

Clean and Sober

The 1988 film *Clean and Sober* stars Michael Keaton as a cocaine addict and Morgan Freeman as an addictions counselor. The film opens when Keaton receives a call from his real estate office about $50,000 in missing escrow funds. Keaton has spent the money on cocaine. Confident that he can talk his way out of the problem, Keaton begins the day by snorting a line of coke. He then offers cocaine to the nude woman lying beside him in bed and discovers that she is comatose from an overdose. Keaton responds to his financial and personal problems by running away. He enrolls in a drug rehabilitation program, not so much for treatment but because it offers a confidential program and a place for him to hide away. Soon, however, he is going

Table 7.3 Criteria for Substance Dependence. Adapted from *DSM-IV*

Criteria	Examples from *Clean and Sober*
1. Tolerance, defined by (a) a need for ever increasing amounts of the substance to achieve intoxication or (b) diminished effect with use of a set level of the substance	Michael Keaton finds that cocaine comes to dominate his life; he snorts it first thing in the morning to get going, and it is a part of almost every social encounter.
2. Withdrawal, defined by (a) specific effects associated with the particular substance being abused or (b) use of the substance to relieve or avoid the withdrawal symptoms (e.g., use of the "hair of the dog that bit you")	Keaton experiences marked withdrawal symptoms (fatigue, insomnia, nausea, and psychomotor agitation) after he enrolls in the Causeway Program and is placed on a detoxification ward.
3. Using the substance in larger amounts or over a longer period than was intended	Keaton's use of cocaine becomes so extensive that he begins to embezzle from his company to pay for his increased use of cocaine.
4. A persistent desire to cut back or eliminate use of the substance	Keaton has failed in his repeated attempts to gain control over his use of cocaine and drugs.
5. A great deal of time is devoted to acquiring the substance or recovering from its effects	When Keaton is unsuccessful in persuading a co-worker to bring him drugs, he drives to his office and demolishes it looking for an envelope in which he has stored cocaine.
6. Important social, occupational, or recreational activities are ignored because of the preoccupation with use of the substance	Keaton is fired from his job and estranged from his family because of his drug and alcohol problems.
7. The substance use is continued despite recurrent physical or psychological problems resulting from its use	Keaton persists in his use of cocaine, despite the fact that his girlfriend has been killed by an overdose in his company.

through the pain of detoxification. Despite this evidence of addiction, Keaton continues to deny the reality of his addiction. However, while in treatment he learns that his girlfriend has died from the overdose, his juggling of the escrow account to cover his drug purchases has been discovered, and he fails in an attempt to cajole money from his mother, who realizes that he will only spend it on drugs.

Morgan Freeman is very convincing as an ex-addict now trying to help others overcome their addictions. Some of the most interesting scenes in the film show Keaton at AA meetings (as mentioned earlier, he is an alcoholic as well as addicted to drugs) and in group therapy.

While in the group, Keaton becomes romantically involved with an attractive woman named Charlie, played by Kathy Baker. Charlie is involved in a pathological and destructive relationship with her live-in boyfriend, and both continue to use drugs when Charlie is discharged from the program. Keaton tries to get her to leave the destructive relationship, and she does briefly. Eventually, she returns to her boyfriend, resumes using drugs, and is killed in a car wreck while high on cocaine. The film ends with Keaton getting his 30-day AA chip, acknowledging to the group that he is both an alcoholic and a drug addict, and realizing that each of us can be responsible only for his or her own behavior.

"Now it's thirty days later. I've been to a funeral, been on about nine million job interviews, I'm $52,000 in debt, and I've got this chip. Suddenly I've got this startling belief that I'm an alcoholic and a drug addict."

Michael Keaton referring to his 30-day sobriety chip from Alcoholics Anonymous in *Clean and Sober*

Substances Depicted in Films

Countless films depict characters abusing substances, and at times it is unclear what substance is being abused. Rather than labeling the character as a "drug addict," it is more important to decipher the

particular substance being abused as each substance has different characteristics (e.g. tolerance, withdrawal, and intoxication levels). Table 7.4 helps make this clarification with some of the best portrayals of substance abuse in films. The number of psi's (Ψ) provides a rating scale, further emphasizing the importance of each—see Appendix G for details on this scale.

Opioids

The best-known opioids are opium, morphine, codeine, methadone, Percodan, and heroin. These drugs are sometimes lumped together under the general rubric of narcotics. Opium is usually smoked; the other drugs are most often ingested or injected. Robert De Niro can be seen smoking opium in both the opening and the ending scenes of Sergio Leone's *Once Upon a Time in America* (1984), and opium plays a significant role in both *Indochine* (1992) and Bernardo Bertolucci's *The Last Emperor* (1987).

Opioids are prescribed as analgesics, anesthetics, or antidiarrheal drugs. All opioids produce significant tolerance, and withdrawal symptoms are common when drug use is discontinued. The marked tolerance is demonstrated by the fact that experienced heroin users frequently require doses in excess of 100 times the amount that was originally necessary to produce a state of euphoria.

A user's response to heroin or other opioids will vary depending on dose level and experience with the drug. During a state of opioid intoxication, the user tends to be euphoric, drowsy, apathetic, and usually indifferent to his or her surroundings. Constipation is common. The user's pupils become markedly constricted, and hallucinations may occur. Judgment is often impaired, although an experienced user may function in routine occupational and social roles. An example of this ability to function despite being very high on drugs can be found in Quentin Tarantino's film *Pulp Fiction* (1994). Vincent (John Travolta) shoots up before going out on a date with his boss' wife, Mia (Uma Thurman), who snorts cocaine before meeting him. The two wind up at "Jack Rabbit Slims" and maintain a coherent—if not stimulating—conversation. They even manage to win a dance contest. Later in the evening, Mia discovers the heroin in Vincent's coat pocket. Believing it to be cocaine, she proceeds to snort a line of the drug and goes into a coma. Vincent eventually manages to save Mia's life by plunging a syringe filled with epinephrine into her heart.

Table 7.4 Substances Abused with Accompanying Film Examples

Abused Substance	Film Example(s)	Comments	Rating
Alcohol	*Leaving Las Vegas* (1995)	Nick Cage giving up	ΨΨΨΨ
	Born on the Fourth of July (1989)	Tom Cruise as a bitter veteran	ΨΨΨΨ
	House of Sand and Fog (2003)	Jennifer Connelly relapsing	ΨΨΨΨΨ
Heroin	*Pulp Fiction* (1994)	Tarantino classic	ΨΨΨΨΨ
	Quitting (2001)	Deterioration and withdrawals	ΨΨΨΨ
Sedatives /Hypnotics	*I'm Dancing as Fast as I Can* (1982)	Valium addiction	ΨΨ
Cocaine	*Traffic* (2000)	Dynamic, integrated drug film	ΨΨΨΨΨ
	Blow (2001)	Johnny Depp as a famous cocaine importer	ΨΨΨ
Crack Cocaine	*MacArthur Park* (2001)	Gripping realism in LA	ΨΨΨ
Methamphetamine	*Requiem for a Dream* (2000)	Ellen Burstyn's role is unforgettable	ΨΨΨΨ
	Spun (2002)	Methamphetamine addiction and lifestyle	ΨΨΨ
Hallucinogens	*Fear and Loathing in Las Vegas* (1998)	Glorifies drug use	ΨΨ
Inhalants	*Love Liza* (2002)	Philip Seymour Hoffman gasoline huffing	ΨΨΨ
Marijuana	*The Big Lewbowski* (1998)	Jeff Bridges as "The Dude"	ΨΨ
Nicotine	*The Royal Tenenbaums* (2001)	Gwyneth Paltrow tries to hide her smoking habits	ΨΨΨΨΨ
Caffeine	*Coffee and Cigarettes* (2003)	Vignettes with both substances	ΨΨΨ
Combination	*Eyes Wide Shut* (1999)	Speedball (cocaine & heroin)	ΨΨΨΨΨ
Polysubstance	*Naked Lunch* (1991)	Bug spray and other substances	ΨΨ

Katharine Hepburn plays a morphine addict with an alcoholic son (Jason Robards) in the film adaptation of Eugene O'Neill's *Long Day's Journey into Night* (1962). Morphine abuse is also portrayed in the science fiction thriller *Pitch Black* (2000).

Opioid withdrawal occurs when use of opioid drugs is discontinued or when an opioid antagonist (any drug that blocks the effects of an opioid) is administered. Naloxone and naltrexone are the most widely used opioid antagonists. Complete withdrawal usually takes three to eight days. Opioid withdrawal can lead to the following symptoms: dysphoric mood, nausea or vomiting, muscle aches, lacrimation (crying) or rhinorrhea (a "runny nose"), diarrhea, yawning, fever, or insomnia. Examples of opioid withdrawal can be seen in the Frank Sinatra film *The Man with the Golden Arm* (1955).

The film, *Quitting* (2001), by Chinese director Zhang Yang, depicts heroin abuse and withdrawal, intermixing both through flashbacks. A young man, Hongsheng, at one time a famous actor, is living with his parents to maintain sobriety from heroin addiction. He is bitter and verbally abusive toward them. Through flashbacks, the viewer learns of his deterioration due to heroin dependence and the ramifications of its abuse; he is left with a renowned career in shambles, loss of several friendships, a delusional obsession with John Lennon, hallucinations, and significant anger outbursts.

"I was fighting with myself. I didn't know what I was fighting about."

Hongsheng in *Quitting*

The classic film about the heroin trade is William Friedkin's *The French Connection* (1971). Friedman won an Oscar for his directing, and Gene Hackman won the Academy Award for best actor for his role as police detective Jimmy "Popeye" Doyle. *The Connection* is a 1961 film about a group of junkies waiting for the arrival of a pusher. A more contemporary, powerful, and realistic presentation of teenage addiction and prostitution is *Christiane F.* (1981) which explores the drug culture of West Berlin. Other film examples of heroin addiction include *High Art* (1998), *Who'll Stop the Rain* (1978), *Mona Lisa* (1986), *Chappaqua* (1966), and *Lady Sings the Blues* (1972).

One of the most powerful drug films ever made is Gus Van Sant's 1989 film *Drugstore Cowboy* starring Matt Dillon as the leader of a group of four addicts who rob drugstores to maintain their habit. The film is especially memorable because of a very realistic cameo of William Burroughs playing an old, burned out, addicted and defrocked priest living in a seedy motel. Dillon sees in Burroughs the image of the man he (Dillon) will eventually become. Dillon's decision to go straight and the dilemmas he faces (including attempts by his girlfriend to seduce him back to the world they formerly shared) seem very realistic.

Sedative-Hypnotics

Sedative drugs produce a calm feeling of well-being in low doses and induce sleep in greater doses. These drugs include barbiturates such as amytal, nembutal, seconal, and phenobarbital, as well as **anxiolytics** (anxiety-reducing drugs) such as the **benzodiazepines** (Valium, Librium, etc.). Xanax, a more recently developed anxiolytic with a short half-life, combines the anxiety-reducing properties of other benzodiazepines with a mild antidepressant effect. It has become one of the most widely prescribed drugs in the United States.

Some of the problems of tranquilizer (Valium) addiction are portrayed in the autobiography and film *I'm Dancing as Fast as I Can* (1982).

Barbiturates are muscle relaxants that induce feelings of well-being in small doses; with larger amounts, the user falls into a deep and profound sleep. Although tolerance develops extremely rapidly with the barbiturates, the dose that is lethal remains relatively constant. This puts the barbiturate abuser at high risk and is one of the reasons barbiturates are rarely prescribed today for anxiety. They remain the medication of choice in some cases of epilepsy.

The effects of barbiturates mimic the effects of alcohol and include symptoms such as slurred speech and staggering gait. These effects may be especially pronounced when barbiturates are combined with alcohol, and this combination is likely to be especially deadly. Marilyn Monroe committed suicide using a combination of alcohol and sleeping pills. In addition, barbiturate withdrawal is generally more difficult and more painful than withdrawal from narcotics, and it is more likely to be life threatening.

Benzodiazepines have largely replaced barbiturates for the treatment of insomnia because they are generally believed to be less addictive and are not as likely to be successfully used in suicide attempts. The benzodiazepines are especially widely prescribed in the United States, and many people feel they are prescribed too frequently.

There is a telling moment at one point in a Woody Allen film when an anxious character begins to hyperventilate in a crowded department store. Allen turns to the crowd and asks, "Quick, has anyone got a Valium?" and 30 people reach for their pockets. Audiences almost inevitably laugh at this pointed comment about the ubiquitous nature of these medications in our daily lives.

Stimulants

Stimulant drugs excite the central nervous system (CNS), fight fatigue, suppress one's appetite, and enhance mood. They are widely available and include relatively unregulated drugs such as caffeine and nicotine. Common amphetamines include **amphetamine** (Benzedrine), **dextroamphetamine** (Dexedrine), and **methamphetamine** (Methedrine). Other stimulants include **methylphenidate** (Ritalin), **khat**, and a variety of appetite suppressants such as Preludin. Cocaine is also best classified as a stimulant drug, although it is considered a narcotic in the current federal drug taxonomy.

Amphetamines are usually taken orally but may be injected. Methamphetamine crystals ("Ice") can also be smoked, producing a high that can last as long as 14 hours. Khat, a shrub grown in Africa and the Middle East, produces leaves that can be chewed to produce an amphetamine-like effect. The use of khat is referred to in *Black Hawk Down* (2001).

Amphetamines are highly addictive, and tolerance for the drugs like methamphetamine develops rapidly. There is a characteristic withdrawal syndrome that includes depression, fatigue, nightmares, insomnia or sometimes hypersomnia, increased appetite, and either psychomotor retardation or agitation. This "crashing" effect appears to be the price the user must pay for the euphoria that accompanies the initial drug use. Amphetamine-induced psychoses often produce symptoms that closely resemble those found with serious mental disorders such as schizophrenia.

The film *Dopamine* (2003) features a lead character who engages in heavy use of stimulants. He gets amphetamine pills from a drug dealer and stays up all night working; in one scene, he has lined up seven cups of coffee next to his computer. Two better films that offer more compelling portrayals of stimulant abuse are *Requiem for a Dream* (2000) and *Spun* (2002).

Requiem for a Dream

The unforgettable *Requiem for a Dream* (2000) tells the stories of four lonely, desperate characters, each on the wrong track and all of them destroying their lives with drugs. Uppers are not the only drug portrayed in the film; essentially, these characters will take any drug available. Drugs take the place of food, sex, life goals, and just about everything else. The effect of drugs on the body and mind is unrelenting. Sara (Ellen Burstyn) takes drugs to lose weight so that she can appear in a live broadcast of a television show. Her son, Harry (Jared Leto), repeatedly steals Sara's television set (even though it is chained to the wall) and pawns it for drugs.

Director Darren Aronofsky uses extreme close-ups to demonstrate the effects of drugs. He shows characters swallowing pills, injecting substances, and snorting drugs followed by predictable physiological effects (e.g. pupil dilation), all with exaggerated sound effects. Vigorous camera-work, editing, and split-screen techniques bring the viewer into the confusion and fast-paced world of addicts abusing "uppers."

In the end, each is left alive and destroyed, well past the point-of-no-return; nevertheless, each is contained by society (hospital, prison, psychiatric institution, and prostitution). Roger Ebert appropriately labels this film as playing like "a travelogue of hell."

Spun

Spun (2002) is a devastatingly realistic portrayal of several methamphetamine addicts. Virtually every main character is a meth addict—Mickey Rourke plays the cook, who sets up meth labs in various shady apartments until they blow up and John Leguizamo plays Spider Mike, the addicted dealer. Another meth dependent is the cook's girlfriend, Nikki (Brittany Murphy), who's dog has turned green due to the meth lab. The lead character, Ross (Jason Schwartzman). is so preoccupied with using and having meth available at all times that he forgets he had chained a woman to his bed during sex. Ross wants to have another chance at a relationship with a different woman, Amy, who left Ross because of his meth abuse and moved on in her life; she is able to see through Ross's denial so patently evident in one of his comments, "You know what the best part is, Amy? I'm not hooked. I can stop at anytime."

"Spoof, dope, crank, creep, bomb, spank, shit, bang, zip, tweak, chard. Call it what you will, it's all methamphetamine. That's what I'm here for."

An opening quote from an addict in *Spun*

These characters are depicted doing meth around the clock—off a girl's body, off a urinal, and "doing a round" while driving. Symptoms of intoxication are represented in each character: inappropriate laughter, jerky, quick body language and movement, and completely trashed living quarters; this is a world in which no one sleeps, everyone talks fast, and no one has a real relationship. The post-intoxication impairment following the repeated pattern of getting high on meth and crashing to sleep after several days of being awake is called being "spun." All these characters surround themselves with meth—they all get spun. The consequences depicted are clear: the meth addict will eventually be jailed, hospitalized, blown up, or (if lucky) he or she will find a way to escape the lifestyle.

As in *Requiem for a Dream*, the camera speeds everything up to let the viewer experience in some small way what it is like to take methamphetamines. A character inhales meth, and a close-up shows his eyes boggy and wide open; cartoon images accentuate thoughts and the drug effects; other close-ups display spinning movements with pupils dilating and contracting.

Cocaine

Cocaine is usually snorted or, more rarely, injected intravenously. Sigmund Freud's recreational and therapeutic use of cocaine is well known and is described in the film *The Seven Percent Solution* (1976), a historical fantasy in which Freud and Sherlock Holmes share their love of cocaine and pool their deductive talents to solve the puzzle of a missing patient.

Other compelling films dealing with cocaine addiction include *The Bad Lieutenant* (1992) starring Harvey Keitel, Martin Scorsese's *Goodfellas* (1990), Brian De Palma's *Scarface* (1983), Johnny Depp in *Blow* (2001), and a tormented Naomi Watts in the Tarantino-like *21 Grams* (2003), directed by Alejandro Gonzalez Inarritu.

Crack cocaine, named after the sound made as the drug is consumed, takes the form of small "rocks" and is smoked. The effects of smoking crack cocaine occur almost immediately, but the high that is produced is relatively brief. Although crack is relatively inexpensive, crack addicts can quickly develop addictions that require hundreds of dollars each day to support. For many people, cocaine addiction leads to prostitution, theft, or violence.

MacArthur Park
The independent film, *MacArthur Park* (2001), depicts Cody, a man addicted to crack and struggling to leave both his addiction and the park where he lives with other homeless crack addicts. He has a reason to leave: a son recently found him and the son has a home where Cody could recover. This film depicts the obstacles of crack addiction Cody must overcome in order to leave.

It is also a story of the world of crack addiction where extensive drug abuse and dependence—as well as drug selling and producing—are depicted. The film's characters use large amounts of crack to cope with their pain and to avoid withdrawal effects. A variety of characters are depicted, and

each has a different relationship with the park's drug world: some are leaving the lifestyle; others are trying to leave, entering the world, deteriorating in it, or have no interest in leaving, while still others are simply "lost causes."

"I'm not homeless I just don't wanna go home."

MacArthur Park

The screenplay was written by Tyrone Atkins, a man who was homeless in LA's MacArthur Park and addicted to crack cocaine; he wrote most of the story while in jail; after leaving jail, he returned to the park before entering a rehabilitation program.

Sweet Nothing
Another film illustrating the degradation associated with crack addiction is *Sweet Nothing* (1996), a true story based on a set of diaries discovered in an abandoned apartment in the Bronx. The film demonstrates the corrosive effects of the protagonist's addiction on his marriage, his relationship with his children, his friends, and his job. At one point, Angelo, the lead character, actually misses his father's funeral because he has an opportunity to get high and this need has come to supersede all others. Angelo loses the ability to become aroused by his wife, and we watch him become increasingly paranoid as the film progresses.

Cocaine has affected the lives and careers of numerous actors and directors. For example, Tommy Rettig (best known as Lassie's master Jeff on the TV series) was sentenced to five years in federal prison for smuggling cocaine; Richard Pryor became badly burned as a result of an explosion related to smoking crack cocaine; and when Rainer Werner Fassbinder, considered by many to be Germany's finest director, died at the age of 37, his death was attributed to heart failure resulting from a combination of barbiturates and cocaine.

Hallucinogens

Hallucinogens, sometimes referred to as psychedelics, are drugs that distort the perception of reality. Users report hallucinations involving all senses, **synesthesia** ("crossed" sensations, such as hearing sights and seeing sounds), and depersonalization.

These drugs can also have profound effects on mood, depending in large part on set and setting.

Hallucinogens can occur in the natural environment but are more often produced synthetically. Naturally occurring hallucinogens include **mescaline**, derived from the peyote cactus, and **psilocybin**, which is present in psilocybe mushrooms. Some Native Americans use psilocybe mushrooms in religious ceremonies.

Mescaline can also be produced in a laboratory. However, the best-known and most widely used of all synthetic hallucinogens is **lysergic acid diethylamide** (LSD). It is most often swallowed as a pill, but it can also be mixed with a fluid, licked off of blotter paper, or swallowed in sugar cubes or gelatin sheets. LSD is colorless, tasteless, and extremely potent. It produces varied symptoms and can result in affective changes that range from euphoria to absolute terror. The most dramatic effects are often sensory in nature: when the drug experience is positive, it allows the user "to see a world in a grain of sand/and a heaven in a wildflower, hold infinity in the palm of your hand/and eternity in an hour" (William Blake, *Auguries of Innocence*). Unfortunately, the experience is not always this benign, and injury or death can result from bad decisions made while under the influence of the drug. Some users have also reported "flashbacks," in which they re-experience the sensory phenomenon associated with previous trips weeks or years after last using the drug. The drug is not addictive, but tolerance develops rapidly.

The renowned director Stanley Kubrick made the following constructive observation about LSD:

> One of the things that's turned me against LSD is that all the people I know who use it have a peculiar inability to distinguish between things that are really interesting and stimulating and things that appear to be so in the state of universal bliss that the drug induces on a "good" trip. They seem to completely lose their critical faculties and disengage themselves from some of the most stimulating areas of life. Perhaps when everything is beautiful, nothing is beautiful.

In the film *In the Name of the Father* (1993), prisoners cope with the monotony of prison life by licking LSD off the back of a jigsaw puzzle. The puzzle is a large world map, and the prisoners get high "one country at a time." The LSD experience is also portrayed in any number of films

from the 1960s that document the youth culture of that period.

Phencyclidine (PCP); also known as angel dust, is another powerful hallucinogen that has been used since the early 1960s. It can be taken in pill form or dusted onto marijuana and smoked. The drug produces symptoms even more marked than those associated with LSD and may result in analgesia, depersonalization, paranoia, rage reactions, or schizophrenia-like psychoses.

Hallucinogen use is also depicted in *Easy Rider* (1969) and *Fear and Loathing in Las Vegas* (1998).

Inhalants

Common substances that inhalant addicts inhale are glue, gasoline, paint thinners, spray paints, cleaners, and spray-can propellants. Methods used to inhale the vapors include soaking a rag with the substance, placing the substance in a paper or plastic bag, inhaling directly from the container, or spraying the substance into the nose or mouth. The chemicals inhaled reach the lungs and bloodstream very rapidly.

Love Liza

In *Love Liza* (2002), Wilson (masterfully acted by Philip Seymour Hoffman) is a computer technician who becomes addicted to inhaling gasoline following his wife's suicide. This is far from a normal bereavement reaction. Wilson is an emotional wreck and puts forth all energies and concerns into "huffing" gasoline. The method he uses is to dilute a rag with gasoline and hold the rag over his face while he inhales. Frequently he is shown bending over to smell the gasoline at the gas station pumps and the opening in his car's tank.

When intoxicated, his speech becomes slurred, distorted, inappropriate, and at times nonsensical. His interpersonal relationship skills dramatically diminish to a level that appears confusing, rude, and distant to the person speaking with him. Cinematic elements enhance the effects of his blurred vision and in one scene, hallucinations. Wilson vacillates from complete euphoria from the gasoline highs which lead to grossly inappropriate behavior of swimming in a lake while remote-controlled boats are racing and cheerfully attempting to converse with other drivers on a highway to severe agitation and anger outbursts evident when he is not huffing or is awakening from a blackout. Wilson becomes more isolated as the film progresses and would probably be completely isolated if it were not for people eager to support him. His judgment is impaired in other ways such as when he supplies two young huffing adolescents who have been banned from gas stations with the intoxicant.

Severe consequences of his huffing include the loss of a new job, the damage of important relationships, and his house burning down. Wilson is experiencing so much pain that he can't bring himself to read his wife's suicide note; instead, he carries it around with him as a constant reminder of her death. Upon eventually reading it, he knows exactly what to do. Overall, this portrayal of addiction is real, honest, and not overdone or melodramatic.

Cannabis

Marijuana is obtained from the hemp plant *Cannabis sativa*. The active ingredient in marijuana is the drug **tetrahydrocannabinol** (THC). The greater the THC content, the more potent the drug. The THC content of marijuana purchased illegally varies widely, but, in general, THC levels have been increasing over the past three decades, and the marijuana used today is approximately five times stronger than that widely available on street corners and on college campuses in the 1960s. The resin of the cannabis sativa plant can be used to produce **hashish**, a stronger form of the drug.

Marijuana has medicinal value, and it can be obtained legally for the treatment of some disorders. The drug enhances appetite and is often helpful in controlling the nausea associated with chemotherapy. Other physical effects include tachycardia, sedation, and psychomotor impairment.

Like the hallucinogens, marijuana can produce markedly varied psychological effects, depending on the mood and situation of the user. Most often, the drug produces mild euphoria, giddiness, and a general sense of well-being. However, at a different time and in a different setting the same drug can produce marked apprehension or paranoia.

Examples of marijuana use can be found in literally dozens of films. One especially memorable scene involves Dennis Hopper, Peter Fonda, and Jack Nicholson sitting around a campfire and smoking marijuana in *Easy Rider* (1969).

The low-budget propaganda film *Reefer Madness* (1936) became a cult classic among young people who smoked marijuana in the 60's, and the Cheech and Chong movies celebrated the drug's use and ridiculed its classification as a narcotic. Other movies emphasizing marijuana include the Coen Brothers' noir, *The Big Lebowski* (1998) and the outlandish comedy *Half Baked* (1998).

Polysubstance Dependence

Polysubstance refers to using three or more groups of substances (excluding nicotine and caffeine) with no particular substance predominating.

Naked Lunch (1991), the David Cronenberg film adaptation of the William Burroughs' book is fascinating albeit not always tightly linked to the novel. William Lee, the protagonist, is a polydrug addict trying to go straight. Unfortunately, both he and his wife are addicted to bug spray, and Bill's job as an exterminator makes it almost impossible for him to avoid this particular drug. The cinematic representation of visual hallucinations in *Naked Lunch* is especially fascinating.

In *Shadow Hours* (2000), a young man working as a gas station attendant is lured back into drug addiction by a wealthy, mysterious writer who advises the young man he must go into the abyss before he can get back to sobriety. They visit dance clubs, drug fests, strip clubs, fight clubs, sadomasochistic clubs, and torture events.

Tobacco

The drug most often portrayed on television and in films is tobacco. Epidemiological studies suggest it is also our most lethal drug. The Centers for Disease Control and Prevention (CDC) estimate that tobacco accounts for 440,000 deaths annually in the United States (approximately one out of every five deaths). Although fatality rates are only one index of the severity of a drug problem, it is clear that none of the drugs typically regarded as our most "serious" are ultimately as dangerous as cigarettes.

In part because of the pain of withdrawal, less than 5 percent of smokers are successful in their attempts to stop smoking, although about 35 percent try to stop each year (and 80 percent express the desire to stop). Some of the symptoms associated with nicotine withdrawal include dysphoric or depressed mood, insomnia, irritability/frustration /anger, anxiety, difficulty concentrating, restlessness, decreased heart rate, and increased appetite or weight gain.

The morbidity and mortality associated with tobacco use have been underscored by a series of reports issued since 1964 by the Office of the

Surgeon General. Partially in response to the massive public education efforts spearheaded by the surgeon general, numerous Americans have stopped smoking. In addition, the American Medical Association and the American Public Health Association have been very vocal in their opposition to tobacco use.

Various films depict people smoking cigarettes. *Coffee and Cigarettes* (2003), directed and written by Jim Jarmusch, explores the use of nicotine and another under-rated addictive substance, caffeine. Several separated vignettes of different characters are connected only by conversation and the use of coffee and cigarettes, some characters using the substances more compulsively than others. There are comical interactions between musicians Iggy Pop and Tom Waits, between actors Alfred Molina and Steve Coogan, between Bill Murray and two members of the Wu-Tang Clan (where Murray drinks coffee straight from the pot), and between Cate Blanchett and herself. Gwyneth Paltrow's character, Margo, is addicted to nicotine and finds creative ways to hide her smoking habits in The Royal Tenenbaums (2001).

Substance Abuse Recovery

Many films depict characters who are former substance abusers in full recovery (e.g., sustained full remission) and are not depicted as abusing or relapsing in the film.

Benicio Del Toro plays a recovery alcoholic and ex-con who is a born-again Christian in *21 Grams* (2003). In *A Mighty Wind* (2003), Eugene Levy's folk singing character, Mitch, has flat affect, slowed speech and thought, and presents with wide-eyed expressions, each assumed to relate to significant drug abuse in his past.

The 12-Steps is a set of guidelines that has become a tradition of numerous support groups. These important beliefs have revolutionized the conceptualization and treatment of substance abusers and have contributed to saving the lives of countless addicts. Table 7.5 reflects the 12-step approach used by Alcoholic's Anonymous, however, the word "alcohol" can be easily replaced by "drugs" (Narcotic's Anonymous), "sex," "gambling," "money," or "food," depending on the person's addiction.

Table 7.5 The Twelve Steps and Twelve Traditions[2]

1. We admitted that we were powerless over alcohol—that our lives had become unmanageable.
2. Came to believe that a power greater than ourselves could restore us to sanity.
3. Made a decision to turn our will and our life over to the care of God *as we understood Him.*
4. Made a searching and fearless moral inventory of ourselves.
5. Admitted to God, to ourselves, and to another human being the exact nature of our wrongs.
6. Were entirely ready to have God remove all these defects of character.
7. Humbly asked Him to remove our shortcomings.
8. Made a list of all persons we had harmed, and became willing to make amends to them all.
9. Made direct amends to such people whenever possible, except when to do so would injure them or others.
10. Continued to take personal inventory and, when we were wrong, promptly admitted it.
11. Sought through prayer and meditation to improve our conscious contact with God *as we understood Him*, praying only for knowledge of His will for us and the power to carry that out.
12. Having had a spiritual awakening as the result of these steps, we tried to carry this message to alcoholics, and to practice these principles in all our affairs.

[2]The Twelve Steps are reprinted with permission of Alcoholics Anonymous World Services, Inc. Permission to reprint the Twelve Steps does not mean that AA has reviewed or approved the contents of this publication, nor that AA agrees with the views expressed herein. AA is a program of recovery from alcoholism only – use of Twelve Steps in connection with programs and activities which are patterned after AA, but which address other problems, or in any other non-AA context, does not imply otherwise.

Critical Thinking Questions

- Can a case be made for the prohibition of alcohol and tobacco, or is this simply a societal experiment that has been tried without success?
- What are the advantages and disadvantages of the 12 Step approach?
- How common is it for patients with psychiatric disorders to have concomitant problems with alcohol or other drugs?
- Are needle exchange programs effective in reducing the incidence of HIV in groups of IV drug users?
- Should intoxication from alcohol and drugs be a mitigating factor in sentencing prisoners for crimes they committed while high (e.g., murder in *Dead Man Walking*)?
- How important is it for therapists treating alcoholism and drug abuse to have been in treatment for these problems themselves? Can a non-addict ever truly understand the needs and problems of the addict?
- What are the arguments for and against the legalization of drugs in the United States?
- How many places do you suppose there are in the world similar to the park in *MacArthur Park*? Does every major city have such a place?
- Whom do you find to be the most sympathetic character in *Requiem for a Dream*? Does your choice change at different points of the film?
- Do most methamphetamine addicts behave in ways similar to the characters in *Spun*?
- What is the difference between "recovered" and "recovering" in addiction terminology?
- If an individual has one definite addiction, how much more likely are they to have a second addiction than a non-addict?
- What is the relationship between drugs and violence? Which drugs have the highest incidence of aggressive behavior? List films to support your answer.

Chapter 8

Sexual and Gender Identity Disorders

I'm not like everybody else. I'm a hermaphrodite.
Teena Brandon's self-diagnosis in *Boys Don't Cry*

Questions to consider while watching *Boys Don't Cry*

- How do films promote gender roles and sexual stereotypes?
- Which actors do you identify as especially masculine or feminine? Why?
- How would you react if you discovered that the person you were flirting with at a bar was actually impersonating someone of a different gender?
- Why are John and Tom so angry when they discover that Teena is actually male?
- Can you imagine yourself falling in love with someone who was a transsexual?
- How should parents decide about how to raise a child if the child is born with ambiguous genitalia?
- Freud once wrote, "anatomy is destiny." Do you agree?
- Are gender identity problems like those illustrated in *Boys Don't Cry* common?
- Do gender identity disorders occur more often in (anatomical) males or females?
- What are the features that distinguish tranvestism, transsexualism and homosexuality?
- Is it accurate to describe Teena Brandon as a lesbian?
- What are the behavioral characteristics that we use to identify whether or not a given individual is male or female?
- Is it more respectful to use masculine or feminine pronouns when referring to someone who is anatomically male but psychologically female?
- Is there any evidence that gender modification surgery contributes to the happiness of transsexuals? If so, should insurance companies be required by law to pay for this surgery if it is desired?
- What is the sexual orientation of a man who has a happy, well-adjusted relationship with a post-surgery male-to-female transsexual?
- Is it likely that someone like Teena Brandon would have been more comfortable and safer living in a large, metropolitan environment like San Francisco or Boston?

Patient Evaluation[1]

Patient's stated reason for coming: "There's something wrong with me. I've got a gender identity disorder."

History of the present illness: Teena Brandon is a 21-year-old female who presents with a self-diagnosed gender identity disorder. She reports feeling "like a boy" since early childhood. This identity as a psychological male has been strong and persistent. Even as a very young child, Teena expressed little interest in playing with girl's toys. She remembers envying boys both their status and their games. Although she has never seen a psychiatrist or psychologist, Teena has read widely about gender identity disorders and she is quite knowledgeable about her current condition. She has told a woman she was dating that she is a hermaphrodite; however, she realizes this is incorrect, and reports she only uses the term because it makes it easier for others to understand her concerns about gender and self-identity. Teena has been—and remains—preoccupied with her wish to be identified as a male and to live as a man.

---

[1] This fictitious interview is based on the character portrayed in the film *Boys Don't Cry*. It is not intended in any way to represent an interview with the real Teena Brandon.

Past psychiatric illness, treatment, and outcomes: There is no significant history of psychiatric illness. Teena has never been hospitalized or treated by a psychologist or psychiatrist. She has frequently contemplated suicide but has never made a suicide attempt or gesture. She saw a guidance counselor in high school when she was believed to be depressed, but she did not share her concerns about gender at that time.

Medical history: The medical history is not significant. According to the patient, she has been examined by several physicians, including gynecologists, all of whom assured her that her genitalia were anatomically and functionally "normal." Menses are regular, although this patient goes to great lengths to hide the fact that she is menstruating. Breasts are small but normal; Teena binds them so they will not show underneath her clothes.

Psychosocial history: Teena Brandon was put up for adoption shortly after she was born, and she has never met her biological parents. She lived with a variety of foster parents; after turning eighteen, she moved to a trailer park in Lincoln, Nebraska where she lived with her older brother until approximately six months ago when she moved to Falls City. Teena was socially isolated and ostracized in school, and she reports that other children always regarded her as "peculiar." At the age of thirteen, Teena began to refer to herself as "Brandon Teena," and this is the name she uses whenever possible. She met normal developmental milestones, but has never had any interest in dating boys. She has been attracted to females since puberty, and typically masturbates to fantasies involving women. Teena does not identify herself as a lesbian, but all of her sexual experiences to date have been with women; most often, these incidents involve either cunnilingus or masturbation. Teena does not allow the woman she dates to touch or view her genitals. There is a history of petty theft and forging checks.

Drug and alcohol history: Teena has been using and abusing both alcohol and drugs since her early teens. The list of abused substances includes marijuana, LSD, and (most frequently) methamphetamine. She has avoided legal difficulties, but acknowledges "black outs" that have occurred on many occasions. Alcohol use occurs almost daily; recreational drugs are typically used on the weekends, in part because Teena cannot afford more frequent use. Teena cannot remember the last time she went 24 hours without drinking beer; however, there is no evidence of withdrawal or other signs of alcoholism.

Behavioral observations: Teena is a slender and attractive young woman who came in for the evaluation dressed in jeans and a flannel shirt. Her hair was closely cropped. She asked that she be called Brandon, although she acknowledges that her legal name is Teena Brandon. She was diffident and quiet, but answered all questions that were asked. She was polite and cooperative. She appeared mildly anxious.

Mental status examination: Teena identified the day of the month as the 23rd rather than the 24th. There were no other errors on the Mini-Mental Status Examination, and this patient earned an overall score of 29.

Functional assessment: Teena is intelligent and friendly. She possesses considerable insight into her gender identity concerns, and she has read widely. Although she has only attained a high school education, it is likely that she could compete successfully in a college setting. Her excellent interpersonal skills and her self-effacing sense of humor will serve her well in a variety of occupational roles.

Strengths: Intelligence, social skills, humor, self-insight.

Diagnosis: Gender Identity Disorder, sexually attracted to females; Alcohol Abuse; R/O Alcohol Dependence.

Treatment plan: Continue to see this patient on a weekly basis to establish rapport and explore her feelings regarding gender. Consult with a specialist in gender identity disorders to see if Teena might be a candidate for hormone therapy or gender reassignment surgery.

Prognosis: Guarded. Teena's intelligence and interpersonal skills make her a good candidate for psychotherapy. She is adamant that she is a male, and no ambivalence is present; however, I continue to be concerned about the deception involved in her current attempts to "pass" as a male, and she continues to misuse alcohol and drugs.

Gender Identity Disorders

Although the *DSM-IV* refers to Gender Identity Disorders, the term **transsexual** is still widely used in clinical practice. Transsexuals are uncomfortable with their anatomic sex and believe they are trapped in the wrong body. There is often a strong desire to replace their genitals with the genitalia of the opposite sex; these urges can be intense enough to lead to self-castration in males. Transsexual identity issues usually originate in childhood; however, the diagnosis is given only after an individual has reached puberty. Transsexuals often suffer from concomitant depression, and suicide attempts are common (APA, 2000).

Boys Don't Cry and Other Gender Identity Films

Hillary Swank is unforgettable as Brandon Teena in Kimberly Peirce's 1999 film *Boy's Don't Cry*, and she won a Best Actress Academy Award for her role in this film. The film is based on a true story which had earlier been portrayed in a 1998 documentary titled *The Brandon Teena Story*.

Boys Don't Cry vividly portrays Brandon's attempts to pass as a male by using a rolled up sock as an ersatz penis, as well as her dismay when she is menstruating. She develops a loving, sensual and happy relationship with Lana, portrayed by Chloë Sevigny. The film accurately presents Brandon's story, and it precisely captures the hatred and homophobia displayed by John Lotter and Marvin Nissen, two men who initially befriended Brandon and later raped and killed her after learning that they had been deceived about Teena's gender identity. The interrogation by a prurient, insensitive and bumbling sheriff is chilling and sadly accurate. The film doesn't glamorize Brandon, and it accurately presents the confusion, dismay, pathos and despair that frequently accompany those situations in which one's anatomical gender doesn't match one's deepest perception of self. The film is required viewing for anyone interested in understanding more about transsexualism.

Other recent films focusing on gender identity disorder include *Normal* (2003) and *Soldier's Girl* (2003). All three of these films show the pain that a person with gender identity disorder faces and the struggles associated with sharing information about sexual identify with loved ones and society. In *Normal*, Roy (Tom Wilkinson) believes he was born in the wrong body and he wants a sex change operation. His wife (Jessica Lange) of 25 years expresses a variety of reactions—denial, shock, anger, rejection, depression, and finally acceptance—as they ultimately work to keep their marriage intact. Roy desires to be accepted by his congregation, co-workers, boss, children, and society, but each presents a different struggle. *Soldier's Girl* is based on the tragic true story of Barry Winchell, a young man who enters the military and falls in love with a transsexual (a man who dressed as a woman in preparation for gender modification surgery).

Interest in the phenomenon of transsexualism burgeoned in the United States and Europe a half century ago after the 1951 gender modification surgery of Christine Jorgensen. (*The Christine Jorgensen Story*, a low-budget and somewhat insipid film, was released in 1970). The mid-1980s witnessed a revival of interest, after widespread publicity and a television movie (*Second Serve*) about the sexual conversion of male surgeon Richard Raskins into a female tennis star, Renee Richards. Other films that have explored transsexualism include *Myra Breckinridge* (1970) (starring film critic Rex Reed), *Dog Day Afternoon* (1975), *The World According to Garp* (1982), and *Come Back to the Five and Dime, Jimmie Dean, Jimmie Dean* (1982). *The Crying Game* (1993) also explores a complex transsexual relationship.

"God meant for me to be somebody else."

Roy in *Normal*

The surgical treatment of transsexuals remains controversial, although tens of thousands of patients have undergone the procedure. Transsexualism occurs more often in biological males than in biological females, and many more males apply for conversion surgery. Transsexuals can be heterosexual, homosexual, or asexual, both prior to and after their surgery. Many professionals who have worked with these patients have been struck by the fact that sexual behavior per se is often a secondary concern; the core issue is one of sexual *identity*, not sexual behavior.

The Range of Normal Sexual Behavior

Few areas of human behavior are as complex, varied, and interesting as sexual behavior. Both social scientists and the public are fascinated by the multitude of possibilities inherent in our sexuality. It is important to appreciate that the range of normal sexual behavior is exceptionally broad, and many behaviors that seem unusual or disturbing to some people do not qualify for a *DSM-IV* label. As a rule, remember that complex or elaborate sexual fantasies are commonplace and do not suggest that any type of psychological disturbance is present. A psychological problem exists when a person acts on his or her fantasies with unwilling partners or behaves in ways that distress other people.

Filmmakers have been quick to exploit our fascination with sexual behavior, and contemporary cinema is replete with examples of sexual psychopathology. A serious student can learn a great deal about abnormal psychology from selective viewing.

Sexual Dysfunctions

The human **sexual response cycle** includes the following four phases:

(1) *Desire*: fantasies related to sex

(2) *Excitement*: arousal, sense of pleasure with physiological changes

(3) *Orgasm*: peaking of sexual pleasure with release of sexual tension

(4) *Resolution*: sense of muscular relaxation and general well-being

There can be a sexual disorder at any level. For example, **Male Erectile Disorder** (impotency) is an excitement/arousal disorder while a male's **Premature Ejaculation** is an orgasm disorder. Other dysfunctions include **Dyspareunia** which is recurrent genital pain during sexual intercourse and **Vaginismus** which is a recurrent involuntary spasm of the outer muscle area of the vagina that interferes with sexual intercourse.

The films *sex, lies, and videotape* (1989), *Italian for Beginners* (2001), *Boxing Helena* (1993), and *Monster's Ball* (2001) each depicts at least one scene where a man becomes impotent and has to face the consequences. *Intimacy* (2000) depicts premature ejaculation.

Kinsey (2004) is an important film about a college professor, Alfred Kinsey (Liam Neeson), who helped reshape the way people viewed sexuality in the middle of the last century. Kinsey published two landmark books based on interviews with tens of thousands of people across the country: *Sexual Behavior in the Human Male* (1948) and *Sexual Behavior in the Human Female* (1953). Many people criticized Kinsey's methodology and research, but his impact on society is undeniable. Kinsey contributed to normalizing homosexuality, premarital sex, and the use of multiple sexual positions; he also debunked numerous misconceptions (e.g., masturbation is harmful). The film portrays Kinsey training his team in conducting interviews that are objective and unbiased, reminding them that "maintaining a nonjudgmental attitude is harder than you think." A

particularly striking scene occurs during Kinsey's straightforward teaching approach in his course on human sexuality where he displays slides of human genitalia. The film also depicts many of the shortcomings of this famous researcher, including his ritualistic compulsiveness (suggesting an obsessive-compulsive personality), barbiturate abuse, lack of personal sexual boundaries, and his superficiality in his interpersonal relations.

Sexual Addictions

Sexual addiction is increasingly being recognized as a growing problem in contemporary society. Patrick Carnes, one of the world's leading authorities on sexual addiction, has written extensively on the topic, addressing sexual compulsivity (*Don't Call It Love* and *Out of the Shadows*), internet sex addiction (*In the Shadows of the Net*), and each of the paraphilias mentioned later in the chapter. There are movies that represent each of these areas.

Good films on sex addicts will not only reveal the behaviors of the addict but also the consequences and realities of the decisions they make. Films about male sex addicts include Ewan McGregor in *Young Adam* (2003), Jude Law in *Alfie* (2004), Johnny Depp in *Don Juan Demarco* (1995), and Michael Des Barres in *The Diary of a Sex Addict* (2001).

The classic Buñuel film, *Belle de Jour* (1967), portrays a married woman who takes a job as a prostitute. The film illustrates female sexual addiction and depicts the creation of a double-life. As the protagonist sinks deeper into her new lifestyle and becomes more comfortable with her lies, she becomes unable to extricate herself. Other female sex addicts are depicted in *Swimming Pool* (2003) and in one segment of *Personal Velocity* (2002).

On-line (2002) examines the serious problem of internet addiction. In the film, a man is abandoned by his fiancé; consequently, he spends countless hours on the internet, partly to help his roommate with a popular pornographic website designed to "link people together with their fantasy." At the end of the film, the viewer learns that the fiancé had been a person online with a webcam whom he watched all day and had never personally met. His compulsive fantasy had become so ingrained that it shaped his personal reality. The film accurately portrays the intense loneliness, isolation, and lack of intimacy or connection that internet addicts and internet sex addicts experience.

An important feature of sex addiction is the secrecy of the behavior. The link between secrecy and sexuality is explored in *Far From Heaven* (2002), *Unfaithful* (2002), and *The Secret Lives of Dentists* (2002). Film directors Pedro Almodóvar, Peter Greenaway, and John Waters are especially known for their creative depiction of sexuality, sexual addiction, and paraphilias.

"As long as you were alone I could bounce that love off your image like a mirror and somehow feel it coming back to me, but now I can't pretend anymore."

An internet addict describes his addiction in *On-line*

The Paraphilias

The *DSM-IV* uses the term **paraphilia** as a substitute for antiquated and emotion-laden expressions such as sexual deviation or perversion. These older labels have strong pejorative connotations and carry a bias that is inappropriate in either research or treatment.

The paraphilias include fetishism, transvestic fetishism, pedophilia, exhibitionism, voyeurism, sexual masochism, sexual sadism, frotteurism, and telephone scatalogia. It is important to reiterate that at some time in their lives most people have had fantasies or have engaged in a behavior that may fit one or more of the categories listed above. However, sexual fantasies *per se* are not a psychological problem—and do not warrant a diagnosis—unless a person has acted on his or her fantasies or is significantly distressed by them. The male who has fantasies about peeping through a window and watching his neighbor undress, for example, is not engaging in deviant behavior. In fact, fantasies of this type are common among males. The behavior would be deviant if the man could be aroused *only* by the fantasy, or if he acted out and actually spied on his neighbor.

Transvestism

Unlike transsexuals, **transvestites** are comfortable with their anatomic sex. However, transvestites derive pleasure and satisfaction from cross-dressing and being identified as a female, and cross-dressing and fantasies about cross-dressing play a prominent role in the sexual lives of transvestites. The transsexual male may cross-dress, but this is not done for purposes of sexual arousal but, rather, because female clothes are important in establishing a female identity. In contrast, the transvestite is likely to be a masculine, heterosexual male who becomes sexually excited when he dresses up in women's clothes. The transvestite does not desire to *be* a woman, but merely wants to be admired as one, or to experience the sexual excitement associated with wearing women's clothes. Brown (1994) maintains that the majority of wives who discover their husband's cross-dressing after marriage come to accept the behavior, and suggests there are no ill effects on children from these marriages. The children of transvestites engage in appropriate sex-role behavior as adults and are unlikely to cross-dress themselves.

As with transsexualism, transvestites may be heterosexual or homosexual, although most are clearly heterosexual. Transvestites cannot be asexual, since sexual arousal is part of the definition of the syndrome.

The cross-dressing behavior of the transvestite almost always begins in childhood, although few little boys who dress up in the clothes of their mother or sister will grow up to have sexual identity problems. While transsexualism is found among both males and females, the diagnosis of transvestism is almost inevitably reserved for males, and there are very few case studies of women who become sexually aroused by wearing men's clothes.

Many transvestites cross-dress only on special occasions, and they may attempt to suppress the behavior, yielding to the impulse only when anxious, during periods of stress, or when separated from a sexual partner. The preferred objects of clothing include nightgowns, panties, bras, hose, and high heels. These garments are often the stimuli associated with fetishes, and in *DSM-IV* transvestism is referred to as transvestic fetishism. It is similar to other forms of fetishism in that sexual arousal is associated not with an individual but, rather, with inanimate objects (women's clothing).

Transvestism is surprisingly common in films, where it is generally treated with humor and almost never as a serious issue. One comedy that addresses cross-dressing is the popular film *Tootsie* (1982), in which an unemployed actor played by Dustin Hoffman pretends to be a woman in order to get an acting job. The counterpart to this film is Blake Edward's *Victor/Victoria* (1982) in which Julie Andrews portrays a starving cabaret singer who gets her big break when she manages to land a job singing as a male female impersonator. Both films are sensitive analyses of the complex relationships linking gender and role.

Other films have explored cross-dressing. *Some Like It Hot* (1959) directed by Billy Wilder and starring Marilyn Monroe, Tony Curtis, Jack Lemmon, and George Raft, is the classic example of this genre. More recently, *Mrs. Doubtfire* (1993) starred Robin Williams as a man who passes himself off as a "nanny" in order to spend more time with his children. The movie Yentl (1983) stars Barbra Streisand as a woman who must dress in male clothes and pretend to be a man in order to achieve an education. *To Wong Foo, Thanks for Everything, Julie Newmar* (1995) is an entertaining film that examines the lives of three transvestites whose car breaks down in a small town filled with bigots. This film stars Wesley Snipes and Patrick Swayze. As Harvey Keitel's authoritarian character regresses and deteriorates, he falls into a sexual obsession and begins to cross dress in Jane Campion's Holy Smoke (1999). Transvestites are also seen in the award winning film *All About My Mother* (1999) and in *House of Fools* (2002).

"I'm the Latina Marilyn Monroe. I've got more legs than a bucket of chicken!"

Miss Chi-Chi Rodriguez in *To Wong Foo*

Unfortunately, some otherwise good films, such as Brian De Palma's *Dressed to Kill* (1980), starring Michael Caine and Angie Dickinson, link transvestism with violence and sociopathy. There is no convincing evidence that transvestites are more likely than the average individual to be homicidal, although, like others whose sexuality may be viewed as deviant by the majority culture, they are somewhat more likely to be victims of crime.

La Cage Aux Folles

Edouard Molinaro's *La Cage aux Folles* (1978) is a comedy that portrays the relationship between two middle-aged homosexual lovers, Renato and Albin. Renato owns and manages La Cage aux Folles, a nightclub in the south of France in which

all the performers are male transvestites who perform as women. Albin, whose stage name is Zaza, is the star performer at La Cage aux Folles, as well as Renato's lover and longtime companion. Albin cross-dresses both on and off stage and has adopted an exclusive feminine identity.

It is important to understand that this film is a farce and not an accurate presentation of either homosexual relationships or transvestites. Albin's role as a drag queen is as exaggerated as his feminine mannerisms, and probably served to perpetuate many of the stereotypes about homosexuality that existed when the film was released in 1978. However, despite reliance on stereotypes, the film can be credited for its presentation of an enduring, loving relationship between its two lead characters. Both men are secure in their sexual identity, even though it does not conform to conventional norms, and they know the life they have made for themselves is the right one for them. At one point Renato remarks, "Yes, I use make–up. Yes, I live with a man. Yes, I'm an old fag. But I know who I am. It's taken twenty years and that deputy isn't going to destroy it."

The film also highlights the sanctimonious hypocrisy of many of those people who are so quick to limit sexual expression in others and illustrates the perils inherent in denial of one's true sexual identity. The film is best viewed as the hilarious farce it is, and one does the film a disservice by insisting that it portray too strong a social message.

Fetishism

An individual has a **fetish** when an inanimate object habitually arouses him or her. A diagnosis is justified only if the sexual arousal associated with the object or fantasies about it are intense, recurrent and last for at least six months. Sex often involves masturbation with the fetish, or the fetish may be incorporated into sexual activity with one's partner. The term *fetish* is used to refer to both the object itself and the inordinate attraction to it. However, the true fetish involves inanimate objects such as panties, silk stockings, garter belts, high heel shoes, or rubber items of clothing or body parts not normally associated with sexual activity (e.g., hair, feet, or the stumps of amputated limbs). Normally the link to sexuality can be surmised, but occasionally a patient will report sexual arousal to stimuli as obscure as file cabinets or baby buggies, and it is difficult to determine (a) how arousal initially could have been paired with the stimulus or (b) the potential symbolic value of the fetish. The fetish is often used for masturbation, but it may also be worn, worshipped, put in the rectum, hoarded, fondled, or sucked (Chalkey & Powell, 1983).

Some authorities have speculated that fetishism is related to the same psychological impulses that trigger transvestism and kleptomania (an overwhelming object to steal, usually trivial or inexpensive objects). The differences among the three conditions seem trivial in comparison with the similarities that link the disorders. The person with a sexual fetish longs to relate to the object sexually, the transvestite longs to wear it, and the kleptomaniac longs to steal it. Anxiety frequently precedes the unusual behavior, and masturbation is common.

A number of films have included either leading or secondary characters with a fetish. One favorite is *Claire's Knee*, a French film directed by Eric Rohmer and released in 1971. This charming movie details the obsession of a soon-to-be-married writer for his friend's daughter—or, more exactly, the daughter's right knee. The erotic elements in the film are handled with delicacy and good taste, and the writer's fixation on the girl's knee soon seems entirely plausible.

"The smell of white paper is like the smell of skin."

Pillow Book

Peter Greenaway's *Pillow Book* (1997) portrays a woman with a fetish for calligraphy. She melds calligraphy with sex, and the calligraphic pen symbolizes the instrument of pleasure. She develops a passion for calligraphy and experiences withdrawal without it. She searches for the ideal mate to write on her; she rules out the old for not having enough energy, and the young for their distracted nature. She captures and tests out a graffiti writer and other random people to write on her in her search. "You're not a writer, you're a scribbler," she tells one candidate.

Another not-to-be-missed film demonstrating a sexual fetish is Steven Soderbergh's *sex, lies, and videotape*. This intelligent film, which won the Best Picture and Best Actor award at the 1989 Cannes Film Festival, was written, directed, and edited by Soderbergh. The film describes how the lives of three people (a man, his wife, and her sister, with whom he is having an affair) are changed forever by the arrival of the man's college roommate, Graham

Dalton. Dalton is an impotent male who now can achieve orgasm only by masturbating while he is watching the videotapes he makes of women discussing the intimate details of their sexual lives. Dalton has decided to live his life with absolute honesty, and he shares the details of his sexual life with Ann, the rejected wife. The two eventually become lovers, and there is a dramatic confrontation between Dalton and his old roommate (Ann's husband). Dalton is transformed through his relationship with Ann, and eventually he is able to move out of his isolation and into an emotionally satisfying and sexually mature relationship.

An equally powerful film is *Equus* (1977). This movie stars Richard Burton as a disillusioned psychiatrist who has lost all traces of passion in his life. The film revolves around Burton's treatment of Peter Firth, who plays a young man arrested for blinding four horses. This cruel act is linked to Firth's fascination with horses; he finds them both threatening and sexually exciting. The film offers some insight into how an animal fetish might develop.

Some films utilize fetishes solely for comic purposes and offer little insight into the paraphilias, as in *Sex and Zen* (1993) and a woman who proclaims to have a "Santa fetish" in *Bad Santa* (2003).

Crash (1996) is a controversial NC-17 David Cronenberg film about people who have developed fetishes for cars and car wrecks. The film is based on a novel by J. G. Ballard, and the opening scene shows a woman rubbing her breasts against the wing of a plane and then licking metal while an apparently anonymous lover enters her from behind. She later relates this experience to her husband, who in turns shares his day's sexual adventures. The husband later becomes involved in a serious car accident in which the driver of the other car is killed. This man's wife, Helen, survives the accident but is hospitalized and has to walk on crutches while she recovers. Shortly after leaving the hospital, she becomes sexually involved with James, the man who had been driving the car that had killed her husband. Helen arouses James by telling him stories about all the men with whom she has had sex in cars. Both individuals find themselves sexually aroused by crashes and the accouterments of highway deaths (ambulances, flares, fire trucks, etc.). They are increasingly drawn into a deviant subculture that shares their sexual fascination with metal, cars, and crashing. This group is led by an unusual man who amuses himself and others by reenacting the 1955 death of James Dean in his sports car "Little Bastard." In addition to its main theme of fetishism, the film involves exhibitionism, voyeurism, triolism (pleasure in having sex in front of others), and homosexuality. The film ends with a suggestion of necrophilia–James deliberately drives his wife's sports car off the road at high speed, and she is thrown from the car. He determines she is alive, and then embraces her unconscious and injured body while muttering, "Maybe the next one, darling, maybe the next one."

Additional Questions for Discussion

- Are the fetishes described in *Crash* simply too far-fetched to be believed?
- Metal, leather, and plastic are all common fetishes. What is it about these particular materials that make them sexually arousing?
- How common is it for a husband and wife to share fantasies about sex with other partners?
- How is it possible for sexual arousal (a positive experience) to so often become linked with pain (a very negative experience for most people)?

Exhibitionism

The exhibitionist's preferred form of sexual gratification is exposing the genitals to unsuspecting strangers. Masturbation often occurs during or after the exposure. The exhibitionist will almost never attempt to have intercourse with the women he intimidates and would likely be intimidated and frightened by an opportunity for an adult sexual encounter. Although reports of exhibitionism in a neighborhood usually result in increased concern about the possibility of rape, exhibitionism and rape are dramatically different behaviors and are almost never linked.

Exhibitionism can occur at any age, but typically develops in males in their mid-twenties. Despite the popular image of a "dirty old man in a raincoat," the incidence of exhibitionism falls off rapidly after the age of 40 and is rare in older males who are cognitively intact. Many exhibitionists have never had meaningful or satisfying adult sexual relationships; others have normal psychosexual development histories.

Reports of true exhibitionism in females are quite rare, although some women may be aroused by exposing their breasts or legs in public. Exhibitionism in females can also be used as a way of establishing dominance in a nonsexual encounter with males. The potential for psychological manipulation through exposure was dramatically portrayed during Sharon Stone's interrogation scene in *Basic Instinct* (1992). A brief scene of

exhibitionistic behavior is depicted in *Natural Born Killers* (1994) and *Movern Callor* (2001).

The Good Mother (1988) raises interesting questions about the boundaries between healthy sexuality and exhibitionism. Diane Keaton plays the divorced mother of a six-year-old daughter. Keaton falls in love with an artist and starts to live a bohemian life that includes nudity in front of her daughter. Keaton's new lover at one point innocently lets the daughter touch his penis when he is getting out of the tub and she expresses natural childhood curiosity. When the ex-husband learns about this event, he sues for custody, and Keaton is forced to renounce her lover in order to maintain visitation rights with her daughter.

Additional Questions for Discussion

- Is it normal for a child to be interested in an adult's genitals?
- If you were the judge in *The Good Mother*, would you have made the same decision?
- Did the bohemian artist in *The Good Mother* make a foolish error of judgment, or was it appropriate to let himself be touched by his lover's daughter?
- How do children who grow up in households where nudity is common adjust sexually and interpersonally?
- What is the link between voyeurism and exhibitionism?
- At what age does it become sexually stimulating to sleep with a parent?

Voyeurism

The **voyeur** is a "peeping Tom" who experiences arousal and derives sexual satisfaction from spying on unsuspecting people, usually strangers, as they are getting undressed, using the bathroom, or having sexual relations. Although it is normal to want to look at the bodies of others (e.g., at the beach), the voyeur goes to great lengths to find surreptitious hiding places from which he or she can watch others without being detected. Arousal is always associated with the clandestine aspects of the situation; voyeurs report little interest in watching pornographic films, visiting topless or nude beaches, or attending topless bars—all experiences where public voyeurism has been sanctioned.

As is the case with exhibitionism and obscene phone calls, it is rare for the voyeur to attempt to initiate sexual relationships with those women he victimizes. The voyeur will most often masturbate while viewing the arousing scene or later, when replaying the scene in memory. Although it is rare for voyeurs to progress to crimes of sexual violence, more than two-thirds of males who commit sex-related murders report early experiences with voyeurism (Ressler, 1986).

An interesting variation of voyeurism is **triolism**, or sexual gratification derived from watching other people have sex (or allowing others to watch oneself engage in sexual activity—behavior more logically linked to exhibitionism than voyeurism). This practice is sometimes referred to as **scoptophilia**. Variations on these themes include the **ménage à trois** ("family of three"), swinging, and couples that have monogamous sex in each other's presence. Swinging or mate swapping is probably widespread, although AIDS and other sexual diseases have presented serious obstacles to this form of sexual expression. A failed attempt at swinging is portrayed in Paul Mazursky's 1969 film *Bob and Carol and Ted and Alice*, starring Robert Culp, Eliot Gould, Dyan Cannon, and Natalie Wood. The film celebrates social permissiveness and the mores of the late sixties more than sexual freedom; in the final scene Bob, Carol, Ted, and Alice, all in bed together, reaffirm their commitment to monogamy.

Breaking the Waves (1996) is a powerful Danish film that examines triolism in a situation in which a formerly virile man paralyzed from an industrial accident insists that his wife have intercourse with other men so he can derive vicarious satisfaction from her stories. The wife, a devout Catholic, goes along with her husband's demands because she is convinced that these voyeuristic pleasures are the only thing keeping her husband alive.

Other films depicting voyeurism include *Lovelife* (1997) and the Canadian film *The Adjuster* (1991). Most films that have dealt explicitly with voyeurism have been misleading presentations that perpetuate common myths. For example, *Peeping Tom* (1960) presents the story of a voyeur (raised by a sadistic psychologist) who tortures his victims and then photographs them as they are dying. This is an example of sexual sadism, not voyeurism. The pain of voyeurism is evident in the film *Voyeur Confessions* (2001).

Some films depict a strong voyeuristic component without depicting explicit sexual fantasy or gratification. Christopher Nolan's debut film, *Following* (1998), tells a creative story about a man who enjoys picking out one person in a crowd and then following them for a day. He is a lonely writer who convinces himself he follows people to get character ideas for his stories. His habit has qualities

of an addiction insofar as it becomes "irresistible" to him, he is unable to keep it under control, he obsesses about it, and he employs various cognitive justifications for maintaining this inappropriate and disturbing behavior.

Another nonsexual (perhaps impotent) voyeur is displayed in Hitchcock's classic film *Rear Window* (1954). Voyeurism is clearly portrayed; Jimmy Stewart's character watches his neighbors incessantly, and he cannot pull away from his window. His whole life revolves around looking into others' lives, and he satisfies his psychological needs in this way. He also resists and rejects a beautiful, caring woman. If the viewer assumes Jimmy Stewart's character is wrong about the murder and that all his behavior was pure voyeurism with no positive, beneficial outcome, it is hard to avoid the conclusion that this is a film about voyeurism.

Sexual Masochism

The **sexual masochist** becomes sexually excited when he or she is humiliated, beaten, bound, or made to suffer. It is important to appreciate that the diagnosis of sexual masochism is made only when patients actually engage in these behaviors. As is the case with other paraphilias, masochistic fantasies are both common and harmless, and moderate sadomasochistic behavior (e.g., scratching and biting) can be a rewarding part of normal sex play.

Masochists allow themselves to be abused in a variety of ways, including bondage, whipping, handcuffing, spanking, cutting, and burning. They are often verbally abused as well as physically mistreated. Humiliation may be necessary for arousal to occur—e.g., a masochist may be forced to wear a diaper, or his partner may defecate or urinate upon the masochist. Whips, chains, leather, and rubber accouterments often play an important role in the sexual activity of the masochist, who is happiest with a (mildly) sadistic partner. A woman who caters to the sexual preferences of masochistic men is referred to as a **dominatrix**. Masochists may be gay or straight, although the majority of sadomasochistic encounters are heterosexual. Among homosexuals, masochists appear to outnumber sadists (Innala & Ernulf, 1992).

Secretary (2002) is an intriguing film about a young woman (Maggie Gyllenhael) who is depressed and seriously self-injurious. She takes a job as a secretary working for a successful attorney (James Spader). She begins to enjoy his harsh criticism of her mistakes and a sadomasochistic relationship develops. Spader's character enjoys spanking her, yelling at her, and engaging in other sadistic behavior, but he prohibits her from injuring herself (paradoxically using his sadism to control her masochism). The film opens with her nicely dressed at work, arms tied to a long bar behind her neck. She picks up items with her teeth or by turning her torso horizontally. Through a variety of sadomasochistic behaviors, she matures, stops her self-abuse, and develops a meaningful relationship with her boss, eventually marrying him.

Quills (2000) depicts the last years of the Marquis de Sade (Geoffrey Rush), who spent years in an institution. The protagonist engages in a variety of paraphilias that give his life meaning and pleasure.

Pedro Almodóvar's *Tie Me Up! Tie Me Down!* (1990) is a provocative investigation of the relationship between a mildly masochistic woman and the man who kidnaps her and holds her hostage, hoping she will eventually come to love him. The theme is ancient, present in other movies, such as William Wyler's 1965 film *The Collector*. However, few directors have developed the concept with as much skill as Almodóvar, who previously directed another complex psychological investigation of the relationships between men and women, *Woman on the Verge of a Nervous Breakdown* (1988).

Tie Me Up! Tie Me Down! tells the story of Ricky, a young man released from a mental institution, whose only ambition is to find a woman, Marina, he had slept with once when he had escaped from the institution. Marina, an actress and a former drug addict, now stars in pornographic movies and has no memory of her former tryst with Ricky. Their interactions after the kidnapping present the viewer with an odd mix of sexual violence and comedy, and the film constantly jumps between the themes of love and control. Love eventually wins out, and Ricky and Marina develop a healthy, satisfying relationship. The movie sounds misogynistic, but Almodóvar very skillfully demonstrates the power Marina maintains throughout her captivity.

The Piano Teacher

In *The Piano Teacher* (2001), Erika Kohut (Isabelle Huppert) is a highbrow, successful pianist. She performs concerts for standing room only crowds and gives demanding lessons to her students. Erika clearly presents as a sexually repressed and conservative woman with a stern, controlling presence. The film takes its time in getting to important themes and core issues, allowing the viewer to be gradually introduced to her world and values. The viewer sees her go to a porn shop briefly in which she chastises a young male student before she leaves. In another scene, she goes into a booth in the shop to watch a video. These scenes progress to acting out sexually with a male student in a public restroom; in this scene, she is mildly sadistic and very controlling. A relationship begins, and it is only then when her deepest fantasies (and true diagnosis) are revealed. She is in fact masochistic. In one scene, she sets up a blockade so her nosey, controlling mother is unable to burst into her room. Erika gives her lover a letter revealing her fantasies about sadomasochistic behavior. As he reads the letter he learns about her desires to be reminded of her powerlessness, to be gagged, and to be hit if she disobeys any of his commands or rules. Next, she reveals her stash of ropes and other sadomasochistic toys. He responds by telling her that he feels both love and repulsion, and that she is "sick" and needs treatment.

"The urge to be beaten has been in me for years."

The Piano Teacher

The film makes inferences about etiology, mostly surrounding a forceful, controlling mother who needs to know every last detail about her adult daughter. The mother is physically controlling, aggressive, and quick to criticize everything from Erika's attire and her piano playing (although Erika is an expert pianist) to a benign conversation she has with a young man. She instructs her daughter, "No one must surpass you, my dear." Erika's father reportedly died of mental illness in an asylum.

Questions to Consider While Watching
The Piano Teacher

- Was Erika's letter to her lover a true expression of love?
- Why is Erika afraid of being seduced?
- How did Erika's mother contribute to her paraphilia?
- Is it typical for masochists sometimes to adopt the role of a sadist?
- How common is it for people to adopt fantasy roles during sex?

Autoerotic asphyxia, using self-strangulation to produce excitement, erections, and ejaculation, is an unusual but not uncommon paraphilia, often related to masochism. Autoerotic asphyxiation results in more than 50 deaths in the United States each year (Rebal, Faguet, & Woods, 1982). Blanchard and Hucker (1991) were able to review the cases of 117 males who died during autoerotic asphyxial activity. Autoerotic asphyxia is especially significant because most of the deaths that result from this practice are assumed to be accidents.

Most of what we know about the practice of autoerotic asphyxia is derived from police reports following death investigations. The victims tend to be young white males. Bondage accouterments are often employed, along with mirrors and cameras. Transvestism is a common practice in these cases. There is often evidence that ejaculation occurred before death.

There is a fascinating portrayal of autoerotic asphyxia in Nigisa Oshima's film *In the Realm of the Senses* (1976). This film documents the sexual obsessions of two Japanese lovers who are preoccupied with sexual pleasure. The woman increasingly resorts to strangulation to prolong the erections of her lover; eventually and predictably, he dies during one of these episodes. In one graphic scene, the woman severs off the man's penis. The film is based on the true story of a woman who accidentally strangled her lover and then wandered around in a daze, carrying her lover's severed penis with her. Oshima was tried for obscenity in Japan when the film was released, but he was eventually acquitted. His stature as a filmmaker was vindicated by the critical and commercial success of the film in Europe and the United States.

Sexual Sadism

Sexual sadism presents the mirror image of sexual masochism. The sadist derives sexual pleasure from the suffering and humiliation of his or her victims. Partners may be consenting or nonconsenting. If the partner is consenting, the diagnosis requires that sexual sadism be "repeatedly preferred or exclusive" and that "bodily injury that is extensive, permanent, or possibly mortal is inflicted in order to achieve sexual excitement."

The terms **sadism** and **masochism** were first used by a German sexologist, Richard von Krafft-Ebing, in the nineteenth century. Krafft-Ebing, who wrote *Psychopathia Sexualis*, the first medical school textbook on sexuality, took the term sadism from the name of French author Marquis de Sade. De Sade's novels and short stories are replete with abuse, torture, and murder, all of

which are linked with sexual gratification. One of his works, *The 120 Days of Sodom*, was made into the movie *Salo or The 120 Days of Sodom*, (1976), directed by Pier Pasolini.

Sadomasochistic sex often involves elaborate sex toys such as chains, whips, rubber and leather garments, and spike heels. Flagellation and bondage are common practices.

Although some sadists are also rapists, it is important to understand that rapists do not derive sexual pleasure from the rape itself. Rape is an act of violence in which sexual arousal may play virtually no role. In contrast, the sexual sadist derives intense sexual pleasure from the suffering of the victim.

Ten to 20 percent of pornographic magazines are devoted to themes of submission and dominance (Dietz & Evans, 1982), suggesting that the prevalence of sexual sadism and masochism is fairly high in the United States. However, it is important to distinguish between *minor* sadism and masochism (sex play involving bondage and discipline or dominance and submission) and *major* sadism and masochism involving torture and the risk of death and bodily injury (Arndt, 1991). There is some evidence that at the minor level there are more women who dominate males; at the extreme level, men are more likely to abuse women.

Films depicting sexual sadism are common in the United States, and they play for large audiences in Europe and Asia as well. Many of these films are heavy-handed and crude and have little social value. A salient exception is David Lynch's *Blue Velvet* (1986).

Blue Velvet

Blue Velvet opens with Bobby Vinton's song of the same name and scenes of a bucolic Midwest neighborhood. This idyllic scene is soon interrupted, and the viewer is never really allowed to relax again until the film concludes.

The plot of the story involves a student, Jeffrey Beaumont, who is home from college to care for his father who has just had a stroke. While walking in a field near his house, Jeffrey discovers a severed ear. It turns out to be the ear of the husband of a cabaret singer (Dorothy). Dorothy's husband and son are being held hostage to force her to comply with the sexual demands of a local gangster, Frank Booth (Dennis Hopper). Dorothy, one of the most complex characters in the film, discovers Jeffrey in her apartment after he goes there in a foolish attempt to solve the crime. Dorothy, in a controversial scene that disturbs many feminists, discovers Jeffrey and uses a knife to force him to have sex with her. Dorothy displays many of the features of masochism previously discussed; these become more prominent later when Frank arrives and proceeds to savagely abuse her. Frank, both obsessed with Dorothy and fixated on the song "Blue Velvet," has cut off a piece of Dorothy's blue velvet bathrobe. It is a fetish that Frank carries with him and uses during other sexual encounters. Hopper is unforgettable as Frank Booth, who is addicted to inhalants as well as sadistic sex.

"I have a part of you with me. You put your disease in me. It helps me. It makes me strong."

A masochistic and troubled Dorothy in *Blue Velvet*

One troubling aspect of the film is that both Dorothy and Jeffrey seem attracted to sadomasochistic sex after they have been exposed to it. A subplot involves Jeffrey's involvement with Sandy, the daughter of a corrupt local detective. The relationship with Sandy seems pale and insipid after the intensity of a sexual encounter with Dorothy.

The film won the National Society of Film Critics award for best film of 1986, and Lynch was selected as best director of the year by the same group. It is a brutally honest film, and not one that will appeal to all viewers. However, it is a film rich in psychopathology and one worth seeing by anyone interested in the complex world of the sexual psychopath (discussed more fully in Chapter 14).

Frotteurism

The **frotteur** is someone who derives sexual pleasure from brushing or rubbing against others in a seemingly inadvertent but clearly sexual manner. Frotteurs frequent crowded stores, escalators, buses, and subways, where their behavior can be attributed to crowding. *DSM-IV* lists frotteurism as an independent paraphilia, although many authors view it as a variation of exhibitionism.

The film *Dummy* (2003) portrays an unemployed man who is a frotteur. The man is balding, and wears thick glasses. He is included in the film purely for laughs. Though his behavior is not depicted cinematically, the correct definition of a frotteur is given.

Pedophilia

The **pedophile** is someone who is sexually aroused by children and who has acted on these desires or who is markedly distressed by them. The pedophile can be attracted to girls, boys, or both, although heterosexual pedophilia appears to be somewhat more common than homosexual pedophilia. The *DSM-IV* stipulates that the child be prepubescent (generally age 13 or younger) for a diagnosis of pedophilia to be appropriate. In addition, the diagnosis is not used unless the perpetrator is at least 16 years old and at least five years older than the child involved.

Although not a formal diagnostic label, the term **ephebophilia** is often used to describe a person who is attracted to post-pubescent adolescents; the ephebophile's attraction is exclusive and specific to this age group (ages 14-17). The phrase "Lolita syndrome" is used to describe men attracted to female adolescents. Though often illegal, ephebophilia is not seen as pathological and is even normative in some societies in which adolescent girls routinely marry older, adult men. Another non-diagnostic variation of pedophilia is the rare condition called **infantophilia**; this term is applied to adults with a primary sexual attraction to children from ages 0 to 5. The movie *Bliss* (1997) includes a scene illustrating infantophilia.

Many pedophiles report being sexually abused as children (Freund, Watson, & Dickey, 1990). Pedophiles who have been attracted to children since adolescence are identified as **fixated pedophiles**. In contrast, if an individual has satisfying adult sexual experiences, but then reverts to a sexual preoccupation with children, the person is classified as a situational or **regressed pedophile**.

There are between 100,000 and 500,000 cases of child sexual abuse in the United States each year, and the number of cases is probably rising (Barnard et al., 1989).

Most people consider the practice of pedophilia reprehensible, perhaps because children are among the most vulnerable members of the human family. However, the widespread availability of "kiddie porn," despite the social opprobrium associated with the practice, suggests that sexual interest in children is as common as most of the other paraphilias. Empirical data document the extent of sexual attraction to children by adults. For example, Briere (1989) surveyed undergraduate males and found that 21 percent acknowledged being sexually attracted to children, 9 percent had sexual fantasies involving children, and 7 percent would consider having sex with a child if certain they could avoid being detected or punished.

Pedophiles and ephebophiles seduce their victims using play, food, or gifts, which are followed by appropriate touching eventually leading to inappropriate touching and assault. The seduction of an adolescent is powerfully and realistically portrayed in *Blue Car* (2003), in which a young, vulnerable girl is seduced by her teacher. Most viewers are not aware that the teacher is manipulating the adolescent from the very beginning of the film. The seduction of adolescents is also depicted in *American Beauty* (1999), *Lolita* (1962), *Lolita* (1997), *Y Tu Mama Tambien* (2001), and *Manic* (2003). In *The Magdalene Sisters* (2002), a priest has sex with a vulnerable, emotionally & physically abused adolescent girl.

Child sexual abuse is portrayed in the powerful and riveting documentary, *Capturing the Friedmans* (2003), as well as in the very dark comedy, *Happiness* (1998). In *Capturing the Friedmans*, a father (Arnold) and his son (Jesse) are accused of pedophilia. When their house was searched, child pornography was found hidden throughout the home. The movie does not fully indict or acquit either individual.

Incest

Incest is treated as a subclass of pedophilia in *DSM-IV*. The term refers to sexual relations between persons too closely related to marry. Russell (1983, 1984) has reported that the incidence of incest for stepdaughters is as high as 16 percent, and stepfathers are seven times more likely to abuse their children than biological fathers. Barnard et al. (1989) report that one out of six women who have stepfathers experienced sexual abuse at some point during childhood.

The prevalence of the various paraphilias can be estimated by surveying pornography and looking at what topics are the most popular. For example, Lebegue (1991) reviewed 3,050 magazine and book titles collected by the 1986 Attorney General's Commission on Pornography. He found that sadomasochism was by far the most common paraphilia; however, incest titles (e.g., *Suzie Loves Her Daddy*) comprised more than 21 percent of 746 titles judged to relate to *DSM-IV* paraphilic diagnoses.

Stanley Kubrick's *Lolita* (1962) is the classic example of incest in a contemporary movie. The film takes liberties with Vladimir Nabokov's novel, but the changes were made with the permission of the great writer, who served as screenwriter for the movie. A psychoanalyst has argued that Nabokov himself was a pedophile as a result of childhood sexual abuse by an uncle (Centerwall, 1992). Considered quite daring when it was released more than three decades ago, the film portrays the love of Humbert (James Mason) for Lolita (played by Sue Lyon). Shelly Winters plays Lolita's mother and Peter Sellers has two roles in the film. Like many actual incestuous stepfathers, Mason's downfall comes from the restrictions he places on his daughter's emerging sexuality and his paranoia about her sexual experience with anyone but him. *Lolita* was remade in 1997 with Jeremy Irons playing the role of Humbert.

There are vivid scenes of bathroom seduction by a stepfather (Karl Malden) in Barbra Streisand's film *Nuts* (1987). The classic example of the combination of pedophilia and sociopathy is found in the Fritz Lang 1931 film *M*, in which Peter Lorre played a child molester stalking the streets of Berlin. A riveting presentation of the fate of child molesters when they are caught and incarcerated is found in the 1977 prison drama *Short Eyes*.

AKA (2002) is a creative film that depicts a father who sexually abuses his son. In *Dolores Claiborne* (1995), a father sexually abuses his daughter in various ways; one memorable scene occurs when the father makes his daughter masturbate him while riding on a boat in the cold weather, claiming her hands are needed to keep him warm.

Other Paraphilias

Telephone Scatologia

Most American women and a considerable number of men have experienced obscene phone calls. DSM-IV-TR identifies the practice as making obscene calls for sexual gratification as **telephone scatologia**. Clinical assessment of 19 male adolescent sexual offenders who had committed exhibitionism or telephone scatologia showed that the majority were maladjusted, had committed numerous sexual offenses and came from multi-problem families. Several of them appeared to be sexually deviant. Anti-social traits, sexual deviance in the family, homosexual conflicts, repressed sexuality and sexual deviance were considered to be contributory factors (Saunders & Awad, 1991)

People who engage in telephone scatologia are generally males with low self-esteem. They often feel sexually inadequate, and the outrage of their victims gives them a feeling of power. These feelings of power are similar to those that accompany exhibitionism; however, the man making obscene phone calls is far less likely to be apprehended, and the practice provides similar thrills with far fewer risks. Obscene phone callers seldom seek out contact with the individuals they call.

Another variation of telephone scatalogia involves "Dial-a-Porn" services. These "900" numbers allow one to engage in paraphilic behavior without risk and with a seemingly enthusiastic partner; however, the costs of calling can quickly escalate. The lead character in Spike Lee's *Girl 6* (1996) and a woman supporting her family in Robert Altman's *Short Cuts* (1994) work as phone sex operators handling such calls. In the latter film, the woman moans, groans, and sighs at the same time she is changing the diapers on her baby and cooking her family's supper. Adam Sandler's character Barry Egan connects with a phone sex company in *Punch Drunk Love* (2002).

Philip Seymour Hoffman portrays a lonely man who is addicted to telephone scatalogia in *Happiness* (1998). He initiates innocuous phone conversations, and then probes for more intimate details while he masturbates.

Miscellaneous Paraphilias

Other paraphilias include **coprophilia** (feces), **urophilia** (urine), **klismaphilia** (sexual pleasure from enemas), **partialism** (exclusive focus on part of the body), **necrophilia** (sex with corpses), and **zoophilia** (animals). Alfred Kinsey investigated zoophilia (bestiality) and found that in some rural areas up to 65 percent of boys had experienced sexual contact with animals.

Necrophilia is believed to be extremely rare, although estimating the prevalence of the disorder is difficult for obvious reasons. In *Kill Bill, Vol. 1* (2003) a hospital aide sells the right to have sex with patients in comas; this behavior would probably be considered to be a form of necrophilia. Public interest in necrophilia was heightened by the arrest of Jeffrey Dahmer, someone who murdered his victims, had sex with their corpses, mutilated their bodies, and ate various body parts. Dahmer was tested with the **Minnesota Multiphasic Personality Inventory** (MMPI), a psychological test widely used to assess psychopathology. A computerized assessment of Dahmer's test results reported, "[This patient] is likely to have significant psychological problems... He typically deals with frustration by acting out in an extrapunitive way... [He is] quite conflicted over sexual issues." *Dahmer* (2002), a film based on the life of Jeffrey Dahmer, has little value as either entertainment or pedagogy.

Necrophilia is commonly portrayed in vampire movies. One of the best of these is *Bram Stoker's Dracula* (1992), directed by Francis Ford Coppola.

There are a number of case studies of people who are aroused by the sight of blood; this phenomenon is frequently referred to as **vampirism**.

Critical Thinking Questions

- Do the *DSM-IV* transgender categories transvestic fetishism and gender identity disorder perpetuate social stereotypes and discrimination against gays and lesbians?
- In *La Cage aux Folles*, would there have been deleterious psychological effects if Renato's son was raised by Renato and Albin? What is your evidence?
- *La Cage aux Folles* suggests that gay men are likely to be especially creative and artistic. Is there any evidence supporting this stereotype? If not, where did it originate?
- The problem of sexual addiction is increasing. What societal factors may contribute to and reinforce this addiction? When is a sex addict most likely to seek treatment? What treatments are available? Are they successful?
- Is pedophilia more common among certain groups, cultures, sexual orientations, or professions? What is the relationship between pedophilia and the priesthood?
- Homosexuality was deleted from the *Diagnostic and Statistical Manual* of the American Psychiatric Association in 1973. What brought about this decision? What have been its effects?
- Body piercing of the genitals and nipples has become common in the 1990s, whereas it was quite rare in the 1950s. Would these behaviors have been viewed as sexual deviance in the 1950s? How do culture and context influence the process of labeling pathology?
- Why is it that women's clothes (e.g., dresses and slips) are distinctly feminine, while men's clothes (e.g., pants and belts) are far less likely to be regarded as exclusively male?
- Is it ethical for therapists to work with gays and lesbians to modify their sexual orientation? If so, under what conditions would it be appropriate?
- What psychological theories have been put forward to explain the development of fetishes and other paraphilias?

Chapter 9

Schizophrenia and Delusional Disorders

"My name is John Nash! I'm being held against my will!
Someone call the Department of Defense!"
Russell Crowe in *A Beautiful Mind*

Questions to consider while watching *A Beautiful Mind*

- What is Paranoid Schizophrenia? What evidence of this disorder is depicted with this patient?
- Are auditory hallucinations more or less common than visual hallucinations in people with schizophrenia?
- What is the etiology of John Nash's illness?
- Describe the course and progression of John Nash's illness as depicted in the film?
- Can mental health providers make accurate predictions about the likelihood of violence in people with mental illness?
- Is there any relationship between John Nash's mathematical genius and the course of his illness?
- What elements of anxiety and depression are present in John Nash and at what points in the film are they heightened?
- Can a patient with schizophrenia comprehend the reality of his or her delusions when they are faced with absolute and contradicting truths?
- John Nash is depicted as having aged quite a bit in the film when compared with his wife and other characters. How can the life-style of someone with an untreated mental illness contribute to aging?
- How were Nash's delusions of paranoia and conspiracy affected by the realities of his job working for the government?
- What treatments are appropriate in addition to medication?
- What clues does director Ron Howard give in the first half of the film to indicate John Nash is in the early stages of schizophrenia?
- How do the cinematic elements, such as lighting and musical score, enhance the depiction of John Nash's schizophrenia?

Patient Evaluation[1]

Patient's stated reason for coming: "They say I've been diagnosed with schizophrenia. I take medicine for this condition. I don't see why I should be here today to talk about my problems. I can find the solution myself. I only came because I promised my wife I would."

History of the present illness: Professor John Nash is a 38-year-old, Caucasian male who presents to this outpatient clinic with a complex history of visual and auditory hallucinations, intense periods of agitation, confusion, paranoia, and delusional thinking. He experiences frequent visual hallucinations that are delusional and usually dangerous, and, on occasion, benign and supportive. The former most commonly take the form of a demanding Department of Defense agent who gives orders. The latter hallucinations are described as a young man and little girl, whom Professor Nash states are an old college roommate and the roommate's niece, respectively. He reported significant delusions of reference and claims he decodes messages from newspapers and magazines as a part of his top-secret work for the Pentagon. This carried into a belief that his psychiatrist, whom at one point

[1] The following fictitious evaluation is written as if John Nash was interviewed shortly after his release from one of his psychiatric hospitalizations.

he assaulted, was a Russian spy and that his hallucinated friend had betrayed him. Professor Nash believes a radium die containing access codes has been implanted in his arm. There is a history of self-mutilation of his left arm in an apparent attempt to remove this device.

Past psychiatric illness, treatment, and outcomes: Professor Nash's symptoms began during his doctoral studies at Princeton University. He first received inpatient psychiatric treatment at the age of 33. He reports a history of two previous hospitalizations and a past diagnosis of "schizophrenia." His most recent hospitalization was ten months ago with a duration of four months. Records of these hospitalizations will be requested. In both instances, he received insulin-shock therapy five times per week for ten weeks.

Medical history: Professor Nash suffers from impotency. This seems to be an effect of the medication he is taking. There is no other significant medical history.

Psychosocial history: Professor Nash quotes his first grade teacher who once said he was "born with two helpings of brain and only a half a helping of heart." He added, "my wife is helping me with the latter." He has been married for eight years. He reports this is a happy marriage and describes his wife as the most beautiful, accepting person he has ever met. They have one child together, a two and a half year old son. Professor Nash earned a Ph.D. in Mathematics from Princeton University. He has a history of various academic awards, including the distinguished Carnegie fellowship.

Drug and alcohol history: Professor Nash denied any significant history of alcohol or drug abuse. He stated he has an occasional beer, and there is a history of binge drinking during graduate school.

Behavioral observations: Professor Nash presented as disheveled and unshaven, with clothes that did not match. He entered and left the office with his head down and a shuffled gait. He occasionally talked to himself in the form of "asides." His eye contact was poor, particularly when answering questions. Mood and affect were dysphoric. Speech was coherent but at times tangential. There was a marked tremor present, possibly a symptom of tardive dyskinesia. Professor Nash has some insight into the nature of his condition but refuses to accept the seriousness of his condition. He seemed to be preoccupied with objects in the office, such as the reflection of the light shining on a water glass.

Mental status examination: Professor Nash scored a 30/30 on the Folstein Mini Mental Status Examination. He was fully oriented at the time of the interview. He was particularly strong with the serial sevens as he swiftly counted backwards from 100 down to 23 accurately, despite the interviewer telling him he could "stop" several times.

Functional assessment: Professor Nash graduated with his Ph.D. ten years ago. He worked as a professor at MIT for six years teaching classes and conducting research. He is currently unemployed. He is a well-known and highly respected scholar in his field. Socially, he is quite withdrawn, has limited social skills, and his current social support consists of two work colleagues and his wife. He states he does not like to socialize but that he enjoys teaching "eager, young minds."

Strengths: This patient is clearly gifted in the areas of science and mathematics. He has conducted seminal work in his field. His love for his wife is strong and apparent. He enjoys stargazing, going on walks, and spending time with his wife.

Diagnosis: Schizophrenia, Paranoid Type. There is clear evidence of both visual and auditory hallucinations and paranoid delusions. There is no evidence of medical conditions or a history of substance abuse that could account for these symptoms. He experiences mild depression as a result of the challenges of rehabilitation, though these do not appear to warrant a separate diagnosis.

Treatment plan: Relapse is highly likely if this patient does not follow up with treatment recommendations, particularly his medication regimen. He could be dangerous if he responds to his delusions. He requires outpatient treatment focused on relapse prevention and regular psychiatric visits to provide medication review and monitoring until his condition further stabilizes. He would likely benefit from a psychiatric rehabilitation approach that emphasizes social skills training, peer support, and facilitated occupational integration into the community.

Prognosis: Good, pending compliance with medication regimen and psychiatric rehabilitation.

Note to the Reader: In this chapter, we avoid examples of hallucinations from relatively healthy characters utilized primarily for cinematic effect. For example, in *Field of Dreams*, Kevin Costner's character, Ray, has auditory hallucinations of "If you build it, he will come" and visually hallucinates a team of famous, dead baseball players with whom he eventually plays ball. The emphasis in this film is on inspirational and spiritual issues, not psychopathology.

Schizophrenia, Rehabilitation, and *A Beautiful Mind*

A Beautiful Mind (2001) depicts the horrors, traumas, and suffering of schizophrenia. It goes beyond this to show the challenges associated with treatment and rehabilitation for a severe mental illness. This film is based on the novel of the same name by Sylvia Nasar, who writes about the life of John Forbes Nash, Jr., who won the Nobel Prize for Economics in 1994. John and Alicia Nash have noted in interviews that they are satisfied with the final film product. Dr. Nash was often on the set in creating *A Beautiful Mind* and consulted with Russell Crowe and Ron Howard in the production process. Although the film is true to the "spirit" and major events of John Nash's life, it does leave out some of the less flattering details such as his divorce and remarriage to Alicia and an arrest history.

"Often what I feel is obligation... or guilt over wanting to leave, rage against John, against God. But then I look at him and I force myself to see the man that I married and he becomes that man. He's transformed into someone that I love and I'm transformed into someone that loves him. It's not all the time but it's enough."

Jennifer Connelly as Alicia Nash in response to a question of how she is coping with her husband's illness

Few films depict the impact of severe mental illness upon healthy family members. The latter part of the film depicts John Nash's wife, Alicia, playing an important role in helping him "live with the realities of schizophrenia." She helps him remember to take his medications. She works longer hours, takes a large role in child rearing, and manages household chores, all in addition to helping in her husband's recovery.

Relapse is common in people with schizophrenia due to numerous challenges, such as depression associated with recovery, the reality of remembering to take medications several times per day, and the multiple unpleasant side effects of the medication. This film is an accurate depiction of the difficulty of compliance with medication regimens and it shows the impact of psychotropic medications on John Nash's ability to work, his struggle in taking care of his son, and his inability to sexually satisfy his wife.

"He's been injected with a serum. I can see him because of the chemicals enlisted in my bloodstream when my implant dissolved. I couldn't tell you, it was for your own protection."

Crowe as John Nash during a relapse after not taking his medication

It is a challenge for the person with schizophrenia to adapt and become integrated into the community. The depiction of John Nash's struggle to adapt is another strength of the film. Stress triggers his delusions, he longs to give up and become further isolated, but he also has moments of grace and connection with others.

The film also shows the fears of the public about schizophrenia. The film delves specifically into the impact on Nash's friends. His best friend goes to Nash's house and is visibly nervous, hesitant in his speech, and laughs uncomfortably. Another friend watches Nash closely when Nash enters the office. Other reactions are more negative: some students at the university make fun of Nash and mimic his awkward gait and posture, while others stare in disbelief at his odd behavior.

The Diagnosis of Schizophrenia

Schizophrenia usually first occurs during late adolescence or early adulthood, but it can begin in childhood or middle/late adulthood. Even though the frequency of the illness occurs equally in both genders, symptoms in males often occur earlier than females.

In order for a person to be diagnosed with schizophrenia, certain symptoms must be present. According to the *DSM-IV*, there must be continuous signs of the disturbance for at least six months and, during one month (the active phase), two or more of the following must be present: delusions, hallucinations, disorganized speech, grossly disorganized or catatonic behavior, or negative symptoms. The individual's ability to function in work, social relations, and self-care decreases during the active phase and rarely returns to the individual's premorbid level of achievement.

Following the active phase of the illness, the following must be present in order to meet diagnostic criteria: marked social isolation or withdrawal, and marked impairment of role function.

"The nightmare of schizophrenia is not knowing what's true. Imagine if you had suddenly learned that the people, the places, the moments most important to you were not gone, not dead, but worse... they've never been. What kind of hell would that be?"

Psychiatrist, Dr. Rosen, educating Alicia Nash about her husband's schizophrenia in *A Beautiful Mind*

Schizophrenia is categorized into five types: Paranoid, Disorganized, Catatonic, Undifferentiated, and Residual.

The **Paranoid Type** is characterized by systematized delusions or frequent hallucinations related to a single theme (e.g., hearing denigrating voices). These individuals are often extremely anxious, angry, or argumentative, and they may become violent. There is not the strong relationship between violence and schizophrenia that many people expect (and which most movies suggest is common). Among people diagnosed with schizophrenia, paranoid patients are the most likely to commit acts of violence. This is a common subtype portrayed in films; it is popularized in films such as *A Beautiful Mind* (2001), *Donnie Darko* (2001), and *Gothika* (2004). The documentary *People Say I'm Crazy* (2004) is a remarkably honest and real portrayal of the daily life of one courageous man with paranoid schizophrenia.

The **Disorganized Type** presents with a picture of incoherent speech and disorganized behavior. These patients rapidly shift from one idea to another; often the ideas are unrelated. They may also express inappropriate emotion, such as laughing on a sad occasion. They usually have very strange mannerisms and are extremely socially impaired. Robin Williams' character in *The Fisher King* (1991) and Geoffrey Rush's portrayal of David Helfgott in *Shine* (1996) have many attributes of this subtype (in addition to Paranoid Type). Ralph Fiennes' character in *Spider* (2002) is one of the best examples of this subtype.

The most salient symptom of the **Catatonic Type** is psychomotor disturbance. For example, catatonic persons may appear to be in a stupor, completely unaware of their environment. They may maintain one posture for a long time (**waxy flexibility**), crawl into a fetal position, hold an arm in a bizarre position, or sit stiffly in a chair; it may be difficult to move the individual because of the muscle rigidity. At times these individuals become very excited or agitated but then slip into the previous mannerisms. At times they are mute. This type of schizophrenia is less common than other types. The film *Awakenings* (1990) is a dramatic portrayal of catatonia (although this particular film depicted a neurological rather than psychiatric condition). Many films depicting psychiatric institutions have one or two characters (often in the background) who have catatonic schizophrenia, as in *K-Pax* (2001) and *House of Fools* (2004).

Schizophrenia of **Residual Type** is a category for persons who do not exhibit any of the symptoms of the active phase (hallucinations, delusions, etc.) but do have other symptoms such as social withdrawal or eccentric behavior (APA, 1994). Eugene Levy's character, Mitch, in *A Mighty Wind* (2003) illustrates this subtype. Mitch sits alone and stares for hours in a drab motel room, displays psychomotor retardation, exhibits blank, distant, and quizzical facial expressions, and has inappropriate social skills, yet he does not appear to be in the active phase of schizophrenia. These are residual effects. The viewer learns Mitch had previously been psychiatrically hospitalized for a severe mental illness relating to previous severe depression, anger outbursts, and eccentric behavior, though the actual diagnosis is never given.

The **Undifferentiated Type** is characterized by psychotic symptoms (delusions, hallucinations, etc.) but lacks the salient characteristics of the other types. The undifferentiated type of the illness is frequently found in inpatient settings. Probably any film with a psychiatric hospital as the setting would have patients on the ward or in the day room that would be diagnosed as Undifferentiated Type.

Family Dynamics

In the 1960s and 1970s, a popular theory implicated ineffective family communication patterns in the etiology of schizophrenia. Communication within the family of a person with schizophrenia was believed to be indirect, unclear, incongruent, and growth impeding. Communication within families was thought of as distorted and based on "double messages," so that the child received two opposing messages from the parent and, thus, was in a **double bind**. For example, a parent might say, "Come here and give me a hug" and, when the child responded, the parent would push the child away. The child then would feel that pleasing the parent was an impossible "no win" situation and would develop schizophrenia behavior in response to this psychological bind. The **schizophrenogenic family** was characterized as being severely fused. Members of these families never adequately separated or developed into individuals; and, thus, the family had no boundaries. This view of distorted family communication has been largely discounted as a cause of schizophrenia.

Despite the fact that no one seriously believes that parents "cause" their children's schizophrenia, this misconception persists in both popular culture and contemporary cinema. Peter Winter's mother in *Clean, Shaven* (1995) is portrayed as cold, aloof, and withdrawn; there is a clear implication that she is at least in part responsible for her son's illness. Likewise, the movie *Shine* (1996), Scott Hick's fascinating film about the life of child prodigy and pianist David Helfgott, clearly implicates David's father as the root of his son's subsequent mental illness. The father is alternately loving and hateful, telling his son, "No one can love you like me!" while at the same time actively working to limit his son's future and potential. A similar theme can be found in the 1962 film *David and Lisa*, where the mother is portrayed as a cold, unresponsive social climber who was totally insensitive to her son's abilities and problems. The father is depicted as passive, distant and was unavailable to David in his younger years. Both parents were ineffective in dealing with David's problems, and the film suggests there is a link between the dysfunctional parental communication and David's mental illness.

Delusional Disorders

A delusional disorder is not a type of schizophrenia and hallucinations are not a predominant feature of delusional disorders. The delusions are not bizarre, rather they involve situations of everyday life, such as being poisoned, followed, or loved, when in fact this is not the case in reality. The delusions can be erotomanic, grandiose, jealous, persecutory, somatic, or a combination of these types. A person with delusional disorder can typically function fairly well in his or her daily life.

Contemporary Films Depicting Schizophrenia and Delusional Disorders

K-Pax

This film provides a fascinating contrast to *A Beautiful Mind* and helps us see the distinction between schizophrenia and delusional disorders.

Kevin Spacey plays Prot, a man claiming to be from the planet K-Pax who has traveled to Earth by light beams. At the onset, we see Prot appear in a busy train station amongst sparkles of light. Soon he is falsely accused of a crime and admitted to a psychiatric institution. The psychiatrist, Dr. Powell (Jeff Bridges), takes an interest in working with Prot when he learns Prot is unresponsive to conventional psychiatric medications. As their relationship progresses, Dr. Powell learns much about the identity of Prot and the differences between K-Pax and Earth. Much of this is evidence for the diagnosis of delusional disorder, such as Prot's extensive (and savant-like) explanations of his planet's rotation patterns, his discussion on how men and women procreate on his planet, and his descriptions of the differences between the planets. The viewer essentially has two options at this point: Prot is either a delusional patient or a spiritual guide from another planet. We can view the film accepting the former as true to help us understand the predicament in which a delusional patient finds himself. He is completely trapped by his delusions and does not have a way out; the painful challenge of this is that the patient is not aware he is delusional.

As Dr. Powell questions Prot on where he comes from and where he has visited on this planet, another diagnostic explanation emerges. We learn through flashbacks and hypnotic regression that Prot is Robert Porter, a man who witnessed the remnants of his murdered and raped wife and child, as well as the trauma of encountering the killer in his home and then breaking the murderer's neck. Prot then washes his bloody hands with a water hose (hence the depicted water phobia) and attempts suicide in a nearby river. The viewer is left to assume Prot was found and taken to the psychiatric hospital. Consequently, additional diagnostic considerations emerge such as PTSD and catatonia.

If we assume that Prot is not from the planet K-Pax, we are left with a strong case of delusional disorder. Prot fits much of the world around him into his delusional framework to help him make sense of both the world and his delusions.

Additional Questions for Discussion (*K-Pax*)

- What diagnoses are appropriate for Prot's character? Explain.
- How does Prot fit the other patients on the ward into his delusional framework?
- What would be appropriate criteria for releasing Prot from the hospital?
- Compare the portrayal of mental illness depicted in this film and in *A Beautiful Mind*.
- Discuss the differences of the role of the psychiatrist and treatment in this film and in *A Beautiful Mind*. How does the time period each film is set in play a role?

Spider

The viewer realizes this is a deeply psychological movie as he/she sees the opening credits. Inkblots, similar to those used with the classic psychological assessment tool, the **Rorschach Psychodiagnostik**, are integrated into the opening. The viewer is thus invited to "interpret" and challenge what he or she is seeing from the onset to the ambiguous ending.

Director David Cronenberg sets the tone of the film in the first scene which depicts "the flow of humanity"—an arriving train, the hustle of activity, and a multitude of people heading toward their own destinations—contrasted with the lead character, Spider, slowly de-boarding the train, disoriented and isolated from everyone else. This dark and dreary film maps out the psychological terrain of a man with schizophrenia. Spider has minimal dialogue so the viewer learns about his inner world through his facial expressions, body language, and utter isolation.

The adult character, Spider, played by Ralph Fiennes, has been discharged from an institution and attempts to integrate into a group home. He has many symptoms of schizophrenia, including

delusions, mumbling and disorganized speech, incoherent and grossly disorganized behavior, an unclean and disheveled appearance, and negative symptoms including severely flattened affect and shuffling gait.

Ingeniously, Cronenberg places the present-day Spider character in all of the memory scenes as Spider tries to reassemble his past. The adult Spider is shown observing his parents and himself as a boy interacting with the world. Some of these memories are false and some are accurate, but neither the viewer nor Spider himself knows the truth. To make matters more complicated, Spider fuses identities of his memories as well as his past and present which results in further confusion and distortion.

This is also a good depiction of **childhood schizophrenia** as we see the young boy distort reality, express paranoia that his father and his father's mistress killed his mother, and the boy's complete isolation from social contact.

"You're by yourself too much. You need some mates. When I was your age I had mates. Every young lad needs... needs some mates."

Gabriel Byrne speaking to his delusional son Spider

Throughout the film, several metaphors are used to portray Spider's struggle to recognize reality and the disintegration of reality into psychosis. In one scene, Spider is carefully putting together a very complex puzzle of hundreds of pieces and in a latter scene after putting together some painful memory fragments, he angrily destroys the puzzle, throwing the pieces to the floor in the day-room. Broken mirrors, pieces of glass, and twine used to create what appears to be a spider-web are symbols representing his mental state.

Additional Questions for Discussion (*Spider*)

- What makes this character's portrayal of schizophrenia so provocative and realistic?
- Are some of the behaviors portrayed by Spider (e.g., collecting little objects from the street, lying in a fetal position in the bathtub) common characteristics of schizophrenia?

- What does this film have to say about the etiology of schizophrenia?
- In interviews, director David Cronenberg has spoken to the potential for multiple endings for this film. Discuss some different options and cite which fits best with this portrayal of schizophrenia.
- Cronenberg states he wants the viewer to "become Spider." Why? Does this happen for you?
- This film obviously deals with a person with schizophrenia. Why isn't the word or any other diagnosis ever mentioned in the movie?

House of Fools

This Russian/Chechnyan film is based on a true story. Set in 1996, during the first Chechen war, the film depicts a psychiatric hospital located on the border of a war torn area. The hospital staff flee due to conflict in Chechnya, leaving the patients to fend for themselves. Soldiers find refuge in the hospital and interact with the patients.

As with most films depicting psychiatric institutions, there is a hodge-podge of psychopathology depicted. One patient, Jana, has hallucinations (or are they day-dreams?) of herself in a video that portrays the famous singer, Bryan Adams, who appears in the film as himself, often singing the lyrics "have you ever really loved a woman?" Jana has a **delusional disorder, erotomanic type**, as she believes Bryan Adams is her fiancé and that he is in love with her. Her room is covered in Bryan Adams posters. In a later scene, she naively believes the mock marriage proposal made to her by a soldier seeking refuge. Soon she finds herself in a bind, struggling to choose between the deceptive solider and the delusion of Bryan Adams. In one scene, Jana is gripping broken glass too hard and her hand becomes cut up and bloodied. She uses a fantasy of Bryan Adams to cope with the pain.

Jana denies her illness, telling people she was once sick but isn't anymore. Furthermore, she believes she is a teacher for her fellow patients, teaching them yoga and how to play the accordion. Jana tries to help other patients when they make mistakes or need guidance. Cinematically, the viewer sees her reality of bright colors and light where the staff and patients are dancing to her music. This cinematic technique—weaving from patient perception to reality—is used frequently in the film.

Other patients include a person with delusions, a psychotic fire starter, a psychotic transvestite, a psychotic midget, and a person who is catatonic.

Additional Questions for Discussion (*House of Fools*)

- Who are the "fools" the film's title is alluding to?
- Are psychiatric patients likely to bond together and collaborate during extreme circumstances such as the one portrayed here? Is their psychopathology likely to be exacerbated at these times?
- Patients with which psychiatric diagnoses would be most likely to escape an institution if given such an opportunity as depicted here?
- Why are psychiatric hospitals often metaphorically represented as a microcosm for society?

The Truman Show

There are no psychotic disorders portrayed in this film. However, this Peter Weir (1998) movie can be a useful teaching tool in understanding delusional disorders. This flips the essence of a delusion on its ear. The film is about the unreal life of Truman Burbank. Everything around him has been created for him (or, better stated, for the viewing public of the reality show)—all the people in the city, the buildings, the street lamps, the water, even the sun! It is all an extensive production set for a television show, yet Truman accepts his town of Seahaven as his reality; it is all he has known from birth to young adulthood. His name is appropriate as he is the only "true man" because everyone else, including his wife, best friend, mother, and father, are set actors. Eventually, Truman senses that he is trapped in a "world within a world" and tries to escape this contrived reality.

Imagine that there was no television show and that Seahaven was like any other town; in this scenario, would Truman's behavior be seen as delusional? All of his behaviors would probably be seen as paranoid: his questioning and threatening of his wife with a knife, his suspicious looking around the store, his pausing in the middle of the street and stopping traffic. Most of the world around him would be incorporated into his delusional framework. He would incorporate various environmental elements into his delusions: the camera equipment that suddenly falls from the sky, the rain water that just rains down on him and then follows him when he steps out of it, the observation of inconsistency in his wife's behavior. Further paranoid behaviors are exhibited when he follows his wife and he questions who he can trust. Truman explains that he believes his whole life is "building to something" and that he needs to escape to Fiji for awhile. We would probably interpret this as delusional thinking.

"We accept the reality with which the world is presented to us."

Ed Harris as Christof in
The Truman Show

Instead, what really happens is Truman does what a delusional disordered person does not typically do. He challenges his own perception of reality, and this is ultimately what sets him free.

Additional Questions for Discussion (*The Truman Show*)

- How can this movie help the therapist or client in understanding the popular treatment approach of Cognitive-Behavior Therapy?
- In some ways, this film is a psychological study. What are the moral and ethical drawbacks and possibilities in creating a research case study in a controlled environment as seen in this film? Will this be done in the future? Would it better society in some way?
- In Truman's world, the society revolves around him. Is this belief common for a person who has symptoms of paranoia, delusions, or schizophrenia?
- As Truman is leaving his world, Christof encourages him not to leave saying "I know you better than you." If Truman were to believe this, would this suggest psychosis? Do most people with a psychotic disorder believe some variation of this?

Other Films Portraying Schizophrenia and other Psychotic Disorders

People with schizophrenia often get stereotyped as being the "crazy person on the street" which generalizes to the misconception that all eccentric behavior is "crazy." Films depict such instances with minor characters that may or may not have much impact on the plot, but nevertheless this misconception helps shape the stigma associated with mental illness. In *Cinema Paradiso* (1988), one man who appears to have schizophrenia makes serious claim to a public square at a certain time each evening. Each day, he runs around a small area of the street he believes he owns exclaiming, "The square is mine. It's twelve o'clock, the square is mine!" refusing to allow anyone to step in this area. Later in the film (many years later), he continues the behavior, claiming "It's my square. It's mine. The square is mine." Though not critical scenes to the film, the eccentricity and subsequent label do not go unnoticed by the viewer.

At times, the psychosis depicted in films is a brief break with reality (i.e., a **Brief Psychotic Disorder**), often with an obvious trigger. Consider Bernardo Bertolucci's most recent film, *The Dreamers* (2003), in which a young man triangulates with a pair of sexually enmeshed fraternal twins (male/female). At one point, when the young man and the female twin are sexually engaged, she begins to hear her brother in the next room with another woman. She breaks with reality screaming "Who are you? What are you doing in my room? Get out!" while pounding on her brother's wall. The next morning, after a restful sleep, she is coherent and once again oriented to reality.

Terry Gilliam's 1991 film, *The Fisher King*, portrays Robin Williams as Parry, an obsessed yet benign street person. Parry believes himself to be a knight whose mission is to save the Holy Grail. Throughout the film, Parry has several hallucinations, including seeing friendly "little people" who communicate with him regularly and give him guidance. The Red Knight is a frightening hallucination that appears at times of extreme stress or when he is reminded of his personal tragedy.

Sophie's Choice (1982) portrays Sophie (Meryl Streep), Nathan, (Kevin Kline), and Stingo (Peter MacNicol). The three become inseparable friends, with Sophie and Nathan maintaining a turbulent romantic/sexual relationship and Stingo eventually falling deeply in love with Sophie. Sophie and Stingo struggle to understand Nathan's eccentric, erratic behavior, which at different times involves intense love, suspiciousness, anger, hostility, and paranoia. Initially, Nathan merely appears to be an unstable, "moody" person who claims to be a Harvard graduate and an overworked research biologist. As the story unfolds, the audience learns that Nathan has been diagnosed with paranoid schizophrenia and he is only marginally coping with life. His symptoms are exacerbated by the use of amphetamines and cocaine, and his psychotic thinking leads to vicious accusations and unpredictable behavior. His bizarre behavior becomes more pronounced as his interpersonal stress increases and his denial is challenged.

Misery is a 1990 Academy Award-winning film directed by Rob Reiner. Kathy Bates plays Annie Wilkes, a delusional, obsessed fan of mystery writer Paul Sheldon (James Caan). Annie gradually becomes more demanding, petulant, and possessive of Paul, who is injured and under her care. Her caretaking shifts to control of his writing and finally descends to violence and abuse as she smashes his ankles with a sledgehammer.

The 1976 film *Taxi Driver* depicts the life of Travis Bickle, an ex-Marine, Vietnam veteran, and taxi driver on the sleazy streets of Manhattan. He suffers from insomnia, works 12 to 14 hours a night, and spends most of his free time in cheap theaters, watching pornographic films.

"You talking to me?!"

**Robert DeNiro as Travis Bickle
in *Taxi Driver***

Travis' behavior suggests an underlying delusional disorder. His delusions that two characters, Betsy and Iris, are innocent victims of unscrupulous men are consistent with the ideas of persecution that accompany a delusional disorder. He stalks characters and places blame on others. At the end of the movie, he is determined to kill someone—anyone.

Psychotic disorders such as schizophrenia and delusional disorders have a long history in film but are rarely depicted accurately. There are literally hundreds of suspense and horror movies about "psychotic killers" who are on a rampage, usually attacking females. While entertaining for some, these films typically have nothing to do with any particular mental disorder, and they perpetuate the stigma associated with mental illness. The term psychotic is used to induce fear and suggest unpredictability. Pictures such as *Alone in the Dark* (1982), *Angel in Red* (1991),

Cape Fear (1991), *The Caretaker* (1964), and *The Silent Partner* (1979) have all helped shape the stigma experienced by people with mental illness. Also, and in part because of films like these, the diagnosis of schizophrenia is often used as a general term that is applied to anyone who has a mental disorder. For example, in the *Psycho* series (1960, 1983, 1986) and in *The Three Faces of Eve* (1957), the protagonists suffer from dissociative identity disorders, not schizophrenia.

A realistic and fairly accurate portrayal of schizophrenia can be found in the film *Benny and Joon* (1993). In two other films, *Sophie's Choice* (1982) and *The Fisher King* (1991), schizophrenia symptoms are evident, but there are other behaviors that do not clearly fit the diagnosis. For example, in *Sophie's Choice*, it is unclear how much Nathan's drug use influences his symptoms. In *The Fisher King*, Parry's cognitive ability is much greater than typical of those with schizophrenia, and it is very unusual for a traumatic experience to precipitate a psychotic episode, especially in someone functioning at a professional level, (as Parry was a college professor). However, all of these films are convincing portrayals of symptoms.

"Ah, but the strawberries! That's, that's where I had them. They laughed at me and made jokes, but I proved beyond the shadow of a doubt, and with, with geometric logic, that, that a duplicate key to the wardroom icebox did exist."

**Captain Queeg in
*The Caine Mutiny***

One of the most vivid cinematic portrayals of psychiatric decompensation occurs in *The Caine Mutiny* (1954). Humphrey Bogart plays Captain Philip Francis Queeg, the obsessive-compulsive skipper of a World War II destroyer. The ship's crew silently watches the deterioration that occurs as Queeg is put under increasing pressure, and eventually a junior officer, Lieutenant Barney Greenwald, takes command. Greenwald is later court-martialed, and the film's most dramatic moment comes when Queeg cracks under the stress of the courtroom examination while playing with steel ball bearings, as he always does when anxious.

The portrayal of delusional disorders tends to be more realistic than most film presentations of schizophrenia. In films such as *Sleeping with the Enemy* (1991), *The Fan* (1981), *Scissors* (1991), *Delusions of Grandeur* (1973), and *The Entertainer* (1960), delusions are clearly involved. None of these films, however, deal with treatment. In contrast, *Benny and Joon* depicts Joon's struggle with her need for independence, as well as with her symptoms. *David and Lisa* (1963) takes place in a treatment setting and reflects the treatment of the time. *I Never Promised You a Rose Garden* (1977) also takes place in a state mental institution and accurately depicts treatment during the 1960s.

International Films: Schizophrenia and Other Psychotic Disorders

See the discussion of *House of Fools* earlier in this chapter, and *The Cook, The Thief, His Wife, and Her Lover* (1989) in the "Violence and Physical and Sexual Abuse" chapter.

He Loves Me, He Loves Me Not

This might be the most effective and clear-cut use of the cinema to depict a delusional disorder. It is the directorial debut of French director Laetitia Colombani. First, the viewer is completely taken in as he/she sees reality from a Angelique's (*Amelie*'s Audrey Toutou) perception of her blooming love relationship with a man named Loic. Mid-way through, the film literally rewinds and flashes back to the beginning of the film and then gives us the vantage point of Loic, who is a married doctor who barely knows Angelique exists. It is only as the second half of the film unfolds that we can then backtrack in our minds to remember how Angelique perceived the relationship and compares it with what Loic sees and experiences. It is the latter that becomes reality. Thus, everything in the first half of the film is Angelique's delusions. The viewer learns she obsessively calls Loic, leaving 23 messages. Her obsessions with drawings, following him around, and writing notes all reinforce and maintain her delusional framework.

The delusional person can readily function in society as shown with Angelique successfully taking care of her house, working a regular job,

wearing appropriate attire, and communicating with others around her. Without knowing her thinking, we would not know she is delusional, particularly with her very sweet, often smiling, and innocent presentation.

The film also depicts the risk in breaking the framework of a person's delusional mind-set. It is here we see the stereotype of the violent psychiatric patient, as Angelique takes on the frame of mind, "If I can't have him, no one will" and attempts to murder two innocent people.

Most films are sympathetic in their depiction of people with delusional disorder, especially when it is ambiguous as to whether the disorder is real or whether the character is being misjudged for his or her idiosyncrasies. However, *He Loves Me, He Loves Me Not* is not at all ambiguous. The film maintains honesty and clarity about the disorder and its purpose in showing drastically different truths where one side is actually much "more real" than the other's.

Angelique's diagnosis of delusional disorder is discussed in the end when she is taken to a psychiatric hospital. The filmmakers knew what they specifically wanted to achieve with this deeply psychological film and they accomplished it.

An Angel at My Table

Jane Campion's film autobiography of New Zealand writer Janet Frame is a compelling story of misdiagnosis and malpractice. Frame, an awkward, anxious, and socially inept adolescent, is misdiagnosed as having schizophrenia after an apparent panic attack and winds up receiving shock treatment and being hospitalized for eight years. She narrowly avoids receiving a frontal lobotomy, a popular treatment at the time.

Critical Thinking Questions

- Consider a quote from Russell Crowe's character in *A Beautiful Mind*: "She never gets old. Marcee can't be real. She never gets old." How common is this kind of insight for a person with schizophrenia or delusional disorder?
- John Nash explains in *A Beautiful Mind* that he won't talk back to his visual hallucinations so as to not feed them and keep them alive. How effective is this approach for most people with schizophrenia?
- Can a parent play a role in the development of mental illness in a child? How?

- Do films such as *Clean, Shaven*, *Shine*, and *David and Lisa* do a disservice to parents by blaming them for what is essentially a biological disorder over which they have no control?
- Films such as *Shine*, *David and Lisa*, and *Benny and Joon* all suggest that love can at least partially offset the deleterious effects of a disease such as schizophrenia. Is there any evidence suggesting this is true?
- In one memorable scene in the film *Clean, Shaven*, Peter Winter is in the library, hitting his head against the stacks. If you had been present, would you have ignored the behavior or tried to intervene and help in some way?
- John Nash's character in *A Beautiful Mind* was a genius, Kevin Spacey's character in *K-Pax* has many savant-like qualities, and Peter Winter's character in *Clean, Shaven* graduated "in the top 5 percent of his high school class." Is there any relationship between schizophrenia, psychosis, and intelligence? Are extremely bright people more or less likely to develop such a disorder?
- What other films can you think of that present good and bad examples of schizophrenia or delusional disorder?

Chapter 10

Neuropsychological Disorders

I have no short-term memory. I know who I am. I know all about myself.
I just—since my injury I can't make new memories.
Everything fades. If we talk for too long I'll forget how we started
and the next time I see you I'm not gonna remember this conversation.
I don't even know if I've met you before. So if I seem strange or
rude or something...I've told you this before, haven't I?

Guy Pearce, *Memento*

Questions to consider while watching *Memento*

- How does Leonard's personality interact with his illness?
- What are the various compensatory strategies Leonard uses throughout the film?
- Even with all the strategies Leonard has developed, is it realistic to believe he could do what he does in this film?
- How does memory for eyewitness testimony compare with Leonard's memory problems?
- How does the filmmaker's depiction of memory speak to more than just those with cognitive disorders?
- What neurological symptoms did this film create for you, the viewer, to experience? Why is this done?
- Leonard exhibits several paranoid traits. Are paranoia and suspicion characteristic of cognitive disorders?
- What clues indicate that Leonard is about to forget something?
- How long could a person with these symptoms survive without constant support and monitoring?
- Do the symptoms of anterograde amnesia improve over time?
- What is the difference between anterograde and retrograde amnesia?

Patient Evaluation

Patient's stated reason for coming: "I need you to help me find out who killed my wife. I was told you could help me. Teddy sent me." (Patient stated this as he referred to notes on a crumpled piece of paper from his pocket).

History of the present illness: Mr. Leonard Shelby is a 29-year-old man who suffered a severe head injury three years ago. He experienced a severe concussion on the left side of his head as he fought with an intruder who broke into his home, raped his wife, and tried to suffocate her. As a result, Mr. Shelby suffers from severe anterograde amnesia, a memory dysfunction that prevents him from converting short-term to long-term memory.

Past psychiatric illness, treatment, and outcomes: According to the available medical records, Mr. Shelby has lived "off and on" at the neuropsychiatric unit of a hospital for the last two years. He has been placed in group-care facilities on two occasions but fled both times within a month. He also escaped from the hospital; each time he flees, it has been "to find out who killed my wife and get revenge." The year immediately after the injury, this patient lived with his wife as they tried to cope with the wife's rape trauma and adapt to Mr. Shelby's head injury. Records indicate Mr. Shelby has killed at least three people, two of whom he believed had raped his wife.

Medical history: Medical records indicate Mr. Shelby has been prescribed several types of antidepressant and mood stabilizing medications; however, he is noncompliant with all medications whenever he is away from the hospital.

Psychosocial history: Mr. Shelby had been married for eight years before his wife died. Medical records indicate Mr. Shelby killed his wife by giving her an overdose of insulin. Apparently, his wife was skeptical of his anterograde amnesia diagnosis and decided to "test" his short-term memory loss. She tested his memory by asking him to give her insulin shots repeatedly, thinking this extreme and life-threatening situation would force him to admit he was "faking." He was not faking, and his wife went into insulin shock and coma, from which she never recovered.

Mr. Shelby graduated from college with an undergraduate degree in Finance. He does not have any children, and he is not currently in a relationship. He has been unemployed since his injury. For eight years prior to the injury, he worked as an insurance claims investigator. He states he enjoyed this work and found it very fulfilling. He began to tell a story about a client he once worked with named Sammy Jenkins; he told parts of this story on three separate occasions during the interview. It may be significant that he has "Remember Sammy Jenkins" tattooed on his left arm.

Drug and alcohol history: There is no significant history of drug or alcohol abuse.

Behavioral observations: Mr. Shelby was 15 minutes late for the interview. He wore a sport coat and slacks that appeared unwashed. Interestingly, he took a photograph of the interviewer upon walking into the examination room, saying "it's so I can remember you" as he wrote down the interviewer's first name and the words "Teddy recommended: Shrink" on the photograph.

Mr. Shelby used numerous compensatory strategies to assist his memory during this interview, including note-cards, handwritten pieces of paper, photographs of people with names and notes written on them, and his own tattoos. The latter, he stated, are for "vital information." He often repeated, "You really do need a system if you're gonna make it work." On two occasions, he began to take off his jacket and shirt to read the tattoos on his chest but the interviewer stopped him and encouraged him to read them later. Frequently, the pieces of paper oriented him to where he was and why he was being examined. He asked himself numerous questions, and he repeated many statements at different points during the interview. This pattern of repetition occurs every 10-15 minutes.

Mental status examination: Mr. Shelby was suspicious and guarded during the evaluation. Mood and affect were labile, quickly shifting from agitation to dysphoria. Anxiety was evident after some questions when the patient appeared to have lost his memory; when this occurred, he would fumble with his photographs and notes, or attempt to read his body tattoos. There was no evidence of flight of ideas, hallucinations, or delusions. There was no current suicidal or homicidal ideation present, although the latter is a significant concern due to his history. Short-term memory is extremely limited. Anxiety and agitation are factors that truncate this range.

Mr. Shelby was oriented to person. He was not oriented to place, time, or situation. However, he was able to figure out each with the help of compensatory strategies. He showed the interviewer some of his notes and writings. Many were phrases and random thoughts, tasks to do, and ideas. These notes serve several purposes: first, they serve as a compensatory strategy to help him stay "on track" long enough to complete tasks; secondly, they help him remember important past events and people, and third, they coach himself along through his difficulties. He forgot my name several times during the interview, but, as we concluded, he quickly referred to his photograph of me, mentioned my name and smiled.

Mr. Shelby was given the Mini Mental Status Examination twice, the first time without the use of notes and the second time with notes. He scored a 15/30 and a 23/30, respectively. Without the use of compensatory strategies, Mr. Shelby struggled with orientation, memory recall, and serial 7's. He was able to following simple commands, name objects in the room, write a sentence, and copy a complex drawing. When using the strategies on the second examination, the main benefit came when he was tested for orientation to date and place.

Functional assessment: Mr. Shelby has almost no ability to convert short-term memory to long-term memory. This has a severe and serious impact on every activity in his life. He has difficulty taking care of himself, and he needs to be reminded to eat meals, change his clothes, and perform other activities of daily living. His injury prevents him from working or going to school and limits his ability to maintain new relationships. Mr. Shelby does not have insight into his actions, speech, emotions, and thoughts, as he forgets them within fifteen minutes.

Strengths: Mr. Shelby is creative, spontaneous, and intelligent. His personality is energetic, engaged, and interesting. He is disciplined and systematic in the organization of compensatory memory strategies. He is highly motivated, and perhaps this motivation can be channeled in prosocial directions. He is aware of his condition insofar and appears to know that he suffers from a problem with the consolidation of memories.

Diagnosis: Amnestic Disorder Due to Head Trauma; Antisocial Personality Disorder

Treatment plan: Mr. Shelby should be monitored closely on the neuropsychiatric unit. In addition, his notes, writings, and photographs should be closely monitored due to the high homicide risk that appears to rise quickly and for no obvious reason.

A complete neuropsychological evaluation is recommended with periodic follow-up testing to assess changes in functional ability, and especially memory. Occupational therapy should also be consulted so the patient can be trained in additional compensatory strategies, particularly ones involving activities of daily living.

Prognosis: Poor.

Memento, Memory, and Viewer Empathy

Memento (2001) is a psychological thriller that centers on the life of Leonard Shelby (Guy Pearce), a man with anterograde amnesia that makes it impossible for him to convert new experiences into long-term memory. The movie chronicles the psychological and social complications associated with this memory disorder, as well as this man's efforts to get revenge. This is the second film of director Christopher Nolan (see also *Following* and *Insomnia*, both discussed in this book), who amazingly created this incredibly complex film in 25 days.

Memento is a cleverly edited film that begins at the end of the story and works backward: the color portions of the film progress backward in approximately ten-minute segments, and these clips are juxtaposed with black & white clips that move forward in time.

Leonard has lost his wife and is struggling to avenge her loss by finding the killer. He does not remember that he was the person who killed her when she "tested" his amnesia by having him administer repeated doses of insulin until she went into insulin shock and coma, and subsequently died. Leonard actually believes the insulin injections were made by Sammy Jenkins, a man whom Leonard believed to be malingering (with anterograde amnesia) when Leonard was an insurance claims investigator. Leonard has fused his story with Sammy's and distorted reality. The film cleverly gives the viewer clues to the truth that Leonard is both denying and forgetting. For example, in one scene, one frame of Leonard is superimposed on the character of Sammy Jenkins, and it is unclear who is actually in the hospital. Another example involves a flashback at the end of the film (the beginning of the story) of Leonard and his wife lying together in bed; the camera focuses briefly on the words "I've Done It" tattooed on his chest, as if to give the viewer one final piece of direct evidence.

The film does a brilliant job of depicting the suffering of someone with a memory disorder, and illustrates the painstaking discipline and detail-oriented approach necessary for someone to cope with a memory disorder using compensatory strategies (e.g., tattoos and Polaroid photographs of people and places). As if Leonard isn't facing enough as a man who has lost the ability to consolidate memories, he must also cope with others determined to take advantage of his illness, manipulating and lying to him. Ultimately, he has no one he can rely on or trust, including himself, as those who appear to help only "use" him (e.g., for drug deals, for murderous revenge, or to make some extra money, all at his expense). Eventually, he is confronted with a harrowing truth. A corrupt police officer, Teddy, tells him: "You don't want the truth…you create your own truth." The viewer eventually comes to realize that Leonard has not known the truth from the beginning, and he is preparing to kill an innocent man.

Perhaps the most remarkable aspect of this film is its ability to force the viewer to experience the world as someone with anterograde amnesia experiences it. The viewer experiences the protagonist's struggles, distortions, lapses, questions, and emotions as he or she tries to put together the scenes going backward while making sense of the juxtaposed black and white scenes that are going forward. The viewer is constantly re-evaluating and re-thinking what has just been seen. The film demands both concentration and memory from the viewer, who almost immediately begins to appreciate the majesty of something most of us take for granted: the ability to convert new information into long-term memory. The viewer experiences the protagonist's confusion as he or she tries to decide who is manipulating whom, and feels what the amnestic patient feels when trying to sort through conflicting distortions of time, place, person, and situation. The viewer questions his or her own memory, and must also adopt some cognitive strategy in order to keep all the confusing aspects of the film straight. The viewer also begins to lose trust in the film's characters, particularly the "unreliable narrator" (Leonard) who comes by the role honestly due to his anterograde amnesia.

This film's complexity extends further to address existential themes about our search for meaning, the loss of identity, finding and operating out of the "shadow," the role of truth and lies (both to oneself and to others), the problem of coping with a cognitive disorder, and the ubiquitous power of denial.

Neuropsychological Disorders

This chapter describes conditions that result in a significant deficit in cognition or memory and consequently have an impact on the individual's ability to function normally. First, general categories of cognitive disorders are discussed—dementia, delirium, and amnesia. Next, specific conditions are covered—head trauma, brain tumors, stroke, and epilepsy.

Dementia

The term **dementia** refers to a collection of brain disorders characterized by memory disturbance, impaired judgment, and personality change. Insidious onset and gradual deterioration of cognitive abilities are also typically found in the dementias. Although some authorities believe the term should be applied only to those conditions that are nonreversible, the more common practice (and that followed by *DSM-IV*) is to use the term descriptively, without any implications for prognosis. Hence, brain dysfunctions relating from causes as diverse as nutritional deficiencies and Cushing's syndrome can be diagnosed as dementias.

Dementia can be caused by any number of medical conditions or they can be substance induced. Some of the more commonly known medical causes are cerebrovascular disease, head trauma, Parkinson's disease, HIV, Huntington's disease, Pick's disease, and Creutzfeldt-Jakob disease. *Awakenings* (1990) offers excellent demonstrations of dementia and catatonia due to Parkinson's Disease. The film is based on the experience of neurologist Oliver Sacks, best known as the author of *The Man Who Mistook His Wife for a Hat*.

The single leading cause of dementia is **Alzheimer's Disease**, responsible for about half of all cases of dementia. Alzheimer's is a public health problem of enormous dimensions, and one that is becoming an increasing problem as the average life span steadily increases.

The brains of patients with Alzheimer's disease are demonstrably different from those of age-matched controls, and they contain **senile plaques** and **neurofibrillary tangles**. Although some neuronal loss is universal with aging, the brain of the Alzheimer's patient shrinks at a more rapid rate. Psychological tests are often the best indicators of the presence of Alzheimer's disease, especially in the early stages, as these patients will often maintain excellent social skills and use these skills to disguise the marked problems they develop with their memory. Other early signs of the insidious onset of Alzheimer's disease include diffuse generalized anxiety and inappropriate social behavior. An official diagnosis of Alzheimer's cannot be made until after the individual has died and an autopsy has been performed.

Iris

Iris Murdoch was one of the greatest writers and thinkers of the 20th century. She wrote 26 novels, six philosophical works, and several plays. The content and purpose of her intricate works can be simplified in one phrase: she wanted to teach humans how to be free and how to be good. Murdoch was a deep, complex, and gifted thinker. It is bitterly ironic to see such a brilliant and well-used brain deteriorate with dementia, as we observe in the film *Iris* (2001).

Some of the early signs of Iris' dementia are seen in her experiences of memory loss—she would forget what she had just said and frequently repeat herself. She then began to talk to herself, exhibit blank stares and flat affect, display further language disturbance (i.e. babbling), and lose her ability to care for herself. Her writing, which had always flowed easily and extensively, came to be constricted and limited, and she would frequently sit at a table with blank pages in front of her. Her care for her home and house became non-existent. The film depicts the development of increasingly serious symptoms, and portrays Iris in serious danger on several occasions—e.g., jumping out of a moving car, trying to control the steering wheel when on the passenger side, and leaving her house to wander in the middle of traffic. The viewer sees Iris slowly retreat into a world of her own; at first, it is for brief periods and she comes back to reality, but she experiences increasingly longer periods of isolation and quiet. She does emerge from her world at times to say "I love you" to her husband in powerful cinematic moments.

The film *Iris* also speaks deeply to the challenges and responses of the caretaker of someone with Alzheimer's. John Bayley, Iris' loving husband, joins Iris in denying her disease at first, saying "she disappears into a mystery world... [but] she always comes back." As he continues to watch his wife display more serious symptoms, his emotions catch up with him and he screams out in anger. Several scenes show John Bayley deep in despair as he sits alone, helpless to do anything to stop the disease. He sadly repeats the phrase: "Love will soon be over." It is fascinating to watch him experience predictable stages of grief: denial, anger, questioning/challenging, sadness, and finally acceptance when he takes Iris to a nursing home.

"She's in her own world now, perhaps that's what she always wanted."

John Bayley on his wife's illness

Dementia vs. Depression

One of the most important tasks confronting clinicians working with older patients is the often-difficult discrimination between dementia and **clinical depression**. Appropriate diagnosis is critical in these cases so that a depressed patient will not go untreated because he or she is inappropriately believed to be suffering from Alzheimer's disease. In the majority of cases, the two disorders will present in ways that are different enough for the alert clinician to distinguish between them. For example, Alzheimer's has a more insidious onset, whereas depression may come on more rapidly. The patient with Alzheimer's always will have genuine cognitive deficits and experience difficulty with learning new tasks.

The depressed patient will lack motivation and may have trouble concentrating but should be able to learn adequately, although slowly. The depressed patient is also more likely to experience loss of appetite and a fluctuating course, and he or she is far more likely to have a history of affective illness.

In addition, depressed patients tend to acknowledge and sometimes even exaggerate their problems. In contrast, patients with Alzheimer's are far more likely to cover up their difficulties, deny that they are having problems, and may be euphoric. Finally, in the later stages of the illness, patients with true dementias will often have abnormal brain images and electroencephalograms.

Another important film portraying Alzheimer's disease is a made-for-TV movie, *Do You Remember Love?* (1985), in which Joanne Woodward plays a college professor who develops the devastating disease. Woodward's portrayal is sensitive and moving. There is also a memorable scene between Jane Fonda's character and her mother in *Agnes of God* (1985). Fonda plays a psychiatrist who goes to visit her mother in a nursing home. The scene opens with the mother watching a children's cartoon program. The disoriented mother gets Fonda confused with her younger sister, who had died years earlier in a convent. Jessica Tandy very convincingly portrays an old woman who eventually develops Alzheimer's disease and is placed in a nursing home in *Driving Miss Daisy* (1989). Tandy won an Academy Award for her performance in this film.

Delirium

Delirium refers to the rapid onset of confusion and disorganized thinking (a "clouding" of cognition) and is often characterized by rambling, incoherent, or inappropriate speech. Emotions are often inappropriate as well; for example, the delirious individual may be extremely anxious or euphoric in situations in which these reactions would be inappropriate. Delirium can also cause illusions, hallucinations, or misinterpretations of sensory stimuli; for example, a doctor's look of concern may be perceived as extreme anger by the delirious patient. Most films depicting dementia will show some examples of delirium as well (e.g., *Iris*).

Delirium most often (but not always) results from a disturbance of the metabolism of the brain, and causes can include infections, insufficient oxygen levels, ionic imbalances, vitamin deficiencies, and kidney disease. One common cause of delirium is either acute intoxication with—or withdrawal from—drugs. **Delirium tremens** is a common problem for alcoholics with a history of problem drinking. Patients experiencing the "DTs" become disoriented, hallucinate, and display marked tremors. Other symptoms may include intense fear, fevers, and sweating. The intensity of delirium tremens is vividly portrayed in Billy Wilder's film, *The Lost Weekend* (1945), and by Nicholas Cage's role in *Leaving Las Vegas* (1995).

Amnesia

Patients with amnesia display marked impairment of short-term memory with relatively intact long-term memory and preserved intellectual functioning. In its extreme form, the disorder results in the total inability to learn new information. A patient with an amnestic syndrome will be unable to recall the doctor's name, no matter how many times it is presented; simple learning tasks such as recalling the names of four objects become virtually impossible. The patient will be able to *repeat* the four items, suggesting intact understanding of the task and good receptive and expressive language skills; however, after dozens of trials the patient will still be unable to recall the four items from memory.

Patients with amnestic syndromes will sometimes **confabulate** and present detailed and plausible explanations for their obvious inability to acquire new information. The patient who can't remember four numbers for more than a few seconds will explain that he was never any good at math, and the patient in a psychiatric hospital may say he is there because of problems with his kidneys. One of our patients with an amnestic syndrome was asked four times during a one-hour, taped interview what he had had for breakfast that morning. The patient responded by supplying four different "menus" during the interview, each equally plausible. On each occasion, he had absolutely no recollection of being asked this question earlier in the interview.

One of the most commonly encountered amnestic syndromes is **Wernicke-Korsakoff syndrome**. Patients with this disorder have great difficulty with new learning, fail to recall recent experiences, exhibit gait disturbances secondary to cerebellar dysfunction, and display a variety of ocular disturbances, including impaired conjugate gaze. This condition is found in older alcoholics after many years of substituting the nutritionally empty calories of alcohol for the protein, carbohydrates, vitamins, and fat found in a normal diet. The disorder is particularly related to deficiencies in thiamin (B1), and some public health experts have recommended "enriching" spirits with vitamins in the same way we enrich bread. Although this could be done with minimal cost, the distillers have not been enthusiastic about this procedure, despite its potential benefit to alcoholics.

A number of films have portrayed characters with amnesia, including *Anastasia* (1956), *Mirage* (1955), *Spellbound* (1945), and *Desperately Seeking Susan* (1985). The 1983 film *The Return of Martin Guerre* and the more contemporary film *Shenandoah* are two movies that creatively explore the limits of memory and the extent to which it can be influenced by motivation and need. Dissociative amnesia (see Chapter 3) needs to be differentiated from amnesia caused by a substance or general medical condition (including head injuries).

Head Trauma

The link between head injuries, amnesia, and movies is very strong. The cinema can relay countless creative stories (discussed below) when someone experiences head trauma and becomes amnestic to the life of their past—they can start over from scratch, they can try to re-discover life with a deeper appreciation, other people can manipulate them, etc.

Although not given a separate rubric in the *DSM-IV* nomenclature, it is common to see references to **dementia pugilistica** (punch-drunk syndrome) in the professional literature and in the medical charts of aging boxers. These patients, after a lifetime of repeated blows to the head (with concomitant brain injuries), often develop difficulty with movement and a tremor similar to that found in **Parkinson's disease**. They develop slurred speech and diminished mental agility, and they become especially sensitive to the effects of alcohol. Dramatic mood swings (referred to as **emotional lability**) are common, and these individuals are quick to become angry, engage in fights, and become paranoid. Many of these symptoms can be seen in Robert De Niro's portrayal of Jake LaMotta in *Raging Bull* (1980).

The repetitive head blows associated with boxing have been shown to cause brain injuries that may not be detected by an MRI. There is evidence that microstructural damage exists in professional boxers when compared to a age- and sex-matched control group (Zhang et al., 2003).

This problem is so serious that the American Medical Association and other professional organizations have called for the elimination of professional boxing as an organized sport. Indeed, it is hard to find redeeming social value in a sport in which the express purpose is to damage the brain of an opponent. However, boxing remains a popular pastime, and this popularity is reflected in films such as *The Great White Hope* (1970), *The Harder They Fall* (1956), *The Joe Louis Story* (1953), *Kid Galahad* (1937/1962), *On the Waterfront* (1954), *Requiem for a Heavyweight* (1962), the ever popular *Rocky* films (1976, 1979, 1982, 1985, 1990), and many others.

"You don't understand! I could've had class. I could've been a contender. I could've been somebody, instead of a bum, which is what I am."

Marlon Brando in
On the Waterfront

When visualizing brain injuries, it is useful to remember that the cranium is a closed, solid container and the brain is soft and consists of a jelly-like substance that moves inside the skull when the head is struck. The brain is actually quite fragile, albeit well protected by the skull and meninges (the three layers of protective covering that are found between the skull and brain).

Head injuries are usually classified as **concussions**, **contusions**, or **open-head injuries**. Concussions occur when the brain is jarred, and amnesia and loss of consciousness are common consequences. Impaired memory and concentration, headaches, fatigue, anxiety, dizziness, and irritability characterize the post-concussion syndrome. Contusions occur when the brain is actually bruised, most often because of an impact between the brain and the skull. Contusions produce more serious neurological consequences than concussions and can result in death. Contusions are characterized as **coup injuries** if the damage is at the site of impact (e.g., at the point where a baseball bat hits the skull). **Contrecoup injuries** occur opposite the point of impact. They most often result from acceleration injuries (such as occur when a moving head hits a stationary steering wheel). Open-head injuries occur when the skull is hit with sufficient force to open it and expose the underlying neural tissue. Open-head injuries from missile wounds are common in wartime, and much of what we know about the organization of the brain is the result of examination of soldiers injured in battle.

Raging Bull

Raging Bull (1980) is a Martin Scorsese film that stars Robert De Niro (who won the Best Actor Academy Award for his role in this film), Cathy Moriarty, and Joe Pesci. This engrossing drama portrays the life of Jake LaMotta, a prizefighter confronted with the need to find purpose and meaning in life once he leaves the ring. LaMotta's marriage fails, his wife takes their children with her, sexual jealousy drives a wedge between him and his brother, and he ultimately is forced to mutilate and then hock the jewels in the belt he received for winning the world middleweight championship. The viewer is never certain whether LaMotta is a pathetic or a heroic figure, but the film ends with reconciliation between the two brothers and with the protagonist successfully performing a Broadway reading of the works of several notable authors. The recitation of one of Marlon Brando's monologues from *On the Waterfront* (a 1954 Elia Kazan film about the life of a down and out prizefighter) is Scorsese's way of paying homage to another great filmmaker and provides a dramatic conclusion for the film.

Raging Bull is replete with examples of LaMotta's poor judgment. Two especially vivid examples are his failure to defend himself in the final round of a fight with Sugar Ray Robinson and his decision to let two 14-year-old girls into his nightclub after each girl kisses him. Impaired judgment is common in aging prizefighters. It also is likely that LaMotta's history of repeated blows to the head (concussions) contributed to his sexual jealousy and paranoia and was responsible for the slurred speech he exhibits in the film as he ages.

Additional Questions for Discussion (*Raging Bull*)

- What actually happens to the brain of a fighter when he is "knocked out?"
- The American Academy of Neurology has supported a ban on professional boxing since 1983. Do you agree with this position?
- What are the characteristic features of chronic traumatic encephalopathy? What features of De Niro's presentation of Jake LaMotta suggest the disorder is present?
- Is the protective headgear used by amateur boxers effective in protecting against head injuries?
- In the film, LaMotta, as an old man, becomes sexually involved with two young girls. Is this an example of impaired judgment?

- LaMotta is incredibly jealous of his second wife, and he becomes convinced she is having multiple affairs. Is this paranoia the result of personality or cerebral impairment?
- What is the "Whore - Madonna" complex? How is it illustrated in the life of Jake LaMotta?

In addition to *Memento*, discussed in detail earlier in this chapter, many films display serious neurological symptoms such as the amnesia that can result from a head injury. One of the best is David Lynch's challenging film, *Mulholland Drive* (2001), which begins with an automobile accident. The amnestic female survivor, Rita (a name she took from a movie poster) finds refuge in the condominium of an aspiring Hollywood actress, Betty (Naomi Watts). The two women befriend each other and Betty takes a particular interest in helping Rita find answers to her identity. The already unique film takes a major surrealistic twist and the viewer is left to either accept the events as they are portrayed or challenge them as illusions. Like *Memento*, Lynch creates a rich atmosphere that allows the viewer to experience the confusion and discomfort of amnesia as he or she increasingly becomes disoriented to person, time, place, and situation. Lynch does not attempt to give answers or insights into amnesia but rather to depict the experience for a character and to give a particular experience to the viewer. It is the viewer who is challenged, like the amnestic character, to accept the film as an experience; this is perhaps more important than a pat explanation for what is happening in the film. This is reinforced at the film's conclusion (and final word) when a character on stage looks at the viewer and with a finger to her lips, says "Silencio."

In contrast to *Memento*'s unforgettable depiction of anterograde amnesia, *The Majestic* (2001) depicts retrograde amnesia. Jim Carrey plays disenfranchised screenwriter, Peter Appleton, who upon being accused of communist ties, goes for a drive away from his Hollywood home. His car topples over a bridge into a river and he subsequently develops retrograde amnesia after he hits his head on a rock in the river and is washed upon the shore of a small town. The townspeople mistake Peter for a former townsperson, Luke Trimble, who had gone to war many years ago and the town proclaims Peter (now Luke) a hero, someone who has been lost for almost a decade after going to war. Not remembering his past, Luke identifies with many of the townspeople and rebuilds the local theater. He does not go through the pain, confusion, mental torture, and frustration that one would expect with retro-

grade amnesia. Instead, Luke readily accepts his new role and does not seriously challenge himself to figure out where he was over the previous ten years. A theory of "double amnesia" is hypothesized where he could have gone to war, experienced PTSD and memory loss, re-established his life for years as a writer, and then upon getting in an accident, experienced amnesia a second time.

Interestingly, two 1991 films address the complexity of amnestic symptoms that result from head injuries, *Regarding Henry* and *Shattered*. *Regarding Henry* is a Mike Nichols film staring Harrison Ford as a high-powered attorney who suffers a major traumatic head injury. After coming out of a coma, he discovers that his life can never be the same. There are interesting scenes in a rehabilitation hospital, and the viewer gets some sense for the sequelae of a head injury. However, the film is flawed by an unrealistic presentation of the deficits following head injury and by the simplistic assumption that someone's personality could be *improved* by a head injury. In *Shattered*, an architect undergoes extensive reconstructive surgery of his face following an automobile accident. Amnesia symptoms mix with his memories (that may or may not be distorted) and the inconsistent stories relayed by various people in his life.

Brain Tumors

Aberrant behavior and abnormal sensations and perception can result from brain tumors (**neoplasms**). The specific behaviors that result will vary across individuals as a function of lesion site, size, type, and rate of growth. Brain tumors often, but not always, result in headaches and seizures. However, less than one out of a thousand people who have headaches will be found to also have a brain tumor.

An individual's premorbid personality will in part determine how he or she reacts to a brain tumor. About half of all patients with brain tumors first complain of psychiatric or behavioral symptoms, especially when the tumor involves the frontal or temporal lobes. Hallucinations, depression, apathy, euphoria, social impropriety, and personality change can all result from brain lesions.

Patients who have **frontal lobe lesions** are likely to display personality changes. They may be passive, apathetic, depressed, and slow to respond. In contrast, frontal lobe lesions can result in irritability and problems with anger control. **Temporal lobe tumors** are often misdiagnosed as psychiatric disorders, and this is especially likely to occur in those cases that result in **psychomotor**

seizures. These tumors can produce hallucinations, stereotyped movements, feelings of unreality, and intense fear. Reports of **déjà vu** (feeling you are re-experiencing a former experience) and **jamais vu** (feeling that familiar settings and situations are now very strange) are common with temporal lobe tumors. Patients with **parietal lobe lesions** often report abnormal sensory experiences (e.g., smelling burning rubber), may have difficulty with simple copying tasks, and **anosognosia** (denial of illness). **Occipital lobe tumors** produce relatively few psychological symptoms, but these lesions may result in visual field defects.

In the Spanish film, *The City of No Limits* (2002), a family patriarch (Max) is dying of a brain tumor. Max displays paranoia and quirky behaviors. Medical doctors describe his psychological state as "verging on derangement." He stares at objects, carefully touches walls, speaks of video cameras watching him, calls a phone number that does not appear to exist, and tries to escape the hospital. He has a concerned and paranoid expression on his face, does not trust others, is constantly fearful, and is dishonest. Some of his comments appear random: "I'll never tell you where they are," and "Don't speak in front of them." He becomes preoccupied with escaping from the hospital to meet with someone named Rancel, wanting to warn him "before it is too late." He is not compliant with his medications. Though the viewer does not know his psychological condition prior to the brain tumor's onset, it is to be assumed most of these symptoms have emerged because of his tumor. Overall, Max's condition waxes and wanes: at times, Max is coherent and oriented; on other occasions, he confuses novels with reality. Important family secrets are uncovered due to Max's seemingly random and ridiculous comments.

"He's alone inside something he invented in his mind."

Victor, the son of a man with a brain tumor in *The City of No Limits*

Stroke

A **cerebrovascular accident** (CVA), more commonly known as a stroke, occurs when there is an inadequate supply of blood and oxygen for the brain. Strokes are characterized by sudden onset and are often fatal. Cerebrovascular disease is currently the third leading cause of death in the United States, following heart disease and cancer. Twenty individuals will experience cerebrovascular accidents for every one who develops a brain tumor.

Infarctions occur when arterial blood flow is blocked. This can occur when a piece of fat or cholesterol becomes lodged in a vessel. This sudden blockage of blood flow is called an **embolus**. Blood flow can also be impeded by the gradual buildup of **atherosclerotic plaque** along the inside of a vessel, resulting in a **thrombus**. Vessels sometimes burst, and the resulting cerebral hemorrhage can be life-threatening. Only about 20 percent of patients survive a cerebral hemorrhage. An **aneurysm** occurs when part of a vessel "balloons" and threatens to burst. Signs of a ruptured aneurysm include painful headaches, nausea, and vomiting.

Transient ischemic attacks (TIAs) are "ministrokes" that last for less than 24 hours. Many patients who experience TIAs will go on to have actual strokes. Other risk factors for cerebrovascular accidents include diabetes, heart disease, and the use of oral contraceptives in women who also smoke. The patient experiencing a TIA will become disoriented, confused, and sometimes amnestic.

In John Steinbeck's novel *The Grapes of Wrath*, Grandpa Joad dies from a stroke. We do not actually see the old man die in John Ford's film adaptation, *The Grapes of Wrath* (1940), but there is a memorable scene in which his relatives bury him alongside the road because they are too poor to do anything else. Henry Fonda writes a short, poignant note to leave at the grave: "This here is William James Joad, died of a stroke, old, old man. His folks buried him because they got no money to pay for funerals. Nobody kilt him. Just a stroke and he died."

David Lynch's *Blue Velvet* (1986) opens with a man watering his yard. As we watch, he has a stroke and falls to the ground. His dog comes over and proceeds to drink out of the hose, and at this point the viewer becomes aware that this will not be an ordinary movie.

Epilepsy

People with **epilepsy** experience uncontrollable attacks of abnormal neuronal activity. These brain "storms" can result from a variety of causes, and it is critical to remember that epilepsy is a symptom of a variety of brain disorders, not a disease in itself.

Head trauma is the most common cause of epilepsy and about half of all penetrating head wounds will result in seizures. **Prodromal symptoms** and auras often precede seizures. Prodromal symptoms are "feelings" that a seizure is about to occur and usually appear several days before the seizure itself. In contrast, an **aura** signals the imminent arrival of a seizure and occurs only minutes before the seizure itself. Auras are often auditory or gustatory sensations.

Jacksonian seizures occur when there is a motoric response, such as twitching or jerking that is confined to one side of the body. A "Jacksonian march" results when minor motor movements in a finger or toe become more exaggerated and spread to other parts of the body on the affected side. If the initially isolated abnormal brain activity spreads to the other hemisphere, the entire body may stiffen or jerk; this attack is referred to as a **grand mal seizure**. Grand mal seizures typically last from two to five minutes and are sometimes referred to as **tonic-clonic** seizures because of their alternating periods of rigidity and jerking. In contrast, **petit mal seizures** (absence seizures), which are relatively common in young children, do not result in falling, jerking, or loss of muscle tone. The child experiencing a petit mal seizure will be, for a very brief period (usually two to ten seconds), very unresponsive to the external environment.

Complex partial seizures (also referred to by the older terms *psychomotor* or *temporal lobe seizures*) are of considerable interest to anyone working in the field of mental health, because these disorders often mimic psychiatric diseases. The patient with complex partial seizures may hallucinate, engage in stereotyped motor behavior, experience feelings of unreality, or become extremely anxious. The sensations of *déjà vu* and *jamais vu* are often reported. The EEG is typically found to be normal in these patients, and about one in five will experience auditory or visual hallucinations. Unlike the hallucinations of the schizophrenic patient, however, auditory hallucinations in the patient with a complex partial seizure will be localized within the head (rather than from an external source); and they will rarely contain bizarre, threatening, or accusatory material.

One of the world's leading experts on epilepsy was fond of relating a story about a patient who had a genuine seizure disorder that could be documented with electroencephalography. However, she only seized when she heard Mahalia Jackson singing "My Heart Has a Life of Its Own." The song could be sung by anyone else, and the patient wouldn't seize. Likewise, she could listen to Mahalia Jackson sing anything else, and she wouldn't experience seizures.

After several weeks in the hospital, someone asked the patient what was so special about Mahalia Jackson singing "My Heart Has a Life of Its Own."

"Didn't you know?" she replied. "That was the song they played at my mother's funeral as her casket was being lowered into her grave."

The made-for-television movie, *First Do No Harm* (1997), stars Meryl Streep and depicts a young boy with a type of epilepsy for which there is no known cause. The film explores particular types of diet in the treatment of epilepsy. The depiction of seizures in movies is fairly common and is portrayed for a variety of reasons: as a response to insulin-shock treatment in *A Beautiful Mind* (2001), ECT in *One Flew Over the Cuckoo's Nest* (1975), and brain surgery in *Molly* (1999).

International Films: Neuropsychological Disorders

The inspirational Argentinean film *Son of the Bride* (2002), which was nominated for Best Foreign Film, follows a man too busy for his family until he suffers a heart attack. This brings him to re-evaluate his life and his relationships, one of which is with his mother who is suffering with Alzheimer's Disease. He had always found his mother to be cynical, controlling, and demanding, and he managed this situation by distancing himself. He is inspired by his father who ritualistically and lovingly visits his wife daily, showing nothing but faithful love and devotion to her despite her rambling speech, distant stares, and frequent inability to recognize her family. This is a touching, realistic, and emotional portrayal of Alzheimer's Disease and the family members' reactions and coping.

In the Finnish film *The Man Without a Past* (2002), a man is robbed and brutally beaten while sleeping outside. He suffers a severe head injury and physicians pronounce him medically dead and walk out of the room; suddenly, the man wakes up, rises, and simply walks out of the hospital. He has retrograde amnesia since the time of the injury and is forced to re-create his life. Although he is an outcast in society, he manages to cope with a greedy landlord, works at the Salvation Army, dates a woman, and finds a trusted companion in a dog and eventually a community. Pieces of memory return to him as he begins to find, reject, and come to terms with his past.

Critical Thinking Questions

- How would a psychologist distinguish between genuine amnesia and malingering?
- Which seems to be more accurate—cinematic portrayals of retrograde amnesia or anterograde amnesia?
- Films like *Memento* and *Mulholland Drive* induce viewer confusion, disorientation, and distortion. Does this help to increase empathy for the character(s)? Does this empathy tend to generalize beyond the screen?
- Should people who have seizure disorders controlled by medication be allowed to drive?
- What are the most current, avant-garde treatment options for Alzheimer's Disease?
- Is it helpful for people who have a family member suffering from Alzheimer's to watch films like *Iris* or *Son of the Bride*?
- Is society obligated to provide care for old people who have dementias that dramatically limit the quality of their lives? What is the alternative?
- How will the aging of the baby boomers affect society? Is it possible to estimate how many people will develop Alzheimer's disease as the baby boom generation ages?
- Should helmets be mandatory for bicycle riders and motorcyclists?

Chapter 11

Disorders of Childhood and Adolescence

He had a human body that he stole off some bogman of a farmer that gave him a lift
but you knew by the twisted sneer that inside he was a fat green blob with tentacles
like an octopus and his face all scales. Make no mistake he says we will control the world
and neither you nor anyone else in this town will stop us.
One of Francie Brady's delusions of alien control in *The Butcher Boy*

Questions to consider while watching The Butcher Boy

- At what point in the film do you first realize that Francie has a mental illness?
- Francie's mother has a history of mental illness, and would "go to the garage" whenever she "broke down." At what age should a parent's mental illness be discussed with a child?
- Does a maternal history of mental illness and suicidality increase the likelihood that Francie will develop a mental illness?
- Francie adopts an alter ego as "Algernon Carruthers." Is this merely a normal childhood fantasy or is it a precursor to the more serious problems that eventually develop?
- What defense mechanism is represented when Francie's father tells Francie, "You did it... You killed Ma."
- Francie is a child of an alcoholic. Does this play a role in the development or likelihood of psychopathology?
- Is Francie's attachment to Joe normal or pathological?
- In the novel, Francie hallucinates that Mrs. Nugent suckles him. What is the significance of this fantasy?
- Why does Francie defecate in the Nugent's living room?
- Francie frequently hallucinates that he sees and talks to the Virgin Mary. Why do hallucinations and delusions so commonly involve religious themes?
- Francie's mother has an obvious history of mental illness. Is there enough history to make a tentative diagnosis?
- Is Francie's illness characterized predominately by positive or negative symptoms?
- How do Francie's symptoms relate to the time (circa 1962) and the prevailing zeitgeist?

Patient Evaluation

Patient's stated reason for coming: "I guess I've broken down and Sergeant Sausage here was told to bring me to the garage so I could get a check-up."

History of the present illness: Francie Brady is a 12-year-old boy who was referred by the court for psychological evaluation after he committed a gruesome murder in the small Irish village of Carn. Francie has exhibited signs of mental illness for approximately two years, and his symptoms have become increasingly salient over the past six months. He presents with an elaborate delusional system in which he relates to people in terms of pigs, and he believes others refer to him and his family as pigs. He also has delusions involving alien control of his community and impending nuclear disaster.

Francie has repeatedly threatened and terrorized townspeople in the small community in which he lives. His paranoid delusions centered on "Mrs. Nugent," a woman he murdered, apparently without provocation. Approximately one year before the murder, Francie was arrested for breaking and entering the Nugent home, destroying property, defacing family heirlooms, and defecating in the family's living room. He had written "Phillip is a Pig" in lipstick on the walls and mirrors; Phillip is the only son of the Nugent family.

Francie's delusions are supported by frequent hallucinations that alternate between invading aliens and visions of the Virgin Mother. There is also a history of hallucinations that involve nursing at the breast of Mrs. Nugent. This child is reported to have lived for several months with the decaying corpse of his deceased father, seemingly oblivious to his father's death. When police discovered the father's body, it was infested with maggots.

Past psychiatric illness, treatment, and outcome: Francie has been considered "odd" for several years. Following the incident in which he vandalized the Nugent home, he was sent to a Catholic boarding home for wayward children (which he refers to as "The School for Bad Boys"). He reports being repeatedly sexually abused by a priest at this school, but we are currently unable to substantiate this history of abuse. After he was discovered having sex with the priest, Francie reports he was encouraged to leave the school and return home.

When Francie returned to Carn, he resumed living with his father. Shortly thereafter, his father died and Francie apparently spent several months living with his father's rotting corpse. When this was discovered, Francie was sent for treatment at a psychiatric hospital. He appears to have been actively psychotic during this time, believing that hospital staff were alien wasps who could be controlled only when they were castrated (i.e., when their "stingers" were cut off).

Hospital records are not yet available for review; however, Francie reports being heavily medicated, and he claims that a lobotomy was performed at the hospital. There are no visible scars supporting this belief. Francie was discharged from the hospital with little apparent evidence of improvement, and with outpatient medication that he immediately threw away after leaving the hospital grounds.

Medical history: There is a history of low birth weight (5 lbs.) and poor nutrition; otherwise, the history is unremarkable.

Psychosocial history: Francie's mother committed suicide approximately one year ago by drowning herself in a lake. Francie experiences considerable guilt about her death, and reports, "she's in the lake, and it was me that put her there." His feelings of guilt are exacerbated by the fact that he had run away from home shortly before her death and was not able to attend her funeral. His father was an alcoholic who blamed his son for the death of the mother. Francie reports only one significant friend, Joe Purcell, but it appears that Joe

has recently spurned Francie's friendship ("Joe was going to leave me and I'd be left with nobody—no ma—nothing"). Francie is fixated upon this relationship, and the fixation appears obsessive and possibly homoerotic.

Francie has had extremely limited experience with girls of his own age. Many of his previous sexual fantasies centered on Mrs. Nugent, the parent of a classmate.

Both parents are now dead, and Francie has limited social support. He reports that he has an uncle on his mother's side who is a successful Dublin businessman. His relationship with his best friend, Joe Purcell, has deteriorated seriously over recent months, and Francie is deeply troubled by this fact.

Francie has worked intermittently over the past six months as a "butcher boy," earning a modest wage that went primarily for the purchase of alcohol. This job involved killing and butchering pigs, and the abattoir bolt gun used to kill Mrs. Nugent was acquired on this job.

After promising to lead the police to Mrs. Nugent's body, Francie escaped, returned home, and set fire to his home. This appears to have been a suicide attempt; however, Francie was rescued by firefighters. He sustained serious burns in the fire. He denies any previous history of fire setting.

Drug and alcohol history: There is a sporadic history of drug use, usually of unspecified drugs ("I use all different kinds and all different colors"). In addition, there is a significant history of alcohol abuse, and despite his youth, Francie was well known in the local pubs in his hometown. He was frequently thrown out of his favorite bar, the Tower, for drunkenness and fighting.

Behavioral observations: Francie was badly burned in a fire and considerable scaring is still present. He was casually dressed and unkempt. He was accompanied for the examination by a police officer. His affect was markedly labile, and he laughed frequently and at inappropriate times. He appears to be oblivious to the serious nature of the crimes he has committed and the likely consequences of his behavior. He stated (cheerfully) that he deserves to be hanged because he is a murderer; when told that hanging had been outlawed in Ireland, Francie exclaimed, "For fuck's sake! What's this country coming to?" There was no evidence of flight of ideas, but loose associations were present (e.g., frequent references to goldfish).

Francie willingly volunteered information about his past difficulties with the legal system and his previous hospitalization. He comfortably discussed two previous suicide attempts—once when he half-heartedly tried to sever his wrists with a fragment from a broken figurine of Jesus, and once when he tried to burn down his home.

Mental status examination: This patient was alert and fully oriented to time, place and person. He paid attention during the interview and responded to all questions asked. He was able to complete all Mini Mental Status Examination tasks without difficulty. Demeanor was consistently cheerful, but clearly inappropriate to situation and circumstance. Speech was rapid but not pressured, and generally coherent. Memory is intact.

This child appears to be quite intelligent, and supremely self-confident. Insight is limited, and Francie appears oblivious to the grim circumstances in which he now finds himself. There is no current suicidal ideation, and he denies any further homicidal intent. Francie's speech is replete with references to aliens and the Virgin Mother, and there is moderate paranoia present. There were no indications of hallucinations during the interview, but Francie freely discussed his history of hallucinations.

Functional assessment: Although Francie dropped out of school at a very early age, he is verbal and intelligent. He has worked intermittently in a butcher shop for the past six months. He has a history of bullying other children, and he reports having few friends. His most significant friend appears to have become frightened by Francie's aberrant behavior and now avoids him whenever possible. Francie's delusions, hallucinations, criminal history, inappropriate affect and history of substance abuse will all limit his personal and vocational options.

Diagnosis: Schizophrenia, Paranoid Type; Conduct Disorder, Childhood-Onset

Treatment plan: Francie Brady was seen for evaluation only. The findings of this assessment will be shared with the court and made available to future treatment providers.

Prognosis: Poor.

Psychopathology and *The Butcher Boy*

Both Patrick McCabe's 1992 novel and the 1997 film Neil Jordan made from the novel offer a chilling introduction to childhood psychopathology. Both works are artistic successes, and Jordan's movie has been compared to classic films in the childhood psychopathology genre, including Stanley Kubrick's *A Clockwork Orange* (1971) and Francois Truffaut's *The 400 Blows* (1959).

> **"Any odd time they'd take me down to the room and hand me bits of paper all blotted with ink. What do you think about that says the doc. You won't be writing any more messages on that paper I says. Why not says the doc lifting the specs. Its destroyed I says, look at it. Hmm hmm. In the school for docs that what they taught them. Lift your specs and repeat after me—hmm hmm!"**
>
> ***The Butcher Boy* (p. 164-165)**

The Butcher Boy protagonist, Francie Brady, comes from a highly dysfunctional family. His mother had a long history of mental illness, and periodically experienced "nervous breakdowns." When Francie and his friend Joe try to make sense of her illness, they find some comfort in the metaphor of a car breaking down, and reason that Annie Brady has simply gone off to a garage to be repaired. The father, Benny Brady, is a drunken musician who spends most of his time in a local pub. The father is less than adequate as a role model—e.g., he responds to a faulty television set by kicking in the screen and threatening to beat up the individual who sold it to him. While a dysfunctional family unit is typically not sufficient to *cause* mental illness, it can clearly *exacerbate* any psychiatric symptoms or conditions that may be present.

Francie Brady's family problems are somewhat offset by a cohesive community structure with clearly defined social roles. However, there are cracks in this foundation. For example, "Uncle Alo," frequently cited as a successful Dublin executive and a role model for Francie, turns out to be a timid and hen-pecked individual who significantly overstates his importance. He is described as someone too shy to reciprocate the love of the only woman who ever genuinely loved him.

The book and film take place in the early 60's, a period of global tension and significant apprehension about the spread of communism. These societal concerns shape Francie's delusions, which focus on global conquest by aliens (a metaphor for communists) and nuclear disaster. Although schizophrenia, Francie's presumed illness, is found across cultures, the exact manifestations of the illness are shaped by cultural experiences and expectations.

In a poignant moment in the film, Francie discovers his mother standing on a table next to a chair, contemplating hanging herself. She eventually commits suicide by drowning in a local lake. Francie, who has run away from home, misses his mother's funeral. Both the townspeople and the father blame Francie for his mother's death, and he blames himself. The incident underscores the penchant children have for attributing misfortune in the family to their own misbehavior, as well as the fact that people who have made previous suicide attempts are at a great risk for actually succeeding in killing themselves in the future.

"Mary had the same face as ma used to have sitting staring into the ashes. It was funny that face it slowly grew over the other one until one day you looked and the person you knew was gone. And instead there was a half-ghost sitting there who had only one thing to say: All the beautiful things of this world are lies. They count for nothing in the end."

The Butcher Boy, p. 212

Francie is eventually hospitalized, receives electroconvulsive therapy, and is threatened with lobotomy. He escapes from the psychiatric hospital and returns to his village and his job as a butcher boy. He subsequently commits a gratuitous murder, is captured, escapes, sets fire to his former home, prepares to perish in the flames, and is then rescued, treated, and hospitalized. He remains a psychiatric inpatient until he is discharged to a half-way house in midlife. In the final scene of the film, Francie Brady is revisited by the Virgin Mary and the viewer is left wondering about the success of treatment and the long-term prognosis for this fascinating character.

Child Mental Health

Psychiatric problems of children are not as easily diagnosed as those of adults, and the symptoms of the mental illness in children often are difficult to distinguish from those changes associated with normal growth and development. For example, an imaginary friend of a four year old is normal, but for an adolescent, an invisible friend would be considered a psychotic hallucination.

Children who receive mental health treatment usually fall in one of the following categories:
1. Children whose behavior does not conform to social norms and is troublesome to others (disruptive behaviors or conduct disorders).
2. Children who experience repeated and excessive depression, anxiety, or states of personal distress.
3. Children whose cognitive or neuromotor development is not preceding normally (developmental disorders).

We will discuss the first two at length in this chapter. For the third category, see Chapter 12: Mental Retardation and Autism.

Schizophrenia in Children

Schizophrenia is a serious illness that alters thoughts, emotions and behaviors. It is a rare diagnosis in children, and is hard to recognize in its early phases. However, it is unquestionably the diagnosis that Francie Brady would have been given.

The features of schizophrenia are fully described in Chapter 9. Some of the specific symptoms that one would look for in a child include seeing things and hearing voices which are not real (hallucinations), odd and eccentric behavior and/or speech, unusual or bizarre thoughts and ideas, difficulty separating television and dreams from reality, confusion, extreme moodiness, and paranoid beliefs. In addition, a child may exhibit age inappropriate behavior (e.g., behaving like a younger child), severe anxiety and fearfulness, difficulty relating to peers and keeping friends, withdrawal and increased isolation, and a decline in personal hygiene (APA, 2000). The movie *Spider* (2002) accurately depicts a child with early symptoms of schizophrenia that follow him into adulthood. The child, nicknamed "Spider," has delusional and paranoid thinking, eccentric behavior, and severe isolation from peers.

The behavior of children with schizophrenia often changes slowly over time, as we note in the case of Francie Brady. The early problems of children who are subsequently diagnosed with schizophrenia are often first noticed by the child's teachers. Schizophrenia is a life long disease that can be controlled but not cured; we see this clearly as a middle-aged Francie Brady prepares to leave the hospital and once again has a conversation with the Virgin Mary.

Child and Adolescent Behavioral Disorders in Contemporary Films

Children and adolescents are frequently being diagnosed with Oppositional Defiant Disorder, Conduct Disorder, and Attention-Deficit/Hyperactivity Disorder (ADD & ADHD). The diagnosis of **Oppositional Defiant Disorder** is given to children and adolescents who have a pattern of negativistic, hostile, and defiant behavior, such as losing their temper, being argumentative, and being easily annoyed and resentful. The diagnosis of **Conduct Disorder**, at times similar in appearance, is given to children and adolescents who violate the basic rights of others or societal norms with aggression to people or animals, destruction of property, theft, deceit, and/or truancy. Children and adolescents with **ADD** or **ADHD** either have marked disturbances in attention, concentration, following directions, and listening (ADD) or are hyperactive and impulsive (ADHD).

In many countries, these diagnostic labels do not exist. Yet behavioral problems are universal, as are the movies that depict them.

Life as a House (2003) and My First Mister (2001)

Two important films portray highly troubled, isolated, suicidal and oppositional adolescents—*Life as a House* with the character of Sam (Hayden Christensen) and *My First Mister* with Jennifer (Leelee Sobieski) as the protagonists. Each film presents a highly troubled and alienated young person who is transformed through meaningful relationships. The major difference between the lead characters is the gender, which provides an opportunity to discuss the relationship between psychosexual development and gender.

In *Life as a House*, we are introduced to Sam, a character with a rebellious, Gothic appearance

as evidenced by his colored hair, lip ring, eye make-up, and tough exterior. In an early scene, he huffs paint while choking himself (autoerotic asphyxiation) in his closet. He resorts to this practice whenever he needs to escape from people and reality: he locks his door, plays loud music (e.g., Marilyn Manson), uses drugs (pills, pot and huffing), and masturbates. With his extreme negativism and oppositional personality, it is easy to see how he believes that no one understands him and why he must come up with complicated ways to isolate himself. At one point in the film, he reveals he has been using drugs since age 12. He earns money to buy drugs through prostitution, finding this preferable to working hard to earn less money. Sam is able to articulate that he wants to become something he is not, and does not know how; this leaves him to feel like "nothing." Beneath his rough exterior is a wounded and isolated adolescent longing for a meaningful connection. He finds the needed friendship and love when he establishes a relationship with his dying father; at that point, Sam's behaviors, attitude, and appearance are transformed.

"I like how it feels not to feel."

Hayden Christensen as Sam in *Life as a House*

My First Mister portrays a similarly troubled youth, 17-year-old Jennifer, who is also gothic in appearance. She wears mostly black and has multiple facial piercings. She is very isolated with no real friends and no genuine interest in her needy mother or distant stepfather. She comments that she has never had a boyfriend or any friends. The closest Jennifer can get to people is when she views them through her binoculars. She fantasizes about living with the Partridge family. She has a blunted, sad affect and is highly negativistic and critical about life. She is preoccupied with death and she writes melancholy poetry about death, hopelessness, and "not existing." She likes to lie on gravesites, and exclaims, "I'm gonna go to hell anyway." Problems that are more serious include self-injurious behaviors (cutting her arm) and visual hallucinations of her deceased grandmother. She finds meaning and purpose in a random, healthy relationship that blossoms with a men's clothing storeowner.

Both films exhibit characters in search of their identities who work through oppositional and conduct problems to find them.

Additional Questions for Discussion
(*Life as a House* and *My First Mister*)

- Contrast the lead characters and the parental figures in each film.
- How likely is it for a teen to undergo rapid, positive transformation as depicted in these films? What type of transformation is most common (i.e., physical, attitudinal, social or emotional)?
- Is there a connection between type of music (e.g., rap, grunge or heavy metal) and adolescent behavior?
- Do body piercings provide any evidence of psychopathology or is this simply a manifestation of healthy adolescent rebellion?
- Both characters live in good homes and had opportunities to thrive in that environment. What could you speculate sends them in the opposite direction we see at each film's onset?
- Both characters engage in some severe self-destructive behavior (e.g., prostitution; self-cutting). How common is such self-destructive behavior in adolescents? In children?
- If a troubled adolescent were to watch one of these films, how likely is it they would change some of their behaviors?

Thirteen (2003)

This film depicts a nightmarish reality for some parents; for others, it may serve as a wake-up call. The film, directed by Catherine Hardwicke, depicts a rapid transformation from childhood to adolescence and the pervasive influence of peer pressure during the teen years.

Tracy, a 13-year-old seventh grader, is eager to be accepted by the "in group" in her school. She earns acceptance from this group when she rejects her current, less popular friends and spontaneously steals money from a woman on the street. She takes her soon-to-be best friend, Evie, on a shopping spree, buying clothing and shoes. A friendship soon develops, and an emotional roller coaster ride begins, characterized by rebellion, acting out, parental opposition, and misconduct. Tracy gets her tongue and belly button pierced, exhibits

self-injurious behavior, abuses substances, tells numerous lies, and lets her grades slip. She also becomes sexually promiscuous. An opening scene (a flash-forward) depicts Tracy and Evie getting high and amusing themselves by punching one other in the face.

"I'll die for you but I won't leave you alone right now."

Holly Hunter to her daughter who has been used and betrayed

As these oppositional behaviors escalate, Tracy becomes more and more isolated from her mother (Holly Hunter). Tracy becomes angry with her mother and resists any attempts to set parental limits on her behavior. The mother makes genuine attempts to establish appropriate boundaries, yet frequently falls short because of her own struggles and limitations as a recovering drug addict. The mother and daughter eventually come to know each other better as a result of their frequent fights. Evie's mother, on the other hand, is a self-absorbed abuse victim who allows and even encourages the girls to drink and smoke. The plot culminates in a bitter betrayal by Evie, demonstrating that peer relationships can end as abruptly as they begin.

Additional Questions for Discussion (*Thirteen*)

- Would one of these two teens benefit more than the other in a juvenile detention program?
- How common is it for seventh graders to use drugs and alcohol, become promiscuous, have their bodies pierced, or practice self-injurious behaviors?
- What does current research say about the social influences of peers? At what age does peer influence peak?
- Does Tracy become involved with an African-American athlete primarily to upset her mother?
- Are peer influences more influential than parental influences?
- How should parents respond when adolescents refuse to accept parental boundaries?

Elephant (2003)

This award-winning (Cannes) independent film, directed by Gus van Sant, is a realistic and artful portrayal of an American high school and the routine life of students just prior to a massive school shooting, reminding the viewer of Columbine and subsequent tragedies. The film is eerie and foreboding in that it is much more about nonverbal behavior than about dialogue; this heightens the importance of the cinematic craft, a craft van Sant has mastered, particularly in his unique camera work and use of **non-diegetic sound** (i.e., sounds whose source cannot be seen in the film). The viewer is taken along as the camera slowly follows several major characters as they go through their daily routines (e.g., walking down long hallways, greeting fellow students), and going in and out of buildings (into danger or safety zones, unbeknownst to them), often with non-diegetic music in the film's background. It is interesting to note the title outside the building reads simply "high school," letting this particular school represent every high school.

Two characters, Eric and Alex, are depicted playing a video shooting game and looking up information about guns on the internet. They order guns and receive them in the mail in a large package without difficulty. Later, these two teens plot their shooting spree with a map of the school, planning to "pick off" as many classmates as possible in the school's high traffic areas.

Although the film is realistic, the viewer is left with more questions than answers about causes, prevention, psychopathology, and etiology. At the same time, this is part of the film's beauty, and each member of the audience is challenged to draw his or her own conclusions.

Additional Questions for Discussion (*Elephant*)

- Why did van Sant choose this title?
- The film provides considerable latitude for viewers to explain the behaviors of Eric and Alex. Which explanations seem most compelling?
- Did Eric and Alex have a history of violent, delinquent, or deviant behavior?
- What is the purpose of the film? How does Gus van Sant's style enhance this purpose?
- What warnings signs are presented in the behaviors of these two characters? Could this shooting have been prevented? How?
- Would stricter gun control laws have minimized the likelihood of the Columbine shootings?

Kids (1995) and *Gummo* (1997)

These two films are listed together because both are extraordinarily disturbing films. Harmony Korine, who wrote the script for Kids, was both writer and director for *Gummo*. Both films provide a frightening perspective on the lives of adolescents, the former in an urban setting and the latter in a small town/rural setting.

Kids, directed by Larry Clark, is a fast-paced film that allows the viewer to experience the thoughts, words, and behaviors of young adolescents as they interact with one another. One unforgettable scene depicts fifteen or so skateboarding teens who brutalize a man who had the temerity to criticize one of the skateboarders. The plot revolves around the character of Telly, a scrawny but confident adolescent who takes tremendous pride in his ability to seduce virgins. Unbeknownst to him, Telly is HIV positive, and he is rapidly spreading the virus to his vulnerable partners, most of whom have never had sex before. Telly is extremely narcissistic, and the viewer assumes he would not change his behavior if he knew his diagnosis. One of Telly's victims, a teenage girl, finds out she has been infected by Telly, and much of the film involves her frantic attempts to get him to stop spreading the disease. The HIV virus is a metaphor for the spread of violence amongst inner-city youth.

Gummo is a realistic and poignant film that portrays lower class, antisocial children and adolescents. The film includes numerous disturbing scenes of animal torture, drug abuse, and bizarre behavior such as that exhibited by one man who has a fight with an inanimate object. The film's two main characters, Solomon and Tummler, bicycle around shooting stray cats and collecting them in garbage bags to sell them to a storeowner so they can get high on glue or have sex with a mentally retarded girl. At times, these two characters are violent just for the sake of violence; they repeatedly whip a hanging dead cat and later take turns shooting a dead cat in the pouring rain. They break into the home of their competitor (another cat-killer), masked with guns and a golf club and unhook the life support of an infirm, elderly woman. Each adolescent is reared by a single parent with limited parenting skills; Solomon's mother threatens to kill him with a toy gun for not smiling, and later washes him in filthy bathwater while serving him spaghetti and milk.

There are many other quirky and disturbed characters in the film, including a boy who dresses like a bunny, urinates on traffic at overpasses, drowns a cat, and fakes his own death, and a developmentally disabled girl who laughs while she shaves her eyebrows and compulsively treats her doll as if it is a real infant. The director, Harmony Korine, has a cameo appearance in the film as a drunken adolescent who randomly pours beer on his head while describing his history of sexual abuse and trying to seduce a gay, African-American midget. Korine's character recollects thowing marbles on his mother's belly when he was a young child—if he hit her navel, he would get five dollars but whenever he hit her arm, he was hit with a rolling pin.

These characters lack insight into their behavior, and they are not able to appreciate the consequences of their acts. Most lack empathy and have little regard for ethical or moral standards; it is reasonable to assume that most will become adults who qualify for a diagnosis of antisocial personality disorder.

Many viewers stay to the end of the credits of *Gummo* to confirm that the animal abuse scenes are simulated, that prosthetic animals are used, and that the characters and situations are fictitious; despite the assurance of the credits, viewers know that for many children, the scenes portrayed are all too real.

Additional Questions for Discussion (*Kids* and *Gummo*)

- What is the value of creating films as shocking as these?
- Compare and contrast potential diagnoses for the main characters in the two films?
- What role does the lack of authority figures play in the lives of these teens?
- What redeeming scenes are included in each film? How do you respond to these?
- What would be appropriate treatment for the characters in these films? Should these children be treated in the juvenile justice system or the mental health system?

Other Portrayals of Behavioral Disorders

In *American Beauty* (1999), one adolescent secretly smokes marijuana and sells it to the neighbors. In *Manic* (2003), the viewer gets an inside look at the adolescent unit of a psychiatric hospital. This well-acted film presents interesting questions about differential diagnosis, friction between various adolescents with clashing behavioral problems (e.g., bipolar

disorder, impulse control problem, and depression), and a good portrayal of group psychotherapy.

My Flesh and Blood (2004) is a documentary about a woman who takes care of special needs children; one child, whose life is explored in detail, has a severe conduct disorder in addition to his cystic fibrosis. His anger outbursts and sexually acting out are at times tempered by a needy softness and emotional vulnerability. His behavioral problems are directly related to the loss of his mother as a caretaker (she continues to visit him), the stress of his environment (one caretaker serves eleven special needs children), and the stress of his illness.

Holes (2002), an excellent Disney feature film, depicts various oppositional and rule-breaking youth who are sent to a working camp because of their behavioral problems. One adolescent steals cars and has a tic disorder.

Child and Adolescent Psychopathology: Depression, Anxiety, and Distress in Contemporary Films

The United States of Leland (2004)

This disturbing film opens with an adolescent, Leland P. Fitzgerald, reflecting on having killed an autistic boy. Leland does not know why he murdered the boy, and he is beginning to regret his behavior: "I think I made a mistake." His attitudes, the motives for his actions, and his methods for coping are often unclear. Throughout the film, Leland has different insights as he struggles to realize and accept that "nothing can make what happened unhappen."

"When I say I don't remember that day, I'm not lying. I wish I did but I just don't. Sometimes the most important stuff just goes away. Goes away so bad it's like it was never there to begin with."

Ryan Gosling as Leland P. Fitzgerald

Leland is very insightful and perceptive; he notices small details in his environment and applies these insights in his interactions with others. Yet, as with many depressed individuals and especially depressed teens, he is unable to articulate his feelings. He states he has not cried since he was a little boy; even then, he was very guarded and concerned with what others would think. Leland clearly suppresses his feelings, such as when he refuses to show hurt or anger toward his girlfriend when she admits she broke up with him so she could date a drug dealer. He does not understand his own sadness, and he denies anger and displays flat affect throughout the film. He even stabs himself in the hand "because I wanted to know what it felt like."

"There's all this sadness and there's nothing you can do about it, and all I wanted was for it to go away."

Leland explaining his suffering

Leland is very detached, and appears to be disinterested in his own fate. His social behavior is quirky; at times, he says very little and appears to be preoccupied with his environment. There are many scenes indicating that Leland does not know how to connect with others. In short, Leland is a profoundly depressed and troubled adolescent.

Additional Questions for Discussion (*The United States of Leland*)

- What diagnosis would you give Leland?
- Do you accept his explanation at the end for why he killed the boy? Is his explanation convincing?
- What is the best treatment approach for a character such as Leland?
- How accurate is memory in recalling traumatic events? Is the depiction in this film accurate?

Other Noteworthy Films Portraying Psychopathology in Children and Adolescents

The Magdalene Sisters (2002) is a somber film based on a true story that depicts the verbal, emotional, and physical suffering of young girls who are sent to a boarding home run by nuns. The girls are forced to work long hours; they endure physical, sexual and verbal abuse, and they are required to turn over all their possessions to nuns who seem far more concerned about money than about character. Many of these girls were sent to the home without legitimate reasons. Humiliation is an institutional norm, and it causes one particularly vulnerable adolescent to have a psychotic break. The girls cope in a variety of ways; one girl takes her revenge on an abusive priest by rubbing a plant on his underwear when she is doing his wash; the plant results in intense itching that dramatically disrupts a religious service the priest is leading.

Pieces of April (2003) depicts a young adult woman who has recovered from severe conduct and oppositional behavioral problems as a youth. April, acted by Katie Holmes, is living alone and away from her family and trying to prepare a final Thanksgiving dinner for her mother (Patricia Clarkson) who is dying from breast cancer. April ultimately succeeds in creating a pleasant meal for a critical, ailing, and dysfunctional family.

Fanny and Alexander, an Academy Award winner for Best Foreign Film, is an excellent 1982 Swedish movie. Touted as one of Ingmar Bergman's finest films, the movie takes place in a Swedish provincial town in the early 1900's and centers on the experiences of two children, Fanny and Alexander, who are growing up within a large, happy extended family. Their father dies and their mother remarries. Their new stepfather is a stern, authoritarian clergyman who is incapable of understanding the feelings of others. Throughout the movie, Alexander has unusual experiences. He periodically has visits from his father' ghost. The viewer is given the impression that his father is watching over him throughout the movie. Alexander's imagination causes a statue to take on a lifelike image and move. He also believes that he has magical powers and, at the end of the movie, Alexander believes that he willed the house fire that caused his stepfather's death.

Films like *The Best Little Girl in the World* (1981) explore specific illnesses such as anorexia nervosa. Truffaut's *The Wild Child* (1970) explores the life of a feral child, and Werner Herzog's *Every Man for Himself and God Against All* (1975) addresses a similar theme in its exploration of the effects of a childhood filled with almost complete isolation, deprivation, and torture.

The exact nature of the illness that causes a teenage boy to blind six horses is never identified in *Equus* (1977), despite the best efforts of psychiatrist Richard Burton, but it is clear the boy is deeply troubled. His problems seem to relate to his emerging sexuality–in one scene he is impotent when confronted with his first sexual opportunity. Likewise, there is no clear diagnosis for the child in *The Tin Drum* (1979) who decides on his third birthday to stop growing, but it is clear that the child is responding to the madness of the world around him and events over which he has no control (like the suicide of his mother).

International Films: Child and Adolescent Psychopathology

City of God

This 2003 Brazilian film looks at children and adolescents growing up in a poor, gang-infested area of Rio de Janeiro (called "The City of God") who must choose between a life consumed with drug dealing, guns, and violence and a life of hope.

These young children quickly learn to show no fear, and they do not seem to care if they live or die. The film depicts very young children (referred to as "runts") running around with guns and talking about achieving revenge by murdering their enemies. The film is especially disturbing because it is based on a true story (it is estimated that at least 100,000 people are involved in drug dealing in Rio), and conduct disorders are the norm for children and adolescents living in "The City of God."

The film contrasts two of the younger boys brought up in this culture: one, the main character, finds passion and meaning in photography and rejects gang-life; the other, named Li'l Zé, meets his life goal of rising to power to take over as drug boss of "The City of God" by killing his competition. The Rio police walk around in fear and largely ignore the drug dealers; before the dealers rose to power, the police would come into homes and pillage.

An interesting and provocative dilemma emerges for the children of "The City of God": A child can either choose an honest occupation and live in poverty or become rich by dealing drugs. If these children choose to deal drugs, there is a well-established career trajectory: first, they act as a drug delivery boy, then as a lookout, then dealer, soldier, and eventually manager. For many of these children, the second option is far more appealing.

Heavenly Creatures

One of the most powerful cinematic portrayals of childhood psychopathology is found in this 1994 New Zealand film, directed by Peter Jackson and starring Kate Winslet. The film is based on the true story of two teenage girls, ages 15 and 17, who conspire to murder the mother of one of the girls. The older girl went on to develop a significant reputation as an author of murder mysteries, writing under the name of Anne Perry. The girl's confusion and mental illness in *Heavenly Creatures* is artistically captured in film through her interactions with life-size clay figures that inhabit a medieval fantasy-land.

Miscellaneous Films

Several high quality foreign films portray normal children living in abnormal or compromised circumstances. *Lilja 4-ever* (2002) is a devastating Scandinavian film about a 16-year-old girl living in a broken-down tenement "somewhere in the former Soviet Union." She is abandoned by her mother and engages in escapism and fantasy with her only friend, an 11-year-old boy. She is betrayed by a man she loves and sold into prostitution in another country where she experiences one tragedy after another.

The Polish film *Island on Bird Street* (1997) is based on a true story about a boy who creates a secret hideout and learns how to survive under traumatic circumstances while he waits for his father's return during the Nazi occupation of Poland. The New Zealand film *Rain* (2002) is another movie that emphasizes the resiliency and endurance of a young person—in this case, a young girl who faces the drowning of her beloved younger brother and the alcoholism, depression, and infidelity of her mother.

Other films explore the ways in which children are affected by poverty. These include *El Norte* (1983), a film about two children escaping poverty in Guatemala and exchanging it for poverty in Los Angeles; *Pixote* (1981), a film that describes the ways in which street children in Brazil are almost inevitably drawn into a squalid life of crime, drugs, and prostitution; and *Salaam Bombay* (1988), a movie that follows the lives and misfortunes of children living on the streets of Bombay. *The Ratcatcher* (1999) is about an adolescent with conduct problems living in Glasgow in an area filled with trash, dead rats, lice, and social decay. A French film fantasy, *The City of Lost Children*

(1995), directed by Jean Pierre-Jeunet & Marc Caro, depicts a young girl, Miette, who is forced to steal on behalf of some evil Siamese-twin sisters. Miette develops a safe, collaborative relationship with a mentally challenged circus strong-man and together they try to stop a mad scientist who kidnaps children and steals their dreams.

In the classic Italian film, *Cinema Paradiso* (1988), a young boy becomes enamored with a local cinema and finds a father figure in the projectionist while growing up in a small town just after WWII. The beautifully simple film *Children of Heaven* (1997) depicts children coping in a poor section of an Iranian city. In the French film, *Monsieur Ibrahim* (2003), an adolescent without a mother resorts to stealing from a local store so he can continue to make meals for his critical father (as well as save up money to purchase the services of a prostitute). The protagonist develops a deep, fatherly friendship in the storeowner despite eventually being abandoned by his father.

The film *Born into Brothels* (2004) portrays the lives of the children of prostitutes living in Calcutta. This film won an Academy Award for being the best documentary of 2004.

Critical Thinking Questions

- Many films portray children who are resilient at very difficult times and in challenging environments. How common is this? Is psychopathology the opposite of resiliency? Can a child be mentally ill and resilient at the same time?
- Should adolescents who commit serious crimes like rape and murder be tried as adults? At what age should a child be held responsible for committing "adult crimes?"
- Before her death, Francie's mother repeatedly played a song about a woman who committed suicide. Do suicidal individuals typically signal their intent like this?
- Benny Brady attempts to spank Francie after his first incident with Mrs. Nugent. Is spanking ever justified? What alternative means of punishment are appropriate?
- The film *Kids* deals with sex, drugs, violence, and AIDS. Is the film accurate in its suggestion that these issues are becoming increasingly salient for very young adolescents?
- The film and the novel *Lord of the Flies* suggest that without adult supervision young children quickly become savages. Do you find this position plausible? Are the kids in *Gummo* simply savages?

- Films often portray stepparents as cold and sadistic. Is there any empirical evidence for this or is it a simple and misguided stereotype?
- Some groups have criticized Director Neil Jordan for Sinead O'Connor's portrayal of the Virgin Mary. Did you find the role offensive?
- Francie repeatedly bullies Phillip Nugent. Is there a relationship between school bullying and future mental illness or antisocial behavior?
- What percentage of children with behavioral problems (e.g., conduct disorders) develop personality disorders (e.g., antisocial personality)?

Chapter 12

Mental Retardation and Autism

What do you mean? Why isn't Lucy going home with me?
I want her to go home with me. I am her father...
Sam (Sean Penn) beginning to realize that
he may lose his daughter in *I Am Sam*

Questions to consider while watching *I Am Sam*

- Is Sean Penn's portrayal of Sam an accurate picture of mental retardation?
- We require a driver's test before we allow someone to drive a car, but people can meet, marry and have children without offering any evidence of competency. Does this make sense to you?
- What specific behaviors lead the protective service worker to conclude that Sam is unable to be an effective parent?
- Is it realistic to think that a man with the intelligence of a 7-year-old could responsibly raise a child?
- What type of social supports would a parent who has mental retardation need in order to be an effective parent?
- What issues will Sam face as a single father raising a daughter through later childhood and early adolescence?
- How was Sam influenced by his own childhood experience in an institution?
- Was Lucy's embarrassment normal behavior for a 7-year-old or did it relate to her father's intellectual limitations?

Patient Evaluation

Patient's stated reason for coming: "I am her... father. I... I want my daughter back."

History of present illness: Sam Dawson is a 35-year-old single, caucasian male who is being seen at the request of the court for a psychiatric evaluation in order to determine his ability to retain parental custody of his 7-year-old daughter, Lucy.

Past psychiatric illness, treatment, and outcomes: Sam has no recent history of psychiatric treatment. He was institutionalized as a child for autistic behaviors and mental retardation. His school records indicate that he has the intellectual ability of a 7 year old. He is not taking any medications.

Medical history: Sam has no known medical disorders or history of medication.

Psychosocial history: Sam lives in an apartment with his daughter whom he has cared for since birth. Lucy's homeless mother abandoned them as they were leaving the hospital after Lucy's

birth and has not been seen since. Sam has assumed total responsibility for raising his daughter with the help of a neighbor. He has not had contact with any family members. He has several friends who also have mental impairments who provide support to Sam and his daughter.

Sam and his daughter are roughly the same intelligence level, and they enjoy playing in the park, singing songs, and reading together. Recently, Lucy surpassed her father's intellectual ability. Sometimes she attempts to protect her father's feelings by denying her own development, but at other times, she is embarrassed by her father's limited cognitive abilities. She struggles to cope with classmates and friends making fun of Sam, and she has frequently told her friends that she is adopted. At a birthday party planned by her father, Lucy became distraught over her father's child-like behavior. Child Protective Services has taken Lucy away from her father.

Sam has no legal history with the exception of a recent instance when he was arrested after being solicited by a prostitute. He was released when police realized that he truly did not understand the purpose of the solicitation.

Drug and alcohol history: Sam denies any history of drug or alcohol use.

Behavioral observations: Sam is a casually, but neatly dressed man who responds appropriately and politely to questions. His speech is slow, but he eventually answers most questions appropriately. He is very cooperative, at times displaying a blank facial expression as if he does not understand the question being asked. He often stares blankly at the ceiling and moves his hands and fingers in a rhythmic motion when he is thinking. He appeared very anxious throughout the interview. He is very eager to retain custody of his daughter and is convinced he is capable of raising her. During the interview, when given various scenarios, he was able to distinguish right from wrong. According to the protective service worker, Sam becomes upset and loud when frustrated, but there was no evidence of aggression or violence during this interview.

Mental status examinations: Sam was alert and oriented to time, place and person. He denied hallucinations or delusions. He was unable to complete serial sevens, and had difficulty with memory recall and copying a complex drawing. He seemed to have no problems with short-term memory questions. He denied suicidal and homicidal ideation. His thinking is concrete, but judgment appears average. He scored a 22 on the Mini Mental Status Examination.

Functional assessment: Sam has been employed at Starbucks for a number of years. He independently maintains his apartment, pays his bills, and provides food, shelter, clothing, school supplies, and arranges transportation for his daughter. His financial resources are very limited, and it is questionable whether he will be able to generate enough income to support his daughter on a long-term basis. His social skills are adequate, but repetitive language and autistic movements often interfere with his ability to interact with others. He appears to be well liked by his friends.

Strengths: Sam is highly committed to the safety and well-being of his daughter. He clearly loves her and is highly motivated to follow the court's directions in order to maintain custody. He has been able to live independently and has developed strategies to compensate for his limited intellectual ability.

Diagnosis: Mild Mental Retardation

Treatment plan: 1) With support from functional adults, Sam could provide his daughter a safe environment and perform parenting functions. 2) Sam's daughter should be routinely evaluated for her devel-

opmental and educational levels in order to ensure that Sam is providing ongoing guidance and discipline. 3) A social worker should make regular home visits to ensure that Sam has the support necessary to function as a single parent and sole caregiver.

Prognosis: Good.

Movies and Persons with Disabilities

Similar to films portraying people with psychological disorders, films depicting individuals with disabilities are often either shocking or overly sentimental. Often stories are created by writers who base their stories on stereotypes, but who have no personal experience with people with disabilities. Their stories are frequently implausible and often emphasize the sentimental. The disability is often used as a plot device, and the character of the person with the disability is not developed fully in the story. Few films present a character who "happens to have" a disability where the disability is treated as just another aspect of the character's life. An exception is French director, Jean Pierre-Jeunet, whose films *Amelie* (2001) and *The City of Lost Children* (1995) depict such characters and suggest their meaningful contributions far outweigh the significance of their disability.

In *Cinema of Isolation: A History of Physical Disability in Film* (1994), Martin Norden writes about the stereotypes of women with disabilities and develops a four-fold typology: the "sweet innocent" in *Stella Maris* (1918), the "obsessive avenger" in *Freaks* (1932), the "civilian superstar" in *Interrupted Melody* (1955), and the "bitter" in *What Ever Happened to Baby Jane?* (1962). Norden also discusses realistic depictions of women with disabilities as in *The Other Side of the Mountain* (1975), *Gaby* (1987), *Passion Fish* (1992), and *The Theory of Flight* (1998).

Diagnosis of Mental Retardation

Below average intelligence and impaired adaptive functioning characterize mental retardation. The diagnosis is made through clinical assessment, historical accounts from parents and teachers, and standardized tests. Diagnosis usually occurs during childhood. Because intelligence tests have been standardized at 100 with a standard deviation of 15, the usual threshold for mental retardation is set at two standard deviations below the mean or lower (i.e., an intelligence quotient of 70 or less). Impaired adaptive functioning is primarily a clinical judgment based upon an evaluation of age-appropriate tasks.

The film *I Am Sam* (2001) depicts an adult with mental retardation with some autistic behaviors who lives independently and who has been able to support his seven-year-old daughter. He thinks very concretely and has difficulty with conceptual thinking. His reading and math ability are very limited.

"You don't know what it is when you try, and you try, and you try and you never get there!"

Sam contemplating the challenges of his life

According to the *DSM-IV*, mental retardation is identified as a mental disorder and is prevalent in one percent of the population. The range of mental retardation extends from mild to profound (see Table 12.1). Before a child is diagnosed with mental retardation, other deficits or impairments in functioning must be present in addition to low scores on an intelligence test. That is, the child does not meet the expected standards for his or her age or cultural group in communication, use of community resources, self-direction, academic skills, leisure, health, and safety.

Even though mental retardation is classified by the *DSM-IV* as a disorder, it is not a disease. The term *mental retardation* denotes the degree to which a person functions below cultural and social norms at a particular time and place. Persons with mental retardation form a heterogeneous group. There are various causes of mental retardation—a few are due

Table 12.1 Levels of Mental Retardation by IQ Range

Category	IQ Level	Approximate % of Persons
Mild	50-55 to 70	85%
Moderate	35-40 to 50-55	10%
Severe	20-25 to 35-40	3-4%
Profound	Below 20-25	1-2%

to drug or alcohol abuse in the mother, chromosomal or genetic disorders, or lack of oxygen during a difficult delivery (Leonard & Wen, 2002).

Down Syndrome, a disorder caused by the individual having three chromosome 21s, has an incidence of 1 per 1,000 live births. These children have distinctive physical characteristics that include hypotonia, hyperflexibility, midface depression, and shortness of ear length. People with Down syndrome are frequently victims of stereotyping and prejudice. In the early 1960s, about 10 percent of all residents who were institutionalized had Down syndrome. They were institutionalized because it was thought that anyone with Down syndrome needed to live apart from the rest of society. This has now been shown to be untrue. Because of the discrimination in the past, families of children with Down syndrome have become pioneers in the understanding of developmental disabilities and vocal critics of social policies that seek to institutionalize people with mental retardation.

Today a child who is diagnosed with mental retardation is usually kept within the family environment. Only those who have profound mental retardation reside in residential care centers. If a child is diagnosed with mental retardation, he or she is best taught in an adaptive learning environment that focuses on discrete skills. The ultimate goal is to help the individual function as independently as possible. With appropriate training, many adults with mental retardation live productive, independent lives.

Ira Wohl's film *Best Boy* (1979) is a documentary that examines the life of Wohl's cousin, Philly, a man with mental retardation who has spent his entire life living with, and being protected by, his parents. The film beautifully documents the concerns of Philly's parents who will take care of him after their death. Philly's father dies while the film is being made, and his mother reluctantly allows Philly to become involved in an adult day services program. The film is deeply moving and very effective in its examination of mental retardation as a social problem. In addition, the film does a beautiful job portraying the emotional richness of Philly's life and the strong bonds that have been formed between this man and his family.

Best Boy illustrates one of the dilemmas confronting Western society as we grow older. As the population ages, the number of aging individuals with mental retardation is also increasing rapidly, although their life expectancy is somewhat lower than that for the population at large. This problem is compounded by the fact that individuals with mental retardation are at greater risk for developing dementia. In the case of Philly, he is forced to leave his parents' home—the only home he has ever known—and learns to cope with the outside world. Older individuals who are **deinstitutionalized** face similar difficulties when they leave the security of large state hospitals, where they have lived for years, and begin to adjust to life in small group homes in community settings.

Ira Wohl produced a moving sequel to *Best Boy* titled *Best Man:"Best Boy" and All of Us Twenty Years Later* (1997). This film brings the viewer up to date on the life of Philly, who now lives in a group home in Queens. He has a full and meaningful life, and he is shown preparing for a significant, albeit delayed, rite of passage—his Bar Mitzvah.

Some films depict a character with a disability who significantly impacts other characters, as in the comedy *There's Something About Mary* (1998). Warren, the brother of Mary (Cameron Diaz), has mental retardation and autistic tendencies. He exhibits **echolalia**, perseverates in his play, displays finger-flicking behavior, and wears earmuffs to block out disturbing sounds. He clearly likes the lead character, Ted (Ben Stiller), but when Ted touches him near his ears, Warren's sensitivity leads to a violent reaction—he picks Ted up and spins him around before throwing him down on the coffee table. It is an upsetting incident, but the whole family realizes that it happened due to a triggering event and was not due to malevolence on Warren's part.

Mary lives near Warren and remains an active part of his life. She volunteers and spends time with Warren and other people with disabilities. Mary is not simply a "do good" personal, she is a good sister. The antagonists in the film attempt to fake being "good" and eventually their manipulations fall short. In addition, although Warren has a significant disability, he does do comical and outrageous things. Since it is a comedy and all the other non-disabled characters do things that are comical, it does not appear that the director has singled Warren out. His behaviors clearly influence the lives of the other characters.

In M. Night Shyamalan's *The Village* (2004), one character (played by Adrian Brody) is a highly stereotypic "village idiot" who exhibits goofy and inappropriate laughter, an inability to control his impulses, an obsession with an attractive girl, and mental slowness. While some of these characteristics apply to people with mental retardation, the character in Shyamalan's film is one-dimensional. He eventually attempts to murder the hero and heroine. This perpetrates both the damaging stereotype that people with mental retardation are inferior to those with normal cognitive functioning as well as the misconception that all people with any kind of mental problem are violent.

Films—like real life—often show persons with disabilities, particularly mental retardation, being taken advantage of by others. In *Amelie* (2001), one character is ridiculed and mistreated by his boss in front of others. Socially, he does not know when to quit and he repeats a particular phrase to the point of screaming laughter. Though he is depicted with borderline intellectual functioning and noted as "slow," his character is more developed as he takes charge of a fruit stand, is competent performing meaningful work, enjoys painting with a friend, and displays a deep appreciation for life. In one of the many disturbing scenes of *Gummo* (1997), an adolescent with mental retardation is sold to young boys for sex. A number of other films have poignantly illustrated the difficulties—and sometimes the beauty—in the lives of people who have mental retardation. Three especially memorable films are *Charly* (1968), *A Day in the Death of Joe Egg* (1972), and *Of Mice and Men* (1992).

Forrest Gump

The now classic film *Forrest Gump* (1994) portrays 40 years in the life of a man who has a marginal IQ of 75 but whose innocence and common sense make him seem wise. Forrest's condition would be classified as **Borderline Intellectual Functioning** today, and he would probably be tested for a learning disability.

This superb film begins with Forrest, played by Tom Hanks, telling his life story. When Forrest was a child, his mother, played by Sally Fields, believed in him and was determined that he would have a full, complete life. Forrest had a weak spine and needed to wear leg-braces. He was forced to run from other children to protect himself, so that even with the leg-braces he became an outstanding runner. Eventually, a local football coach spots Forrest and signs him to play college football. He begins a brilliant career that eventually leads him to the army and service in Vietnam. He wins a medal and becomes a table-tennis star. After being discharged from the army, Forrest goes into the shrimp business and becomes a millionaire. Forrest has a life-long friend, Jenny Curran, who often came to his aid as a child. As an adult, he is able to help her as she and her son cope with disability and death resulting from AIDS.

Even with a limited intelligence and modest academic ability, Forrest is able to feel good about himself and who he is, a simple man who leaves his mark on the world. The development of his self-esteem has its roots in his childhood and his mother's confidence in him. The friendship with Jenny encourages him. Because of the support of these two women, Forrest never realizes that he could not succeed.

Drill Sergeant: "Gump! What's your sole purpose in this army?" Forrest Gump: "To do whatever you tell me, drill sergeant!" Drill Sergeant: "God damn it, Gump! You're a goddamn genius! This is the most outstanding answer I have ever heard. You must have a goddamn I.Q. of 160. You are goddamn gifted, Private Gump."

Forrest Gump **(1994)**

Radio

Inspired by a true story, *Radio* (2003) is the story of Coach Harold Jones (Ed Harris) who takes in a young man, Radio (Cuba Gooding, Jr.), and makes him an assistant coach for the football team. Though he is never given a diagnosis in the film (other than as the label "slow"), Radio, like Forrest, would probably be diagnosed with "Borderline Intellectual Functioning." At the beginning of the film, Radio barely speaks a word, mostly uttering sounds, is hunched over in posture, and walks around with a shopping cart for several miles to get groceries. He lives alone with his mother and is almost completely isolated. He is never given a chance at life. Early in the film, Radio is cruelly ridiculed and mistreated by several football players. One particular player continues his cruel taunting of Radio, but he accepts the criticism without complaining. Given an opportunity to help out the football team, Radio agrees and begins to talk much more, interacts interpersonally, and helps out the team in significant ways; in fact, he becomes a symbol of inspiration for the players and his whole life changes.

Coach Jones goes out of his way to help give Radio opportunities; he defends Radio in front of the community, and integrates him into the school system. When the coach is asked why he is helping Radio, he responds, "It's the right thing to do." The story speaks to the courage and sacrifices of two men who influence one another and in turn grow in courage and dedication. Coach Jones admits part of his dedication and care for Radio arises from childhood shame for not taking action to protect a boy with a disability who was being tortured.

Autistic Disorder

An **autistic disorder** is usually diagnosed before the age of three. This condition occurs four to five times more frequently in males than in females and is prevalent in four to five per 10,000 children under 15 years of age. Approximately 75 percent of persons with autistic disorder have mental retardation, and about half do not communicate verbally. Autism is a complex problem and requires special treatment and family support.

Problems in social interaction and communication are the primary symptoms of autistic disorder. Many children with autism are not able to maintain eye-to-eye gaze, respond with facial expressions, or use normal body posture and gestures. As children with autism grow older, they do not typically develop peer relationships that are appropriate to their developmental level. They often do not express pleasure in other people's happiness or participate in interpersonal "give or take." These children can be very frustrating to their parents because of their lack of emotional warmth.

Children with autism have major problems in communication. There is a delay or sometimes a complete lack of development of spoken language. If there is speech, there is impairment in the ability to initiate or sustain a conversation with others. Their use of language is often repetitive or idiosyncratic. As children, they may not be able to engage in make-believe play or social imitative play appropriate to their developmental level.

Other symptoms of autism are repetitive and stereotyped patterns of behavior, interests, and activities. There is often an encompassing preoccupation with one or more stereotyped and restricted activities; this preoccupation is abnormal in its intensity and focus. In children, preoccupation with moving, circulating objects is common. Stereotyped, repetitive motor mannerisms may also be present. For example, children may rock for hours, twist their fingers, rub their hands on their legs, spin, or repeat complex body movements. People with autism compulsively adhere to specific, often nonfunctional, routines or rituals. The children are frequently preoccupied with objects rather than people. A child with autism may be fascinated with a motor, a piece of equipment, or a model automobile. The child may literally spend hours taking the object apart and putting it together again.

Most adults with autism continue to be inattentive to social convention, lack social skills, have few or no friends, and often do not marry. They may also be troubled by chronic anxiety. Their repetitive behavior and movements usually continue (Micaki, Chakrabarti, & Fombonne, 2004).

In addition to treatment with medication, behavior modification, and individualized educational approaches, the family plays a critical role. Most families need help in order to deal with special children, and need to learn to implement treatment programs conducted within the home in order to help the child generalize from an academic setting to the home. Parents learn how to teach their children appropriate social and communication skills, as well as behavior modification techniques. Family therapy is recommended in order to help the family cope with problems associated with raising a disabled child.

The prognosis for children with autism is mixed. If they begin to acquire language, are socially responsive, and improve their cognitive skills by the ages of five to seven, they have a better prognosis than those children who do not. Approximately 25 percent of children with autism develop seizures, usually in early adolescence. During puberty, they may experience behavioral changes, including a negativism that sometimes leads to aggression. Most do not develop hallucinations or delusions. However, their behavior and thinking may continue to be peculiar and concrete and their affect flat.

Rain Man and Autism

Rain Man (1988) won Academy Awards for Best Actor, Best Director, Best Picture and Best Original Screenplay. The film stars Dustin Hoffman as Raymond Babbitt and Tom Cruise as Raymond's younger brother, Charlie. The drama opens with Charlie, a cynical hustler in his mid-twenties, unemotionally learning of his father's death. Charlie and his father had been estranged for many years. Charlie's father only left a 1949 Buick to his youngest son, but he left $3 million in a trust fund for a secret beneficiary.

Charlie traces the beneficiary and discovers that he has an older brother, Raymond, who is autistic. Raymond's world is bound by the rituals of watching television programs and eating certain foods on certain days. The books and baseball memorabilia in his room must be in order, or Raymond becomes agitated and begins reciting the Abbot and Costello routine, "Who's on First." When the sanitarium administrator refuses to give Charlie half of the inheritance, Charlie removes his brother.

Charlie wants to return to the coast, but Raymond refuses to fly. The story unfolds as Charlie and Raymond cross the country in their father's Buick. Their adventures include viewing an accident, after which Raymond refuses to travel on interstate highways and a day in a motel because Raymond refuses to go out in the rain. Raymond has many idiosyncrasies, such as having maple syrup on the table before the pancakes are served, insisting upon snacks of apple juice and cheese balls, imitating any noise he hears, and being preoccupied with television. One of Raymond's most significant symptoms is his repetitive language as he is continually repeating himself.

Charlie: "He's not crazy, he's not retarded but he's here?"
Dr. Bruner: "He's an autistic savant. People like him used to be called idiot savants. There are certain deficiencies, certain abilities that impair him."
Charlie: "So he's retarded."
Dr. Bruner: "Autistic. There are certain routines, rituals that he follows."
Charlie: "Rituals, I like that."
Dr. Bruner: "The way he eats, sleeps, walks, talks, uses the bathroom. It's all he has to protect himself. Any break from this routine leaves him terrified."

Rain Man (1988)

Raymond has **savant** abilities, which occur in about 10% of people with autism. With this problem, the individual usually scores low on standardized IQ tests but has one or two outstanding talents, such as calculating dates, drawing, or musical performance. Raymond has unusual memory and mathematical skills that Charlie plans to use to recoup his business losses through gambling in Las Vegas. When Raymond inadvertently makes a date with a prostitute, Charlie teaches his brother how to dance. When the woman fails to show up, Raymond dances with Charlie's girlfriend, Susan, who gives Raymond his first kiss.

Charlie develops an appreciation for the complexity of the illness when Raymond becomes upset after being frightened by the noise of a smoke detector. The movie ends when Charlie, who has developed a sensitivity and love for his brother, turns down a $250,000 settlement and lets his brother voluntarily admit himself back into Wallbrook.

Overall, this is a technically correct portrayal of a character with autism—Raymond has all the correct mannerisms, tics and tendencies of any number of real-life people with autism. The story surrounding the characters is also realistic—many families were separated by institutionalization as people with disabilities were simply erased from family memory. (For example, Charlie had completely forgotten he ever had an older brother).

Rain Man does perpetuate the misconception that "it's an institution or nothing" for people with significant disabilities. Consequently, we question the assumption that someone like Raymond would be happiest in a large institution. Although the familiarity and smooth routines often occurring in an institutional setting enhance Raymond's comfort and adaptation, people like Raymond can also live quite fully, successfully and happily in their own homes, with individualized supports as needed and with housemates of their own choosing. Paid relationships need not be their only choices for companionship. Some states (e.g., Michigan) no longer admit people with developmental disabilities into state hospitals, and only a few hundred people with developmental disabilities remain in this sort of environment and efforts are underway to integrate them into the community. While this generally means transitioning into group homes, there is a newer movement that helps people with even the most significant disabilities live in their own homes with housemates they choose.

Additional Questions for Discussion (*Rain Man*)

- Is the scene in which Raymond calculates complex square roots but cannot make change for a dollar realistic?
- Why is Raymond unable to appreciate the humor in Abbott and Costello's "Who's on First" routine?
- Would Raymond realistically be "a voluntary admission free to leave at any time," as Dr. Bruner maintains?
- Would it have been an example of sexual exploitation if Charlie Babbitt's girlfriend, Susanna, had sex with Raymond? Why or why not?
- Identify examples of repetitive behavior in the film. Are these behaviors more likely to occur when Raymond is stressed?
- Why is Raymond's favorite word "definitely"?

- Raymond smiles at one point and appears to appreciate the ironic humor involved in asking for maple syrup when it is already on the table. Is the appreciation of subtle humor like this characteristic for someone with autism?
- How would you rate the quality of care provided for Raymond at Wallbrook?
- Raymond's knowledge of trivia serves him well when watching the quiz show "Jeopardy." What sorts of games or activities would Raymond find the most difficult?

The United States of Leland (2003) portrays a boy with autism who fidgets, cries, and has limited eye contact; he spends most of his time staring off into space or keeping his head down. His most notable trait is his frequent repetition of the phrase "sing a song." He has limited communication with everyone, including his sister to whom he is closest.

This film was extremely controversial within the autism community. In the film, the lead character, Leland, stabs the autistic brother of his girlfriend without a clear explanation other than cryptic comments, such as "there's all this sadness and there's nothing you can do about it and all I wanted was for it to go away." Many disability activists believe the film promotes themes of mercy killing of people with disabilities, moral euthanasia, and the message that disability is a fate worse than death.

Leonardo DiCaprio plays the autistic younger brother in *What's Eating Gilbert Grape?* (1993). This character is not a savant, and he certainly is no saint; however, he is realistically portrayed as a needy, younger sibling growing up in a family that loves him.

In the classic *To Kill a Mockingbird* (1962), a young Robert Duvall makes his film debut as Boo Radley, a neighbor with autism who kills a man to protect two young children. His diagnosis is not mentioned and it probably would not have been recognized as autism at the time the film was made.

Molly (1999) is a disappointing film about a woman with autism. Molly (played by Elisabeth Shue) undergoes experimental surgery that temporarily brings her back to normal functioning; her brain eventually rejects the cells used in the operation and she returns to her pre-surgery levels of functioning. Molly's brother, Buck, initially avoids and fears his sister and agrees to try anything to make her better, but this enthusiasm is followed by disappointment in the surgery's failure. The film ends with a stereotypic "change-of-heart" ending when Buck arranges for Molly to live with him.

Asperger's Disorder

Asperger's Disorder is a pervasive developmental disorder often referred to as "high functioning autism." It is a subgroup of what are normally called autism spectrum disorders or pervasive developmental disorders. People with Asperger's disorder have very limited social interactions, and restricted, repetitive, and stereotyped patterns of behavior, interests, and activities are present. They are frequently labeled as odd and eccentric. However, language skills are generally intact, and cognitive development is not delayed.

American Splendor (2003) is about Harvey Pekar, a comic book writer whose friend and co-worker is a man (Toby Radloff) with Asperger's. Toby is socially awkward, has a monotone voice, and restricted patterns of interest and behaviors. Toby is a self-proclaimed "world-class nerd" who wears a button reading "Genuine Nerd" and proudly recounts once driving over 200 miles to see the movie *Revenge of the Nerds*. Overall, the portrayal is realistic and challenges the viewer's stereotypes about Asperger's.

Other Disorders Usually First Diagnosed in Infancy, Childhood, or Adolescence

Two other pervasive developmental disorders include: (1) **Childhood Disintegrative Disorder** in which there is normal development for at least the first two years, then language, social, motor, or play skills are lost, and (2) **Rett's Disorder**, which appears primarily in girls who exhibit normal development for at least the first six months, but between the ages of 5 and 48 months show a deceleration of head growth and loss of previously acquired purposeful hand movements, with the development of stereotyped hand movements and a loss of social engagement. Other developmental delays include severely impaired expressive and receptive language with severe psychomotor retardation development.

Other disorders evident early in life with film examples include a learning disorder in *Cinema Paradiso* (1988), a communication disorder (stuttering) in *The Straight Story* (1999) and *Liam* (2000), **Tourette's disorder** in *Niagara, Niagara* (1997), **pica** in *The Princess and the Warrior* (2001), and a rare genetic disorder, **progeria**, in *Jack* (1996). The latter film accurately depicts some of the developmental issues a child with progeria is likely to face; however, the film is not fully accurate in its clinical depiction of the disorder.

Critical Thinking Questions

- Howard Gardner describes seven kinds of intelligence (verbal, visual, physical, musical, mathematical and logical, introspective, and interpersonal) in his book *Frames of Mind* (1983). How does this model help you understand individuals such as Raymond Babbitt, Sam Dawson, and Forrest Gump?
- Some films, such as *I Am Sam*, have actors with disabilities playing important roles in the film. How much does this enhance the overall film?
- Explain how films that portray autism such as *Molly* and *Rain Man* do a disservice to people with autism.
- Is there anything a person with a disability cannot do that a person without a disability can?
- How are persons with mental retardation and other disabilities stigmatized in today's society? In your town or city?
- In *The United States of Leland*, if the autistic child in the film was substituted for a child without a disability, would this change the story and the film's meaning?
- How have the parents of children with autism been stigmatized in the past? Are there comparable examples of inappropriate stigma today for the parents of children with different conditions?
- Do people with mental retardation experience sexual feelings like everyone else? If so, how can health professionals support natural sexual expression while at the same time avoiding exploitation and abuse?
- Which labels are more useful: specific terms such as *autism* or more generic labels such as *pervasive developmental disorder*?
- Why does it matter what labels are used to refer to people with disabilities?
- Do people who are at greater genetic risk for having children with severe developmental disorders have a moral obligation not to have children?

Chapter 13

Sleep, Eating, Impulse Control, and Adjustment Disorders

Let me sleep...just let me sleep.
Al Pacino in *Insomnia*

Questions to consider while watching *Insomnia*

- How long can a person go without sleep?
- Is insomnia more often a primary condition or it usually secondary to other psychological disorders?
- What are the most common psychological disorders to which insomnia is a symptom?
- How common is the degree of insomnia Will Dormer's character experiences?
- How does stress contribute to Dormer's insomnia?
- What are the physical and psychological causes of insomnia depicted in the film?
- What is the impact of Dormer's insomnia on his mental status and interpersonal relationships?
- How is the condition of insomnia expressed through the film's landscape and cinematography?
- What coping strategies does Dormer use in attempting to get to sleep? What are some strategies he did not try?
- What is the psychological role of guilt in the film? Who is really guilty? What is guilt's role in Dormer's mental status?
- Is Dormer a "good" cop or a "bad" cop? Is his character redeemed in the end?
- Is it appropriate for non-medical therapists to prescribe over the counter medications like melatonin and Kava Kava?
- Should psychologists be permitted to recommend sleep medications like Ambien for patients with insomnia?

Patient Evaluation

Patient's stated reason for coming: "I can't sleep. It's too bright in this place. I haven't slept for days. You got any tricks up your sleeve?"

History of the present illness: Detective Will Dormer is a 52-year-old caucasian male who is self-referred to this clinic because of serious problems with insomnia. Detective Dormer arrived from out-of-town five days ago for a murder investigation he is leading. He has not slept in five and a half days. Prior to this episode of insomnia, he reports some problems sleeping for about a month or two, sleeping an average of five hours per night. He frequently awakens during the night, unable to get back to sleep; overall, his sleep is not restful. As the current insomnia symptoms have worsened, he has experienced concentration problems, forgetfulness, and several visual and auditory hallucinations. He states he has experienced all of these symptoms in the past, but only as a consequence of insomnia. Work performance has been seriously affected, and he believes if he continues without sleep he risks losing his job. He is not interested in social relationships—the insomnia only contributes to this lack of interest.

Three days ago, Detective Dormer's partner was murdered while on duty. Detective Dormer feels significant guilt and responsibility, and he believes he should have saved his partner or somehow prevented the murder.

Past psychiatric illness, treatment, and outcomes: Detective Dormer has no previous psychiatric history. He reports he has battled insomnia throughout his adult life with the longest span of no sleep being three days prior to the present episode of insomnia.

Medical history: Detective Dormer reports he may have **sleep apnea**, but he has never been formally tested for sleep problems. He reports previously being diagnosed as hypertensive, but this is untreated. He has no history of psychiatric medication, severe medical illness, or diseases. He has been injured twice on the job. On one occasion he was shot in the arm, and on another occasion he was cut on the neck with a knife; the resulting scar was visible during the interview.

Psychosocial history: Detective Dormer has worked as a criminal investigator for the police department for thirty years. He states, "I've always worked in the city so I've seen everything. I've caught a lot of scum." He was married for ten years but divorced fifteen years ago. He maintains occasional, friendly communication with his former wife. He has not remarried. He has no children. He has few meaningful friendships. From time to time, he isolates himself from others; however, this behavior does not appear to be related to depression.

Drug and alcohol history: Detective Dormer denied a history of drug abuse. He drinks alcohol frequently after work. He reports having two drinks each evening to relieve the tension and stress he experiences on his job. He drinks to the point of intoxication about twice per month. He denies significant problems due to his alcohol use.

Behavioral observations: Detective Dormer was appropriately dressed. His overall appearance was unkempt. He appeared exhausted with bags under his eyes, slightly open mouth, and poor eye contact. He intermixed periods of blank stares and periods of frequent blinking as if he was trying to keep his eyes open. At times, he slurred his speech; this appeared to be due to fatigue. Detective Dormer's mood and affect were agitated. He also reported some apathy about the case on which he is currently working.

Mental status examination: Detective Dormer scored a 28/30 on the Mini Mental Status Examination. His concentration was appropriate for serial 7's and other tasks. He did not recall all three objects at first but then suddenly exclaimed, "It's all in the details," and he remembered two of the three. He chose not to copy the drawing, stating, "I'm too exhausted to put forth that kind of effort."

Functional assessment: Despite the extreme fatigue and sleeplessness Detective Dormer has recently experienced, he continues to function at work. He reports his concentration and attention have worsened. He continues to drive a vehicle despite his fatigue and difficulty with concentration.

Strengths: Detective Dormer is a very adaptable, strong-willed man. He is an experienced and hard-working police officer.

Diagnosis: Primary Insomnia

Detective Dormer reported experiencing symptoms of insomnia over the last one to two months, and these symptoms have exacerbated over the past week.

Treatment plan: (1) Detective Dormer was cautioned about driving anywhere before he gets some sleep, and in fact he was encouraged to take a taxi home. We called a cab from the office. (2) Discussed the principles of stimulus control, with instructions to begin sleep hygiene practices this evening. (3) Suggested he consider taking Melatonin, 3 mg at bedtime beginning immediately. (4) Referred Detective Dormer to a local psychiatrist for sleep medication and further assessment. (5) Recommended making an appointment with a university based sleep lab when he returns home to rule out other sleep-related conditions.

Prognosis: Good

Insomnia

Insomnia (2002), a remake of a well-done, 1997 Norwegian film of the same name, is deeply psychological with multiple layers of complexity. One of these layers is the deteriorating mental status of Al Pacino's character, Will Dormer. Director Christopher Nolan accurately depicts this deterioration, documenting both the realities and dangers of the sleep disorder, primary insomnia. This film provides a quality prototype of the disorder.

"A good cop can't sleep because a piece of the puzzle's missing, and a bad cop can't sleep because his conscience won't let him."

Hillary Swank to Al Pacino

A Los Angeles police officer, Detective Will Dormer, flies to Alaska to lead a murder investigation. He arrives in Alaska already tired at a time of year where the sun never sets ("white nights") so it never gets dark outside. Throughout the case, Dormer lies in bed with his eyes open, struggling to get some sleep. Under internal pressure to sleep, Dormer employs various strategies, such as blocking all light coming into the room, drinking water, hiding the alarm clock, chewing gum, and turning the phone off. As his insomnia worsens, he sees flashes and trickles of light that become associated with flashes of memory. His vision becomes blurry; he nods off during conversation, often has an unkempt appearance, and frequently stares blankly into space. The longer Dormer goes without sleep, the more severe the consequences; he begins to hallucinate, his agitation develops into anger outbursts, he nearly runs a woman over with his car, and he begins to hallucinate. Ultimately, Dormer goes six nights without sleep.

Dormer's insomnia symptoms are clearly exacerbated by the psychological pressure he is experiencing. Two major stressors include the pressures of the murder case and his guilt about killing his partner and lying about it to protect himself in the coming Internal Affairs investigation. His current guilt triggers memories of other events of his life about which he feels guilty.

Insomnia is a powerful metaphor in the film. Director Christopher Nolan has discussed the challenges involved in making a film about insomnia that will not tire viewers; to avoid this problem, Nolan utilized various images in the film to symbolize the experience of insomnia. At the film's onset, the viewer is shown miles and miles of Alaskan glaciers—representing something of a dreamscape, followed by endless green trees covered by moving fog. Other examples of sleep imagery include empty streets with blinking traffic lights, flashes of light, tunnels and escape hatches, and things as mundane as trance-inducing windshield wipers. These all symbolize haziness, drifting, mental confusion, and disorientation.

Sleep Disorders

Sleep disorders are categorized into dyssomnias and parasomnias. **Dyssomnias** involve abnormalities in the amount, quality, or timing of sleep. These include insomnia, hypersomnia, and narcolepsy. **Parasomnias** involve abnormal behavioral or physiological events occurring in association with the sleep cycle. These involve problems with nightmares, night terrors, and sleepwalking.

Most sleep researchers recognize five **sleep stages**: stages 1 through 4 and REM (Rapid-Eye-Movement sleep). Each of the first four stages of sleep gets progressively deeper and each has distinct differences on an EEG. Stage 1 is a transition stage from wakefulness (light sleep), stage 2 occupies about 50% of the time spent asleep, and stages 3 and 4 (slow-wave sleep) are the deepest levels of sleep. REM is where most dreams are reported, it occurs cyclically throughout the night, and alternates about every hour and a half with NREM (the first four stages). Individuals with insomnia will typically have increases in stage 1 sleep and decreases in stages 3 and 4. In narcoleptic individuals, the onset of REM sleep is more rapid after sleep onset and there is an increase in REM.

Sleep laboratories are used to conduct sleep studies to ascertain accurate diagnoses. **Polysomnography** (PSG) is the most common sleep test and measures EEG, EKG, respiratory effort, leg movements, and other physiological activities during sleep. The PSG helps to diagnose different forms of **sleep apnea** (most often the cause of the psychological and medical diagnosis, Breathing-Related Sleep Disorder). The **Multiple Sleep Latency Test** (MSLT) is used by sleep labs to diagnose narcolepsy. Referrals to sleep labs are usually done through physician prescription which can often be encouraged by mental health professionals.

Film depictions of sleep disorders are rare. When depicted, they are usually either very brief or flawed. The film *Insomnia* is certainly an exception.

Insomnia

Primary insomnia is characterized by difficulty initiating or maintaining sleep or nonrestorative sleep for one month which causes significant problems in certain areas of functioning. In any given year, 30-40% of adults will have complaints of insomnia; sometimes this is a symptom of another disorder or a transient reaction to a stress and not "primary" insomnia.

The symptoms of insomnia are experienced by the two characters in *Lost in Translation* (2003), played by Bill Murray and Scarlett Johansson. Both characters are Americans who have traveled to Japan and experience apathy and loneliness in this unfamiliar setting. Both deal with their insomnia symptoms by going to the hotel bar and watching late-night television. Eventually they meet and build a friendship. One important scene depicts them lying awake in bed together at night; director Sofia Coppola seems to be showing they are facing their symptoms (symbolized by being awake in bed) in a nonsexual, healthy way through communication.

Edward Norton's character in *Fight Club* (1999) suffers from serious insomnia. The insomnia may be a symptom caused by **Circadian Rhythm Sleep Disorder, Jet Lag Type**, due to his work which requires frequent travel. He states he feels as though he is never awake or asleep and that he loses weight because he cannot sleep. He exhibits blank stares and his body language suggests that he is exhausted. It may be that jet lag exacerbates a preexisting problem with primary insomnia. His experience of sleeplessness triggers a break with reality leading to the development of Dissociative Identity Disorder. It is important to note that individuals with prolonged, severe insomnia may experience dissociative symptoms or psychotic states, but there is no evidence it will cause DID.

"With insomnia, nothing's real. Everything's far away. Everything's a copy of a copy of a copy."

**Edward Norton
in *Fight Club***

The effects of insomnia are also graphically portrayed in *The Machinist* (2004); Christian Bale lost 60 pounds to play the role of Trevor Reznik in this film.

Hypersomnia

Primary hypersomnia is excessive sleepiness evidenced in prolonged sleep or daytime sleep episodes for at least one month, which causes significant problems in areas of functioning. Like insomnia, hypersomnia can be a symptom of other disorders (e.g., depression) or a separate entity itself.

In *American Splendor* (2003), Harvey Pekar's girlfriend moves in with him and sleeps all day. She seems to have an agitated depression that manifests itself in irritability and in sleeping on the couch well into the middle of the day. This may reflect hypersomnia; her long hours in bed may also be a symptom of depression.

Narcolepsy

Narcolepsy is a devastating sleep disorder in which the individual experiences uncontrollable and unwanted daily "sleep attacks." People with narcolepsy can fall asleep while talking, eating or walking. The disorder is frequently accompanied by **cataplexy** (sudden loss of muscle tone without loss of consciousness). A rare but fair portrayal of narcolepsy occurs in the character River Phoenix plays in *My Own Private Idaho* (1991).

The portrayal of narcolepsy in movies is often brief, uncompassionate, and superficial with the sole intent being humor. This type of humor is highly predictable as it almost always involves a character falling asleep at an inopportune, unexpected, or embarrassing moment. Though the portrayals are not entirely inaccurate (since sleep attacks in narcolepsy are of rapid onset and can be triggered by an emotional experience), they are grossly exaggerated and almost uniformly unflattering. Minor characters in *Moulin Rouge* (2001), *Deuce Bigalow: Male Gigolo* (1999), *Rat Race* (2001), and *Bandits* (2001) have narcolepsy. In *Rat Race*, Rowan Atkinson (aka Mr. Bean) falls asleep at a critical moment when he is about to win a race, and in *Bandits*, a bank manager, being robbed by the characters of Bruce Willis and Billy Bob Thornton, falls asleep due to the stress of the experience.

Nightmares

Nightmare Disorder is a parasomnia in which an individual repeatedly awakens from sleep recalling a frightening dream. When waking, the individual quickly becomes alert and oriented. Themes of the nightmare usually involve threats to survival, security, or self-esteem.

"Don't you know that when you sleep with someone, your body makes a promise whether you do or not."

**Cameron Diaz to Tom Cruise
in *Vanilla Sky***

Countless movies depict characters experiencing nightmares, yet only a handful would qualify for the diagnosis of nightmare disorder. Many filmmakers enjoy manipulating the plot in such a way that the viewer is never sure if a film is a dream (or nightmare) or reality. This plot device is used in Cameron Crowe's *Vanilla Sky* (2001). Sometimes the character awakens from a nightmare the viewer may or may not have known was happening; other films leave the viewer confused as to what has actually been experienced or just occurred. David Lynch is famous for the use of this approach; the strategy can be seen in his films *Blue Velvet* (1986), *Lost Highway* (1997), and *Mulholland Drive* (2001). The latter film is very confusing, and the second half of the film is usually assumed to reflect a character's dream.

Sleep Terrors

Sleep Terror Disorder is a parasomnia in which the individual experiences recurrent episodes of abrupt awakening from sleep, often with a panicky scream. The person experiencing sleep terror disorder shows signs of significant distress (e.g., rapid breathing, sweating) and is generally disoriented and unresponsive to attempts to comfort him or her. The individual does not recall the dream itself or the experience of screaming.

Some films illustrate sleep terrors when a character screams in his or her sleep only to wake up unaware of what they were dreaming. This is depicted by an amnestic woman in *Dead Again* (1991), in an adolescent girl screaming during sleep while on an inpatient unit in *Manic* (2003), in a woman on a psychiatric unit of a woman's prison in *Gothika* (2003), and in a young boy who has been cloned partially with cells taken from a murderous child in *Godsend* (2004).

Sleepwalking

Sleepwalking (somnambulism) is a parasomnia involving repeated episodes of rising from bed and walking around during sleep. During these episodes, the person has a blank stare, is unresponsive to others, and can only be awakened with great difficulty. The person does not remember the episode and there is no impairment in mental activity or behavior upon awakening.

In *Secondhand Lions* (2003), Robert Duvall's character sleepwalks each night and goes to stand near a pond; sometimes he acts out an imaginary battle. Michael Caine's character warns others not to awaken the sleepwalker, particularly because Duvall's character will fight in his sleep if he is disturbed. The film suggests that Duvall's character is searching for a love who has died. A young adolescent, played by Haley Joel Osment, enjoys watching Duvall but is anxious about his safety.

In *Donnie Darko* (2001), the lead character, Donnie (Jake Gyllenhaal) hallucinates and is discovered by his psychiatrist to be a sleepwalker, often following his hallucinations outside when sleeping or napping.

"The trick is to combine your waking rational abilities with the infinite possibilities of your dreams. Because, if you can do that, you can do anything."

Guy Forsyth in *Waking Life*

Waking Life (2001) blends animation and drama in a surrealistic film with the feel of a lucid dream. The movie addresses existential themes and questions our own wakefulness during the day, utilizing the metaphor of humans as "sleepwalking" through the days often unaware of what is going on around them. The film explores dream-states, reality, and the insights that can be reached with each. Many important questions and issues are raised for the viewer to reflect upon, with themes of "creating one's own life," reality vs. illusion, lucid dreaming, free will vs. determinism, mindfulness vs. automatic pilot, destiny, and the experience of suffering in life. Similar themes are explored in the 2004 film *Sleepwalking*.

Eating Disorders

There are two major categories of eating disorder: anorexia and bulimia. Other problems with eating include the diagnosis of **obesity**, which is a general medical condition, and disorders of feeding and eating usually diagnosed in infancy or early childhood such as **rumination disorder** and pica. For a graphic depiction of an adult with **pica**, see the film, *The Princess and the Warrior* (2000), which portrays an adolescent psychiatric patient chewing and swallowing glass.

Anorexia Nervosa

In anorexia, the individual refuses to maintain an appropriate body weight for his or her age and height and has an intense fear of gaining weight or becoming fat even though he or she is underweight. The anorectic patient also has a distorted perception of his or her weight and shape. Many symptoms are similar to that of starvation, such as amenorrhea, abdominal pain, and lethargy. Depression and obsessive-compulsive features associated with food are quite common co-occurring disorders. Anorexia presents serious health risks and may lead to death by starvation, suicide, or electrolyte imbalance.

Big budget films rarely portray anorexia; however, this disorder is portrayed accurately in television movies (which often can be rented at video stores). A compelling examination of anorexia and its treatment is found in the film *The Best Little Girl in the World* (1981). Jennifer Jason Leigh dropped down to 90 pounds for her role in this movie. Other films depicting anorexia include *For the Love of Nancy* (1994) which stars Tracey Gold, *Dying to Be Perfect* (1996), *Dying to Dance* (2001), and *Hunger Point* (2003).

Bulimia Nervosa

Bulimia is characterized by **binges**, which are self-indulgent and unrestrained eating episodes. In addition, some behavior is used to prevent weight gain, such as **purging** (self-induced vomiting), misuse of laxatives, diuretics, enemas, or medications, fasting, and/or excessive exercise. Bulimics are preoccupied with their body weight or shape. Depression, anxiety, substance abuse, and borderline personality are the most common co-occurring diagnoses.

In *Center Stage* (2000), one of the dancers, Maureen, suffers from bulimia. She has a very controlling mother who is trying to relive her life through her daughter. The mother talks about little other than dance opportunities for Maureen. Maureen has been restricted as a child, not allowed her to play tennis or play games with other children. To please a new boyfriend, she eats junk food and later purges to stay fit for the dance competitions. Elements of denial are evident when she is on a boat with her boyfriend who hears her purging; Maureen claims she is simply experiencing motion sickness. Her boyfriend later confronts her about "hurting her body." An element of insight emerges when Maureen sees another dancer fall and hurt themselves thus becoming unable to dance in the competition; she finds herself wishing she'd have been the one who was injured because then the intense pressure both externally (her mother) and internally (herself) would be gone.

In *Life is Sweet* (1990), a rebellious adolescent girl, Nicola, is bulimic, binging and purging on chocolate bars hidden in her bedroom. She attempts to include the chocolate into her sex life by rubbing it over her body. It is clear she lives in a dysfunctional family entrenched in themes of food, cooking, and the restaurant business.

In *Elephant* (2003), numerous characters are shown going through a typical day before a school tragedy occurs. Three adolescent girls, Brittany, Jordan, and Kelly, focus on the caloric contents of their lunch food. After eating, they walk into the bathroom together and, each using separate stalls, collectively purge. They do it quickly and without a word about the behavior—acting nonchalantly in the middle of their conversation. They are depicted as attractive with slender bodies, and the three girls obviously want to maintain their appearance. Purging together provides social support for their aberrant behavior.

Although 90% of people with bulimia are females, the prevalence seems to be rising in males. The film *Seabiscuit* (2003) displays a male horse-racing jockey (Tobey Maguire) who forces himself to throw up in order to maintain his low weight so he can ride faster. Ben Stiller's narcissistic, male-model character in *Zoolander* (2001) refers to purging after meals to lose weight, to look better, and keep his job.

Bulimic themes are also evident in *Heathers* (1989), *Girl, Interrupted* (1999), the Korean film *301, 302* (1995), *Angus* (1995), *When Friendship Kills* (1996), and *Drop Dead Gorgeous* (1999).

Body Image and Eating Disorders

Body image is one of the most significant problems with regard to both anorexia and bulimia. Many films, however, display characters struggling with their body image though not all of them suffer from formal eating disorders. Often the use of a mirror or reflective surface shows characters viewing and assessing themselves to convey the character's beliefs about his or her body image. Many times the image in the reflection is shown as distorted, blurred, formless, or unclear to emphasize self-hate, self-deprecation, or self-distortion.

Soldier's Girl (2003) and *I've Heard the Mermaids Singing* (1987) depict characters with problems with body image who stand in harsh self-judgment in front of a mirror. Toward the end of the acclaimed docudrama, *What the Bleep Do We Know?!* (2004), the lead character (Marlee Matlin) stares in the mirror at her body, wearing only underwear, examining it with distaste, distortion, and rage.

Impulse Control Disorders

Impulse control disorders are categorized into the following categories: intermittent explosive disorder, kleptomania, pyromania, pathological gambling, and trichotillomania.

Intermittent Explosive Disorder

Anger is a normal emotion all humans experience. At times, it is a healthy indicator of internal stress, a sign that deeper emotions are being tapped, or a cue someone has offended us. In many instances, the anger turns from thoughts and feelings into behaviors and is acted out in some form. Anger can be extraordinarily destructive and this destructiveness comes across verbally or physically. Intermittent explosive disorder occurs when there are several discrete episodes of aggressive impulses that result in serious assaults or property destruction. Several good films depict intermittent explosive disorder.

"But you know what scares me the most? When I can't fight it anymore, when it takes over, when I totally lose control... I like it."

Bruce Banner in *Hulk*

Acclaimed director Ang Lee's *Hulk* (2003) is a commentary on anger and, more specifically, intermittent explosive disorder. The whole film is about raw anger: anger being unleashed, the dangers and detrimental effects of anger, the build-up and development of anger, and family of origin issues in regard to anger. When Bruce Banner transforms into the hulk, there is enormous destruction of property and this occurs in intermittent episodes of rage as he shifts into the role

of Hulk and then back to the scientist role after his anger subsides. If this film is viewed with intent to understand the psychological phenomenon of anger better, it becomes an educational and fascinating movie to watch.

In *Punch Drunk Love* (2002), Adam Sandler plays the quirky, serious character of Barry Egan who alternates from extreme passiveness (often to his sisters' requests) to brief explosions of anger. Interestingly, when he is confronted with danger, he either runs away or explodes with rage (illustrating the "fight or flight" response).

In *Manic* (2001), an adolescent, Lyle, is sent to an adolescent inpatient unit for what appears to be intermittent explosive disorder: while angry, he had smashed a peer's head with a baseball bat. Though Lyle does begin to relate and connect with others as well as understand himself in a deeper way, he continues to explode periodically with his rage directed towards others. Lyle is sporadic in his anger management attempts—sometimes he stops his anger choosing not to fight and other times he both fights and provokes fights. Lyle reflects the cause of his anger is that his father was physically abusive and his peers made fun of him because of this. An authoritative psychologist (Don Cheadles) utilizes an intervention that involves telling Lyle he is "just like dad" with regard to his anger outbursts.

Mateo, a man dying of AIDS, frequently screams and destroys property in his apartment in *In America* (2003). Another man dying of AIDS, Keifer Sutherland's character in *Behind the Red Door* (2001), has repressed rage from the diagnosis and from a family history of anger and abuse. His outbursts emerge verbally and at seemingly random times (e.g., when his rice is not fully cooked).

In a remarkable Norwegian film, *Elling* (2002), the character Kjell, upon being released from the hospital, has explosive bouts of anger at times of stress and frustration. Antwone in *Antwone Fisher* (2002) exhibits explosive anger, attacking his fellow sailors in response to minor provocation. The viewer later learns that beneath the anger lies intense internal pain and unresolved abuse issues.

Kleptomania

Kleptomania is the recurrent failure to resist impulses to steal objects that are not needed for personal use or for their monetary value. Feelings of tension precede the theft act, and pleasure or relief occurs at the time of the theft.

It is uncertain whether the characters in the following films meet the full *DSM-IV* criteria for kleptomania, but they are at least interesting to consider: *Niagara, Niagara* (1997), *Female Perversions* (1996), and *Mortal Transfer* (2001). In *Mortal Transfer*, one of the psychiatrist's patients is undergoing psychoanalysis and cannot resist her impulses to steal, including taking objects from her psychiatrist's desk.

"I steal to stop me from killing myself."

Maddie Stevens in
Female Perversions

Pyromania

Pyromania is deliberate and purposeful fire setting on more than one occasion, in which there is tension prior to the act, pleasure or relief after it, and a fascination and curiosity with fire itself.

In *House of Fools* (2002), one of the patients at a psychiatric hospital, Mamud, is a veteran with pyromania. After burning the curtains down in the hospital, he quickly exclaims, "it wasn't me!" Mamud is restricted from having any fire-setting materials and even the patients are instructed to not give him matches. Francie in *Butcher Boy* (1997) sets fires, but he would not qualify for this diagnosis insofar as his aberrant behavior is better explained by other diagnoses.

Pathological gambling

Pathological gambling is diagnosed when there is persistent, recurrent gambling behavior. The prototypical gambler with this diagnosis has made several unsuccessful attempts to stop gambling, gambles with increased amounts of money, "chases" losses, lies to cover up the problem, and escapes from personal problems or internal pain by gambling.

Gambling is fairly frequent in movies. Although not all depictions would meet criteria for a gambling addiction (pathological gambling), one film is as clear of a depiction as any—*Owning Mahowny* (2002).

Owning Mahowny

This film is based on true events that occurred in Toronto from 1980-1982; the movie tells the story of a man who stole 10.2 million from his employer to support his gambling addiction. He eventually served a 6-year prison term for fraud.

Philip Seymour Hoffman stars as Dan Mahowny, a man described at the onset as having three lives: (1) a public life, (2) a private life, and (3) a secret life. Mahowny has a loving, dedicated girlfriend and at work he is the youngest in his position as a loan officer, someone described as having an "impeccable record" and "excellent judgment." His secret life involves his very serious, self-destructive gambling problem.

Psychologist: "How would you rate the thrill you got from gambling, on a scale of one to 100?"
Dan Mahowny: "Um... a hundred."
Psychologist: "And what about the biggest thrill you've ever had outside of gambling?"
Dan Mahowny: "Twenty."

***Owning Mahowny* (2002)**

Mahowny accumulates a debt of $10,300 by placing bets with shady bookies. He decides to writes fake loans in order to pay off his debt. He then begins to gamble with this money at casinos to pay off the debt more quickly. He flies to Atlantic City numerous times to gamble. Along the way, he tells various lies to his girlfriend (Minnie Driver) and his boss in order to keep his secret life hidden. While gambling, Mahowny appears to be in a trance—very focused and absorbed in the experience, losing track of time. His losses progressively increase; he loses $15,000 one night and then $100,000 another night, unsuccessfully attempting to "chase" losses by doubling-up on his bets. His denial is obvious to the viewer such as when he frequently convinces himself that he is "in the zone." Mahowny deteriorates psychologically and behaviorally as his behavior becomes erratic, his appearance disheveled and unkempt, and his self-care poor. At one point, he gives a friend money to hold, making him promise not to give it back to him no matter what; soon Mahowny is screaming at his friend to "give me my money and stay away from me." Scenes like this powerfully display the intensity and power of addiction. Mahowny is alone and depressed, he does not get enough sleep, and he even falls asleep while driving. The film is a dramatic depiction of the despair of someone caught in the throes of a gambling addiction.

The casino realizes its potential profit and goes to great lengths to keep Mahowny gambling, following him, watching him, trying to entice him, offering him food, drinks, a free hotel stay and women, and even sending him a "friend" to shadow him and keep him there. Mahowny rejects the women and alcohol; he is referred to as a "purist" in his gambling addiction because he does not mix sex, alcohol, or drugs with his gambling.

The addiction worsens when Mahowny takes his girlfriend on a special vacation and then neglects her; when she confronts him about this while he is gambling, he simply begs for a "few more minutes," ultimately choosing gambling over his girlfriend. This scene illustrates the huge disparity that has developed in their relationship; she continues to be focused on the relationship, while his addiction leaves him too engrossed in gambling to even care what happens to her.

Additional Questions for Discussion (*Owning Mahowny*)

- How common is it for someone to have a "secret life"?
- What is the difference between having a debt problem and having a gambling problem? How does each apply to Mahowny?
- What addictions typically co-occur with gambling? What is the percentage of gamblers who are purists?
- At what point does Mahowny's behavior become unmanageable and out of control?
- In what ways does Mahowny lie to himself?
- What treatments and support groups are available for someone like Dan Mahowny?

In *Dinner Rush* (2001), a cook at an upscale New York City restaurant is unable to control his betting on sports teams. This greatly affects his work performance, interpersonal relationships, and his ability to focus. He exhibits the common gambler's behavior of attempting to "chase" his losses. The impact on his life and functioning is clear: he continues to upset more and more people around him, and eventually he puts his life in danger.

Trichotillomania

Trichotillomania is the recurrent pulling out of one's hair to such an extent that it results in noticeable hair loss. There is an increase in tension prior to pulling the hair, and pleasure or relief upon pulling the hair out.

Trichotillomania is rarely depicted or even referred to in movies. It is one of the least represented psychological disorders in film.

An experience with similar dynamics to trichotillomania is compulsive skin picking. The film *Personal Velocity* (2002) depicts an adolescent boy who skin-picks his fingers, arms, and other areas of his body. Many of the areas are infected. The boy appeared to have been severely abused and is running away by hitchhiking; he presented as severely withdrawn.

Adjustment Disorders

An adjustment disorder is diagnosed when a person develops significant emotional or behavioral symptoms in response to a particular psychosocial stressor; the response exceeds what would typically be expected in such a situation. Social, academic, or occupational functioning may be affected. Adjustment disorders are usually associated with depression, anxiety, disturbance of conduct, or some mixture of each.

A very high percentage of feature films depict some character struggling with a conflictual situation or problem and adjustment disorder symptoms often are evident. Many films depicting relationship stress or those addressing problems with work often display characters with adjustment disorder symptoms, such as Jack Nicholson's anxiety in *Something's Gotta Give* (2003) and Matt Dillon's disturbance of conduct in *Beautiful Girls* (1996). Films that integrate several vignettes or stories are almost certain to have at least one character with an adjustment disorder. Some good examples include *Lantana* (2001), *The Last Kiss* (2001), and *13 Conversations About One Thing* (2001).

It is important to distinguish Adjustment Disorders from bereavement. **Bereavement** is not a psychological disorder. It is the expected response to the death of a loved one, whereas an adjustment disorder occurs when the reaction to a death is in excess of or more prolonged than what is expected. This may be a challenge to distinguish as it seems inappropriate and inhumane to put an arbitrary time limit or label on the time it takes to recover from a painful loss. Toni Collette's character in *Japanese Story* (2003) and a young girl in *Ponette* (1996) both experience protracted bereavement.

In each of the following three films the bereaved character copes by immediately going on a journey in reaction to his or her pain: Jack Nicholson as Warren loses his life-long wife in *About Schmidt* (2002), a young woman loses her beloved father in *Searching for Paradise* (2002), and another young woman loses her boyfriend to suicide in *Movern Callor* (2002).

One example of symptoms going well beyond bereavement and meeting criteria for at least an adjustment disorder is found in the film, *Mother Ghost* (2002). A man begins to have significant conflicts with his wife, ignores his son, numbs his pain by getting drunk, is unable to sleep, and his deceased mother's jewelry begins to appear. The reactions to deaths in both *Truly, Madly, Deeply* (1991) and *In the Bedroom* (2001) seem to go beyond healthy bereavement and consequently would warrant a diagnosis, though by the end of each film, the viewer gets the sense that the characters have found healing and have learned to cope with their losses.

Critical Thinking Questions

- Consider any category of psychological disorders and discuss the impact of sleep deprivation on the disorder's symptoms. Are any of your examples portrayed in movies?
- What are the ways in which insomnia and hypersomnia can be managed psychologically? Are there any films depicting these techniques?
- The ingenious film *Waking Life* explores the question (noted on the DVD cover), "Are we sleep-walking through our waking state or wake-walking through our dreams?" What is this question asking and how does one go about answering it? What is the clinical utility of such a question?
- What role does society have in causing and maintaining eating disorders (e.g., anorexia and bulimia)? Are there some countries where these disorders do not occur?
- Does social class influence bulimia and anorexia?
- What are the similarities and differences between impulse control disorders and addictions? How can movies help in making the distinction?

- Considering how fascinating the impulse control disorders are, why are they not depicted in movies more frequently?
- Is trichotillomania categorized better as an obsessive-compulsive disorder or as an impulse control disorder?
- Can adjustment disorders be more severe than other major psychiatric disorders? At what point should they be treated with medication?
- Can adjustment disorders last for years, or is this contrary to the definition?

Chapter 14

Violence and Physical and Sexual Abuse

When I woke up, I went on what the movie advertisements
refer to as a roaring rampage of revenge.
I roared and I rampaged and I got bloody satisfaction.
I've killed a hell of a lot of people to get to this point.
But I've only one more...the last one...the one I'm driving to right now.
The only one left. And when I arrive at my destination, I am gonna kill Bill...
Uma Thurmond in *Kill Bill: Vol. 2*

Questions to consider while watching *Kill Bill: Vols. 1 and 2*

- What is the murder rate in the United States? In your hometown?
- Is the rationale for the revenge of Uma Thurmond's character, the bride, justified?
- What would you say to someone intent on getting revenge via murder?
- Following a four-year coma, how long should it typically take to work through muscle atrophy in the legs? Can a person "will" their toes to move as the bride does in *Kill Bill, Vol.1*?
- What is the role of violence in these two films? Does it change from one film to the next?
- Director Quentin Tarantino works hard to develop characters who are violent and dangerous. What is he trying to express in doing so?
- Tarantino blocks out the bride's real name for much of both films. What is the psychological relevance of this?
- There are several seriously violent characters in this film. How are their motives and world-views different from one another? How are they similar?
- One scene involves a deviant hospital worker prostituting coma patients for money. How frequently does something like this occur?
- Tarantino engages the viewer in feeling compassion for a serial killer. How does he do this? Do you feel manipulated by this?

Patient Evaluation

Patient's stated reason for coming: "I have only one thing on my mind...revenge. As soon as I get out of here, I'm gonna kill Bill!"

History of the present illness: Ms. Beatrix Kiddo is a 34-year-old, caucasian woman being evaluated to assess her mental status and to ascertain treatment recommendations. She was caught by police three days ago driving a stolen vehicle owned by a man who was murdered in the hospital she was staying at. She is a suspect in several murder investigations, including a mass murder of over fifty people. She is currently placed in isolation at the county jail. She did not provide details regarding any homicides; however, she was adamant about her plan to kill five people, of which, according to Beatrix, only one remains. The person who remains is her ex-boyfriend and former boss, "Bill."

Past psychiatric illness, treatment, and outcomes: Beatrix does not have a history of psychiatric problems. She denied post-traumatic stress symptoms. She denied depression, anxiety, hallucinations, and delusions.

Medical history: Beatrix was hospitalized in a coma for four years following a severe head injury from a gunshot to her head. She awoke from the coma suddenly, immediately remembering the events that lead her to the hospital. Shortly thereafter she overheard a conversation noting she was raped several times while in the coma by a hospital worker who had been prostituting her to various men. She has been out of the coma for about two weeks.

Beatrix has no history of taking psychiatric medication. She denied a history of other injuries, illnesses, or medical disorders, other than "occasional bumps and bruises from kung fu training and fighting."

Psychosocial history: Beatrix would not disclose her complete occupational history; however, did state she "helped rid the world of scum." Following this job, she worked at a music store and became engaged. On the night of the wedding rehearsal, her fiancé and his family were killed and she states she was beaten and shot by the five people mentioned earlier and she was shot in the head by "Bill." She believes this was revenge taken upon her for leaving her previous job. She was pregnant at the time she was shot. She states this caused her to lose the baby and put her in a coma. This disclosure brought tears to her eyes.

Beatrix has never been married. She graduated from high school and then traveled around the world receiving training in various forms of specialized martial arts. Beatrix states she does not have any friends, but paradoxically states that she makes friends easily.

Drug and alcohol history: Beatrix denied any significant substance use history. She occasionally drinks alcohol (twice per month) and smokes marijuana (once per month).

Behavioral observations: Beatrix presented as pleasant, charming, and engaging. She was quite relaxed throughout the interview. She expressed considerable intensity when she spoke of the revenge she hoped to achieve. Mood and affect were euthymic. Speech was normal, evenly paced, and coherent. She seemed to be very clear in her choice of words as she frequently placed emphasis on particular words. No tangential or circumstantial speech was noted. No psychotic processes were evident. No dissociative symptoms were observed. She appeared guarded throughout the evaluation, but she cooperated fully, and the results of the examination are believed to be valid. There were no inconsistencies in her story that might indicate dishonesty, malingering, or other form of manipulation.

Mental status examination: Beatrix was oriented to place, person, time, and situation. She appears to be very intelligent, both socially and intellectually. She scored 30 out of a total of 30 possible points on the Mini Mental Status Examination. No cognitive, attention, concentration, or memory problems were noted, despite the severe head injury and coma in her fairly recent past.

Functional assessment: Beatrix is very bright and clever. She clearly knows how to take care of herself and get her needs met. She does not appear to experience any after-effects from the head injury and coma, other than an intense anger and preoccupation for revenge. Though she ruminates and plans revenge, this does not get in the way of getting her needs met. She states she lacks "mercy, compassion, and forgiveness," but that she has a high dose of rationality. She does present as rational; this rationality is not congruent with the allegations of serial killing and her revenge plans involving murder.

Strengths: Beatrix is direct, assertive, and succinct in her communication. She is talented in martial arts and well-skilled in self-defense.

Diagnosis: Adjustment Disorder with Disturbance of Conduct; Antisocial Personality Disorder

Treatment plan: (1) It is recommended Beatrix not be released at this time due to her significant threats to harm others. (2) Request personality and projective psychological testing to provide a more complete evaluation (e.g., MMPI, Rorschach). (3) Request hospital records from her four-year hospitalization following her head injury. (4) Offer the option of individual psychotherapy to work with decision-making, provide support, and discuss coping strategies.

Prognosis: Guarded

Violence, Revenge, and *Kill Bill*

Kill Bill: Vol. 1 (2003) and *Kill Bill: Vol. 2* (2004) both involve dramatic depictions of violence. Some viewers will argue these are two of the most artistic action films ever made. Others will see their violence as overly graphic and gratuitous. Still others will speak of the role of violence influencing today's culture and today's youth and argue that despite the artistry, the violent imagery that defines these films cannot be beneficial for youth or adults. Others will speak to the glorification of murder and the purposeless nature of revenge. Finally, some will note the film is not to be taken "literally," and that it is to be seen for entertainment, distraction, appreciation, and even inspiration (e.g., the theme of a woman's courage and bravery). Each of the above perceptions is valid and at least partially accurate.

In an interview, David Carradine (who played the character Bill) stated "The essence of a Tarantino movie is not the violence, not the action.

It's the inside look at the mind, the heart, of violent people." This insight emphasizes looking more deeply at all people and looking beyond violent acts to better understand them. There are a variety of violent characters in the film; each is portrayed as unique, with different backgrounds, motivations, thought processes, and actions. Rather than a one-dimensional "bad guy," Tarantino develops all of his characters, showing their flaws, strengths, nuances, and everyday interactions behind their violent presentation.

Some people will be offended by the frequency and intensity of the violence in the films. This is not unjustified, for in many ways these are quintessential violent movies. Scores of people are killed, arms are chopped off, blood sprays, and eyes are ripped out of their sockets. The bride is buried alive, she is raped while in a coma, and other characters are tortured as the killer watches them suffer and die. One of the most violent sequences occurs in *Kill Bill, Vol. 1* and is presented completely in animation; this episode presents the traumatic history of one assassin, who as a girl watched her father and mother brutally murdered in front of her. Tarantino does not do this for gratuitous purposes—not solely to sell movie tickets and just to be graphic—for there are real depths to these characters, an intricate story to be told, and beautiful cinematic artistry to appreciate. The dramatic mixture of violence and cinematic genius is reminiscent of Stanley Kubrick's classic, *A Clockwork Orange* (1971), which was berated as being overly violent and degrading of woman, neither of which was Kubrick's intent.

Tarantino's other films involve similar themes and use violence as a communication medium: *Reservoir Dogs* (1992), *Pulp Fiction* (1994), and *Jackie Brown* (1997). He also wrote the screenplay for the film *From Dusk Till Dawn* (1995).

Violence and Movies: A Meaningful Purpose

In the majority of current action and horror movies, the purpose of the violence is to stimulate, dazzle, and entertain the viewer for a brief period. This helps the viewer escape from his or her present reality and magically enter a more exciting world. Ultimately, the violence in this type of action film (usually a Hollywood product) is unrealistic, unnecessary, and/or gratuitous. It is merely a means to an end—the overriding purpose is to sell movie tickets, not to enhance the cinematic art, to relay an important message to the viewer, or to engender insights.

The following are several exceptions to the above form of film as each creates and depicts violence for what seems to be a more meaningful purpose. The following films are grouped around seven themes and all use violence to support their cinematic intent.

(1) Depicting a Particular Reality

Often violence is the most succinct and honest way to portray the reality of a particular situation, problem, or conflict. In *City of God* (2003), violence is a part of the everyday life of children, adolescents, and adults in a poor section of Rio de Janeiro. Gangs and drugs are a normal part of existence for these children. This type of film is often a shock to viewers who live a very different life and are unaware of the daily poverty and dangers other people face. In *Elephant* (2003), the reality of violence in schools is depicted. Director Gus van Sant portrays the typical everyday life of several students who are unaware of the danger and violence about to take place.

Sometimes the reality portrayed is of actual historical events, e.g., *Schindler's List* (1993). War films depict not only historical events, but can be generalized to illustrate the atrocities and violence of present day wars. For example, *Saving Private Ryan* (1998) reveals the realities of war, de-glamorizing it while not denigrating the sacrifices the men made. Antiwar films reveal similar realities emphasizing the futility of war. *No Man's Land* (2001), a film that won an Academy Award for Best Foreign Film, is one good example; likewise, Stanely Kubrick made three excellent, anti-war films: *Paths of Glory* (1957), *Dr. Strangelove: or How I Learned to Stop Worrying and Love the Bomb* (1964), and *Full Metal Jacket* (1987).

(2) Showing the Ridiculous and Futile Nature of Violence

Two recent films, *2LDK* (2002) and *Series 7: The Contenders* (2001) are almost entirely about violence. Their purpose, though they go about it in very different ways, is to demonstrate the futility and folly of violence. In *2LDK*, a competition rises between two girls rooming together as both audition for an acting role. Growing anger, resentment, and negative and hateful thoughts develop in each girl, artfully shown as they speak and act one way with voice-overs revealing their true thoughts.

Eventually they come face-to-face and an exchange of slaps and damage to each other's personal property turns into physical assaults in the forms of electrocution, spraying cleaner fluid in the face, and attacking with a fire extinguisher.

Series 7: The Contenders is a tongue-in-cheek, fictional reality television show where six people are randomly chosen from their government issued numbers and forced to hunt and kill the others while cameras film them for the television audience. The narrator excitedly describes "real people, real murders" and states that "the rules are as simple as life and death." Dawn, a pregnant woman, is "the longest running contender;" she continues with each new episode enhancing the theme of "kill or be killed." Her success fails to impress her family, and her sister labels her as an "animal, whore, addict, murderer, and thief."

(3) Revealing the Psyche of Violent People

As discussed earlier in the chapter, most of Quentin Tarantino's films embody this theme. Serial killer movies (discussed in more detail later) sometimes attempt to attain this level, but they rarely succeed. In *American Psycho* (1999), assuming the violence is all in Patrick Bateman's mind, the purpose of the violence is to depict the inner psyche and violent fantasies of a disturbed man. The film illustrates a fundamental contradiction as Bateman spends hours daydreaming about violent acts while his body, attire, job, business cards, selection of social outings, and overall presentation are virtually perfect. Thus, the film gets at what no one else in Bateman's world would be privy to—his mind. Something similar occurs when the violent thief in Peter Greenaway's *The Cook, the Thief, His Wife, and Her Lover* (1989) is revealed to be psychotic.

(4) Showing How Violence Is a Cyclical Trap

In *American History X* (1998), one of the purposes of the violence is to show its cyclical nature. This film relates the following sequence of events: man gets involved in a violent group, man gets out of the group but not before consequences of his involvement emerge, man tries to challenge and resolve these new conflicts, but ultimately must face that it is too late and violence ensues completing the circle. The message: Do not get involved with violence in the first place.

In Wim Wenders' *The End of Violence* (1997), Bill Pullman plays an action/violence film director who hides out from society and starts a new life after he is almost murdered. While his character promotes violence in his movies, he also fears violence as evidenced in a high level of paranoia leading him to believe his enemies can come from anywhere—land, water, and sky. A contrasting character (Gabriel Byrne) tries to prevent violence as a secret government officer working a program that oversees the city with thousands of cameras watching over every interaction. Violence's cyclical nature is evident in both the man who directs violent movies only to become an attacked victim of violence and the man trying to prevent violence through spying who is himself killed.

(5) Projecting a Dangerous Future

The message associated with these films is clear: if society keeps heading in a particular direction, a dangerous future is inevitable. *A Clockwork Orange* (1971), in a very artistic way, speaks to this theme with regard to youth violence, the role of the prison system, and the predominate psychological approach at the time, behaviorism. Rather than denigrating such a film and labeling it as offensive, it is more helpful to see the film as a message and motivator to promote change in the present.

(6) Showing the Potential Danger of Authority Roles and Group Contagion

Das Experiment (2001) depicts a research study in a prison setting where subjects are divided into either prisoners who waive their civil rights or guards who are instructed to maintain peace and order. This film bears some initial structural similarity to one of the most well known psychological experiments ever conducted, the Zimbardo Prison Experiment; however, it in no way portrays it accurately as the film's violence goes well beyond what actually occurred in Zimbardo's study. It is clear the violence in this film, though at times overdone, is employed to show the danger of group contagion and the power of the authority role. Shortly into the study, the guards collude and decide they need to humiliate the prisoners to regain control. Prisoners are stripped, ridiculed, called names, denigrated, urinated on, and even beaten and left to bleed to death. One guard captures and rapes the female psychologist. The prisoners experience depression, extreme helplessness, psychosis, and panic attacks. It is difficult for an American viewer to see this film and not be reminded of the shocking reports of prisoner abuse that occurred at Abu Ghraib prison in Baghdad.

(7) Demonstrating Obstacles People Must Face with Courage and Sacrifice

Jesus and Gandhi look directly in the face of violent crowds in *The Passion of the Christ* (2004) and *Gandhi* (1982), respectively. Both show the enormous sacrifice and courage that is often necessary in order to confront oppression and defeat violence.

The Impact of Violence in Films

Contemporary films and television programs are replete with violence, and it is difficult to avoid violence in the media or to briefly catalogue the most egregious examples of violence in recent films. According to the American Academy of Pediatrics, the typical American youngster will have witnessed about 200,000 acts of violence on television by the age of 18, and is likely will have witnessed several thousand additional acts of violence in films such as *Rambo III* (1988) or any of the *Halloween* films.

Several studies have examined the role of violence in television and movies and explored its impact on aggression, attitudes, and behavior. Many articles have emphasized the impact of movie violence on children and adolescents and often the attempt is made to link this violence with violent acts committed by teens. However, while viewing violent movies does appear to contribute to higher acts of aggression, the degree of influence is unclear as many other factors are involved (e.g., video games, parental upbringing, level of poverty, education level, etc.)

Often the person committing the violent act in movies is mentally ill; some estimates note as many as 70% of movie characters with mental illness are dangerous. This certainly contributes to the misconception that all people with mental disorders are violent. Some films are able to appropriately make the distinction between violence and mental illness, such as Roman Polanski's *Repulsion* (1965), Martin Scorsese's *Taxi Driver* (1976), and *Raging Bull* (1980) (Zimmerman, 2003).

Violence and Groups

Group contagion occurs when the individual's identity is lost amongst the group and the individuals conform to the group as a whole. This process of **deindividuation** can be linked with increases in aggressive behavior as people feel more anonymous acting within a group rather than alone. These social psychology themes can clearly be seen in *A Clockwork Orange*, *Fight Club*, *Amores Perros*, *Das Experiment*, and gang related movies such as *South Central*. It also occurs in larger numbers as in the persecution of religious figures, where crowds and major groups of people turn against Gandhi in *Gandhi* and Jesus in *The Passion of the Christ*.

These themes are also present with gang behavior, which is frequently portrayed in movies. *City of God* (2003), a Brazilian drama/documentary about a poor area of Rio de Janeiro, portrays how gangs can take over much of a major city through group violence leaving the individual with few options other than joining the drug lords or dying. In *South Central* (1992), the gangs portrayed take over at night, implement rules to keep their power, emphasize controlling the "hood" by killing, and enforce the idea that "nothing goes on without we saying so." The film emphasizes three alternatives to gang-life: (1) Kill the enemy, (2) Turn against oneself and go crazy, or (3) Change. The film also speaks to anger and hate in the lead character, Ali, who must change and influence others to break his own "hate cycle," thus removing his "badge of shame." This theme is reinforced in a non-gang film, *Antwone Fisher* (2002), in which a young African-American man must face his own anger-abuse cycle deep within him that can be traced generations back to the time of slavery.

Gang-related films often explore issues of racism and the link between racism and violence; this is the case in films such as *South Central* and *8 Mile* (2002). Gangs of violent skin-heads promoting hate are depicted in four powerful and unforgettable films: *American History X* (1998), *The Believer* (2001), *MacArthur Park* (2001), and *Hate* (1995).

In the psychologically complex film, *Fight Club* (1999) men gather one-on-one to physically and brutally fight one another until one of the combatants can no longer stand. An entirely underground fight club movement grows and moves from city to city. The violence is depicted as a way to express anger and repressed rage, as an alternative to the monotony of everyday life, as an antidote to consumerism and depression, and as a way to feel "really alive."

Serial Killers

People have been fascinated with the topic of serial killers since Jack the Ripper strangled and cut the throats of five London prostitutes in 1888. More recent serial killers include Albert De Salvo (the Boston Strangler), David Berkowitz (the Son of Sam killer), Henry Lee Lucas, John Wayne Gacy, Ted Bundy ("the Preppie killer"), Wayne Williams, Charles Manson, and Jeffrey Dahmer, a harmless-looking young man who killed dozens of other young men, ate their body parts, and kept other parts in his refrigerator. The FBI defines a serial killer as anyone who has committed three or more separate murders. It seems that if a serial killer is fairly well-known, a movie will eventually follow; consider the recent films, *Dahmer* (2002), *Ted Bundy* (2002), *Gacy* (2003), *Monster* (2003), and *Summer of Sam* (1999).

Anthony Hopkins plays one of the most terrifying serial killers ever filmed in *The Silence of the Lambs* (1991), *Hannibal* (2001), and *Red Dragon* (2002). *American Psycho* (2000) is a quality film depicting a serial killer if the film is taken literally by the viewer. Another valid vantage point is to consider all of the killings of the fictional character, Patrick Bateman, as fantasies rather than reality; there are numerous cinematic elements to support this hypothesis, although few viewers leave the theater with this impression.

Contrary to media presentations and popular opinion, few if any serial killers are psychotic. (David Berkowitz was a salient exception.) In contrast, many are sexual sadists who derive sexual excitement from the murders they commit; most are sociopaths who experience little remorse or regret for their crimes. Both John Wayne Gacy and Jeffrey Dahmer were homosexual pedophiles.

Some serial killers commit multiple murders for utilitarian reasons—i.e., they are "hit men" who kill for money. This is the kind of serial killer portrayed by Jack Nicholson in *Prizzi's Honor* (1985). Two quality documentaries addressing the lives of sociopathic serial killers have been *In Cold Blood* (1967) and *Henry: Portrait of a Serial Killer* (1990). The latter is loosely based on the life and confessions (since called into question) of Henry Lee Lucas. Henry shares a cheap room with Otis, a man he had met in prison in Vandalia. The film is controversial because it presents graphic details of several murders, including one in which Henry and his roommate, Otis, pretend their car isn't running and then kill a man who stops to help. In a subsequent scene, Henry and Otis videotape the murder of an entire family. The film develops a triangular sexual tension between Henry, Otis, and Becky, Otis' sister, a woman down on her luck who has come to live with her brother. In the final scene of the movie, Henry decapitates Otis. The movie is especially powerful insofar as it seems to trivialize murder, as in the scene in which Henry and Otis murder two prostitutes, then go out and casually share an order of French fries.

Physical and Sexual Abuse in Films

Domestic Violence and Films

Domestic violence is a serious, ubiquitous, and under-reported problem in our society. Violence sufficient to cause death or serious injury will occur in about 1 in 25 families, and hitting, slapping, or punching will occur in approximately one in four families. It is unfortunate that some men feel that marriage gives them special license to hit, hurt, or rape their spouse. (Whether or not a man can be charged with raping his wife is one of the themes explored in the 1959 film *Anatomy of a Murder*.) Two out of three female victims of violence know their attackers; however, they frequently will not report their abuse because they desire to protect their assailants or because they fear reprisals (Abbey, 2005).

The film *Personal Velocity* (2002) studies three very different, vulnerable, and courageous women, each in separate segments. One segment addresses issues of domestic violence; Delia (Kyra Sedgwick) is physically abused by her husband. She is slapped hard in the face at the kitchen table in front of their children for saying the wrong thing, and she is frequently beaten. Delia develops enough motivation to leave when she realizes the pain of what her children are going through; this helps her to "break through the inertia." When speaking to her child, she says she stayed with her husband because he needed her more; this speaks to the irrational self-sacrificing of the victim. In looking back, Delia admits that she and her husband never talked about their problems. In a later scene, a memory of her husband triggers a catharsis. Delia struggles to create a new life, depending on compassionate people, such as a counselor at a women's shelter and an old acquaintance who houses Delia and her children.

Men who abuse their wives are also at high risk of abusing their children. Alcohol or other drugs are commonly involved in cases of domestic violence, and this relationship is clearly present in *Once Were Warriors* (1994).

Once Were Warriors

This remarkable film documents the life of a New Zealand Maori family and the devastating effects of alcoholism and domestic violence on every member of the family, including the husband/father/perpetrator. The film is especially effective in portraying the effects of domestic violence on the children in the family: one son responds by returning to his Maori roots, while a sensitive, poetry-writing daughter responds by committing suicide.

Additional Questions for Discussion (*Once Were Warriors*)

- What role does alcoholism play in the violence we witness in this family?
- To what extent is violence an important part of Maori culture?
- Should a therapist be sensitive to the fact that family violence may be judged appropriate and justified in some cultures?
- If you were Beth's therapist, would you actively encourage her to leave Jake, or would you leave this decision to Beth (knowing she has always decided to stay with him in the past)?

Rape and Films

Rape is included in this section rather than in the chapter on sexual and gender identity disorders because rape is an act of violence and an act of sexual abuse, *not* an act of sexual passion. Incest is discussed in the Sexual and Gender Identity Disorders chapter.

The statistics on rape are sobering. The United States has one of the highest rates of rape in the world—four times higher than Germany, 13 times higher than England, and 20 times higher than Japan. It is estimated that one out of three women will be sexually assaulted in her lifetime, and one out of seven will be raped by her husband. Sixty-one percent of rape victims are under the age of 18, and 78 percent of rape victims know their attacker. One in four college women have either experienced rape or have been exposed to attempted rape, and the majority of both men and women involved in acquaintance rape had been drinking or using drugs at the time. About a third of the victims of rape develop a rape-related post-traumatic stress disorder sometime in their lifetime. It is estimated that only about 16 percent of rapes are reported to the police in the United States, usually because women feel that nothing can be done or because they feel it is a private matter between them and their assailants. When compared with women who have not experienced rape, rape victims are found to be more than nine times more likely to attempt suicide.

Rohypnol (flunitrazepam), a powerful benzodiazepine often referred to as the "date rape drug" is about 10 times more powerful than diazepam (Valium). It is used to treat insomnia and to take the edge off the crash that accompanies withdrawal from binge use of other drugs. Women who have passed out after unwittingly taking Rohypnol have found that the profound sedation and memory impairment that accompany its use have made it very difficult for them to prosecute their assailants.

Rape has been a recurrent theme in contemporary American films. There were significant rape scenes in *A Clockwork Orange* (1971), Ken Russell's *The Devils* (1971), and *My Old Man's Place* (1972). Marlon Brando rapes a passive and indifferent Maria Schneider in *Last Tango in Paris* (1973). There is a vicious and unforgettable rape scene in *Blue Velvet* (1986). Farrah Fawcett takes control of the situation and exacts revenge on a rapist in *Extremities* (1986); Dustin Hoffman gets revenge following his wife's graphic rape in Sam Peckinpah's violent film *Straw Dogs* (1971); and two independent women inadvertently kill a man who tries to rape one of them in *Thelma and Louise* (1991). Vietnamese women are raped in several of the Vietnam War films, most notably in *Casualties of War* (1989). Harrison Ford is wrongly accused of rape in *Presumed Innocent* (1990). Date rape occurs in the 1995 film *Higher Learning*; gang rape is portrayed in *Last Exit to Brooklyn* (1989); and there are homosexual rapes in *Deliverance* (1972) and *American History* (1998). A nun is raped in *Bad Lieutenant* (1992), but the nun forgives her assailant and refuses to press charges against him. Two children play a game of rape in *Welcome to the Dollhouse* (1996). Ingmar Bergman takes up the theme of the rape of innocence in *The Virgin Spring* (1959), and two rapes occur in the gritty Dutch film *Antonia's Line* (1995), one of which involves a man who rapes his sister who is mentally retarded. *Dead Man Walking* (1995) presents the viewer with difficult choices about the appropriateness of capital punishment in a case of rape and murder, and we are forced to think about whether or not drug intoxication is a mitigating circumstance in this case and others like it.

Attempted rape of a man by a woman is discussed extensively in the film adaptation of Michael Crichton's novel *Disclosure* (1994). When Michael Douglas rebuffs Demi Moore, the new female boss, she lies and manipulatively accuses her new subordinate of sexual harassment.

Perhaps the most troubling portrayals of rape occur in those films in which rape is shown to be a woman's fantasy, or in those films in which a woman who is being raped becomes aroused by the experience or attracted to the rapist. There are elements of these themes in two otherwise remarkable movies, Pedro Almodovar's *Tie Me Up! Tie Me Down!* (1990) and Lina Wertmuller's *Swept Away* (1975).

Victims of Physical and Sexual Abuse

Every act of violence or abuse has both a perpetrator and a victim. Both are depicted in films but for emphasis of story, character development, or artistic integrity, one is often emphasized over the other.

If there was ever a character who is a victim of abuse, it would be Lilja in *Lilja 4-Ever* (2002). This remarkable Denmark/Swedish film develops the character of Lilja, a 16-year-old girl who seems to encounter just about every form of abuse and exploitation a person can experience. She is lied to and abandoned by her mother, rejected by her family, manipulated and sold into prostitution by a man she had hoped to live with, gang raped, physically and sexually abused, and ruthlessly prostituted. She is completely tossed away by society as the viewer clearly sees at the onset where Lilja is depicted walking the streets, bloodied and beaten up, with no safe place or person to turn to. Nevertheless, Lilja does not take on the victim role of helplessness and fear, but instead pushes forward. Her resiliency is commendable and inspirational, but every human has a breaking point and the viewer sees this as Lilja contemplates suicide.

Antwone Fisher (2002) is based on the true story of a young man, Antwone Fisher (Derek Luke), who enlists in the Navy and begins to have problems with anger and assault. He is sent to a Navy psychiatrist (Denzel Washington) and eventually opens up his traumatic past, which includes a history of significant physical and sexual abuse.

Some films depict entire groups, cultures, or ethnicities that are victims of physical or sexual abuse. *The Magdalene Sisters* (2002), based on a true story, depicts the lives of a large group of young girls sent away for behavior problems and forced to endure daily physical hardships, abuse, and humiliation. Each adolescent sent to this Catholic workhouse is abused by nuns who seem oblivious to the pain they inflict.

Mystic River and Sexual Abuse

In *Mystic River* (2003), director Clint Eastwood depicts three boyhood friends (Sean Penn as Jimmy, Tim Robbins as Dave, and Kevin Bacon as Sean) who re-unite following the death of Jimmy's daughter. At the film's onset, the three boys are approached by a man in a car who intimidates them and identifies himself as a cop. Only Dave gets in the car with the man who turns out to be a pedophile. Dave is sexually abused and escapes from his abductors after four days. The story moves ahead about 30 years and the viewer sees the adult Dave, now married with a son. Dave has never fully recovered from the abduction.

Tim Robbins, who won an Academy Award for Best Supporting Actor for his role as Dave, provides a stunning portrayal of a sexual abuse survivor. Dave is passive, timid, unassuming, and unemotional, yet appears to have a happy family life. In what can be viewed as an unfortunate consequence, Dave sees a man abusing a young boy and his own abuse history is triggered; trying to free the boy and (metaphorically) himself, Dave snaps, killing the man and allowing the boy to escape. Consequently, Dave is plagued with confusion and pain that he is unable to share with his wife; he tells her a different story, and he becomes a suspect in the murder of Jimmy's daughter who had died the same night. Dave becomes more distant (thus appearing more guilty), increasingly quirky, and begins to talk to himself. In one dramatic scene, he seems to hallucinate, hearing voices in his head.

The Accused and Rape

The Accused (1988) is based on a true story of gang rape on a pool table in a blue-collar bar. The crime was especially despicable insofar as more than a dozen spectators stood by clapping and cheering while a woman was repeatedly raped. No one attempted to stop the rape or assist the victim. The complacency of the bystanders in the film is in part attributed to the fact that Jodi Foster's character,

Sarah Tobias, had been drinking heavily and smoking pot earlier in the evening, had openly flirted with one of the men, was provocatively dressed, and had engaged in a sensuous dance immediately before being raped. Her defense is weakened by the fact that she had jokingly referred to one of the men earlier in the evening, telling her girlfriend, "I should take him home and fuck his brains out." The attorneys for the defense argue that Tobias is simply "trailer park trash" who was an enthusiastic and willing participant in everything that occurred.

Some of the most vivid scenes in the film occur during an insensitive gynecological examination by a woman doctor who asks detailed questions about Sarah's sexual history ("Have you ever made love to more than one man at a time?") and recent experiences. The insensitivity is compounded by the questions of the assistant district attorney, who wants to know how Sarah was dressed and when was the last time she experienced intercourse before the rape.

Tobias loses the first legal round, when the three rapists are convicted but have their sentences reduced from rape to "reckless endangerment." However, she is eventually successful in convicting several of the men who witnessed the rape and did nothing. The film concludes with two sobering facts: (1) in the United States, a rape is reported every six minutes, and (2) one out of every four rape victims is attacked by two or more assailants.

Neglect and Abandonment

Many films depict the neglect of children by their parents. One particular poignant film where neglect plays an important role is the Russian film *The Return* (2003). Two boys are abandoned and neglected by their father for 12 years when suddenly and without warning the father returns. He is quick to leave them again for business, but then changes plans and takes them on a trip. The boys are pushed physically and emotionally to survive his challenges (e.g., they are left to do the work of figuring out how to set up a tent, push a car out of the mud, and row a boat in challenging waters) and continued abandonment (e.g., one boy is left in the middle of nowhere in the pouring rain because he asked too many questions about fishing). The father is an enigma throughout the film: taciturn in speech with comments of "Get in" and

"Get out," cryptic in his behavior, and secretive about his occupation. Among many other themes, one theme is clear: many issues arise from abandonment and neglect by a parent, and one cannot simply "return" and expect everything to be normal.

Critical Thinking Questions

- Some movies (e.g., *Pulp Fiction*, *True Romance*) depict people who commit extremely violent acts but do not suffer the consequences. What kind of meaning and impact does this have on the viewer?
- Do therapists have an obligation to respect cultural values and practices that may be harmful or degrading (e.g., slapping children for misbehaving or female genital mutilation)?
- What is the relationship between pornography and violence against women?
- Did your views of pornography change after watching *The People vs. Larry Flynt*?
- Should alcohol or drugs be considered mitigating circumstances in cases of rape or murder (e.g., *Dead Man Walking*)?
- Is it possible to develop accurate "psychological profiles" that can help identify serial killers?
- Are there common factors that characterize the childhood experiences of those individuals who grow up to become serial killers?
- How do the media perpetuate violence in American society?
- Should a woman's dress or provocative behavior be treated as extenuating circumstances in a rape case?
- What conformity studies in social psychology can be used to understand the behavior of the bystanders in The Mill bar who did nothing to help Sarah Tobias in *The Accused*?
- What steps could police officers and hospitals take to ensure rape victims are treated humanely and compassionately?
- In *Mystic River*, how different would you hypothesize the character of Tim Robbins to be emotionally and behaviorally if he had not gotten in the car?

Chapter 15

Treatment

You have to use that energy to better yourself.
Denzel Washington in *Antwone Fisher*

Questions to consider while watching *Antwone Fisher*

- How is the portrayal of the psychiatrist, Jerome Davenport, realistic or unrealistic?
- Describe how Davenport's approach changes over time? Why does he change his methods?
- Which of Davenport's interventions is most effective?
- Are there empirically validated techniques that Davenport does not use? How would these change based on Antwone's diagnosis?
- Is Davenport an ethical psychiatrist despite the boundary violations we observe?
- Davenport is a psychiatrist, but medication is not used. In a military setting, would Antwone realistically have been seen by a psychiatrist or by another mental health professional?
- How long does Antwone's treatment last? Is this realistic?
- Are any of the sessions Davenport has with Antwone outside of the office justified?
- When is it healthy for someone to confront his or her abusers? When is it unhealthy or inappropriate?
- How much of what occurs in this portrayal of psychotherapy exaggerated for cinematic purposes?

Evaluation of Treatment in *Antwone Fisher*

Treatment modality: Individual psychotherapy

Treatment facility: Outpatient clinic at a U.S. Naval Base

Role of treatment facility: To evaluate and screen Navy personnel for psychological issues that might impair service and to provide brief therapy for psychological disorders.

Psychiatrist portrayed: Dr. Jerome Davenport is a 45-year-old, African-American, Navy psychiatrist, who evaluates and treats a number of sailors and naval officers with various psychological struggles. The focus of this report will be his work with one particular patient, Antwone Fisher.

Theoretical orientation: Eclectic and integrative (psychodynamic, behavioral, interpersonal process, humanistic, and spiritual approaches are blended).

Therapeutic structure: Dr. Davenport schedules one to three sessions with each patient to complete an evaluation and make recommendations.

Initial session: Dr. Davenport greets Antwone as "Seaman Fisher." He is cordial yet makes little attempt to establish rapport. He starts the assessment with the question, "I understand you like to fight" and offers to talk about it further. When Antwone resists, he initially accepts the resistance and instructs Antwone to return next week. Dr. Davenport appears to be casual in his approach to counseling, but he accepts no nonsense from his clients; he appears to be somewhat authoritarian, but this style is appropriate in a military setting.

Follow-up sessions: Antwone skips the second scheduled session, and Dr. Davenport has officers escort him to the appointment the following week. Antwone shows significant resistance; Dr. Davenport responds by patiently waiting and doing other work or eating while Antwone sits or stands in silence. A paradoxical intervention is set up when Dr. Davenport stated that their three sessions do not begin until Antwone starts talking. This is an indirect form of showing respect for the client insofar as it gives Antwone the space and time necessary to open up; it also puts the responsibility for treatment success upon Antwone.

Toward the end of the fifth session of going into the office and not speaking for 50 minutes,

Antwone finally begins to talk. Dr. Davenport utilizes gentle questioning, helping him to explore a variety of interpersonal issues in a comfortable way. He is authoritative and continues to avoid putting pressure on Antwone. He asks appropriate but probing questions at appropriate times in the counseling sessions.

After their three official sessions are finished, Dr. Davenport terminates his work with Antwone. This is appropriate based on the boundaries set in the initial meeting; however, it is inappropriate insofar as there are therapeutic issues that remain unsettled and Antwone is experiencing many new emotions that have not been processed. As a likely response to termination, Antwone acts out by attacking a peer. At a later week, Antwone goes to the office and explodes in the waiting room, mocking Dr. Davenport in front of several other patients. Dr. Davenport watches and waits for the highly inappropriate behavior to end before asking, "Would you like to step in my office?" He is then firm and forceful as he sets new boundaries; he also listens to Antwone's explanation for his misbehavior. Antwone states he is sorry, and he opens up, admitting "I don't know what to do."

Dr. Davenport later seeks Antwone out and admits his mistake in insisting on early termination; he agrees to see Antwone in weekly psychotherapy sessions. The psychotherapy process shifts to a more casual and supportive approach, and sessions are held in a variety of settings. At one point, Dr. Davenport uses the word "son" in addressing Antwone; this may actually reflect **countertransference** on the part of the therapist; in any case, it has powerful metaphorical implications since Antwone's father was murdered before he was born and Dr. Davenport is clearly a father figure. When Antwone is arrested, Dr. Davenport holds a session in the jail. When the sensitive topic of childhood sexual abuse arises, Dr. Davenport is careful and patient, asking probing but not leading questions, and he is careful not to make unwarranted assumptions. He is sensitive to Antwone's embarrassment and his difficulty in sharing the personal and painful issues.

Interventions utilized: Paradoxical intention; role-playing; self-disclosure; exploring family history; processing emotions; anger management strategies; relationship building; bibliotherapy; supportive therapy and advice giving. Spiritual interventions include processing forgiveness, making amends with the past, enhancing resiliency, and alluding to courage, letting go, and hope within almost every therapy session.

Boundary assessment: Dr. Davenport initially sets a three-session limit for his work with Antwone. After making a shift to ongoing weekly psychotherapy, the boundaries of the relationship loosen significantly. Dr. Davenport continues a conversation after the time boundaries of a session to give advice and initiate a role-playing exercise. The boundaries are stretched much further when he states, "I'm gonna give you my phone number. If you have any problems, any questions at all, you can call me...any time of day or night. Have fun; give me a call, ok?" This leads to Antwone making a surprise visit to Dr. Davenport's home, after which new boundaries are quickly set. Dr. Davenport then breaks his client's confidence by telling his wife several (superficial) details about Antwone using information that had come out of previous therapy sessions.

Dr. Davenport later blurs the boundaries of therapy by inviting Antwone to his home for a therapy session that is conducted in the living room with the door open and with his wife in the house. Antwone is subsequently invited to Thanksgiving dinner. This experience triggers Antwone's dormant feelings of abuse and neglect. Dr. Davenport also conducts psychotherapy sessions in a jail cell (appropriate for the situation) and in a men's room (highly inappropriate for the situation). In the latter location, Dr. Davenport attempts once again to terminate his work with Antwone, Antwone's abandonment issues are triggered, and he responds by describing another traumatic incident. Dr. Davenport listens and then terminates, instructing Antwone to contact him after he re-locates his family. Davenport's final words are "I love you, son."

Self-disclosure: Dr. Davenport speaks openly about his wife when asked. He is comfortable with self-disclosure and uses it in a balanced way. He also speaks to his own nervousness in situations to normalize his client's anxiety.

Management of personal issues: It is clear Dr. Davenport is struggling with problems with his wife; however, these problems do not appear to intrude on the sessions. After psychotherapy has terminated, he informs Antwone of the impact Antwone had on his life, suggesting that the experience of working with Antwone in therapy has made him a better doctor and husband.

Types of issues discussed: Some of the topics discuss include Antwone's lack of family, the experiences of physical and sexual abuse, Antwone's current interactions with peers, his past friendships, his relationship with a new girlfriend, and the cultural acceptance of abuse that was passed down through generations.

Flexibility and openness: Dr. Davenport's high flexibility, candor, and humanistic approach open Antwone to share stories of his abuse and mistreatment.

Ethics: Dr. Davenport is an ethical, competent psychiatrist with no intent to do harm or take advantage of his patient or others in any way. Nevertheless, there are potential ethical violations in failing to maintain his client's confidentiality and allowing a dual relationship to develop.

Diagnosis of patient: Adjustment Disorder, with Disturbance of Conduct; Intermittent Explosive Disorder (Rule Out)

Treatment outcome: Positive. Antwone met and confronted his mother, confronted two abuse perpetrators from his childhood, established a healthy intimate relationship, earned a promotion, and reunited with his family. He has also completed his work in therapy.

Prognosis: Excellent.

Referrals: None necessary at the current time. After the initial 3-session evaluation, psychotherapy should have been recommended.

Therapist quote: "It's not what I want you to say, it's what you want to tell me."

Patient quote: "You may be able to make me come here but you can't make me talk."

Overall portrayal of psychologist/psychiatrist: Balanced. [Considering this is a cinematic presentation, the portrayal is actually quite good since there are no gross ethical violations; however, many of the boundary violations that we see in the film would be troubling if they occurred in a real psychotherapeutic setting.]

Treatment Modalities

Individual Psychotherapy

Individual psychotherapy is the most common treatment modality depicted in movies. Sometimes it is quite accurate; at other times, it is preposterous.

The most frequently portrayed theoretical orientation continues to be **psychoanalysis**, though it is also the most stereotyped approach to therapy. Both the frequency of cinematic depictions of psychotherapy and many of the stereotypes can be credited to director Woody Allen, who has portrayed psychoanalysts in his films from the late 1960s through 2003. Interestingly, the psychologist portrayal in the recent film *Anything Else* (2003) is one of his most stereotypic (i.e., he is a therapist who refuses to respond to important

patient questions). One of the least stereotypic portrayals occurred the previous year when Allen directed *Hollywood Ending* (2002), a film about a man hired to direct a picture being produced by his ex-wife. The protagonist develops a case of psychosomatic blindness, and his therapist is portrayed as someone who accurately diagnoses the conversion disorder and offers helpful suggestions. Other orientations illustrated by films include a humanistic and supportive approach in *Lantana* (2001), and what appears to be Transactional Analysis in *Good Will Hunting* (1997). (Note the titles of the books when Robin Williams pins Matt Damon to the wall.) Interestingly, one of the most widely used, popular and empirically validated approaches, Cognitive-Behavior Therapy, is very rarely depicted in films.

"My father was an alcoholic. Mean fuckin' drunk. He'd come home hammered, lookin' to whale on somebody. So, I had to provoke him so he wouldn't go after my mother and little brother."

Matt Damon described his childhood in a therapy session with Robin Williams

---

Antwone Fisher (2002) depicts multiple sessions of individual psychotherapy. Antwone (Derek Luke) and his psychiatrist, Dr. Jerome Davenport (Denzel Washington), slowly work through the topics of anger, physical abuse, sexual abuse, and trauma. The film is framed around the psychotherapy sessions, and the plot deepens whenever Antwone opens up in a deeper way. The sessions can be divided into phases of resistance and exploration: first Antwone refuses to share anything, later he begins to open up sharing his physical abuse, next his sexual abuse, and finally his feelings as he witnessed the murder of his best friend. These four therapy phases are appropriately juxtaposed with relevant narrative components.

The psychiatrist also changes because of his therapy sessions with this patient. Dr. Davenport had not realized the full extent of his isolation, and he was not aware of how he also needed to change.

Dr. Davenport was humble enough to recognize his own weaknesses as he watched his patient's courage and resiliency grow.

In addition to *Antwone Fisher*, other recent balanced individual psychotherapy portrayals can be seen in *Good Will Hunting* (1997), *K-Pax* (2001), *The Sixth Sense* (1999), *Gothika* (2004), and *Elling* (2002) while unbalanced individual psychotherapy portrayals can be seen in *Normal* (2003), *Lantana* (2001), and *Vanilla Sky* (2001) (Niemiec & Wedding, 2005).

Successful individual treatment is also portrayed in films such as *Sybil* (1976), *David and Lisa* (1963), and *Ordinary People* (1980). In *Ordinary People*, Conrad, the surviving son, begins therapy with a psychiatrist (played by Judd Hirsch) who demonstrates warmth and caring and allows his young patient to examine painful family relationships within the safety of individual therapy. In *Equus* (1977), Richard Burton plays a psychiatrist who treats a very disturbed young man played by Peter Firth. During psychotherapy, the true depth of the psychological disturbance is revealed. In some instances, as in *Best Boy* (1979), a rehabilitation program is portrayed.

Films also often portray mental health professionals behaving unethically. For example, breaches in confidentiality are evident in *Equus*, and sexual relationships between clients and psychiatrists are depicted in *Bliss* (1997), *Mr. Jones* (1993), and *Prince of Tides* (1991).

Group Psychotherapy

In *Manic* (2003), group psychotherapy is depicted on an inpatient unit for adolescents. It is accurate and appropriate as a portrayal of group intervention, perhaps helped by the inclusion of some actual psychiatric patients. The psychiatrist (Don Cheadles) has his hands full with severely depressed individuals, those who are self-injurious, threatening and violent patients, and those with explosive personalities. He attempts to include everyone in group discussions, and he cleverly reframes patient experiences in a positive, balanced way.

In stark contrast, the group therapy sessions portrayed in the film, *Wilbur Wants to Kill Himself* (2002), are disappointing and unrealistic. One of the psychiatrists is overly supportive, obsequious, and flirtatious with patients while the other psychiatrist smokes during sessions, sets himself apart from the group, and makes jokes about not wanting to be there.

Psychiatric Hospitalization

Mental health treatment settings are most often portrayed in films as capacious institutions, and their depiction is almost always negative. Psychiatric hospitals are usually portrayed as dark, gloomy, and unwelcoming places with considerable background noise (often screaming), staff nurses dressed in white, and patients with nothing to do other than to walk the halls of the institution acting odd. It is immediately obvious to the viewer when a movie scene takes place in such an institutional setting. From a cinematic perspective, this stereotyped presentation makes sense inasmuch as the viewer is more likely to remember a majestic, foreboding hospital exterior than a simple clinical office. These hospitals typically have stunning architecture, winding corridors, and an interesting activities room.

Some movies with these dreary though memorable settings include *The Snake Pit* (1948), *One Flew Over the Cuckoo's Nest* (1975), *Instinct* (1999), *Twelve Monkeys* (1995), *Sling Blade* (1996), *Girl, Interrupted* (1999), *Don Juan Demarco* (1994), *A Beautiful Mind* (2001), and *Analyze That* (2002). *One Flew Over the Cuckoo's Nest* is the classic film that depicts the violation of human rights in mental institutions, but it was certainly not the first. *The Snake Pit* was one of the earliest films to raise consciousness about the treatment of persons with mental illness. It depicted the institution metaphorically as a zoo in which patients were fenced in, and as a place for visitors to tour, and a place where patients were "herded" into their own cages (rooms). One important difference between the two films is that the character of Virginia in *The Snake Pit* is truly mentally ill, whereas Randle Patrick McMurphy is not. *Chattahoochee* (1989) also describes the plight of those who disagree with institutional authority and power, and *Nuts* (1987) portrays a woman's struggle to avoid being committed to an institution.

House of Fools (2002), a film reminiscent of *King of Hearts* (1966) but based on a true story, takes place in a psychiatric institution in a war-torn country (Chechnya). When the town is about to be taken over by the enemy, the staff evacuates, the patients stay, and the soldiers find refuge in the hospital. The movie raises questions about the insanity of war, and it uses the hospital as a metaphor for the insanity of a world at war.

The film *K-Pax* (2001) moved away from some of the stereotypes of the psychiatric hospital environment. It depicts an institution in New York that has adequate light, numerous windows, and meaningful activities for both staff and patients. The patients contact and communicate easily with one other. Although the film loses this focus at times, such as when the patients begin to run about in a frenzy, their excitement is not "crazy" and random but grows out of support for one another. Overall, *K-Pax* portrays a less dehumanizing environment than many older films.

As the closing of psychiatric hospitals continues, there will be fewer institutions to portray in films, and eventually the only portrayals of massive psychiatric institutions in movies will be in period films.

A Clockwork Orange

Stanley Kubrick's *A Clockwork Orange* (1971) does not take place in a psychiatric institution, but instead at a specialized hospital running a research program for the prison system. This film remains a prototype in the cinematic exploration of the ethical issues associated with behavioral treatment. In the film, Malcolm McDowell plays Alex, the leader of a vicious gang. Alex and his friends are psychopathic personalities: they thrive on violence and commit both rape and murder without any evidence of remorse. However, at the same time that audiences are repulsed by Alex's violence, they find themselves attracted by his high-spirited personality and his love of classical music.

Alex is captured after being set up by his friends, who have come to resent his authority. He is convicted of murder and sentenced to 14 years in prison; however, he is given the option of early release if he is willing to participate in a conditioning experiment. In scenes almost as horrifying as the earlier rape scenes, Alex is injected with a nausea-inducing drug and repeatedly forced to watch scenes depicting rape and violence while Beethoven symphonies are played in the background.

The conditioning proves to be highly successful, and Alex cannot even think about a violent incident without becoming ill. He is released from prison, but finds himself totally unable to cope with life on the streets. He eventually attempts suicide. While he is recovering in the hospital, a reform movement occurs in the government, and Alex is portrayed as a guinea pig who was abused by the previous administration. The treatment is reversed, and Alex is once again able to fantasize happily about rape and murder. The film dramatically presents the conundrum faced by society as it contemplates treatments that attempt to improve society by limiting personal freedom (e.g., mandatory injections of drugs such as **Depo-Provera** that diminish sex drive in men convicted of sexual crimes).

Additional Questions for Discussion (*A Clockwork Orange*)

- Can Alex accurately be described as evil? Is the concept of evil meaningful for mental health professionals?
- How accurate are the behavior modification practices portrayed in the film? What behavioral treatments most resemble those applied to Alex?
- Are fantasies about rape or murder significant mental health problems? Under what conditions does their presence warrant intervention?
- What diagnostic label in *DSM-IV* would be most appropriate for Alex? For the others in his gang?
- Is Alex treatable? If so, what theoretical orientation, treatment approach, and interventions are likely to be of most help for Alex?
- Can you think of real-life examples of situations in which health professionals have exploited prisoners?

Treatment Interventions

Hypnosis

It is interesting to discuss hypnosis in a book about movies because the film viewer goes in and out of light trance states throughout the movie-viewing experience. However, we have grown so accustomed to the habit of viewing movies and television shows that we rarely realize when we have entered a trance state. Hypnosis has been portrayed in numerous films, but it is rarely given an accurate or realistic portrayal.

Hypnosis has remained a popular intervention for over 100 years and is an empirically validated technique for both psychological and medical disorders. Hypnosis continues to fight a battle against public misconception, part of which unfortunately is perpetrated by movies (and by stage hypnotists).

A common misconception is that hypnosis represents a form of mind control through which a person can be programmed to do things against his or her will. This myth is perpetrated by films like *The Manchurian Candidate* (1952) and its recent (2004) remake. In the more recent film, a character, upon hearing the designated cue word, immediately comes under the hypnotist's spell (cinematically accompanied by changes in ambient light) and is at once fully controlled by the voice of the hypnotist. Through flashbacks, other characters are shown killing while in a trance. One character is depicted going fully against his own values when he smothers his long-time lover following a trance suggestion. Of course, this is cinematic nonsense.

"I was a damn good shrink. Nineteen years I worked with a lot of people through a lot of shit. OK, I slept with a patient or two. It's not like I didn't care about them. I loved being a doctor. I used to not charge half my patients. Then the fucking state comes along, they send in some bitch undercover, and I'm fucked. Life isn't fair, is it?"

Robin Williams reviews his life as a hypnotherapist in *Dead Again*

In films like Kenneth Branagh's *Dead Again* (1991) and Woody Allen's *The Curse of the Jade Scorpion* (2001), hypnosis is used as a blatant form of manipulation for malevolent purposes. In the former film, a hypnotist (who is also an antiques dealer) takes advantage of vulnerable people by asking them questions in the trance state about where rare antiques can be found in their home or at their work sites; he then gives the suggestion that the person will have total amnesia for the experience. In the latter film, hypnosis is used to steal jewels; here too, subjects are told they will be totally amnestic for the hypnosis episode. Films like these convince viewers that hypnosis can be used to make people do things that are illegal, unethical, and immoral.

Some people believe that hypnosis may be painful and destructive. *The Butterfly Effect* (2003) perpetuates this misconception by having

a young man replay his past under hypnosis; when he does, we see him squirming in pain, his nose bleeds, and he falls onto the floor only to become amnestic for the experience.

"Just think of your mind as a movie, you can pause, rewind or slow down any details you want."

A hypnotherapist's advice in *The Butterfly Effect*

Often times professionals are depicted as incompetent in their use of hypnosis, such as the psychologist in *Donnie Darko* (2001) who uses hypnosis with a patient who has schizophrenia; this diagnosis would actually be a contraindication for hypnosis. The patient in *Donnie Darko* begins to masturbate while in a trance.

Even when the intent to use hypnosis is justified and well-intentioned, it is most often depicted in an overly dramatic manner; for example, in many films the hypnotic technique of "age regression" is employed, and the patient is shown reliving very painful experiences or past traumatic events. The psychiatrist played by Jeff Bridges in *K-Pax* (2001) explains hypnosis, performs an induction, and begins to explore his patient's past. The patient screams in agony and nearly goes into shock. In reality, hypnosis is rarely this dramatic.

In each of these films, the subject is depicted as helpless and under the control of the hypnotist. These depictions hardly represent the well established therapeutic truism that "all hypnosis is self-hypnosis."

Medications

The use of contemporary medications began in 1952 with the introduction of **chlorpromazine** (Thorazine), first used as an antihistamine. Several compounds with similar properties were subsequently synthesized. Thorazine was believed to be a miracle drug that would empty all of our mental hospitals. These medications did enable many patients to live in the community; unfortunately, they were often indiscriminately prescribed, and dosages were usually excessive. Because of a lack of knowledge about the drug and its consequences, excessive sedation and **extrapyramidal side effects** (muscle cramps of the head and neck, restless pacing or fidgeting, and stiffening of muscular activity in the face, body, arms, and legs) were common. In *One Flew over the Cuckoo's Nest*, the patients were receiving excessive dosages of medications that sedated them and put them at high risk for debilitating side effects.

Today there are several different classifications of pharmacological agents. **Antipsychotic medications** are given to treat thought disorders, such as schizophrenia, and some mood disorders. **Antidepressants** are given for the mood disorders and some anxiety disorders, and **lithium** is a common medication choice for bipolar disorders. **Anxiolytic** (antianxiety) medications are carefully prescribed for patients with anxiety disorders. Some of these drugs, such as Xanax, Valium, and Librium, can be addictive. These drugs are also the ones most often used in combination with alcohol and recreational drugs. The 1982 movie *I'm Dancing as Fast as I Can* stars Jill Clayburgh as the award-winning TV producer Barbara Gordon, who becomes addicted to Valium but eventually recovers.

"You know, our bodies are capable of incredible things when they're subjected to anxiety and stress. I found my ex-best friend's cufflinks in my wife's purse one time. I couldn't get an erection for a year and a half."

Inappropriate self-disclosure by a psychiatrist in *Garden State*

In the recent film *Garden State* (2004), the overly sedated lead character, who has been taking various medications for a mood disorder for over a decade, decides on his own to discontinue taking medication after learning of the death of his mother. He prospers without the medication, meets a wonderful woman, learns to be assertive when dealing with his controlling psychiatrist father, and feels genuinely happy for the first time in years. While this film is meant to be inspirational and liberating, it also imparts an inappropriate, mixed message to countless people who are taking similar medications.

Electroconvulsive Therapy (ECT)

In the 1950s, both electroshock and insulin shock became accepted treatment methods to induce seizures, and many psychiatrists were convinced that seizures could be used to protect patients from mental illness. By the 1960s, electrical stimulation, called **electroconvulsive therapy** (ECT), was well established as the safest way to induce seizures.

Originally, ECT was used for many psychiatric illnesses, including schizophrenia. However, more effective pharmacological approaches were ultimately developed for most of these disorders. Today, severe depression, mania, and occasionally some types of thought disorders are treated with ECT, but only when other approaches have failed. The procedure is accompanied by the administration of short-acting general anesthesia and muscle paralytic agents that prevent the muscle contractions associated with seizures. Then a very mild electrical stimulus is passed through the brain, which causes the seizure. A series of 8-10 treatments is usually administered before clinically significant results are obtained.

In the past, ECT was used frequently and indiscriminately, often with excessive voltage. In films such as *One Flew over the Cuckoo's Nest* (1975) and *An Angel at My Table* (1990), ECT is pictured as a painful, lengthy treatment, with the hapless patient strapped to a table by sadistic attendants. In reality, contemporary use of ECT takes about 5–10 minutes from start to finish and rarely results in a visible seizure. There are also very clear practice guidelines regulating when ECT is appropriate and when it is not. In *One Flew over the Cuckoo's Nest*, ECT was used as punishment for patients who challenged the authority of Nurse Ratched (ranked fifth on the American Film Institute's list of the 50 all-time greatest movie villains; see Appendix B). Its use was just as inappropriate when used to treat New Zealand novelist Janet Frame, as portrayed in *An Angel at My Table*. Another controversial film biography, *Frances* (1982), depicts the 1930s Hollywood actress Frances Farmer and her confinement in mental institutions for rebellious behavior. *Frances*, played by Jessica Lange, received both shock treatment and a lobotomy.

In *A Beautiful Mind* (2001), John Nash receives **Insulin Shock Therapy** and not ECT, although many viewers don't make this distinction. When insulin shock therapy is used, insulin is injected, the body goes into a state of shock and convulsions ensue. *A Beautiful Mind* shows Nash receiving multiple treatments over several weeks.

Treatment of Anxiety Disorders

There are numerous approaches to the treatment of anxiety, and all of them are at least partially efficacious. Education can be a critical first step in therapy, and it is often tremendously therapeutic for the patient with an anxiety disorder simply to realize that he or she is not going insane and that these disorders are commonplace and almost always respond to treatment. In addition, patients need to realize that their symptoms are not life-threatening, that they will not pass out or fall down no matter how bad they feel, and that many people experience similar symptoms but assign different labels (**attributions**) to these sensations (e.g., a tingling sensation in your stomach before you give a speech can be interpreted as anticipatory excitement and a signal that you're going to do a good job).

It is also critical to assess carefully a patient's prior use of alcohol or drugs as ways of coping with his or her anxiety symptoms. Many of these patients have learned to use substances to modulate their anxiety levels: for example, alcoholism is common in veterans with post-traumatic stress disorders (as portrayed in *Born on the Fourth of July*). In addition, it is necessary to assess the consumption of coffee, soft drinks, and nicotine. All three exacerbate the symptoms of anxiety.

Psychotherapy may be helpful with some patients with anxiety. In particular, behavior therapy is the treatment of choice for many phobic disorders, and some patients have been helped by behavioral methods after years of insight therapy. Almost all behavior therapies will involve exposure to the feared stimulus or situation. *In vivo* **exposure with response prevention** is an empirically-validated approach (and the treatment of choice for OCD and other anxiety disorders) involving a graduated exposure hierarchy of anxiety arousing stimuli. The patient is prevented from avoiding the stimulus and must use anxiety-reducing coping skills instead. **Flooding** and **implosion** are related techniques that involve massive exposure to the feared stimuli. Mindfulness, relaxation training, and hypnosis may also be used as adjunctive therapies in the treatment of anxiety.

Movies themselves can be powerful stimuli when developing an **exposure hierarchy** for a person with an anxiety disorder. Particular movies can be tailored to the individual's fears, obsessions, and dysfunctional belief patterns. The individual will typically be asked to watch a film or a particular scene (often repeatedly) while practicing anxiety management techniques. For example, a person with a contamination fear of dirt might be asked to watch a war film where dirt, dust, and blood are prominent, such as *Saving Private Ryan* (1998), and the individual will be trained to use coping skills to manage their anxiety as it rises during parts of the film. The individual who is homophobic and afraid of contamination with the AIDS virus might be asked to watch *Kissing Jessica Stein* (2002) and *The Birdcage* (1995), and those afraid of getting in an accident or seeing an accident could watch action films containing multiple crashes as in the *Lethal Weapon* series (1987-1998). Some other potential films that could be used for desensitization purposes include *Cast Away* (2000), *Philadelphia* (1993), and *Super Size Me* (2004) for fear of, respectively, isolation, contamination and throwing up in public. Children or adolescents afraid of being rejected might be asked to watch *A Bug's Life* (1998), *Shrek* (2001), or *Hercules* (1997), and those afraid of the dark might watch particular scenes from *Harry Potter and the Sorcerer's Stone* (2001). These uses of films in therapy are explored further in Wedding and Niemiec (2003).

Cognitive therapy which includes the practice of **cognitive restructuring** is often employed in the treatment of anxiety disorders. Cognitive therapy helps patients identify and understand the internal statements and irrational thoughts that may trigger arousal in certain situations and settings (Beck & Emery, 1985). Medication may also be used as a treatment or, more commonly, as an adjunct to therapy. Widely used classes of drugs include **beta-blockers** (often used to treat social phobias, panic disorder and agoraphobia) and **selective serotonin reuptake inhibitors** (SSRIs) (for OCD and comorbid depression issues). **Benzodiazepines** are also widely used in the treatment of anxiety symptoms, and include lorazepam (Ativan), and alprazolam (Xanax). It is interesting to note that the human brain has been shown to have specific receptor sites for benzodiazepine molecules. In addition, there is growing interest in the use of over-the-counter herbal remedies such as **Kava** (available from health food stores) and **Valerian Root** in the treatment of mild to moderate anxiety.

Treatment of Mood Disorders

Lithium carbonate is often the treatment of choice for the bipolar disorders. This agent is a naturally occurring element that has been found to be effective in correcting the chemical imbalance associated with this illness. No one is sure how or why lithium works, but it is believed that it either alters neurotransmitters or inhibits viruses that affect DNA. If lithium carbonate is not effective, other mood stabilizers can be used (e.g., **Depakote**).

Cognitive-Behavioral Therapy (CBT), which addresses the defective thinking process, is particularly helpful for patients with depression. This approach to psychotherapy forces the patient to examine the evidence for his or her negative beliefs, and the therapist encourages patients to reframe their beliefs based on the evidence presented in therapy. Once beliefs change, patients begin to perceive the world in a more balanced way, which has an impact on future behaviors. This technique has been very successful and is generally believed to be as efficacious as antidepressants in the treatment of mild to moderate depression.

Treatment of Alcoholism

The first stage of treatment is **detoxification**, or "drying out." This process can vary from several days to a month in duration and is usually extremely unpleasant for the person involved. Vitamins are routinely prescribed in the treatment of addictions. Benzodiazepines (primarily Librium and Valium) were often administered to help an individual cope with the physiological distress that accompanies detoxification; however, this approach to treatment has always been controversial and is less common now.

"The last time I seen my father, he was blind and diseased from drinking. And every time he put the bottle to his mouth, he don't suck out of it, it sucks out of him until he shrunk so wrinkled and yellow even the dogs didn't know him."

Chief Bromden describes his father's alcoholism in One Flew Over the Cuckoo's Nest

---

Antabuse (disulfiram) blocks the metabolism of alcohol and may help some alcoholics avoid resumption of drinking after detoxification. An individual taking Antibuse will become violently ill if exposed to even a very small amount of alcohol and will experience nausea, vomiting, sweating, and accelerated respiration and heart rate. Antibuse is most useful in the first months of sobriety, when the craving for alcohol is most intense.

Alcoholics Anonymous, a self-help fellowship founded in 1935, is widely regarded as an important part of treatment for most alcoholics. More than a million people in the United States belong to this self-help group, and there are more than 1.5 million members worldwide. Almost every town of any size has a local chapter of Alcoholics Anonymous, and many large cities have meetings in different chapters every evening of the week. These meetings involve self-disclosure, social support, and a commitment to the disease model of alcoholism. The well-known 12 Steps of Alcoholics Anonymous are presented in Table 7.3 of Chapter 7. The founding of Alcoholics Anonymous is described in the film *My Name Is Bill W.* (1989), and the movie *Drunks* (1995) offers an opportunity to see a realistic presentation of how an AA meeting is conducted.

Al-Anon is a related group for families and friends of alcoholics. The program is modeled on Alcoholics Anonymous and uses a 12-step model. **Alateen** is a similar affiliated group designed to serve teenage children of alcoholic parents.

Although most providers in the substance abuse community are quick to praise the good work done by Alcoholics Anonymous, there is surprisingly little empirical evidence supporting the program. In addition, some individuals find the quasi-religious philosophy of the organization distasteful.

Treatment of Drug Addiction

Before treatment can begin, **detoxification** must occur. In general, the severity of detoxification from narcotic drugs depends on the health status of the addict and the purity of the drugs he or she has been taking. Withdrawal from barbiturates tends to be more serious than withdrawal from heroin, cocaine, or alcohol. Detoxification is potentially life threatening and should occur in a structured, medical setting. The film *Quitting* (2001) depicts the challenges and pain of detoxifying outside of a structured, hospital environment. Anxiolytics such as Xanax, Ativan and Librium are sometimes used to reduce the severity of the effects of detoxification.

Methadone is a synthetic narcotic that is taken orally rather than injected. It is administered on a daily basis, usually in an outpatient setting. The drug itself is addicting; however, it is longer lasting, and with daily use the addict is able to avoid the symptoms of withdrawal that typically occur a few hours after use of drugs such as heroin. In addition, the drug blocks the reinforcing effects of other narcotics. With methadone treatment, there is a reduction in intravenous drug use and a concomitant reduction in crime. In addition, the likelihood of needle sharing and AIDS is dramatically reduced. Despite these benefits, methadone maintenance programs remain controversial, and there are some clear disadvantages to methadone maintenance therapy, including the development of a large underground market for methadone, the fact that many people drop out of methadone treatment because of side effects (sweating, impotence, constipation, and insomnia), and the fact that many people are philosophically offended by the idea of giving addicts another addicting drug in the name of treatment.

Some programs have used **narcotic antagonists** such as **Naloxone** or **naltrexone** to treat opioid addiction. These drugs block the reinforcing effects of narcotics; in effect, the addict may still take drugs but they no longer produce a "high." However, because of the potential for precipitating withdrawal reactions, these programs are complex and costly and require medical supervision.

Programs such as **Narcotics Anonymous** (NA), modeled after Alcoholics Anonymous, advocate total abstinence from drugs. These programs are often associated with therapeutic communities in which a highly structured program and frequent group therapy are core components of treatment. Former addicts who serve as powerful role models for residents often staff these programs. Therapy is often confrontational and may involve spouses and significant others. The film *Clean and Sober* (1988) presents an excellent example of the kind of treatment that occurs in a **therapeutic community**, with Morgan Freeman in the role of a recovered addict and counselor.

Antidepressant medications are sometimes used to assist in the treatment of amphetamine or cocaine addiction. However, in general all treatment programs for stimulant addiction have unimpressive success records.

The success of smoking cessation programs has been more notable. Nicotine gum, transdermal nicotine patches and some antidepressants hold considerable promise as important aids in comprehensive treatment packages. Behavior modification and hypnosis are two other techniques that have helped many individuals overcome their addiction to nicotine.

Despite the success of some treatment programs, it is clear that the only real solution to the drug problem is prevention. Prevention will involve limiting the flow of drugs to the United States and educating the public about the deleterious effects of drug use.

Ethical Issues and the Right to Humane Treatment

Films such as *One Flew over the Cuckoo's Nest* attempt to show the human injustices that once existed and occasionally are still found in the mental health system. In this film, once McMurphy moved from the prison system into the mental health system, he lost almost all civil rights, including his right to refuse treatment. The issues addressed by the film are not the usual problems faced by large institutions such as inadequate facilities, problems maintaining cleanliness, too few staff, or organizational communication. Instead, the film addresses fundamental issues of autonomy and paternalism. The treatment team has ultimate control over McMurphy's treatment and discharge. A rigid, overly controlled nurse engages in an ongoing power struggle with a patient whom she perceives as a threat to her control of the unit. She uses her position and knowledge of the system to gain control over McMurphy. McMurphy's **lobotomy** is the ultimate abuse of psychiatric power.

One Flew over the Cuckoo's Nest was not the first movie to portray patients' lack of control over treatment. One of the first movies to address mental illness seriously was *The Snake Pit* (1948), a film directed by Anatole Litvak that starred Olivia de Havilland. The movie portrays a woman trying to overcome her illness in a crowded mental institution. The horrifying conditions portrayed in the film actually mobilized state legislators to improve the level of care provided in institutions. This movie was especially effective in portraying the lack of power females have traditionally had in inpatient psychiatric settings. In *The Snake Pit*, Virginia truly has a mental illness and is taken for treatment by a caring husband. However, many women who did not have mental illnesses were placed in psychiatric hospitals and kept there as a convenience for husbands who had grown tired of them (Geller & Harris, 1994).

A more recent film, *Chattahoochee* (1990), not only depicts the horrible conditions in a Florida state hospital during the 1950s but also one patient's campaign to change these conditions. In this film, Korean War veteran Gary Oldham (played by Emmett Foley) loses many of his rights because of his protests against authority. This film, based on a true story, begins when Gary Oldham becomes depressed by unemployment and tries to provoke the police into killing him after he shoots up the neighborhood. He wants his wife to receive the life insurance she would be denied if he committed suicide. Instead, he is sent to Chattahoochee, a prison for people with mental illness. The conditions in Chattahoochee are deplorable. With the support of a friend (played by Dennis Hopper), he begins a letter-writing campaign to protest the conditions. When his writing privileges are taken away, he starts writing in a Bible and surreptitiously slipping pages to his sister. A state commission is formed, hearings are held, and conditions improve as a result.

Movies illustrate the ongoing struggles for civil and human rights that have occurred in the mental health system. They also reflect the prevailing stigma toward persons with mental illness. Our language characterizes individuals with these illnesses as crazy, nuts, or wacky. The people who treat them are called shrinks, do-gooders, or bleeding hearts (Trachtenberg, 1986). The media portray patients as clowns, buffoons, or harmless eccentrics (Hyler, Gabbard, & Schneider, 1991). In *The Dream Team* (1989) and *The Couch Trip* (1988), a little bit of freedom proves adequate to cure mental illness. Other films, such as the *Psycho* (1960-1990) series, depict individuals with mental illnesses as homicidal maniacs. In John Carpenter's *Halloween* series (1978–1998), an escaped psychiatric patient serially kills teenagers who have engaged in sexual experimentation. When Tommy Lee Wallace directed *Halloween III* (1982), the central villain was portrayed as a madman toy maker who made wicked Halloween masks programmed to harm children. However, the original madman on the loose from a mental hospital returned in *Halloween IV* and *V* (1988, 1989). These films and others have misled the public about the dangerousness of psychiatric patients.

Critical Thinking Questions

- Why do films continue to perpetrate psychotherapy misconceptions such as "only psychiatrists practice psychotherapy" and "the most common type of treatment for mental disorders is psychoanalysis?"

- How common is it for a mental health professional to commit a boundary violation? Why is this so frequently depicted in movies?
- What psychotherapy techniques and interventions are rarely portrayed?
- What diagnostic categories are given the most accurate and realistic treatment approach in movies?
- It has been suggested that on a college campus, the only thing separating harmless eccentricity from mental illness is tenure. How does one's environment shape expectations about what is or is not appropriate behavior?
- Vincent van Gogh was a genius, but he was also mentally ill, and his life was tragically cut short by suicide. Would the world be better off if this illness had been diagnosed and treated? Would you take the same position if you knew psychotropic medication would rob van Gogh of his creative spirit and his passion for art?
- Is it ever ethical to treat someone who refuses treatment? If so, who should be empowered to make these decisions?
- There is a clear asymmetry of power and knowledge when doctors meet with family members to discuss treatment options. How does this fact influence the principles of informed consent and patient autonomy?
- Do you think it is ethical to offer early release to prisoners who have committed sexual offenses if they allow themselves to be castrated? What if they simply agree to take medications that eliminate all sexual drive? Are the courts ever justified in mandating treatments of this sort?
- What can mental health professionals (or the public) do to change the stereotypes and misconceptions often perpetrated in films?

Appendix A

The American Film Institute's
100 Best of 100 Years[1]

1. *Citizen Kane* (1941)
2. *Casablanca* (1942)
3. *Godfather, The* (1972)
4. *Gone With the Wind* (1939)
5. *Lawrence of Arabia* (1962)
6. *Wizard of Oz, The* (1939)
7. *Graduate, The* (1967)
8. *On the Waterfront* (1954)
9. *Schindler's List* (1993)
10. *Singin' In the Rain* (1952)
11. *It's A Wonderful Life* (1946)
12. *Sunset Boulevard* (1950)
13. *Bridge On the River Kwai, The* (1957)
14. *Some Like It Hot* (1959)
15. *Star Wars* (1977)
16. *All About Eve* (1950)
17. *African Queen, The* (1951)
18. *Psycho* (1960)
19. *Chinatown* (1974)
20. *One Flew Over the Cuckoo's Nest* (1975)
21. *Grapes of Wrath, The* (1940)
22. *2001: A Space Odyssey* (1968)
23. *Maltese Falcon, The* (1941)
24. *Raging Bull* (1980)
25. *E.T. the Extra-Terrestrial* (1982)
26. *Dr. Strangelove* (1964)
27. *Bonnie & Clyde* (1967)
28. *Apocalypse Now* (1979)
29. *Mr. Smith Goes to Washington* (1939)
30. *Treasure of the Sierra Madre, The* (1948)
31. *Annie Hall* (1977)
32. *Godfather Part II, The* (1974)
33. *High Noon* (1952)
34. *To Kill a Mockingbird* (1962)
35. *It Happened One Night* (1934)
36. *Midnight Cowboy* (1969)
37. *Best Years of Our Lives, The* (1946)
38. *Double Indemnity* (1944)
39. *Doctor Zhivago* (1965)
40. *North by Northwest* (1959)
41. *West Side Story* (1961)
42. *Rear Window* (1954)
43. *King Kong* (1933)
44. *Birth of a Nation, The* (1915)
45. *Streetcar Named Desire, A* (1951)
46. *Clockwork Orange, A* (1971)
47. *Taxi Driver* (1976)
48. *Jaws* (1975)
49. *Snow White & the Seven Dwarfs* (1937)
50. *Butch Cassidy & the Sundance Kid* (1969)
51. *Philadelphia Story, The* (1940)
52. *From Here to Eternity* (1953)
53. *Amadeus* (1984)
54. *All Quiet on the Western Front* (1930)
55. *Sound of Music, The* (1965)
56. *M*A*S*H* (1970)
57. *Third Man, The* (1949)
58. *Fantasia* (1940)
59. *Rebel Without a Cause* (1955)
60. *Raiders of the Lost Ark* (1981)
61. *Vertigo* (1958)
62. *Tootsie* (1982)
63. *Stagecoach* (1939)
64. *Close Encounters of the Third Kind* (1977)
65. *Silence of the Lambs, The* (1991)
66. *Network* (1976)
67. *Manchurian Candidate, The* (1962)
68. *American in Paris, An* (1951)
69. *Shane* (1953)
70. *French Connection, The* (1971)
71. *Forrest Gump* (1994)
72. *Ben-Hur* (1959)
73. *Wuthering Heights* (1939)
74. *Gold Rush, The* (1925)
75. *Dances With Wolves* (1990)
76. *City Lights* (1931)
77. *American Graffiti* (1973)
78. *Rocky* (1976)
79. *Deer Hunter, The* (1978)
80. *Wild Bunch, The* (1969)
81. *Modern Times* (1936)
82. *Giant* (1956)
83. *Platoon* (1986)
84. *Fargo* (1996)
85. *Duck Soup* (1933)
86. *Mutiny on the Bounty* (1935)
87. *Frankenstein* (1931)
88. *Easy Rider* (1969)
89. *Patton* (1970)
90. *Jazz Singer, The* (1927)
91. *My Fair Lady* (1964)
92. *Place in the Sun, A* (1951)
93. *Apartment, The* (1960)
94. *Goodfellas* (1990)
95. *Pulp Fiction* (1994)
96. *Searchers, The* (1956)
97. *Bringing Up Baby* (1938)
98. *Unforgiven* (1992)
99. *Guess Who's Coming to Dinner* (1967)
100. *Yankee Doodle Dandy* (1941)

The American Film Institute's Top 50 Heroes and Villains[1]

Heroes

1. **Atticus Finch**
    To Kill a Mockingbird
2. **Indiana Jones**
    Raiders of the Lost Ark
3. **James Bond**
    Dr. No
4. **Rick Blaine**
    Casablanca
5. **Will Kane**
    High Noon
6. **Clarice Starling**
    The Silence of the Lambs
7. **Rocky Balboa**
    Rocky
8. **Ellen Ripley**
    Aliens
9. **George Bailey**
    It's a Wonderful Life
10. **T. E. Lawrence**
    Lawrence of Arabia
11. **Jefferson Smith**
    Mr. Smith Goes to Washington
12. **Tom Joad**
    The Grapes of Wrath
13. **Oskar Schindler**
    Schindler's List
14. **Han Solo**
    Star Wars
15. **Norma Rae Webster**
    Norma Rae
16. **Shane**
    Shane
17. **Harry Callahan**
    Dirty Harry
18. **Robin Hood**
    The Adventures of Robin Hood
19. **Virgil Tibbs**
    In The Heat of the Night
20. **Butch Cassidy & the Sundance Kid**
    Butch Cassidy & the Sundance Kid
21. **Mahatma Gandhi**
    Gandhi
22. **Spartacus**
    Spartacus
23. **Terry Malloy**
    On the Waterfront

Villains

1. **Dr. Hannibal Lecter**
    The Silence of the Lambs
2. **Norman Bates**
    Psycho
3. **Darth Vader**
    The Empire Strikes Back
4. **The Wicked Witch of the West**
    The Wizard of Oz
5. **Nurse Ratched**
    One Flew Over the Cuckoo's Nest
6. **Mr. Potter**
    It's a Wonderful Life
7. **Alex Forrest**
    Fatal Attraction
8. **Phyllis Dietrichson**
    Double Indemnity
9. **Regan MacNeil**
    The Exorcist
10. **The Queen**
    Snow White and the Seven Dwarfs
11. **Michael Corleone**
    The Godfather: Part II
12. **Alex De Large**
    Clockwork Orange
13. **HAL 9000**
    2001: A Space Odyssey
14. **The Alien**
    Alien
15. **Amon Goeth**
    Schindler's List
16. **Noah Cross**
    Chinatown
17. **Annie Wilkes**
    Misery
18. **The Shark**
    Jaws
19. **Captain Bligh**
    Mutiny on the Bounty
20. **Man**
    Bambi
21. **Mrs. John Iselin**
    The Manchurian Candidate
22. **Terminator**
    The Terminator
23. **Eve Harrington**
    All About Eve

24. **Thelma Dickerson & Louise Sawyer**
    Thelma & Louise
25. **Lou Gehrig**
    The Pride of the Yankees
26. **Superman**
    Superman
27. **Bob Woodward & Carl Bernstein**
    All The President's Men
28. **Juror #8**
    12 Angry Men
29. **General George Patton**
    Patton
30. **Luke Jackson**
    Cool Hand Luke
31. **Erin Brockovich**
    Erin Brockovich
32. **Philip Marlowe**
    The Big Sleep
33. **Marge Gunderson**
    Fargo
34. **Tarzan**
    Tarzan the Ape Man
35. **Alvin York**
    Sergeant York
36. **Rooster Cogburn**
    True Grit
37. **Obi-Wan Kenobi**
    Star Wars
38. **The Tramp**
    City Lights
39. **Lassie**
    Lassie Come Home
40. **Frank Serpico**
    Serpico
41. **Arthur Chipping**
    Goodbye, Mr. Chips
42. **Father Edward**
    Boys Town
43. **Moses**
    The Ten Commandments
44. **Jimmy "Popeye" Doyle**
    The French Connection
45. **Zorro**
    The Mark of Zorro
46. **Batman**
    Batman
47. **Karen Silkwood**
    Silkwood
48. **Terminator**
    Terminator 2: Judgment Day
49. **Andrew Beckett**
    Philadelphia
50. **General Maximus Decimus Meridus**
    Gladiator

24. **Gordon Gekko**
    Wall Street
25. **Jack Torrance**
    The Shining
26. **Cody Jarrett**
    White Heat
27. **Martians**
    The War of the Worlds
28. **Max Cady**
    Cape Fear
29. **Reverend Harry Powell**
    The Night of the Hunter
30. **Travis Bickle**
    Taxi Driver
31. **Mrs. Danvers**
    Rebecca
32. **Clyde Barrow & Bonnie Parker**
    Bonnie and Clyde
33. **Count Dracula**
    Dracula
34. **Dr. Szell**
    Marathon Man
35. **J.J. Hunsecker**
    Sweet Smell of Success
36. **Frank Booth**
    Blue Velvet
37. **Harry Lime**
    The Third Man
38. **Caesar Enrico Bandello**
    Little Caesar
39. **Cruella De Vil**
    One Hundred and One Dalmatians
40. **Freddy Krueger**
    A Nightmare on Elm Street
41. **Joan Crawford**
    Mommie Dearest
42. **Tom Powers**
    The Public Enemy
43. **Regina Giddens**
    The Little Foxes
44. **Baby Jane Hudson**
    Whatever Happened to Baby Jane
45. **The Joker**
    Batman
46. **Hans Gruber**
    Die Hard
47. **Tony Montana**
    Scarface
48. **Verbal Kint**
    The Usual Suspects
49. **Auric Goldfinger**
    Goldfinger
50. **Alonzo Harris**
    Training Day

---

[1]Reprinted with permission of the American Film Institute. http://www.afi.com/tvevents/100years/handv.aspx

Appendix C

Internet Movie Database (IMDb) Top 250 Movies[2]

1.	*Godfather, The* (1972)
2.	*Lord of the Rings: Return of the King, The* (2003)
3.	*Shawshank Redemption, The* (1994)
4.	*Godfather: Part II, The* (1974)
5.	*Seven Samurai* (1954)
6.	*Schindler's List* (1993)
7.	*Casablanca* (1942)
8.	*Lord of the Rings: Fellowship of the Ring, The* (2001)
9.	*Lord of the Rings: Two Towers, The* (2002)
10.	*Star Wars* (1977)
11.	*Citizen Kane* (1941)
12.	*One Flew Over the Cuckoo's Nest* (1975)
13.	*Star Wars: Episode V - The Empire Strikes Back* (1980)
14.	*Pulp Fiction* (1994)
15.	*Rear Window* (1954)
16.	*Dr. Strangelove or: How I Learned to Stop Worrying and Love the Bomb* (1964)
17.	*Raiders of the Lost Ark* (1981)
18.	*Usual Suspects, The* (1995)
19.	*Memento* (2000)
20.	*The Good, the Bad and the Ugly* (1966)
21.	*12 Angry Men* (1957)
22.	*North by Northwest* (1959)
23.	*City of God* (2002)
24.	*Lawrence of Arabia* (1962)
25.	*Psycho* (1960)
26.	*It's a Wonderful Life* (1946)
27.	*Amelie* (2001)
28.	*Silence of the Lambs, The* (1991)
29.	*Goodfellas* (1990)
30.	*Once Upon a Time in the West* (1968)
31.	*Sunset Blvd.* (1950)
32.	*American Beauty* (1999)
33.	*Vertigo* (1958)
34.	*Matrix, The* (1999)
35.	*Apocalypse Now* (1979)
36.	*To Kill a Mockingbird* (1962)
37.	*Eternal Sunshine of the Spotless Mind* (2004)
38.	*Pianist, The* (2002)
39.	*Third Man, The* (1949)
40.	*Fight Club* (1999)
41.	*Paths of Glory* (1957)
42.	*Spirited Away* (2001)
43.	*Taxi Driver* (1976)
44.	*Some Like it Hot* (1959)
45.	*Double Indemnity* (1944)
46.	*Singin' in the Rain* (1952)
47.	*The Boat* (1981)
48.	*Chinatown* (1974)
49.	*M* (1931)
50.	*L.A. Confidential* (1997)
51.	*Maltese Falcon, The* (1941)
52.	*Se7en* (1995)
53.	*All About Eve* (1950)
54.	*Requiem for a Dream* (2000)
55.	*Bridge on the River Kwai, The* (1957)
56.	*Kill Bill: Vol. 1* (2003)
57.	*Rashômon* (1950)
58.	*Monty Python and the Holy Grail* (1975)
59.	*Saving Private Ryan* (1998)
60.	*Raging Bull* (1980)
61.	*Alien* (1979)
62.	*American History X* (1998)
63.	*Léon* (1994)
64.	*Wizard of Oz, The* (1939)
65.	*Manchurian Candidate, The* (1962)
66.	*Mr. Smith Goes to Washington* (1939)
67.	*Sting, The* (1973)
68.	*Treasure of the Sierra Madre, The* (1948)
69.	*Modern Times* (1936)
70.	*Life Is Beautiful* (1997)
71.	*Reservoir Dogs* (1992)
72.	*Touch of Evil* (1958)
73.	*2001: A Space Odyssey* (1968)
74.	*Clockwork Orange, A* (1971)
75.	*On the Waterfront* (1954)
76.	*Ran* (1985)
77.	*Amadeus* (1984)
78.	*Great Escape, The* (1963)
79.	*Finding Nemo* (2003)
80.	*Apartment, The* (1960)
81.	*Annie Hall* (1977)
82.	*Jaws* (1975)
83.	*Metropolis* (1927)
84.	*Aliens* (1986)
85.	*High Noon* (1952)
86.	*Braveheart* (1995)
87.	*Crouching Tiger, Hidden Dragon* (2000)
88.	*City Lights* (1931)

89. *Shining, The* (1980)
90. *Fargo* (1996)
91. *Donnie Darko* (2001)
92. *Strangers on a Train* (1951)
93. *The Seventh Seal* (1957)
94. *General, The* (1927)
95. *Blade Runner* (1982)
96. *Cinema Paradiso* (1989)
97. *Great Dictator, The* (1940)
98. *Sixth Sense, The* (1999)
99. *Princess Mononoke* (1997)
100. *Duck Soup* (1933)
101. *The Bicycle Thief* (1948)
102. *Best Years of Our Lives, The* (1946)
103. *Full Metal Jacket* (1987)
104. *Yojimbo* (1961)
105. *Princess Bride, The* (1987)
106. *Big Sleep, The* (1946)
107. *Rebecca* (1940)
108. *Notorious* (1946)
109. *Kill Bill: Vol. 2* (2004)
110. *Terminator 2: Judgment Day* (1991)
111. *Forrest Gump* (1994)
112. *Butch Cassidy and the Sundance Kid* (1969)
113. *Run Lola Run* (1998)
114. *Patton* (1970)
115. *It Happened One Night* (1934)
116. *Toy Story 2* (1999)
117. *Graduate, The* (1967)
118. *Deer Hunter, The* (1978)
119. *Hero* (2002)
120. *Once Upon a Time in America* (1984)
121. *Cool Hand Luke* (1967)
122. *Glory* (1989)
123. *Unforgiven* (1992)
124. *Manhattan* (1979)
125. *Philadelphia Story, The* (1940)
126. *Star Wars: Episode VI - Return of the Jedi* (1983)
127. *Mystic River* (2003)
128. *Ben-Hur* (1959)
129. *Elephant Man, The* (1980)
130. *African Queen, The* (1951)
131. *Searchers, The* (1956)
132. *Green Mile, The* (1999)
133. *Talk to Her* (2002)
134. *Bringing Up Baby* (1938)
135. *Dogville* (2003)
136. *Stalag 17* (1953)
137. *Wild Strawberries* (1957)
138. *Grapes of Wrath, The* (1940)
139. *Amores perros* (2000)
140. *Back to the Future* (1985)
141. *Indiana Jones and the Last Crusade* (1989)
142. *Shrek* (2001)

143. *Night of the Hunter, The* (1955)
144. *Platoon* (1986)
145. *Hustler, The* (1961)
146. *Gone with the Wind* (1939)
147. *Gold Rush, The* (1925)
148. *Christmas Story, A* (1983)
149. *Straight Story, The* (1999)
150. *Wild Bunch, The* (1969)
151. *Arsenic and Old Lace* (1944)
152. *All Quiet on the Western Front* (1930)
153. *Battleship Potemkin* (1925)
154. *Lost in Translation* (2003)
155. *Big Fish* (2003)
156. *His Girl Friday* (1940)
157. *Young Frankenstein* (1974)
158. *Die Hard* (1988)
159. *The 400 Blows* (1959)
160. *Adventures of Robin Hood, The* (1938)
161. *Life of Brian* (1979)
162. *The Grand Illusion* (1937)
163. *Man Who Shot Liberty Valance, The* (1962)
164. *Witness for the Prosecution* (1957)
165. *Monsters, Inc.* (2001)
166. *Spartacus* (1960)
167. *Grave of the Fireflies* (1988)
168. *Gladiator* (2000)
169. *The Celebration* (1998)
170. *Roman Holiday* (1953)
171. *Day the Earth Stood Still, The* (1951)
172. *Sling Blade* (1996)
173. *Ed Wood* (1994)
174. *Magnolia* (1999)
175. *Ikiru* (1952)
176. *Conversation, The* (1974)
177. *Charade* (1963)
178. *Garden State* (2004)
179. *Killing, The* (1956)
180. *Streetcar Named Desire, A* (1951)
181. *Toy Story* (1995)
182. *To Be or Not to Be* (1942)
183. *All the President's* Men (1976)
184. *Brazil* (1985)
185. *Almost Famous* (2000)
186. *Three Colors: Red* (1994)
187. *Night at the Opera, A* (1935)
188. *Nosferatu the Vampire* (1922)
189. *Insider, The* (1999)
190. *In America* (2002)
191. *Shadow of a Doubt* (1943)
192. *Who's Afraid of Virginia Woolf?* (1966)
193. *Gandhi* (1982)
194. *21 Grams* (2003)
195. *Pirates of the Caribbean: The Curse of the Black Pearl* (2003)
196. *Dog Day Afternoon* (1975)

197. *Twelve Monkeys* (1995)
198. *Harvey* (1950)
199. *Exorcist, The* (1973)
200. *Oldboy* (2003)
201. *Groundhog Day* (1993)
202. *Stand by Me* (1986)
203. *Trainspotting* (1996)
204. *The Passion of Joan of Arc* (1928)
205. *Terminator, The* (1984)
206. *Being John Malkovich* (1999)
207. *Mulholland Dr.* (2001)
208. *Sunrise: A Song of Two Humans* (1927)
209. *The Road* (1954)
210. *Miller's Crossing* (1990)
211. *Lion in Winter, The* (1968)
212. *Laura* (1944)
213. *Before Sunset* (2004)
214. *This Is Spinal Tap* (1984)
215. *Network* (1976)
216. *8½* (1963)
217. *Right Stuff, The* (1983)
218. *Rain Man* (1988)
219. *King Kong* (1933)
220. *Station Agent, The* (2003)
221. *Snatch* (2000)
222. *39 Steps, The* (1935)
223. *Big Lebowski, The* (1998)
224. *Midnight Cowboy* (1969)
225. *Bonnie and Clyde* (1967)
226. *Lock, Stock and Two Smoking Barrels* (1998)
227. *Whale Rider* (2002)
228. *Stagecoach* (1939)
229. *Adaptation* (2002)
230. *Rio Bravo* (1959)
231. *Thin Man, The* (1934)
232. *Persona* (1966)
233. *Untouchables, The* (1987)
234. *In the Heat of the Night* (1967)
235. *Sullivan's Travels* (1941)
236. *Bride of Frankenstein* (1935)
237. *Planet of the Apes* (1968)
238. *Judgment at Nuremberg* (1961)
239. *X2* (2003)
240. *Children of Paradise* (1945)
241. *Fanny and Alexander* (1982)
242. *Being There* (1979)
243. *Others, The* (2001)
244. *Kind Hearts and Coronets* (1949)
245. *The Killer* (1989)
246. *Last Samurai, The* (2003)
247. *Heat* (1995)
248. *In the Mood for Love* (2000)
249. *Barry Lyndon* (1975)
250. *Sleuth* (1972)

---

[2]Information courtesy of The Internet Movie Database (http://www.imdb.com). Used with permission.

Appendix D

Recommended Websites

Internet Movie Data Base (the largest movie database)
www.imdb.com

Movie Review Query Engine (over 42,000 movie titles; over 420,000 reviews)
www.mrqe.com

American Film Institute
www.afi.com

Independent Movie Resources
www.indiewire.com

Comprehensive movies lists, awards, and resources
www.filmsite.org

Rotten Tomatoes (movie database)
www.rottentomatoes.com

Danny Wedding's Home Page (filmography link)
www.mimh.edu/danny_wedding

Film Listing by Health Topics
http://webcampus.med.drexel.edu/whep/womenshealth.htm

Psychiatrist, Roland Atkinson on Film
www.atkinsononfilm.com or www.psychflix.com

Susan Nicosia: Movies and Mental Illness: Psychology, Psychiatry and the Movies
http://faculty.dwc.edu/nicosia/moviesandmentalillnessfilmography.htm

Hollywood Entertainment Corporation
www.reel.com

Movie Monologue Page (Quotes)
www.whysanity.net/monos/

Internet Movie Network
www.movieweb.com

Movie reviews, updates, news
www.moviefreak.com

Appendix E

Common Misconceptions About Mental Illness Perpetuated by Movies

Misconception	Film Examples
Love alone conquers mental illness	*Wilbur Wants to Kill Himself;* *Matchstick Men;* *Benny & Joon*
People with mental illness are violent	*Nightmare on Elm Street*
Parents cause schizophrenia, autism, etc. (the myth of the schizophrenogenic parent)	*Clean, Shaven;* *Shine*
All mental illness has a traumatic etiology	*The Fisher King;* *The Snake Pit;* *The Three Faces of Eve;* *K-Pax;* *Nurse Betty*
Schizophrenia is the same as Dissociative Identity Disorder, Gender Identity Disorder, etc.	*Me, Myself, and Irene;* *Dressed to Kill*
People in psychiatric hospitals are merely eccentric, not sick (society is suppressing them)	*One Flew Over the Cuckoo's Nest;* *King of Hearts;* *House of Fools*
Psychiatric treatment (e.g., ECT, medications) blocks creativity and intelligence	*A Beautiful Mind*
It is liberating to discontinue psychiatric treatment at one's will (e.g., medications)	*Garden State*

Appendix F

Portrayals of Psychotherapists in Movies

Balanced Portrayals

Antwone Fisher (2003)
Manic (2003)
Identity (2003)
Elling (2002)
Hollywood Ending (2002)
K-Pax (2001)
Gothika (2004)
The Sixth Sense (1999)
Girl, Interrupted (1999)
Good Will Hunting (1997)
Don Juan DeMarco (1994)
Ordinary People (1980)
Equus (1977)
Psycho (1960)

Unbalanced Portrayals

Wilbur Wants to Kill Himself (2002)
Normal (2004)
Anything Else (2003)
Vanilla Sky (2001)
I Am Sam (2001)
Analyze This (1998)
Bliss (1997)
Mr. Jones (1993)
Final Analysis (1992)
The Prince of Tides (1991)
The Silence of the Lambs (1991)
What About Bob? (1991)
High Anxiety (1977)
One Flew Over the Cuckoo's Nest (1975)

See Niemiec & Wedding (2005) for more details.

Appendix G

Films Illustrating Psychopathology

Key to Ratings

Ψ   Description provided for your information only; don't bother with the film
ΨΨ   Mildly interesting and somewhat educational; probably worth your time
ΨΨΨ   A good film relevant to your education as a mental health professional
ΨΨΨΨ   Highly recommended both as art and as professional education
ΨΨΨΨΨ   A must-see film that combines artistry with psychological relevance

---

Anxiety Disorders

Adaptation (2002) Comedy/Action ΨΨΨΨ
Multi-layered Spike Jonze film in which Nicholas Cage plays twin brothers, one of whom is a neurotic screenwriter struggling to write a story based on a book about orchids.

Analyze That (2002) Comedy/Action ΨΨ
The follow-up film to *Analyze This*, in which a panic-disordered mob boss (De Niro) malingers to get released from prison, tries to maintain an ordinary job, and is convinced to return while stringing along his psychiatrist (Crystal).

Analyze This (1999) Comedy/Action ΨΨ
The original Billy Crystal/Robert De Niro comedy where Deniro plays the lead thug in a New York mafia group who develops panic attacks. De Niro sees a psychiatrist (Billy Crystal) for treatment.

Arachnophobia (1990) Comedy/Horror ΨΨ
A story about a doctor with a paralyzing fear of spiders. (Actually, the spiders in this film are pretty intimidating, and fear appears to be a perfectly reasonable response.)

As Good As It Gets (1997)
Romance ΨΨΨ
Jack Nicholson won his third Academy Award as Best Actor for this film, in which he portrays a homophobic, racist novelist with an obsessive-compulsive disorder.

Aviator, The (2004) Drama/Biography ΨΨΨΨ
Martin Scorsese portrayal of Howard Hughes (Leonardo Dicaprio), a wealthy and psychologically complex eccentric. Hughes suffered from obsessive-compulsive disorder. Former APA CEO and President Raymond Fowler conducted a psychological autopsy for the Hughes estate.

Big Parade, The (1925) Romance/War ΨΨΨΨ
Epic film about World War I gives the viewer a sense of the stress of combat and the trauma of returning to civilian life minus a leg or an arm.

Black Rain (1989) Drama ΨΨΨ
Black-and-white film by Japanese filmmaker Shohei Imamura about the aftermath of the bombing of Hiroshima and its long-term psychological effects.

"Who's gonna love me, Dad? Whoever's going to love me?"

Ron Kovic in
Born on the Fourth of July

Born on the Fourth of July (1989)
Drama/War/Biography ΨΨΨ
Oliver Stone film about the anger, frustration, rage, and coping of paralyzed Vietnam veteran Ron Kovic (Tom Cruise). Kovic was thrown out of the 1972 Republican convention, but went on to

address the Democratic convention in 1976. The film has especially memorable VA hospital scenes.

Casualties of War (1989) War ΨΨΨ

Brian De Palma film about five GIs who kidnap, rape, and murder a young Vietnamese girl. The film deals with themes of guilt, stress, violence, and, most of all, the dehumanizing aspects of war.

Coming Home (1978) Drama/War ΨΨΨΨ

Jon Voigt plays a paraplegic veteran who becomes Jane Fonda's lover in this sensitive anti-war film. Fonda's Marine Corps husband winds up committing suicide. Interesting analysis of the different ways different people respond to the stress of war.

Copycat (1995) Suspense/Thriller ΨΨ

Sigourney Weaver plays a criminal psychologist who struggles with agoraphobia symptoms as she helps police track down a serial killer (Harry Connick, Jr.).

Coyote Ugly (2000) Comedy/Drama ΨΨ

A young woman moves to New York City to try to make it as a songwriter. She takes a job as a "coyote" bartender at a wild, interactive bar and the experience helps her overcome her social anxiety.

Creepshow (1982) Horror ΨΨ

A man with an insect phobia winds up being eaten alive by cockroaches. Directed by George Romero, who also directed the classic film *Night of the Living Dead*. Stephen King wrote the screenplay, and the film is actually better than one might initially expect.

Deer Hunter, The (1978) War ΨΨΨΨΨ

Robert De Niro in an unforgettable film about how Vietnam affects the lives of three high school buddies. The Russian roulette sequences are among the most powerful scenes in film history. Psychopathology themes include drug abuse, PTSD, and depression. The movie won five Academy Awards, including one for best picture, and De Niro has described it as his finest film.

Dummy (2002) Comedy/Drama ΨΨ

A predictable film starring Adrian Brody as Steven, an aspiring ventriloquist, who is unemployed, naïve, passive, and socially awkward but finds meaning and social support through his "dummy." Interesting metaphor of the socially phobic person finding their "inner voice." All ventriloquism in the film is actually performed by Adrian Brody.

The DVD features interviews and comic classes with champion ventriloquist Jeff Dunham.

"I'm not sure there is any help for you."

The dummy's comment to his ventriloquist Steven in *Dummy*

Elling (2001) Drama ΨΨΨΨ

Norwegian film about two men released from a psychiatric hospital and must prove themselves capable of coping with everyday life. Oscar nominee for Best Foreign Film.

Feardotcom (2002) Thriller/Horror Ψ

Various characters access a deadly website that makes their deepest fears or phobias come true (e.g., one has a phobia of beetles and soon is covered by them).

Fearless (1993) Drama ΨΨ

Jeff Bridges in an engaging film that portrays some of the symptoms of anxiety in airline crash survivors. Interesting vignettes showing group therapy for PTSD victims.

Fisher King, The (1991) Drama/Fantasy/Comedy ΨΨΨ

Jeff Bridges plays a former talk show personality who unwittingly encourages a listener to go on a shooting spree. Bridges' withdrawal, cynicism, and substance use can all be interpreted and understood in the context of a post-traumatic stress disorder.

"If you ladies leave my island, if you survive recruit training... you will be a weapon, you will be a minister of death, praying for war. But until that day you are pukes."

Drill instructor Hartman in *Full Metal Jacket*

Full Metal Jacket (1987) War ΨΨΨ

Stanley Kubrick's Vietnam film. The first half of the film is devoted to life in a Marine boot camp, and it is a good illustration of the stress associated with military indoctrination. One of the recruits kills his drill instructor and then commits suicide in response to the pressure of boot camp.

Hamburger Hill (1987) War ΨΨ
A graphic presentation of the stress and horror of war.

High Anxiety (1977) Comedy ΨΨ
Mel Brook's spoof of Hitchcock classics about a psychiatrist who works at "The Psycho-Neurotic Institute for the Very, Very Nervous." The film is better if you've seen the Hitchcock films on which the parody builds.

House of Games (1987) Crime ΨΨ
Lindsay Crouse in the lead role plays a psychiatrist who has just written an important book on obsessive-compulsive disorders. She becomes obsessed with confidence games and is slowly drawn into the criminal life.

In Country (1989) Drama ΨΨ
Bruce Willis plays a Vietnam veteran with post-traumatic stress disorder who is unable to relate meaningfully to the world around him until he visits the Vietnam memorial.

In the Bedroom (2001) Drama/Suspense ΨΨΨΨ
Introspective film with a talented cast that examines grief, despair, and revenge after the murder of someone deeply loved. Marisa Tomei's character develops an Acute Stress Disorder following the trauma. The film makes good use of silence; these scenes underscore the tension, unspoken feelings, and underlying pain associated with the death of a loved one.

"What does your therapist think of all this," "Oh, I would never tell my therapist," "Why not?" "Because it's private."

Dialogue in Kissing Jessica Stein

Inside Out (1986) Drama ΨΨ
A little known but interesting film in which Elliott Gould plays a man with agoraphobia. He sends out for food, sex, and haircuts but finds that he cannot meet *all* his needs without leaving home.

Jacob's Ladder (1990) Drama ΨΨ
Complex film about a Vietnam veteran who has dramatic hallucinations of indeterminate etiology (possibly the result of military exposure to experimental drugs).

Kissing Jessica Stein (2002) Comedy ΨΨΨ
Quality independent film about a neurotic, young woman who in exploring her sexuality and intrapersonal life is able to extend beyond her rigidity and generalized anxiety.

"Take it all but in the name of humanity, let me out of this cage."

Olivia de Havilland as a Lady in a Cage

Lady in a Cage (1964) Drama/Suspense ΨΨ
Olivia de Havilland plays an upper class woman trapped inside her home elevator. The film melodramatically represents claustrophobia and panic.

Manchurian Candidate, The (2004) Drama/Suspense ΨΨΨ
The new version of this classic film stars Denzel Washington as a Gulf War veteran with PTSD, paranoia, and memories he cannot understand, which lead him to unravel a conspiracy involving brain washing and political maneuvering.

Manchurian Candidate, The (1962) Drama/Suspense ΨΨΨ
Original version stars Frank Sinatra as the veteran who experiences flashbacks and PTSD symptoms.

M*A*S*H (1970) Comedy/War ΨΨΨ
Wonderfully funny Robert Altman film about military surgeons and nurses who use alcohol, sex, and humor to cope with the stress of war. The portrayal of Hawkeye Pierce, half-drunk but always ready for surgery, is troubling.

"I've got things a certain way."

Nicolas Cage in Matchstick Men

Matchstick Men (2003) Comedy ΨΨΨΨ
Nicholas Cage plays a con man with OCD, agoraphobia with panic, tics, and antisocial personality in

this interesting Ridley Scott film. Upon meeting his estranged daughter things begin to change for Cage.

Obsession (1976) Thriller Ψ
Brian De Palma version of Hitchcock's *Vertigo*. The De Palma film doesn't live up to the original.

Panic Room (2002) Drama/Suspense ΨΨ
David Fincher film about a woman (Jody Foster) and her young daughter who become trapped in a full-proof "panic room" when three men break into their home. Despite the title, the film teaches little about genuine panic disorder.

"Sergeant, I want you to arrange for the immediate transfer of this baby out of my regiment. I won't have any of our brave men contaminated by him."

Paths of Glory

Paths of Glory (1957) War ΨΨΨΨΨ
Kirk Douglas in an early Stanley Kubrick film about the horrors and stupidity of WWI. There is a memorable scene in which a general repeatedly slaps a soldier, trying without success to bring him out of his shell-shocked state. The scene was repeated in the 1970 film *Patton*.

Pawnbroker, The (1965) Drama ΨΨΨ
Rod Steiger plays a concentration camp survivor who watched his wife being raped and his children being murdered; he copes by becoming numb. Interesting flashback scenes. Steiger lost the 1965 Academy Award for best actor to Lee Marvin in *Cat Ballou*.

"I want you to remember that no bastard ever won a war by dying for his country. He won it by making the other poor dumb bastard die for his country."

George C. Scott in *Patton*

Patton (1970) War/Biography ΨΨΨ
George C. Scott is perfect in the role of the controversial general who was relieved of his command after slapping a crying soldier who had been hospitalized for combat fatigue, or what we would probably now call post-traumatic stress disorder. The film won an Academy Award as best picture and George C. Scott won the Oscar for best actor.

Phobia (1980) Horror/Mystery Ψ
Canadian film about the systematic murders of phobic psychiatric patients.

Princess and the Warrior, The (2000) Drama ΨΨΨΨ
A nurse at a psychiatric hospital is hit by a truck and saved by a crook who cuts a hole in her throat and breathes for her. Upon recovering, the nurse goes on a journey of purpose to find this man. A minor character has PTSD. One intensely graphic and chilling scene depicts a kind-hearted adolescent with **pica**; believing the nurse has rejected him, the teenager eats glass.

Raiders of the Lost Ark (1981) Adventure ΨΨ
Steven Spielberg film with Harrison Ford as anthropologist Indiana Jones, who is forced by the situational demands of heroism to overcome his snake phobia.

San Francisco (1936) Romance/Disaster ΨΨΨ
This is one of the greatest disaster films ever made, and the special effects give the viewer some appreciation for the acute stress one would experience in a real earthquake. Clark Gable and Spencer Tracy have unforgettable roles in this film.

Shoah (1985) Documentary ΨΨΨΨΨ
Widely praised nine-hour documentary about the Holocaust. The film offers some insight into the behavior of both the German officials and their victims and illustrates antisocial personalities and post-traumatic stress disorders.

Something's Gotta Give (2003) Comedy ΨΨ
Jack Nicholson stars as a man who experiences panic attacks while grappling his interest in relationship with a woman played by Diane Keaton.

Twelve O'Clock High (1949) War ΨΨΨ
Gregory Peck in an interesting presentation of the stress of combat and the ways in which leaders can influence the behavior of those they lead.

Unmarried Woman, An (1978) Drama/Comedy ΨΨΨ
Tender, sensitive, and funny film about Jill Clayburgh learning to cope with the stress of being a single

parent after her husband abandons her. Her friends, a psychiatrist, and an affair with Alan Bates all help.

"I have this acrophobia. I wake up at night and I see that man falling."

Jimmy Stewart describing his symptoms in *Vertigo*

Vertigo (1958) Thriller ΨΨΨΨ
Wonderful Hitchcock film in which Jimmy Stewart plays a character whose life is dominated by his fear of heights. He attempts a self-styled behavior modification program early in the film without success.

Waiting for Ronald (2003) Short Film/Drama ΨΨΨ
This film about a man who leaves a supervised residence to live with a friend in the community depicts OCD with a hand-washing compulsion.

Walking on Water (2002) Drama ΨΨ
Australian film about a man who becomes haunted by intrusive memories and deteriorates into self-destructive behavior after suffocating a gay friend who was dying of AIDS.

What About Bob? (1991) Comedy ΨΨ
Bill Murray plays an anxious patient who cannot function without his psychiatrist, played by Richard Dreyfuss. Not a great film, but a fun movie that explores the doctor-patient relationship and the obsessive-compulsive personality.

"As a four limb person, I don't feel incomplete. It's more of a feeling that my body doesn't belong to me."
"The relief from the 50 years of torment I had was indescribable."
"I'm complete now."

Comments from individuals who want or have had healthy limbs removed in *Whole*

Whole (2003) Documentary ΨΨ
Fascinating documentary about individuals who

have a strong desire to have one of their limbs amputated, despite being totally healthy. Presents interesting differential diagnostic questions. Is this OCD, Body Dysmorphic Disorder, an identity disorder, or self-mutilation? One psychiatrist, who interviewed 53 people with this condition, proposed the rubric "Body Integrity Identity Disorder."

Dissociative and Somatoform Disorders

3 Women (1977) Drama ΨΨΨ
Strange but engaging Robert Altman film about two California women who seem to exchange personalities.

Agnes of God (1985) Mystery ΨΨΨ
Good performances by Anne Bancroft, Meg Tilly, and Jane Fonda. Fonda plays a court-appointed psychiatrist who must make sense out of pregnancy and apparent infanticide in a local convent. Good examples of *stigmata,* an example of conversion.

Altered States (1980) Science Fiction ΨΨ
Not entirely satisfying film based in part on the sensory deprivation experiments of Dr. John Lilly. The scientist (William Hurt) combines isolation tanks with psychedelic mushrooms to induce altered states of consciousness. Good special effects.

"This is poetry, and don't you deny it. Come back to me when you've written something really perverse, really depraved."

An editor reviews Isabelle's work in *Amateur*

Amateur (1994) Drama/Comedy ΨΨ
Hal Hartley film in which a man who is amnestic as a result of a traumatic head injury takes up with a nun who has left the convent to write pornographic novels. Almost every character in the film has a complex double identity and is uncertain about who he or she *really* is.

Anastasia (1956) Drama ΨΨΨΨ
Yul Brynner, Helen Hayes, and Ingrid Bergman star in this film about an amnestic woman who is

believed to be the lost princess Anastasia, daughter of the last czar of Russia.

Bandits (2001) Comedy ΨΨ
Loosely based on a true story about two criminals who rob banks in a non-violent way. One of the men (Billy Bob Thornton) is hypochondriacal. In interviews, Thornton stated it was not much of a "stretch" to play this role—he has a well-documented phobia of antique furniture.

Black Friday (1940) Horror ΨΨ
Boris Karloff and Bela Lugosi star in this film about transplanting a gangster's brain in a college professor's cranium.

Butterfly Effect, The (2003) Drama/Suspense ΨΨ
A young man (Ashton Kutcher) tries to change his traumatic past with unpredictable and increasingly problematic consequences. When he reflects on blackouts, he enters the memory and is able to change it for the long-term but must face the consequences of the change each time. The film attempts to depict chaos theory, and opens with a famous quotation.

Cyrano de Bergerac (1990) Romance ΨΨΨ
Gerard Depardieu stars as the inimitable Cyrano, a man obsessed with the size of his nose and convinced it makes him forever unlovable.

Dark Mirror, The (1946) Thriller Ψ
Olivia De Havilland plays both parts in a story of twin sisters, one of whom is a deranged killer.

Dead Again (1991) Mystery/Romance ΨΨΨ
Emma Thompson costars with her husband, Kenneth Branagh (who also directed the film). The movie illustrates traumatic amnesia and its treatment through hypnosis. The hypnotist, an antique dealer, is not the most professional of therapists!

Despair (1979) Drama ΨΨΨΨ
Fassbinder film based on a novel by Vladimir Nabokov. A Russian Jew émigré in Germany who runs a chocolate factory kills another man who looks like him, and tries to pass it off as his own suicide. When his plan fails, he becomes psychotic.

Devils, The (1971) Drama/Historical ΨΨΨ
Ken Russell film adapted from Aldous Huxley's book *The Devils of Loundun*. The film traces the lives of seventeenth-century French nuns who experienced highly erotic dissociative states attributed to possession by the devil.

Double Life of Veronique, The (1991)
Fantasy/Drama ΨΨ
The lives of two women turn out to be linked in complex ways the viewer never fully understands.

Double Life, A (1947) Crime ΨΨ
Ronald Coleman plays an actor who is unable to sort out his theatrical life (in which he plays Othello) and his personal life.

Dr. Jekyll and Mr. Hyde (1932) Horror ΨΨΨ
Fredric March in the best adaptation of Robert Louis Stevenson's classic story about the ultimate dissociative disorder. Stevenson was an alcoholic, and alcohol may be the model for the mysterious liquid that dramatically transforms Jekyll's personality.

Exorcist, The (1973) Horror ΨΨ
Linda Blair stars as a 12-year-old girl possessed by the devil in William Friedkin's film based on the William Peter Blatty novel. One of the most suspenseful films ever made.

"It's only after we've lost everything [that] we are free to do anything."

A premise of *Fight Club*

Fight Club (1999) Drama/Suspense ΨΨΨ
A disillusioned, insomniac (Edward Norton) meets a dangerous, malcontent part of himself in the character of Brad Pitt. Norton then establishes "fight clubs" in which men can unload their aggressions onto one another. Interesting look at Norton's deterioration.

Freud (1962) Biography ΨΨΨ
Montgomery Clift in an interesting account of the early year's of Freud's life. The film illustrates paralysis, false blindness, and a false pregnancy, all examples of somatization disorders.

Great Dictator, The (1940) Comedy ΨΨ
A satire of Adolph Hitler, with Charlie Chaplin in the role of a Jewish barber who suffers amnesia and eventually finds himself assuming the personality of Adenoid Hynkel, the dictator of Tomania.

Hannah and Her Sisters (1986)
Comedy/Drama ΨΨΨ
Mickey (Woody Allen) is a hopeless hypochondriac

who was formerly married to Hannah (Mia Farrow). Mickey spends his days worrying about brain tumors, cancer, and cardiovascular disease.

"Every husband should go blind for a little while."

Woody Allen in *Hollywood Ending*

Hollywood Ending (2002) Comedy ΨΨΨ
Woody Allen film about a struggling film director (Allen) who develops a conversion disorder (hysterical blindness) and has to direct the film blind.

Home of the Brave (1949) Drama/War ΨΨ
A black soldier develops a conversion disorder following his return from combat.

Identity (2003) Suspense/Thriller ΨΨΨ
A serial killer with a dissociative identity disorder is at his final hearing before receiving the death penalty. This story juxtaposes with another tale of several people suddenly stuck at an isolated motel and living in terror as they are killed one by one. These two components are cleverly weaved together as the people represent DID alters being killed off.

Last Temptation of Christ, The (1988) Religious ΨΨΨ
Challenging and controversial Martin Scorsese film in which Jesus, while on the cross and in great pain, has a dissociative episode in which he imagines himself as an ordinary man who married Mary Magdalene and lived a normal life.

Lizzie (1957) Drama ΨΨ
Eleanor Parker, a woman with dissociative identity disorder is treated by psychiatrist Richard Boone.

Method (2003) Suspense/Thriller Ψ
An actress studying and playing the role of a past serial killer tries too hard to "feel her character" and she dissociates and takes on her model's past behavior.

Mirage (1965) Drama ΨΨ
A scientist who makes an important discovery develops amnesia after viewing the death of a friend.

My Girl (1991) Drama/Comedy ΨΨ
The film centers on an 11-year-old girl whose mother has just died and whose grandmother has

Alzheimer's disease. The child responds by developing a series of imaginary disorders. Strong performances by Dan Aykroyd and Jamie Lee Curtis.

Overboard (1987) Comedy ΨΨ
Goldie Hawn plays a haughty millionairess who develops amnesia and is claimed by an Oregon carpenter as his wife and forced to care for his children.

Paris, Texas (1984) Drama ΨΨΨ
Wim Wenders film about a man found wandering in the desert with no personal memory.

Persona (1966) Drama ΨΨΨΨΨ
Complex, demanding, and absolutely fascinating Bergman film starring Liv Ullmann as an actress who suddenly stops talking after one of her performances. Ullmann is treated by a nurse, and the two women appear to exchange "personas." Highly erotic description of a beach memory.

"I have not spoken since I was six years old. Nobody knows why, least of all myself."

Ada's thoughts at the beginning of *The Piano*

Piano, The (1993) Drama ΨΨΨΨΨ
Jane Campion film about a woman who had voluntarily stopped speaking as a child. She communicates with written notes and through playing the piano, a pleasure forbidden to her by her New Zealand husband. There are scenes of extraordinary sensuality between Harvey Keitel and Holly Hunter and a dramatic suicide attempt.

Poison Ivy (1992) Drama Ψ
Newcomer into a pathological family plans to take over the role of wife and mother. The father is alcoholic, the mother a hypochondriac.

Prelude to a Kiss (1992) Comedy/Romance ΨΨ
The ultimate example of a dissociative disorder. A beautiful young woman and a sad old man kiss on her wedding day and exchange bodies. The film makes this extraordinary event seem almost plausible.

Primal Fear (1996) Drama ΨΨΨ
Richard Gere stars in this suspenseful drama about a man who commits heinous crimes, ostensibly as

a result of a dissociative disorder. The film raises useful questions about the problem of malingering and differential diagnosis.

> "Mother, my mother, uh, what is the phrase? — she isn't qu-quite herself today."
>
> **Norman Bates in *Psycho***

Psycho (1960) Horror/Thriller ΨΨΨΨΨ
Wonderful Hitchcock film starring Anthony Perkins as Norman Bates, who vacillates between his passive, morbid personality and his dead mother's alter ego. In the final minutes of the film, a psychiatrist offers a somewhat confused explanation for Bates' behavior. The shower scene is one of the most famous shots in film history.

Queen Margot (1994) Drama ΨΨ
Period film set in 1572 France at a time of heavy religious warfare (Catholic vs. Protestant). The king in the film is highly somatic to stress and various situations.

Raising Cain (1992) Thriller/Drama Ψ
Confusing De Palma film about a child psychologist with multiple personalities who begins to kill women and steal their children for experiments.

Return of Martin Guerre, The (1982) Historical ΨΨΨ
Gerard Depardieu as a sixteenth-century peasant who returns to his wife after a seven-year absence. His true identity is never made clear. This film, the basis for the American movie *Sommersby,* is based on a true story.

Safe (1995) Comedy/Drama ΨΨΨΨ
A rare film almost exclusively focusing on a woman (Julianne Moore) with a somatoform disorder, various treatment approaches, and the effects on her family. This satirical film is cleverly directed by Todd Haynes.

Secret of Dr. Kildare, The (1939) Drama Ψ
The good Dr. Kildare works hard to cure a patient's conversion disorder (blindness) in this dated but still interesting film.

Secret Window (2004) Drama/Suspense ΨΨΨ
Mort Rainey (Johnny Depp) finding his wife cheating on him in a motel; the film jumps forward

six months to a scene in which Mort is an isolated writer in a house in the woods and now separated from his wife. He is visited and threatened by an odd psychopath (John Turturro). Based on the Stephen King short story, "Secret Window, Secret Garden." *Identity* meets *The Sixth Sense.*

Send Me No Flowers (1964) Romance/Comedy Ψ
Rock Hudson plays a hypochondriac convinced he will die soon. Hudson sets out to find a suitable replacement so his wife will be able to get along without him.

Seventh Veil, The (1945) Drama ΨΨΨ
Psychological drama about a pianist who loses the ability to play. Hypnotherapy makes it possible for Ann Todd to play the piano again and sort out her complex interpersonal relationships.

Sisters (1973) Thriller/Horror ΨΨ
De Palma film about Siamese twins separated as children; one is good, the other quite evil. The use of Siamese twins is a Hitchcock-like twist on the theme of multiple personality.

Sommersby (1993) Drama ΨΨ
Richard Gere returns to wife Jodie Foster after a six-year absence during the Civil War. Gere is remarkably changed, so much so that it appears he is a different man.

Sorry, Wrong Number (1948) Thriller ΨΨ
Barbara Stanwyck and Burt Lancaster in a murder film. Stanwyck is a rich heiress who is bedridden with psychosomatic heart disease and paralysis.

Spellbound (1945) Thriller ΨΨΨΨ
Ingrid Bergman and Gregory Peck star in this Hitchcock thriller. Peck is an amnestic patient who believes he has committed a murder; Bergman is the psychiatrist who falls in love with him and helps him recall the childhood trauma responsible for his dissociative state.

Steppenwolf (1974) Drama ΨΨ
Film adaptation of Herman Hesse's remarkable novel about Harry Haller (played by Max von Sydow), a misanthropic protagonist who wrestles with the competing forces of good and evil within himself.

Stigmata (1999) Suspense/Horror Ψ
Beautician begins to have episodes of visions, seizures, and stigmata wounds on her body after her mother sends her a sacred rosary from Brazil.

Suddenly, Last Summer (1959) Drama ΨΨΨ
Adaptation of a Tennessee Williams story about an enmeshed and pathological relationship between a mother (Katharine Hepburn) and her homosexual son and a dissociative amnesia in a cousin who witnessed the son's death. Among its other virtues, the film includes a fascinating discussion of the benefits of lobotomy.

"He-he was lying naked on the broken stones... It looked as if-as if they had devoured him!... As if they'd torn or cut parts of him away with their hands, or with knives, or those jagged tin cans they made music with. As if they'd torn bits of him away in strips!"

Suddenly, Last Summer

Sullivan's Travels (1941) Comedy/Drama ΨΨΨΨ
Joel McCrea plays a movie director who goes out to experience life as it is lived outside a Hollywood studio. He winds up getting a head injury, becoming amnestic, and being sentenced to six years on a chain gang.

Sybil (1976) Drama ΨΨΨ
Made-for-TV movie in which Joanne Woodward, the patient in *The Three Faces of Eve,* plays the psychiatrist treating a woman with 16 different personalities.

Three Faces of Eve, The (1957) Drama ΨΨΨΨ
Joanne Woodward won an Academy Award for her portrayal of a woman with three personalities (Eve White, Eve Black, and Jane); based on the book by Thigpin and Cleckley.

Twelve O'Clock High (1949) War ΨΨΨΨΨ
Gregory Peck plays the role of General Frank Savage, an effective leader who develops a conversion disorder (psychosomatic paralysis) in response to his role in the death of several of his subordinates. The film is based on a true story.

Up in Arms (1944) Musical/Comedy/War Ψ
Danny Kaye plays a hypochondriac in the Army.

Voices Within: The Lives of Truddi Chase (1990) Drama ΨΨ
Made-for-TV movie about a woman with multiple personality disorder; based on the best selling-book *When Rabbit Howls*.

Whatever Happened to Baby Jane? (1962) Drama ΨΨΨ
Bette Davis and Joan Crawford star as two elderly sisters who were formerly movie stars. Jane (Bette Davis) had been a child star, but her fame was eclipsed by the renown of her talented sister, now confined to a wheelchair. Jane torments her sister and experiences a dramatic dissociative episode in the final scene in the movie.

Zelig (1983) Comedy ΨΨ
Quasi-documentary about Woody Allen as Zelig, a human chameleon whose personality changes to match that of whomever he is around. He is treated by psychiatrist Mia Farrow, whom Zelig eventually marries. Watch for Susan Sontag, Saul Bellow, and Bruno Bettelheim.

Psychological Stress and Physical Disorders

12 Angry Men (1957) Drama ΨΨΨΨΨ
Henry Fonda stars in this fascinating courtroom drama that illustrates social pressure, the tendency toward conformity in social settings, and the stress associated with noncompliance with societal norms.

Alive (1993) Action/Adventure/Drama ΨΨ
The survivors of a plane crash in the Andes survive for more than 70 days by eating the passengers who died. The film is a vivid portrayal of traumatic stress and its consequences.

All Quiet on the Western Front (1930) Drama ΨΨΨΨΨ
This remarkable film illustrates the horror of war and celebrates pacifism as its only solution. The film poignantly documents that it is young men who fight our wars and shows the folly of jingoism and blind patriotism.

Barbarian Invasions, The (2003) Drama /Comedy ΨΨΨΨ
Friends and family gather to support a stubborn, outspoken man suffering from a terminal illness. The film vacillates from light to heavy, from the

somber to the humorous. This Canadian film won an Academy Award for Best Foreign Film.

"Oh, God! why did they do this to us? We only wanted to live, you and I. Why should they send us out to fight each other? If they threw away these rifles and these uniforms, you could be my brother, just like Kat and Albert. You'll have to forgive me, comrade. I'll do all I can. I'll write to your parents."

Paul attempts to comfort a man he has killed in
All Quiet on the Western Front

Best Years of Our Lives, The (1946) Drama ΨΨ
Sam Goldwyn film about servicemen adjusting to civilian life after the war. One of the sailors has lost both hands.

Blue (1993) Drama ΨΨΨ
British filmmaker Derek Jarman's last film; he died from AIDS shortly after the movie was completed. Jarman reviews his life and analyzes the ways in which his life has been affected by his disease.

Bone Collector, The (1999) Suspense/Thriller ΨΨ
Denzel Washington is a crime scene specialist with quadriplegia.

Brief History of Time, A (1992) Biography ΨΨΨ
A documentary about the life of Stephen Hawking, a theoretical physicist coping with amyotrophic lateral sclerosis.

Cactus (1986) Romance ΨΨΨ
Australian film about a woman who loses one eye and considers giving up sight in the other in order to more fully understand the world of her blind lover.

Children of a Lesser God (1986) Romance ΨΨΨ
The film examines the complications involved in a love relationship between William Hurt, a teacher in a school for the deaf, and Marlee Matlin, a young deaf woman who works at the school. Much of the conflict in the film revolves around Matlin's refusal to learn to lip-read. Matlin won an Academy Award as Best Supporting Actress for her role in this film.

Chinese Roulette (1976) Drama ΨΨ
Fassbinder film about a disabled girl and the ways in which she dominates and manipulates her family.

Cinema Paradiso (1988) Drama ΨΨΨΨ
A young boy is mesmerized by a movie theater in a small, post-WWII, Italian town, and befriends a crusty yet warm-hearted projectionist who goes blind after a fire accident. Classic Giuseppe Tornatore film.

Common Threads: Stories from the Quilt (1989) Documentary ΨΨΨ
This HBO film examines the lives of five individuals linked by a common illness—AIDS. The movie won the Academy Award for Best Documentary Feature in 1989.

Crash of Silence (1953) Drama ΨΨ
Mother agonizes over whether to keep a hearing impaired daughter at home or send her to a special school.

Cure, The (1995) Drama ΨΨ
Two adolescent boys become best friends. One has AIDS from a blood transfusion, leading the boys to set off in search of a miracle cure.

Deaf Smith and Johnnie Ears (1973) Western ΨΨ
A deaf Anthony Quinn teams up with Franco Nero to cope with the challenges of life in rural Texas.

Doctor, The (1991) Drama ΨΨΨ
William Hurt plays a cold and indifferent physician whose approach to treatment changes dramatically after he is diagnosed with throat cancer.

"Why don't you ask me probing questions about my childhood?"

Julie Andrews queries her therapist in *Duet for One*

Duet for One (1986) Drama ΨΨ
Julie Andrews plays a world class violinist who learns to cope with multiple sclerosis. Good illustration of the effects of chronic illness on psychological health. Max von Sydow plays the role of Andrews' therapist.

Dummy (1979) Drama ΨΨ
Made-for-TV movie about a hearing impaired and mute teenager who is charged with murder and defended by a deaf attorney.

Early Frost, An (1985) Drama ΨΨΨ
Excellent made-for-TV movie (available on videocassette) that explores the pain and anguish involved as a young man explains to his family and friends that he is gay and has AIDS.

Eating (1990) Comedy ΨΨΨ
An extended conversation that examines the relationship among life, love, and food.

"I am NOT an animal! I am a human being!"

John Merrick in *The Elephant Man*

Elephant Man, The (1980) Drama ΨΨΨ
David Lynch film about the life of John Merrick, a hideously deformed man who is befriended by a London physician. The film is effective in forcing the viewer to examine his or her prejudices about appearance.

Eye, The (2002) Suspense/Thriller ΨΨΨ
A young, blind woman regains her sight through a cornea transplant. She immediately begins to see ghosts which she identifies as the souls of the dead. Pang Brothers film in the tradition of *The Sixth Sense* and *The Ring*.

Falling Down (1994) Drama ΨΨΨ
Good presentation by Michael Douglas of the cumulative effects of stress on a marginal personality. The film does not give us enough information to clearly diagnose the character played by Douglas, but he displays enough symptoms to justify an Axis II diagnosis of paranoid personality disorder.

Gabby—A True Story (1987) Biography ΨΨΨ
A true story about a woman with cerebral palsy who goes on to become a respected author. Contrast this story with the life of Christy Brown told in *My Left Foot*.

Glengarry Glen Ross (1992) Drama ΨΨΨ
A hard-hitting and powerful presentation of job-related stress and interpersonal conflict in the real

estate business. Wonderful cast, with Jack Lemmon playing a figure whose despair with his job is reminiscent of Willy Lomax in Arthur Miller's *Death of a Salesman*.

Heart Is a Lonely Hunter, The (1968) Drama ΨΨ
Alan Arkin stars in this adaptation of Carson McCuller's sad, poignant novel about a simple friendship between two men. One of the men is deaf; the other is mentally retarded. If you have to choose between the film and the novel, read the novel.

Honkytonk Man (1982) Drama Ψ
Clint Eastwood produced, directed, and starred in this film about a country and western singer with leukemia who hopes to make it to Nashville before he dies.

Hunchback of Notre Dame, The (1939) Horror ΨΨΨΨΨ
Charles Laughton plays Quasimodo in this film adaptation of the Victor Hugo novel. The film is a classic in the genre examining the relationship between body image and self-concept.

I Sent a Letter to My Love (1981) Drama ΨΨΨ
French film about a sister caring for her paralyzed brother. They each seek romance by writing to a newspaper personals column; without realizing what is happening, each winds up corresponding with the other.

Ikiru (1952) Drama ΨΨΨΨ
Existential Akira Kurosawa film about a man dying from cancer who finds meaning in the last days of his life by helping a group of mothers build a playground for their children.

In America (2003) Drama ΨΨΨΨ
Irish family immigrates to the United States to Hell's Kitchen. They befriend a Nigerian painter who is suffering with AIDS.

In for Treatment (1979) Drama ΨΨΨ
Dutch film about the indignities suffered by a cancer patient who has to deal with an impersonal health care system.

Italian for Beginners (2002) Comedy/Drama ΨΨΨ
In a hodge-podge of interrelated stories, one character has pancreatic cancer and suffers extraordinary pain.

It's My Party (1996) Drama ΨΨΨΨ
Sensitive film about a man with AIDS who throws one last party before killing himself. Much of the

film centers on the issue of voluntary suicide and the ethics of euthanasia.

Jacquot (1993) Biography ΨΨ
Moving film about the life of French director Jacques Demy, who died from a brain tumor shortly after the film was released.

Johnnie Belinda (1948) Drama ΨΨ
Jane Wyman (who was Ronald Reagan's wife at the time) earned an Academy Award for her performance as a deaf-mute woman who is stigmatized and raped. The film is dated but still offers insights into the ways in which people who are hearing impaired are perceived.

La Symphonie Pastorale (1946) Drama ΨΨΨΨ
French adaptation of André Gide novel about a Swiss minister who falls in love with his blind protégée and abandons his wife to be with her. When the blind girl later regains her sight, she is tormented by the decisions he has made because of her.

Leap of Faith (1992) Drama ΨΨ
Steve Martin plays itinerant evangelist Jonas Nightengale, whose faith healing stunts require technological support from backstage assistant Debra Winger. Contrast Martin's role with that of Burt Lancaster in *Elmer Gantry* (1960) and the documentary *Marjoe* (1972).

Life on a String (1991) Drama ΨΨΨ
Lyrical movie about a blind Chinese musician who believes his sight will be restored when he breaks his thousandth banjo string. He grows old and wise while he waits.

Light That Failed, The (1939) Drama ΨΨ
Adaptation of Kipling novel about a great artist who goes blind as a result of an injury while in Africa.

"Let go. It's all right. You can let go now."

**Bruce Davison comforts
his dying lover in
*Longtime Companion***

Living End, The (1992) Comedy ΨΨ
Two HIV positive men hit the road and explore what it means to live purposively with their disease.

Longtime Companion (1990) Drama ΨΨΨ
This film explores the ways in which AIDS has affected a group of gay friends and traces the love and loss that is shared between two men as one of them dies from the disease.

Man Without a Face, The (1993) Drama ΨΨ
Mel Gibson directs and stars in this film about a man whose face becomes terribly disfigured after an automobile accident. He becomes reclusive but finds redemption in his relationship with the 12-year-old boy he tutors.

Marvin's Room (1996) Drama ΨΨΨΨ
A compelling examination of the way in which chronic illness affects caregivers and families.

Mask (1985) Drama ΨΨΨ
Cher stars in this film about her character's son, Rocky Dennis, a spunky teenager whose life has been dramatically affected by craniodiaphyseal dysplasia, a disorder that distorts the shape of his skull and face. This is a feel good movie that succeeds. The thwarted love relationship between Rocky and a blind girlfriend underscores our tendency to judge people by their appearance.

Men, The (1950) Drama ΨΨΨ
Marlon Brando in his first film role plays a paralyzed WWII veteran full of rage about his injury and his limitations.

Miracle Worker, The (1962) Biography ΨΨΨ
Patty Duke and Anne Bancroft star in this well-known film about the childhood of Helen Keller and the influence of a gifted teacher.

My Flesh and Blood (2004) Documentary ΨΨΨ
Moving documentary about Susan Tom, who adopted 11 special needs children and raised them on her own. The children suffer in a variety of ways; their problems include cystic fibrosis, severe burns, developmental disabilities, the absence of legs, and a genetic skin disorder that causes severe pain.

My Left Foot (1989) Biography ΨΨΨΨ
The inspiring life story of Christy Brown, an Irish writer who triumphs over cerebral palsy. Daniel Day-Lewis received a Best Actor Academy Award for his role as Brown.

My Life (1993) Drama ΨΨ
Michael Keaton learns he is dying from cancer and makes a series of videotapes for his still-unborn

son, including one in which he teaches his son how to shave.

My Life Without Me (2003) Drama ΨΨΨ
A 23-year-old woman is diagnosed with ovarian cancer and decides not to tell her family but instead live her life more fully and prepare them for when she is gone.

Niagara, Niagara (1998) Drama ΨΨ
Two teenagers on the lam encounter multiple problems en route. Reminiscent of *Bonnie and Clyde*, the film is chiefly memorable because it is one of the few films in which Tourette's syndrome is sympathetically and realistically portrayed.

"My whole life disappeared with you that morning"

Grieving in
Open Hearts

Open Hearts (2003) Drama ΨΨΨ
Danish film about a random car accident that leaves a man paralyzed from the neck down. He lashes out in anger unable to accept the reality of his losses. His girlfriend begins an affair with the driver's husband.

Passion Fish (1992) Drama ΨΨΨΨ
The stress of disability and the demands a disabled person can make on caregivers are nicely chronicled in this film about a querulous paraplegic actress and her caretaker/companion.

Patch Adams (1998) Comedy ΨΨ
Robin Williams plays a medical student, nicknamed Patch, who defies the medical institution and crosses boundaries in using humor and holistic medical practices with various patients throughout a hospital. Some humorous and touching scenes occur on the children's cancer ward and with other suffering patients.

Phantom of the Opera, The (1925) Horror ΨΨΨ
A disfigured music lover, played by Lon Chaney, lives in the bowels of the Paris opera house, unable to achieve romantic love because of his hideous face. He is eventually hunted down and killed by an angry mob.

Philadelphia (1993) Drama ΨΨΨ
Tom Hanks won an Academy Award for his portrayal of an AIDS-afflicted attorney who is fired from a prestigious law firm once his illness becomes known to the partners. There is a particularly moving scene in which Hanks plays an opera and explains to Denzel Washington why he loves the music so passionately.

Joe Miller: "What do you love about the law, Andrew?"
Andrew Beckett: "I... many things... uh... uh... What I love the most about the law?"
Joe Miller: "Yeah."
Andrew Beckett: "It's that every now and again - not often, but occasionally - you get to be a part of justice being done. That really is quite a thrill when that happens."

Philadelphia

Pieces of April (2003) Drama/Comedy ΨΨΨ
A young woman, estranged from her family, is determined to impress them with a Thanksgiving dinner. She has a particularly tenuous relationship with her cynical mother who is dying of cancer.

Places in the Heart (1984) Drama ΨΨ
Sally Field won an Academy Award for Best Actress for her role in this film about a widowed woman struggling to keep her farm and her family in a small Texas town during the Depression. The film is memorable for bringing together John Malkovich as a blind World War I veteran and Danny Glover as a hapless drifter. The standoff between a blind Malkovich and the local chapter of the Ku Klux Klan is especially memorable.

Promises in the Dark (1979) Drama ΨΨ
Melodrama about a young woman dying from cancer.

Proof (1992) Drama ΨΨΨΨ
Australian drama about a blind man who takes photographs to document his life and its meaning.

Savage Nights (1993) French Drama /Biography ΨΨΨΨ
This controversial film was directed by French filmmaker Cyril Collard, who died from AIDS three

days before *Savage Nights* was selected as the Best French Film of the Year. The movie deals with the existential decisions made by a bisexual antihero who continues to have unprotected sex even after learning he has AIDS.

Shadowlands (1993) Biography ΨΨΨ
Wonderful Richard Attenborough film about the late-life romance of C. S. Lewis (Anthony Hopkins) and Joy Gresham (Debra Winger). Lewis must come to grips with the meaning of pain, suffering, and loss when Joy develops cancer.

Shootist, The (1976) Western ΨΨ
John Wayne's last film, about an aging gunfighter dying from cancer. Also stars Jimmy Stewart, Lauren Bacall, Ron Howard, Harry Morgan, John Carradine, Hugh O'Brian, and Richard Boone. John Wayne, a heavy smoker, died from lung cancer after making this film.

"You aim to do to me what they did with John Wesley Hardin. Lay me out and parade every damn fool in the state past me at a dollar a head, half price for children, and then stuff me in a gunny sack and shovel me under."

John Wayne confronts the undertaker in *The Shootist*

Shop on Main Street, The (1965) Drama ΨΨΨΨ
Czechoslovakian film about a man appointed as the "Aryan controller" of a button shop in World War II. He befriends and hides the Jewish owner of the shop, who does not understand the situation because she is deaf. She assumes the new arrival has been sent as her assistant; when he later hides her to avoid deportation to the death camps, she smothers. Overcome with remorse, he kills himself. Selected as the Best Foreign Film of 1965.

Tell Me That You Love Me, Junie Moon (1970) Comedy ΨΨ
Otto Preminger film in which three unusual roommates come together as a family. Liza Minnelli is disfigured; another has epilepsy; the third is wheelchair-bound.

Terms of Endearment (1983) Comedy ΨΨΨ
Shirley MacLaine, Debra Winger, and Jack Nicholson star in this poignant but funny movie about relationships, caring, and cancer.

Test of Love, A (1984) Drama ΨΨ
An Australian film based on a true story of a teacher's successful attempt to reach out to a disabled girl.

Unbreakable (2000) Drama/Suspense ΨΨΨΨ
Samuel L. Jackson plays Elijah, a comic book collector, who was born with a rare genetic bone disease which makes him highly susceptible to injury. Bruce Willis, on the other hand, plays a security officer who is in a train wreck and is the one survivor and does not have even a scratch on him. Second mainstream film by master story-teller, M. Night Shyamalan.

Vanilla Sky (2001) Drama/Suspense ΨΨΨ
Cameron Crowe film in which Tom Cruise plays a wealthy businessman in NYC who has a car accident and must re-establish his life with a severe facial deformity. This changes his interactions especially with a woman he is falling in love with (Penelope Cruz). He begins to break down further as his dead friend (Cameron Diaz) reappears.

"Got you in a halo, huh. I call that thing a crown of thorns. I thought they was gonna screw it into my brain."

A paralyzed patient describes his rehabilitation in *The Waterdance*

Waterdance, The (1992) Drama ΨΨΨΨ
Realistic film about the way spinal cord injuries have changed the lives of three men who meet in a rehabilitation hospital.

Whales of August, The (1987) Drama ΨΨΨ
Vincent Price and Ann Sothern support Lillian Gish and Bette Davis in a remarkable film about what it means to grow old. Davis plays the blind and embittered sister who is still loved by Gish.

Whatever Happened to Baby Jane? (1962) Drama ΨΨ
Bette Davis and Joan Crawford portray two elderly sisters. Crawford is wheelchair-bound as a result of an automobile accident possibly caused by her

sister. Davis is obviously demented and terrorizes her younger sister. Surprise ending.

White Heat (1949) Crime ΨΨΨΨ
James Cagney plays a ruthless gangster who has debilitating migraine headaches that only his mother can cure. The film ties into the psychoanalytic ideas of the day and features a famous ending in which Cagney blows up an oil tank.

"Cody Jarrett. He finally made it to the top of the world. And it blew up in his face."

White Heat

Whose Life Is It Anyway? (1981) Drama ΨΨΨΨ
Richard Dreyfuss plays a sculptor paralyzed from the neck down after a car crash. He argues convincingly for the right to die.

Woman's Tale, A (1991) Drama ΨΨΨΨ
An Australian film directed by Paul Cox about the final days in the life of a 78-year-old woman dying of cancer.

Mood Disorders and Suicide

American Splendor (2003) Comedy/Drama/Documentary/Animation ΨΨΨΨ
Small time comic book writer and curmudgeon, Harvey Pekar, reaches cult status including several appearances on the David Letterman show. This film integrates a narrative about a depressed couple trying to get along and manage life's stressors, comic book animation, and documentary of the real Harvey Pekar.

"Right now I'd be glad to spare some growth for some happiness."

Harvey Pekar in *American Splendor*

Anna Karenina (1935) Drama ΨΨΨΨ
Greta Garbo leaves her husband (Basil Rathbone) and son to follow a new love (Fredric March); when she sees him kissing another woman, she commits suicide by stepping into the path of an oncoming train. Based on a Tolstoy novel.

Bell Jar, The (1979) Biography Ψ
An unsuccessful attempt to capture the spirit of Sylvia Plath's autobiographical novel *The Bell Jar*. Plath eventually committed suicide by putting her head into an oven and turning on the gas.

Cooler, The (2003) Drama ΨΨΨ
Unlucky, depressed man (William H. Macy) walks around the casino as "the cooler," someone paid to bring bad luck to successful gamers by appearing near their gambling tables. He is paying off his enormous gambling debts owed to the casino owner Alec Baldwin.

Crossover (1983) Drama Ψ
A male nurse is plagued by self-doubts after one of the psychiatric patients commits suicide.

Eye of God (1997) Drama ΨΨ
Some of the scenes in this film address a boy who witnesses his mother's suicide, experiences acute stress disorder, and kills himself at age 14.

Field, The (1990) Drama ΨΨ Ψ
Dramatic presentation of the suicide by drowning of a young man who finds he cannot live up to his father's expectations.

Fox and His Friends (1975) Drama ΨΨΨΨ
Werner Fassbinder's scathing indictment of capitalism revolves around the life of a poor gay circus performer who wins money, only to lose it through the exploitation of those he assumes are his friends. He responds by committing suicide.

Garden State (2004) Drama/Comedy ΨΨΨ
A young man flies to his hometown in New Jersey for his mother's funeral. He has been estranged from his family for several years. Without his "bipolar" medication for the first time, he begins to experiment with life and find love.

Good Morning, Vietnam (1987) Comedy/Drama/War ΨΨ
Robin Williams as an Air Force radio announcer in Vietnam. Williams has a funny, frenetic style that could be described as hypomanic.

Hairdresser's Husband, The (1992) Comedy/Drama ΨΨΨ
A woman chooses to commit suicide rather than face the incremental loss of love that she believes

will accompany aging. This is a beautiful movie, despite the somewhat grim ending.

Horse Feathers (1932) Comedy ΨΨ
Groucho Marx plays a manic college president who displays flight of ideation and pressured speech.

Hospital, The (1971) Comedy/Drama ΨΨΨ
George C. Scott is first rate as a disillusioned and suicidal physician despondent in part because of the ineptitude he sees everywhere about him. There is an especially memorable scene in which Scott is interrupted as he is about to commit suicide by injecting potassium into a vein.

House of Sand and Fog (2003) Drama ΨΨΨΨΨ
Jennifer Connelly and Sir Ben Kingsley play opposite one another in a gripping and deeply poignant story about two seemingly very different people, each with a legitimate claim to ownership of the same house. The film accurately portrays depression, alcohol abuse, suicide attempts, and suicide.

Hours, The (2002) Drama ΨΨΨΨΨ
Well-acted and well-crafted tapestry integrating three stories from different times—Nicole Kidman as the renowned novelist, Virginia Woolf, struggling to write her novel *Mrs. Dalloway*; Julianne Moore, who is reading the novel decades later; and Meryl Streep who embodies many of Mrs. Dalloway's characteristics. Each of the four main characters (the three aforementioned and Ed Harris) struggles with some form of mood disorder.

"You cannot find peace by avoiding life."

Nicole Kidman as Virginia Woolf in *The Hours*

Inside Moves (1980) Drama ΨΨ
A man who has failed in a suicide attempt makes new friends in a bar and regains the will to live. Mainly notable as the comeback film for Harold Russell, the double amputee from *The Best Years of Our Lives* (1946).

It's a Wonderful Life (1946) Drama ΨΨ
A Christmas tradition. The film actually presents Jimmy Stewart as a complex character who

responds to the stress of life in Bedford Falls by attempting suicide.

"You see, George, you've really had a wonderful life. Don't you see what a mistake it would be to throw it away?"

Clarence in *It's A Wonderful Life*

Juliet of the Spirits (1965) Drama ΨΨΨ
Frederico Fellini film about a bored, lonely, depressed, and menopausal homemaker who hallucinates about the life of the exotic woman next door.

Last Days of Disco, The (1998) Drama Ψ
One of the characters has bipolar disorder and is stereotyped as "looney" and "crazy"; however, he is depicted as compliant with Lithium, and his life is stable and balanced. Interesting contrast to the frequently portrayed stereotypes of bipolar disorder.

Last Picture Show, The (1971) Drama ΨΨΨΨ
Peter Bogdanovich adaptation of Larry McMurtry's novel describing the events—and personalities—involved in the closing of the town's only movie theater. There is a striking presentation of the symptoms of depression in the coach's wife.

Life Upside Down (1965) Drama ΨΨΨ
French film about an ordinary young man who becomes increasingly detached from the world. He is eventually hospitalized and treated, but with little success.

Mishima (1985) Biography ΨΨΨ
A fascinating film about one of the most interesting figures in contemporary literature, Yukio Mishima. Mishima, a homosexual, traditionalist, and militarist, committed ritual suicide *(seppuku)* before being beheaded by a companion.

Mommie Dearest (1981) Biography ΨΨ
Biographical film based on the book by Joan Crawford's adopted daughter. Faye Dunaway plays Crawford. The film suggests the great star was tyrannical, narcissistic, and probably bipolar.

Monsieur Ibrahim (2003) Drama/Comedy ΨΨΨ
An elderly widower and troubled teen form a unique friendship while living in Paris in the 1960s.

A secondary character, the boy's father, suffers from agitated, masked depression, and eventually abandons his son (who had already been abandoned by his mother) and commits suicide.

Monster's Ball (2002) Drama ΨΨΨΨ
Emotionally jarring film about two lost, self-hating people who begin to experience emotion and face their pain through their relationship. Stars Billy Bob Thornton and Halle Berry, the latter who won an Academy Award for Best Actress for her role in this film.

"It takes a human being to really see a human being."

Monster's Ball

Mosquito Coast, The (1986) Adventure ΨΨΨ
Harrison Ford is an eccentric American inventor who flees the U.S. for Central America because of his paranoia. His diagnosis is never clearly stated, but Ford appears to be bipolar (although almost continually manic in the film).

My First Wife (1984) Drama ΨΨ
A moving and well-directed Australian film about a man who falls apart after his wife decides to leave him.

Network (1976) Drama ΨΨΨ
A veteran anchorman who has just been told he is being fired announces on national TV that he will commit suicide on the air in two weeks. Ratings soar. He eventually reneges on his promise but becomes the leader of a national protest movement.

"... I'm as mad as hell, and I'm not going to take this anymore!"

Newscaster Howard Beale in *Network*

Nightmare Alley (1947) Crime ΨΨ
Tyrone Power's favorite film. Power plays a carnival huckster who teams up with an unethical psychologist to dupe the public. Memorable carnival "geek" scenes include biting the heads off chickens.

Ordinary People (1980) Drama ΨΨΨΨ
This film was Robert Redford's debut as a director. It deals with depression, suicide, and family pathology and presents a sympathetic portrayal of a psychiatrist, played by Judd Hirsch. Conrad, the protagonist, would probably meet *DSM-IV* criteria for PTSD as well as depression.

Outcry, The (1957) Drama ΨΨΨ
Antonioni film about a man who becomes depressed and confused when he is rejected by his lover.

Pollock (2000) Drama ΨΨΨ
Ed Harris portrays the troubled painter, Jackson Pollack, who struggles with alcoholism and bipolar disorder.

Rain (2001) Drama ΨΨ
Coming-of-age New Zealand film about a young girl whose mother is a depressed alcoholic.

Scent of a Woman (1992) Drama ΨΨΨ
Al Pacino plays Colonel Slade, a depressed blind veteran who seems to have lost all meaning in his life until he is challenged by a younger man.

Seventh Veil, The (1945) Drama ΨΨ
Psychological drama about a gifted musician who loses the ability to play the piano and becomes depressed and suicidal. Hypnotherapy makes it possible for Ann Todd to play again, as well as to sort out her complex interpersonal relationships.

Station Agent, The (2003) Drama/Comedy ΨΨΨΨ
Heartwarming, honest story of three lonely and disparate characters who form a unique friendship with one another. The three characters are a schizoid dwarf whose only desire is isolation, a woman who has repeated conflicts with her husband and attempts suicide, and a talkative man from New Jersey. Good mix of both healthy and unhealthy coping approaches to loneliness and depression.

Suicide Club (2002) Drama/Suspense ΨΨΨ
Fifty-four young girls collectively jump in front of an oncoming subway train, which triggers individual and group suicides around the country. This mysterious Japanese film raises questions of cause, documenting links between suicide and adolescence, violence, and consumerism.

Summer Wishes, Winter Dreams (1973) Drama Ψ
Joanne Woodward is a bored, depressed housewife searching for meaning and purpose in her life. The

film includes dreams that may be hallucinations, and a possible somatoform disorder.

Sylvia (2003) Drama ΨΨ
Gwenyth Paltrow portrays the life of respected American poet, Sylvia Plath, who committed suicide in 1963.

Tenant, The (1976) Horror ΨΨΨΨ
Roman Polanski film in which a man rents an apartment previously owned by a woman who committed suicide. The man begins to assume the personality of the woman and becomes suicidal himself.

Umberto D. (1952) Drama ΨΨΨΨΨ
Classic Vittorio De Sica film about an indigent old man in Rome who is being evicted and must face the prospects of homelessness and isolation. The old man fails a suicide attempt and finds a reason for living to continue to care for his dog.

Vincent (1987) Biography/Documentary ΨΨΨ
An interesting examination of the life of Vincent van Gogh. The focus is on the artist's work rather than his mental illness.

Vincent & Theo (1990) Biography ΨΨΨ
This Robert Altman film deals sensitively with van Gogh's troubled relationships with Gauguin and Theo, the incident with the prostitute and his ear, van Gogh's hospitalization, and finally his suicide.

Virgin Suicides, The (1999) Drama ΨΨ
Sofia Coppola's directorial debut about a repressed family with five daughters, who in response to their mother's control, repression, and forced group isolation, decide to commit suicide.

Wilbur Wants to Kill Himself (2002) Drama/Comedy ΨΨ
Disappointing and highly stereotypic movie of both suicide and boundary-crossing psychotherapists. Perpetrates the misconception that love can conquer mental illness (in this case, multiple, severe suicide attempts).

Woman Under the Influence, A (1974) Drama ΨΨΨ
A John Cassavetes film in which Gena Rowlands plays a homemaker who has to be hospitalized because of a mental illness that appears to be bipolar disorder. Peter Falk plays her sympathetic but mystified husband.

Wrong Man, The (1956) Crime ΨΨ
Hitchcock film in which a man and his wife (Henry Fonda and Vera Miles) become depressed in response to an unjust accusation of murder.

Personality Disorders

25th Hour (2002) Drama ΨΨΨΨ
A Spike Lee film about a young man (Edward Norton) about to go away to prison for 7 years for marijuana trafficking. In making the most of his final hours, he meets with his "recovering alcoholic" father, girlfriend, friends, and an "underground" boss and his henchmen. Look for tributes to 9/11 throughout the film (it was the first film to use Ground Zero as a film scene).

Accidental Tourist, The (1988) Comedy ΨΨΨ
William Hurt plays a withdrawn, unemotional writer whose isolation is compounded when his 12-year-son is senselessly murdered in a fast-food restaurant.

Aguirre: The Wrath of God (1972) Historical/Drama ΨΨΨΨΨ
Klaus Kinski stars in this Werner Herzog film about the growing delusion of a grandiose Spanish conquistador obsessed with finding the lost cities of gold in the South American Amazon.

Alfie (2004) Comedy ΨΨΨ
Jude Law stars as a man with a narcissistic personality who prides himself in being a womanizer and not committing in relationships. Law's asides to the audience provide insight into his narcissistic thinking. By the end of the film, Alfie begins to face the impact of his behavior on others.

Amelie (2001) Comedy/Romance ΨΨΨΨΨ
Audrey Tautou stars as Amelie, an avoidant woman who wants an intimate relationships with others but is unable to be direct. Upon deciding to change her life by making a difference in others' lives, she adopts extreme and creative measures to bring joy to others and make connections. Brilliantly directed by the Frenchman Jean Pierre-Jeunet.

American Beauty (1999) Comedy/Drama ΨΨΨΨΨ
Kevin Spacey has the lead role in this remarkable film about a very dysfunctional family and the ennui that accompanies life in suburbia. Annette Bening plays a woman with a classic Histrionic

Personality Disorder. Almost every character exhibits some degree of psychopathology. The film is a compelling examination of what Freud called the psychopathology of everyday life.

American History X (1998) Drama/ Suspense ΨΨΨ
Edward Norton plays an antisocial, white supremacist who decides to change his life when he sees his younger brother is following his example.

American Psycho (1999) Drama/Suspense ΨΨΨ
Christian Bale is Patrick Bateman, a narcissistic Wall Street executive, who emphasizes excess and style over substance in everything from business cards and facial cleansers to restaurant selection and conversation. He is depicted as a serial killer who saves the victim's heads in his refrigerator. However, there is enough cinematic evidence to suggest that there were no murders at all, and everything in the film simply reflects the fantasies of an antisocial mind.

Anatomy of a Murder (1959) Drama ΨΨΨΨ
Jimmy Stewart as an attorney defending a man accused of murder. His case rests on the contention that the defendant could not help behaving as he did because the man he murdered had allegedly raped his wife. The film raises interesting questions about the irresistible impulse defense.

Anything Else (2003) Comedy ΨΨ
Woody Allen film about a young man with dependent personality who falls for an erratic young woman (Christina Ricci).

"See where I'm standing? That's where I'm from."

Robert Duvall as Sonny in *The Apostle*

Apostle, The (1997) Drama ΨΨΨΨ
Robert Duvall directs, writes, and stars as a philandering but dedicated minister who flees his hometown after committing a violent act. His redemptive journey takes him to a small town where he builds a ministry until his past catches up with him.

Apt Pupil (1998) Drama/Suspense ΨΨΨ
A high school student becomes fascinated with his discovery of a man (Ian McKellan) who was formerly a Nazi henchman for Hitler. McKellan is living (and hiding out) in a local town. The student manipulates the man to tell him detailed stories of the man's previous work.

"To the whole world I am a monster."

Ian McKellan as an escaped Nazi in *Apt Pupil*

Arsenic and Old Lace (1944) Comedy ΨΨ
Frank Capra film about Cary Grant's two aunts who practice mercy killing by giving their gentlemen guests poisoned elderberry wine. Grant worries about the fact that mental illness not only runs in his family, it gallops!

Bad Santa (2003) Comedy Ψ
This Terry Zwigoff film stars Billy Bob Thornton as a rule breaking, crass alcoholic who works as Santa Claus at a department store. The female co-star has a "Santa fetish."

Bad Seed, The (1956) Drama Ψ
Interesting examination of whether or not evil is congenital.

Bartleby (2001) Comedy ΨΨΨΨ
This dark comedy brilliantly casts Crispin Glover as the aloof, quirky clerk, Bartleby, who repeats the same phrase "I would prefer not to" when asked to work. Ironically colorful set design and a hodgepodge of quirky personalities as supporting cast. This is clearly a "love it or hate it" film, based on a short story by Herman Melville. Bartleby's character is a classic depiction of a person with a schizoid personality.

Bartleby (1970) Comedy ΨΨΨ
Original, black and white, version of the Herman Melville short story, Bartleby the Scrivener. More slow, dark, and dreary than its recent counterpart, yet still an excellent depiction of schizoid personality.

Believer, The (2001) Drama ΨΨΨ
Fascinating character study of Danny Burrows who is living his life in an impossible contradiction as a Jewish Nazi. As he faces his true self, his ruthless antisocial characteristics begin to crumble.

Based on a true story of events that occurred in Burrows' life in the Fall of 1965.

Box of Moonlight (1996) Drama ΨΨΨ
A rigid, orderly, rule-obsessed man, played by John Turturro, takes extra time off from his blue-collar, managerial position and from his family to re-discover his lost adolescence. The title becomes a beautiful, transformational metaphor in the film.

Bruce Almighty (2002) Comedy Ψ
Whimsical comedy about a man (Jim Carrey) given the opportunity to "be God" for a day.

Butley (1974) Drama ΨΨΨΨ
Alan Bates in a Harold Pinter film adaptation of a London play about the life of a British university professor. Bates' wife and lover are both leaving him, and his colleagues are estranged. Bates seems to fail in every interpersonal encounter.

Caine Mutiny, The (1954) Drama ΨΨΨ
Humphrey Bogart is the ship's paranoid captain, who decompensates under the pressure of testimony when he is called to the witness stand. Humphrey Bogart plays the role of Captain Queeg.

Catch Me If You Can (2002) Drama ΨΨΨ
Steven Spielberg directs Leonardo Dicaprio who plays the role of a manipulative con man with an antisocial personality. He repeatedly changes his identity while defrauding banks and keeping FBI agent (Tom Hanks) one step behind him. Based on the true story of Frank Abagnal, Jr.

"That boy, I'll strangle him for nine tenths and the last tenth will make him strong."

Dreverhaven describing his son in *Character*

Character (1998) Drama ΨΨΨ
Best Foreign Film winner (Dutch) about a young man's personal and financial struggle to be free of his antisocial father. His mother appears to have a schizoid personality disorder.

Come Back to the Five and Dime, Jimmy Dean, Jimmy Dean (1982) Drama ΨΨ
A Robert Altman film in which Sandy Dennis plays a local woman in a small Texas town who is convinced she bore a son by James Dean when he was in town filming *Giant*.

Conspiracy Theory (1997) Drama ΨΨ
Mel Gibson plays a cab driver with virtually no personal life, who is obsessed with a woman, and who writes a newsletter on conspiracies. His paranoia takes him to every possible place and situation, including one conspiracy that turns out true.

Conversation, The (1974) Drama ΨΨΨ
A Francis Ford Coppola film in which Gene Hackman plays a surveillance expert with a paranoid personality.

The Crush (1993) Drama/Suspense Ψ
Alicia Silverstone plays a 14-year-old temptress who is obsessed with a 28-year-old man who is simply not interested in her. This is an interesting portrayal of a character who is likely to qualify for a diagnosis of Antisocial Personality Disorder (as soon as she turns 18).

Dementia 13 (1963) Horror Ψ
Third rate film about an ax murderer; interesting primarily because it is Francis Ford Coppola's first "serious" film.

Divine Secrets of the Ya-Ya Sisterhood (2002) Drama/Comedy ΨΨ
A group of friends teach a young woman (Sandra Bullock) about her troubled mother. Ellen Burstyn and Ashley Judd play the erratic, labile, and abusive mother.

Dogville (2003) Drama ΨΨΨ
Nicole Kidman stars as a woman on the run who finds refuge in a small, isolated town. If a town could be diagnosed, this one would clearly be "antisocial" as group contagion results in manipulation, deceit, and abuse. Unique set design of a town without any houses or doors and is set as if on a theater stage.

Dream Lover (1994) Drama Ψ
A sociopathic woman plots to marry a man and then have him committed to an insane asylum.

End of Violence, The (1997) Drama ΨΨΨ
Wim Wenders film about a paranoid personality played by Bill Pullman.

Evita (1997) Drama/Musical ΨΨ
Madonna portrays Argentina's first lady, Eva Peron, and depicts her rise from poverty and scandal to

fame, fortune, and the adulation of a nation. Eva (Evita) does what it takes to climb the ladder of success, eventually marrying military leader Juan Peron. She speaks out on his behalf, mobilizes the people of Argentina, frees him from jail, and helps him get elected. Antonio Banderas plays her alter ego with running commentary, warnings, criticism, and song.

Family Man, The (2000) Family/Comedy ΨΨ
Corporate executive (Nicholas Cage) obsessed with money, fame, and power gets an opportunity to see how his life would have turned out if he had married his college sweetheart. The film includes obvious parallels with *It's a Wonderful Life*.

Fatal Attraction (1987) Thriller/Romance ΨΨΨ
Glenn Close displays classic characteristics of borderline personality disorder, including fears of abandonment, unstable interpersonal relationships, impulsivity, suicidal gestures, inappropriate and intense anger, and affective instability. This remarkable film is flawed by a contrived and artificial ending.

Finding Forrester (2000) Drama ΨΨ
A high school student befriends an aloof, retired professor and writer who has avoided people for years. Their relationship is "rocky," taking many turns, yet each individual has a profound impact on the other.

Five Easy Pieces (1970) Drama ΨΨΨ
Jack Nicholson, raised in an upper class and gifted family, is a talented pianist who left his affluent life to work in the oil fields. The plot is thin, but the character Nicholson plays is complex and fascinating.

Freaks (1932) Horror ΨΨΨΨ
Fascinating film about a "normal" trapeze artist who marries a midget and then tries to poison him. When his friends find out, they kill her strong-man lover and turn her into one of them.

From Dusk Till Dawn (1995) Horror Ψ
Quentin Tarantino and George Clooney portray psychopaths who rendezvous at a biker bar that turns out to be run by vampires. The film is actually two very different movies combined—the first is Tarantino-like in character interaction and dialogue, and the second half is a horror show. Robert Rodriguez directs the films.

From the Life of the Marionettes (1980) Drama ΨΨΨ
Bergman film in which an executive rapes and kills a prostitute.

Girl, Interrupted (1999) Drama ΨΨ
A depressed, young woman (Winona Ryder), sent to a psychiatric hospital and labeled with Borderline Personality Disorder, encounters a dangerous patient (Angelina Jolie) with an Antisocial Personality Disorder.

God is Great and I Am Not (2003) Comedy ΨΨ
Audrey Tautou plays a dependent woman who obsessively conforms to the religion of any man she is dating.

Grifters, The (1990) Crime ΨΨΨΨ
Anjelica Huston stars in this fascinating introduction to the world of the con. Contrast this film with a movie almost as good, David Mamet's *House of Games* (see Treatment section).

Heavy (1995) Drama ΨΨΨ
An obese, schizoid man loses his mother (whom he has lived with) and becomes even more withdrawn as he grieves.

I, Robot (2004) Action/Suspense ΨΨ
Surprisingly high quality action film about an agent who battles robots threatening to take over the world. Will Smith's role illustrates paranoid personality traits.

"I did it because I could."

Aaron Eckhart as Chad in
In the Company of Men

In the Company of Men (1997) Comedy ΨΨΨ
Misogynistic satire of two men (with varying levels of narcissism) who deliberately seduce the same vulnerable girl, lead her on, and then abandon her. Directed by Neil LaBute.

Knife in the Water (1962) Drama ΨΨΨΨ
One of Roman Polanski's earliest films. A man and his wife on a sailing holiday pick up a hitchhiker. There is mounting sexual tension between the older man and his younger rival. The younger man eventually makes love to the wife after a complex turn of events that occur when the couple becomes convinced the young man has drowned.

La Cage aux Folles (1978) Comedy ΨΨΨ
Zaza (Albin), the transvestite nightclub performer, is a wonderful example of a histrionic personality.

He is dramatic and flamboyant and threatens suicide when things do not go his way.

Ladies Man, The (2000) Comedy Ψ
Tim Meadows plays a narcissistic talk-show host and "player." Spin-off of a successful Saturday Night Live skit.

Ladykillers, The (2004) Comedy ΨΨ
Tom Hanks leads a group of thieves in a caper to steal money from a casino by digging underground from an oblivious, good-hearted, elderly woman. Good portrayal of how people with antisocial personalities can use language to manipulate. Directed by the Coen Brothers.

Le Boucher (1969) Thriller ΨΨΨ
Claude Chabrol film in which a butcher who is also a murderer commits suicide when the woman he loves realizes he is a criminal.

Leave Her to Heaven (1945) Romance/Crime ΨΨ
Protagonist commits multiple murders, watches her brother-in-law drown, and terminates her pregnancy by throwing herself down a flight of stairs with no sense of shame or remorse. Dated but interesting portrayal of an antisocial personality.

Lemony Snicket's A Series of Unfortunate Events (2004) Comedy/Drama ΨΨΨ
Jim Carrey plays a comical psychopath who adopts multiple disguises in an attempt to inherit a family fortune that rightfully belongs to three orphans whose parents have died in a fire.

Levity (2003) Drama ΨΨΨ
Billy Bob Thornton plays a "recovered antisocial," who, after his release from prison, tries to make amends with a family member (Holly Hunter) of a boy he killed decades ago. Morgan Freeman plays an antisocial preacher.

Lovelife (1997) Comedy ΨΨ
Film about a group of friends and their struggles in relationships, many with symptoms of disorders that prevent them from connecting—the depressed intellectual, the dependant woman, and the neurotic voyeur—but the standout is the narcissist professor.

Mad Love (2002) ΨΨ
Spanish film about a princess who marries and later becomes queen and is nicknamed "Joan the Mad" because of her worries about her philandering husband.

Man from Elysian Fields, The (2001) Drama ΨΨΨ
Married man (Andy Garcia) becomes an escort and his life falls apart.

Man Who Cried, The (2000) Drama ΨΨ
Slow-moving film of a young woman (Christina Ricci) who left a very poor Russian family years ago to make it as a dancer in the theater. Sub-par film with an all-star cast including Johnny Depp (in another vagrant role), Cate Blanchett, and John Turturro as a grandiose opera singer.

Man Who Wasn't There, The (2001) Drama ΨΨΨ
This Coen Brothers' film noir is a fascinating character analysis of Ed Crane (Billy Bob Thornton) who is an aloof, taciturn, and unemotional barber struggling to find purpose.

Marriage of Maria Braun, The (1978) Drama/War ΨΨΨ
This Fassbinder film, an allegory about postwar Germany, portrays the dehumanizing effects of war and its aftermath as we watch the commercial success and personal failures of Maria Braun. There is an explosive finale.

Minus Man (1999) Drama ΨΨ
Owen Wilson stars as a charming, kind, drifting serial killer. The film does not explain his behavior, which he claims is spontaneous.

Monster (2004) Docudrama ΨΨΨΨ
Graphic, disturbing film based on the life of Aileen Wuornos, a prostitute and drifter turned serial killer. Charlize Theron won an Oscar for her powerful performance as Wuornos.

Naked (1993) Drama ΨΨΨΨΨ
Fascinating story about an "existential antisocial," Johnny, wandering the streets of London exchanging philosophical beliefs with various quirky characters. Comedy, love, drama, and violence flow throughout this film. Written and directed by renowned British director Mike Leigh.

Odd Couple, The (1968) Comedy ΨΨΨ
Jack Lemmon is magnificent as the obsessive-compulsive Felix Unger, who uses air freshener and leaves notes on the pillow of housemate Walter Matthau.

One Hour Photo (2002) ΨΨΨ
Robin Williams in a quirky, dramatic, and disturbing role as the personality disordered, Sy the Photo

Guy. Sy collects photographs from a customer's family and finds meaning through their lives until he discovers they are not the perfect family.

"The things we fear the most have already happened to us."

Robin Williams as Sy, the Photo Guy in *One Hour Photo*

Paper Moon (1973) Comedy/Drama ΨΨ
Fun Peter Bogdanovich film, with Ryan O'Neal and daughter Tatum working together as a pair of con artists in the early 1930s.

Pacific Heights (1990) Drama/Suspense ΨΨΨ
Michael Keaton plays a classic antisocial personality who becomes a tenant of a Victorian home and refuses to leave or pay rent, reaping significant havoc.

Phone Booth (2003) Action/Suspense ΨΨ
A one-dimensional, narcissistic New Yorker begins to unravel as he is manipulated and forced to stay on the phone on the busy streets of Manhattan with a serial killer (Kiefer Sutherland). Worth seeing for the ending which cinematically shows the deep wounds underlying many narcissistic personality disorders.

Pumpkin Eater, The (1964) Drama ΨΨ
Most memorable for the scene in which Anne Bancroft, responding to the stress of eight children and an unfaithful husband, breaks down in Harrods.

Rampage (1992) Drama/Thriller ΨΨΨ
A film that explores the insanity defense, sociopathy, and mass murder. Directed by William Friedkin, who was also the director for *The Exorcist*.

Remains of the Day (1994) Romance /Drama ΨΨΨΨ
Anthony Hopkins plays a butler whose rigid personality will not allow him to experience intimacy or genuine love. Few films have been more effective in presenting this reserved, over-controlled, and limiting personality type.

Rick (2003) Comedy/Drama ΨΨΨ
Satirical comedy starring Bill Pullman as Rick, a narcissistic corporate executive who is self-serving, misanthropic, and cruel. The film has strong independent cinema elements.

Roger Dodger (2002) Comedy ΨΨΨ
Manhattan executive teaches his 16-year-old nephew about women in one night by taking him to the streets of New York. Great portrayal of narcissism.

Royal Tenenbaums, The (2001) Comedy ΨΨΨΨ
Dark comedy classic about highly dysfunctional Tenenbaum family where the parents (Gene Hackman and Angelica Huston) raise three genius children (Ben Stiller, Gwenyth Paltrow, and Luke Wilson) who develop significant problems (paranoia/anger, depression/incest, dependency/suicidal thoughts/incest, respectively). The family is reunited when the narcissistic father returns home stating he is dying of stomach cancer. We are left to see the dysfunctional dynamics of the family take place in comical form. Schizotypal personality is also portrayed (Owen Wilson)—a cinematic rarity.

Séance on a Wet Afternoon (1964) Crime ΨΨΨΨ
A British film in which Kim Stanley plays a medium who persuades her husband (Richard Attenborough) to kidnap a child so they can then use her power of clairvoyance to "find" the missing child.

Servant, The (1963) Drama ΨΨΨ
Joseph Losey film in which a wealthy British gentleman and his manservant wind up switching roles. There are strong homosexual overtones in the relationship between the two men, and a complex relationship develops with two women. The film is an interesting examination of dominance and submission.

Sexy Beast (2001) Drama ΨΨΨ
Ben Kingsley portrays a brutal antisocial personality who is anything but sexy.

The Shape of Things (2003) Comedy ΨΨΨ
Disturbing comedy of a woman who helps transform an anxious, insecure man through physical alteration and love only to later reveal it was all a manipulative, self-serving project. Another film by director Neil LaBute who has been appropriately nicknamed by some film critics as Neil La-Brute because of his often brutal character portrayal of people or society.

Shattered Glass (2003) Drama ΨΨΨ
Based on a true story of a young journalist for the popular New Republic magazine, Stephen Glass (well acted by Hayden Christensen), who in 1998

made up several of his published stories. He was fraudulent with people, places, and events, making up fake business cards, notes, websites, numbers, and voice mails. Great depiction of "the antisocial in trouble," where the person becomes neurotic and remorseful. The "real" Glass, a self-proclaimed "pathological liar" in reference to the events in the film, admits that 27 of his 41 published magazine stories were partially or completely made up.

"I wanted every story to be a home run."

The real Stephen Glass in a "60 Minutes" interview, speaking of being out of control and doing anything to please the readers

---

Silence of the Lambs, The (1991) Personality Disorders ΨΨΨ
Sir Anthony Hopkins plays one of film history's greatest antisocial personalities, psychiatrist and cannibal Hannibal Lector. Jodi Foster is the FBI agent.

"A census taker once tried to test me. I ate his liver with some fava beans and a nice Chianti."

The Silence of the Lambs

Sleeping with the Enemy (1991) Suspense ΨΨ
Julia Roberts plays the battered wife of a possessive and sadistic husband played by Patrick Bergin. Roberts fakes her death and assumes a new identity in a desperate attempt to escape.

Small Time Crooks (2000) Comedy Ψ
Woody Allen plays a "foolish antisocial" who devises a plan to rob a bank with his not-so-bright pals. Hugh Grant plays a manipulative, charming, self-serving narcissist.

Sneakers (1992) Drama/Comedy ΨΨ
This film has a star cast that includes Dan Akroyd, who plays an ex-convict with paranoid traits who sees conspiracy in almost every situation.

Speed (1994) Drama ΨΨ
Dennis Hopper plays a deranged sociopath who programs a bomb to explode if a city bus slows to less than 50 miles per hour.

Stagecoach (1939) Western ΨΨΨ
Classic John Ford movie, with Thomas Mitchell playing a drunken physician. Mitchell won an Academy Award for Best Supporting Actor for his role.

Strangers on a Train (1951) Thriller ΨΨΨΨ
Classic Hitchcock film in which Farley Granger is unable to extricate himself from his involvement with sociopath Robert Walker.

Streetcar Named Desire, A (1951) Drama ΨΨΨΨ
Elia Kazan film starring Marlon Brando and Vivian Leigh. Blanche DuBois offers a striking example of a histrionic personality. Brando is unforgettable in the role of Stanley Kowalski.

"They're dead, they're finished! There was a time in this business when they had the eyes of the whole wide world. But that wasn't good enough for them. Oh, no. They had to have the ears of the world, too. So they opened their big mouths, and out came talk. Talk! Talk!"

Sunset Blvd.

Sunset Blvd. (1950) Drama ΨΨΨ
Billy Wilder film in which a narcissistic, histrionic, and delusional Gloria Swanson clings to the memories of her former greatness as a silent screen star. William Holden plays a young man who exchanges attention and sexual favors for security.

Swimfan (2002) Drama/Suspense Ψ
Girl's one-night-stand with a fellow classmate shifts from infatuation to the "If I can't have you, no one will" belief.

Swimming With Sharks (1994) Comedy ΨΨ
Dark comedy with Kevin Spacey as a nasty, heartless, business executive who is held hostage and tortured by an employee he has verbally abused over the years.

Swimming Pool (2002) Drama/Mystery ΨΨΨΨ
Mystery writer leaves London to find peace, quiet, and inspiration at her publisher's secluded home in a French village. She overcomes her writer's block by writing about the adventures of a seductive, provocative young woman, the publisher's daughter, who has spontaneously moved in.

"I always thought it would be better to be a fake somebody than a real nobody."

Tom Ripley describing his secretive, double-life in *The Talented Mr. Ripley*

The Talented Mr. Ripley (1999) Drama ΨΨΨΨΨ
Matt Damon is the deceitful, charming, clever, impersonator, Tom Ripley, who manipulates anyone in his path until he sees enough of his "shadow" that he can no longer turn away. Breakthrough film for supporting actor Jude Law.

Tao of Steve, The (2000) Comedy Ψ
Self-serving, amateur philosopher uses some ideas from Buddhist philosophy to pursue and sleep with women.

Tape (2001) Drama ΨΨΨΨ
Creative, engaging, and honest story of how people manipulate other to meet their own desires and how they react when their secrets are exposed. It also shows what can happen when someone has unresolved psychological issues. The entire film takes place in one motel room with only three characters—all young veterans—Ethan Hawke, Robert Sean Leonard, and Uma Thurmond.

Taxi Driver (1976) Drama ΨΨΨΨΨ
The premorbid personality of Travis Bickle illustrates delusional paranoid thinking. Bickle would probably meet the criteria for a diagnosis of schizotypal personality disorder.

Thin Blue Line, The (1988) Documentary ΨΨΨ
Gripping documentary examining the unjust incarceration of a man accused of the murder of a Texas policeman.

Toto le Heros (1991) Drama/Comedy ΨΨΨΨ
An old man in a nursing home reviews his life and

his lifelong hatred for his next-door neighbor, who appeared to have every advantage. Wonderful example of a paranoid personality disorder.

"You talkin' to me? [slower] You talking to me? You talking to me? Well, then, who the hell else are you talking— you talking to me? Well, I'm the only one here."

Travis Bickle rehearsing in *Taxi Driver*

Unfaithful (2002) Drama/Suspense Ψ
Married man (Richard Gere) finds out his wife (Diane Lane) is having an affair and he seeks revenge.

Violette Noziere (1978) Biography/Crime ΨΨ
Claude Chabrol film based on the true story about a teenage girl who poisoned her parents, eventually killing her father, whom she claimed had raped and abused her.

Wannsee Conference, The (1984) Historical/War ΨΨΨ
Recreation of the Berlin meeting in which Nazi officers first outlined the "final solution" for dealing with the "Jewish problem."

Whisperers, The (1966) Drama Ψ
Dame Edith Evans stars as a lonely old woman, divorced from her husband and estranged from her son, who devotes her days to worry and paranoid ramblings.

"Loneliness is the human condition. Love humiliates you. Hatred cradles you."

Michelle Pfeiffer as Ingrid, teaching her philosophy to her teenage daughter Astrid in *White Oleander*

White Oleander (2002) Drama ΨΨΨΨ
Young girl is tossed around from home to home when her mother is incarcerated. Range of mother figures played by Michelle Pfeiffer (Antisocial),

Renee Zellweger (Dependent), and Robin Wright-Penn (Histrionic). Fascinating dynamics of a young girl's resilience with each personality disordered mother-figure.

Wild at Heart (1990) Comedy/Drama/ Romance ΨΨΨ
David Lynch film with ex-con Nicolas Cage and his lover, Laura Dern, as two antisocial personalities (despite their apparent commitment to each other). Won the Palme d'Ore at Cannes, but not all critics were impressed. Too violent for some tastes.

Willard (2003) Drama ΨΨ
Crispin Glover plays a schizoid man whose only contact is his critical mother and numerous rats living in his basement. He uses the rats for revenge until they turn on him.

Wise Blood (1979) Drama ΨΨΨ
John Huston's adaptation of Flannery O'Connor's gothic Southern novel about an obsessed preacher.

Zoolander (2001) Comedy Ψ
Absurd, over-the-top depiction of a narcissistic model who is brainwashed to become an assassin. Ben Stiller directed, co-wrote, and starred in this film.

Substance Use Disorders

Alcoholism

Arthur (1981) Comedy ΨΨ
Dudley Moore as a drunken millionaire who falls in love with Liza Minnelli. A genuinely funny film, but upsetting in its cavalier approach to alcoholism and drunken driving.

Susan: "A real woman could stop you from drinking."
Arthur: "It'd have to be a real BIG woman."

Arthur

Barfly (1987) Comedy/Romance/Drama ΨΨΨΨ
Faye Dunaway and Mickey Rourke play two alcoholics whose lives briefly touch. Good examination of skid row alcoholism; based on a story by cult poet Charles Bukowski.

Basketball Diaries, The (1995) Drama ΨΨΨ
Adolescent basketball stars succumb to drug abuse in this film that stars Leonardo Dicaprio and Mark Wahlberg. Adapted from a Jim Carroll novel.

Beloved Infidel (1959) Biography Ψ
Gregory Peck plays F. Scott Fitzgerald and Deborah Kerr is columnist Sheila Graham, who tries to save Fitzgerald from his alcoholism.

"You're a T6—paralyzed from the mid-chest down . . . . you'll be in a wheelchair for the rest of your life."

Ron Kovic's grim prognosis in *Born on the Fourth of July*

Born on the Fourth of July (1989) Drama/War/Biography ΨΨΨΨ
Tom Cruise plays paralyzed and alcoholic Vietnam veteran Ron Kovic in Oliver Stone's film. Stone won an Oscar as best director for this film.

Cat Ballou (1965) Comedy/Western Ψ
Light-hearted film, with Jane Fonda playing a schoolteacher turned outlaw. Lee Marvin got an Oscar for his role as an alcoholic gunman. The film perpetuates the myth of the down-and-out drunk whose shooting skills return after he has had a few drinks. Marvin won an Oscar as Best Actor for his role in this film.

"Big Daddy! Now what makes him so big? His big heart? His big belly? Or his big money?"

Cat on a Hot Tin Roof

Cat on a Hot Tin Roof (1958) Drama ΨΨΨ
Paul Newman, Elizabeth Taylor, and Burl Ives in a subdued adaptation of Tennessee Williams' play about "mendacity." Alcohol plays a prominent role in the life of almost all the character's lives.

Come Back, Little Sheba (1952) Drama ΨΨΨ
Burt Lancaster and Shirley Booth in a film about
alcoholism and marriage. Booth won an Academy
Award for Best Actress for her role.

Come Fill the Cup (1951) Drama ΨΨ
James Cagney and Jackie Gleason star in this serious examination of the problems of alcoholism in
an ex-newspaperman.

Dark Obsession (1989) Drama/Mystery ΨΨ
Five drunken British military officers are involved in
a hit-and-run accident in which the victim dies. The
five men take a vow of silence; one is troubled by the
decision. Interesting analysis of responsibility for
one's behavior while intoxicated.

Days of Wine and Roses (1962) Drama ΨΨΨΨ
Blake Edwards film starring Jack Lemmon and
Lee Remick. Lemmon teaches Remick how to
drink. Lemmon is saved by AA; Remick is unable
to stop drinking, despite the consequences.

> **"You see, the world looks so
> dirty to me when I'm not drinking.
> Joe, remember Fisherman's
> Wharf? The water when you
> looked too close? That's
> the way the world looks to
> me when I'm not
> drinking."**
>
> **Kristen describes why
> she continues to drink
> in Days of Wine and Roses**

Drunks (1995) Drama ΨΨΨΨ
This film is the best available introduction to
Alcoholics Anonymous. It is highly recommended
for any student who will be working with substance abuse issues.

Educating Rita (1983) Drama ΨΨ
Michael Caine as an alcoholic college professor
who takes on the task of educating a working-class
woman.

Fire Within, The (1963) Drama ΨΨΨΨΨ
French filmmaker Louis Malle's remarkable
account of alcoholism, suicide, and the existential
choices that confront us all.

Gervaise (1956) Drama ΨΨΨ
French film based on Emile Zola's story about a
young Parisian woman with an alcoholic husband.

> **"Mrs. Robinson, you're trying to
> seduce me. Aren't you?"**
>
> **The Graduate**

Graduate, The (1967) Drama/Comedy ΨΨΨ
A telling indictment of the shallow values of the
time (e.g., "plastics"). Mrs. Robinson's alcoholism
impairs her judgment and ruins her life.

Great Man Votes, The (1939) Drama ΨΨ
John Barrymore plays an alcoholic college professor
fighting to maintain custody of his children.

Harvey (1950) Comedy ΨΨ
Jimmy Stewart is a happy drunk who goes drinking
with Harvey, an invisible six-foot rabbit. When
hospitalized, Stewart frequently switches places
and counsels his psychiatrist, Dr. Chumley.

Iceman Cometh, The (1973) Drama ΨΨ
Lee Marvin in an adaptation of Eugene O'Neill's
play about alcoholism and the pathos of dreams
unfulfilled.

I'll Cry Tomorrow (1955) Biography ΨΨΨ
Singer Lillian Roth (Susan Hayward) attempts sui-
cide as a way of coping with her alcoholism before
AA support helps her find her way.

Ironweed (1987) Drama ΨΨΨΨ
Jack Nicholson and Meryl Streep in compelling
roles as homeless alcoholics. The film, a very realistic portrayal of life on skid row, should be contrasted with another excellent film made the same
year, *Barfly*.

Key Largo (1948) Crime ΨΨΨ
Claire Trevor won Best Supporting Actress for her
role as an alcoholic singer forced to beg gangster
Edward G. Robinson for a drink during a hurricane
in Key West.

Last Night at the Alamo (1983) Drama ΨΨΨ
Fascinating examination of bar culture in a small
Texas town. Unforgettable characters, most of
whom are coping with alcoholism and adultery.

Leaving Las Vegas (1995) Drama ΨΨΨ
Nicholas Cage delivers a stunning performance as an alcoholic who has no interest in quitting. He develops a relationship with a prostitute (Elisabeth Shue) who is the first to truly understand him. Gripping alcohol dependence portrayal with painful delirium tremens on screen.

"You can never, never ask me to stop drinking. Do you understand?"

Nicolas Cage gives instructions to Elisabeth Shue in *Leaving Las Vegas*

Legend of Bagger Vance, The (2000) Drama/Inspiration ΨΨΨ
Matt Damon plays Rannulph Junuh, a talented golfer whose game has deteriorated because of his war experiences. He isolates himself, drinks heavily, and plays cards all night. He returns to golf in a promotional event against the top two golfers in the game with the help of an inspirational caddy and mentor, Bagger Vance (Will Smith).

Lonely Passion of Judith Hearne, The (1987) Romance ΨΨ
Maggie Smith plays a lonely alcoholic who mistakenly believes she has a last chance to find love and meaning in her life.

Long Day's Journey into Night (1962) Drama ΨΨΨΨΨ
Alcohol is a part of daily life for this deeply troubled family. Numerous examples of family pathology, conflict between father and sons, and denial.

Lost Weekend, The (1945) Drama ΨΨΨΨΨ
Billy Wilder classic starring Ray Milland as a writer struggling to overcome his alcoholism. Some scenes were filmed at Bellevue, and the examples of delirium tremens are very convincing. Polanski borrowed scenes from *The Lost Weekend* as models for his film *Repulsion*.

Love and Diane (2002) Documentary ΨΨ
A mother recovers from an addiction to crack as she attempts to start a new life and connect with the children she had abandoned.

Maria, Full of Grace (2004) **Drama** ΨΨΨ
Fascinating, independent film depicting the realities and dangers young girls from Colombia face as they take jobs as "mules," smuggling drugs into the United States by swallowing them in large latex packages. While this film is not about substance abuse, it depicts the drug trade and problems related to ingesting drugs for illegal purposes.

"It shrinks my liver, doesn't it, Nat? It pickles my kidneys, yeah. But what it does to the mind? It tosses the sandbags overboard so the balloon can soar. Suddenly I'm above the ordinary. I'm competent. I'm walking a tightrope over Niagara Falls. I'm one of the great ones."

Don Birnam talking to his bartender about what it feels like to be drunk in *The Lost Weekend*

My Favorite Year (1982) Comedy ΨΨΨ
A great actor (modeled after John Barrymore and Errol Flynn) who has become a pathetic drunk must confront one of the greatest challenges of his career—a live television performance.

My Name Is Bill W. (1989) ΨΨ
Made-for-TV movie about the founding of Alcoholics Anonymous.

National Lampoon's Animal House (1978) Comedy ΨΨ
One of the best of a hundred or so college films that portray fraternity life as a series of beer busts interspersed with an occasional class. At one point, John Belushi, not the brightest of the fraternity brothers, chugs a fifth of Jack Daniels.

Night of the Iguana, The (1964) Drama ΨΨ
Richard Burton and Ava Gardner star in John Huston's adaptation of Tennessee Williams' play. Burton plays a very convincing alcoholic and erstwhile clergyman.

Pay It Forward (2000) Drama/Inspiration ΨΨ
Haley Joel Osment plays a seventh grader implementing a class assignment that has profound

effects on the people around him. His mother (Helen Hunt) is a struggling alcoholic.

"Think of an idea to change our world... and put it into action."

Kevin Spacey giving his students an assignment in *Pay It Forward*

Proud and the Beautiful, The (1953) Romance ΨΨ
A film about a woman who helps an alcoholic physician overcome his problems and regain some sense of dignity. Filmed in France and Mexico.

Ray (2004) Drama/Biography ΨΨΨΨ
Story of Ray Charles' rise to fame and the numerous obstacles he faced after witnessing his brother's death and the subsequent loss of his sight. As an adult, Ray Charles struggled with addictions to heroin and sex, and he lived several different lives (e.g., family man with wife and children, lover with his mistress, a secret life as a drug abuser, a life as a famous singer and musician). Stellar performance by Jamie Foxx.

Skin Deep (1989) Comedy ΨΨ
A funny Blake Edwards film about an alcoholic writer who continues to deny his alcoholism long after it has become apparent to everyone else.

Smash-Up, the Story of a Woman (1947) Drama ΨΨ
Melodramatic Susan Hayward film about a movie star who must come to grips with her alcoholism.

Streamers (1983) Drama ΨΨΨ
Robert Altman film about three soldiers waiting to go to Vietnam. The film deals with themes of homosexuality, violence, and racism, but also illustrates the alcohol abuse that is pervasive in military life.

Sweet Bird of Youth (1962) Drama ΨΨ
Paul Newman in an adaptation of Tennessee Williams' play about a has-been actress (played by Geraldine Page) addicted to alcohol and drugs who takes up with a young, vital Newman.

Taxi Blues (1990) Drama ΨΨΨ
Alcoholic jazz musician becomes friends with an anti-Semitic taxi driver. This Russian film won the prize for Best Director at Cannes. Fascinating

examination of the role of alcohol in the daily lives of the protagonists in Moscow society.

Tender Mercies (1983) Drama ΨΨΨΨΨ
Sensitive and optimistic film in which Robert Duvall plays a successfully recovering alcoholic songwriter. Duvall won an Oscar for this almost perfect performance.

Trees Lounge (1996) Comedy ΨΨΨΨ
Steve Buscemi wrote and directed this compelling film, and he plays the lead character, a 31-year-old unemployed auto mechanic. Few contemporary films present a more vivid picture of the problems associated with alcoholism.

Under Capricorn (1949) Drama Ψ
A little-known Hitchcock film starring Joseph Cotton and Ingrid Bergman. Bergman is a wealthy socialite whose life is ruined by her alcoholism.

Under the Volcano (1984) Drama ΨΨΨΨ
John Huston directing Albert Finney; excellent portrayal of chronic alcoholism.

Edward J. Concannon: "Why wasn't she getting oxygen...?"
Dr. Robert Towler: "Well, many reasons, actually..."
Edward J. Concannon: "Tell me one?"
Dr. Robert Towler: "She'd aspirated vomitus into her mask..."
Edward J. Concannon: "She threw up in her mask. Let's cut the bullshit. Say it: She threw up in her mask."

The Verdict

Verdict, The (1982) Drama ΨΨΨΨ
Paul Newman in a wonderful role as a disillusioned alcoholic lawyer who becomes genuinely involved with a brain-injured client who is the victim of medical malpractice. He wins the case but continues to drink. Interesting analysis of codependency.

Vital Signs (1986) Drama ΨΨ
Ed Asner in a surpassingly good made-for-TV movie about a father and son, both surgeons, fighting the twin problems of alcoholism and drug abuse.

What Price Hollywood? (1932) Drama ΨΨ
Alcoholic director helps Hollywood waitress become a star. The figure of the alcoholic director may have been modeled after John Barrymore.

When a Man Loves a Woman (1994) Drama ΨΨ
Meg Ryan as a middle-class alcoholic. This is a melodramatic and somewhat predictable film, but an interesting introduction to AA and Al-Anon. The film explores the role of codependency and a husband's role in his wife's alcoholism.

Drug Abuse

21 Grams (2003) Drama/Mystery ΨΨΨΨ
Complicated, well-integrated stories of an ex-con and recovering alcoholic (Benicio Del Toro), a cocaine addict (Naomi Watts), and a terminal man awaiting a transplant (Sean Penn), all brought together by an accidental death.

"They say we all lose 21 grams at the exact moment of death… everyone. The weight of a stack of nickels. The weight of a chocolate bar. The weight of a hummingbird."

21 Grams

Bad Lieutenant (1992) Drama ΨΨΨ
Harvey Keitel stars in one of his most powerful roles as a police lieutenant addicted to cocaine, alcohol, and prostitutes. The film illustrates stark abuse of power and the deterioration of family life that accompanies addiction. Keitel's character at one point has a hallucination in which Jesus Christ comes to him.

Big Lebowski, The (1998) Comedy ΨΨ
Coen Brothers film portraying The Dude (Jeff Bridges), a cannabis-smoking, unemployed drifter in this entertaining, film noir comedy.

Bird (1988) Biography ΨΨ
Clint Eastwood directed this biographical film of the life of jazz great and drug addict Charlie "Bird" Parker. Parker was an addict for all of his adult life, and his addiction killed him at the age of 34.

Blow (2001) Drama ΨΨΨ
Johnny Depp stars as George Jung, a man who claimed to have imported about 85% of all cocaine in America in the late 1970s.

Born on the Fourth of July (1989)
Drama/War/Biography ΨΨΨΨ
Antiwar film by Oliver Stone starring Tom Cruise as Ron Kovic, who uses alcohol and drugs to cope with the frustration of paralysis. One of the best of its genre.

Chappaqua (1966) Drama Ψ
Heroin addict checks in for treatment. The film is most notable for short roles by William Burroughs, Ravi Shankar, and Allen Ginsburg.

Christiane F. (1981) Drama ΨΨΨ
Powerful and frightening examination of the life of a teenage drug addict in West Berlin. Based on a true story, the film is still gripping almost two decades after it was made.

Clean and Sober (1988) Drama ΨΨΨ
Good portrayal of AA, cocaine addiction, and alcoholism.

"The best way to break old habits is to make new ones."

Morgan Freeman giving advice in *Clean and Sober*

Cocaine Fiends, The (1936) Drama Ψ
Another "word of warning" film that portrays the dangers of cocaine. Made in the same year as *Reefer Madness*. The message in this film is exaggerated and histrionic but somewhat more realistic in its estimate of the dangers of the drug.

Coffee and Cigarettes (2003) Comedy ΨΨΨ
Various conversational skits (starring a variety of talents, including Bill Murray, Roberto Benigni, Cate Blanchett, Iggy Pop, and Steve Buscemi) linked through the characters' use of coffee, tea and smoking. Portrayals of compulsive use of each, side effects, and the desire to quit or avoid the substance.

Connection, The (1961) Drama ΨΨΨ
Heroin addicts in New York wait for their pusher.

Dopamine (2003) Drama/Comedy ΨΨ
Independent film explores the chemistry behind male-female relationships. One character uses amphetamine pills and large quantities of caffeine. Interesting debate on how physical attraction emerges.

"Most people don't know how they're gonna feel from one moment to the next. But a dope fiend has a pretty good idea. All you gotta do is look at the labels on the little bottles."

Matt Dillon reflects on the pleasures of drugs in *Drugstore Cowboy*

Drugstore Cowboy (1989) Drama ΨΨΨΨ
Matt Dillon leads a group of junkies who rob pharmacies to support their habit. William Burroughs plays a junkie priest.

Easy Rider (1969) Drama ΨΨΨ
Classic film of the late 1960s with Jack Nicholson as an alcoholic lawyer and Peter Fonda and Dennis Hopper as marijuana-smoking, LSD-using free spirits. The film is dated but still worth seeing.

Fear and Loathing in Las Vegas (1998)
Fantasy ΨΨ
Terry Gilliam's adaptation of Hunter S. Thompson's Gonzo journalism classic. The book is better than the film; although the movie does not glorify drug use, it clearly models the behavior and tacitly condones the practice of driving while intoxicated.

Half Baked (1998) Comedy Ψ
Exaggerated comedy about smoking "weed." Interesting for its classification of different types of marijuana smokers: "you should have been there smoker," the "scavenger," the "enhancer," the "medicinal," the "after school special," the "father, I'm 40 and still cool," the "MacGyver smoker," the "straight-up potheads," and the "I'm only creative if I smoke" smoker.

Hatful of Rain, A (1957) Drama ΨΨ
Melodramatic film about the life and problems of a drug addict. This was one of the earliest films to honestly examine the problem of drug addiction.

High Art (1998) Drama/Comedy ΨΨ
Realistic, well-acted independent film about several people who's lives intersect for drugs, support, and conversation in a New York City apartment.

I Don't Buy Kisses Anymore (1992)
Comedy/Romance Ψ
Lightweight but entertaining film about an obese male who falls in love with a woman using him as a subject for her master's thesis.

I'm Dancing as Fast as I Can (1982) Drama ΨΨ
Jill Clayburgh plays the role of a high-powered documentary filmmaker who becomes addicted to Valium and requires hospitalization in a special program for addicts. Based on a true story.

Jungle Fever (1991) Drama/Romance ΨΨΨ
Interesting film about race relations and sexual stereotypes, with a subplot involving Gator, the crackhead brother of the protagonist, who is destroying his middle-class family.

"The governor of Louisiana gave me this. Madame Tinkertoy's House of Blue Lights, corner of Bourbon and Toulouse, New Orleans, Louisiana. Now, this is supposed to be the finest whorehouse in the south. These ain't no pork chops! These are U.S. Prime!"

Jack Nicholson plans for his trip to New Orleans in *Easy Rider*

La Femme Nikita (1990) Action/Drama ΨΨ
Sociopathic and drug-addicted woman is sentenced to die for murder and then is transformed into a government agent. Most memorable for the drugstore robbery that opens the film.

Lady Sings the Blues (1972)
Biography/Musical ΨΨ
Diana Ross plays heroin addict Billie Holiday.

Long Day's Journey into Night (1962)
Drama ΨΨΨΨΨ
Katharine Hepburn plays a morphine-addicted, histrionic mother with an alcoholic son (Jason Robards). One of O'Neill's greatest plays; one of Hepburn's greatest roles. Hepburn's character is a good illustration of a histrionic personality disorder.

Love Liza (2002) Drama/Comedy ΨΨΨ
Philip Seymour Hoffman skillfully plays a man who huffs gasoline in response to his wife's suicide. A rare and tremendous depiction of inhalant abuse and intoxication.

Luna (1979) Drama Ψ
Disappointing Bernardo Bertolucci film, with Jill Clayburgh playing the mother of a drug addict son. The film hints at an incestuous relationship between mother and son.

MacArthur Park (2001) Drama ΨΨΨ
A crack addict struggles to leave drug dependence and his home in the park to live with his estranged son. A quality independent film.

"What the fuck do I need to be sober for so I can see how fucked up shit really is, please. High is how I am gonna be. I'm high till I die"

A crack addict in *MacArthur Park*

Man with the Golden Arm, The (1955)
Drama ΨΨ
Frank Sinatra and Kim Novak in a dated but interesting portrayal of drug addiction. Good example of the challenge of "cold turkey" withdrawal.

Mask (1985) Biography ΨΨΨ
Bogdanovich film with Cher as the mother of deformed but spunky teenager Rocky Dennis. Sympathetic portrayal of motorcycle gangs. Cher struggles with her angry father and her compulsive use of alcohol and drugs as she works hard to be a good mother.

Mighty Wind, A (2003) Comedy ΨΨ
Hilarious Christopher Guest parody of folk music. One character displays significant remnants of years of drug abuse.

Naked Lunch (1991) Drama/Science Fiction/Fantasy ΨΨ
This film is based on the novel by William Burroughs and deals with drug abuse, paranoia, and homicide.

New Jack City (1991) Action/Crime ΨΨ
Wesley Snipes and Ice-T in a realistic movie about the business of drugs. Good introduction to cocaine addiction and Narcotics Anonymous.

"If the First Amendment will protect a scumbag like me, it will protect all of you."

Larry Flint on free speech in *The People vs. Larry Flint*

People vs. Larry Flynt, The (1996)
Biography/Drama ΨΨΨ
A good movie about a controversial figure, the film forces the viewer to examine his or her views on pornography and free speech. The film is included in this section because of the effects of drugs on the lives of Flynt and his wife, Althea (Courtney Love), after he is shot and becomes addicted to narcotics.

Platoon (1986) War ΨΨΨΨ
Vietnam veteran Oliver Stone directed *Platoon,* one of the most realistic of dozens of war movies. There is an interesting juxtaposition of "boozers" (those who use alcohol to escape) and "heads" (those who take refuge in marijuana and other illegal drugs).

Postcards from the Edge (1990)
Comedy/Drama ΨΨΨ
Mike Nichols' adaptation of a Carrie Fisher story about life as the daughter of a famous actress. The mother is alcoholic; the daughter abuses multiple drugs, including cocaine and sedatives. There are brief scenes of therapy and a terrific cast.

Pulp Fiction (1994) Drama ΨΨΨΨΨ
Quentin Tarantino film about drugs, crime, depravity, the underworld, and life in urban America. One especially memorable scene involves John Travolta smashing an adrenaline-filled needle into Uma Thurman's chest

to revive her after she inadvertently overdoses on heroin.

> "What now? Let me tell you what now. I'ma call a coupla hard, pipe-hittin' niggers, who'll go to work on this soon-to-be-dead hillbilly rapist here with a pair of pliers and a blow torch. You hear me talkin', hillbilly boy? I ain't through with you by a damn sight. I'ma get medieval on your ass."
>
> **Marsellus plans his revenge in *Pulp Fiction***

Quitting (2001) Drama ΨΨΨ
Slow-moving but interesting Chinese film about a one-time famous actor who deteriorates due to a heroin addiction. The emotional and psychological withdrawals depicted are memorable. This is an important film on addiction and withdrawal.

Reefer Madness (1936) Drama Ψ
Camp film depicting the dangers of marijuana. Ironically, several thousand college students have gone to see this film high on the very drug the film condemns.

Requiem for a Dream (2000) Drama ΨΨΨΨ
Greatly disturbing film about four drug addicts whose lives deteriorate. Unforgettable performances and critically acclaimed. Cinematically crafted with excellence by Darren Aronofsky.

> "I'm somebody now, everybody likes me."
>
> ***Requiem for a Dream***

Rose, The (1979) Musical ΨΨ
Bette Midler portrays Janis Joplin and her problems with Southern Comfort and drugs.

Rush (1991) Crime/Drama ΨΨΨ
Two undercover narcotics agents find addiction to be an occupational hazard.

Scarface (1983) Crime ΨΨΨ
Brian De Palma movie starring Al Pacino as a Cuban immigrant mobster who becomes addicted to the cocaine he is marketing. This long film, which tends to be loved or hated, is based on a 1932 Howard Hawks classic with the same name.

Seven Percent Solution, The (1976) Mystery ΨΨ
Sigmund Freud treats Sherlock Holmes' cocaine addiction. Creative idea and historically accurate in documenting Freud's early enthusiasm for cocaine.

> "Dog had a litter of about 8, and my Mother was bending over killing each one of these little puppies in the bathtub. I remember I said 'why?'... She said 'I'm just killing what I can't take care of.' Then my momma said to me, she looked at me and she said, 'I wish I could do that to you.'"
>
> **A recollection by the cook in *Spun***

Shadow Hours (2000) Drama Ψ
Wealthy man manipulates a young gas station attendant into drug relapse and fraternizing with three types of "night owls": (1) those who find their prince charming or princess and end at midnight, (2) vampires—prostitutes, drug dealers, (3) and Mr. Hydes—those that can't sleep.

Sid and Nancy (1986) Biography ΨΨΨΨ
Compelling biography of Sid Vicious of the Sex Pistols; offers insight into the worlds of drugs and rock and roll.

Spun (2002) Drama/Comedy ΨΨΨ
A well-done, intense film about methamphetamine addiction.

Stardust (1975) Drama Ψ
British film about a rock star whose success is tarnished by drug addiction and mental illness.

Sweet Nothing (1996) Drama ΨΨΨ
An effective examination of the futility, desperation, and violence associated with crack addiction. This is a true story based on diaries found in a Bronx apartment in March of 1991.

Synanon (1965) Drama ΨΨ
Interesting only insofar as the film documents the treatment methods practiced in this highly praised treatment program.

Traffic (2000) Drama ΨΨΨΨ
Steven Soderbergh film thematically intersects the lives of a newly hired government drug czar (Michael Douglas), his daughter who experiments with crack, police officers struggling with drug cartels, and a suburban wife of a drug lord.

Trainspotting (1996) Drama/Comedy ΨΨΨ
A realistic and disturbing film about the heroin scene in Edinburgh. The film presents accurate depictions of cold turkey withdrawal. There is one memorable scene in which a young mother's baby dies while she is high, and she immediately needs a fix to cope with her grief. Several scatological scenes seem gratuitous and unnecessary.

"I've been known to sniff it, smoke it, swallow it, stick it up my arse and inject it into my veins. I've been trying to combat this addiction, but unless you count social security scams and shoplifting, I haven't had a regular job in years."

Trainspotting

Veronika Voss (1982) Drama ΨΨ
Rainer Werner Fassbinder film about a German movie star who becomes addicted to morphine. Fassbinder himself died from abuse of alcohol and heroin.

Wasted (2002) Drama ΨΨ
Teens, covering up inner pain, fear, and loneliness, battle their heroin addiction.

What's Love Got to Do with It? (1993) Musical/Biography ΨΨ
Excellent film biography of singer Tina Turner includes some memorable scenes of husband Ike strung out on cocaine.

Who'll Stop the Rain? (1978) Crime/Drama ΨΨ
Also known as *Dog Soldiers,* this film explores the world of drug smuggling and addiction.

Sexual and Gender Identity Disorders

Adjuster, The (1991) Drama ΨΨΨ
This interesting Canadian film explores voyeurism and exhibitionism.

"Being a man one day and a woman the next isn't an easy thing."

Bernadette complaining about life as a transsexual in *Adventures of Priscilla, Queen of the Desert*

Adventures of Priscilla, Queen of the Desert (1994) Comedy ΨΨ
Terence Stamp plays an aging transsexual who joins with two friends to travel from Sidney to Alice Springs in the Australian outback to perform a lip-synching routine. Much of the film revolves around the prejudice and homophobic hostility the three transsexuals encounter.

AKA (2002) Drama ΨΨΨ
Fascinating artistry where most of the screen is split into three where the viewer is simultaneously shown past & present, different character reactions, different camera angles, and even the internal thoughts & behaviors of a character. The lead character, sexually abused by his father, escapes on a journey exploring his sexual and psychological identity. As in *Memento*, the viewer must pay close attention throughout the film.

All About My Mother (1999) Drama/Comedy ΨΨ
Pedro Almodovar film about a nurse who tragically loses her beloved son and in her grief and travels meets a transvestite prostitute and a pregnant nun (Penelope Cruz). Winner of an Academy Award for Best Foreign Language Film.

Angels and Insects (1995) Drama ΨΨΨ
Complex drama about social class, passion, and hidden sexual secrets in a wealthy Victorian household.

Another Time, Another Place (1983) Drama ΨΨΨ
Sensitive film in which a Scottish woman in an unhappy marriage has a brief affair with an Italian

prisoner of war working as a laborer on the farm. The man is accused of a rape he did not commit; his lover can save him, but only at the cost of revealing her adultery.

Bad Timing: A Sensual Obsession (1980) Drama ΨΨ
Art Garfunkel (playing a psychology professor), Harvey Keitel, and Theresa Russell star in a provocative and explicit film about a psychiatrist who becomes sexually obsessed with a young woman after she makes a suicide attempt.

Basic Instinct (1992) Suspense/Thriller ΨΨ
Psychological thriller about a novelist (Sharon Stone) who is a sex addict that entangles an investigator (Michael Douglas) into a complex mystery of murder, sex, and fascination.

Psychologist: "Nick, when you recollect your childhood, are your recollections pleasing to you?" Nick: "Number 1, I don't remember how often I used to jerk off, but it was a lot. Number 2, I wasn't pissed off at my dad, even when I was old enough to know what he and mom were doing in the bedroom. Number 3, I don't look in the toilet before I flush it. Number 4, I haven't wet my bed for a long time. Number 5, why don't the two of you go fuck yourselves; I'm outta here."

Michael Douglas threatened by a psychological interview in *Basic Instinct*

Beginner's Luck (1983) Comedy ΨΨ
Lightweight comedy about a law student who becomes involved in a *ménage à trois*.

Belle de Jour (1967) Drama ΨΨΨΨ?
Luis Buñuel film with Catherine Deneuve playing a bored housewife who amuses herself by working in a brothel from two until five every afternoon, at least until her sexual obsessions begin to complicate her life. Buñuel may be filming what is just an erotic dream.

Birdcage, The (1996) Comedy ΨΨΨ
Mike Nichols and Elaine May's remake of *La Cage aux Folles*. This film is almost as good as the original, thanks to strong performances by Robin Williams and Gene Hackman.

"Al, you old son of a bitch! How ya doin'? How do you feel about that call today? I mean the Dolphins! Fourth-and-three play on their 30 yard line with only 34 seconds to go!"

Armand trying to act masculine in *The Birdcage*

Blame It on Rio (1984) Comedy ΨΨ
Two men take their teenage daughters to Rio's topless beaches, and one of the men, 43 years old, has an affair with the 15-year-old daughter of the other. The film has a vaguely incestuous theme and is modeled after the French film *One Wild Moment*.

Bliss (1997) Drama Ψ
Very fragile woman with a borderline personality disorder goes to a charming sex therapist who sleeps with his patients. The husband finds out; when he confronts the therapist, the husband converts and becomes his disciple. The film illustrates numerous ethical violations, and it demeans sacred Hindu tantric practices.

Blue Angel, The (1930) Drama ΨΨΨΨΨ
Classic film about a phlegmatic professor who loses everything because of his obsession with a cabaret singer.

Blue Car (2002) Drama ΨΨΨ
Independent film about an adolescent girl who is tutored by her teacher. Good depiction of the disturbing, subtle aspects of seduction and sexual exploitation.

Blue Velvet (1986) Mystery ΨΨΨΨ
A powerful and engrossing David Lynch film about drugs, sexual violence, and sadomasochism. Dennis Hopper portrays Frank Booth, one of the most sociopathic and sadistic villains in film history.

Bound (1996) Suspense/Drama ΨΨ
A tough female ex-con and her new female lover

concoct a scheme to steal mob money. This film noir is The Wachowski Brothers' directorial debut.

Boys Don't Cry (1999) Drama ΨΨΨ
One of the best films to ever depict the pain and problems that can emerge from gender identity disorder. A brutal, powerful film.

"Are you sleeping with other men just to feed his sick fantasies?"

A question put to Bess in *Breaking the Waves*

Breaking the Waves (1996) Drama ΨΨΨ
A Danish film in which a devout Catholic wife submits to sexual degradation to satisfy the voyeuristic demands of her paralyzed husband.

Cabaret (1972) Musical/Drama/Dance ΨΨΨΨ
Liza Minnelli in a film about sadomasochism, bisexuality, and the relationship between sex and power. *Cabaret* won Oscars for Best Actor, Best Actress, and Best Director. One scene in the film is as unforgettable as the classic confession of incest in *Chinatown*.

Caesar and Rosalie (1972) Comedy/Romance ΨΨ
Lighthearted and amusing examination of a ménage à trois.

"Don't worry, you've got everything under control."

A therapist's comments to a pedophile who was worried he might molest his own children; he later molested numerous children in a class he taught out of his home in *Capturing the Friedmans*

Capturing the Friedmans (2003) Documentary ΨΨΨΨ
Extraordinarily disturbing and emotional documentary about a father and son accused of pedophilia. Important film to see regarding sex addiction,

pedophilia, and the importance of not casting judgment too quickly.

Carnal Knowledge (1971) Drama ΨΨ
This Mike Nichols film traces the sexual lives of two college roommates, played by Jack Nicholson and Art Garfunkel, as they age and become increasingly disenchanted with sex, love, and the possibilities inherent in relationships.

Chinatown (1974) Mystery ΨΨΨΨ
A film about power, incest, and the complexity of human relationships. Actors includes Jack Nicholson, Faye Dunaway and John Huston.

"You see, Mr. Gettes, most people never have to face the fact that, at the right time and in the right place, they are capable of anything."

John Huston comment to Jack Nicholson in *Chinatown*

Claire's Knee (1971) Drama ΨΨΨ
An intelligent film in which a middle-aged man becomes obsessed with a young girl's knee.

Close My Eyes (1991) Drama ΨΨ
A British film about brother-sister incest.

Closer (2004) Comedy/Drama ΨΨΨ
A quality film with good dialogue and superb acting by Jude Law, Natalie Portman, Julia Roberts, and Clive Owen. Important issues related to sexuality are portrayed, including deceit, infidelity, the failure to self-disclose, dependency, the impact of guilt and shame, and relationship testing. One scene depicts an amusing online conversation between two men sending erotic instant messages.

Collector, The (1965) Drama ΨΨΨ
Terence Stamp stars as a young man who collects butterflies. He becomes obsessed with Samantha Eggar, kidnaps her, and winds up inadvertently killing her.

Crash (1996) Drama ΨΨΨ
A David Cronenberg film about people who become sexually aroused by automobile accidents.

The film presents a plausible hypothesis; people have developed fetishes for stranger things, and there are erotic overtones to both cars and speed.

"You couldn't wait for me? You did the Jane Mansfield crash without me!"

One of many strange interactions in David Cronenberg's *Crash*

Crime of Father Amaro, The (2002) Drama ΨΨΨ
A young priest, newly ordained, goes to a small, Mexican town to serve a parish. He witnesses his pastor having sex with women and he falls for a woman whom he secretively uses for sex until she becomes pregnant.

Cruising (1980) Crime Ψ
Controversial William Friedkin film starring Al Pacino as an undercover police officer who infiltrates gay bars and bathhouses. Gay activists condemned the film because it perpetuates stigma and stereotypes.

Crying Game, The (1992) Drama ΨΨΨΨ
This Neil Jordan film explores homosexuality, transsexualism, interracial sexuality, and the ability of two human beings to love one another deeply in an asexual relationship. Too complex to explain simply, the film must be seen to be fully appreciated.

Damage (1992) Drama ΨΨΨ
A Louis Malle film starring Jeremy Irons as a man who develops a sexual obsession for his son's fiancée. Both the father and the son's girlfriend seem powerless to control their erotic attachment despite its inevitable consequences.

Day in the Country, A (1936) Romance ΨΨΨΨ
Jean Renoir's adaptation of a short story by Guy de Maupassant that describes the seductions of a man's wife and daughter.

Diary of a Sex Addict, The (2001) Drama ΨΨ
Depiction of a classic sex addict who denies, rationalizes and continues a series of affairs until he finally can deceive no longer. He continues his compulsive behavior, even after the consequences

of this behavior are almost fatal. The film offers a realistic portrayal of a sex addict.

Therapist: "Which one is really you? The family man or the other guy?"
Patient: "Both"

The Diary of a Sex Addict

Door in the Floor, The (2003) Drama ΨΨ
A couple separates after the death of their twin sons. The catalyst for the breakup is Eddie, a 16 year old who takes a job as Jeff Bridges' assistant. Eddie is infatuated by Kim Bassinger and masturbates using her photos and undergarments to become aroused. Bassinger eventually seduces Eddie, who reminds her of her dead sons. Based on a novel by John Irving.

Dreamers, The (2003) Drama ΨΨΨ
Fraternal twins take in a roommate in this Bernardo Bertolucci exploration of politics, the cinema, and sexuality. The dynamics become complicated when the new roommate falls in love with the female twin, taking her virginity and challenging her enmeshment with her brother.

"A filmmaker is like a peeping Tom, a voyeur. It's as if the camera is the key to your parent's bedroom and you spy on them and you're disgusted and you feel guilty but you can't... you can't look away."

The Dreamers

Everything You Always Wanted to Know About Sex *But Were Afraid to Ask (1972) Comedy ΨΨΨ
Woody Allen classic includes vignettes on crossing-dressing, bestiality, sex in public, and the inner workings of the brain during sexual excitement.

Evil Alien Conquerors (2002) Comedy Ψ
Painfully bad film in which Saturday Night Live star, Chris Parnell, has a foot fetish.

Eyes Wide Shut (1999) Drama ΨΨΨΨΨ
The final Stanley Kubrick film about a man (Tom Cruise) who discovers a sexual underworld after his wife (Nicole Kidman) tells him of her fantasies and previous sexual encounters. Depiction of ephebophilia (sexual attraction of adults to adolescents), orgies, sexual rituals, exhibitionism, prostitution, infidelity, sexual fantasy, seduction, and betrayal. Mythological and Jungian psychology themes are omnipresent.

Far From Heaven (2002) Drama ΨΨΨ
Julianne Moore, living in a conservative area in a conservative time, finds out her husband is a homosexual. Interesting film that explores racism, stereotypes, and secrets.

Fellini Satyricon (1970) Historical ΨΨΨΨ
Controversial Fellini film about the decadence of ancient Rome. The film is visually stunning and explores human vices ranging from homosexual pedophilia to cannibalism. The film can be a springboard for a discussion of hedonism.

Female Perversions (1996) Drama ΨΨΨ
Confused and often confusing examination of the relationship between women, power, sexuality, and psychopathology. Based on a scholarly book with the same title by psychoanalyst Louise J. Kaplan.

Fetishes (1996) Documentary ΨΨΨ
True examination of the clients of Pandora's Box, an elite club catering to the sexual fetishes of New York City.

Fist in His Pocket (1966) Drama ΨΨΨ
Italian film about a dysfunctional family with multiple examples of psychopathology including epilepsy, murder, and incest.

Flawless (1999) Drama/Comedy ΨΨ
Philip Seymour Hoffman plays a drag queen named Rusty who is saving money for a gender modification operation; Robert DeNiro is the homophobic neighbor who takes voice lessons from Rusty following a stroke.

Fried Green Tomatoes (1991) Comedy/Drama ΨΨΨ
Presents a positive, healthy, loving view of an (assumed) lesbian relationship. We are quickly caught up in the complex and intertwined story of these two women.

Girl 6 (1996) Drama/Comedy Ψ
Spike Lee film about a woman who takes a job as a phone sex operator for the money.

God's Little Acre (1958) Drama Ψ
Buddy Hackett and Michael Landon star in this adaptation of Erskine Caldwell's tale of depravity and Georgia farm life.

Good Mother, The (1988) Drama ΨΨΨ
A provocative film in which Diane Keaton plays the divorced mother of a six-year-old daughter. Keaton falls in love with an iconoclastic artist, who allows the daughter to touch his penis when she sees him in the bath and expresses normal childhood curiosity. Keaton is eventually forced to denounce her new lover in order to maintain a relationship with her daughter.

Joe: "What do you think would happen if I got him a professional... you know..."
Bill: "A professional?"
Joe: "Hooker. You know, the kind that can teach things... first-timers, you know... break him in."
Bill: "But Joe, he's 11."
Joe: "You're right, you're right. It's too late."

Cultures clash in *Happiness*

Happiness (1998) Comedy/Drama ΨΨΨ
Disturbing dark comedy portraying a variety of quirky characters. The most striking are the pedophiliac psychiatrist who rapes his son's best friend and Philip Seymour Hoffman as a man who is obsessed with telephone scatalogia. Director Todd Solondz has a cameo as a doorman.

Harold and Maude (1972) Comedy ΨΨΨ
A cult film that examines sexual and romantic attraction across generations; this movie will force you to reexamine your feelings about age and death.

Henry & June (1990) Drama ΨΨ
Adaptation of Anais Nin diary detailing her *ménage à trois* with novelist Henry Miller and his wife June.

Holy Smoke (1999) Drama ΨΨΨ
Jane Campion film about a family who believes their daughter (Kate Winslet) is under the power of a cult leader. They hire a renowned "cult exiter"

(Harvey Keitel) whose role is to isolate the subject, provoke them, and then reintegrate them into the family. His power role reverses and he finds himself developing a sexual obsession.

In the Realm of the Senses (1977) Drama ΨΨΨ
A sadomasochistic relationship intensifies into highly graphic and unforgettable scenes of autoerotic asphyxiation and the severing of an adult penis.

Intimacy (2000) Drama ΨΨ
Depressed man and woman meet for anonymous sex in a dilapidated apartment once a week. The man becomes curious about the woman and follows her to learn more about her. Slow, dark film that depicts the double life of the addict.

Ju Dou (1990) Drama/Historical/Romance ΨΨΨΨ
Wonderful, visually stunning film examining the complex links that bind a husband, his wife, her lover, and the son of the illicit union. Good illustrations of sexual passion and sexual torment.

Jules and Jim (1961) Drama ΨΨΨΨΨ
Beautiful and engaging Truffaut film about a complex *ménage à trois* and an ultimate suicide. The film deals with far more than sexuality; it explores fundamental dimensions of human relationships and the boundaries of friendship and love.

"Love is the answer, isn't it? But, sex raises a lot of very interesting questions."

Liam Neeson as Alfred Kinsey in *Kinsey*

Kinsey (2004) Drama/Biography ΨΨΨΨ
Examination of the life of Alfred Kinsey, a sex researcher who revolutionized the way Americans viewed sexuality. The film depicts Kinsey's obsessive-compulsive personality, his inability to connect in deep way, and the failure to set boundaries for his own (and his research team's) sexual practices.

Kiss of the Spider Woman (1985) Prison ΨΨΨΨ
A homosexual and a political activist share a prison cell and grow to understand and appreciate each other. William Hurt won an Academy Award for his performance.

Kissed (1996) Drama ΨΨΨ
A controversial but sensitive film dealing seriously with necrophilia. Molly Parker is the protagonist, a young woman obsessed from childhood with death. She gets a job in a mortuary and has ritualistic sex ("crossing over") with the bodies she embalms. Her boyfriend commits suicide in an attempt to compete for her affection and attention.

"I told them my father was a Cultural attaché. What will they think when they find out he lives with a drag queen?"

Renato's son in *La Cage aux Folles*

La Cage aux Folles (1978) Comedy ΨΨΨ
A gay man and his transvestite lover manage a popular St. Tropez nightclub. Much of the humor revolves around sex roles and the folly of trying very hard to be something you're not.

Last Exit to Brooklyn (1989) Drama ΨΨ
A film based on a controversial book about life in a sordid Brooklyn neighborhood. The film deals with rape, prostitution, homosexuality, and transvestism, but mostly with the sad and bleak reality of the lives of its characters.

Last Tango in Paris (1973) Drama ΨΨΨΨ
Marlon Brando stars in a classic Bernardo Bertolucci film about a man who begins a casual sexual liaison on the day his wife commits suicide. The two lovers never exchange names. The film includes themes of depression, sexuality, loneliness, and cynicism.

Lianna (1983) Drama ΨΨΨ
Sensitive film portraying the emotional life of a woman who leaves her husband and two children after she becomes romantically involved with a lesbian professor teaching a night course in child psychology.

Lolita (1962) Drama ΨΨΨΨ
James Mason and Sue Lyons star in a loose adaptation of Vladimir Nabokov's novel about pedophilia and murder. Laurence Olivier turned down the role of Humbert Humbert. Directed by

Stanley Kubrick; watch for Peter Sellers as Dr. Zempf, the Beardsley High School psychologist.

"What drives me insane is the twofold nature of this nymphet... this mixture in my Lolita of tender, dreamy childishness and a kind of eerie vulgarity."

Humbert Humbert in *Lolita*

Luna (1979) Drama ΨΨ
A Bertolucci film that explores mother-son incest and addiction. The film is not Bertolucci's best effort.

Magenta (1996) Drama Ψ
Happily married physician crosses boundaries sexually with his sister-in-law, creating havoc in his family.

Manhattan (1979) Comedy/Romance ΨΨΨΨ
Classic Woody Allen film in which his former wife, played by Meryl Streep, has taken a lover, found happiness, and written a book to tell the world about Allen's kinky habits. Allen's character (in an example of art imitating life) is consumed with guilt over the fact that he is living with a teenage girl.

Mark, The (1961) Drama ΨΨΨΨ
A British film about a pedophile who serves his sentence and is released, supposedly cured. However, a journalist who reveals the man's past hampers his rehabilitation. Interesting film in light of recent court decisions about sex offenders.

Matador (1986) Comedy/Drama ΨΨ
Almodovar film about a bullfighter who acts in snuff films.

Menage (1986) Comedy ΨΨ
A French film that examines sex roles, sexual stereotypes, and the need for novelty and excitement in sexual relationships.

Midnight Cowboy (1969) Drama ΨΨΨΨΨ
Jon Voight leaves Texas to make his fortune in New York City working as a stud; instead, he winds up hanging out with Ratso Rizzo, who dies before the two can escape to Florida. This film is a fascinating and complex character study.

"Well, I'll tell you the truth now. I ain't a real cowboy, but I am one helluva stud."

Jon Voight as Joe Buck in *Midnight Cowboy*

Midsummer Night's Sex Comedy, A (1982) ΨΨ
Excellent Woody Allen film about friends and acquaintances who gather at a country house in the woods at the turn of the century. Sexual boundaries blur in this homage to Shakespeare, Renoir, and others.

Mona Lisa (1986) Crime ΨΨΨ
Interesting Neil Jordan film about prostitution, exploitation, drug addiction, and love. Filmed in Soho, the film gives some insight into the two different worlds of prostitution: that of the call girl and that of the streetwalker.

Montenegro (1981) Drama ΨΨ
A Dusan Makavejev film about a bored housewife slowly becoming psychotic. She becomes sexually liberated and then murders her lover. Despite its psychopathological theme, the film is really about politics and social class.

"Well, I hope you're up for a little competition. She's got a power tool in the bedroom, dear. It's her own personal jackhammer. She could break sidewalks with that thing. She uses it and the lights dim, it's like a prison movie. Amazed she hasn't chipped her teeth."

Mrs. Doubtfire tries to discourage Stu, his ex-wife's new lover in *Mrs. Doubtfire*

Mrs. Doubtfire (1994) Comedy ΨΨ
Robin Williams cross-dresses as an English nanny to have time with his children.

Murmur of the Heart (1971) Comedy ΨΨ
A sensitive, intelligent, and funny French film about an incestuous relationship between a young mother and her adolescent son.

My Beautiful Laundrette (1985) Drama ΨΨ
The two lead characters are homosexuals, although this fact is almost incidental to the story about alcoholism, street gangs, race relations, and social class.

My Favorite Season (1993) Drama ΨΨΨ
A French film dealing with adolescent sexuality, family dynamics, and love between a brother and sister.

My Life to Live/Vivre sa Vie (1963) ΨΨΨ
Jean-Luc Godard's 12-part examination of the life of a prostitute, starring Anna Karina.

My Own Private Idaho (1991) Drama ΨΨ
River Phoenix, who subsequently died of a drug overdose, plays a homosexual prostitute.

Mystery of Alexina, The (1985) Drama ΨΨ
A story about the psychological sequelae of the decision to raise a male child as a female.

Nine and ½ Weeks (1986) Drama/Suspense ΨΨ
Excellent character portrayals by Mickey Rourke and Kim Basinger who meet at a grocery store and later engage in sensual sexual exploration and mild sadomasochism.

Normal (2003) Drama ΨΨΨ
A man (Tom Wilkinson) after 25 years of marriage tells his wife (Jessica Lange) he is a woman trapped in a man's body and he wants gender modification surgery.

Nos Amours, A (1984) Drama ΨΨΨ
A French film exploring the sexuality of a 15-year-old girl and the way it affects her family.

Of Human Bondage (1934) Drama ΨΨ
Bette Davis stars in this film about the sexual obsession of a club-footed physician for a cruel, vulgar, and manipulative waitress. Based on a novel by Somerset Maugham. This film is far superior to the two adaptations that followed it.

On-line (2002) Drama ΨΨΨ
A film about internet addiction. Emphasis on the lack of connection and relational intimacy of the addict. Depicts an obsession with fantasy that becomes confused as reality.

"You dirty swine! I never cared for you... It made me sick when you kissed me. I only did it because you drove me crazy. And after you kissed me I always used to wipe my mouth – wipe my mouth!"

Bette Davis berates Leslie Howard in *Of Human Bondage*

Oscar Wilde (1960) Biography Ψ
Robert Morley plays Oscar Wilde, the wit and playwright who was convicted of sodomy.

Peeping Tom (1960) Thriller ΨΨΨ
Controversial film about a sexual psychopath who photographs his victims as they are dying. Look for the full-length version of the film, which was released in 1979.

Personal Best (1982) Sports ΨΨΨ
Fascinating film that explores the sexual relationship that develops between two women competing for a position on an Olympic team.

"It's being aware of what it means to lose oneself before being completely abandoned."

The Piano Teacher

Piano Teacher, The (2001) Drama ΨΨΨΨ
This is a powerful French film about a prominent, masochistic piano teacher who becomes sexually involved with one of her pupils. The film makes sexual obsession understandable and plausible.

Pillow Book (1997) Drama ΨΨΨ
Complex Peter Greenaway film about a woman who becomes sexually obsessed with calligraphy. This film is a meditation on love, art and imagination, eroticism, order, and decay.

Pretty Baby (1978) Drama ΨΨ
This Louis Malle film about pedophilia introduces Brooke Shields as a 12-year-old New Orleans prostitute.

Pretty When You Cry (2001) Drama/Suspense Ψ
Mostly flashbacks as detectives follow up a murder investigation with a young man who tells the story of his infatuation and love for a beautiful woman who was in an abusive relationship. The masochistic-sadistic relationship is portrayed, as well as physical, verbal and emotional abuse.

Princesa (2001) Drama Ψ
Brazilian transvestite moves to Italy and earns money as a prostitute in order to get money for his sex change operation.

Private Parts (1997) Comedy Ψ
Inside look at radio personality Howard Stern and his obsession with sex and outlandish comedy.

"Look, maybe your method of massage differs from mine, but touchin' his lady's feet, and stickin' your tongue in her holiest of holies, ain't the same ballpark, ain't the same league, ain't even the same fuckin' sport. Foot massages don't mean shit."

Jules and Vincent discuss foot massage in *Pulp Fiction*

Pulp Fiction (1994) Drama ΨΨΨΨΨ
Quentin Tarantino film depicts an underworld sadomasochistic den of iniquity run by two sexual sadists in the basement of an Army surplus store. A masochistic slave dressed totally in leather lives in a box in the back of the room.

Quills (2000) Drama ΨΨΨ
Depiction of the last years of the Marquis de Sade (well played by Geoffrey Rush) who was sent to the Charenton Asylum for the Insane as punishment for his erotic writings. Interesting portrayal of various paraphilias.

Reflections in a Golden Eye (1967) Drama ΨΨ
A John Huston film in which Richard Burton plays the role of a repressed homosexual Army officer

serving on a small Georgia military base. Elizabeth Taylor is his sadistic and sexually liberated wife. The film was banned by the Catholic Film Board.

Rita, Sue and Bob Too (1986) Comedy ΨΨΨ
British film about a married man who winds up in a sexual relationship with the two working-class teenage girls who baby sit for his children. Interesting examination of the appropriate age for consent and issues of sexual exploitation.

Rocky Horror Picture Show, The (1975) Comedy/Horror/Musical/Dance Ψ
A fun film about a Transylvanian transsexual. From a psychological perspective, the film is not nearly as interesting as those fans who have turned it into a cult classic.

Sailor Who Fell from Grace with the Sea, The (1976) Drama ΨΨΨΨ
Interesting story of adult romance and child psychopathology; based on a Mishima novel.

Salo or **The 120 Days of Sodom** (1975) Horror Ψ
Pasolini's adaptation of de Sade's famous novel. Set in the fascist Italy of World War II, this violent film is an interesting introduction to the practice of sadism.

Secretary (2002) Drama ΨΨΨ
A self-injurious, depressed woman is hired as a secretary after leaving a mental hospital; she takes a new job and begins to enjoy the criticism and punishment of her boss. They develop a sadomasochistic relationship in the work setting and eventually fall in love and marry.

"In one way or another I've always suffered. I didn't know why exactly. But I do know that I'm not so scared of suffering now. I feel more than I've ever felt and I've found someone to feel with. To play with. To love in a way that feels right for me."

Maggie Gyllenhaal reflects on her new fascination with masochism in *Secretary*

Sergeant, The (1968) Drama ΨΨ
Rod Steiger plays an Army sergeant sexually obsessed with a young private in his outfit. Filmed in France.

Sex and Zen (1993) Comedy Ψ
Second rate film about a Buddhist who leaves his master and new wife to seek out a life of debauchery and erotic pleasures.

sex, lies, and videotape (1989) Drama ΨΨΨ
The film revolves around an impotent young man who can achieve orgasm only when masturbating while watching videotapes of women whom he has persuaded to share the most intimate details of their sexual lives. This film won the top award at the Cannes Film Festival.

Short Cuts (1993) Drama ΨΨ
Most memorable for a scene in which a bored woman talks dirty on the phone to earn a few dollars while she changes her baby's diapers. Her husband wonders why she never talks to *him* like that.

Short Eyes (1977) Prison ΨΨΨΨ
A powerful film about life in "The Tombs," New York City's Men's House of Detention. Short Eyes is prison slang for a child molester.

Sliver (1993) Drama Ψ
William Baldwin plays a voyeur who is the landlord of an apartment complex with high tech cameras set up in the tenants' rooms.

"The imagination is the most powerful force known to mankind. And it is my imagined self, the one who is beautiful and loving and worthy of being loved, that has been my guiding force. My inspiration. I can only hope to become the person Barry imagined me to be. I pray for the courage it will take to become a real, live soldier's girl."

Lee Pace as Calpernia Addams
in *Soldier's Girl*

Soldier's Girl (2003) Drama/Biography ΨΨΨ
Based on the true story of Barry Winchell who entered the military and fell in love with a transsexual dancer at a club. Military peers find out about the secret relationship and the situation ends tragically.

Some Like It Hot (1959) Crime/Comedy ΨΨ
Tony Curtis and Jack Lemmon pass for women musicians to avoid detection by the mob.

Something About Amelia (1984) Drama ΨΨ
Popular made-for-TV movie about father-daughter incest.

Strange One, The (1957) Drama ΨΨ
Ben Gazzara stars in this film about homosexuality and sadism in a Southern military academy.

Swept Away (1975) Drama/Comedy ΨΨΨ
Lina Wertmuller's examination of sex roles. A rich woman and a poor deckhand are marooned on an island and find sexual excitement and satisfaction in the new roles each assumes.

That Obscure Object of Desire (1977)
Drama ΨΨΨΨ
Surrealistic film by Luis Buñuel about violence, love, and sexual obsession in a middle-aged man. The film is complex, intriguing, and full of symbolism.

This World, Then the Fireworks (1997) Drama ΨΨ
This film traces the development of incestuous twins who eventually become con artists.

Tie Me Up! Tie Me Down! (1990)
Comedy/Romance ΨΨΨ
A Pedro Almodovar film about a former mental patient, kidnapping, masochism, and sex roles. Some critics have maintained that the film trivializes the problem of sexual violence and denigrates women.

Director: "I'd like to make her look a little more attractive, How far can you pull back?"
Cameraman: "How do you feel about Cleveland?"

Tootsie

Tootsie (1982) Comedy/Romance ΨΨΨΨ
Funny Dustin Hoffman film in which an unsuccessful actor finds success when he impersonates a woman. He learns from the process, and the audience learns some important lessons about gender, sex roles, and human relationships.

Torch Song Trilogy (1988) Drama ΨΨΨ
Anne Bancroft and Matthew Broderick in a film adaptation of Harvey Fierstein's play about a homosexual drag queen and his lovers, enemies, and mother.

Two Women (1961) Drama/War ΨΨΨ
Classic Vittorio De Sica film starring Sophia Loren. The film is about love, war, rape, and a mother's love for her teenage daughter.

Unbearable Lightness of Being (1988) Romance ΨΨΨ
A highly sensual film about a Prague neurosurgeon and his inability to separate sex and love. The film is based on the novel of the same name by Milan Kundera.

Unfaithful (2002) Drama/Suspense ΨΨ
Richard Gere finds his wife (Diane Lane) is cheating on him and plots revenge.

Victor/Victoria (1982) Musical/Comedy ΨΨ
Blake Edwards film with Julie Andrews as a down-on-her-luck singer who becomes a sensation when she pretends to be a male-female impersonator.

Viridiana (1961) Drama ΨΨΨΨ
This complex Luis Buñuel film tells the story of a young woman who returns home to visit her uncle just before taking vows as a nun. She resembles her dead aunt, and her uncle drugs her while she is wearing her aunt's wedding dress. He plans to rape her but is unable to commit the act. He commits suicide; she inherits his estate and devotes her life to serving the poor.

Visiting Desire (1996) Documentary ΨΨ
Twelve strangers are brought together to act out their sexual fantasies.

"Stealing images from life is my life."

A voyeur describes himself in *Voyeur Confessions*

Voyeur Confessions (2001) Drama ΨΨ
This film captures the pain associated with the life of the voyeur. The movie touches on the etiology of voyeurism, and helps serious students better understand the paraphilias.

Warm Water Under a Red Bridge (2001) Drama/Comedy ΨΨΨ
A Japanese fable about a woman with a supernatural sexual condition in which water builds up in her body and can only be released by sex. Directed by Shohei Imamura.

We Don't Live Here Anymore (2004) Drama ΨΨΨ
Two couples (played by Peter Krause, Naomi Watts, Mark Ruffalo, and Laura Dern) find both their marriages failing, in part due to adultery. The movie includes themes of deceit, manipulation, lack of integrity, and the excitement of secrecy. Each couple battles against boredom and idleness, using sex to escape the emptiness of their lives.

Wild Orchid 2: Two Shades of Blue (1991) Drama Ψ
Disappointing film about the daughter of a heroin addict who becomes a prostitute to support her father's habit while maintaining a double identity.

World According to Garp, The (1982) Comedy/Drama ΨΨ
John Lithgow plays transsexual Roberta Muldoon in a film in which troubled sexuality is commonplace.

Yentl (1983) Musical ΨΨ
Barbra Streisand directed and produced this film, and she has the lead role as a young woman in Eastern Europe who has to pass herself off as a man in order to get an education. Interesting examination of sex roles; terrific performance by Streisand.

Young Adam (2003) Drama ΨΨ
Ewan Macgregor as a sexual addict who acts out sexually with his boss' wife, her sister, and a woman he meets at a ship's port.

Schizophrenia and Other Psychotic Disorders

13 Moons (2002) Drama ΨΨ
Three priests, a bail bondsman, a musician, and two clowns cross paths on night-time city streets. One character, a drug addict needed for an organ transplant, is blatantly psychotic throughout the film.

Alone in the Dark (1982) Suspense Ψ
A psychiatrist's family is besieged by a psychotic patient during a citywide blackout.

Amadeus (1984) Biography/Musical ΨΨΨ
The film opens with the court composer Salieri, now old, mad, and suicidal, wondering if he murdered Mozart. Salieri is obsessed with the genius of Mozart and can never forgive his rival for his talent or himself for his mediocrity.

Angel at My Table, An (1990) Biography /Drama ΨΨΨΨΨ
Jean Campion's biography of New Zealand novelist Janet Frame, who was misdiagnosed with schizophrenia and mistreated with electroconvulsive therapy.

Angel Baby, An (1995) Drama ΨΨΨ
Australian film about two mentally ill people who meet in an outpatient clinic, fall in love, and try to face life together. Unfortunately, their lives fall apart as a consequence of an ill-fated decision to mutually discontinue their medication.

Angel in Red (1991) Suspense Ψ
A psychotic pimp goes gunning for his former employee after she turns to a rival pimp for protection.

Benny & Joon (1993) Comedy ΨΨΨ
A generally sympathetic portrayal of schizophrenia, with a vivid example of decompensation on a city bus; the film trivializes the problem of schizophrenia by suggesting love alone is enough to conquer the problem.

Berlin Alexanderplatz (1980) Drama ΨΨΨΨΨ
This film, a 15-hour Fassbinder masterpiece, traces the gradual moral and mental disintegration of a man who leaves prison resolved to live a good life. The film explores exploitation of women, violence, homosexuality, and mental illness.

Betrayed (1988) Political/Thriller Ψ
Debra Winger plays an undercover agent who falls in love with a seemingly simple farmer, actually a right-wing, paranoid fanatic.

Betty Blue (1986) Drama ΨΨΨ
Artistic, erotic French film about two young lovers and their passions that lead from poverty to violence and destruction. One particularly shocking scene depicts self-mutilation resulting from psychosis.

Bill of Divorcement, A (1932) Comedy ΨΨ
A mentally ill man is discharged from a psychiatric hospital and returns home to his wife and daughter. Katharine Hepburn's debut as a film actress.

Birdy (1984) Drama/War ΨΨΨΨ
Nicolas Cage tries to help his friend, Matthew Modine, who is a catatonic inpatient in a military hospital. Both men are Vietnam veterans, but Modine's problems seem to predate the war.

Boxing Helena (1994) Drama ΨΨ
Eminent surgeon is rebuffed by a beautiful woman. His obsessions of her turn delusional as he captures her and eventually amputates her arms and legs while paradoxically fawning over her. Interesting dynamic of his forcing the woman to be physically dependent upon him emerging from his psychological dependence on her. Directorial debut of Jennifer Chambers Lynch, daughter of distinguished filmmaker, David Lynch.

"I am still haunted by my love for her… those dreams."

Eerie quote by character Nick Cavanaugh in *Boxing Helena*, leaving the viewer to ponder how much of the film is delusion, reality, or a dream

---

Camille Claudel (1988) Biography ΨΨΨ
Biographical film of the mistress of Rodin, who spent the last 30 years of her life in an asylum.

David and Lisa (1963) Drama ΨΨΨ
Story of two institutionalized teenagers who become romantically involved. Based on a story by psychiatrist Theodore Isaac Rubin.

Dead of Night (1945) Horror ΨΨΨΨ
Five short episodes loosely linked together. The last of these, "The Ventriloquist's Dummy," stars Michael Redgrave, who has to be hospitalized after he becomes convinced that he and his dummy are exchanging personalities (and, in fact, they are).

Delusions of Grandeur (1973) Comedy Ψ
In seventeenth-century Spain, a wily servant saves his king from the intrigues of a tax collector.

Don Juan Demarco (1995) Drama ΨΨΨ
Marlon Brando plays a compassionate psychiatrist to Johnny Depp who plays a delusional man who thinks he is the legendary Don Juan.

"I am the world's greatest lover!"

Don Juan Demarco

Donnie Darko (2001) Drama ΨΨΨ
Although this film is about a delusional college student who frequently hallucinates a "demon bunny" instructing him that the end of the world is near, the film is fairly complex with important comments on fear, the pain of mental illness, and the nature of reality.

Don't Say A Word (2001) Suspense/Mystery ΨΨ
Michael Douglas plays a psychiatrist whose daughter is kidnapped for the ransom of a 6-digit code locked in the brain of a very disturbed psychiatric patient (Brittany Murphy).

Dressed to Kill (1980) Thriller Ψ
Popular film in which Michael Caine plays Angie Dickinson's psychiatrist. The film confuses transsexuality and schizophrenia, but it is exciting, if not always accurate.

Entertainer, The (1960) Drama Ψ
This film, starring Laurence Olivier and Albert Finney, portrays Olivier as a third-rate vaudevillian whose delusions of grandeur alienate people around him.

Fan, The (1982) Horror Ψ
A Broadway star played by Lauren Bacall is terrorized by an embittered fan.

Fan, The (1996) Drama Ψ
Robert De Niro and Wesley Snipes are wasted in this tired film about a baseball fan who is obsessed with a Giants center fielder.

Final (2001) Drama ΨΨΨ
Well-acted performance by Denis Leary who plays "Bill" in this Campbell Scott film. Bill awakens from a coma in an isolated, bright room of a psychiatric hospital. He has frequent paranoid delusions, anger outbursts, and hallucinations as his therapist helps him remember flashbacks of his car accident and his father's death. Interesting portrayal of the "doctor-patient" relationship, presenting many questions about boundaries, ethics, and relational dynamics.

Fisher King, The (1991) Drama/Fantasy/Comedy ΨΨΨ
Terry Gilliam film in which Robin Williams plays a homeless, mentally ill man who is befriended by a disillusioned former disc jockey. The movie is funny but confusing, and it misleads the public with its suggestion of a traumatic etiology for schizophrenia.

Frailty (2001) Drama/Suspense ΨΨΨ
Bill Paxton plays a serial killing, religious zealot with a delusional disorder who believes he's on a mission from God to fight off demons (his human victims).

"Now you stay down here until you see the truth. Pray to god, Fenton. Pray for a vision. Only he can help you now!"

Bill Paxton's character in *Frailty*

Gothika (2004) Suspense ΨΨ
Halle Berry plays Dr. Miranda Grey who works to unravel the mystery of her patient's (Penelope Cruz) psychopathology and is confronted by disturbing secrets and the supernatural.

Goya in Bordeaux (1999) Drama /Biography ΨΨΨ
Spanish film, depicting the famous painter, Francisco de Goya on his deathbed, who recalls major events of his life, hallucinates, and experiences severe migraines. Addresses themes of psychosis and creativity, integrity vs. despair, and the interrelationship of life and death.

He Loves Me, He Loves Me Not (2002) Drama ΨΨΨΨ
A must-see film for depiction of delusional disorders that is so unique that it could only be done cinematically. First, the viewer sees reality from the young woman's perception and flashes back to the beginning giving the viewer the vantage point of the man she loves. This French film stars *Amelie*'s Audrey Tautou.

House of Fools (2002) Drama ΨΨΨΨ
Based on a true story: the staff in a mental institution flee due to conflicts in Chechnya, leaving the patients to fend for themselves. Soon soldiers occupy the hospital and the viewer is left with various questions of war, politics, mental health treatment and which is most "crazy." Loaded with psychopathology examples, including a fire-starter, all the schizophrenia subtypes, and a woman who believes she is the fiancé of singer, Bryan Adams (who appears in the film).

Housekeeping (1987) Drama ΨΨΨΨ
An eccentric aunt comes to care for two sisters in the Pacific Northwest after the suicide of their mother. The girls can't decide if their aunt is simply odd or seriously mentally ill. The viewer confronts a similar dilemma.

I Never Promised You a Rose Garden (1977) Drama ΨΨΨΨ
Accurate rendition of the popular book by the same name. The patient has command hallucinations that tell her to kill herself. There is a sympathetic portrayal of psychiatry and treatment; a breakthrough occurs when the protagonist first realizes she is able to feel pain.

Images (1972) Drama ΨΨΨ
Robert Altman's examination of the confused life of a woman with schizophrenia. A difficult film, but interesting, with a heuristic presentation of hallucinations.

K-Pax (2001) Drama ΨΨΨΨ
Multi-layered film in which Kevin Spacey plays Prot, a man claiming he's from a far away planet who is able to give convincing evidence for his case to astrophysicists. The viewer is left to hypothesize whether the character is delusional, experiencing PTSD, or an enlightened spiritual being; whichever the case, the portrayal and diagnostic criteria are convincing for each.

La Dolce Vita (1960) Drama ΨΨΨ
Vintage Fellini film with an interesting vignette in which hundreds of Roman citizens develop a mass delusion following reports of a sighting of the Virgin Mary.

Lunatics: A Love Story (1992) Comedy ΨΨΨ
A former mental patient spends six months hidden away in his apartment. The lead character has been described in reviews as agoraphobic, but a more serious diagnosis seems appropriate, especially in light of the patient's delusions and hallucinations.

Lust for Life (1956) Biography ΨΨΨΨ
Kirk Douglas as Vincent van Gogh and Anthony Quinn as Paul Gauguin. The film portrays the stormy relationship of the two men and van Gogh's hospitalization and eventual suicide. Contrast with *Vincent* (1987) and Robert Altman's *Vincent and Theo* (1990).

Madness of King George, The (1994) Historical Biography ΨΨΨ
Nigel Hawthorne as King George III in an adaptation of a stage play examining the reactions of the court and family as the king becomes increasingly demented (due to porphyria, a genetic metabolic disorder).

"One may produce a copious, regular evacuation every day of the week and still be a stranger to reason."

An observation by a court doctor in *The Madness of King George*

Magic (1978) Thriller ΨΨ
Anthony Hopkins' talents are largely wasted in this Richard Attenborough film about a ventriloquist obsessed with his dummy. Not nearly as good a film as the 1945 movie *Dead of Night*.

Misery (1990) Horror ΨΨ
Kathy Bates plays an apparently delusional woman who becomes convinced she is justified in capturing a novelist and forcing him to rewrite his latest novel to meet her tastes. The movie, like Wagner's music, is better than it sounds.

Nurse Betty (2000) Drama ΨΨΨ
Director Neil LaBute film about a woman (Renee Zellweger) who views a traumatic event and becomes delusional, believing the characters from her favorite soap opera are real and that she was once engaged to the character she most admired. With her delusional framework becoming more solidified, she journeys to Los Angeles where this character lives.

Outrageous! (1977) Comedy ΨΨ
Canadian film about a gay hairdresser and a woman with schizophrenia who is pregnant.

People Say I'm Crazy (2003) Documentary **???**
Cinema verite styled documentary of the daily life of a man with paranoid schizophrenia. Interesting for discussions on differentiation of schizophrenia, schizoaffective disorder, and mood disorders. Deeply honest, enlightening, and inspiring.

"I cannot trust my own perceptions."

**John Cadigan who directs
and plays himself
in *People Say I'm Crazy***

Perfect Strangers (2003)
Drama/Suspense ΨΨ
A mysterious man (Sam Neill) invites a woman he has just met to his private island home and then kidnaps her. The two become romantically involved, and she nurses him back to health after he is injured. His obsessions transfer to the woman who frequently hallucinates after her lover dies.

Possessed (1947) Drama ΨΨΨ
Joan Crawford stars in a suspenseful film depicting catatonic schizophrenia with examples of waxy flexibility and numerous other symptoms of severe mental illness.

Promise (1986) Drama ΨΨ
A made-for-TV movie, starring James Garner, about a man who honors a commitment made to his mother to care for his brother with schizophrenia. Excellent illustrations of the symptoms of schizophrenia.

Repulsion (1965) Horror ΨΨΨΨΨ
Powerful, unforgettable film about sexual repression and psychotic decompensation. Memorable examples of hallucinations (e.g., arms reaching out from walls); the film culminates in an unforgettable murder scene. This was Roman Polanski's first English language film.

Ruling Class, The (1972) Comedy ΨΨΨΨ
Brilliant British black comedy in which a member of the House of Lords inadvertently commits suicide and leaves his fortune and title to his son who is delusional and has schizophrenia (Peter O'Toole), who believes he is Jesus (at first) and later Jack the Ripper.

Saint of Fort Washington, The (1993)
Drama ΨΨΨ
A man with schizophrenia is evicted from his home winds up in a shelter, where he is befriended by a street-wise Vietnam veteran. Good portrayal of the life of people who are both mentally ill and homeless.

Santa Sangre (1989) Horror/Thriller ΨΨΨΨ
A disturbing film about a young man forced to witness the mutilation of his mother and the suicide of his father. We never know if these events are real or simply delusions of a patient. The film is complex and visually stunning.

Scissors (1991) Suspense Ψ
The paranoid delusions of a traumatized young woman take on a frightening reality when she finds her assailant dead.

Scotland, PA (2001) Comedy ΨΨ
Dark comedy that's a subtle parody of Macbeth, about greed, power, love, and "going crazy." A young couple who take over the work at a restaurant after killing the owner, begin to deteriorate with rumination, guilt, and poor coping as police detective (Christopher Walken) investigates the murder case.

**"David, if you go you will never
come back to this house again.
You will never be anybody's son.
The girls will lose their brother. Is
that what you want?... You want
to destroy the family... if you love
me you will stop this nonsense."**

**David Helfgott's father
admonishes him about leaving
home in *Shine***

Shine (1996) Biography/Drama ΨΨΨΨ
True story of David Helfgott, an Australian prodigy whose brilliant career is interrupted by the development of an unspecified mental illness that is probably schizophrenia. The film not so subtly suggests that David's domineering father was directly responsible for his mental illness and conveys the misleading but endearing message that love and hope can conquer mental illness.

Shock Corridor (1963) Drama ΨΨ
Journalist feigns insanity in order to get a story from a man admitted to a psychiatric hospital; later the journalist begins to lose touch with reality.

Snake Pit, The (1948) Drama ΨΨΨ
One of the first films to document the treatment of patients in a mental hospital.

Sophie's Choice (1982) Drama ΨΨΨ
Meryl Streep won an Academy Award for her portrayal of a concentration camp survivor infatuated with Nathan, who is described as having paranoid schizophrenia but who may suffer from a bipolar disorder. Based on William Styron's novel.

Spider (2002) Drama ΨΨΨΨ
Ralph Fiennes, a patient with schizophrenia, disorganized type, is released from the hospital to a group home. It's a dark, bleak, psychologically complex film and a brilliant portrayal of the isolation and inner world of schizophrenia. Directed by David Cronenberg. The DVD cover reads: "The only thing worse than losing your mind, is finding it again."

Spiderman (2002) Fantasy/Drama ΨΨ
Sam Raimi classic based on the Marvel comic book series. The Green Goblin (Willem Dafoe) hears voices and seems to be mentally ill. The film perpetuates the myth that people who are mentally ill are also violent.

Story of Adèle H., The (1975) Biography ΨΨ
François Truffaut story about the sexual obsession of the daughter of Victor Hugo for a young soldier she can never marry.

Stroszek (1977) Comedy ΨΨ
Offbeat Werner Herzog comedy about three Germans who come to America in search of the American dream. They fail to find it in Railroad Flats, Wisconsin. One of the three has schizophrenia.

Summer of Sam (1999) Drama/Documentary ΨΨΨ
This Spike Lee film succeeds artistically and presents interesting insights into ethnic dynamics and the process of scapegoating; however, it provides little insight into the motives or the mental illness that drove serial killer David Berkowitz, the highly publicized "Son of Sam," to commit multiple murders. The emphasis is on the fear and psychological trauma of people living in New York City who know a serial killer is still loose.

Sweetie (1989) Comedy ΨΨΨΨ
Director Jane Campion paints a memorable and realistic picture of a woman with schizophrenia and the difficulties her illness presents for her and her family.

Sylvia and the Phantom (1945) Drama ΨΨΨ
French film about a young woman who must distinguish between reality and fantasy, hallucination and phantom, love and illusion. Her many seducers include a narcissist, a lover, a criminal, and a phantom.

Tarnation (2003) Documentary ΨΨΨ
Poignant, disturbing, dramatic, and realistic film chronicles the life of a family plagued by mental illness. *Tarnation* illustrates schizophrenia and depersonalization disorder as well as the effects of brain damage and traumatic abuse. The film integrates home movies, photographs, short videos, diaries, and pop culture artifacts into a striking visceral experience. If you can find this independent film, you should watch it.

Taxi Driver (1976) Drama ΨΨΨΨ
Robert De Niro becomes obsessed with Jodi Foster and determines to rescue her from prostitution.

"Someday a real rain will come and wash all the scum off the streets."

Taxi Driver

Tenant, The (1976) Horror ΨΨΨ
Roman Polanski film about an ordinary clerk who moves into an apartment in which the previous owner committed suicide. The new owner assumes the personality of the old owner, becomes paranoid, and commits suicide in the same way as the previous owner.

Through a Glass Darkly (1962) Drama ΨΨΨΨ
Powerful and memorable Bergman film about a recently released mental patient who spends the summer on an island with her husband, father, and younger brother.

Truman Show, The (1998) Drama ΨΨΨΨ
This Peter Weir film stars Jim Carrey as Truman Burbank, who unbeknownst to him, has had his entire life broadcast on a popular television

show where all the people in his life are actors and his home and town are part of an elaborate production studio. This film provides a fascinating setup for a discussion of delusional disorders.

Who's Afraid of Virginia Woolf? (1966) Drama ΨΨΨ
A Mike Nichols film, with Elizabeth Taylor and Richard Burton, who appear to have a shared psychotic disorder involving a son who never really existed; the film also portrays alcoholism and interpersonal cruelty. Elizabeth Taylor and Sandy Dennis both won Academy Awards for their performances in this film.

"Now that we're through with Humiliate the Host... and we don't want to play Hump the Hostess yet... how about a little round of Get the Guests?"

Who's Afraid of Virginia Woolf?

World Traveler (2001) Drama ΨΨ
Julianne Moore has a supporting role as an alcoholic with a delusional disorder.

Neuropsychological Disorders

50 First Dates (2004) Comedy Ψ
Adam Sandler plays a veterinarian and womanizer who falls in love with a woman (Drew Barrymore) with a fictional cognitive disorder in that she has no long-term memory as she awakens each morning forgetting everything from the day before (so she repeats the same activities each day, enabled by her family). A flawed *Memento*.

Awakenings (1990) Drama ΨΨΨ
Robin Williams as neurologist Oliver Sacks treats patient Robert De Niro in a Bronx hospital. The film documents the use of L-Dopa in the treatment of patients with advanced Parkinson's disease. Good portrayal of the daily life of a mental hospital.

City of No Limits, The (2002) Drama ΨΨΨ
The patriarch of a Spanish family is dying of a brain tumor and displays symptoms of paranoia, dementia, and depression. One son discovers that

amidst his father's confusion, there are family secrets and lies to be uncovered.

"This is not a hospital. They are not doctors or nurses. Didn't they tell you? They all believe that the city has got no limits."

Dying Max's confusion and paranoia in *The City of No Limits*

Dark Victory (1939) Drama ΨΨΨ
Bette Davis, George Brent, and Humphrey Bogart star, but watch for Ronald Reagan. Davis has a fatal brain tumor. She spends what little time she has left with her brain surgeon husband. The "dark victory" refers to living life well, even when facing death. Remade (not very effectively) with Susan Hayward in *Stolen Hours* (1963).

Death Be Not Proud (1975) Biography ΨΨ
A made-for-TV film based on John Gunther's moving account of his son's struggle with a brain tumor, which killed the boy at the age of 17. The book provides considerable insight into the neurology of brain lesions.

Do You Remember Love? (1985) Drama ΨΨ
Joanne Woodward won an Emmy for her portrayal of a middle-aged college professor who develops Alzheimer's Disease.

Harder They Fall, The (1956) Sports ΨΨΨΨ
Humphrey Bogart in his last film, made the year before his death. The movie is very critical of the sport of boxing and the exploitation of fighters by promoters. A slow-witted boxer has a brain clot and is almost killed in his last fight.

Iris (2001) Drama/Biography ΨΨΨΨ
Based on the life of the famous British novelist and philosophical writer, Iris Murdoch (played by Judi Dench), who deteriorates because of her Alzheimer's Disease. Oscar-winner, Jim Broadbent plays John Bayley, Iris' extraordinarily loving husband. A powerfully realistic and emotional film.

Lorenzo's Oil (1992) Drama ΨΨΨ
True story of the Odone family and their desperate struggle to save their son's life. The boy has a rare

neurological disease that they are told is ultimately fatal. Good illustration of the effects of chronic illness on family functioning.

Majestic, The (2001) Drama ΨΨ
Jim Carrey plays a disenfranchised screenwriter who develops amnesia after his car topples over a bridge. He washes on the shore of a small town whose citizens take him in as a lost war hero.

Man Without a Past, The (2002) Drama ΨΨΨ
A man is severely beaten while sleeping outside and is proclaimed dead. He awakens with amnesia and begins to create a new life for himself before eventually discovering parts of his old life.

Memento (2001) Suspense/Mystery ΨΨΨΨ
Christopher Nolan directs this one-of-a-kind, exquisitely crafted masterpiece about a man suffering from anterograde amnesia. The film demands the viewer have very good short-term memory as the major plot progresses backwards scene by scene while juxtaposing past events (going forward) in black-and-white. This is a film not to be missed.

"How am I supposed to heal if I can't feel time?"

Guy Pearce in *Memento*

Memories of Me (1988) Comedy ΨΨ
Henry Winkler directs Billy Crystal, a high-powered surgeon who has just had a heart attack, and Alan King, his actor father who may have Alzheimer's. It turns out that an aneurysm is present, and father and son eventually learn to care for one another.

Mercy or Murder? (1987) Drama ΨΨ
Made-for-TV movie about a Florida man who went to prison after killing his wife because she had advanced Alzheimer's Disease. The film raises interesting questions that society will increasingly be forced to confront.

Mulholland Drive (2001)
Mystery/Drama/Suspense ΨΨΨΨ
David Lynch film about a woman who experiences a head injury from a car accident, becomes amnestic, and finds refuge in an aspiring Hollywood

actress' condominium. This is characteristic Lynch in its non-linearity and themes of reality vs. illusion, identity confusion, and nightmarish dream sequences.

My Girl (1991) Comedy ΨΨ
Eleven-year-old girl is a hypochondriac with a mortician for a father and a grandmother who has Alzheimer's disease.

"You was my brother, Charley, you should've looked out for me just a little bit so I wouldn't have to take them dives for the short-end money."

**Marlon Brando
in *On the Waterfront***

On the Waterfront (1954) Drama ΨΨΨΨ
Classic Elia Kazan film starring Marlon Brando as Terry Malloy, a prizefighter of limited intelligence who is exploited by almost everyone around him. Brando won an Oscar as Best Actor for his performance as Terry Malloy, who took a dive and spent the rest of his life regretting it.

Pride of the Yankees (1942) Biography ΨΨΨ
Gary Cooper stars in this Samuel Goldwyn film about legendary Yankees' first baseman Lou Gehrig, who had to give up baseball due to amyotrophic lateral sclerosis, which came to be known more widely by the eponym "Lou Gehrig's disease."

"Some people say I've had a bad break, but I consider myself to be the luckiest man on the face of the earth."

**Lou Gehrig giving up baseball in
*Pride of the Yankees***

Private Matter, A (1992) Biography ΨΨ
Provocative made-for-TV movie starring Sissy Spacek as a TV personality who gets national attention after her decision to abort a child likely to be affected by the drug thalidomide.

Raging Bull (1980) Biography/Sports ΨΨΨΨ
Powerful film depicting the psychological, moral, and mental decline of a prizefighter. Robert De Niro won an Oscar for his portrayal of Jake LaMotta.

Regarding Henry (1993) Drama ΨΨ
Attorney has his life permanently altered following a head injury; his values change as well as his personality.

Shattered (1991) Mystery/Suspense ΨΨ
A man in a near-fatal car accident experiences amnesia and undergoes reconstructive facial surgery. He begins to find inconsistencies in stories from loved ones about his past and his own memories, only to face a shocking truth.

Son of the Bride (2002) Drama/Comedy Romance ΨΨΨΨ
Moving drama from Argentina with many inspirational and comic moments about a man too busy for his families who reevaluates his life after he has a heart attack. A major sub-story is the man's aging father, who steadfastly expresses unconditional love to his wife who is deteriorating with Alzheimer's Disease.

Tuesdays with Morrie (1999) Drama /Inspiration ΨΨ
Made-for-TV movie based on the best-selling Mitch Albom book about a journalist who befriends and finds inspiration from a man dying of ALS.

Disorders of Childhood and Adolescence

Ali Zaoua: Prince of the Streets (2000) Drama ΨΨΨ
Four young homeless boys, living in poverty on the streets of Morocco, rebel against their gang leader's oppressive rule.

Best Little Girl in the World, The (1981) Drama ΨΨ
Good made-for-TV movie in which a psychiatrist treats a girl who is suffering from anorexia nervosa.

Butcher Boy, The (1997) Comedy ΨΨΨΨ
Dark comedy about a schizophrenic boy, Francie Brady, living in Ireland in the 1960s. Francie's behavior ranges from absurd and humorous to delusional and dangerous.

"He took me, with the stink of filthy roadhouse whiskey on his breath, and I liked it. I liked it! With all that dirty touching of his hands all over me. I should've given you to God when you were born, but I was weak and backsliding, and now the devil has come home."

A psychotic Francie Brady in
The Butcher Boy

Carrie (1976) Horror ΨΨ
This Brian De Palma film is based on a Stephen King novel and depicts the cruelty of adolescents and some of the stresses associated with caring for a mentally ill mother. Sissy Spacek's performance is remarkable.

City of God (2003) Drama/Foreign ΨΨΨΨ
Painful, sobering and graphic examination of the violence associated with gang-life, drug trafficking, and poverty in Rio de Janeiro. This film depicts of young children and adolescents who grow up in an environment in which guns and murder are commonplace.

City of Lost Children, The (1995) Fantasy/ Comedy ΨΨΨΨ
A mad scientist is aging prematurely so he tries to capture children to steal their dreams. Implicit in the film is the use and abuse of children; film critics have commented that this kind of film could not have been made in the United States. The movie is a black comedy that has been praised for its cinematic craft, creative set design, and the use of quirky, unique characters.

Dangerous Lives of Altar Boys, The (2002) Drama/Comedy ΨΨ
High school outcasts express rebellion in a variety of ways, including abuse of an authoritarian nun (played by Jodie Foster).

Elephant (2003) Drama ΨΨΨΨΨ
Well-crafted, foreboding, eerie Gus van Sant film addressing the tragedy of recent school shootings.

Powerful parallels with Columbine. Winner of the Palm award at Cannes for Best Picture and Best Director.

"And most importantly, have fun, man!"

Final words of an adolescent to his co-assassin preparing to enter a school building in
Elephant

Equus (1977) Drama ΨΨΨ
Richard Burton examines the meaning and purpose of his own life as he attempts to unravel the psychosexual roots that led an adolescent to blind six horses. Wonderful soliloquies by Burton.

Every Man for Himself and God Against All (1975) Biography ΨΨΨΨΨ
Werner Herzog film based on a true story about a man who spent an isolated childhood virtually devoid of stimulation. This movie should be contrasted with Truffaut's film *The Wild Child* and the more recent film *Nell*.

Face to Face (1976) Drama ΨΨ
Bergman film in which Liv Ullmann plays a suicidal psychiatrist estranged from her husband and 14-year-old daughter. During a coma that results from an overdose of sleeping pills, Ullmann dreams about a childhood experience in which she was punished by being locked in a closet.

Fanny and Alexander (1983) Drama ΨΨΨΨΨ
Bergman film about two young children and the ways in which their lives change when their father dies and their mother remarries. The film is sensitive, tender, and haunting and shows how the world looks through the eyes of a 10-year-old.

Firestarter (1984) Drama/Suspense Ψ
Early Stephen King film in which Drew Barrymore portrays a young girl with pyrokinetic, telekinetic, and telepathic powers. Barrymore is able to sets fires simply by staring at whatever she wants to set on fire.

Forbidden Games (1951) War/Drama ΨΨΨΨ
This beautiful French film is about two children who create and share a private fantasy world. The movie juxtaposes the innocence of childhood with the horror of war.

Four Hundred Blows, The (1959)
Drama ΨΨΨΨΨ
Semiautobiographical film by François Truffaut about a 13-year-old boy who is caught up in a life of truancy and petty crime. His mother sleeps around; his father is preoccupied and distant. *Four Hundred Blows* is reported to be Truffaut's favorite film.

**Psychiatrist: "Your parents say you're always lying."
Antoine Doinel: "Oh, I lie now and then, I suppose. Sometimes I'd tell them the truth, and they still wouldn't believe me, so I prefer to lie."**

Antoine explains his behavior to a psychiatrist in ***The 400 Blows***

Gummo (1997) Independent ΨΨΨ
This extremely disturbing and unforgettable film directed by Harmony Korine depicts life in a small, rural town after its destruction by a tornado. Despite the lack of a coherent plot, the film gets high marks for its honesty and realism. Various types of psychopathology are presented with an emphasis on conduct disorders.

Holes (2002) Family ΨΨΨ
One of the better non-animated Disney films about troubled youth who are sent to a work camp to dig deep holes in the middle of the desert to help three criminals find a lost treasure. Sigourney Weaver has a memorable role in this film.

Innocents, The (1961) Horror ΨΨΨ
Deborah Kerr plays a governess hired to care for two precocious children. Is she hallucinating or delusional, or are there really ghosts in the house? Interesting sexual tension develops between Kerr and the boy. Based on the Henry James novella *Turn of the Screw*.

Island on Bird Street (2000) Drama ΨΨΨ
Polish film about an adventurous, high-spirited boy who escapes from Nazi control; inspired by Robinson Crusoe, he creates a hide-out and waits for his father's return.

Kids (1995) Drama ΨΨΨ
Gritty and disturbing film about urban adolescents, sex, drugs, and violence. The main character is a teenager with AIDS who preys on young adolescent girls, taking particular pride in seducing virgins.

"If you deflower a girl... you're the man. No one can ever do that again. You're the only one. No one, no one, has the power to do that again."

Telly describes his fascination with virgins in *Kids*

Leolo (1992) Comedy ΨΨΨΨ
Leo, an adolescent boy growing up in a very dysfunctional family in Montreal, is unable to accept the reality of his genetic heritage and concocts a fantasy in which he was accidentally conceived by sperm that crossed the Atlantic in a Sicilian tomato. (The film is better than this brief synopsis suggests.)

Life as a House (2001) Drama ΨΨΨ
Touching film about the transformation of the relationship between a rebellious, addicted adolescent (Hayden Christensen) and his terminally ill father (Kevin Kline).

Lilja 4-ever (2002) Drama ΨΨΨ
Heartbreaking film about a girl, rejected by her family and society, who seems to meet with tragedy just when it appears she is headed in the right direction. Lilja is physically, emotionally, and sexually abused in the film.

Little Man Tate (1991) Drama ΨΨΨ
Jodi Foster directed this film about a child prodigy and the tensions that arise between his mother and the psychologist to whom the child's education is entrusted. Foster acknowledged that the film is partly autobiographical.

Lord of the Flies (1963) Drama ΨΨ
Film adaptation of William Goldman's novel about a group of schoolchildren who quickly shed the thin veneer of civilization and become savages. Both the film and book raise interesting questions about nature and nurture. Remade in 1990.

Los Olvidados/The Young and the Damned (1950) Drama ΨΨΨ
Luis Buñuel film about juvenile delinquency in the squalid slums of Mexico City.

Magdalene Sisters, The (2002) Docudrama ΨΨΨ
Troubled adolescent girls are sent to a dehumanizing boarding home where they are abused, mistreated and exploited by the nuns who run the home. One particularly abused adolescent sexually acts out with a priest and later becomes psychotic.

Manic (2001) Drama ΨΨΨ
A psychologist played by Don Cheadle tries to help an angry adolescent. Interesting group therapy sessions and inpatient hospital scenes with adolescents who have bipolar disorder, intermittent explosive disorder, major depression, self-injurious behavior, and night terrors.

Mommie Dearest (1981) Biography ΨΨ
A film about the pathological relationship between Joan Crawford and her adopted daughter. The movie suggests that Crawford suffered from bipolar disorder.

"What are wire hangers doing in this closet? Answer me! I buy you beautiful dresses, and you treat them like they were some dishrag. You do! Three hundred dollar dress on a wire hanger!"

Joan Crawford in a manic state berates her daughter in *Mommie Dearest*

Monsieur Ibrahim (2003) Drama ΨΨΨ
Heart-warming French film about an adolescent boy raised by a critical, neglecting father; he develops a meaningful friendship with a local store-owner.

My First Mister (2001) Drama ΨΨ
Adolescent girl struggles with severe isolation, depression, self-injurious behavior, and other acting out behaviors until she befriends a 49-year-old man. The teen has a host of behavioral problems including

"huffing," autoerotic asphyxiation, isolation from her family, and prostitution.

My Flesh and Blood (2004) Documentary ΨΨΨ
Moving story of Susan Tom, who adopted 11 special needs children and raised them on her own. One has cystic fibrosis and severe anger and oppositional behaviors directed at most people around him.

Nell (1994) Drama ΨΨΨ
Jodi Foster plays a feral child raised in isolation in the North Carolina woods. She is terrified of the doctor who discovers her and eventually learns her own odd language. The doctor consults an expert on child psychology. Interesting examination of Rousseau's concept of the "natural savage."

Noi the Albino (2003) Drama ΨΨΨ
A film about a troubled but gifted teen who struggles with conduct problems in Iceland. The movie provides a realistic evaluation of a gifted adolescent who is out of place in both school and life.

Pelle the Conqueror (1986) Drama ΨΨΨΨΨ
Moving film about lust, passion, dreams, aging, hope, pragmatic romance, and, most of all, the love between a father and his son. The film won the Grand Prix at the Cannes Film Festival and an Academy Award as Best Foreign Film.

Pieces of April (2003) Comedy ΨΨΨ
Previously troubled adolescent estranged from her family tries to create a pleasant, memorable experience for her dysfunctional family's Thanksgiving dinner. Well-acted by Katie Holmes and Patricia Clarkson.

Pixote (1981) Drama ΨΨΨΨΨ
A powerful film about the squalid, depressing lives of street children in Sao Paulo. In the film, the child, Pixote, commits his first murder at the age of 10. Ironically, the child star actually was shot and killed by the police five years after the film was released.

Ratcatcher, The (1999) Drama ΨΨΨ
Young adolescent living in Glasgow has to cope with trash-covered streets, lice, and dead rats. He acts out as he tries to cope with poverty.

Rebel Without a Cause (1955) Drama ΨΨΨ
Dated but still interesting examination of teenage alienation, violence, and family pathology. James Dean is the rebellious protagonist. All three stars (Dean, Natalie Wood, and Sal Mineo) met violent deaths (a car wreck, a drowning, and a murder).

"Boy, if, if I had one day when I didn't have to be all confused, and didn't have to feel that I was ashamed of everything"

James Dean
in *Rebel Without a Cause*

Salaam Bombay! (1988) Drama ΨΨΨ
Remarkable story about the way indigent children manage to survive to adulthood on the mean streets of Bombay.

Cole Sear: "We were supposed to draw a picture, anything we wanted. I drew a man who got hurt in the neck by another man with a screwdriver."
Malcolm Crowe: "You saw that on TV, Cole?"
Cole Sear: "Everyone got upset. They had a meeting. Mom started crying. I don't draw like that any more."
Malcolm Crowe: "How do you draw now?"
Cole Sear: "Draw... people smiling, dogs running, rainbows. They don't have meetings about rainbows."

A child figures out how to game the system in *The Sixth Sense*

Sixth Sense, The (1999) Drama ΨΨΨ
Bruce Willis plays a Philadelphia child psychologist treating a child who sees himself surrounded by dead people. If this child were seen at a clinic, he would probably be diagnosed with childhood schizophrenia. The film has a surprise ending and offers some insight into a troubled marriage, but it offers little to help us understand child psychopathology.

Splendor in the Grass (1961) Drama ΨΨ
A teenage girl unable to come to grips with adolescent sexuality winds up in a psychiatric hospital.

Thirteen (2003) Drama ΨΨΨΨ
Important film about the rise and fall of teen friendships, sexual promiscuity, self-hate, rebellion, and the intense need adolescents fill to fit in and be accepted. Holly Hunter plays the recovered alcoholic mother struggling with the delicate balance between giving her daughter appropriate levels of freedom and setting limits.

Tin Drum, The (1979) Drama/War ΨΨΨΨ
Political allegory about a child who decides to stop growing. Based on a Gunter Grass novel, the film won an Academy Award as Best Foreign Film. The film recently received considerable attention because a scene in which the child has oral sex with an adult was judged to be obscene under Oklahoma law.

"She did something that in our society is unspeakable. She kissed a black man. Not an old uncle, but a strong, young Negro man. No code mattered to her before she broke it, but it came crashing down on her afterwards."

Atticus Finch speaking to the jury in *To Kill a Mockingbird*

To Kill a Mockingbird (1962) Drama ΨΨ
Robert Duvall makes his film debut as Boo Radley, a man with mental retardation who kills another man in order to protect two children.

Tree Grows in Brooklyn, A (1945) Drama ΨΨΨ
Elia Kazan film about a poor Irish family living in Brooklyn at the turn of the century. The family's problems are complicated by the father's alcoholism.

United States of Leland, The (2004) Drama ΨΨΨ
Interesting story about Leland P. Fitzgerald (Ryan Gosling), an adolescent who kills an autistic boy but can't explain why. His emotions are blunted, his social behavior is quirky, yet his thoughts are often insightful and perceptive. Kevin Spacey co-stars.

Welcome to the Dollhouse (1996) Comedy ΨΨΨ
Interesting examination of families, emerging sexuality, and the cruelty of adolescents.

Wild Child, The (1969) Drama ΨΨΨ
François Truffaut's engaging film about the life of a feral child, the "Wild Boy of Aveyron." Based on a true story and the journal of Jean Itard, the doctor who set out to educate the child. Truffaut himself plays the role of Itard.

Willy Wonka and the Chocolate Factory (1971) Family ΨΨ
Five lucky children win a free tour of a wonderful chocolate factory. Four of the five children (excluding the hero, Charlie) are either oppositional, obsessed, or enormously selfish.

Wish You Were Here (1987) Drama ΨΨ
A teenage girl coming of age in Great Britain in the early 1950s must come to grips with her emerging sexuality.

Mental Retardation and Autism

Antonia's Line (1995) Comedy ΨΨΨ
A film with unforgettable characters, including Loony Lips and Dede, two mentally challenged people who fall in love and get married. The film is a joyful celebration of life and family.

Being There (1979) Comedy ΨΨ
Peter Sellers plays the role of a gardener with mild mental retardation who finds himself caught up in a comedy of errors in which his simple platitudes are mistaken for wisdom. This film is a precursor to *Forrest Gump*.

Best Boy (1979) Documentary ΨΨΨΨ
Ira Wohl's moving tribute to his cousin (who has mental retardation) examines the options facing the young man when his father dies and his aging mother is no longer able to care for him. This film won an Academy Award as Best Documentary film.

Best Man: "Best Boy" and All of Us Twenty Years Later (1997) Documentary ΨΨΨ
A sequel to the 1979 film documenting that director Ira Wohl's cousin has a rich, full and meaningful life, despite his cognitive limitations.

Bill (1981) Biography ΨΨ
Mickey Rooney won an Emmy for playing a man

with mental retardation who was forced to leave an institution after 46 years in this made-for-TV movie.

Boy Who Could Fly, The (1986) Fantasy ΨΨ
Love story about the affection that develops between a teenage girl whose father has just committed suicide and a new neighbor who is autistic.

"Why is that people who would never dream of making fun of a blind man or a cripple will make fun of a retard?"

Charly wonders about the cruelty of people in *Charly*

Charly (1968) Drama ΨΨ
Cliff Robertson won an Oscar for his role as man with mental retardation who is transformed into a genius, only to find himself reverting to a state of retardation. (Compare this film with *Molly* [1999].)

Child Is Waiting, A (1963) Drama ΨΨ
Burt Lancaster and Judy Garland star in this film about the treatment of children with mental retardation living in institutions.

City of Lost Children, The (1995) Fantasy/Drama ΨΨΨΨ
A mad scientist is aging prematurely so he tries to capture children to steal their dreams. The circus strongman named One, who has a developmental disability, teams up with a bold, bright young girl to save the children.

Dangerous Woman, A (1993) Drama ΨΨ
Debra Winger plays a woman with mild mental retardation who becomes involved with an itinerant alcoholic.

Day in the Life of Joe Egg, A (1972) Comedy ΨΨ
British black comedy that examines the issue of mercy killing.

Dodes'ka-den (1970) Drama ΨΨΨ
Akira Kurosawa film about a boy with mental retardation living in the slums of Tokyo. This was Kurosawa's first color film. Although now regarded as a classic, this film was not well received by the public or by critics when it was released, and

it's failure led to Kurosawa's attempt to commit suicide by slashing his wrists in 1971. Kurosawa died in 1998 in Tokyo.

Dominick and Eugene (1988) Drama ΨΨΨΨ
A man with mild mental retardation works picking up garbage so he can send his brother to medical school. The story revolves around the relationship between the two brothers and provides good insight into the quality of life possible for someone who is mildly mentally retarded.

Forrest Gump (1994) Fantasy ΨΨΨΨ
Traces the life of Forrest Gump, who triumphs in life despite an IQ of 75 and a deformed spine. The film will make you examine your stereotypes about mental retardation.

**Forrest Gump: "Lieutenant Dan, what are you doing here?"
Lieutenant Daniel Taylor: "I'm here to try out my sea legs."
Forrest Gump: "But you ain't got no legs, Lieutenant Dan."**

Forrest Gump

House of Cards (1993) Drama Ψ
Tommy Lee Jones is wasted in an insipid movie about a young girl who becomes autistic and withdrawn.

I Am Sam (2001) Drama ΨΨΨ
Sean Penn portrays a man with mild mental retardation who fights for custody rights for his daughter.

Larry (1974) Biography ΨΨ
Dated but still interesting film about a man discharged from a psychiatric hospital and forced to cope with the outside world. The film suggests the patient himself isn't really ill but still acts strange because he has grown up in a world where everyone acts a little odd.

Molly (1999) Drama Ψ
This film tries hard to be *Rain Man* with a female autistic character (Elisabeth Shue) but ends up being highly stereotypic, unrealistic, and unhelpful in educating the public about autism.

Of Mice and Men (1992) Drama ΨΨ
John Malkovich as Lenny, a farmhand with mental retardation. This is a wonderful film, but see the 1939 original as well.

"He's a nice fella. Guy don't need no sense to be a nice fella."

A comment about Lenny's personality in *Of Mice and Men*

Other Sister, The (1999) Drama ΨΨ
Carla (Juliette Lewis), after spending her adolescent years at a special institution, is determined to move away from home, become independent, and develop her relationship with her boyfriend (Giovanni Ribisi). Both Lewis' and Ribisi's characters would probably be diagnosed with mild mental retardation and the film uses stale stereotypes to define these two characters.

Radio (2003) Drama ΨΨΨ
Cuba Gooding Jr. plays a mentally challenged man who when given a chance by the coach (Ed Harris) of the local football team, inspires and influences many lives. With regard to the portrayal of disabilities, the pros outweigh the cons in this heart-warming, true story.

"I know you're in there somewhere."

Charlie Babbitt responds to his brother Raymond in *Rain Man*

Rain Man (1993) Drama ΨΨΨΨ
Dustin Hoffman plays an autistic man who is also a savant, initially exploited by an older brother. Hoffman read widely about autism and worked with autistic people when preparing for this role.

Sling Blade (1996) Drama ΨΨΨΨΨ
Billy Bob Thornton wrote the screenplay, directed the film, and played the lead in this remarkable film, which examines the life of a 37-year-old man with mental retardation who has been incarcerated in a mental hospital for the past 25 years after killing his mother and her lover. The fact that Childers winds up committing a third murder after being released perpetuates the myth that people who have mental retardation are potentially dangerous.

"I reckon I got no reason to kill no one. Uh, huh."

Carl Childers in *Sling Blade*

There's Something About Mary (1998) Comedy ΨΨ
Ted (Ben Stiller) tries to track down and rekindle love with Mary (Cameron Diaz). Mary has a brother with a developmental disability who plays a significant role in the story.

Tim (1979) Drama ΨΨ
In this Australian film, an older woman has an affair with a man with mild mental retardation.

Unforgotten: 25 Years After Willowbrook (1996) Documentary ΨΨΨΨΨ
Geraldo Rivera follows up on the original Willowbrook State School expose and contrasts the grim reality of institutional life with the current success of some survivors, including Bernard Carabello, a man abandoned by his parents at age three because he had cerebral palsy, who spent 18 years at Willowbrook.

Village, The (2004) Drama/Suspense ΨΨ
Director M. Night Shyamalan's latest "surprise-genre" film about a village surrounded by forest containing the highly feared "those we don't speak of." Adrian Brody's character is a purposefully stereotypic portrayal of a developmental disability—the "village idiot." The least powerful of Shyamalan's four films.

What's Eating Gilbert Grape (1993) Drama ΨΨΨ
Johnny Depp stars in this interesting portrayal of the dynamics of a rural Iowa family and small town America. Depp's life revolves around the care of his brother (who has mental retardation) and his morbidly obese mother.

Sleep, Eating, Impulse Control, and Adjustment Disorders

12 Monkeys (1995) Science Fiction/Suspense ΨΨ
Terry Gilliam film about a time traveler (Bruce Willis) trying to save the world from a deadly plague. Brad Pitt co-stars as a character with paranoid schizophrenia. At times, the film seems to take on a cinematic representation of a nightmare.

Behind the Red Door (2001) Drama ΨΨ
Keifer Sutherland plays a man dying of AIDS who exhibits explosive anger.

Best Little Girl in the World, The (1981) Drama ΨΨ
Good made-for-television movie in which a psychiatrist treats a girl who is suffering from anorexia nervosa.

Best in Show (2000) Comedy ΨΨ
A couple entering their beloved dog in a competitive dog show continuously fight, and their fights escalate in response to the tension and anxiety associated with the show. They later cure themselves of their "adjustment" problem by blaming their dog for being self-deprecating and purchasing a new dog who does not mind watching them have sex.

Bookies (2003) Drama ΨΨ
Three college roommates, obsessed with gambling, secretly launch a "bookie" operation.

California Split (1974) Comedy ΨΨ
Robert Altman movie starring George Segal and Elliott Gould as two compulsive gamblers. Not as strong a film as *The Gambler*.

Casino (1995) Drama ΨΨ
Martin Scorsese film explores the mafia's relationship to Las Vegas and gives an inside look at casinos and some gambling addiction. A strong cast includes Robert De Niro, Joe Pesci, Sharon Stone, and James Woods.

Center Stage (2000) Drama ΨΨ
A woman fights her way to the top role as a dancer and performs well despite encouragement to drop out. One dancer has bulimia and the portrayal is accurate and well-done; however, the film is clichéd and predictable.

Cooler, The (2003) Drama ΨΨΨ
Unlucky, depressed man (William H. Macy) walks around the casino as "the cooler" carrying bad luck to successful gamblers by appearing near their gambling tables. He is paying off his own enormous gambling debts and appears to have given up the behavior.

Deuce Bigalo, Male Gigolo (1999) Comedy Ψ
Rob Schneider takes a job as a male escort—one of his "calls" is for a woman with Tourette's Disorder and the other is a woman with narcolepsy. The latter falls asleep in the middle of her bowling stride.

Dinner Rush (2001) Drama/Comedy ΨΨ
In New York City sits an upscale restaurant frequented by high brow customers, self-centered art critics, hoodlums from Queens, and casual customers. One of the cooks has a gambling problem.

Elling (2001) Drama ΨΨΨΨ
Norwegian film about two men released from a psychiatric hospital who must prove themselves capable of coping with everyday life. One man suffers from intermittent anger episodes. Oscar nominee for Best Foreign Film.

Gambler, The (1974) Drama ΨΨΨΨ
James Caan plays a university professor of literature who can't control his compulsive gambling. One of the best film portrayals of pathological gambling.

Godsend (2004) Suspense/Thriller Ψ
Highly disappointing film starring Robert DeNiro as a genetics researcher cloning human beings. He clones a child who begins to experience night terrors, hallucinations, delusions, and murderous behavior.

Good Thief, The (2002) Drama ΨΨ
Nick Nolte plays a junkie gambler.

House of Games (1987) Drama ΨΨ
A psychiatrist specializes in the treatment of gambling addiction. Fascinating introduction to the world of the con.

Hulk (2003) Action/Drama ΨΨΨ
Ang Lee converts the famous "Incredible Hulk" comic series to film and in doing so creates a wonderful representation of anger and intermittent explosiveness.

Insomnia (2002) Drama/Mystery ΨΨΨΨ
Al Pacino stars as Will Dormer, a cop tracking down a minor writer (Robin Williams) in a murder

investigation. Dormer deteriorates with insomnia as he battles guilt, stress, and an Alaskan environment where the sun doesn't set. Directed by Christopher Nolan.

"Guess I'm a little cranky, lack of sleep, ya know."

Al Pacino in *Insomnia*

Life is Sweet (1990) Drama ΨΨΨ
Mike Leigh film about a dysfunctional British family. One of the twin girls binges and purges on chocolate bars.

Lost in Translation (2003)
Drama ΨΨΨ
Two Americans (Bill Murray and Scarlett Johansson) "stuck" in Japan find solace, excitement, and friendship in one another. Both characters suffer with severe insomnia symptoms.

Machinist, The (2004)
Drama/Mystery ΨΨΨ
Christian Bale lost 60 pounds to play the role of the gaunt, troubled Trevor Reznik. Trevor has experienced insomnia for over a year and begins to experience what could be hallucinations.

"I'll be rejected if I meet a good person."

Lyle, defending his façade of anger in *Manic*

Manic (2003) Drama/Action ΨΨΨ
Adolescent inpatient unit has patients with intermittent explosive disorder, bipolar disorder, major depression, self-injurious behavior, and night terrors.

Marnie (1964) Thriller/Romance ΨΨ
Hitchcock film about a sexually frigid kleptomaniac who dominates her new husband. As in other Hitchcock films, the protagonist's problems are found to be rooted in childhood trauma. Watch for the use of a word association test.

Matrix Reloaded, The (2003) Action ΨΨΨ
Keanu Reeves is Neo in this first sequel of the daring Trilogy by the Wachowski Brothers. Neo suffers from insomnia though on a more important level, his insomnia functions as a metaphor for being "awake" and "alive." He also experiences nightmares and frequently worries at night about decisions he needs to make the next day.

Maverick (1994) Western/Drama ΨΨ
Mel Gibson and Jodi Foster star as charming gamblers and cons in a game of high stakes poker.

Melvin Goes to Dinner (2003) Comedy ΨΨΨ
Interesting dialogue film about an unplanned get-together between four people. They discuss religion, God, faith, ghosts, affairs, and sex. The character Melvin probably has an adjustment disorder.

Mortal Transfer (2001)
Mystery/Drama ΨΨΨΨ
French film depicting one of a psychoanalyst's patients undergoing psychoanalysis and struggling with her kleptomania.

Mother Ghost (2002) Drama ΨΨΨ
A man (Mark Thompson) begins to have significant adjustment problems after his mother's death (she died a year ago) resulting in marital conflict, increased alcohol use, and other personal problems. Interesting interaction and therapy with a radio psychologist (Kevin Pollack) on the air.

My Own Private Idaho (1991) Drama ΨΨ
River Phoenix stars as a young male prostitute who has narcolepsy. He is befriended by Keanu Reeves, and the two leave Portland and travel together. Interesting presentations of dreams that occur during narcoleptic episodes.

Owning Mahowny (2003) Drama ΨΨΨ
Philip Seymour Hoffman, one of today's finest character actors, plays a pathological gambler. Great portrayal of the addictive cycle and elements of denial, deterioration, and self-destruction. The film is based on a true story.

Punch Drunk Love (2002)
Drama/Comedy ΨΨΨ
Adam Sandler in a serious role about a man who alternates from an awkward passivity to explosive anger. Falling in love changes him. Quirky cinematic elements are added by director Paul Thomas Anderson.

Rat Race (2001) Comedy Ψ
Several characters travel long distances in a competition for monetary reward. One character, played by Rowan Atkinson, has narcolepsy.

Rounders (1998) Drama ΨΨ
Matt Damon stars as a poker player who has gambled away his life savings to a Russian mobster, gives up gambling, and is lured back into the game by his friend (Edward Norton).

Seabiscuit (2003) Drama ΨΨ
Tobey Maguire plays a disc jockey with bulimic symptoms in order to keep his weight down and compete in horse-racing championships. Bulimic symptoms are fairly common among jockeys, though this is not an emphasis in the film.

Secondhand Lions (2003) Family ΨΨ
A young adolescent (Haley Joel Osment) is forced to live with his two rich uncles (Robert Duvall and Michael Caine), one of whom often sleepwalks.

Secret Lives of Dentists, The (2002) Drama ΨΨ
A married couple, both dentists, is unable to adjust to both living and working together. One begins an affair while the other stews in anger.

Story of Us, The (1999) Comedy/Drama ΨΨ
Bruce Willis and Michelle Pfeiffer star as a couple on the brink of separation after 15 years of marriage. Directed by Rob Reiner.

To Live (1994) Drama ΨΨΨΨ
This epic film by Zhang Yimou follows a Chinese family through tragic and wonderful times. One of the early struggles of the lead character, Fugui, is gambling, he loses his family home and his fortune gambling with dice.

Waking Life (2001) Drama/Animation ΨΨΨ
This unique, creative film follows a character searching for answers to life's most important questions in a world that seems surreal and dream-like. The film is a surrealistic blend of animation and drama with a heavy philosophical and existential bent. The film questions whether we are sleepwalking through our days and our lives, and whether we are more awake when we interact with others or when we dream.

Wrong Man, The (1956) Drama/Crime ΨΨ
Hitchcock film in which a man and his wife (Henry Fonda and Vera Miles) become depressed in response to an unjust accusation of murder.

Violence and Physical and Sexual Abuse

2LDK (2002) Drama/Action ΨΨΨ
A little known but striking independent film about two girls rooming together temporarily as they compete in an acting audition. A simple argument turns into an outrageously violent battle between the two roommates. The methods of violence are unique and extraordinary, despite being contained in one apartment.

8 Mile (2002) Drama ΨΨ
Director Curtis Hanson depicts the struggles, racism, and abuse of rapper, Eminem. "8 mile" is a road in Detroit that represents several cinematic themes: it is the borderline and boundary between black and white, city and suburbia, and the authentic and non-authentic.

Aileen: Life and Death of a Serial Killer (2003) Documentary ΨΨΨ
Nick Broomfield directed this documentary about serial killer Aileen Carol Wuornos, a highway prostitute who was executed in Florida in 2002 for killing seven men. The film includes the filmmaker's testimony at Wuornos' trial. (See also *Monster*.)

Accused, The (1988) Drama ΨΨΨΨ
Jodi Foster won an Academy Award for Best Actress for her role as a woman who is gang raped in a bar. Her character chooses to prosecute for rape rather than aggravated assault; and the film examines the legal relevance of lifestyle (alcohol, drugs, and promiscuity) to the event and the complicity of bystanders. Based on a true story.

American History X (1998) Drama/Suspense ΨΨΨ
Edward Norton plays a former skinhead who has decided to leave gang-life but must also convince his younger brother.

American Psycho (1999) Drama/Suspense ΨΨΨ
Christian Bale plays Patrick Bateman, a narcissistic Wall Street executive, who emphasizes excess and style over substance in everything from business cards and facial cleansers to restaurant selection and conversation. He also has a pathologically violent mind.

Amores Perros (2000) Action/Suspense ΨΨΨ
Mexican film with a non-linear plot with various hit men, murderers, and other perpetrators of highly

graphic violence. Abuse and senseless killing of humans and animals are depicted.

Anatomy of a Murder (1959) Drama ΨΨΨΨ
Classic courtroom drama in which Jimmy Stewart plays a prosecuting attorney in a case involving rape and promiscuity. The film presents an interesting analysis of the "irresistible impulse" defense.

Antonia's Line (1995) Comedy ΨΨΨΨ
Remarkable film about the resiliency of the human spirit, the power of love, and the importance of families. It is included here because of its treatment of a rapist, but also because of its treatment of people with mental retardation, the suicide of a major character, the film's open acceptance of sexual differences, and its healthy attitudes about aging and death.

"Every man has got a breaking point. You and I have. Walter Kurtz has reached his. And, very obviously, he has gone insane."

An Army general tries to describe the aberrant behavior of ColonelKurtz in
Apocalypse Now

Apocalypse Now (1979) War ΨΨΨΨΨ
Francis Ford Coppola produced and directed this classic war film, which stars Marlon Brando, Robert Duvall, and Martin Sheen. The film is loosely based on Joseph Conrad's *Heart of Darkness* and was designed to drive home the madness of war, as well as its folly. Perhaps the best-known line in the film is "I love the smell of Napalm in the morning."

Bad Lieutenant (1992) Drama ΨΨΨ
Cocaine-addicted, alcoholic police officer who abuses his position and his family reexamines his life and values after investigating the case of a nun who refuses to identify the man who has raped her.

Badlands (1973) Crime/Drama ΨΨΨ
Film based on a true story about a sociopathic young man who takes up with a 15-year-old girl and goes on a killing spree. The film effectively portrays the lack of guilt and remorse that in part defines the antisocial personality.

Blue Velvet (1986) Mystery ΨΨΨΨ
A powerful and engrossing film about drugs, sexual violence, and sadomasochism. Dennis Hopper plays Frank Booth, a sociopathic and sadistic drug addict who appears to be evil personified.

"He kidnapped them to control her, to make her do things. Then she wanted to commit suicide so he started cutting off ears as a warning to her to stay alive. I'm not kidding. Frank loved blue. Blue velvet."

Blue Velvet

Bonnie and Clyde (1967) Crime ΨΨΨ?
Perhaps the best of its genre, this landmark film examines the lives of five of the most fascinating characters in the history of crime.

"I ain't much of a lover boy. But that don't mean nothin' personal about you. I never saw no percentage in it. Ain't nothin' wrong with me. I don't like boys..."

**Clyde Barrow to Bonnie Parker
in *Bonnie and Clyde***

Boston Strangler, The (1968) Crime ΨΨ
Tony Curtis, George Kennedy, and Henry Fonda in a film that attempts to portray the inner life of a serial killer.

Bridge on the River Kwai, The (1957) Drama ΨΨΨΨ
Alec Guinness plays an Academy Award-winning role as a British colonel who becomes so obsessed with building a bridge that he loses sight of his loyalty and allegiance to the allied forces.

Cape Fear (1991) Thriller ΨΨΨΨ
Interesting Scorsese remake of a 1962 classic. This version includes Nick Nolte playing a sleazy attorney and Robert De Niro is a sociopathic ex-con out

to get revenge by hurting Nolte and his family and seducing his teenage daughter.

"Do not speak to me of rules. This is war. This is not a game of cricket. He's mad, your Colonel. Quite mad."

The Bridge on the River Kwai

Casualties of War (1989) Drama ΨΨΨ
Sean Penn leads a group of five soldiers who kidnap and rape a Vietnamese girl and subsequently kill her. Michael J. Fox subsequently shows the moral courage to confront the four rapists and murderers. Based on a true story.

City of God (2003) Drama ΨΨΨΨ
Painfully sobering and graphic look at violence associated with child and adolescent gang-life, drug trafficking, and poverty in a section of Rio de Janeiro, Brazil. Depiction of young children and adolescents walking around with no fear, guns, and only revenge on their minds.

Clockwork Orange, A (1971)
Science Fiction ΨΨΨΨΨ
Stanley Kubrick's masterpiece about "ultraviolence," stereotypes, Beethoven, pathological youth, the future of society, the evils of aversion therapy, good vs. evil, the rehabilitation of prisoners, and free will vs. determinism is regarded by many film experts as one of the greatest films ever made.

Cold Mountain (2003) Drama/Romance ΨΨ
Amidst a dramatic love story (between characters played by Jude Law and Nicole Kidman) is a lot of antisocial behavior, violence, immoral behavior, attempted rape, and senseless tortures and killings.

Compulsion (1959) Crime ΨΨΨ
Two homosexual law students kidnap and kill a young boy. Based on the Leopold-Loeb case, the film examines the morality of capital punishment and features Orson Wells in the role played by Clarence Darrow in the actual case.

Cook, the Thief, His Wife & Her Lover, The (1989) Drama ΨΨΨΨ
Peter Greenaway film far too complex to capture in a sentence or two. Full of psychopathology, the

film deals with passion, deceit, gluttony, murder, cannibalism, and man's inhumanity to man.

Copycat (1995) Drama ΨΨΨ
Sigourney Weaver plays a forensic psychologist trying to understand the psyche of a serial killer who models his murders after those committed by infamous murderers, such as Son of Sam and the Boston Strangler.

Das Experiment (2001) Drama/Suspense ΨΨΨ
Depiction of psychological research experiment in a prison setting where subjects are divided into prisoners who waive their civil rights and guards who are to maintain peace and order. While this film bears some initial structural similarity to the famous Zimbardo Prison Experiment, it in no way portrays it accurately as the film's violence goes well beyond actual events.

"They got me on a greased rail to the Death House here."

Sean Penn
in *Dead Man Walking*

Dead Man Walking (1995) Drama ΨΨΨΨ
Susan Sarandon and Sean Penn star in this dramatic examination of a nun's need to understand and help a man sentenced to die for the rape and murder of two teenagers. The film skillfully examines the death penalty, family dynamics, themes of redemption, and the mitigating role of drugs without ever providing easy answers. Sarandon won an Academy Award for her performance in this film.

Deliberate Stranger, The (1986) Drama Ψ
Made-for-TV movie about serial killer Ted Bundy.

"Lewis, don't play games with these people."

Deliverance

Deliverance (1972) Adventure ΨΨΨΨ
Jon Voight, Ned Beatty, and Burt Reynolds on a white water rafting trip in Appalachia. Beatty

winds up being sodomized, and Reynolds kills the rapist, using a bow and arrow. Based on a James Dickey novel, the film raises interesting questions about personal responsibility and social justice.

Disclosure (1994) Drama ΨΨ
A less-than-illuminating film about reverse sexual discrimination. Stars include Demi Moore and Michael Douglas; based on a novel by Michael Crichton.

Dog Day Afternoon (1975) Crime ΨΨΨ
Al Pacino holds up a bank to get enough money to fund a sex-change operation for his homosexual lover. Good illustration of a basically good person caught up in an stressful situation.

Down and Dirty (1976) Drama ΨΨ
An interesting examination of the effects of poverty, squalor, and alcoholism on an Italian family.

Dressed to Kill (1980) Thriller Ψ
The film confuses transsexualism and schizophrenia but offers good suspense. Mimics Hitchcock.

Elephant (2003) Drama ΨΨΨΨΨ
Well-crafted, foreboding, eerie Gus van Sant film that attempts to explain a tragic school shooting. Powerful parallels with Columbine. Winner of the Palm award at Cannes for Best Picture and Director.

End of Violence, The (1997)
Drama/Suspense ΨΨΨ
Bill Pullman plays an action/violence film director who is almost murdered so he hides out from society and starts a new life. While his character both promotes and greatly fears violence, a secret government worker (Gabriel Byrne) tries to prevent violence by watching over the city with thousands of cameras.

Executioner's Song, The (1982)
Made for TV Drama ΨΨ
Tommy Lee Jones plays serial killer Gary Gilmore. Based on a story by Norman Mailer.

Extremities (1986) Drama Ψ
Farrah Fawcett plays a victimized woman who gets revenge on the man who rapes her.

Fight Club (1999) Drama/Suspense ΨΨΨΨ
A disillusioned, insomniac (Edward Norton) meets a dangerous, malcontent part of himself in the character of Brad Pitt. Norton then establishes

"fight clubs" where men can violently release their aggressions by fighting one another.

"The great war is a spiritual war; the great depression is our lives."

Fight Club

Gangs of New York (2002) Drama/Action ΨΨΨ
Martin Scorsese picture of the turbulence of New York City in the mid-1800s.

Godfather, The (1972), **The Godfather, Part II** (1974), and **The Godfather, Part III** (1990) Drama ΨΨΨΨ
The three-part gangster trilogy, directed by Francis Ford Coppola, examines violence, corruption, and crime in America.

"We'll make him an offer he can't refuse."

The Godfather

Halloween I–V and H2O (1978, 1981, 1982, 1988, 1989, 1998) Horror Ψ
Infamous mass murderer depicted as an escaped mental patient and a deranged toy maker. These films have contributed significantly to the negative stereotypes of mental illness.

Hand That Rocks the Cradle, The (1992) Thriller/Drama Ψ
Sociopathic woman seeks revenge for the suicide of her husband by moving in and taking over the family of the woman she holds responsible for her husband's death. Predictable performances, but still an engrossing film.

Heavenly Creatures (1994) Drama ΨΨΨΨ
A New Zealand film directed by Peter Jackson and based on the true story of two adolescent girls who grow up sharing a fantasy world. When the mother of one of the girls decides to separate the children, they murder her. One of the girls, Ann Perry, now lives in England and writes mystery novels.

Henry: Portrait of a Serial Killer (1990)
Crime/Horror ΨΨΨΨ
A violent, controversial film about mass murderer and sociopath Henry Lee Lucas. A scene in which Lucas and his roommate videotape one of their murders is especially unnerving.

"She'd make me watch it... She'd beat me when I wouldn't watch her... She'd make me wear a dress and they would laugh."

Henry Lee Lucas describing abuse by his prostitute mother in *Henry: Portrait of a Serial Killer*

Honeymoon Killers, The (1970) Crime Ψ
A very realistic black-and-white film based on the true story of a couple who lured, exploited, and then killed lonely women. Both the man and the woman were executed at Sing-Sing Prison.

I Spit on Your Grave (1980) Horror Ψ
A terrible film in which a woman systematically gets revenge on the four men who raped her.

"They all felt physically inferior or sexually inadequate. Their childhood was violent... They couldn't distinguish between fantasy and reality. They didn't hate their victims, they didn't even know them."

A doctor describes serial killers in *In Cold Blood*

In Cold Blood (1967) Biography/Crime ΨΨΨ
This film is based on a Truman Capote biographical novel about two sociopaths who kill a Kansas family. The film explores the family dynamics that in part lead to the senseless murders.

Kill Bill: Vol. 1 (2003) Action/Suspense ΨΨΨΨΨ
Dynamic Tarantino story of a samurai bride (Uma Thurmond) betrayed by her ex-lover and boss. This first film sets up the mythology and the world of the characters. It has more extensive graphic violence than Vol. 2 and an "eastern" martial arts emphasis.

"I've kept you alive for two reasons. First reason is information... But I am gonna ask you questions and every time you don't give me answers, I'm gonna cut something off. And I promise you they will be things you will miss!"

Uma Thurmond as the Bride in *Kill Bill: Vol. 1*

Kill Bill: Vol. 2 (2004) Action/Suspense ΨΨΨΨ
Tarantino's conclusion to the revenge story of The Bride. This part emphasizes the unfolding of the stories and further deepening of characters amongst a more "western" style.

"I'm a killer. I'm a murdering bastard and there are consequences for breaking the heart of a murdering bastard"

David Carradine as Bill in Kill Bill: Vol. 2

Killing Fields, The (1984) Drama ΨΨΨ
Gripping film about the horrors of war and the particularly gruesome and cruel practices of the Khmer Rouge in Cambodia following the evacuation of American soldiers from Vietnam in 1975.

Lilja 4-Ever (2002) Drama ΨΨΨ
A powerful depiction of the cruelty of violence. An adolescent girl experiences neglect, abandonment, rejection, physical and sexual abuse, gang rape, exploitation, and forced prostitution, all by the age of 16.

Looking for Mr. Goodbar (1977) Drama ΨΨ
Diane Keaton plays a special education teacher with a compulsive need to pick up men in bars and engage in sadomasochistic sex. There are numerous examples of family pathology in the film, and it is interesting to remember how casual sexuality was in a time before AIDS.

M (1931) Crime/Drama/Horror ΨΨΨΨ
A must-see Fritz Lang film (his first "talkie") starring Peter Lorre as a sexual psychopath who molests and murders little girls. When tried by a vigilante jury, he pleads irresistible impulse, but the jury is not impressed.

Magdalene Sisters, The (2002)
Docudrama ΨΨΨ
Troubled adolescent girls are sent to a dehumanizing, boarding home where they are treated by nuns who run the home with abuse, neglect, and humiliation. The film follows four girls in particular as they experience and respond differently to the highly abusive situation.

Midnight Express (1978) Biography ΨΨΨ
True story about an American college student who is busted for trying to smuggle two kilograms of hashish out of Turkey and is treated brutally in Turkish prisons before eventually escaping.

Monster (2003) Drama ΨΨΨΨ
A powerful film based on the life of Aileen Carol Wuornos, a highway prostitute who was executed for killing seven men in the state of Florida during the 1980s. (See also *Aileen: Life and Death of a Serial Killer.*)

Murder in the First (1995) Drama ΨΨ
A man imprisoned in Alcatraz for petty theft in the 1930s is put in solitary confinement for three years, becomes deranged, and then kills a guard. The film suggests the system is to blame for the crime. Based on a true story.

"Insane, no. Psychotic, yes. A menace to living creatures, yes. But to suggest that they're insane gives the impression that they don't know right from wrong. Mickey and Mallory know the difference between right and wrong. They just don't give a damn."

A psychiatric opinion in *Natural Born Killers*

Natural Born Killers (1994) Crime/Drama ΨΨΨ
A violent Oliver Stone film based on a story written by Quentin Tarantino and starring Woody Harrelson

and Juliette Lewis. The film depicts a couple who celebrate their roles as mass murderers and find their new status as cult figures a welcome reprieve from the dreariness of the life they left behind.

Night Porter, The (1974) Drama/War ΨΨ
A former Nazi officer who sexually abused a 14-year-old girl in a concentration camp has the tables turned on him when she shows up at the hotel in which he works. This is one of several films linking Nazi practices with sadomasochistic sex.

No Man's Land (2001) Drama/Suspense ΨΨΨΨ
A Bosnian escapes a firing attack and finds himself in "No Man's Land" between enemy lines. A Serb goes to ensure there were no survivors and finds himself in a standoff with the Bosnian. Another Bosnian survivor, barely alive, awakes on top of a land mine that will explode if he rises. Heated debates, murder attempts, threats, desperation, and hopelessness characterize each of the three men.

"It's the same old story. I've got to learn to keep my mouth shut."

Beth blaming herself for the beating she has received from her husband in *Once Were Warriors*

Once Were Warriors (1994) Drama ΨΨΨΨ
Important New Zealand film about substance abuse and domestic violence among urban Maori tribes people. The film will help you understand a different culture, as well as the ways in which alcoholism interacts with spousal and child abuse in almost every society.

Passion of the Christ, The (2004)
Drama/Biography ΨΨΨΨΨ
Mel Gibson film depicting the violent torture and suffering of the final hours of Jesus Christ. This highly controversial film is intensely graphic and visual in its portrayal of violence. It is interesting to note that it is Mel Gibson's hand that nails Jesus to the cross.

Peeping Tom (1960) Thriller ΨΨΨ
Controversial film about a psychopathic murderer who photographs his victims as they die.

Personal Velocity (2002) Drama ΨΨΨ
Independent film about three strong women divided into three segments. One segment addresses issues of domestic violence.

"She imagined going back to him like she had done so many times before but this time her body wouldn't follow."

Narration on the escape from an abusive husband in Personal Velocity

---

Play Misty for Me (1971) Thriller ΨΨΨ
The first film directed by Clint Eastwood. A California disc jockey becomes involved with a listener who is clinging, dependent, fanatical, and ultimately homicidal. Interesting portrayal of sexual obsession.

Prick Up Your Ears (1987) Biography ΨΨΨΨ
A film showing the homosexual relationship and eventual murder/suicide of playwright Joe Orton and his lover.

Rampage (1992) Thriller ΨΨΨ
This movie, directed by William Friedkin, challenges many of the assumptions educated people are likely to hold about the insanity defense.

Rashomon (1950) Drama ΨΨΨΨΨ
Classic Akira Kurosawa film in which a rape-murder is described from four different perspectives by the four people involved. The film makes the point that reality is subjective and that truth, like beauty, is truly in the eye of the beholder.

Reservoir Dogs (1992) Drama ΨΨΨ
Extremely violent but powerful Tarantino film with a graphic and realistic torture scene in which a sociopathic sadist derives great pleasure from using a razor to slowly torment a bound and gagged undercover police officer.

River's Edge (1986) Drama ΨΨΨΨ
A riveting film based on a true-life incident in which a young man kills his girlfriend and then shows the decomposing body to a series of friends. It takes days before one of his friends finally notifies authorities about the murder.

Rope (1948) ΨΨ
Experimental Hitchcock film about two young homosexual men who kill a friend for sport and then hide the body in a room in which they are hosting a cocktail party. Based on the Leopold-Loeb case.

Santa Sangre (1989) Horror ΨΨΨΨ
A controversial but unquestionably powerful Jodorowsky film about a boy growing up in bizarre circumstances. There are strong themes of violence and incest. Roger Ebert called this film "a collision between Freud and Fellini."

Saving Private Ryan (1998) War/Action ΨΨΨ
Steven Spielberg World War II film regarded by some as the most realistic and powerful war film ever made.

Series 7: The Contenders (2001) Suspense/Comedy ΨΨΨ
Highly violent, tongue-in-cheek film about a reality television show where the contestants must seek out and kill one another.

"Now I'm not gonna bullshit you. I don't really care about what you know or don't know. I'm gonna torture you for a while regardless. Not to get information, but because torturing a cop amuses me. There's nothing you can say, there's nothing you can do. Except pray for death."

The sadistic Mr. Blonde in Reservoir Dogs

Seven (1995) Drama ΨΨΨ
Morgan Freeman and Brad Pitt star in this engrossing film about a serial killer (Kevin Spacey) who is obsessed with the seven deadly sins (pride, envy, gluttony, lust, anger, covetousness, and sloth) and who kills his victims accordingly (e.g., a man who is gluttonous is forced to eat until he dies from overeating).

Seven Beauties (1976) Comedy/Drama ΨΨΨ
Lina Wertmuller film in which the protagonist (the brother of the seven sisters alluded to in the title) must perform degrading sexual acts for the female

commandant of a German prison camp to survive the war.

Shelter Island (2003) Drama/Suspense Ψ
A lesbian couple goes to get away at an island house to relax. A stranger (Stephen Baldwin) appears on their doorstep during a storm and things are not what they seem. Simplistic psychology that is not well-applied or developed.

Sleepers (1996) Drama ΨΨΨ
Guards at a reform school physically and sexually abuse young boys. After the boys grow up, they avenge their abuse and attempt to manipulate the courts to avoid sentencing. Many stellar actors including Robert De Niro, Dustin Hoffman, Brad Pitt, and Kevin Bacon.

South Central (1992) Action/Suspense ΨΨ
A man is released from prison and tries to lead a "clean," gang-free life.

Stone Boy, The (1984) Drama ΨΨ
Robert Duvall and Glenn Close star in this slow-moving but intelligent film about a young man who accidentally shoots his brother and the effect the shooting has on the entire family.

Straw Dogs (1971) Crime ΨΨΨ
Provocative and violent Sam Peckinpah film, with Dustin Hoffman as a peace-loving mathematician who resorts to violence after his wife is raped.

Tattoo (1981) Drama Ψ
Mentally ill tattoo artist kidnaps a model and uses her body as a canvas for his art. This is the type of movie that perpetuates stigma and prejudice about mental illness.

Thelma and Louise (1991) Drama/Comedy ΨΨΨ
Two women friends on the road for a weekend lark wind up fleeing from the law and end their lives in a defiant suicidal act. Powerful feminist film.

Time to Kill, A (1996) Drama ΨΨΨ
Samuel Jackson plays an angry father who murders two white men who have raped his daughter. The film explores themes of racial and social injustice, temporary insanity, and justifiable homicide.

Treasure of the Sierra Madre, The (1948) Drama ΨΨΨΨ
Tremendous John Huston film starring Humphrey Bogart. The movie explores obsessive greed, the folly of avarice, and the ways in which love of money can come to be the dominant force in one's life. Bogart's character is an example of a paranoid personality disorder.

"Badges? We ain't got no badges! We don't need no badges. I don't have to show you any stinkin' badges!"

The Treasure of the Sierra Madre

Triumph of the Spirit (1989) Biography ΨΨΨ
Story of Auschwitz concentration camp during World War II. Good introduction to the horrors and stress of concentration camp life.

Two Women (1961) War/Drama Ψ
This Vittorio de Sica film starring Sophia Loren examines war, rape, coming of age, and mother-daughter relations. Loren won an Academy Award as Best Actress for this film.

Virgin Spring, The (1959) Drama ΨΨΨ
An Ingmar Bergman film examining the rape and murder of a young girl by three bandits.

Vulgar (2002) Drama ΨΨ
A man working as a clown for children decides he can make more money working as a clown at bachelor parties. He is tortured, gang raped, and blackmailed by a psychopath and his two sons. The film graphically depicts trauma and violence, but there are also comic moments.

Treatment

Antwone Fisher (2003) Drama/Biography ΨΨΨ
Troubled and angry sailor gets in fights and is referred to a psychiatrist (Denzel Washington). Their relationship develops and he becomes comfortable sharing his history of childhood abuse and trauma; he makes amends with his past and healing begins. Fair and balanced portrayal of a psychiatrist.

Article 99 (1992) Comedy Ψ
Unsuccessful M*A*S*H*-like attempt to ridicule the quality of care provided in Veterans Administration medical centers.

Bad Timing: A Sensual Obsession (1980)
Drama ΨΨ
Interesting and provocative film in which a psychiatrist becomes sexually involved with a troubled and self-destructive woman.

Badlands (1973) Crime/Drama ΨΨΨ
This film is based on a true story about a sociopathic young man who takes up with a 15-year-old girl and goes on a killing spree. The film effectively portrays the lack of guilt and remorse that in part defines the antisocial personality.

"Without treatment, John, the fantasies may take over entirely."

Psychiatrist Dr. Rosen attempting to educate John Nash on the importance of continuing his treatment regimen in
A Beautiful Mind

Beautiful Mind, A (2001) Drama ΨΨΨΨΨ
Based on Sylvia Nasar's biography with the same name. Russell Crowe portrays John Forbes Nash, a mathematical genius and Nobel Prize laureate in Economics, who battles schizophrenia and is treated with antipsychotics and insulin-shock therapy.

Beautiful Dreamers (1992) Drama/
Biography ΨΨΨΨ
True story about poet Walt Whitman's visit to an asylum in London, Ontario. Whitman is shocked by what he sees and persuades the hospital director to offer humane treatment. Eventually, the patients wind up playing the townspeople in a game of cricket.

Beyond Therapy (1987) Comedy Ψ
Disappointing Robert Altman film about New York yuppies and their psychiatrists.

Butcher's Wife, The (1991) Romance/
Fantasy ΨΨ
Greenwich Village psychiatrist Jeff Daniels finds Demi Moore, the butcher's wife, is giving advice at least as good as his own.

Cabinet of Dr. Caligari, The (1919)
Horror ΨΨΨΨΨ
German expressionistic film about hypnosis and the power of a hypnotist to induce others to do his bidding. One of the earliest stereotypic presentations of the madman who runs a psychiatric hospital.

Captain Newman, M.D. (1963) Comedy/
Drama ΨΨΨ
Sympathetic story about an Army psychiatrist (Gregory Peck) taking on the military bureaucracy to provide effective treatment for Bobby Darin. Darin is clearly manic and ultimately commits suicide.

Carefree (1938) Musical/Dance ΨΨ
Fred Astaire is a psychiatrist who was talked out of being a dancer. Ginger Rogers is referred to him for treatment (hypnosis) so she can learn to love one of Astair's friends; he complies with her request, but predictably falls in love with her himself.

Caretakers, The (1963) Drama Ψ
Second-rate film that documents life in a West Coast psychiatric hospital and portrays some of the problems associated with introducing innovations in hospital settings.

Chattahoochee (1990) Drama ΨΨΨ
Korean War veteran with a post-traumatic stress disorder is hospitalized and treated. Dennis Hopper has a major role as a fellow patient.

Clockwork Orange, A (1971)
Science Fiction ΨΨΨΨ
Fascinating interpretation of Anthony Burgess' novel. The portrayal of aversion therapy is somewhat heavy-handed but raises legitimate questions about the appropriate limits of behavior modification.

"There was me, that is Alex, and my three droogs, that is Pete, Georgie, and Dim. . . and we sat in the Korova Milkbar trying to make up our rassoodocks what to do with the evening."

Alex in ***A Clockwork Orange***

Color of Night (1994) Drama Ψ
Bruce Willis plays a disillusioned psychologist who gives up his practice after a patient commits suicide. Willis discovers he is no longer able to perceive the color red. Much of the plot revolves around a patient with multiple personalities who

is simultaneously a group therapy patient (as a male) and, unknown to Willis, his lover (in a core personality named Rose).

Couch Trip, The (1988) Comedy Ψ
Dan Aykroyd plays the role of a psychiatric patient who escapes from an institution and then passes himself off as a Beverly Hills psychiatrist. The film reinforces the notion that psychiatry is mainly pretentious language and social manipulation.

Dark Past, The (1948) Crime ΨΨΨ
A psychologist who is taken prisoner tries to use his training to help his captor. Remake of the film *Blind Alley*.

Dead Man Out (1989) Drama ΨΨ
Superior and timely made-for-TV movie about a psychiatrist treating a convict so the man will be sane enough to be executed. The film raises meaningful questions about ethical issues and the appropriate limits of professional practice.

Jack McDermott: "What about dinner? Who's gonna get us our dinner?"
Billy: "... aren't you the same guy who changed water into wine? Huh? J.C.? Ain't the son of God good for a burger in his town? You get us something!"

The Dream Team

Dream Team, The (1989) Comedy ΨΨ
Four psychiatric patients are being taken to a game in Yankee Stadium when their doctor/escort is knocked unconscious and hospitalized. The entire film appears to be based on the well-known (and better done) shipboard outing by Jack Nicholson and his friends in *One Flew Over the Cuckoo's Nest*.

Face to Face (1976) Drama ΨΨΨΨ
Liv Ullmann plays a psychiatrist whose life is falling apart. She attempts suicide by taking an overdose and winds up in a coma. Interesting dream sequences with Bergman's usual presumption of childhood trauma as the trigger for adult unhappiness.

Fear Strikes Out (1957) Biography/Sports ΨΨΨ
Anthony Perkins as baseball player Jimmy Piersall, who suffers a mental breakdown as a result of his inability to please a domineering, demanding father. Piersall was successfully treated with psychotherapy and ECT and eventually staged a comeback.

"Just repeat the last two words they say and phrase it like a question."

Psychiatrist Richard Gere jokes about his profession in *Final Analysis*

Final Analysis (1992) Thriller/Drama ΨΨ
A complex film that pays homage to Hitchcock; interesting issues of childhood sexual abuse, repressed memories, professional responsibility, and the doctor-patient relationship.

Fine Madness, A (1966) Drama ΨΨΨ
Sean Connery plays Samson Shillitoe, an eccentric and unconventional poet who is hospitalized and lobotomized because of his sexual peccadilloes and the fact that he can't conform to societal expectations. The film was ahead of its time in raising important issues about the rights of people with mental illness.

Flame Within, The (1935) Drama Ψ
Dated and insipid film about a psychiatrist who falls in love with a patient.

Frances (1982) Biography ΨΨΨΨ
A vivid portrayal of the life of actress Frances Farmer, including her institutionalization, lobotomy, and alcoholism.

Good Will Hunting (1997) Drama ΨΨΨ
Robin Williams won an Academy Award as Best Supporting Actor for his role as a counseling psychologist teaching at a community college and treating a troubled young man who is extraordinarily gifted mathematically.

High Anxiety (1977) Comedy ΨΨ
Mel Brooks spoofs Hitchcock films and introduces The Psycho-Neurotic Institute for the Very, Very Nervous.

Home of the Brave (1949) Drama/War ΨΨΨ
Black soldier suffers a mental breakdown and is treated by a sympathetic psychiatrist. One of the first films to deal honestly with racism and bigotry.

House of Games (1987) Crime ΨΨ
A David Mamet film about a psychiatrist specializing in the treatment of gambling addiction. Fascinating introduction to the world of the con.

House of Fools (2002) Drama ΨΨΨΨ
Based on a true story: the chief psychiatrist and treatment staff of a mental institution flee due to conflicts in Chechnya, leaving the patients to fend for themselves. Soon soldiers occupy the hospital and the viewer is left with various questions of war, politics, mental health treatment and which is more crazy—the mentally ill or the politics of war. The film is loaded with examples of psychopathology.

Inside/Out (1997) Drama ΨΨΨ
A Rob Tregenza film about life in a psychiatric hospital that was well received at the 1998 Sundance Film Festival. The film documents that both patients and staff find it hard to cope with the difficult demands of life.

Intimate Strangers (2004) Drama ΨΨΨ
This French film shows what happens when a nervous woman with an attention deficit disorder and marital problems mistakenly enters the wrong office and begins telling her personal problems to a man she assumes is a psychiatrist. The man, a tax accountant, is used to hearing problems and giving advice, and he is so fascinated by his new client that initially he cannot bring himself to correct her mistake.

King of Hearts (1966) Comedy/Drama /War ΨΨΨΨ
A Scotsman separated from his unit wanders into town, abandoned by all except the inmates of the local insane asylum. Must-see film for those interested in public attitudes about mental illness.

Ladybird, Ladybird (1993) Drama ΨΨΨΨ
Dramatic presentation of the clash between the rights of a parent and society's need to protect children.

Lilith (1964) Drama ΨΨ
Strong cast (Peter Fonda, Gene Hackman, Warren Beatty, and Kim Hunter) supports a weak script about a psychiatric inpatient who seduces a neophyte therapist.

Lost Angels (1989) Drama ΨΨ
Donald Sutherland plays a psychiatrist treating a Los Angeles adolescent who is angry and troubled but probably not mentally ill.

> **"When insurance paid for a year in a place like this, we said it took a year to help a kid. Now insurance pays for three months, and, presto, it takes three months to turn a kid around."**
>
> **Donald Sutherland complaining about the system in *Lost Angels***

Ludwig (1973) Biography Ψ
Long and somewhat tedious film about the mad King Ludwig of Bavaria. Good costumes and scenery, but the film teaches us little about mental illness or Ludwig himself.

Macbeth (1971) Drama ΨΨΨ
Powerful Roman Polanski adaptation of Shakespeare's play. It is interesting to speculate about the obsessions of Lady Macbeth and to compare Polanski's version with the earlier Orson Welles' adaptation.

Man Facing Southeast (1986) Drama ΨΨΨΨ
Fascinating Argentine film about a man without identity who shows up at a psychiatric hospital claiming to be from another planet. It seems that this is not just another patient, and neither the hospital staff nor the film's audience ever figures out exactly what is happening. (In a line that is meaningful to one viewer in a thousand, Bill Murray's character in *What About Bob?* pays homage to this film by asking if he can arrange his bed so it faces southeast.)

Man Who Loved Women, The (1983) Comedy Ψ
A remake of the François Truffaut film of the same name. This film involves long sequences in which Burt Reynolds unburdens himself to his psychiatrist.

Marat/Sade (1966) Drama ΨΨΨΨ
In the early 1800s, the inmates of a French asylum put on a play directed by the Marquis de Sade (a patient) based on the bathtub assassination of Jean Paul Marat. The play incites the patients to riot.

Mine Own Executioner (1947) Drama ΨΨ
Confused and troubled psychoanalyst tries to help out a schizophrenic veteran.

Mr. Deeds Goes to Town (1936) Comedy ΨΨΨ
Frank Capra film in which Gary Cooper inherits $20 million and is judged insane when he decides to give it all away to needy farmers.

Mr. Jones (1993) Drama/Comedy ΨΨΨ
Richard Gere portrays a bipolar patient treated by a psychiatrist who falls in love with him. This film raises interesting questions about the therapeutic relationship and boundary issues in psychotherapy.

No Time for Sergeants (1958) Comedy Ψ
Andy Griffith stars; Don Knotts plays an Army psychiatrist.

No Way Out (1950) Drama ΨΨΨ
This was Sidney Poitier's first film. Poitier plays a black physician treating two racist hoodlums. When one dies, his brother (Richard Widmark) incites a race riot. The film was one of the earliest serious examinations of racism in postwar America.

Nobody's Child (1986) Biography ΨΨ
Marlo Thomas won an Emmy for her role as a woman who experiences tremendous personal and professional success when she is released after spending 20 years in a mental hospital.

"Oh Jerry, don't let's ask for the moon. We have the stars."

**Bette Davis as Charlotte Vale
addressing her married lover
in *Now, Voyager***

Now, Voyager (1942) Drama ΨΨΨ
Her psychiatrist and inpatient treatment help sexually repressed Bette Davis find meaning and purpose in her life by serving as a surrogate mother for the daughter of a man she loves. The title comes from Walt Whitman's *Leaves of Grass* ("The untold want by life and land ne'er granted / Now voyager sail thou forth to seek and find.")

Nuts (1987) Drama ΨΨΨ
Barbra Streisand plays a prostitute who has killed a patron. She is resisting an insanity defense, and

through flashbacks we learn that she was sexually abused as a child. Interesting examination of civil liberties and forensic psychiatry.

"They was giving me ten thousand watts a day, you know, and I'm hot to trot! The next woman takes me on's gonna light up like a pinball machine and pay off in silver dollars!"

Randle P. McMurphy commenting on ECT in *One Flew Over the Cuckoo's Nest*

One Flew Over the Cuckoo's Nest (1975) Drama ΨΨΨΨΨ
Classic film with Jack Nicholson as Randle P. McMurphy, who takes on Nurse Ratched and the psychiatric establishment. The film offers good insight into life on an inpatient ward, although the portrayal of ECT is stereotyped and inaccurate; in addition, the suicide of Billy seems to be simplistically linked to his domineering mother. This film took all five of the top Oscars in 1975: Best Picture, Best Actor, Best Actress, Best Director, and Best Screenplay.

Passion of Joan of Arc, The (1928) Historical ΨΨΨ
Historically important silent film that portrays the burning of Joan of Arc as a heretic. The mental status of Joan of Arc remains a controversial subject for historians interested in psychopathology.

President's Analyst, The (1967) Spy/Comedy ΨΨ
James Coburn plays a psychoanalyst working for the President of the United States.

Pressure Point (1962) Drama ΨΨΨ
A black psychiatrist (Sidney Poitier) treats a racist patient (Bobby Darin). Based on a case from Linder's *The Fifty-Minute Hour*.

Prince of Tides, The (1991) Drama/Romance ΨΨΨ
Barbra Streisand plays a psychiatrist who becomes sexually involved with the brother of one of her patients (Nick Nolte). The film raises interesting questions about the proper limits of the doctor-patient relationship.

Quills (2000) Drama ΨΨΨ
Geoffrey Rush stars in this Philip Kaufman film about the notorious French author who is responsible for the word sadism. The film depicts the abuses that occurred in the eighteenth century in the Charenton Insane Asylum, a mental hospital located in the suburbs of Paris. The Marquis de Sade died at Charenton in 1814.

"I write of the great, eternal truths that bind together all mankind. The whole world over, we eat, we shit, we fuck, we kill and we die."

The Marquis de Sade describes his views on literature in *Quills*

Rampage (1992) Drama/Thriller ΨΨΨ
William Friedkin film about a sociopath who is arrested and tried for murder. The film raises important questions about capital punishment, the not guilty by reason of insanity (NGRI) plea, and the role of the expert witness in the courtroom.

See You in the Morning (1989) Drama ΨΨ
A film about a Manhattan psychiatrist with multiple problems, including a failed first marriage. Interesting group therapy sequences and lots of speculation about motivation and purpose.

Shock Corridor (1963) Drama ΨΨ
Samuel Fuller film in which a journalist has himself admitted to an insane asylum in order to get an inside story on a murder but soon becomes psychotic himself. The film is better than it sounds.

"Good night and sweet dreams... which we'll analyze in the morning."

Dr. Alex Brulov in *Spellbound*

Spellbound (1945) Thriller ΨΨΨΨ
Ingrid Bergman plays a psychiatrist treating Gregory Peck's amnesia. Salvador Dali helped design the film's dream sequence. Producer David Selznick wanted the film to be based on his own experiences with psychotherapy and he used his own analyst as a technical advisor. Watch for the Hitchcock cameo.

Still of the Night (1982) Thriller Ψ
A psychiatrist becomes romantically involved with a woman who may have murdered one of his patients.

Teresa (1951) Drama Ψ
Notable only because it stars Rod Steiger in his first role. Steiger plays a psychiatrist in the film.

Through a Glass Darkly (1962) Drama ΨΨΨΨΨ
Classic Bergman film that follows the life of a mentally ill woman after she is treated with ECT and released from a mental hospital.

Touched (1983) Romance Ψ
Two patients on a psychiatric ward fall in love and try to set up a life together after they escape.

"I'm not a shmuck Bob, and I'm not going to let you breeze into town and steal my family away just because you're crazy enough to be fun."

Dr. Leo Marvin to patient Bob Wiley in *What About Bob?*

What About Bob? (1991) Comedy Ψ
Bill Murray plays Bob Wiley, a patient who becomes overly dependent on his therapist, Leo Marvin, played by Bill Murray. The film is very funny, and it raises interesting questions about transference and countertransference. Note the inane discussion of potential psychotropic medications.

Whispers in the Dark (1992) Thriller/Drama ΨΨ
This murder mystery revolves around a psychiatrist who becomes overly involved in the lives of her patients. Mainly useful as a vehicle for discussion of professional issues and lessons on how *not* to behave in therapy.

References

Abbey, A. (2005). Lessons learned and unanswered questions about sexual assault perpetration. *Journal of Interpersonal Violence, 20*, 39–42.

Alper, G. (2004). *Like a movie: Contemporary relationships without the popcorn.* St. Paul, MN: Paragon House.

American Psychiatric Association (APA). (1994). *Diagnostic and statistical manual of mental disorders* (4th ed.). Washington, DC: Author.

American Psychiatric Association. (2000). *Diagnostic and statistical manual of mental disorders* (4th ed., text revision). Washington, DC: Author.

Arndt, W. B., Jr. (1991). *Gender disorders and the paraphilias.* Madison, CT: International Universities Press.

Banks, G. (1990). *Kubrick's psychopaths: society and human nature in the films of Stanely Kubrick.* Found at www.gordonbanks.com/gordon/pubs/kubricks.html, accessed on December 29, 2004.

Barnard, G.W., Fuller, A.K., Robbins, L., & Shaw, T. (1989). *The child molester: An integrated approach to evaluation and treatment.* New York: Brunner/Mazel, Inc.

Beck, A. (1976). *Cognitive therapy and the emotional disorders.* New York: Meridian.

Beck, A., Steer, R., Beck, J., & Newman, C. (1993). Hopelessness, depression, suicidal ideation, and clinical diagnosis of depression. *Suicide and Life–Threatening Behavior, 23,* 139–145.

Blanchard, R., & Hucker, S. J. (1991). Age, transvestism, bondage, and concurrent paraphilic activities in 117 fatal cases of autoerotic asphyxia. *British Journal of Psychiatry, 159,* 371–377.

Bordwell, D., & Thompson, K. (1993). *Film art: An introduction.* New York: McGraw-Hill, Inc.

Briere, J. (1989). University males' sexual interest in children: Predicting potential indices of "pedophilia" in a nonforensic sample. *Child Abuse and Neglect, 13,* 65–75.

Brown, G. R. (1994). Women in relationships with cross-dressing men: A descriptive study from a nonclinical setting. *Archives of Sexual Behavior, 23,* 515–30.

Canby, V. (1981). Review of *Arthur. New York Times* (July 17, p. 10).

Cape, G. S. (2003). Addiction, stigma and movies. *Acta Psychiatrica Scandinavica, 107,* 163–169.

Casson, I. R., Siegel, O., Sham, R., Campbell, E. A., Tarlau, M., & DiDomenico, A. (1984). Brain damage in modern boxers. *The Journal of the American Medical Association, 251,* 2663–2667.

Classen, C., Koopman, C., & Spiegel, D. (1993). Trauma and dissociation. *Bulletin of the Menninger Clinic, 57,* 178–194.

Denzin, N. K. (1991). *Hollywood shot by shot: Alcoholism in American cinema.* New York: Aldine De Gruyter.

Dietz, P. E., & Evans, B. (1982). Pornographic imagery and prevalence of paraphilia. *American Journal of Psychiatry, 139,* 1493–1495.

Fleming, M., & Manvell, R. (1985). *Images of Madness: The Portrayal of Insanity in the Feature Film.* Rutherford, NJ: Fairleigh Dickinson University Press.

Fullerton, C. S., Ursano, R. J., & Wang, L. (2004). Acute stress disorder, posttraumatic stress disorder, and depression in disaster or rescue workers. *American Journal of Psychiatry, 161,* 1370–1376.

Gabbard, K., & Gabbard, G. (1999). *Psychiatry and the cinema.* Washington, DC: American Psychiatric Press.

Geller, J., & Harris, M. (Eds.). (1994*). Women of the asylum: Voices from behind the walls, 1840–1945.* New York: Doubleday.

Giannetti, L. (1993). *Understanding movies.* Englewood Cliffs, NJ: Prentice Hall.

Goldstein, A. (1996). *Violence in America.* Palo Alto, CA: Davies-Black Publishing.

Hiller, W., & Fichter, M. M. (2004). High utilizers of medical care: A crucial subgroup among somatizing patients. *Journal of Psychosomatic Research, 56,* 437–443.

Hyler, S. E. (1988). DSM–III at the cinema: Madness in the movies. *Comprehensive Psychiatry, 29,* 195–206.

Hyler, S. E., Gabbard, G. O., & Schneider, I. (1991). Homicidal maniacs and narcissistic parasites: Stigmatization of mentally ill persons in the movies. *Hospital and Community Psychiatry, 42,* 1044–1048.

Jamison, K.R. (1993). *Touched with fire: Manic–depressive illness and the artistic temperament.* New York: The Free Press.

Kieseppa, T., Partonen, T., Haukka, J., Kaprio, J., & Lonnqvist, J. (2004). High concordance of bipolar I disorder in a nationwide sample of twins. *American Journal of Psychiatry, 161,* 1814–1821.

Konigsberg, I. (1987). *The complete film dictionary.* New York: Meridian.

Kuo, W. H., Gallo. J. J., & Eaton, W. W. (2004). Hopelessness, depression, substance disorder, and suicidality: A 3-year community-based study. *Social Psychiatry Psychiatric Epidemiology, 39,* 497–501.

Lazarus, R. S. (2000). Toward better research on stress and coping. *American Psychologist, 55*, 665–673.

Leonhard, H., & Wen, X. (2002). The epidemiology of mental retardation: Challenges and opportunities in the new millennium. *Mental Retardation and Developmental Disabilities, 8*, 117–134.

Mann, C. E., & Himelein, M. J. (2004). *Psychiatric Services, 55*, 185–187.

McCabe, P. (1992). *The butcher boy*. London: Picador.

Micali, N., Chakrabarti, S., & Fombonne, E. (2004). The broad autism phenotype: Findings from an epidemiological survey. *Autism, 8*, 21–37.

Mueser, K. T., Salyers, M. P., Rosenberg, S. D., Goodman, L. A., Essock, S. M., Osher, F. C., & Swartz, M. S. (2004). Interpersonal trauma and posttraumatic stress disorder in patients with severe mental illness: Demographic, clinical, and health correlates. *Schizophrenia Bulletin, 30*, 45–57.

National Institute of Mental Health. (January, 2001; revised May, 2003). *In harm's way: Suicide in America* (NIH Publication Number 03-4594). Retrieved on December 29, 2004, from the National Institute of Alcohol Abuse and Alcoholism: http://www.nimh.nih.gov/publicat/NIMHharmsway.pdf.

National Institute on Alcohol Abuse and Alcoholism. (July, 1990; revised October 2000). Alcohol Alert. *Children of alcoholics: Are they different?* (NIH Publication Number 09- PH 288). Retrieved on December 29, 2004 from the National Institute of Alcohol Abuse and Alcoholism: http://www.niaaa.nih.gov/publications/aa09.htm.

Niemiec, R., & Wedding, D. (2005). The role of the psychotherapist in movies. *Advances in Medical Psychotherapy and Psychodiagnosis, 13*.

Norden, M. (1994). *The cinema of isolation*. New Brunswick, NJ: Rutgers University Press.

North, C., & Smith, E. (1992). Posttraumatic stress disorder among homeless men and women. *Hospital and Community Psychiatry, 43*, 1010–1016.

Peake, T. H. (2004). *Cinema and life development: Healing lives and training therapists*. Westport, CT: Praeger

Piper, A., & Merskey, H. (2004). The persistence of folly: A critical examination of dissociative identity disorder. Part I. The excesses of an improbable concept. *Canadian Journal of Psychiatry, 49*, 592–600.

Putnam, F. (1985). Multiple personality disorder. *Medical Aspects of Human Sexuality, 19*, 59–74.

Rebal, R. F., Faguet, R. A., & Woods, S. M. (1982). Unusual sexual syndromes. In C. T. H. Friedmann & R. A. Faguet (Eds.), *Extraordinary disorders of human behavior* (pp. 121–54). New York: Plenum.

Saunders, E. B., & Awad, G. A. (1991). Male adolescent sexual offenders: Exhibitionism and obscene phone calls. *Child Psychiatry and Human Development, 21*, 169–178.

Steinberg, M. (1991). The spectrum of depersonalization: Assessment and treatment. In A. Tasman & S. Goldfinger (Eds.), *Review of psychiatry, volume 10* (pp. 223–247). Washington, DC: American Psychiatric Press.

Szasz. T. S. (1974). *The myth of mental Illness: Foundations of a theory of personal conduct*, Revised Edition. New York: Harper Row.

Szasz, T. S. (1977). *Psychiatric slavery: When confinement and coercion masquerade as cure*. New York: Free Press.

Trachtenberg, R. (1986). Destigmatizing mental illness. *The Psychiatric Hospital, 17*, 111–114.

Uhde, T., Tancer, M., Black, B., & Brown, T. (1991). Phenomenology and neurobiology of social phobia: Comparison with panic disorder. *Journal of Clinical Psychiatry, 52*, 31–40.

Van Ameringen, M., Allgulander, C., Bandelow, B., Greist, J. H., Hollander, E., Montgomery, S. A., Nutt, D. J., Okasha, A., Pollack, M. H., Stein, D. J., & Swinson, R. P. (2003). World Council Association recommendations for the long-term treatment of social phobia. *CNS Spectrums, 8* (Suppl 1), 40–52.

Veitia, M. C., & McGahee, C. L. (2001). Nicotine and alcohol addiction. In D. Wedding (Ed.) *Behavior and medicine* (3rd ed.) (pp. 247–261). Seattle, WA: Hogrefe & Huber Publishers.

Wahl, O., & Lefkowits, J. (1989). Impact of a television film on attitudes toward mental illness. *American Journal of Community Psychology 17*, 521–528.

Wahl, O. (1995). *Media madness: Public images of mental illness*. New Brunswick, NJ: Rutgers University Press.

Wedding, D., & Niemiec, R. (2003). The clinical use of films in psychotherapy. *Journal of Clinical Psychology 59*, 207–215.

Wedding, D. (2001). The portrayal of alcohol and alcoholism in the western genre. *Journal of Alcohol & Drug Education 46*, 3–11.

Zhang, L., Ravdin, L. D., Relkin, N., Zimmerman, R. D., Jordan, B., Lathan, W. E., & Ulug, A. M. (2003). Increased diffusion in the brain of professional boxers: A preclinical sign of traumatic brain injury. *American Journal of Neuroradiololgy, 24*, 52–57.

Zimmerman, J. N. (2003). *People like ourselves: Portrayals of mental illness in the movies*. Lanham, MD: Scarecrow Press, Inc.

A Handbook
for Garden
Designers

A Handbook for Garden Designers

ROSEMARY ALEXANDER FRSA
with Karena Batstone

WARD LOCK

A WARD LOCK BOOK

First published in the UK 1994
by Ward Lock
Wellington House, 125 Strand
London WC2R 0BB

A Cassell Imprint

Reprinted 1994
First Paperback edition 1996
Reprinted 1998, 1999

Copyright © Text Rosemary Alexander and
Karena Batstone 1994
Copyright © Illustrations Karena Batstone 1994,
unless otherwise indicated

Distributed in the United States
by Sterling Publishing Co. Inc.
387 Park Avenue South, New York, NY 10016-8810

A British Library Cataloguing in Publication Data block
for this book may be obtained from the British Library

ISBN 0 7063 7476 2

Typeset by Litho Link Ltd, Welshpool, Powys, Wales
Printed and bound in Great Britain by The Bath Press, Bath

Cover photograph: Derrick Witty

Contents

Acknowledgments

The authors would like to thank all who have helped in compiling this book, in particular the staff, tutors and students at the English Gardening School, especially Diana Abbott for typing and retyping the text. We also thank those who have allowed us to design their gardens – the plans for many of which appear here, and the following, whose work has been used in this book:

Georgina Bryson (pp. 63, 77, 103); Elizabeth Cochrane (p. 101); Hallie Cohn (p. 95); Zal Davar (p. 64); Anthony du Gard Pasley (p. 104); Ayuko Inoue (p. 119); IPC Magazines Ltd/Robert Harding Syndication/National Trust (p. 104); Sarah Janson (p. 63); Fred Jennett (pp. 17, 18); John Keyes, Keyes Landscape and Graham Rose (p. 21); Pamela Lane-Smith (pp. 75, 80, 102); Gwyn Lewis (p. 109); Candace Long Brewer (pp. 64, 97, 109); Helen Miller (pp. 78, 94); Geoff Moring (p. 64); Tara Owens (p. 79); Partridge Office Equipment (p. 13); Graham Slocombe, Landscape Software (p. 20, 22, 23); Ann Springford (p. 63); Helen Tindale (p. 98), Susanna Yeatman Biggs (p. 120).

Preface

In writing this book, we have tried to explain the surveying, draughting and planning techniques that we use as garden designers, and that we teach at the English Gardening School in London. No two designers will work in exactly the same way, and the intention of this book is to show what should be done, and how to do it, although we anticipate that most readers will adapt our suggestions to their own needs and environment.

In the past, garden plans were drawn individually for each client or garden, the work being executed in ink by skilled draughtsmen on cartridge paper as copying machines were not available. Today original work can be easily reproduced and all work, including the design process, must be carried out quickly and efficiently, as time spent on a project by the desiger will be reflected in the client's bill.

We have tried to show that, as in most professions, there are certain aids, such as the grid, which can help inspire the most inhibited designer. We have tried to show simple and speedy drawing techniques, and as we expect most of our readers to draw their own plans, we do not attempt to compete with the graphics of design consultants who may employ specialists to execute their beautiful and often complex plans.

After understanding and experimenting with your own drawings, we hope you will become more critical and analytical of the work of other designers, often adapting a particular technique to your own style. We hope you enjoy your work, and that we may help you to express your intentions clearly to persuade your clients to build beautiful gardens.

Rosemay Alexander

Karena Batstone

Introduction

Garden design is not simply a matter of choosing plants and arranging them on site. It is the culmination of a process that begins with the soil and the seasons and that involves everything from the construction of the garden to the way in which the client will use the space.

Although garden design is now a recognized profession, many of the most admired gardens, such as Sissinghurst in England, were laid out not by garden designers but by the owners of the properties themselves. Other gardens have evolved gradually, consecutive owners making alterations according to their needs or tastes. Frequently, fashion plays a part in these changes, people being influenced by magazines, television and other media. The increasing number of people visiting gardens over recent years has led to a greater interest in gardening and in garden design, with people trying to create in their own gardens what they have admired elsewhere. In Britain, many private gardens are open to the public, allowing other people to see what has been done and to ask how and why.

Home owners are now aware that a garden that is well laid out and well planted is an asset to be enjoyed and exploited, rather than a luxury to be considered if time and resources allow. These home owners may have admired the gardens of their friends and neighbours, but they are often themselves inexperienced in horticulture or too busy to design and plant their own gardens.

Garden centres can offer the materials, tools and plants, but the staff, even if they are qualified to do so, can rarely spare the time to visit the site and advise on garden layout. Home owners who want to redesign their gardens would save both time and money by calling in a garden designer, who will plan the space according to a client's requirements and the limitations of the site. Garden designers are often also used by house or hotel developers and by interior designers, who realize that their specialist expertise can greatly enhance a property.

Normally a garden designer will be responsible not only for designing the garden but also for suggesting a competent firm of builders to construct it. The designer will usually oversee the work, liaising with the owner about any alterations to the plan, supervising the planting and arranging for future maintenance. In some cases the clients may want only a planting plan or they may wish to construct the garden themselves, and most designers are accustomed to complying with the individual requirements of their clients. In many cases a designer will continue to advise a client as the garden develops.

1

Necessary equipment

In order to communicate ideas to a client the designer will usually survey the site and then draw up the survey to scale as the basis for a future design. Both surveying and draughting equipment will be necessary, and although a professional surveyor may sometimes be used, the designer will learn much more about the site by taking the survey personally.

Surveying equipment

You will need:

■ **30m (100ft) tape measure**, preferably the modern, plasticized version, or two measures if the site is large (1) ....☐

■ **metal skewer** secured with wire to the end of the tape (2) ....☐

■ **damp cloth** for cleaning the tape ....☐

■ **2m (6ft) or 10m (33ft) rigid spring tape or measuring rod** for taking short dimensions, such as the height of steps or low walls (3) ....☐

■ **double clip board** to keep out the wind or rain when making notes (4) ....☐

■ **graph paper** to help keep the lines straight when taking measurements (5) ....☐

■ **note book**, A4 (11²⁄₃ × 8¼in) (6) ....☐

■ **pencils, eraser and pens** in a case (7) ....☐

■ **ball of smooth, thick string** for setting out lines that may be too long for the tape measure, plus garden canes (8) ....☐

■ **spirit level, pegs and a wooden plank** if simple levelling is required (9) ....☐

■ **camera**, spare film and batteries, and a tripod (optional) (10) ....☐

■ **compass** to ascertain the north (11) ....☐

■ **existing plans**, maps and plans for any proposed house extension or conservatory if available (12) ....☐

■ **trowel and plastic bags and labels** for taking soil for pH testing (13) ....☐

■ **suitable clothing**, warm and waterproof if necessary ....☐

■ **bag** or holdall to keep all the equipment clean and dry ....☐

How to use the equipment

Tape measure Before you buy a tape measure, make sure that all measurements are clear and easy to read and that the tape itself is strong and winds in easily. At the end of the tape there is usually a metal ring or hook, which can be slipped over a cane, hooked on to something or held by an assistant. Make sure that you count this ring as part of the measurement, otherwise all your dimensions will be slightly out. Keep the tape clean by always winding it in between a piece of damp cloth so that any dirt or dust picked up from the site is removed. If this is not done the inside of the case can easily become clogged. If you are unfamiliar with using a tape measure, practise measuring simple heights and widths and noting them down. In this way you will become familiar with the figures and will be less likely to make mistakes when measuring a real site.

Metal skewer This should be about 150mm (6 in) long and should be fastened with wire or string to the ring or hook at the end of the tape. It can then be stuck into any convenient crack or into the soil or lawn and obviates the need for an assistant to hold the end of the tape measure.

Rigid spring tape This is particularly useful and quick for measuring vertical dimensions, such as steps or walls, where a long tape measure would be inconvenient. Again, take care to avoid getting dirt inside the casing.

Double clip board This is invaluable for protecting notes, graph paper or plans from wind or rain when you are on site, because the upper side can be used as a shield when you are writing notes. A tough, plasticized, wipe-clean material is preferable.

▲ Surveying equipment.